KU-356-906

# LANGTON'S AUSTRALIAN FINE WINE GUIDE

5th EDITION

Authors
Andrew Caillard
Stewart Langton

Design
Sharon McGrath

Cover Design
Juliana Tufegdzic

Editor
Peter Ching

Marketing Director
Stephen Balme

Printer
Phoenix Offset &
Bookbuilder

Publisher
Media21 Publishing Pty Ltd
30-36 Bay Street
Double Bay NSW 2028
Tel: (02) 9362 1800
Fax: (02) 9352 9500
Email: m21@media21.com.au
(ACN 090 635 073)

ISBN 1-876624-94-9

This book is copyright and no part may be reproduced without written permission from the publisher. Enquiries should be made in writing to the publisher.

© 2002
Media21 Publishing Pty Ltd

# CONTENTS

# INTRODUCTION

*This book, now in its fifth edition, exists because any meaningful market requires monitoring and analysis. It is one of the pillars of an organised market. Price realisations and pricing data are the foundation of this information.*

*Important too are market sentiments. In the sharemarket, fluctuations relate to confidence, profitability, and potential. In the secondary wine market they relate to vintage, producer and wine reputation, past performance, and potential.*

*As the secondary wine market grows we have become increasingly aware that many of the wines traded encapsulate in some way the dreams and aspirations of winemakers and their families.*

*Achieving something unique and special – in a commercial world – is a difficult pathway. Fine wine production often requires sacrifice. Yields are purposely kept low to maintain quality. Winemaking now embraces more philosophical approaches.*

The sudden appearance of the cult wine scene in 2000 challenged the long-held market principles of wine investment. Reputation and track record, always considered critical factors, suddenly seemed unimportant.

One wine writer, apparently vexed by the wide acceptance of *Langton's Classification of Australian Wine*, relished the anticipated demise of this benchmark listing of Australia's top performing wines at auction. It should therefore be a salutary lesson to this observer that the cult scene – at its height, no more than an attention-grabbing feature of the auction market – is now deathly quiet. Its rapid rise and fall illustrates the extraordinary possibilities and dangers of the ultra-fine wine scene.

The whole point of the *Classification* is that it transcends market dalliances and short term speculative plays.

Australia is producing a wide range of interesting and exquisite wines from diverse regions. In our entire history, never have we been making better wines. The sheer quality, diversity, and regional expression is remarkable. But along with success, comes baggage in the form of expectations propelled by the cultures of envy, greed, and adding shareholder value (at the expense of consumer value).

As many producers rise to prominence, the temptation that goes with short supply/strong demand increases. But unreasonable price hikes can damage the reputation and fortunes of a wine. Wynns 1998 *John Riddoch Cabernet Sauvignon* – arguably their best vintage ever –

was de-valued/re-priced by the producer because of market perceptions – a painfully difficult but ultimately positive move. We'll no doubt see this sort of tactic used again, in various guises, by other overpriced wine labels, when the market gets carried away from reality. Another market variable emerges when wine companies, Lake's Folly for example, change hands. Immediately, perceptions of inherent quality change.

The Australian wine industry has become rather polarised in some respects. The commercial wine industry has had a successful decade, capturing increased market share in major export markets. The proliferation of new brands is quite astonishing. This is an industry obsessed with building brand names and achieving 'shareholder value'.

Yet this same industry is sometimes accused of making 'boring and bland' wines. It's a sector like any other form of fast moving consumer good in that prices are a reflection of production costs plus margin.

The Australian wine industry now claims $2 billion in exports. This is a remarkable success story, based on strong brand marketing and high volume sales, largely dominated by wine giants Foster's, BRL Hardy, Southcorp, and Beringer Blass.

BRL Hardy chief Stephen Millar was quoted recently as wishing to make his company the 'Coca-Cola of wine', illustrating the commercial orientation of this overwhelming sector of the market place.

New passionless brands built on the persona of Australian sports stars and celebrities are another new feature. The Greg Norman brand has been enormously successful, especially in the United States. The new Koala Blue brand of Olivia Newton John, apparently a non-drinker, also cashes in on the reputation of Australian wine.

Homogenisation of our wines in some form has been suggested in recent articles by U.K. wine writers Tim Atkin and Jancis Robinson. They are both right and wrong. The 'wine show' system has done much to lift quality, but in many respects, it has also done much to encourage mediocrity. The larger wine companies are responsible for foisting upon us wines with names more suited to apartment blocks, and with false and unimaginative mythologies. Their quest to 'value add' through pretentious (sometimes shameless) and lazy marketing is a crown of thorns that threatens the extraordinary reef of our remarkable Australian wines.

The sheer volume and overall success of commercial Australian wines rather overwhelms the much smaller ultra-fine Australian wine market, especially in Europe and the U.S. The challenges for many of our best producers is how they deal with change and how they market their wine.

The obsession with wealth creation is seeing production-oriented wineries transforming into market-oriented producers. Witness the spate of new 'icon' wine labels, many of which provide the consumer with absolutely no intrinsic added value. The worst such offender is Coonawarra. The region has devalued its excellent now standard wines in the pursuit of making high margins with strongly flavoured, sometimes overly concentrated wines.

In a world currently embracing wines with strong single vineyard or regional provenance, some of these wines seem to miss the mark, with plenty of winemaking skill but little sense of place.

Larger wine companies also try to cash in on marketing tactics, adding value through slick winemaking techniques such as fractional draining. We're not sure the market is completely taken by overtly concentrated wines, yet some winemakers seem to think that concentration and power are the major elements of quality at the highest level. This may well explain the penchant of some well-capitalised wineries for not releasing wine in a particular vintage.

The desire for quality at the very highest level seems to verge on fanaticism. If we are to believe in concepts such as distinguished vineyard site, shouldn't we also understand vineyard character in all its light and shade?

Notwithstanding the overlapping and intertwining of the wine industry overall, fine wine making is generally run by production-oriented standards, where few compromises are made in the vineyard or the winery. These are relatively limited productions usually based on single vineyards and/or strongly focused ideas of quality.

The best winemakers – usually blessed or annointed with great generosity of spirit – can bring a palpable sense of place to their wines. Ultimately, the wine, not the words, should capture the imagination of the wine consumer!

While *Langton's Classification of Australian Wine* reflects today's market conditions, there is no question that the order of things will change. Achieving quality is a lifelong commitment. It requires constant refinement, innovation, and at times painful decisions.

It's not uncommon for Australian wine makers to declassify their own wines. Penfolds did not make a 2000 *Penfolds Bin 707*, and Clarendon Hills poured its 2000 *Astralis* down the plug hole, both because they didn't meet quality standards. While this practice creates the issue about 'light and shade', can you imagine any other industry doing this?

The secondary wine market is evolving in ways we could never predict five years ago. There are more players than ever before. The emergence of wine investment brokers, wine exchanges, and specialist wine advisors, has broadened a field once dominated by wine auction houses. Cellars are now called "wine investment portfolios" and a new wine release is called an "investment opportunity".

The battle to capture the hearts and minds of the wine collector comes at a price. Over-enthusiasm, wishful thinking, lack of knowledge, and a degree of greed, all combine to create a world full of cul-de-sacs, pot holes, and crevasses.

*Langton's Australian Fine Wine Buying And Investment Guide* is a unique resource that draws on our collective, and considerable, experience in the secondary market. The Australian wine industry continues to surprise and unfold a wonderful array of wines, many of which are yet to claim a market presence.

This fifth edition of the *Guide* is completely revised, giving up-to-date and comprehensive information on the secondary wine market and ultra-fine Australian wine. While this book focuses on wine buying and investing, it should be remembered that wine is something to be enjoyed rather than something to covet. *Langton's Australian Fine Wine Buying And Investment Guide*, therefore, represents just a small journey in a much greater voyage of discovery.

*ANDREW CAILLARD, MW*

*STEWART LANGTON*

# THE PHENOMENON
# The Australian Wine Investment Story

*The secondary wine auction market is like the air above – where clear skies can belie the complex air currents that move within it – as you'll see in this story of Australian wine investment. The issues at play in the market help explain why one wine captures the imagination of buyers, while another sits in the doldrums.*

**The Story begins**

The fine wine market is today's modern spice trade. And over recent years, growth in the Australian wine investment market has been significant. Penfolds *Grange*, once the only serious investment wine, now leads a remarkable list of Australian wines traded regularly on the secondary market… for profit and for pleasure.

Limited supply, reputation, and sheer quality, have thrust many of Australia's best wines onto the world's wine auction and exchange markets. Hyperbole, greed, and speculation, are now added features of this dynamic and interesting market. So too the cult wine phenomenon which, fuelled by influential American wine critic Robert Parker Jr, recently had the market paying over $1,000 a bottle for almost unheard of wines.

**Market in evolution**

The secondary market is in rapid evolution, driven by more buyers and sellers than ever before. New entrants, new market mechanisms, growing international recognition for high quality Australian wine, and new investment wines, make the market increasingly complex and hazardous. The emergence of 'tin-shack' cult wines has also become a small, but attention-grabbing, feature.

While track record and reputation are core market factors, some traditional 'blue chip' wines do get downgraded. The wine investor who understands the market is better equipped to know where it is likely to go.

**Modest beginnings**

Until the late 1980s, wine auctions in Australia attracted only a few buyers and sellers – mainly focused on imported wine, particularly Bordeaux, Burgundy, and Champagne. Favourable exchange rates made Australia an important export market for European producers from the late 1970s to the early 1980s. As the dollar weakened, things began to change. Quality imported wines became comparatively expensive. Australian buyers turned to their own backyard.

The 1980s was a period of great enlightenment with rapid growth in small quality-oriented new wineries. The Australian wine industry enjoyed a golden age in technology and capitalisation. And enthusiasts were drawn to the growing number of remarkable, likeable and innovative winemakers, viticulturists, and marketers. This was a period of new ideas, new wine regions, of new small 'boutique' wineries proliferating, and the beginning of a highly successful export market.

**A formative market**

The low dollar proved an effective incubator, as an emerging local market took interest in fine Australian wine, Penfolds *Grange* and Seppelt *Para Liqueur Port* principal among the early secondary market performers. Quickly the numbers grew, with early winning form shown by Balgownie, Cape Mentelle, Lake's Folly, Mount Mary, Penfolds, Petaluma, Redman, Tyrrell's, Virgin Hills, Wynn's Coonawarra Estate, and Wolf Blass.

Over the last 20 years, some wines have gone from strength to strength. Others have fallen by the wayside. The evolution viewed in hindsight, is amusing. Barossa Shiraz, now a cornerstone of the market, was considered old fashioned and the district too hot for premium wine! Wines thought to have no future on the secondary market now look important and convincing, thanks to the concept of low-yielding single vineyard distinguished sites and regional diversity.

**Australian wine investment recognised**

In 1991, Langton's published its first *Classification of Australian Wine*, also the first positive indication to potential wine investors that wise money could be invested in Australian wines. There was the new essence of Coonawarra Cabernet – Wynn's *John Riddoch* to consider. And recognition of specialised small wineries such as Henschke, Yarra Yering, and Mount Mary. Cabernet Sauvignon was king, with Coonawarra Cabernet among the most prominent in the emerging market. This was recognised by the market in 1991 when Langton's put on its first ever event sale – 'Classic Coonawarra'.

**New directions**

By 1994, interest in the market started to come from overseas – at first from ex-patriot Australians. Asian and U.S. markets followed. Acclaim for Australian wines from influential wine critics and international wine publications, helped position Australia as a major fine wine producer. Interest in Australian shiraz, particularly Barossa and McLaren Vale styles, was a feature.

In 1996, the rise in prominence of Australian shiraz was confirmed by Langton's second *Classification* –

particularly South Australian Shiraz, but also by omission, the demise was noted of Australian Vintage Port as a secondary market performer.

**A coming of age**

From 1997 to 2000, Langton's embarked on a program to promote Australian wine internationally with a series of event auctions: 'The Great Wine Estates of Western Australia', 'Shiraz Australia', and 'Golden Summers – A Vintage Australian Decade 1990-1999'. These reaped significant interest, buoyant sales results, and created new overseas buyers.

The Australian Shiraz juggernaut continued to gather momentum, drawing attention particularly for the international celebrity brands, Penfolds *Grange* and Henschke *Hill of Grace*. The heightened interest in Australian Shiraz and the emerging importance of regional defined wines such as Margaret River Cabernet and Chardonnay, and Barossa and McLaren Vale Shiraz, was highlighted in Langton's *Classification* III.

**A force to be reckoned with**

In early March 2000, *The Australian* newspaper predicted a battle between traditional wine auction houses and the new 'dot.com' ventures. Secondary market activity the preceding year, had been strengthening, with more buyers and sellers than ever before. Wine investment, previously a relatively minor feature, surged to prominence in the market. E-commerce opportunities, aggressive investment strategies, and new entrants changed the market terrain in an extraordinary way – even though the 'dot.com' phenomena failed to fulfil its promise.

**Shifting sands**

The secondary market now embraces the established, emerging, and cult wine scenes. Robert Parker Jr, the world's most influential wine writer, championed several new-fashioned wines that were almost unheard of in the auction market. Clarendon Hills *Astralis*, Torbreck *The Run Rig*, Three Rivers, and Wild Duck Creek *Duck Muck Shiraz* are just a few examples of wines that suddenly drew a storm of interest from Parker's extensive readership in Asia and the U.S. The impact at one point, threatened the investment dominance of Australia's top marquees. However, by the end of 2001, *Grange* was shining brightly, as the cult scene waned under crushing uncertainty following the September 11th crisis.

Market conditions aside, these wines and many others, represent a shift in the sands. The ultra-fine wine scene in Australia is more diverse and interesting than ever before, with an astonishing array of beautifully made wines.

**A broader market of buyers**

Both wine investors and traditional wine enthusiasts flock to the secondary market. Contrary to popular opinion, most wine investors are extremely knowledgeable and passionate about wine. Some, from the financial community, see opportunities in a rising and increasingly more organised market. These individuals challenge and expand, through secondary market channels, almost every aspect of buying and selling wine.

Today we have a larger more educated market, and more wine enthusiasts who are more keen than ever before. They appreciate wine, not just as a drink, but an experience. And they're prepared to pay more for wines that have been either cellared or difficult to find.

**The future is more change.**

The last two years have taught us that while track record and reputation are very important considerations, we live in a brash world of dynamic change and junk culture. The wine investment paradigm has moved to also embrace the enthusiasms of newer, younger buyers – some pre-occupied with status and health. It also caters to the idiosyncrasies of emerging regional markets, as well as to the palpable expectations of personal wealth building.

The developing secondary wine market underscores, even validates, the achievements of our best winemakers and producers. In a world seemingly obsessed with ownership and statistics, greatness is generally measured in terms of price and value. Nevertheless it always has been – in wine at least – since Roman times.

**What is wine investment?**

Investment wines are those that will mature and increase in value – either in the short, medium, or long term. They are invariably perceived as being high quality, usually produced in limited quantity, and having potential to develop and improve with cellaring.

Critical opinion, wine show results, rarity value, reputation, and past performance – all have influence on the market.

Massaged and hyped by wine critics and public relations machines, the market is a minefield of entrenched prejudices, popular wine mythologies, and more than a little wishful thinking.

*Langton's Classification of Australian Wine* is a form guide to wines that have performed strongly and consistently on the auction market. It is a reactive assessment that neither predicts a wine's performance in the future, or singles out particular vintages. Crystal ball gazing is both the fun and frustration of wine investment – the more you read, the more confounded you become.

**Wine investment issues**

Important issues underlying wine investment are discussed in detail below.

- *Limited product* – Wine is an agricultural commodity. Adverse weather can affect yield and quality. Each year production fluctuates with grape supply. Vintage reputation and wine availability are key concerns. Investors generally buy on the basis of 'good vintage/short supply', hoping the market will rise through 'strong demand'.
- *Provenance* – embraces the key concerns of reputation, 'regionality', and past cellaring conditions.
- *Reputation* – relates to brand definition, consistent quality, and cellaring potential. This is a key investment factor and invariably related to track record. Years of consistent strong demand on the secondary market are a good indication. Reputations are earned through favourable criticism and word of mouth – only sometimes through wine show successes. Penfolds *Grange*, Henschke *Hill of Grace*, *Mount Mary Cabernet*, are good examples. Time ultimately levels the playing field. An authoritative indication of reputation is a listing in Langton's *Classification*.
- *Regionality* – the Australian term that evokes the French concept of *terroir*, noting that a wine's character can reflect the spirit of its place. The vast Australian landscape harbours a myriad of topographies, micro-climates, soil types, as well as vineyard and winery practices. This is linked inextricably to the suitability of grape variety. Hence the proven track records of Barossa Shiraz, Margaret River Cabernet, and Coonawarra Cabernet – all have strong regional provenance.
- *Storage* – Conditions under which wine is stored prior to its sale, is becoming very important. This is especially so with increasing international interest in Australian wines. Repatriation of wine cellared in Asian countries, for instance, is a major concern. There is a consensus that wine should be cellared at between 14° and 18° Celsius with 70-75 per cent relative humidity.

The dusty, cobwebbed, underground cellar is a thing of the past. These days, buyers want wines in pristine condition: minimal ullage, perfect labels and capsules, and perfect past cellaring conditions. Future market expectations will no doubt include the availability of documented cellaring records.

Past cellaring conditions are not easy to determine when the immediate past owner is not known. Older vintages of course may have changed hands more than once. Documented cellaring records can support more accurate valuation. The only serious option for vendors without recognised cellaring bona fides, may well be high-quality, commercial wine storage.

There is also the issue of faked wines. In the past two years, Penfolds *Grange* and *St Henri* have been counterfeited. News of faked wines grabs media attention but it is, in fact, a minor problem. Nevertheless, the message is clear – buyers should only purchase from reputable suppliers.

• *Wine Shows* – the plethora of wine shows in Australia is extraordinary. The major, long established shows are run by agricultural societies, and were originally conceived as comparative, critical forums, not as aids to marketing.

Sometimes (but less so nowadays), winning a trophy such as Melbourne's Jimmy Watson, can automatically confer secondary market credentials.

There are simply too many shows, with too many classes, and too many trophies, for any single award to mean much at the level of wine investment. Further complicating the issue, there are now many other, more obviously promotional, wine awards and competitions. Show success can still bring prestige, especially when good results continue over years.

Many of Australia's ultra-fine wine producers simply do not enter the shows – out of pride, or because they don't need to, or because they suspect the inevitable silvers and bronzes might crack their gold quality image, or just because their stocks are too limited to meet entry criteria.

Inevitably, the Australian wine show system has become a champion of commercial and corporate wine.

• *Larger Formats* – Wine comes in varying bottle sizes. Large format bottles (magnums and over) are generally quite rare. In these bottles, wines age more slowly than in standard 750ml and half (375ml) bottles.

Buyers may pay an extra premium for these larger formats, if from a recognised vintage. Penfolds *Grange* and Henschke *Hill of Grace* magnums trade well over double the price of standard bottles of the same vintage.

Half bottles, especially from highly regarded vintages and producers, may also carry a premium, although the outlay is still less than a single 750ml bottle.

• *Australian vintages* – Australia's enormity means a wide variety of climatic conditions. Regionality – the notion that a specific region can produce wines of individual and unique quality – has become a catchword of the contemporary wine scene. Barossa Shiraz is quite different from Hunter Valley Shiraz, just as Coonawarra Cabernet is different from Margaret River Cabernet.

Vintages can differ markedly even within one state. For instance, the 1995 vintage in Coonawarra was a damp squib, despite drought conditions prevalent in the Barossa Valley. So-called 'distinguished vineyard sites' can also outperform other vineyards in good and indifferent years.

• *Ageing qualities* – Mature, ultra-fine Australian wine has become a highly sought commodity over the past 10 years. Although fashion played a major role, technology has undoubtedly improved quality in the vineyard and the winery. Australian winemakers are used to good ripening conditions. Indeed there is a belief that ripeness is the key to the development of critical flavour and aroma components.

Barossa Valley Shiraz for instance, needs an alcohol level of 13-14 per cent, to bring on those concentrated, beautifully direct, aniseed, liquorice, and blackberry characters. The wines become more meaty and complex as they develop. Some can age for 20 years or more – notably Penfolds *Grange* – but most are delicious to drink after five or six years in bottle. Depending on the vintage and the philosophy behind the wine, they can still drink beautifully for another 10 or so years.

Hunter Valley Shiraz is in the process of reinventing itself. The 1965 *Lindemans Bin 3110* is still drinking well, although it is an aberration. Most Hunter Shiraz is quite light in colour and develops complex, leathery, earthy aromas, and more palate weight, as it ages. This style is often cellared for too long. It is best after three years in bottle, although examples from top producers in the best vintages can age for longer.

Central Victorian Shiraz is proving to have good ageing potential. Some will age for as much as 20 years, although most are ready to drink after six or seven.

Hunter Valley Semillon, picked relatively early, is one of the lowest-alcohol wines made in Australian (about 11-12 per cent). When young, the style is tightly structured and rather simple and linear in style, but over time, it develops richness and complex flavours. From a good vintage, these wines can age for 20 years or more.

Coonawarra Cabernet Sauvignon has two guises. The essence-of-Cabernet, super rich, over-concentrated style, needs substantial bottle development – at least seven years – to soften. The classic Coonawarra style however, needs only about four years to come around, and makes an immensely enjoyable drink for many more years after that.

Margaret River Cabernet Sauvignon is very structured, with fine-grained tannins and restrained fruit. The style blossoms after about five years, and the best examples prove to have excellent cellaring potential.

Clare Valley Riesling has brilliant ageing potential. Purity of fruit and indelible acidity, provide the strong spine necessary for long life. Over time, the wines develop complex toast-and-honey characters. Expect wines from a year like 1997, to age gracefully for 30 years. Although they are so beautiful when young, there will no doubt be few bottles in their late 20s left to enjoy.

Australian Chardonnay is a more difficult subject about which to generalise. Vintage and producer are extremely important. The 2000 Leeuwin Estate *Art Series Chardonnay* has the restraint and power, together with focused fruit and acid cut, to justify ageing. However most Chardonnays are so complex and worked when young, that they seem to get brassy and almost one-dimensional within three to five years of vintage. Adelaide Hills, Margaret River, and Melbourne Dress Circle Chardonnays are showing promise, and other wines such as Tyrrell's *Vat 47 Hunter Valley Chardonnay*, have shown excellent cellar life.

Ultimately, any wine's ageing potential relates directly to the drinker's palate. If you like primary fruit characters, drink wine young. Makers of fine wine constantly experiment to improve quality. The best insight is gained by using your cellar properly – as a drinking resource. Your wine cellar should not be, nor should it become, a museum – although if you are serious only about investing, not enjoying the wine as well, this may well be what unfortunately happens.

• *Models of wine investment success* – Why do perfectly good wines flounder while others charge on to the market confidently? Although winemakers chase quality in the vineyard and in the winery, success relies on a critical mass of perceptions, encompassing all sorts of elements. Regardless of personal opinions, virtually universal agreement on quality is the common factor.

• *Reputation* – Wines that have achieved an extraordinary reputation for quality over a period of time include Penfolds *Grange* and *Bin 707*, Cullen *Cabernet Sauvignon-Merlot*, Henschke *Hill of Grace*, Jasper Hill *Georgia's Paddock*, Moss Wood *Cabernet Sauvignon*, and Howard Park *Western Australian Cabernets*.

• *Trickle-Down Effect* – dovetailing new wines into an existing structure – is, according to some, difficult, if not impossible, to achieve. Examples do exist however, the obvious being new Penfolds wines such as *Magill Estate Shiraz*, *Bin 407 Cabernet Sauvignon*, and *RWT Barossa Valley Shiraz*. Rosemount and Grant Burge are also using this strategy.

• *Consumer Demand Shift or Fashion* – The consumer's love affair with Shiraz is enough to put pressure on supply. Is Australian Pinot Noir next? Wines with apparently no investment potential can flourish almost overnight. Examples are Pinot Noir and Clare Valley Riesling. Watch out for Viognier and Pinot Gris – although with white wines, potential is likely to be short term. Wines also fall out of fashion.

• *Regionality* – The developing reputation of a region can change fortunes. Examples are Xanadu in Margaret River, Charles Melton and Torbreck in the Barossa Valley, Yering Station in Victoria's Yarra Valley, and Majella and Penley Estate in Coonawarra.

• *Limited Production Wines* – (either real or perceived) are attractive propositions for collectors, especially if the wines derive from highly regarded vineyards/wineries and carry some status. Also involved is a combination of good luck, fashion, and shrewd marketing. Rockford *Basket Press* and Rockford's new single vineyard shirazes, Henschke *Hill of Grace*, Brokenwood *Graveyard Vineyard*, Jim Barry *The Armagh*, Bass Phillip *Reserve Pinot Noir*, and Penfolds experimental bin range, are examples from a wide range.

• *Parkerisation* – Robert Parker Jr, the influential American wine writer, is in a league of his own. His pronouncements can not only confer star status on a single wine but can have a powerful impact on the evolution of regional style – for better or worse. *Three Rivers Barossa Valley Shiraz*, Torbreck *The Run Rig*, Wild Duck Creek's *Duck Muck*, and Greenock Creek *Roennfeldt* are examples. Continuing success for Parkerised' wines relies on the buoyancy of the international economy and limited production levels.

** Some wines encompass one or more of the above models.*

**Global investment in Australian wine**

Liquor laws, especially in the U.S., will continue to slug the growth of the world market for Australian investment-quality wine. However, high end buyers are prepared to pay extra duties and freight for what is perceived as great wine.

The secondary market is value-sensitive, not necessarily price-sensitive. There is some elasticity however. Because their perception of value is dictated by their own market and currency, foreign investors often pay higher prices than domestic buyers. There is also a trend toward international buyers storing wine in the market of origin, further reducing costs to the investor.

The wine investment movement challenges the traditional wine market. There are those who believe that wine investment is a force of darkness. In reality, it merely reflects the belief of many, that Australia is able to make some of the finest wines in the world. Why can't a Barossa Shiraz or a Margaret River Cabernet, for instance, be as good as a Vosne Romanee, a first growth Bordeaux, or a Napa Valley Cabernet?

We are seeing unprecedented levels of confidence in Australian wine, from an entire generation of Australians and indeed, an enthusiastic and growing church of international followers.

**Words of Caution**

• *Understand the market:* 'Buy early', 'buy low', 'buy cheap' are concepts common to all investments. This means buying wine at release, negotiating the lowest price possible from a retailer, or buying from what is essentially a wholesale wine auction market. Occasionally, investors can buy 'futures' barrels, particularly at auction. This is a market in its infancy. Be aware that the secondary wine market also embraces the high-valued rarity market – "must have" wines, usually classic, difficult to find vintages, or limited production tin-shack cult wines. These can attract speculative prices.

• *Don't judge a wine by its packaging:* Every man and his dog is vying for recognition at the top of the market. Producers invent stories and modern mythologies – easily done in this 'Information Age'. Not all succeed in capturing the imagination of consumers, but some do. And, as with collectors' ports of the 1970s and 1980s, some investors will be disappointed. Potential, no matter how sure it may seem today, may not be realised in the future. A plethora of supposedly high-quality wines simply don't deliver in terms of reputation or value.

• *Don't always believe the newspapers:* The media plays its part in communicating the greatness of Australian wine. But it can also send wrong messages. Each year, Australian economic analyst Access Economics, releases a paper on Australia's best investments. Wine has headed the list for some years, and is said to outperform Australian shares, bonds, racehorses, art, and even taxi-plates. Closer scrutiny reveals that what has been analysed is the secondary market performance of 1971 Penfolds *Grange*. The fact that this is but one particular vintage with so few bottles in the market, is not reported by the media.

*Langton's Australian Fine Wine Index* – based on a basket of 28 wines and three rolling vintages – is now used by Access Economics, and gives potential investors a clearer picture.

Academic analysis of the market, while worthy, will also show that wine investment is not a sure thing. However, if you pick your wines well, you may indeed achieve your financial objectives.

**The Five Wine Investment Maxims**

1. Understand the market.
2. Buy only good vintages.
3. Beware of hyperbole.
4. Cellar conditions are very important.
5. Read more than one wine critic.

## CULT WINES

*Cult Wines are celebrity wines. Fanned by the hyperbole of influential wine writers, these wines are slavishly followed by a relatively small circle of wine investors with near-religious zeal.*

*The Cult Wine movement emerged during the 1980s, gathering pace with the development of the super-premium Californian wine industry and the information technology boom of the 1990s. The rise of Californian wine names like Screaming Eagle, Bryant Family, and Harlan Estate – some selling at US$1,000 or more at the height of the boom – spurred a movement that challenged the order of the fine wine market in almost every serious winemaking country.*

The current Australian Cult Wine market was largely generated by the influential American wine writer Robert Parker Jr and *Wine Spectator* magazine. Driven by wealthy American and Asian buyers, it arrived with a bang in 1999. However, it arrived in the midst of the international market's Indian Summer. By late 2001, the market in Australia slumped as buyers pulled back from paying ever-increasing prices. At the same time blue-chip wines, particularly those in Langton's *Classification*, showed resilience, either maintaining or increasing their value.

The prominence of Australian Cult Wines has had enormous impact on the overall market. The most recent wave beneficially changed the way many Australians regard their own wine, overturning entrenched views of wine quality.

Over the years, the 'Wine Show' system, almost a closed shop in Australia, has overseen the homogenisation of Australian wine style. Australian wine judges and reviewers have been far too technical and prescriptive about wine style.

The irresistible rise of Australian Cult Wines has been a very healthy phenomenon. It brought back a level of debate and passion that will ensure diversity of wine style, highlight winemaking as a craft, and show that the dream of creating exceptional wine is not just a pursuit for the rich.

In various guises, Australian Cult Wines have arguably been with us for over 50 years. In the 1950s, before the dominance of the 'Wine Show' system, and when most Australians were largely drinking fortified wines, a small group of Australian buyers supported producers like Leo Buring, Woodley's, Mount Pleasant and Penfolds. During the 1960s, Chateau Reynella, d'Arenberg, Hardy's, Henschke, Lindemans, Orlando, Seppelt, Tyrrell's, Wynns, and Yalumba became prominent.

In the 1970s and 1980s, a number of new wine producers captured the hearts and minds of wine buyers, e.g. Balgownie, Hickinbotham, Mitchell, Mount Mary, Moss Wood, Petaluma, Piper's Brook, Redman, Taylor's, Virgin Hills, Wirra Wirra, and Yarra Yering. By the late 1980s, the secondary wine market, as we now know it, began to evolve. In 1991 Langton's introduced its first *Classification of Distinguished Australian Wine* to bring order to this market.

Mergers, acquisitions, tragedy, and triumph have all played roles in the evolution of the market. Some wines from the 1970s, 1980s, and even the 1990s, have already fallen by the wayside. Others have become established classics, deserving their place in Langton's *Classification*.

Today, Cult Wine prices can overwhelm quality issues. Three Rivers began as a wine enthusiast's curio, a sought-after wine among a small number of buyers who enjoyed something different. Robert Parker Jr's high scores and rave reviews launched Three Rivers onto the international market, rocketing prices up by 400 per cent within a single year.

Excessive demand on limited supply can have a powerful effect on price. Fox Creek, Torbreck, Noon, Greenock Creek, and Wild Duck Creek followed a similar path.

Currently the market is in dramatic slump, almost to the point of inactivity. Sellers' price expectations are unrealistic. *Three Rivers Shiraz*, once attracting AUD$1,400 a bottle, is now impossibly difficult to sell. However this wine has excellent intrinsic quality and could yet become a classic (albeit at more reasonable prices). Wild Duck Creek's *Duck Muck Shiraz* had a brief spell in the limelight but probably needs continuing positive reviews to retain its cachet. Greenock Creek *Roennfeldt Road Shiraz* still attracts interest.

The strongest Cult Wines in the market are Clarendon Hills *Astralis Shiraz* and Torbreck *Run Rig Shiraz* (which are comparatively well-priced) and *Noon Reserve Shiraz* which, until 2002, was released at a mere AUD$25 (it is now AUD$60). The market still looks on favourably at these wines, largely because prices remain realistic.

However wine investors should be very careful investing in Cult Wines. Their track record is erratic. Some buy these wines simply to drink them, some for investment, and others to hold them as trophies.

From an investor's point of view, the Cult Wine market illustrates the maxim that the only certainty is change. The best advice is to learn from the experience of the most recent wave and invest in wines that could attract enthusiasm in the future. This means vintage year, size of wine make, regional provenance, and a certain amount of luck. Track record is also something of an issue. Buyers have, in the past, mistakenly clung to pseudo-provenance – a mixture of the real, such as the appeal of old vines, and the unreal – the gushing levels of marketing hype and the promise of easy returns.

In 1999, offshore buyers supported the entire market. Another wave of frantic buying could easily occur with the strengthening of the US economy, the low Australian dollar, and the perception of exceptional 2001 vintages in South Australia and Victoria.

Ultimately this is a very difficult corner of the investment market. Cult wines are generally speculative stocks. Nevertheless the following is a list of the leading Australian Cult Wines past and present as Langton's sees it.

*Caveat Emptor!*

**MT. PLEASANT (McWilliams) Maurice O'Shea wines, Lower Hunter Valley**

Maurice O'Shea is often regarded as the father of the Australian table wine industry. His wines (1921 to 1956) were remarkably good, begging the question, why has the Hunter Valley not achieved its early promise in the market?

**WOODLEY'S Treasure Chest Series, Shiraz Blends, Coonawarra**

Fabulous series of wines from 1949 to 1956. All Shiraz-based. All brilliantly packaged. Made in the building that now houses Wynns Coonawarra Estate. Still eagerly sought.

**1955 WYNN'S Michael Hermitage (Shiraz), Coonawarra**

A great Coonawarra vintage. This wine was considered a freak and was apparently matured in old fortified wine casks. Impossibly rare.

**1963 MILDARA Peppermint Patty Cabernet Sauvignon, Coonawarra**

Another freak wine, which won the Jimmy Watson Trophy in Melbourne. *Peppermint Patty* (not named after a person - rather the smell of a chocolate/peppermint sweet) was the wine's nickname. Occasionally comes up for sale.

**1959 LINDEMANS Bin 1590 Burgundy (Shiraz), Lower Hunter Valley**

Legendary Hunter Valley Shiraz showing the Hunter Valley paradox. Very rare. (The paradox is that the Hunter Valley is able to make the greatest Australian wine – but only once in a blue moon… about every 20 years.)

**1965 LINDEMANS Bin 3110 & 3100 Hunter River Burgundy (Shiraz), Lower Hunter Valley**

Arguably one of the greatest Australian Shirazes ever made. Still showing plenty of life in all its complex glory. Two bottlings – *Bin 3100* and *3110* – released from the winery at varying times.

**1970 LINDEMANS Bin 3875 Hunter River Chablis**

The most successful wine to appear on the Australian Wine Show circuit. Judges would spot it every time and award top points. Beginning to fade, but a real 'show-stopper'.

**1962 PENFOLDS Bin 60A Kalimna Shiraz – Coonawarra Cabernet Sauvignon**

Considered by many as one of the greatest Australian wines ever made. Perhaps Penfolds' most successful wine on the Australian Wine Show circuit. Increasingly rare, however most bottles are still holding up well.

**1962 PENFOLDS Bin 60 Kalimna Shiraz, Coonawarra Cabernet Sauvignon**

A reverse blend of *Bin 60A*. Never achieved the same accolades, but still very rare and holding up well.

**1963 PENFOLDS Bin 64 Cabernet Sauvignon, Barossa Valley**

Experimental wine, the precursor of the highly regarded *Bin 707*. Coming towards the end of its life. Very rare.

**1966 PENFOLDS Bin 620 Cabernet Sauvignon Shiraz, Coonawarra**

A Coonawarra Cabernet Shiraz blend which now needs drinking. Some good bottles. Very rare.

**1967 PENFOLDS Bin 7 Coonawarra Cabernet Sauvignon, Kalimna Shiraz**

Recognised as one of the great Australian wines of the 1960s. Still holding up well. Not getting quite the same kudos as *Bin 60A*. Very rare.

**1980 PENFOLDS Bin 80A Coonawarra Cabernet Sauvignon, Kalimna Shiraz**

Made in the mould of *Bin 60A*. One of the cult wines of the local Australian market but now settled as a stable performer although its value reflects healthy market respect.

**1982 PENFOLDS Bin 820 Cabernet-Shiraz, Coonawarra**
In hindsight, the lesser of the two special releases. 1982 was seen as a remarkable year at the time but has since been reassessed as a freak year giving unusual flavour profiles. Worth seeking out and attracting healthy market support.

**1990 PENFOLDS Bin 90A Coonawarra Cabernet Sauvignon, Barossa Valley Shiraz**
Fabulous wine that immediately sparked the market. Sits in the shadow of 1990 *Grange* and *Bin 707*, but has similar attributes. Curiously undervalued.

**1990 PENFOLDS Bin 920 Cabernet-Shiraz, Coonawarra**
Classic Penfolds blend with excellent regional provenance. Sits in the shadow of *Bin 90A*, but highly regarded.

**1996 PENFOLDS Bin Block 42 Cabernet, Kalimna**
Superb wine from Penfolds' mother vineyard at Kalimna. A great vintage, arguably as good as *Grange*. Attracted considerable hype at release. Not much made and minute quantities come up for sale.

**BASS PHILLIP Reserve Pinot Noir, Gippsland**
Strong market presence driven by this producer's reputation for making superb Pinot Noir.

**BURGE FAMILY WINEMAKERS Draycott Reserve Shiraz, Barossa Valley**
A Robert Parker Jr recommended wine which has attracted strong support in the past.

**CLARENDON HILLS Astralis Shiraz, McLaren Vale**
Australians were astonished with Robert Parker Jr's high ratings. It precipitated a paradigm shift in winemaking thought. Can do extremely well – most market interest from Asia and the U.S.

**GREENOCK CREEK Roennfeldt Road Shiraz, Barossa Valley**
Impossibly small parcel of wine. Robert Parker Jr deified it by associating Chris Ringland with Greenock Creek.

**NOON Reserve Shiraz, Langhorne Creek**
Speculative but high quality stock frenzied by Robert Parker Jr's pronouncements.

**NOON Reserve Cabernet, Langhorne Creek**
Speculative but high quality stock frenzied by Robert Parker Jr's pronouncements.

**THREE RIVERS Shiraz, Barossa Valley**
Impossibly small production made by Rockford's talented winemaker Chris Ringland. Australia's *Screaming Eagle* or *Le Pin*.

**TORBRECK Run Rig Shiraz, Barossa Valley**
A scion of the Barossa Shiraz style with moderating interest. Excellent regional provenance and winemaking credentials may see this wine going down the *Astralis* route – fast becoming an establishment wine!

**VERITAS Hanisch Shiraz, Barossa Valley**
A wine sold almost entirely into the U.S. and overseas markets. The wines look terrific.

**VERITAS Heysen Shiraz, Barossa Valley**
Strong regional provenance and the wand of Robert Parker Jr has seen market support.

**WILD DUCK CREEK Duck Muck Shiraz, Heathcote**
Australian humour meets U.S. seriousness.

# EMERGING WINES

*The secondary market is in constant evolution. Emerging wines are those beginning to have some form of definition or market presence at auction. These wines comprise both the old and new – wines with relatively long term reputations, and new marques that have captured the hearts and minds of the wine enthusiast in a relatively short time frame.*

Wines with an up-and-coming profile on the secondary wine market are described as 'emerging wines'. Some may have been around for some time, attracting stronger levels of market sponge, with higher volume bidding and more stable results. Others, newer to the market, can perform erratically on the secondary market. Generally, emerging wines have unique properties – both tangible and intangible – and carry a high perception of quality.

Reputation, consumer demand, regional definition, and limited production, play a major role in propelling wines onto the secondary market. The developing renown of a region can also foster emerging wines. This is happening with all the major established regions. Torbreck in the Barossa, Yering Station in the Yarra Valley, and Balnaves in Coonawarra, are good examples.

Micro blends and wines 'perceived' as limited releases also appeal to collectors, especially if the wines are derived from highly regarded wineries. Penfolds *Experimental Bins*, Rockford *Single Vineyard Shirazes*, and Noon *Reserve Shiraz* are good examples.

Emerging wines are neither classified, or cult wines, but they trade regularly (or even irregularly) on the secondary wine market. It is important to point out that the emerging category is not a classification – it's more of a vinous purgatory where performance will, in the end, decide its fate on the secondary market. Only the most consistent performers will eventually become classic wines and find their way into *Langton's Classification*. Conversely, there are others that may just fall into a cul-de-sac. The emerging wine scene only suggests a market presence.

The investment nature of Australian wine is still in its infancy. Returns of around 15 to 30 per cent are not uncommon. If you are looking to invest in wines from the emerging category, be careful and apply the usual wine investment advice – stick to good vintages, carry out plenty of research, be prepared, and be open to risk.

A number of wines in the emerging category are wines that missed the cut for *Langton's Classification III* (2000).

These may be well regarded on the wine auction market, but lack the track record of vintages to qualify for Classification. Parker Coonawarra Estate *First Growth* is a good example. In many respects it has not entered the *Classification* due to the winery's pursuit of quality – 1992, 1995, and 1997 vintages were not made. Yalumba *Octavius* is another example.

'Emerging' also includes wines that have appeared on the market in recent years, often without much of a track record, but which have made a strong impression on the consumer. Often these wines are vintage specific. A good example is Penfolds *RWT Shiraz*, a new Barossa Shiraz with strong regional and producer provenance, yet no specific track record. *Majella Cabernet Sauvignon* and *Clonakilla Shiraz–Viognier* are other examples.

Emerging wines are driven by both domestic and international markets. In the last five years, wines unheard of on the local market, have become primary market forces in the U.S. and Asia. Many of these wines are yet to acquire a meaningful presence on the Australian secondary market – mainly because much of the wine is exported. However wines like Henry's Drive and Killibinbin could quite possibly earn an established market presence in the future. Australian Shiraz is the emerging market's strongest force, particularly from recognised regions such as McLaren Vale and the Barossa.

A subset of the emerging category is the U.S.-driven "emerging" wine scene which are "pseudo-cult" wines – generally Shirazes and usually cult wannabes.

New wines seem to appear out of the woodwork too often these days – usually with a string of endorsements from *Wine Spectator* or Robert Parker Jr. These pseudo-cult wines – especially made for the wonderment of influential American wine critics – further confuse and blur the market. Enthusiasm for these wines is usually based on one vintage. The marketer's cranked-up hyperbole will turn fragments of positive sentiment into vainglorious spin.

The sheer level of consumer enthusiasm and the unquestioning acceptance of 'endorsed' Australian Shiraz is a feature of the primary market and secondary market. A single vintage, however, does not equate to a wine track record, although it's a good start.

Non-U.S. wine commentators sometimes deride the enthusiasms of critic-led American and Asian markets. However, it should be pointed out, these markets can buy wine from other countries. They don't have to buy Australian wine. Indeed their participation challenges established ideas and entrenched viewpoints. While the order of things may change in the future, their support of ultra-fine Australian wine has been crucial. It has brought excitement, opportunity, and plenty of soul searching. This enthusiasm has also created impetus in the ultra-premium European markets.

It's likely, over the next 10 years, that more emerging wines will derive from single vineyards. The concept of regional definition will refine its focus into issues of sub-regional definition and vineyard character. This will have a massive impact on vineyard valuations, which in turn, could see values of ultra-fine Australian wine increase. The Barossa is a good example. Winemakers now frequently speak of the differences between northern, central, and southern Barossa Shirazes. A fledgling Margaret River movement also attempts to define sub-regional characters. Even Coonawarra winemakers see north/south differences.

As Australia churns out more and more commercial and brand oriented wines, an understanding of sub-regional and vineyard differences will become a market imperative – especially for smaller producers.

The ultra fine wine scene is in constant flux. Wines that reek of potential today, may fall by the wayside tomorrow. It has happened before, especially when smaller wineries are taken over and accountants start making the wine.

Time will ultimately sort the wheat from the chaff. Wines we've never heard of will find their place, as the ultra-fine Australian wine market evolves and expands internationally.

## EMERGING WINES

**Bannockburn SRH Chardonnay, Geelong**
Rarely seen at auction. Highly valued by collectors.

**Bannockburn Serre Pinot Noir, Geelong**
Hardly seen at auction. Highly valued by collectors.

**Balnaves Reserve Cabernet, Coonawarra**
Peter Bissell's skilful winemaking is instrumental in reshaping the fortunes of Coonawarra Cabernet Sauvignon and helping to lead Coonawarra back into secondary market relevance Relatively new Reserve label. Could perform well in the future.

**Balnaves Cabernet Sauvignon, Coonawarra**
Wine with superb regional definition.

**Bailey's 1920 Block Shiraz, Glenrowan**
More traditional style based on very old vine material. Likely to be pulled up by the market.

**Bailey's 1904 Block Shiraz, Glenrowan**
More traditional style based on very old vine material. Likely to be pulled up by the market.

**Bass Phillip Reserve Pinot Noir, Gippsland**
So rare but just so fine. All too academic – the most profoundly interesting Australian Pinot Noir.

**Best's Thomson Family Shiraz, Grampians**
A dark horse cantering, on the back of strong regional provenance, into the secondary wine market. Superb old vine material. Wonderful family history. Strong market presence. Extraordinary recent interest driven by superb quality.
**Bethany GR Reserve Shiraz, Barossa Valley**
Super wines – produced in better vintages - showing strong regional provenance.
**Bindi 'Block 5' Pinot Noir, Macedon Ranges**
From a relatively new producer with a strong sense of place and a commitment for making something different and unique in the pantheon of Australian Pinot Noir.
**Bindi 'Original Vineyard' Pinot Noir, Macedon Ranges**
Parker gave the 1998 vintage 95 points, catapulting this wine to success on the market.
**Brand's 'Stentiford's Reserve Shiraz, Coonawarra**
A leading secondary market producer in the early 1980s, this wine could do well as Coonawarra redefines itself.
**Branson 'Coach House' Shiraz, Barossa Valley**
A 'Parker wine'. Minimal market presence at this stage.
**Cape d'Estaing Shiraz, Kangaroo Island**
A 'Parker wine'. Minimal market presence at this stage.
**Charles Cimicky 'Signature' Shiraz, Barossa Valley**
Seasoned producer making classic Barossa Shiraz.
**Clarendon Hills 'Liandra' Shiraz, McLaren Vale**
Not much market presence at the moment, but impressive, particularly in a classic vintage.
**Clonakilla Shiraz Viognier, Canberra District**
Highly regarded at home and abroad. The great red hope of New South Wales, breaking through that state's glass ceiling to show that inherent quality and strong regional potential can ultimately win the hearts and minds of the fine wine consumer. Commanding strengthening interest and prices.
**d'Arenberg 'The Dead Arm' Shiraz, McLaren Vale**
Sprang onto the market with ease some years ago through wonderful vineyard resources, outstanding winemaking, and clever marketing.
**d'Arenberg 'Ironstone Pressings' Grenache-Shiraz-Mourvedre, McLaren Vale**
Well regarded wine – its success linked to fortunes of *The Dead Arm*.
**Dalwhinnie 'Eagle' Shiraz, Pyrenees**
A *tete de cuvee* Shiraz that has attracted growing support.
**De Bortoli 'Melba Vineyard' Cabernet Sauvignon-Shiraz-Cabernet Franc-Merlot, Yarra Valley**
Impressive wine. Could well become a classic.
**Devil's Lair Chardonnay, Margaret River**
Southcorp producer and member of the Great Wine Estates

of Western Australia. One of the top Chardonnays coming out of Margaret River.

**Devil's Lair Cabernet Sauvignon, Margaret River**
Southcorp producer. Member of the Great Wine Estates of Western Australia. Quality wine with plenty of potential.

**Diamond Valley 'Close Planted' Pinot Noir, Yarra Valley**
One of the top Pinot Noirs in the country.

**Dutschke 'Oscar Semmler' Shiraz, Barossa Valley**
Very impressive new Barossa producer making rich classic Barossa Shiraz. Very stylish and beautifully made. Based on older vine material and craftsman-like winemaking. Unknown on the secondary market but with all the class required for entry.

**Dutschke 'St Jakobi Shiraz', Barossa Valley**
Very impressive new Barossa producer making rich classic Barossa Shiraz.

**Freycinet Pinot Noir, East Coast Tasmania**
Highly regarded Tasmanian Pinot Noir producer.

**Fox Creek 'Reserve' Shiraz, McLaren Vale**
Lovely wines boosted immensely by Robert Parker Jr. Already had some form of presence on the market. The style is in evolution but is a serious McLaren Vale contender.

**Glaetzer Shiraz, Barossa Valley**
A wine with superb credentials. Colin Glaetzer, the creator of *E&E Black Pepper Shiraz*, knows the veins along the back of the Barossa's hand. Watch this space.

**Grant Burge 'Meshach' Shiraz, Barossa Valley**
One of the largest vineyard holder in the Barossa with some extraordinary resources. The best fruit, the best oak, and plenty of love and care, behind this label. Has done well on the secondary market although prices have been erratic in more recent years. Strong regional provenance. When released commanded quite a lot of hype. Plenty of potential.

**Greenock Creek 'Seven Acre Block' Shiraz, Barossa Valley**
Extraordinary interest led by Robert Parker and the rolling stone interest in Australian Shiraz.

**Greenock Creek 'Creek Block' Shiraz, Barossa Valley**
Lovely wines swept along by the gushing enthusiasms of Robert Parker Jr.

**Greenock Creek 'Apricot Block' Shiraz, Barossa Valley**
Extraordinary interest led by Robert Parker and the rolling stone interest in Australian Shiraz.

**Hanging Rock Shiraz, Heathcote**
Heathcote is an important emerging wine region. Hanging Rock, around for a while now, has attracted interest.

**Henry's Drive Reserve Shiraz, Padthaway**
Barely known on the Australian market, this wine was

discovered by Robert Parker Jr. Has no real track record on the secondary market.

**Henschke Abbott's Prayer Merlot-Cabernet Sauvignon, Eden Valley**

The antithesis of *Hill of Grace*. This wine is elegantly proportioned with superb fruit definition, supple tannin structure and flavour length. A first class wine. Impressive beginnings on the secondary market, however in more recent times, it has been shaded by the prevailing hysteria for Shiraz. It retains a very solid good following.

**Houghton 'Jack Mann' Cabernet-Shiraz-Malbec, Great Southern**

A regular trophy winner on the Australian wine show circuit. A very solid local secondary market performer

**Hollicks 'Ravenswood' Cabernet Sauvignon, Coonawarra**

Sits on the outside of the secondary market paradigm but, as Coonawarra becomes fashionable once again, has all the bone fides to do well. A brilliantly seductive wine loaded with fruit but balanced beautifully with oak. One of the wines that is redefining Coonawarra.

**Jim Barry 'McCrae Wood' Shiraz, Clare Valley**

A Clare Valley Shiraz that is emerging as an auction staple.

**Katnook Estate 'Odyssey' Cabernet Sauvignon, Coonawarra**

Lovely wines with strengthening domestic following. Katnook is making some of the best Cabernet in the country, combining excellent vineyard resources and intuitive wine-making with business acumen. The *Odyssey* is only a notch up from the brilliant Katnook *Cabernet Sauvignon*, but sits comfortably in the firmament of ultra-fine Australian wine.

**Katnook 'Prodigy' Shiraz, Coonawarra**

A top notch Coonawarra Shiraz that has plenty of potential.

**Kays Amery Block 6 Shiraz, McLaren Vale**

A long term producer of classic McLaren Vale Shiraz – unrecognised until put under the spell of Robert Parker Jr.

**Killibinbin Shiraz, Langhorne Creek**

An emerging producer.

**Leasingham Classic Clare Shiraz, Clare Valley**

Classic Clare Valley Shiraz. Emerging as an auction staple.

**Lengs and Cooter 'Reserve' Shiraz, Clare Valley**

Emerging. Another anointment from Robert Parker Jr. The 1998 vintage scored 96 points.

**Maglieri Steve Maglieri Shiraz, McLaren Vale**

Has achieved secondary market presence but is unlikely to move beyond a modest auction staple.

**Main Ridge Pinot Noir, Mornington Peninsula**

Fastidious maker of very high quality wine.

**Majella 'Mallaea' Shiraz Cabernet, Coonawarra**
A producer with strong regional provenance, a very fine intuitive winemaker, and wonderful fruit resources. Absolute blue chip in the making.

**Majella Cabernet Sauvignon, Coonawarra**
As above, and an example of how generosity of spirit and a sense of place combine to make something extremely special. Bruce Gregory is a remarkable winemaker.

**Maxwell 'Lime Cave' Cabernet Sauvignon, McLaren Vale**
Barely known on the Australian market, this wine was discovered by Robert Parker Jr. Has no real track record on the secondary market.

**McWilliams Lovedale Semillon, Lower Hunter Valley**
Sits on the very edge of the secondary wine investment scene. Best described as very good old fashioned wines with only modest potential. Good vintages of *Lovedale Semillon* – simply the best expression of Hunter Valley – can spark enthusiasm. Admired rather than followed.

**Charles Melton Shiraz, Barossa**
A wine with impeccable quality and market credentials.

**Mitchell 'Peppertree' Shiraz, Clare Valley**
A producer around for a very long time, making super wines at relatively inexpensive prices. The *Peppertree Shiraz* is an excellent expression of Clare Shiraz.

**Mitchell Riesling, Clare Valley**
Clare Riesling at its very best. While Grosset is king – this is a worthy consort – especially when you consider the release price.

**Mitchelton 'Print Label' Shiraz, Goulburn Valley**
An utterly beautiful wine that has somehow been missed by the punters. For sheer quality, it's breathtaking.

**Noon 'Solaire' Reserve Grenache McLaren Vale**
Speculative but high quality stock frenzied by Robert Parker's pronouncements.

**Noon 'Eclipse' Grenache-Shiraz, McLaren Vale**
An example of credit given where it is due. Robert Parker Jr turned this tiny struggling producer into a superstar.

**Paringa Estate Pinot Noir, Mornington Peninsula**
Small producer in the Mornington Peninsula setting the standard for Shiraz. Very vintage dependent, but very good.

**Parker Coonawarra Estate 'First Growth' Cabernets, Coonawarra**
Narrowly missed inclusion in *Langton's Classification* due to the number of vintages released. This wine has led Coonawarra out of the wilderness with a strong regionally defined wine with all the class of a First Growth.

**Penley Estate Cabernet Sauvignon, Coonawarra**

One of Robert Parker Jr's favourite producers. Plenty of love and attention given to this wine. Strong regional provenance. Established by Kim Tolley, a scion of the Penfold clan. In recent years has been seen as one of the wines bringing Coonawarra back into focus as a wonderful producer of Cabernet Sauvignon.

**Peppertree Reserve Cabernet, Coonawarra**
Has attracted considerable attention, including winning the Jimmy Watson Trophy – but is yet to transpire into something solid on the secondary market.

**Peppertree Reserve Merlot, Coonawarra**
Has attracted considerable attention but is yet to transpire into something solid on the secondary market.

**Penfolds RWT Shiraz, Barossa Valley**
A new Barossa Shiraz. Excellent producer and regional provenance.

**Pierro Cabernets, Margaret River**
Strong regional provenance with vineyards adjacent to Moss Wood.

**Peter Lehmann 'Eight Songs' Shiraz, Barossa Valley**
A producer with some of the best resources in the Barossa. Definitive Barossa Shiraz with fabulous packaging.

**Penfolds 'Yattarna' Chardonnay, South Australia**
Swings considerably in the market. Hailed as white *Grange* but does not appear to have the keeping power. May improve in years to come.

**Randall's Hill Shiraz 1910, Barossa Valley**
Not really an emerging wine – rather a pseudo cult wine – essentially de-classified *Three Rivers Shiraz*. Absolutely minuscule production and only produced in lesser Barossa Vintages. Followed however by Chris Ringland devotees.

**Reynell Basket Pressed Shiraz, McLaren Vale**
An old Australian wine family name, now owned by BRL Hardy. Classic Shiraz that is emerging as an auction staple rather than a meteoric performer.

**Rockford Black Shiraz, Barossa**
Fabulous old-fashioned sparkling Shiraz style. Disgorgement dated rather than vintage. Small but strong following.

**Rockford Single Vineyard Series including Flaxman Valley Shiraz, Hoffman Shiraz and Moorooroo Shiraz, Barossa Valley**
Reputation, provenance, and limited production will drive these wines forward on the market.

**Rosemount 'Balmoral' Shiraz, McLaren Vale**
A very well regarded and beautifully made wine with presently erratic secondary market interest.

**Rosemount 'Mountain Blue' Cabernet-Shiraz, Mudgee**
While the highly respected and established Huntington Estate

missed out on the secondary market, Rosemount, a relatively new entrant to the Mudgee scene, has shown that it is possible to make a wine with strong secondary market credibility.

**Saltram No 1. Shiraz, Barossa Valley**

Excellent regional provenance but rather shrouded in corporate grey.

**Stoniers Reserve Pinot Noir, Mornington Peninsula**

A leading producer of this variety. Moderate and medium term potential.

**Summerfield Reserve Shiraz, Pyrenees**

A bit of a market secret. Strong regional provenance and quality wine making could see this wine emerge.

**Tahbilk Reserve Shiraz 1933 Vines, Nagambie Lakes**

Dark horse wine with superb class. Incredibly strong regional provenance and made for long term cellaring.

**The Mcalister Cabernet-Cabernet Franc-Merlot, Gippsland**

A bit of an enigma to the market in general, but with a crowd of strong devotees nevertheless. Rarity value alone gives this wine plenty of potential.

**Tarrawarra Pinot Noir, Yarra Valley**

A no-expenses spared operation that has been focusing on Pinot Noir for some time.

**Tim Adams 'Aberfeldy' Shiraz, Clare Valley**

Outstanding vineyard resources, considerable winemaking flair, and consistency of quality are behind this strongly focused regional Shiraz.

**T'Gallant 'Tribute' Pinot Gris, Mornington Peninsula**

Definitely not an investment wine, but a celebration of the increasing diversity of Australian wine. Probably has limited secondary market potential, but the quality is superb.

**Torbreck ' The Steading', Grenache-Mataro-Shiraz, Barossa Valley**

Modestly valued in this company, the wine is eagerly sought by those who are keen to find out what Torbreck is all about.

**Torbreck Descendant Shiraz-Viognier and The Factor Shiraz, Barossa Valley**

Torbreck is the most exciting new winery to emerge from the Barossa. While its *Run Rig* enjoys a cultish status, the *Factor* and the *Descendant* are wines that combine strong regional provenance with highly intuitive and clever wine making. Immensely seductive and brilliantly conceived, these wines are highly individual, yet have all the hallmarks of strong regional style.

**Turkey Flat Shiraz, Barossa Valley**

A Barossa producer with strong regional provenance

**Vasse Felix 'Heytesbury' Cabernet Sauvignon, Margaret River**

Starting to attract a stable following. Impeccable bone-fides.

**Vasse Felix Shiraz, Margaret River**

Probably the most convincing of Margaret River Shirazes. Excellent fruit definition and chocolaty tannin structures.

**Voyager Estate Chardonnay, Margaret River**

One of the best Chardonnays coming out of Margaret River.

**Wild Duck Creek Spring Flat Shiraz, Heathcote**

Heathcote producer known for its *Duck Muck Shiraz*. This is probably a better wine.

**Yalumba 'The Octavius' Shiraz, Barossa Valley**

Limited release, based on outstanding vineyard resources in Eden Valley and Barossa floor and matured in octaves. Super wine. One of the emerging Barossa Shirazes. Plenty of potential here.

**Yalumba 'The Virgilius' Viognier, Barossa Valley**

Yalumba has pioneered this grape variety very successfully. A wonderful wine style, but with limited secondary market potential.

**Yering Station Reserve Cabernet Sauvignon, and Reserve Pinot Noir, Yarra Valley**

Probably the most exciting wines to come out of the Yarra Valley since Mount Mary, Yeringberg, and Yarra Yering.

**Zema Estate Family Selection Cabernet Sauvignon, Coonawarra**

A wine producer with excellent regional provenance and a very fine reputation. Very good market credentials.

*Clearly, the market has an emphasis on red wine. Some few white wines perform well. Sparkling wines are yet to make an impact, with the occasional exception of a specific vintage, or in the case of a highly-prized sparkling shiraz.*

*Fortified wines in the form of non-vintage tawny ports, muscats, and tokays are ludicrously under-valued at auction, but have no real future until they are vintage-dated. Even vintage-dated fortified wines have come off the boil, except for a number of classics. These are virtually exclusive to Chateau Reynella, Hardy's, and Penfolds.*

*Although the secondary market has thrived in recent years, there are still bargains to be found and undiscovered wines to be enjoyed. The beaten track is well worn, but just off it are some excellent wines. From an investment point of view however, going bush is risky, as always.*

## LANGTON'S CLASSIFICATION OF DISTINGUISHED AUSTRALIAN WINE

**Exceptional:** The most highly sought and prized Australian wines on the market.

**Outstanding:** Super-seconds of the Australian wine market. Benchmark quality wines with a strong market following.

**Excellent:** High-performing wines of exquisite quality, achieving slightly lower values and market strength.

**Distinguished:** Secondary market staples or emerging classics. Sometimes under-valued by the market.

## MARKET STRENGTH

**Strong** – Strong volume of interest.

**Moderate** – Consistent, moderate volume of interest.

**Weak** – Weak volume of interest.

## EXPLANATION OF TERMS

**Ullage:** Loss of wine from a bottle by reason of leakage or evaporation. Ullage levels are described as follows:

*Into neck:* Close to original fill level. Perfectly good for wine of any age. Outstanding for wine aged 10 years or more.

*Very high shoulder:* Quite acceptable level in any wine over 15 years old, expecially if there are no signs of leakage.

*High shoulder:* The limit of acceptability. Both the Penfolds Wine Clinics and the Henschke Quality Assurance Program show a high proportion of wine in good condition, despite this level of ullage. The warmer the climate in which the wine has been stored, the greater the risk of damage.

*Mid-high shoulder:* Purchasers should inspect the wine or obtain a condition report in order to assess the risk of further ullage.

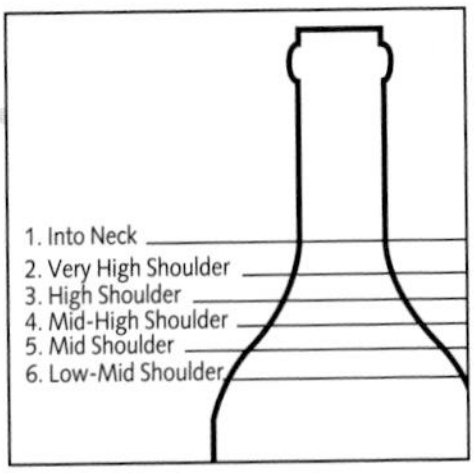

1. Into Neck
2. Very High Shoulder
3. High Shoulder
4. Mid-High Shoulder
5. Mid Shoulder
6. Low-Mid Shoulder

*Mid-shoulder:* In important wines from older vintages, these bottles can be attractive as curios in a collector's cellars. Otherwise avoid.

**Original Timber Case:** Some wines are packed in timber cases, e.g. Penfolds *Grange* (since 1987), Jim Barry's *The Armagh*, Penfolds *Grange* magnums, Howard Park. These lots are very attractive to collectors. In the current market, a timber case can value-add up to 10 per cent to the lot.

**Cellar-Damaged Label:** Labels soiled by dust and dirt, or marked by racking wires, humidity or water. Can be an indication of poor cellaring conditions. Langton's policy is to cull wines that are clearly in bad condition.

**Penfolds Wine Clinics:** Penfolds wines, 15 years and older, may be assessed, topped up, re-corked, and re-capsuled at biennial Wine Clinics held in state capitals. Bottles in acceptable condition are given labels signed by a Penfolds winemaker, certifying the wine has been topped up and re-corked under proper supervision. Langton's will not sell wine if it fails to meet Clinic standards. For all but the most rare vintages, the market for re-corked bottles is no different from the market for those with original corks.

**Henschke Quality Assurance Program:** Similar to the Penfolds clinics above – an in-house re-corking program for older Henschke red wines. But with a different market response. Re-corked bottles of *Hill of Grace* 1972, 1973, 1975, and 1976 do not fetch the values that more recent vintages do. Why? Because the *Hill of Grace* phenomenon begins from 1978, when Stephen and Prue Henschke took over the family winery.

## BOTTLE DESCRIPTIONS

| | | |
|---|---|---|
| **HB** | Half bottle | 375ml |
| **B** | Bottle | 750ml (standard bottle) |
| **M** | Magnum | 1,500ml or 1.5 litres |
| **DM** | Double magnum | 3000ml or 3 litres |
| **J** | Jeroboam | 3,000ml or 3 litres (sparkling wine bottle format) |
| **J** | Jeroboam | 4,500ml or 4.5 litres (Bordeaux wine bottle format) |
| **I** | Imperial | 6,000ml or 6 litres |
| **MET** | Methuselah | 6,000ml or 6 litres (sparkling wine bottle format) |

# WINE REGIONS

*Regional definition or Regionality is inextricably linked to the development of the Australian Fine Wine Industry. With the exception of notable multi-regional wines such as* Penfolds Grange *and* Howard Park Cabernet Merlot, *most established and emerging ultra-fine wines are linked to either a single vineyard or single region.*

*The reputation of region has a major impact on the efficacy of emerging wine brands and substantially underpins the credibility of established wines. For instance Barossa Shiraz and Margaret River Cabernet Sauvignon are considered classic Australian regional wines. It is more likely for a new Barossa Shiraz label to make an impact on the market – than say an Orange Merlot.*

## WESTERN AUSTRALIA

### Margaret River, W.A.

*Warm maritime climate/Elevation about 90 metres*

A report published by John Gladstones in 1965, found that this area's warm, maritime climate was similar to Pomerol or St Emilion, with low frost risk, plenty of sunshine and equable temperatures within the growing season, promoting even ripening. Serious vineyard development began in the late 1960s. Essentially the soils derive from granitic and gneissic rock over which laterite has formed. The region can be divided in three sub-regions: the cooler south between Yallingup and Karridale with predominantly lateritic gravelly loamy sands and sandy loams; the warm and sunnier Willyabrup in the centre with predominantly gravelly loams, but some gritty sandy loams and granitic gravels; and Margaret River in the north with similar soils, but slightly cooler temperatures. This is entirely consistent with style – wines from Willyabrup being more generous than the highly structured wines of the north and the elegant styles of the south. The region is also subject to southeast trade winds.

The Bordeaux grape varieties have thrived, particularly Cabernet Sauvignon and Merlot. Although Chardonnay has problems with fruit set, the wines are generally outstanding. Vintage takes place between the end of February and mid-April. The region has established an astonishing reputation in 30 years, illustrating a consistency in quality and a strongly focused winemaking culture.

- *Shiraz*

Margaret River, better known for its Cabernet Sauvignon, makes some very approachable, but structured, Shiraz styles. These are elegantly proportioned and medium concentrated wines with intense spice, black cherry, cinnamon and raspberry aromatics, textured ripe tannins and plenty of length.

- *Cabernet Sauvignon*

These wines are less opulent, but more structured than Coonawarra's. Cedar and cassis aromas, wonderful purity of fruit, pronounced, yet fine, gripping tannins and acidity, and superb length, are all hallmarks of high-quality producers. Cape Mentelle, with its 1982 and 1983 Jimmy Watson Trophy-winning Cabernets, put the region on the map. Xanadu, Moss Wood, Cullen, Leeuwin Estate and Vasse Felix are making some great wine. Unlike Coonawarra, with its range of Cabernet styles, Margaret River producers seem to have reached consensus on what Margaret River Cabernet Sauvignon should be. The wines are rarely over-oaked, often restrained, and the idea that a particular vineyard site brings uniqueness to the wine is enthusiastically embraced. There is a strong belief that Cabernet from the northern area around Cowaramup shows slightly riper expressions than that from other areas. Cabernets from the south have more sinewy structures.

- *Chardonnay*

Despite the curses of 'poor set' by the viticulturists, Chardonnay has a huge following here. Leeuwin Estate leads the way with the benchmark *Art Series Chardonnay*. Its classical tropical fruit, limey and melon-like aromas, hints of cashew nut, new oak and creamy, tropical fruit flavours combined with searing natural acidity, tightly-knit structure and overall persistence, have given the wine an enviable reputation. Pierro is making equally seductive, although slightly more alcoholic, Chardonnay. Cullen is outstanding, but is more restrained, and Cape Mentelle has made some beautifully defined examples in recent years. The 1995 and 1997 Leeuwin Estate *Art Series Chardonnays* have consolidated Leeuwin's position at the very top of Australia's Chardonnay tree.

**Pemberton, W.A.**

*Cool climate/Elevation 170 metres*

Pemberton is a pioneering wine region with apparently great potential, located in the southwest of Western Australia in the heart of karri forest country, where the deep red loams and high rainfall give rise to Western Australia's tallest, most majestic forest. The first grapes were planted in 1977, with commercial plantings expanding throughout the 1980s. The climate here is markedly cooler and slightly wetter than the Margaret River growing season. The region experiences slightly fewer sunshine hours, although it is also maritime influenced. Soils are typically brown loams derived from gneissic rock. The terrain is quite undulating with stands of karri. This region is unproven, although Pinot Noir is particularly promising. It is also well suited to the production of refined Bordeaux style wines.

- *Pinot Noir*

Pemberton Pinot Noir is another example of an emerging wine style. Many believe this could be something quite special, although it is far too early to pin down regional characteristics. Many show classic cherry strawberry aromas and silky palate structure. Others can show some stalky or vegetal characters.

### Great Southern (Albany, Mt. Barker, Frankland River), W.A.

*Cool climate/Elevation 60–250 metres*

The underbelly of southwest Western Australia, known as the Lower Great Southern, is Western Australia's coolest wine-growing region. The Department of Agriculture planted the first experimental vineyard in the late 1960s at Forrest Hill. Successful trials encouraged Tony Smith of Plantagenet Wines to plant the first commercial vineyard of Cabernet Sauvignon and Shiraz in 1968. In the south around Denmark, the climate is maritime influenced becoming more continental inland. The result is quite a variation of temperatures in the growing season particularly around Mount Barker and Frankland River. Inland vineyards are generally located on higher elevations above the salty water table. Rainfall becomes increasingly unreliable towards the northern edge and frost risk increases. The soil types are derived from granitic and gneissic rock, mostly laterite gravelly loams or sandy loams.

The overall ripening season is similar to the Medoc. It is therefore no surprise that Cabernet Sauvignon, and even Merlot, do particularly well, especially around Mount Barker and Porongurup. Frankland River has a strong reputation for its Riesling, more on account of low vigour and moderate ripening conditions. Rainfall is significantly higher around Denmark, although southeast trade winds during the summer reduce susceptibility to fungal disease. This district is particularly suitable to Chardonnay.

- *Cabernet Sauvignon*

Plantagenet at Mount Barker (one of Australia's first subregions) is leading the way with this variety, with its strong cassis-like aromas and fruit-sweet, but well-structured, palate. Howard Park is probably the most exciting winery, although its philosophy is similar to Penfolds – the Cabernets have a major Lower Great Southern component, but also contain fruit from all over W.A. It is a brilliant wine, with extraordinary fruit definition and depth.

- *Shiraz*

Shiraz is a promising variety from this region, although it is difficult to define. Plantagenet is yet again a promising producer with its elegant, but well focused, style. These wines show plenty of white pepper, red berries and forest floor nuances developing richness over time. Howard Park *Scotsdale Vineyard Shiraz* is an impressive newcomer.

## SOUTH AUSTRALIA

### Clare Valley, S.A.

*Warm to hot climate/Elevation 400-500 metres*

John Horrocks was the first settler in the region and encouraged his servant James Green to plant the first vines in 1842 at Penwortham. Edward Gleeson founded Clare in the 1840s and also planted the Inchiquin vineyards. The development of Clare, however, was uneven. When the Broken Hill Proprietary Company Limited was established at Broken Hill in 1885, Clare became a major transit centre for supplies. By 1897, the region had over 580 hectares of vines in production. The climatic data suggests that Clare is essentially continental with hot summers and cool/cold winters. However, the vineyards are mostly located at higher elevations than the weather stations. For instance, Petaluma's Hanlin Hill is at about 500m. During the growing season moderating cool breezes funnel up the Clare's corrugation of hills and gullies from the south. The soils are red brown, chocolaty loams over shale allowing excellent drainage. Although snow is rare, the chill factor is something to behold.

Some of the older vines are planted in the valley floor, originally to take advantage of the deep water holding capacity of the soils, as rainfall is relatively low. With the advantages of supplementary irrigation, many of the best vineyard sites are located on higher elevations or towards the south of the valley. Polish Hill and Watervale are important sub-regions. The Clare Valley has become particularly famous for its fruit-pure Rieslings and tightly-knit Shirazes. Cabernet Sauvignon also performs quite well.

- *Shiraz*

Clare Valley Shiraz is rarely as opulent as Barossa Shiraz: concentrated, yes, but with spicier, cracked pepper and anise aromas over ripe, prune-like fruit and a slightly more structured palate with angular tannins. Jim Barry's *The Armagh* is a rare beast making intensity, immensity and density a seamless combination. *Wendouree Shiraz* is particularly idiosyncratic with its iron-fisted tannins.

Leasingham is making very impressive wine – witness its gobsmacking 1994 *Classic Clare Shiraz* – yet this label is under-valued, considering its quality. Tim Adams (especially *The Aberfeldy*) and Mitchell are also very impressive producers who are yet to make their run.

- *Riesling*

After Hunter Valley Semillon, this is one of the most recognisable wines of Australia, which makes the Clare Valley one of the classic wine regions of the world. Indeed, these wines are often thrown into a Master of Wine tasting exam. When young they have a very strong lime/citrus/floral aroma, moderate to high alcohol, incredible fruit purity and an indelible, minerally acid cut. They are devastatingly thirst-quenching. Over time they develop toast-and-honey characters, with the palate fleshing out and becoming a little oily. There is strong evidence to suggest that there are differences between *Watervale* and *Polish Hill*, the latter showing more intensity and definition. The best performers in the secondary market are Grosset and Petaluma. Mitchell, Wilson Vineyard and Mount Horrocks are well regarded but have yet to impress investors. Old Leo Burings are fabulous wines; 1975 *DWE 17* was brilliant, but the bin numbering system is difficult to understand. Orlando's Richmond Grove label hosts some great Clare Valley Riesling, but is yet to develop brand definition. It is interesting to note that many Clare Valley producers are now embracing the use of 'Stelvin' closures as an alternative to cork.

**Barossa Valley, S.A.**

*Warm climate/Elevation 270 metres*

Colonel William Light, the South Australian colony's Surveyor-General, named the Barossa in 1837 after the site of an English victory over the French in the Spanish Peninsular War. Silesian and English immigrants in the mid-1800s settled it. Wherever you go in the Barossa Valley, you can find the Germanic influence in the architecture, the name of its communities and leading families in the district. The region incorporates the whole gamut of the wine dream, from the micro to macro-winery. The Barossa comprises two distinct sub-regions: Eden Valley and the warmer Barossa Valley floor at 270m. The Barossa Valley is comprised of rich brown soils and alluvial sands. Cool sea breezes from the Gulf of St Vincent and elevation modify temperatures. However, hot northerly winds can occasionally dominate creating considerable vine stress. The region is also known for its relatively low rainfall. Many of the vineyards are dry-grown on single wire trellising. Supplementary irrigation is also used extensively. The Barossa is famous for its Shiraz-based wines, but can also make some beautifully rich and chocolaty Cabernet Sauvignons. Semillon and Chardonnays are generally more commercial propositions on the Barossa floor.

- *Shiraz*

Often combined with American oak, seasoned and coopered in Australia, classic Barossa Shiraz has complex, opulent aromas of plums, licorice, chocolate and vanillin, a palate packed with fruit sweetness, massive concentration, ripe tannins and exceptional length. The wines age beautifully. Mature Barossa Shiraz can often show a meaty, chocolate and fruit cake-like bouquet and spectacular richness on the palate. Penfolds is a shining light. *Grange* is almost entirely a Barossa wine these days with 1983, 1986, 1990, 1991, 1996, and 1998 the best recent vintages. There is increasing recognition of the difference between the more tightly-knit Eden Valley Shiraz style and the looser-knit Barossa Valley floor style – an exciting development – but further complicated by the increasing acceptance of sub-regional variation on the floor itself! The wines to the north are more perfumed with mulberry fruit characters and slinky tannins. The wines get heavier and more chocolaty towards the south. Peter Lehmann *Stonewell Shiraz* and Yalumba *Octavius* are impressive wines. Rockford *Basket Press Shiraz*, St Hallett *Old Block* and Charles Melton are all making highly individual, but classic, Barossa Shiraz. The lesser known Three Rivers, Greenock Creek, and Torbreck, are so-called 'tin shack' producers who have wowed the American market with their extraordinarily opulent fruit definition and relatively high alcohol levels. Barossa Shiraz is becoming excitingly more diverse and interesting. Really, the sky is the limit.

### Eden Valley, S.A.

*Cool climate/Elevation 450 metres*

Eden Valley is the cooler and elevated sub-region of the Barossa (a part of the Mount Lofty Ranges) averaging 450m and is situated in the Barossa Range to the east, overlooking the Barossa Valley. Together, these valleys comprise what is today known as the Barossa zone. Slope, aspect and particularly a degree of protection from wind are as important as is the correct match of site and variety. It produces a range of excellent wines because the topography is so varied and the climate neatly balanced. The soils in the Eden Valley are derived from schistic and sedimentary rock. They are mostly red clay soils and sandy, silty loams interspersed with schistic gravels. This region is widely known for its Shiraz and Riesling. The high altitude and cool climate of the region produces wines with great complexity and capacity for long-term cellaring. Eden Valley is also emerging as an important area for Cabernet Sauvignon and Merlot. The spread of vineyards is limited by water availability.

- *Riesling*

This area is given classic status almost entirely on the basis of many high-quality Leo Buring Rieslings. Henschke also makes a very fine wine – now called *Julius* – and Penfolds has attracted attention with its new *Eden Valley Reserve Riesling*. They are all very similar to Clare Rieslings, though perhaps not quite as fine or spectacular. A recent release of 1984 *Seppelt Eden Valley Riesling* is wonderfully pure and intense, showing that extraordinarily good wines can be made. The new Grosset/Yalumba joint venture wine – *Mesh* – based on two specific Riesling vineyards, will no doubt thrust this region further into the limelight.

- *Shiraz*

The iconic Henschke *Hill of Grace* and Henschke *Mount Edelstone* are classic examples of Eden Valley Shiraz or, rather, what the area might aspire to. These wines derive from very old contorted vines – some of the oldest in Australia. Eden Valley Shiraz (which can be labelled as Barossa Shiraz is a little tighter and cooler in flavour spectrum than the Barossa floor. They have raspberry/blackberry aromas, fine firm tannin structures, but plenty of fruit sweetness and length. Barrel fermentation and use of American oak provide further complexity. *Three Rivers Shiraz*, a wine made by Chris Ringland – and lionised by Robert Parker Jr – is technically an Eden Valley wine, but also shows how creating regional paradigms can be confusing.

**Adelaide Hills (Lenswood, Piccadilly Valley), S.A.**

*Cool climate/Elevation 450-550 metres*

The Adelaide Hills run in a north-south direction and belong to the Mount Lofty Ranges. To the north of the Adelaide Hills lies the Eden Valley and immediately to its west is Adelaide. The area was settled initially as a summer retreat from the searing hot summers of Adelaide. The pressure of urbanisation on market gardening and viticulture is palpable. The region is cool to very cool with most vineyards at an elevation of 450 to 550m (Mt Lofty rises to 700m). However the region is a jigsaw of meso-climates, the best vineyards facing north or north-east in protected positions. These seem to be centred around Piccadilly Valley and Lenswood. Rainfall is relatively high and spring frosts are a problem. The best sites appear to correlate to good orchard country, many located on steep slopes and at altitudes above 500m. This area is not immune to hot northerly winds. In 1983, the Adelaide Hills experienced terrible bush fires. The soils are derived from schistic and sedimentary rock, typically well-drained sandy loams over red clay interspersed with schistic gravels.

The region is well suited to Chardonnay and Pinot Noir with Sauvignon Blanc and Merlot showing great promise. Petaluma has done much for the reputation of this region and significant capital has been invested in the last 15 years.

- *Chardonnay*

Adelaide Hills is another emerging classic Chardonnay region. Many wines have tropical fruit and grapefruit-like aromas with complex, grilled nuts bouquet and a creamy, flavoursome palate with fine acidity. With Nepenthe, Petaluma, Penfolds, Geoff Weaver, Shaw and Smith, Tim Knappstein and Henschke all making Adelaide Hills Chardonnay, this area will become increasingly important. Indeed, it is likely that Adelaide Hills, Margaret River and the 'Melbourne Dress Circle' will soon be seen as Australia's finest Chardonnay regions. Both Petaluma (*Tiers*) and Penfolds (*Yattarna*) have released ultra-Chardonnays based on Adelaide Hills fruit. The investment market, after initial enthusiasm, has shown sluggish interest in these wines.

**McLaren Vale, S.A.**

*Warm climate/Elevation 50-200 metres*

John Reynell began a tradition of viticulture and winemaking in 1838 by planting the first vineyard at Reynella in South Australia. Thomas Hardy, who was employed briefly by John Reynell in the 1840s, bought the Tintara winery at McLaren Vale in 1876 from Dr A.C. Kelly. A quirk of fate saw Hardy's (now BRL Hardy) buy Chateau Reynella in 1982. In 1912, Joseph Osborn, a teetotaller and director of Thomas Hardy and Sons, purchased the well established Milton Vineyards in the hills just north of the townships of Gloucester and Bellevue, now just known as McLaren Vale. Climatically this region is warm and maritime with elevations of between 50m to 200m. Temperatures do vary around the region. The best sites are those protected from the prevailing afternoon southerly breezes. Rainfall is relatively low so supplementary irrigation is used, although there are many dry-grown vineyards. There are three distinctive soil types: the sandy loams of Blewitt Springs; the darker soils of McLaren Flat; and the terra rossa over limestone soils further back near Chapel Hill. McLaren Vale, sometimes called the Southern Vales, is often referred to as Australia's mid-palate because of the mid-palate richness of its Shirazes. Famous for its Shiraz, this region also makes good Cabernet Sauvignons and Chardonnays.

• *Shiraz*

The best have immense blackberry and licorice aromas, often modified a little by American oak, fleshy palates with concentrated, ripe tannins, not dissimilar to Barossa Shiraz. Coriole *Lloyd Reserve* is a beacon of quality. d'Arenberg and Chapel Hill follow slightly behind, while Clarendon Hills is re-defining McLaren Vale Shiraz with individual vineyard wines. Hardy's *Eileen Hardy Shiraz* has a proportion of McLaren Vale fruit and is making strong progress in the investment market. Rosemount *Balmoral* already impresses with its opulent fruit, American oak and ripe tannins. The tiny Noon winery is also making spectacular Shiraz and enjoys a cult following in the U.S.

**Padthaway, S.A.**

*Cool maritime climate/Elevation 50 metres*

When you reach Padthaway, about three hours' drive south of Adelaide, the land undulates and the eucalypt trees are taller. The landscape is richer and prettier. First established as a viticultural area in the 1960s, Padthaway was soon recognised as a premium, cool-climate region. Originally planted in 1968, Orlando purchased the first Padthaway vineyard in the 1980s. The vineyards are located on the shoreline of an ancient sea-bed and comprise deep, free-draining sandy loams over red brown clay and limestone-based soils. Frosts are a problem in spring and hot weather over summer can stress the vines. Padthaway is close enough to the sea to benefit from cool moderating afternoon sea breezes. Irrigation is used extensively. Although rainfall averages about 500mm, falling mostly during winter and spring, there is ample ground water.

Padthaway is becoming an important region. Pressure to increase levels of production, combined with competition for old vine material, has forced larger makers to look for new sources of very high quality fruit. Padthaway is now increasingly supplying grapes into well-known, ultra-fine house brands.

• *Shiraz*

Padthaway Shiraz – typified by Orlando *Lawson's Shiraz* – shows attractive choc-menthol characters over very bright, blackberry liquorice fruit and plenty of palate richness. The wines develop plenty of complexity over time. In recent years, Padthaway Shiraz has become a highly important component of many ultra-fine wines including Penfolds *Grange* and Hardy's *Eileen Hardy Shiraz*. This is an area to watch carefully, although it is in danger of being seen as a corporate region, much in the same way as Coonawarra was looked upon until recently.

- *Chardonnay*

It is far too early to define Padthaway Chardonnay, although it has shown its promise in the highly commercial, but extremely well made, Lindemans *Padthaway Reserve Chardonnay*. At the top end of the scale, Hardy's *Eileen Hardy Chardonnay* draws some fruit from this region.

**Coonawarra, S.A.**

*Cool climate/Elevation 60 metres*

The Coonawarra fruit colony was established 108 years ago and began a century of grape growing. Bill Redman once said "from 1890 to 1945 you can write failure across the face of Coonawarra". His family had been supplying bulk wine to Woodleys since 1920, enabling it to produce the prized *Treasure Chest* series of wine in the early 1950s. By 1951, David Wynn established Wynns Coonawarra Estate at the disused Chateau Comaum stone winery. It was the first winery in Australia to use the word 'Estate'. Coonawarra is today one of the most famous red wine regions in Australia. Its weathered limestone terra rossa soils, relatively cool climate and overall water availability make it a unique vineyard site. The region, however, is extremely flat and unprotected. Consequently, it can be exposed to the swinging influences of the cool Great Southern Ocean and hot, dry northerly winds. Spring frosts are a major problem and have been known to wipe out crops. Mechanical and machine harvesting is widely used in Coonawarra, although smaller producers prefer to tend their vines by hand.

The region is best known for its Cabernet Sauvignon, although its Shiraz can be particularly smart. There are some Coonawarra Rieslings and Chardonnays, but these don't have the same impact as the red wines of this region.

- *Cabernet Sauvignon*

Coonawarra is one of the classic Cabernet-producing regions of Australia, once described as the 'Medoc of the Southern Hemisphere' and, truly, Coonawarra Cabernet Sauvignon can be disarmingly like Bordeaux when young. The 1986 Wynns *Coonawarra Estate Cabernet Sauvignon* is an example, typically highly perfumed, with striking blackcurrant, licorice, cedary fruit characters and a beautifully structured palate with fine-grained tannins. Bowen Estate, Hollick, Katnook, Leconfield, Lindemans, Orlando St Hugo, Majella, Penley Estate, Petaluma, Rouge Homme, and Rymill all fall more or less in the same category. Since 1982 we have also had the super-concentrated, often soupy style of Wynns Coonawarra Estate *John Riddoch*. This has been described as the essence of Cabernet and investors and collectors have shown great interest in it. The 1982, 1986 and 1990 are usually successful in the market, while the 1988 has never fired. Orlando *Jacaranda Ridge* is another example of this style.

Some of Coonawarra's 'golden oldies' are the 1949-1956 Woodley *Treasure Chest* series, 1963 Mildara *'Peppermint Pattie'*, 1966 Penfolds *Bin 620* and, arguably, the 1980 Lindemans *St George*. Investors should generally avoid the 1995 vintage, although the 1995 Petaluma *Coonawarrra* transcends the vintage record. Recently Coonawarra has experienced four outstanding or above average vintages in a row – 1998, 1999, 2000, and 2001. This gift of nature has given the ammunition this region needs to bring back focus to its wonderful Cabernets.

- *Shiraz*

Wynns Coonawarra Estate *Michael* is the alter ego of *John Riddoch*, a richly concentrated wine with pronounced spicy, blackberry and licorice aromas and substantial oak. Investor confidence in this style has waned over the last few years as buyers seek greater regional definition. Most other Coonawarra Shirazes are more elegant and refined. Bowen Estate, Zema Estate and Majella are examples. They can be mistaken for Cabernets, as they often show blackcurrant-like fruit. The palate is usually the giveaway, with much riper and less-structured tannins. Interestingly, it was Shiraz that put Coonawarra on the map – the original 1955 Wynns *Michael* is one of Australia's most famous wines.

## VICTORIA

### Grampians, Vic.

*Warm climate/Elevation 240-350 metres*

The Grampians, in western Central Victoria, was settled during the gold rush of the 1850s. Indeed Seppelt at Great Western was built at the end of the gold rush when out-of-work prospectors excavated its extensive drives and cellars. The Grampians encompasses the viticultural centres of Great Western and Ararat at elevations of 240 to 350m. The region is essentially cool but has long sunshine hours and low rainfall. Supplementary irrigation is needed. The best vineyard sites are on protected, but north-east facing, slopes. Strong continentality means that spring frosts can be particularly severe. Birds can also be a problem (some vineyards use netting). Soils in the Grampians range from weathered volcanic soils to sandy and red clay loams interspersed with ironstone.

The region is particularly suited to Shiraz and, to a lesser extent, Cabernet Sauvignon. Some excellent Chardonnays are also being produced.

- *Shiraz*

In a good vintage the Grampians area, as typified by Mount Langi Ghiran and Seppelt Great Western, can produce some of the best Shirazes in the country. These are quintessential Australian cool-climate Shirazes with intense, pepper/spice aromas, fine tannins, concentration and lovely fruit purity. The wines develop a complex matrix of aromas, the best showing an earthy, gamy, peppery bouquet and beautifully rich and textured palates. These are profoundly important wines, an outstanding foil to the richer and opulent Shirazes of McLaren Vale and the Barossa.

**Pyrenees, Vic.**

*Warm climate/Elevation 350-450 metres*

The Pyrenees is located in western Central Victoria and was settled during the gold rush of the 1850s. The Australian Pyrenees, at the most southerly part of the Great Dividing Range, are located about 70km northwest of the Grampians. Many of the vineyards are planted at an altitude of around 350 to 400m on quartz and decomposed slatey soils over friable clay with easterly aspect. Rainfall is generally quite low necessitating drip irrigation. Late afternoon southerly breezes moderate temperatures during the growing season.

This region is particularly suited to Shiraz and, to a lesser extent, Cabernet Sauvignon. Some excellent Chardonnays are also being produced.

- *Shiraz*

Encompassing the Bendigo and Pyrenees districts of Victoria, these Shirazes show immense pepper-and-spice aromas and massive fruit concentration with quite finely structured tannins. They often develop meaty, gamy bouquets and silken palates. There are, however, differing styles. In the Pyrenees district, the philosophy is for more restrained, structured wines. The 1996 *Taltarni Shiraz* is quite Rhone-ish, with intense, ripe, blackberry and raspberry aromas, indelible acidity and pronounced tannins. In time, the wine will develop a quite pruney, licorice and earthy bouquet and the palate will soften out. Dalwhinnie is a similar but far more concentrated style with a strong following.

- *Cabernet Sauvignon*

Pyrenees Cabernet is an evolving style and is in some respects in the shadow of Shiraz. The *Dalwhinnie Cabernet Sauvignon* is an elegantly structured wine, with earthy, cassis-like aromas and underlying oak, ripe tannins and fruit sweetness balanced by marked acidity. Taltarni is going through a period of experimentation at all levels as it redefines its style – the fruit is being picked at riper levels of sugar and flavour, vinification is being refined and attention has now been given to oak treatment. Older vintages have been restrained and elegant with earthy tones and plenty of interesting complexity. The best is probably yet to come.

**Heathcote, Vic.**

*Warm climate/Elevation 130-300 metres*

The Heathcote wine region is located in Central Victoria about 100km north of Melbourne and 50km west of the Goulburn Valley. This is classic rolling Australian countryside punctuated by eucalypts and rounded hills. The best vineyards are located on the Heathcote red snake – a strip of Cambrian-derived soils of friable red brown gravelly loams that run in a thin north-south non-continuous direction. The region is warm with strong continentality, but enjoys an even temperature range during ripening. Vineyards are elevated at about 300m and rainfall is limited. The best vineyard sites are probably yet to be discovered, although its wines – particularly Shiraz – have already captured the imagination of a whole generation of wine drinkers.

- *Shiraz*

Jasper Hill, at Heathcote, produces a Shiraz that is concentrated and oak driven. *Georgia's Paddock* and *Emily's Paddock* are both outstanding examples. They are complex, ripe, plummy, meaty wines with abundant fruit, ripe, but pronounced, tannins and concentration. Wild Duck Creek has also become recognised for its rich opulent Shirazes. Its curiously named, but delightfully silly, *Duck Muck Shiraz* drew gushing enthusiasm from the highly influential Robert Parker Jr, making this wine one of the most expensive Australian Shirazes on the secondary market. Heathcote Shiraz is still in evolution and difficult to define. There are certainly more elegantly structured styles. However, what makes Heathcote so exciting is that it can make fabulous wines already.

**Macedon Ranges, Vic.**

*Cool Climate/Elevation 500-690 metres*

The first vines were planted in the Macedon region (also known as the Macedon Ranges) by Tom Lazar at Virgin Hills above Kyneton. The area was also pioneered by Knight's Granite Hills and Cope-Williams. The Macedon region, an hour's drive north west of Melbourne, is regarded as one of the coolest mainland wine regions, so cool that viticulture was considered a risky venture. By the early 1980s a number of enthusiasts had already debunked the theory and planted vineyards, mostly to the early ripening varieties Pinot Noir and Chardonnay. This is a region that is, for Australia, at relatively high elevation. Mount Macedon is 1000 metres high. The region is largely of volcanic origin with skeletal soils ranging from grey granitic sandy loams to weathered basalt clay. The topography is undulating, sometimes steep, with the best sites in the lee of the prevailing winds. Most of the vineyards are elevated to around 500 metres with frost risks fairly high in early spring and late autumn. Elevated at 690 metres Mount Macedon is the highest vineyard. In some colder sites vignerons use overhead sprinklers. Rainfall is around 890mm per year. Ripening is the major issue. Some early plantings of Cabernet have been grafted over to Pinot Noir.

The region has become noted for its Chardonnay, Pinot Noir, Pinot Gris and sparkling wines. Bindi, Hanging Rock and Virgin Hills are the most prominent secondary market wines although Cope-Williams, Cleveland, and Rockford are also well regarded.

- *Pinot Noir*

Macedon is quickly achieving a strong cult following for its beautifully aromatic, well- concentrated and balanced Pinot Noirs. Bindi and Rockford are leading the way. The region is yet to show a strong body of work.

- *Cabernet Sauvignon, Shiraz, Merlot and Malbec Blend*

The only Cabernet-driven wine making an impression is Virgin Hills. Its vineyard is planted on a marginal site. New ownership and a commitment to improving quality may indeed bring this wine back to its glory days. They are restrained styles with blackcurrant/cedar aromas and a compact palate structure.

**Sunbury, Vic.**

*Cool climate/Elevation 35 metres*

Sunbury is a cool region of gently undulating plains located close to greater Melbourne's north-west boundary. It leans towards continentality consequently frost risk is greater. Most vineyards are planted on the alluvial river flats, the soil essentially sand over river stones. This area was first planted in 1863, although the local industry disappeared in the late 1920s to later reappear in the 1970s. The vineyards are mostly vertically shoot positioned to increase exposure to sunlight. The growing season is relatively cool and dry compared to the Yarra Valley. Vintage takes place around mid-April/early May.

- *Shiraz*

Sunbury Shiraz, as typified by Craiglee, is a more restrained style of Shiraz with earthy raspberry notes, some white pepper nuances and fine structured/elegant palate. These wines develop richness with age. Craiglee *Sunbury Shiraz* is regarded as one of the top Shirazes in Victoria. There are other producers, but this is really a very new wine region despite its interesting early history.

**Geelong, Vic.**

*Cool maritime climate/Elevation 10-100 metres*

Geelong is located about 80km southwest of Melbourne and was initially established by Swiss immigrants in 1842. It was one of Victoria's pioneering wine districts and enjoyed considerable success during the 1860s and 1870s. The chill factor over winter is bone crunching. In spring, blustery cool winds are quite prevalent and can affect flowering and fruit set. Soils are diverse, mostly volcanic over limestone with some lesser quality black soils. Rainfall is moderate and even throughout the calendar year. Blustery weather during spring can affect ripening. By the late 1870s, phylloxera was discovered. Vignerons were told to uproot their vines by the Legislative Assembly, bringing the wine industry to a virtual halt. The area was re-established in the late 1960s. It is Bannockburn Vineyards, however, that put this region on the quality map in the mid 1980s.

As a wine region Geelong is disparate with too few standout wines to define its style. The best wines seem to be made from Pinot Noir, Chardonnay and Shiraz.

- *Pinot Noir*

The region is very cool, which is ideal for Pinot Noir. Bannockburn's Pinot Noirs are exceptional. Its tete de cuvee *Serre Pinot Noir* and classified Pinot Noirs are beacons of quality. *Scotchman's Hill* is also making an impression.

- *Chardonnay*

Bannockburn's Chardonnays are also of exceptionally high quality. Its tete de cuvee *SRH Chardonnay*, as well as its classified Chardonnay, are likewise highly prized.

**Mornington Peninsula, Vic.**

*Cool maritime climate/Elevation 1-200 metres*

Mornington Peninsula is located to Melbourne's south. The region is virtually frost-free, but is susceptible to high winds. Rainfall is moderate, even through winter and the growing season. Most of the vineyards are located between just above sea level and 200 metres. Soils range from weathered volcanic soils to sandy loams and friable well-drained clays. The Bordeaux varieties do better at altitudes below 100m, unless in particularly warm and protected sites.

Vintages can be variable but, in good years, Mornington can make some of the most sublime Pinot Noirs and Chardonnays. Cabernet Sauvignon, Merlot and Pinot Gris also show potential.

- *Chardonnay*

It is too early to recognise this region as the producer of a defined Chardonnay style. Ssome of Australia's most seductive and beautifully made Chardonnays, without question, come from around Melbourne. The Burgundian model is again often on show. The best producers make classically proportioned Chardonnay with complex, cashew nut and tropical fruit aromas and plenty of new oak vanillin. Mornington Peninsula is as unreliable as Burgundy itself, often failing to ripen fruit adequately. Chaptalisation (addition of sugar to the ferment) is not an option in Australia, so producers can struggle. The tiny Main Ridge is making some of the best Chardonnay in the country, but it is hard to get. Stonier *Reserve* is also impressive.

- *Pinot Noir*

Mornington Peninsula is probably doing more for Pinot Noir than anywhere else. In a good vintage, this region is capable of making some of the most aromatic and silky Pinot Noirs in Australia. Stoniers, Port Phillip Estate, Main Ridge, Mooruduc, Massoni, Red Hill Estate, and Paringa Estate are examples of high achievers.

**Yarra Valley, Vic.**

*Cool climate/Elevation 50-400 metres*

The Ryrie brothers, who pioneered a way through the Snowy Mountains to the Yarra Valley, planted grapes there in 1838, only three years after John Batman founded Melbourne. A wine industry, developed by Swiss settlers (particularly Hubert de Castella and Baron Guillaume de Pury) in the 1850s, thrived during the gold rush and heyday of the 19th century. In the early 1920s, Yarra Valley's wine industry died. It was kick-started again in the 1970s. The region, probably Australia's best known cool-climate area, is really a patchwork of meso-climates. The more exposed sites are subject to severe spring frosts and winds. The area has relatively high rainfall and is known for its temperature extremes during ripening. Site selection seems a major issue - the best appear to be where vines were once planted – generally on sandy clay loams and gravels. Hence Yeringberg and Yarra Yering have enjoyed apparent consistency. Mount Mary, on similar soils, has achieved an almost mythical reputation. Some vineyards, planted on more fertile red volcanic soils, however, don't seem to show the same degree of success. The topography of the Yarra Valley creates an incredible set of variables. Vineyards are planted on elevations of 50 to 400m on varying aspects and management programs.

The Yarra Valley is well known for its Cabernet Blends, but this is based on the performance of just a few producers. Pinot Noir and Chardonnay can be quite exquisite, while Shiraz is variable. Sparkling wine production has become extremely important. The Yarra Valley produces some of Australia's best.

• *Cabernet Sauvignon*

After many years of decline, if not wine death, the Yarra Valley has emerged as an important Cabernet Sauvignon producer. The idiosyncratic trio of Mount Mary, Yarra Yering, and Coldstream Hills reflects the enormous range of Cabernet style and character that this region brings. The *Yarra Yering Dry Red No. 1* style is dense and powerful, with enormous depth and balance, and needs years to come together. The 1986 vintage is now ready to drink, with a lovely meaty complexity and textured palate. The *Mount Mary Quintet* is a more restrained style with the emphasis on structure. The 1990 is brilliant, with extraordinary fruit definition, blackcurrant/cassis, cedary aromas, fine-grained tannins, concentration and length. Arguably the finest Cabernet of the entire Australian 1990 vintage. A string of good recent vintages, particularly 1998, should bring new wines into focus.

• *Pinot Noir*

Yarra Valley is emerging as a new classic region for Pinot Noir. In fact, regions dotted around Melbourne – the so-called 'Melbourne Dress Circle' – have good potential. They include Geelong and Mornington Peninsula. It is probably premature to describe Yarra Valley Pinot Noir as a classic style. Mount Mary and Yarra Yering have been making them for years and they are completely different from each other. The *Mount Mary* is more classical, showing good fruit definition and purity, whereas *Yarra Yering* is a very individual, highly concentrated, if not soupy style. Coldstream Hills Reserve Pinot Noir, De Bortoli, Yarra Ridge, and Tarrawarra have done much to impress Pinot-philes. These wines are quite Burgundian in style, indeed, almost caricatures. Recent auction results show a strong interest in Australian Pinot Noir, with the name of the producer most important.

• *Chardonnay*

It is too early to recognise the Yarra Valley as the producer of a defined Chardonnay style. Again, the Burgundian model is often on show. The best producers make classically proportioned Chardonnay with complex, cashew nut and tropical fruit aromas and plenty of new oak vanillin. Coldstream Hills (especially the *Reserve*) makes classic Burgundian style Chardonnay, while Mount Mary makes a highly individual complex style with proven cellaring potential. Yarra Yering Chardonnays are variable and fail to inspire. De Bortoli and Tarrawarra are making some really lovely complex wines, although their investment value still lies in the pleasure of drinking.

### Goulburn Valley, Vic.

*Warm climate/Elevation 130-300 metres*

The Goulburn wine region is located in Central Victoria about 100km north of Melbourne and 50km east of Heathcote. The newly named Nagambie Lakes is a sub-region. The Goulburn Valley, which centres on the towns of Seymour and Nagambie, has a warm climate with strong continentality. The lazy Goulburn River dissects the region and has washed the red and brown sandy clay loams with alluvial sands. Most of the vineyards are located on old river flats close to the river. Temperatures fluctuate enormously during the growing season creating a stressful environment for vines. Rainfall is low, although the region has experienced the occasional vintage washout. The most suited variety is Shiraz as typified by Mitchelton and Tahbilk.

- *Shiraz*

From a secondary market perspective, Tahbilk and Mitchelton dominate this region. Tahbilk *1860s Vines Shiraz* – made from fruit grown on a small patch of pre-phylloxera vines – is a rarity indeed and is arguably the most famous wine of this region. A wine of immense proportions, it has earthy plum, mulberry-like aromas, pronounced rusty tannins and plenty of structure. Its *Reserve Shiraz* – from 1933 vines – has a plumper style and is very impressive. The hugely likeable Mitchelton *Print Shiraz* is a more classic modern style with partial barrel fermentation. It shows more intense plum blackberry aromas, underlying oak, some meaty complexity, pronounced, but riper, tannins and plenty of concentration and length.

### Rutherglen, Vic.

*Warm climate/Elevation 160 metres*

Rutherglen in north-east Victoria – known for its fortified wines, particularly its Muscats and Tokays – has produced a distinctive Australian style. The region was first discovered in 1836. George Frederick Morris established his vineyard in 1859. During the late 1880s, Rutherglen enjoyed a substantial export market to the U.K., but experienced harder economic conditions during the 20th century. It is the sheer quality of the wine that has kept the region going. The climate here is warm to hot, with a high degree of continentality and low relative humidity. The soils range from gravels to red and sandy alluvial loams. It is generally considered that the best vineyards are located on red loamy soils. Most of the vineyards, at around 160m, are on gentle slopes and close to the Murray River.

- *Liqueur Muscat & Liqueur Tokay*

These are opulent and luscious fortified wines. Because they have no vintage dates, they rarely perform on the secondary market. These styles are blends of several vintages. Often base material will be as old as 50 or 60 years. They are phenomenal wines and will bring joy to any serious wine lover with their rich, rancio aromas and decadently luscious flavours. The only profit is happily in the drinking.

**Beechworth, Vic.**

*Cold climate/Elevation 400-500 metres*

Beechworth has attracted considerable interest in recent years, generated by the enthusiasm for the reclusive Giaconda wines. The vineyards, taking into account Beechworth's high level of sunshine hours, are generally planted at altitudes of around 400m. The region is cool with high continentality so site selection is vitally important. The best sites are located away from higher altitude, cold-air drainage channels, with the risk of frost high in both spring and autumn. The soils are granitic loams over decomposed gravels and clays. While north or north-easterly slopes may generally be favoured, Giaconda's vines are planted on protected south-facing slopes.

- *Pinot Noir*

Beechworth Pinot Noir is yet to appear as a regional style. In the meantime, it is entirely expressed through the wines of Giaconda. The style is highly regarded and keenly sought. The wines have plenty of strawberry/dark cherry/meaty aromas and flavours with fine attenuated tannins. More recent vintages are impressive.

- *Chardonnay*

Giaconda's *Beechworth Chardonnay* is a Helen of Troy. Its sheer beauty has launched a scramble of suitors wishing to emulate this wine. It is hardly a regional style yet, although it must reflect its vineyard site and the sheer potential of this region. Giaconda's *Chardonnay* is a classic style with excellent fruit definition and creamy flavours, all balanced by deft oak handling and fine acid cut. The wines appear to benefit from cellaring, which puts them into the elite league of Australian Chardonnay. This is an exciting wine with so much complexity and interest.

**Gippsland, Vic.**

*Cool climate/Elevation 30-100 metres*

Gippsland is named after a former Governor of Victoria and comprises the south-eastern underbelly of Victoria extending from Phillip Island in the south to the southern border of New South Wales to its northeast. Topographically, it is comprised of coastal plains and the predominantly south-facing slopes of the foothills of the Great Dividing Range.

The area is similar in size to Belgium with varying meso-climates and soil compositions. The coastal regions comprise silty and chocolaty loams over sedimentary and volcanic derived rock. The foothills – largely undeveloped – are made up of sedimentary and weathered granitic and volcanic soils. South Gippsland, the coolest and wettest sub-region, is located about 100km east of Melbourne. Its climate is similar to the Yarra Valley, although there is a greater maritime influence. The best sites are in more elevated and protected positions planted on deep silty loams with a high iron content and northeasterly aspects. This is an emerging region with a reputation largely forged by Phillip Jones of Bass Phillip. Here is an example where meso-climate is modified by the human factor. His vineyards are close-spaced and each vine is given inordinate attention. East Gippsland, which lies between two prevailing weather patterns, can experience periods of drought and, at times, heavy rainfall during ripening. This sub-region shows some promise for its Cabernet Sauvignon driven wines.

- *Pinot Noir*

It is not really possible to define Gippsland Pinot Noir. Bass Phillip near Leongatha makes some of Australia's most extraordinary Pinot Noir, yet it is made in painfully small quantities. At the esoteric end, the wines are extraordinarily intense and perfumed with black cherry/meaty/floral aromas and flavours and beautifully textured palates. Yet these wines reflect extremely low-cropping levels and intensive care. Commercial reality inevitably means a spectrum of wine quality. Gippsland is an emerging wine region with plenty of potential.

## NEW SOUTH WALES

### Hunter Valley, N.S.W.

*Hot climate/Elevation 75-250 metres*

The Hunter Valley is the most important quality wine-producing region in New South Wales, even though it represents only eight per cent of the State's production. Established in the early 1800s, the first vignerons recognised that the coastal fringe north of Sydney was just too wet and humid, so moved into the hinterland. Edward Tyrrell planted his first vines in 1858, and had his first vintage in 1864, beginning a family tradition of winemaking in the Hunter Valley. Indeed Tyrrell's still harvests Shiraz fruit from blocks planted in 1879 and 1892 which together represent almost five hectares of century-old vines. Although it can be particularly hot, the cloud and rainfall patterns modify the micro-climate remarkably. The area is maritime influenced with afternoon sea breezes funnelling up through the Hunter River/Goulburn River Gap. Rainfall is very erratic and can arrive at the most inopportune time. Soils are generally rich volcanic and alluvial soils. The best vineyard sites appear to be located within sight of the imposing Brokenback Range that is exposed to the cool sea breezes. Further inland the maritime influence gives way to a greater degree of continentality. The area is hotter and drier, although it can often experience rain towards vintage. The wine industry here competes with the local coal industry. Hunter Valley Shiraz and Semillons can be exceptional. Some producers have been successful with Cabernet Sauvignon and Chardonnay.

- *Cabernet Blends*

When Max Lake first planted Cabernet Sauvignon in the Hunter Valley, local vignerons and growers said that the Lower Hunter was totally unsuited to this variety. Opinion is polarised. Some suggest that the micro-climate – if you take into account the length of daylight during summer – is not too far from warmer European regions such as Bordeaux or the Rhone. The proof, however, is in the pudding. Hunter Cabernet lurches from the classic cedary, fine-grained styles like Lake's Folly to more opulent fruit bomb styles. It's all weather-dependent really as, in some years, this early ripening variety can be caught in the rain resulting in dilute wines. In a classic vintage, the wines do have good ageing potential. Some of the Lake's Folly Cabernets are brilliant as aged wines.

- *Semillon*

The best Hunter Valley Semillons are invariably unoaked and are some of the lowest alcohol wines produced in Australia. When young they show herbaceous, tropical fruit aromas, quite lean palates and good acid backbone. The ageing process sees these wines develop remarkably. The primary aromas give way to a complex, honeyed, straw-like bouquet. The palate fleshes out with concentrated honey/straw flavours, apparent fruit sweetness, cutting acid and great length. This is a misunderstood style favoured by passionate wine enthusiasts and many in the wine trade. Yet it has generally failed to ignite interest in the secondary market except for specific vintages and wines: 1970 *Lindemans*, 1979 *Rothbury Estate*, 1984 McWilliams *Lovedal*e and 1986 *Tyrrell's Vat 1* are all classic wines.

- *Shiraz*

Once seen as the classic red wine of Australia, Hunter Shiraz may well bounce back as buyers seek a variety of Shiraz experiences. Its reputation has been somewhat tarnished over the years as the region has become more commercialised. Tyrrell's, Brokenwood, Tamburlaine, Rothbury

Estate and others are doing much to win back the confidence of fine wine buyers. The early leaders, Lindemans and McWilliams, after rather dull performances in the 1980s, are on the comeback trail, too. Classic Hunter Valley Shiraz shows an opulent, complex, plummy/earthy/leathery bouquet with concentrated, earthy flavours, plenty of fruit sweetness, ripe tannins and length. The term 'sweaty saddle' has often been used to describe old Hunters. The smell of an old Chesterfield sofa is another description. Too much of these characteristics, I think, destroy the wine. The best Hunters can age for decades. Witness the dense and brooding 1965 Lindemans *Bin 3100 Hunter River Burgundy*. Some of the old Maurice O'Shea wines from the late 1940s and early 1950s have also stood the test of time. More recent classics are the 1986 and 1991 *Tyrrell's Vat 9*. The 1998 Brokenwood *Graveyard* is a very great wine.

- *Chardonnay*

Hunter Valley Chardonnay comes in a plethora of styles from the innocuous to the refined. From the rich and unctuous, deep yellow, oaky darlings to the tightly structured and beautifully defined *Tyrrell's Vat 47*, it is a wine with proven ageing capacity. Rosemount *Roxburgh* is a marketing-driven wine that is found in the fridge or on board the boat of many a captain of industry. Indeed, Rosemount *Show Reserve* may well be the better wine with its excellent varietal definition, fruit sweetness and balance. Lake's Folly makes a punter's Chardonnay rather than a critic's choice. Wine writers often slam it, yet it can be excellent. Cork taint problems in the early 1990s have been no help. Most Chardonnays from this region, however, are early drinking styles.

### Mudgee, N.S.W.

*Warm climate/Elevation 500-600 metres*

Mudgee, in the central west of New South Wales, is an up-and-coming Shiraz region. Located in the crater of an extinct volcano, this area has a viticultural history spanning almost 150 years. The first vines were planted in 1858 during the gold rush of that time. Curiously, however, the region came to prominence only in the 1970s.

Huntington Estate, established in the late 1960s, has produced some exceptional Shiraz-based wines. The last decade has seen significant capital investment ploughed into this region. Rosemount and Orlando are particularly active. The climate is warm to hot, with a high degree of continentality, and spring frosts are a problem. Soils are generally sandy loams and red sandy clay loams. The best vineyard sites are located at elevations of around 500m on slopes. Rosemount has done much to attract attention to this region. Mudgee has witnessed an astonishing amount of new plantings.

- *Chardonnay*

Some of the oldest Chardonnay vines can be found in Mudgee with plantings dating back to the 1930s and earlier. However, the Hunter Valley – through Tyrrell's *Vat 47 Chardonnay* – began the inexorable pathway to success. Mudgee Chardonnay ranges from the elegantly structured to the thick milkshake style. The arrival of Rosemount, known as Chardonnay specialists, has given an upbeat feeling about this region.

- *Shiraz*

The wine capitalists somehow bypassed Mudgee during the 1960s and 1970s. Most went to the Hunter Valley leaving a small, dedicated group of winemaking pioneers to do all the hard work. Mudgee Shiraz has had a keen niche market for years, but the style is actually difficult to define. The wines certainly have plenty of blackberry liquorice fruit, concentration and pronounced gravely tannins. Better vintages show plenty of chocolaty flavours and palate softness. Mudgee could well express the ultimate Australian marriage of Shiraz and Cabernet Sauvignon.

- *Shiraz-Cabernet Sauvignon*

In the last five years, Mudgee Shiraz-Cabernet Sauvignon is turning heads. It is a classic story of how people value things once they are packaged in a particular way. Mudgee's reputation is swathed in the reflected glory of Rosemount's marketing and winemaking flair. Yet Huntington Estate has been making some excellent wines for years. The fruit opulence and sweetness of Shiraz is meshed in with the fine, grainy tannin structure of Cabernet Sauvignon bringing wines with plenty of ageing potential. Mudgee has never looked so exciting.

**Southern N.S.W. (Canberra District & Hilltops)**

The Hilltops, Canberra District. and Tumbarumba wine regions, in southern New South Wales, are located on the flanks of the Great Dividing Range, a spinal cord of foothills, tablelands, and mountain ranges, that lies along the eastern seaboard of Australia. This area was largely opened up by European graziers during the 1830s and is world famous for its merino sheep and quality of its wool. Gold was discovered during the 1850s, progressively opening up new settlements and attracting immigrants. This is also classic 'bushranger country' with its vast undulating and crumpled landscape, hidden valleys, and timbered wilderness. More recently, this area has attracted market gardening, fruit growing, tourism, and light industry. The bushrangers have been replaced by Australia's Federal seat of government at Canberra. Wine growing is relatively recent, the first vineyards being planted in the late 1960s. Generally, the area is quite elevated, with vineyards between 300 and 800 metres. The climate is largely continental and although the heat summation index suggests a cool climate, summers are often hot with prolonged sunshine hours. The geological history of Southern New South Wales is extremely complex and spans two billion years. Active continental growth has seen widespread volcanic activity, sedimentation, granite intrusions, and intense folding and faulting. The Hilltops region is located on south-western slopes; is largely granitic-based, and attracts greater summer rainfall. McWilliam's Barwang vineyard is an exemplary site. The Canberra district, on elevated tablelands (about 500m), is much drier during the growing season and requires irrigation. Spring frosts can be a problem – although most vineyards have been rigorously sited. Soils are granitic to sedimentary. Clonakilla *Shiraz-Viognier* epitomises the potential of this district. Tumbarumba lies in the western foothills of the Snowy Mountains and is much cooler with a mean January temperature of only 19° C. (Hilltops is 23° C). Much of the fruit – Chardonnay and Pinot Noir is used for premium Australian sparkling wine.

**Riverina (Murrumbidgee), N.S.W.**

*Hot dry climate/Elevation 140 metres*

The Riverina district was settled by Italian immigrants and returned soldiers who established large-scale market gardening and grape growing in an area supplied by the Murrumbidgee Irrigation Scheme. Although some wine producers claim to have established themselves earlier, this region didn't really get going until the 1950s. The Riverina is famous for inexpensive fortified and table wines. In 1982 De Bortoli released its *Botrytis Semillon 'Sauternes'* creating consternation among wine critics. It appeared ludicrous that this region could make a dessert wine of such finesse and quality. The wine, with almost two decades of production, continues to enhance its reputation with sheer consistency and quality. The region is hot and dry with plentiful sunshine and vines planted on medium to heavy clay loams. The vineyards are managed to ensure a high level of humidity between the vines to promote botrytis.

- *Botrytis Semillon*

The Riverina is better known as a broad-acre vineyard region producing wines of very commercial quality. De Bortoli pioneered the botrytis Semillon style in the early 1980s with others following suit. The De Bortoli *Noble One* style has become an Australian classic very quickly. The wines show lovely deep yellow colour, apricot-honey aromas and a luscious tremendously concentrated palate with plenty of dried apricot/peach/honey flavours. This is all balanced by fine attenuated acidity that brings life, length and lasting power to the wine.

## TASMANIA

Tasmania is an island State which is separated from the southeast coast of mainland Australia by Bass Strait. These vineyards are Australia's most southerly, the first vineyard planted in 1823 near Hobart. The emerging wine industry petered out during the late 1880s due to difficulties with climate and economic pressures.

**Northern Tasmania**

*Cool to cold climate/Elevation 15-200 metres*

The arrival of Andrew Pirie and the planting of vineyards around Pipers Brook near Launceston in Tasmania's north really kicked off northern Tasmania's wine industry. The vineyards are all located in cool to cold maritime areas. The warmest and sunniest part of the island is in the north. At Pipers Brook most of the vineyards are located on slopes at elevations of around 100 to 140m on basalt-derived gravelly soils with relatively high iron content. Pipers Brook vineyards are close spaced on north-facing vineyards but quite exposed to wind. Riesling has thrived, while Chardonnay and Bordeaux varieties are a mixed bag, and Pinot Noir is showing great potential. Meso-climate and individual sites differ markedly around Tasmania. The Tamar Valley, close to Pipers Brook, is estuarine influenced. In terms of wine investment, Tasmania has a very small presence. Despite a strong commitment by BRL Hardy in sparkling wine production and a few relatively large-scale ventures, Northern Tasmania has still to find its feet. This is illustrated by the change of ownership of several enterprises – Pipers Brook being the most recent.

- *Riesling*

Riesling has shown the most promise in this marginal wine-growing region. They have pronounced limey aromas with a touch of dried herb/spice nuances, fine acidity and plenty of concentration and length. Vintage is important

- *Chardonnay*

Chardonnay has struggled. The climate is extremely marginal and botrytis seems to be a perennial problem in some vineyards. Producers are able to make leaner Burgundian styles, but many seem to have a herbal edge to them. Sparkling wine producers (specifically Hardys and Domaine Chandon) value the fruit highly, which is where its ultra-fine future probably lies in the medium term. *Pipers Brook Chardonnay* was once one of Australia's leading wines, but is now lost in a sea of Australian Chardonnays. However it can only get better!

- *Pinot Noir*

Some good expressions of Pinot Noir are produced in these parts. Pipers Brook and Tamar Ridge are making Burgundian styles, although vintage is an important consideration.

**Eastern Tasmania**

*Cool to cold climate/Elevation 5-35 metres*

This beautiful stretch of coastline may well become Australia's pre-eminent Pinot Noir region. Certainly the wines of Freycinet illustrate the extraordinary promise of this capricious grape variety. Centred near the fishing port of Bicheno, famous for abalone, and the early penal colony of Maria Island, the soils are generally granitic with a high iron content. The best vineyards lie in protected slopes as the prevailing cold south and southeast winds can hinder growth. The Moulting Lagoon, a substantial body of water, moderates the micro-climate particularly in autumn. Frost is non-existent and rainfall is erratic.

- *Pinot Noir*

It is far too early to point to regional style. However, Freycinet is making the most exquisitely beautiful Pinot Noir showing plenty of ripe cherry, meaty aromas and silky textured palate.

**Southern Tasmania**

*Cool to cold climate/Elevation 5-55 metres*

The Tasmanian wine industry re-emerged in the late 1950s with the establishment of Moorilla Estate on the outskirts of Hobart in Tasmania's south. The vineyards located close to the Derwent Estuary and Coal River near Hobart and planted on a range of sandstone and alluvial soils. They are protected from wind, enjoy long hours of sunshine and maritime influence. The nearby large body of water moderates temperatures during autumn. However, supplementary irrigation is needed because of low rainfall. The Huon Valley is yet to make its mark. Moorilla Estate is perhaps the most important producer. Certainly it is making some very good Pinot Noir, Merlot and Riesling. Its Gewürztraminer is highly regarded, too, but none of these wines performs on the secondary market. The small Domaine A, located at Campania near Coal River, is also showing potential.

# WINERIES & CLASSIFICATIONS

*Reviews of Australia's important fine wine producers. The market is quick to recognise a producer's improvement or loss in quality. These are the leading current market performers, emerging stars and cult wineries. Omission does not necessarily mean no secondary market presence. The cult wine scene, for instance, embraces a plethora of new (and sometimes established) wine labels, but which are still relatively unknown in Australia.*

## WESTERN AUSTRALIA

### CAPE MENTELLE, MARGARET RIVER

*Langton's selections – Cape Mentelle Cabernet Sauvignon, Cape Mentelle Chardonnay, Cape Mentelle Shiraz, Cape Mentelle Zinfandel*

The Cape Mentelle winery and original vineyard lie between the town of Margaret River and the Cape from which it takes its name. The original Mentelles were French geographer Edmunde and his cartographer brother Francois-Simon, who lived in Paris in the early 1700s.

*Cape Mentelle Cabernet Sauvignon* began impressively, with Jimmy Watson Trophies for both the 1982 and 1983 vintages. But a number of ordinary vintages followed. By the late 1980s, the quality began to improve enormously.

"I want to make one of the defining styles of Margaret River Cabernet – a great Australian Cabernet – a wine that outlasts me and helps consolidate the region as a premium wine producer for future generations," says winemaker David Hohnen.

In the 1990s, the wine emerged as a classic West Australian style. Restrained and elegant when young, these wines age beautifully, developing complexity and richness. The cedary, roasted coffee aromas, ripe tannins, and textured palate are central to the overall style.

Displaying regional definition, *Cape Mentelle Chardonnay* is emerging as one of Margaret River's classic wines. The result is a rich blending of options – typically, excellent, ripe, Chardonnay fruit expression with plenty of nutty, lanolin complexity, concentration, and fine acidity.

*Cape Mentelle Shiraz* is a quintessential West Australian Shiraz and an excellent foil to the rich, ripe, deeply concentrated Shirazes of South Australia. It shows raspberry, peppery aromas with touches of cherry, gravelly tannins and toasty oak – a style in evolution.

*Cape Mentelle Cabernet Sauvignon* is a pacesetter; *Cape Mentelle Shiraz* is emerging as another important benchmark. The *Zinfandel* is quirky but highly seductive. The *Chardonnay* is at last hitting its straps and could well join the Margaret River elite.

- *CAPE MENTELLE Cabernet Sauvignon, Margaret River W.A. – Outstanding*

The Walcliffe Vineyard was planted between 1970 and 1973, on gravel laterite soils derived from decomposed ironstone over gravel/clay subsoils. The vines are trellised on a traditional narrow T-trellis system or trained on a modified Scott Henry trellis. Irrigation is used only sparingly.

The fruit is hand-picked, usually at the end of March/April, de-stemmed and lightly crushed, before fermentation in steel. After fermentation, it is pressed and racked twice, before going into French oak barrels from Nevers, Alliers, and Troncais. It is bottled after 21 months in new (30%) and used oak.

- *CAPE MENTELLE Chardonnay, Margaret River W.A. – Distinguished*

*Cape Mentelle Chardonnay* displays all the hallmarks of regional definition. Core fruit component is sourced from the low-yielding McHenry vineyard, with its deep gravelly loams and north-easterly aspect near the Margaret River. The remaining fruit is sourced from the Maiolo and Ironstone vineyards further to the north. The vines are all cane pruned and vertical shoot positioned. As with many vineyards in this area, birds are a major problem that can reduce yields.

Vintage is typically in mid-February/early March. A portion of the fruit is crushed, chilled, and gently pressed, before cold-settling in stainless steel, after which it is inoculated with Montrachet yeast. A few days later, it is transferred to approximately 45 per cent new, and 55 per cent one and two year old French oak. The remaining portion is whole-bunch pressed, then racked into barrels to await fermentation by indigenous yeasts. About a third of the blend goes through malo-lactic fermentation.

Medium term cellaring prospect.

- *CAPE MENTELLE Shiraz, Margaret River W.A. – Distinguished*

The fruit is sourced from Cape Mentelle's Walcliffe Vineyard. The vines are all trained on Scott Henry and TK2 trellis systems to enhance exposure to sunlight and to control vigour. Fruit is cropped at about two tonnes per acre.

The blend also comprises a touch of Grenache sourced from the Emerald Park vineyard, planted on a ridge of quartz gravel loams at Donnybrook, about 80km north of Margaret River. Typically, the fruit is picked during March/April. 25 per cent of the fruit is whole bunch fermented to increase the spectrum of aromas and flavours. Thirty per cent of the wine is aged in a combination of French and American oak, the remainder matured in large oak vats.

Oak plays a supporting role in the wine. The wines show raspberry, peppery aromas with touches of cherry, gravelly tannins, and toasty oak.

A style in evolution with medium term cellaring prospects.

## CULLEN, MARGARET RIVER

*Langton's selections – Cullen Cabernet Sauvignon-Merlot, Cullen Chardonnay*

In 1966, Diana and Dr Kevin Cullen planted a trial one acre (now 71 acre) vineyard on their sheep and cattle property at Willyabrup in the Margaret River. The wines are made by the 15-year formidable mother daughter partnership of Di and Vanya Cullen.

In 1989, Vanya, a Roseworthy trained winemaker, assumed prime winemaking responsibilities. Vanya was *WINE Magazine's* 2000 Winemaker of the Year, a significant achievement. Her eye for detail and uncompromising approach has seen *Cullen Cabernet Sauvignon-Merlot* emerge as one of the great Australian Cabernets. Fruit definition and overall balance are extraordinary. Here is a wine that is pure, bottled philosophy.

*Cullen Chardonnay* is made from estate-grown fruit, with cropping levels as low as about two tonnes per acre. The fruit is whole-bunch pressed. Eighty to 100 per cent of the wine is barrel fermented with wild yeast strains, and matured in new French oak – the remainder in steel tanks to allow blending options.

*Cullen Chardonnay* is quite lean when first released, but opens up after a short period in the cellar. It is not so prevalent in the market, but is always well subscribed.

Cullen enjoys a strong following on the secondary market. Some vintages – particularly the 1995 – attract significant bidding.

- *CULLEN Cabernet Sauvignon-Merlot, Margaret River W.A. – Outstanding*

The Cabernet Sauvignon vines were planted in 1971 and are trained on a Scott Henry trellis system, which increases the exposure of leaf and grape area to the sun. The Merlot and Cabernet Franc vines were planted in 1976.

In recent years, small plantings of Petit Verdot and Malbec have been added to the vineyard, illustrating a constant quest for refinement of style. Fruit is picked at about 13° Baume on flavour development. The grapes are fermented in static fermenters until dryness, then drained, pressed, and finally racked into a proportion of new one and two year old new French oak for up to 22 months, depending on vintage. A portion of the wine may see partial barrel fermentation.

This estate style is about freshness and complexity, structure and suppleness. When young, the wines have pronounced cassis and cedar aromas and a supple palate, with fine, ripe tannins. Earthy, anise-like, gamy aromas and flavours develop with age.

- *CULLEN Chardonnay*
  *Margaret River W.A. – Distinguished*

The Chardonnay fruit is picked at sugar levels of varying Baume (between 13° and 14.5°) to achieve varying aromas and flavour characteristics. It is whole-bunch pressed 'to increase fruit flavours and longevity and to reduce the level of phenolics', then allowed to ferment using wild yeasts. This fermentation, according to Vanya Cullen, gives the wine 'better mouth-feel and length on the palate'.

The wine is kept on lees for six months with regular lees stirring (*battonage*) to achieve further complexity. Whole-bunch pressing seems to make the wines finer and more elegant, certainly improving cellaring potential.

This is a wine, unlike many Australian Chardonnays, which needs a period of time in bottle. It is very tight and focused when young, with melon/cashew nut-like aromas and flavours, rapier-like acidity, and tremendous length. A touch of bottle age sees richness on the palate and the opening up of aromas and flavours. This is what Australians call a 'dark horse' – just when the race seems over, a dark horse comes through to beat the field.

## DEVIL'S LAIR, MARGARET RIVER

*Langton's selections – Devil's Lair Chardonnay, Devil's Lair Cabernet Sauvignon*

Phil Sexton established Devil's Lair in 1985, with his first vineyard plantings in 1981. The vineyards are located on varying Margaret River soils from pockets of gravelly loams (ideal for Cabernet Sauvignon), to loamy soils (especially suited to Chardonnay). The vines are all trellised on a simple vertical shoot positioned system, mostly in protected north-easterly aspects. Fruit is machine- and hand-picked, depending on site and wine style.

New winemaker Stuart Pym (ex Voyager Estate) harvests on optimum ripeness and flavour development, which can mean varying fruit profiles to increase complexity and blending options.

The *Cabernet Sauvignon* is fermented in static, stainless steel pump-over tanks at relatively warm ferments.

Extended skin maceration is given to 50 per cent of the blend before it is drained and pressed into 50 per cent new- and 50 per cent one year old oak to mature for two years. Two-year-and-older barrels are used for Devil's Lair's Fifth Leg brand. The *Chardonnay* is classically made with 30 per cent of its hand-picked fruit whole-bunch pressed. The juice is cold-settled before barrel fermentation in new French oak. Regular *battonage*, extended lees contact, and 11 months' maturation in new oak completes the picture.

The *Chardonnay* is brilliantly focused, with all the signs of cellaring potential. The *Cabernet Sauvignon*, which comprises a proportion of Merlot, Cabernet Franc, and Petit Verdot, is yet to be bolted down in terms of a winemaking philosophy. With Stuart Pym at the helm, and all the resources at hand, expect a rapid evolution. Devil's Lair is a member of the Southcorp stable.

## HOWARD PARK, MARGARET RIVER & DENMARK (GREAT SOUTHERN)

*Langton's selections – Howard Park Cabernet Merlot, Howard Park Riesling, Howard Park Chardonnay*

Howard Park was established by Jeff Burch and John Wade in the mid-1980s and quickly achieved acclaim for its wines. Well-respected and highly innovative winemaker, John Wade made the first wines.

In the late 1990s, after considerable success in the market place, Howard Park moved its red wine production to Margaret River to take advantage of its reputation and proximity to a larger population base. Winemaker Michael Kerrigan replaced Wade, maintaining continuity and indeed improving style.

*Howard Park Cabernet Sauvignon-Merlot*, first vintage 1986, is a multi-region five-vineyard West Australian blend. Noted for its intense, blackcurrant, blackberry, briary aromas, balance and structure, this wine needs several years to meld. The *Chardonnay* fruit comes from vineyards around Denmark in the Lower Great Southern. These wines show excellent fruit definition and creamy complexity. *Howard Park Riesling* is made only from Riesling grown in the Great Southern and, more specifically, around Mt. Barker and the Porongurup Ranges. This is one of the few recognised Rieslings outside the Clare and Eden Valleys.

Howard Park recently launched a *Scotsdale Cabernet Sauvignon* (*and Scotsdale Shiraz*) based on Lower Great Southern fruit. The *Cabernet* is matured for 18 months in 100 per cent French oak barrels. *Leston Vineyard Shiraz* (a *Leston* Cabernet is also made) is 100 per cent Margaret River Shiraz, matured in predominantly new (65%) and used French oak, for about 18 months. Both wines are presumably aimed at the emerging investment markets.

Howard Park also owns the brand Madfish Bay.

- *HOWARD PARK Cabernet Sauvignon-Merlot, W.A. – Excellent*

*Howard Park Cabernet Sauvignon-Merlot* is a West Australian blend, made with fruit sourced from the Lower Great Southern and Margaret River regions – most coming from Mount Barker and Porongurup. The fruit is sourced from five different vineyards, each site performing differently each year. Some of Howard Park's best Cabernet Sauvignon is sourced from Spring View Vineyard, in the rain shadow of the southern side of the Porongurup Ranges. Wines made from its fruit are described by Michael Kerrigan as being very complex, perfumed and textural. His Wildwood Road Vineyard, on the northern edge of Margaret River, brings chocolaty aromas and mid-palate richness. All his vineyards are planted on 'gravelly, mean' soils.

Once the fruit achieves a certain level of ripeness, it is picked on flavour development. More recent vintages are a touch higher in Baume level. The fruit is chilled for a few days at about 10-12° C, before batch fermenting in open static fermenters. The fermenting wine is regularly pumped over with a splash-and-return system and aerated to polymerise and resolve tannin structure. At dryness, the wine is given extended maceration for 20 to 30 days, before ageing in well-seasoned, fine grained, Seguin Moreau French oak for 24 months. Barrel selection on the concept of best of vintage and house style, takes place before final blending.

Opulence without soupiness, restraint with underlying power and concentration, are hallmarks of the Howard Park style. The wines evolve over 8-10 years – reaching a plateau of complexity, developing a mature bouquet of cedar and polished leather, but still showing freshness and intensity of fruit. The palate is highly concentrated and fleshy, balanced by pronounced acid and fine-grained tannins.

## LEEUWIN ESTATE, MARGARET RIVER

*Langton's selections – Leeuwin Estate Art Series Chardonnay, Leeuwin Estate Art Series Cabernet Sauvignon*

Established in 1974 by Denis and Tricia Horgan, with initial help from Californian winemaker Robert Mondavi, Leeuwin Estate has emerged as one of Australia's benchmark Chardonnay producers.

A formidable team comprising winemaker Bob Cartwright and viticulturist John Brocksopp, plus a succession of brilliant vintages and great consistency of style, have made Leeuwin Estate *Art Series Chardonnay* the most highly prized Australian white wine on the secondary market. It now sits with Penfolds *Grange* in the Exceptional category of *Langton's Classification*. The 1987, once considered the definitive Australian Chardonnay, is only just starting to tire. The 1995 and 1997 vintages are wondrous.

The *Cabernet Sauvignon* is finally emerging as one of the best from the region. Since the early 1990s, this wine has become more consistent in style – one of the top Margaret River Cabernets with pronounced blackcurrant/cassis, earthy, leafy characters. It has a highly concentrated palate with fine, but pronounced tannins, underlying new oak and indelible acidity. The *Pinot Noir* is less interesting.

- *LEEUWIN ESTATE Art Series Chardonnay, Margaret River W.A. – Exceptional*

Leeuwin Estate Chardonnay, widely considered Australia's finest, illustrates the extraordinary promise of Margaret River. On free-draining laterite gravel soils over ancient base rock, the Chardonnay vineyards – including the mother vineyard, Block 20 – are planted to the low-yielding Gin Gin Chardonnay clone (from the U.S.A. originally, brought to W.A. as a virus indicator by the Department of Agriculture). Cropped at around one-and-a-half to two tonnes per acre, this clone gives highly concentrated flavours, but is susceptible to *millerandage* (or 'hen and chicken') where bunches of grapes have berries ripening unevenly. Birds, particularly Silver Eyes, are a problem. Partial vineyard netting and the introduction of cereal rye and sunflowers as alternative food sources, have reduced crop loss. Most of the fruit is destemmmed, crushed and drained, sometimes after skin contact. The must is then pumped into stainless steel tanks and cold settled. Clarified juice is racked from solids approximately three days later, inoculated with yeast culture (Simi white), and transferred to new French oak barrels where fermentation continues. To bring more complexity, partial malo-lactic fermentation is encouraged, according to vineyard lots. The wine spends up to 14 months in oak with extended lees contact, and further time in stainless steel tanks, before bottling and further maturation, prior to release. The style is complex and well defined, with pineapple, melon, roasted nuts, leesy and vanillin aromas, fruit definition, and a natural, indelible acidity across the mid-palate.

A succession of brilliant vintages and proven cellaring potential, make this wine one of the most highly prized (and expensive) Australian white wines.

- *LEEUWIN ESTATE Art Series Cabernet Sauvignon, Margaret River W.A. – Distinguished*

Leeuwin Estate *Art Series Cabernet Sauvignon* has been overshadowed by the extremely fine *Art Series Chardonnay*. In recent times however, it has become one of the top 10 Margaret River Cabernets. The vineyard, 30-60 metres above sea-level, is located on deep gravel and loamy soils over sandy gravel sub-soils, with sufficient water-holding capacity. Vines are trellised to a single vertical hedge and rod pruned to approximately 50 buds. Trimming and leaf plucking are routine necessities. Grapes are harvested on flavour profile with a cursory eye to the basic rules of analysis. Yields are about two to three tonnes per acre. The fruit is crushed and de-stemmed, then transferred to closed fermenters with regular pumping over and fermentation controlled at approx-imately 30° C. The wine is left on skins for up to three weeks before pressing. After malo-lactic fermentation, the vineyard components are blended and racked into 40 per cent new French oak and used Chardonnay barrels. A proportion of Petit Verdot (structure and colour), Malbec (mid-palate richness), and Merlot (softness) is added for complexity. About two years' maturation in barrel, then a further year or so in bottle, prior to release. These are highly structured wines that demand cellaring for the medium to long term. Recent vintages are more likely to soften out.

### MOSS WOOD, MARGARET RIVER

*Langton's selections – Moss Wood Cabernet Sauvignon, Moss Wood Chardonnay, Moss Wood Semillon, Moss Wood Pinot Noir*

Moss Wood was established in 1969 by Dr Bill Pannell, at what is one of the choicest and most beautiful vineyard sites in Australia. Clare and Keith Mugford bought the property in 1985 and have taken Moss Wood to the pinnacle of Australian Cabernet Sauvignon. The wine is elegant in style with pronounced cassis-blackcurrant aromas, hints of cedar and leafiness, and a finely-structured palate.

The *Reserve Cabernet Sauvignon* was discontinued in favour of a single wine, the highly respected *Cabernet Sauvignon*, now elevated in *Langton's Classification* to Exceptional status. The *Margaret River Pinot Noir* is perfumed and supple, arguably the region's best, and much better than the almost identically labelled *Moss Wood Pemberton Pinot Noir* – a pleasant but early-drinking style.

The *Chardonnay* is yet another reason why Margaret River is a leading region for this variety. And the *Semillon* is a brilliant foil to the Hunter Valley style, with fresh, lemony, herbal aromas and flavours, and thirst-quenching acidity. *Moss Wood Cabernet Sauvignon* is a highly important secondary market performer.

- *MOSS WOOD Cabernet Sauvignon, Margaret River W.A. – Exceptional*

The five hectare vineyard, at Willyabrup, is planted on gentle north-east facing slopes, in soils ranging from sandy loam to gravelly red-brown loam over clay. Vines, mostly on a Scott Henry Trellis, are unirrigated and low yielding. The combination of site, vineyard management, and soil conservation, has been the key to ultimate fruit quality. More recently, attention has been given to winemaking and refinement of style. This has included longer skin contact time during fermentation and a change in *encepagement* (varietal blend). Adding Cabernet Franc (5%), Petit Verdot (5%), and Merlot (0.05%) to the wine, has given it deeper colour and more perfume and texture. As of the 1996 vintage, all *Moss Wood Cabernet Sauvignon* sees extended oak ageing (24 months, rather than 18 months) in French *barriques*. First vintage (250 cases produced), was in 1973.

These wines age brilliantly, revealing more site-specific aromas and flavours, a touch of earth and briar character on the bouquet, and suppleness on the palate.

## PIERRO, MARGARET RIVER

*Langton's selections – Pierro Chardonnay, Pierro Cabernet*

There is something special about the Pierro Vineyard. Its natural beauty draws the eye in to the textured landscape of stony outcrops and rounded hillocks. Tall gum trees skirt the vines and protect them from winds. Below, the Willyabrup River, sometimes only a trickle, cuts through the property, reaching a man-made lake beside the new concrete/earth winery. The site was selected not by soil analysis or water availability, rather because of its proximity to Dr Mike Peterkin's romantic interest – his wife Shelley (Cullen). The vineyard was originally to be planted to Riesling, but a need for vineyard expertise accompanied by offer of an 5,000 Chardonnay cuttings, changed the course of Pierro's fortunes.

Vineyard management is an important concern here. This is a classically proportioned wine with extraordinary complexity and concentration. It has an indelible acid-cut across the mid-palate, creaminess, good length of flavour, and is sometimes quite high in alcohol, but has the balance to age. *Pierro Cabernet*, a classic Bordeaux blend, is also an impressive wine, but is yet to prove itself in the secondary market. The *Chardonnay* is considered one of Australia's best and, correspondingly, attracts good demand.

- *PIERRO Chardonnay, Margaret River W.A. – Outstanding*

Vineyard management is the key. The vines (same Gin Gin clone as at Leeuwin Estate) are closely spaced, which increases relative humidity among them. With this practice, fruit exposure is a critical component. The vineyard is stony which means, at night, heat radiates into the clusters of Chardonnay berries, effectively burning off excessive levels of malic acid. *Pierro Chardonnay* is vinified in Burgundian fashion with barrel fermentation in new French oak, lees stirring (*battonage*), and lees contact.

## PLANTAGENET, MOUNT BARKER (GREAT SOUTHERN)

*Langton's selections – Plantagenet Cabernet Sauvignon, Plantagenet Shiraz*

Original owner Tony Smith (from the prominent British bookseller family), set up a sheep farm in Western Australia's isolated Great Southern region. It took him years to realise the future was in ultra-fine wine rather than ultra-fine wool.

The vineyards are the oldest in the Mount Barker subregion and produce outstanding quality fruit. Extraordinarily well made, this wine expresses the riper spectrum of Cabernet Sauvignon with bright cassis aromas, underlying oak, ripe, fine-grained tannins, and high concentration. The *Shiraz* is seen as a leading West Australian example.

Plantagenet also produces a nicely made Chardonnay – but don't confuse it with the rather hit-and-miss *Omrah*, an unwooded style. Plantagenet has established a very fine reputation for its *Cabernet Sauvignon* and *Shiraz*. It has a moderate profile on the secondary market, but its inclusion in *Langton's Classification* illustrates a solid base.

- *PLANTAGENET Cabernet Sauvignon, Mount Barker W.A. – Distinguished*

The heart of *Plantagenet Cabernet Sauvignon* comes from the original vines planted at Bouverie in 1968. A portion of Merlot and Cabernet Franc is blended with the wine to give mid-palate richness. The wine is batch vinified in static fermenters with regular pumping over. At dryness, the wine is allowed an extended maceration on skins to polymerise and resolve tannin structure. Some batches are partially barrel fermented to achieve further complexity. By the time the wine is bottled, *Plantagenet Cabernet Sauvignon* has spent approximately two years in one and two year old French oak, roughly 30-50 per cent of it new.

"We are looking for balance and structure," says winemaker Gavin Berry. "By balance, I mean that the wine shows a complete harmony between fruit, oak and tannin. By structure, I mean underlying but ripe, finely grained tannins, and fine acidity."

*Plantagenet Cabernet Sauvignon* is a beautifully complex wine with gamy, dark chocolate aromas and flavours, and a supple tannin structure. These wines are very seductive and they age extremely well.

**VASSE FELIX, MARGARET RIVER**

*Langton's selections – Vasse Felix Cabernet Sauvignon, Vasse Felix Shiraz*

Vasse Felix was the first commercial vineyard and winery established at Margaret River. Its name derives from French seaman Vasse, drowned last century while exploring the coast on the ship Geographe under Captain Freycinet. Second half of the name is a French for luck. Vasse Felix is seen as a pioneering producer of Cabernet Sauvignon that, after a decade of rather disappointing vintages, has been completely revitalised thanks to the watchful eye of Clive Otto, and a cash injection from owner Janet Holmes a Court.

These superbly made wines show intense cranberry, blackcurrant aromas and cedary complexity, with plenty of fruit sweetness and lacy tannin structure.

Vasse Felix has embraced the concept of an ultra-fine icon, best-of-vintage wine, with its Heytesbury label. This is now a Bordeaux blend of Cabernet Sauvignon, Merlot, and Cabernet Franc, with increased exposure to new French oak and extended maturation. Heytesbury could well eclipse the current *Cabernet Sauvignon*. The *Shiraz* is excellent, and could even become a classic with its slightly funky, meaty aromas, and plenty of flavour and balance. The Chardonnay is well made, but is yet to define itself.

- *VASSE FELIX Cabernet Sauvignon, W.A. – Distinguished*

*Vasse Felix Cabernet Sauvignon* is a multi-regional, but Margaret River-driven West Australian blend, with a small proportion of Shiraz, Malbec, and Merlot to add freshness and complexity. Fruit is sourced from the estate and from contract growers. The Vasse Felix vineyard is 120 metres above sea-level, with red gravel loam soils over clay. Vintage takes place late March to early April, cropping at under three tonnes per acre. The fruit is de-stemmed, crushed, and pumped into a rotary fermenter that is spun for about an hour prior to the start of fermentation. Further regular spinning washes the fermenting must over the skins. The must ferments at up to 28° C, before cooling to less than 25° C. Towards the end of fermentation, the cap is kept just wet. Rack and returns, pumping air into the ferments, and micro-oxygenation are also used to increase flavour complexity and to resolve tannin structures. Extended maceration and partial barrel fermentation in mainly French oak *barriques* follows. After fermentation, the wine is matured in a combination of French and American (20%) oak.

## VOYAGER ESTATE, MARGARET RIVER

*Langton's selections – Voyager Estate Chardonnay, Voyager Estate Cabernet Sauvignon, Voyager Estate Tom Price Cabernet Sauvignon*

The Voyager Estate winery – in sumptuous Cape Dutch style, complete with slave bell – is a reminder that the first vines planted in Western Australia in 1829 were South African in origin.

The first vines at Voyager were planted in 1978 and gradual vineyard expansion has followed, predominantly on gravelly loams over clay, with excellent moisture-holding capacity. Drip irrigation is used, but only as a management system. Vines are trellised on a vertical shoot position system and are harvested by hand or machine, depending on wine style. The *Chardonnay* is whole-bunch pressed and given a touch of oxidative handling to impart complexity. In new oak for 11 months, the maturing wine receives plenty of lees contact. This wine is now tightening up and beginning to show tremendous form.

The *Cabernet Sauvignon* is made with some Merlot, Cabernet Franc, and Petit Verdot. Vinification focuses on tannin management. Before fermentation, about 10 per cent of the juice is run off, to increase skin to juice ratio. During fermentation, the must is regularly pumped over, racked and returned to break up the skin cap. About 30 per cent of the wine is given extended skin maceration to soften tannins and increase complexity. About five per cent is partially barrel fermented. The wine then matures for two years in 50 per cent new, 50 per cent two year old, tightly grained oak.

Voyager's *Tom Price Cabernet* – named after Mt. Tom Price, source of the owner's iron ore royalties – is a 10 barrel selection of wine made from specially selected fruit and given a further six months' maturation. Voyager also produces a *Tom Price Sauvignon Blanc-Semillon* blend. The *Chardonnay* is delicious and the *Cabernet Sauvignon* is very promising. Certainly worth a look.

## XANADU, MARGARET RIVER

*Langton's selections – Xanadu Cabernet Reserve*

Adjacent to Cape Mentelle, Xanadu is in a hurry to make an impact on the ultra-fine wine market. Expanding rapidly in the last few years, its vineyard capacity has increased from the original 17 hectare Lagan Estate, to total holdings of 129 hectares. John Lagan and family established Xanadu in the late 1970s. During the mid-1980s and 1990s, its wines attracted a strong following.

The *Cabernet Reserve*, first released in 1989, is from the John Lagan Vineyard, a collection of 20 to 25 year old vines, on well-drained, red-brown gravelly sandy-loams with a sandy clay subsoil. The vineyard is interspersed with boulders and blocks that range from fist sized to the size of a car. Xanadu pursues an organic philosophy as much as possible, using its own organic fertilisers and permaculture. Vinification follows Bordelais lines. Fermentation takes place in static overhead fermenters with regular plunging and lees work. Gentle pressing is also central to wine-making practice. The *Cabernet Reserve* receives extended maceration for up to 30 days before maturation – around 22 months in tightly grained French oak.

"Our Reserve wines are refined styles," Conor Lagan says. "We are not into fruit power, nor into excessively tannic wines. We seek balance and complexity, not boring opulent fruit, over-oaked, Cabernet styles".

The tremendous changes at Xanadu could well influence market perceptions. The *Cabernet Reserve*, a superior wine to the standard Cabernet Sauvignon, deserves to be followed. It shows plenty of regional definition and structure to go the distance. The wine has an erratic following on the secondary market but it performs well in such events as the 'Great Wine Estates of Western Australia'. The next few years will show us whether the wine will be seen in the same light as other important and classified wine producers.

- *XANADU Cabernet Reserve,*
  *Margaret River W.A. – Distinguished*

Surrounded by tall eucalypt trees, Xanadu was established in the late 1970s, just outside the township of Margaret River, quite close to Cape Mentelle winery. Its *Cabernet Reserve*, first released in 1989, is made off the reserve block – now called the John Lagan Vineyard, with its 20 to 25 year old vines and well-drained gravelly sandy loams and sandy clay subsoil.

Xanadu favours an organic philosophy, using its own organic fertilisers and perma-culture. The fruit is hand-picked in early April. Fermentation in static fermenters, receives regular plunging and lees work. The wine sees an extended maceration for up to 30 days. Towards dryness, some of the wine is free run into barrel to complete fermentation and add complexity to the wine. At dryness, the wine is transferred to tightly grained French oak from various coopers, for around 22 months' maturation. The wine is matured in bottle for a further two years prior to release to the market.

Jurg Muggli says, "We have fundamentally retained the same winemaking philosophy since our first *Cabernet Reserve* vintage in 1989. I always work the wine, stirring the lees during fermentation to achieve more complexity.

The blending component is an essential feature. Cabernet Franc and increasingly, Merlot, are used to fill out the wine, giving a seamless impression on the palate. These wines are classic cellaring styles."

This wine has been renamed *Xanadu Lagan Estate Cabernet Reserve*.

## SOUTH AUSTRALIA

### BALNAVES, COONAWARRA

*Langton's selections – Balnaves Cabernet Sauvignon*

The Balnaves family, shopkeepers originally, arrived in the Penola district in 1854 from Scotland. Doug Balnaves began planting grapes in 1975, after taking over farm management from his father Ian who had earlier used the farm for sheep grazing. Doug was vineyard manager for Hungerford Hill's Coonawarra vineyards from 1971 to 1990. The first Balnaves wines, from its own vineyard at the southern end of Coonawarra, were released in 1990.

The 120 acre vineyard, in classic *terra rossa* country, is a matrix of sub-divisions, each block managed according to soil profile, clonal selection, and trellis system. Vines are mostly machine pruned and harvested. Fruit is fermented in vinimatics and open-topped static fermenters. Maturation for 18 to 22 months takes place in tight-grained new and used French oak *barriques* (from various coopers) and hogsheads. Around 500 tonnes of fruit is processed, most of it contract grown, but only about 140 tonnes is used for the Balnaves label.

On the secondary market, Balnaves is an emerging name and its *Cabernet Sauvignon* is well regarded. Its prospects are linked to the skills of winemaker Peter Bissell and the likely market resurgence of Coonawarra.

### BAROSSA VALLEY ESTATES, BAROSSA VALLEY

*Langton's selections – Barossa Valley Estates E&E Black Pepper Shiraz*

Barossa Valley Estates was established by 50 grape growing members of the Valley Growers Co-operative, many from the dry-grown northern Moppa and Ebenezer sub-regions of the Barossa. BVE is now partially owned by the burgeoning, resource-rich BRL Hardy empire. A new winery has been completed at Seppeltsfield in time for the 2002 vintage.

The *E&E Black Pepper Shiraz*, originally conceived by Colin Glaetzer, comprises the best fruit from the vintage. *Black Pepper Shiraz* is considered a benchmark Barossa *Shiraz*, with its plush rum'n'raisin/aniseed nose, ripe tannins, deep-set fruit, and skilful oak handling. This wine has the balance and structure to age well.

Barossa Valley Estates also produces a variant – the sparkling *E&E Shiraz*. These two wines attract healthy interest on the secondary market, although the latter is extremely specialised. The modestly valued *Ebenezer Shiraz* also has a good following.

- *BAROSSA VALLEY ESTATES E & E Black Pepper Shiraz – Barossa Valley S.A. – Excellent*

Barossa Valley Estates *E&E Black Pepper Shiraz* is sourced from some of the best dry-grown vineyards in the Barossa – 30 to 100 year old vines (average about 60 years). Although this wine is essentially a *tete de cuvee* reflecting the power, richness, and flavour of regional Barossa Shiraz, most of its fruit is from low-yielding vines in the north-east corner of the Barossa Valley. The wine is made in traditional style – picked at optimum ripeness and fermented in open headed down fermenters. At dryness, the wines are drained and pressed into a combination of new and one and two year old American and French oak, maturing for 12 to 18 months.

## BRL HARDY, REYNELLA (McLAREN VALE)

*Langton's selections – Hardy's Eileen Hardy Shiraz, Hardy's Tintara Shiraz*

Hardy's had top end market success in the 1990s, and a trail of winemaking quality has been blazed by the likes of David O'Leary (now a Clare Valley winemaker), Peter Dawson, and Steve Pannell.

Hardy's *Eileen Hardy Shiraz*, named after Eileen Hardy, a matriarch who inspired excellence, has evolved into one of the country's best Shirazes. The wine is based on fruit from Clare, Padthaway, and McLaren Vale – each region bringing different characters in varying proportions, according to season. Vinification uses traditional winemaking techniques. At dryness, it is drained and pressed in traditional basket presses.

"By shovelling Shiraz pressings into a basket press," says Steve Pannell, "we avoid slurrying and over-maceration of the wine. And this brings out beautiful tannin structures."

When young, *Eileen Hardy Shiraz* has gamy, blackberry/liquorice intensity, with plush, well-integrated new oak, fine, pronounced tannins, and plenty of length. Yet to prove its longevity, this wine has the elements of a classic.

The *Tintara McLaren Vale Shiraz* also has great potential. Packaging is excellent and, more importantly, the wines are elegantly structured but have tremendous fruit sweetness. Hardy's *Thomas Hardy Coonawarra Cabernet Sauvignon* is a finely textured wine with excellent fruit definition. *Eileen Hardy Chardonnay* performs well at shows, yet is sluggish at auction. Hardy's *Vintage Port* is a definitive example of the style, but over the last five years, interest in vintage Port has waned significantly. Hardy's also produces excellent sparkling wines, especially its *Arras*.

On the secondary market, Hardy's performance has been erratic, although its *Eileen Hardy Shiraz* has recently emerged with a strong loyal following. Recent moves into DNA tagging of its wines, hardly driven by consumer greed or counterfeiting, begs the question: Is it a case of the tail wagging the dog, or a red herring for uncertain consumers?

- *HARDYS Eileen Hardy Shiraz, S.A. – Excellent*

First released in 1970, *Eileen Hardy* was originally made from Shiraz and then Cabernet Sauvignon. It is now made exclusively from the best parcels of Shiraz fruit from Padthaway, McLaren Vale, and Clare Valley – each bringing essential characters.

Technically, the wine is vinified traditionally. Fermentation takes place in small open fermenters, which allows the winemaker to bring out the natural fruit characters of Shiraz and build backbone and structure. At dryness, the wine is drained and pressed in traditional basket presses. Since the 1995 vintage, the wine has progressively moved to approximately 20 months' maturation in 100 per cent French oak. A barrel selection process eliminates all but the best casks for the *Eileen Hardy* label. The wine is then assembled and aged another four months in oak, before bottling.

"*Eileen Hardy Shiraz* is a living breathing beast," says Pannell. "I seek opulence and perfume from our McLaren Vale vineyards, texture and richness from Padthaway, and spice and elegance from Clare. We are moving towards a very high proportion of French oak, as it plays a more subtle role in the wine."

## BETHANY, BAROSSA VALLEY

*Langton's selections – Bethany Shiraz*

Bethany winery is on the site of an old quarry, in one of the most picturesque corners of the Barossa Valley, overlooking the family vineyards and the historic hamlet of Bethany. The Schrapels have been in the Barossa for five generations. Johann Gottlob Schrapel, a Silesian immigrant, arrived in 1844, just eight years after the colony was settled. He established a mixed farm and planted a vineyard in 1852.

Subsequent generations continued building the farming enterprise and the vineyards gradually expanded, along with the growing Barossa wine industry. The Schrapel family became important Barossa growers supplying wine to co-operatives, particularly Kaiser Stuhl.

Although the vineyards have turned over at least three times, the older vines are between 60 and 80 years old. Economic conditions, vine age, and changing market demand have influenced the vineyard varietal mix. During the late 1940s, for instance, many of the vines were planted to Palomino and Pedro Ximenez to satisfy the burgeoning fortified wine industry.

The vineyards, at the north-eastern edge of the Barossa Valley, under Menglers Hill, in what locals call the Hill Space Zone, are in the path of cool gully winds and on-shore breezes of the Great Southern Ocean. The 30 hectare vineyard in Bethany comprises the Bethanien block, the Old Manse block, and the Homestead block. On a range of well-drained loamy topsoils to red clays over vertical seams of granite, bluestone, and sandstone, these vineyards – planted to Shiraz, Cabernet Sauvignon and Merlot – represent a mixed palate of characters. The Shiraz vines are trellised on single wires, many of them self-supporting.

The wines are vinified in the traditional Barossa manner, with open top, headed down fermenters, partial barrel fermentation, and around 18 months' maturation in a mix of American and French oak (about 20% new).

The *GR Family Reserve Shiraz* is a rigorous selection of the best fruit, batch-vinified, partially barrel fermented, and matured for two years in a combination of 60 per cent new and used French medium toasted Cadoux oak. Bethany's overall vineyard resources are some of the best in the Valley and its Shiraz wines are highly under-valued. It also produces a number of commercially well-received wines.

## BOWEN ESTATE, COONAWARRA

*Langton's selections – Bowen Estate Cabernet Sauvignon, Bowen Estate Shiraz*

The Bowen Estate vineyards, established in 1971 by Joy and Doug Bowen, now comprise about 32 hectares. Their daughter Emma Bowen, is now actively involved in the winemaking, illustrating a family commitment to Coonawarra. Since the first vintage in 1975, Bowen Estate has built a reputation for producing opulent well-crafted *Cabernet Sauvignon*. Its vineyards lie towards the southern end of Coonawarra. The winery is a prominent feature in this flat landscape and looks European.

In the last five years or so, Doug Bowen's wines have risen a notch, with more concentration, colour, and fruit sweetness. The *Cabernet Sauvignon* is reliable and well priced. Bowen Estate makes quintessential Coonawarra Cabernet Sauvignon with ripe, blackcurrant, and vanillin aromas, and a beautifully balanced palate. The alcohol level in some vintages can suggest moderate cellaring potential. The *Cabernet Sauvignon-Merlot-Cabernet Franc* is a more restrained style. In good vintages particularly, it can deliver more than the sum of its parts. The *Shiraz* reflects Coonawarra *terroir* well, with plenty of ripe, blackcurrant pastille fruit characters, and touches of pepper. The palate is typically generous and ripe, with plenty of squashy fruit, fine tannins, and length. Bowen Estate has been a solid performer, although vintage reputation is important. The Estate recently released a wine called *Ampelon* Shiraz.

- *BOWEN ESTATE Cabernet Sauvignon*
  *Coonawarra S.A. – Distinguished*

The famed *terra rossa* over limestone soils, cool climate, a winter rainfall pattern, and a good supply of underground water make Coonawarra the ideal place to grow Cabernet Sauvignon. The vineyard is planted on a two-wire arched cane trellis system, hand-pruned (50-60 buds per vine), and cropped at around two tonnes per acre. Winter and spring frosts are major threats. Grapes are machine harvested, then crushed immediately. After five days' vinification in vinimatics, the wine is transferred to new French oak *barriques* (approximately one-third new oak) to complete fermentation.

- *BOWEN ESTATE Shiraz*
  *Coonawarra S.A. – Distinguished*

Shiraz is usually harvested after Cabernet Sauvignon. After fermentation in vinimatics, the wine is transferred to new and used oak. A portion of the wine is matured in new American oak *barriques* to give complexity of flavour.

### BRAND'S OF COONAWARRA

*Langton's selections – Brand's of Coonawarra Stentiford's Reserve Old Vines Shiraz, Brand's of Coonawarra Patron's Reserve Cabernet Shiraz Merlot*

Brand's original Laira vineyard was established in 1896 by Captain Stentiford, a merchant navy man who named his property after a 'holed' square-rigger that once worked the coastlines of Australia and New Zealand. The remaining original plantings, some of the oldest in Coonawarra, miraculously still bear fruit. Eric and Nancy Brand purchased the property from father-in-law/father Bill Redman in 1965. Until then, they'd sold their fruit to local wineries. Their sons, Bill and Jim, began making wines under the Brand's own Laira label in the mid 1960s, enjoying quick success.

In 1990, McWilliam's, one of Australia's oldest family companies, joined forces with the Brand family, re-invigorating the business through winery upgrading and new vineyard developments, including Kirkgate and Station Block within the Coonawarra boundary.

Brand's *Stentifords Reserve Old Vines Shiraz* – entirely made from 100 year old vine material – shows plenty of mulberry fruit characters, new oak, and bristling tannins when young, but appears to have excellent ageing potential. Brand's *Patron's Reserve Cabernet Shiraz Merlot*, named after Eric Brand ('first patron of Coonawarra'), is profoundly deep in concentration with fine chocolaty tannins and well-integrated oak. This is a very convincing style. About 500 cases each of these wines are produced each year.

The moderately priced *Shiraz*, *Cabernet Sauvignon*, and *Limited Release Merlot*, all illustrate strong commitment to quality. Brand's of Coonawarra should be doing a lot better on the secondary market. Their top wines are not yet well known, but they do have what it takes to go the distance.

## CHAPEL HILL, McLAREN VALE

*Langton's selections – Chapel Hill Reserve Shiraz, Chapel Hill Shiraz*

Built in 1865 as a parish church and school, the now deconsecrated Chapel serves these days as a tasting room. Complementing the original stone construction, the winery is built into the hillside. Behind its façade is a state of the art winemaking facility, pristine and well ordered.

Vineyards are located at Blewitt Springs (on deep alluvial sands and clays), at Chapel Hill's own maritime-influenced hilltop vineyards (on red/brown clay over shale with ironstone), and at Kangarilla, and Baker's Gully in McLaren Vale east (on sand and mottled clays). Vines are trellised on a modified VSP 'west down, east up' system. Fruit quality is optimised during ripening by shading fruit on the hotter western canopies and exposing fruit on the wetter eastern canopies. Fruit is picked for optimal flavour and ripeness, with each vineyard having unique qualities. Vinification includes partial barrel fermentation and maturation for around 20 months in a combination of new and used French and American oak, depending on the wine. Chapel Hill imports its American oak and seasons it under Australia's scorching sun. Wines are made by noted winemaker Pam Dunsford.

When produced, *Chapel Hill Reserve Shiraz* is a ripe expression of McLaren Vale Shiraz with opulent, plummy, spicy, vanillin aromas, ripe, structured tannins, high concentration and flavour. The *Chapel Hill Shiraz* is a traditional style with mulberry/plum/raspberry punnet, even spicy aromas, underpinned by American oak. With its highly defined fruit and integrated oak, this richly flavoured wine is a quintessential McLaren Vale Shiraz-style. *Chapel Hill The Vicar* is a traditional Shiraz-Cabernet Sauvignon blend with a soupçon of Merlot.

Permafix, a global investment company with vineyard interests in California, Argentina, and Switzerland, now owns Chapel Hill. Yet to fire the market's imagination, Chapel Hill's current focus on ultra-fine Australian wine could well change this. Quality and commitment are there. Hazel Murphy, who's partly responsible for Australia's export success in the U.K. and Europe, recently joined this organisation.

## CHARLES MELTON, BAROSSA VALLEY

*Langton's selections – Charles Melton Nine Popes Shiraz-Grenache-Mourvedre, Charles Melton Shiraz*

Gifted winemaker Charlie Melton, is the man behind some of the most highly-prized and undervalued wines in the country. His winery, on Krondorf Road, just along from Rockford and St Hallett, has a certain eccentricity. Weatherboards are greying and the place looks a little battered by the elements. It sits below curvaceous hills, almost bare of trees, but is extraordinarily evocative.

Melton is often seen at the cellar door swapping yarns with loyal customers. The current micro-winery set-up is bursting at the seams, so a new winery is being constructed. Melton's approach, like his wines, is generous and embracing. As expected, great emphasis is placed on fruit quality – *Nine Popes* to *Grenache*, and *Mourvedre*, are what *Grange* is to *Shiraz*. Erroneously named after *Chateauneuf-du-Pape*, *Nine Popes* (first vintage 1988) has become the doyen of Australian Rhone blends. This is a very Australian wine, with ripe penetrating musky/plummy aromas, deep-set fruit and flavour.

The Barossa *Shiraz* is a classic Barossa style with perfumed blackberry, plum, dark cherry and chocolate aromas, underpinned by vanillin oak. Very much a 'heartland' style, the palate is big and plump with immense fruit and weight. The fruit is sourced from low-yielding vines, many of them gnarled old veterans. The dry-grown Barossa vineyards, often cropped at below one-and-a-half tonnes per acre, are scattered throughout the Barossa Valley floor from Williamstown in the south to Ebenezer in the north. The combination of sub-regional and varietal nuances brings complexity to all the wines.

Charles Melton's wines are moderate performers on the secondary market attracting solid market demand. These are staple auction wines, enthusiastically followed, but not at all costs. Just the way Charlie Melton would like it!

- *CHARLES MELTON Nine Popes Shiraz-Grenache-Mourvedre, Barossa Valley S.A. – Excellent*

Fruit is from low-yielding dry-grown Barossa vineyards. Sub-regional and varietal nuances bring complexity to the wine. Whole bunch fermentation, open fermentation, *pigeage*, and indigenous fermentation, are some of the wine-making techniques used to increase blending options. The wine is matured in 25 per cent new French and American oak. The perfume of Grenache, the richness of Shiraz, the structure of Mourvedre, and the savoury notes of oak are all melded together to produce a wine of great complexity and flavour. Alcohol is rarely above 14.5 per cent. These wines are best enjoyed relatively young. Only the best vintages will develop over the long term.

**CLARENDON HILLS, McLAREN VALE**

*Langton's selections – Clarendon Hills Astralis Shiraz, Clarendon Hills Hickinbotham Shiraz, Clarendon Hills Piggott Ranges, Clarendon Hills Sandown Cabernet Sauvignon, Clarendon Hills Liandra Shiraz*

Clarendon Hills is the original new breed cult winery. Its highly controversial *Astralis Shiraz* polarised critical Australian wine opinion. A few believed it to be the vinous equivalent of the Second Coming; most thought the style sailed close to the wind from a technical point of view. Depending on the source, many believed the wine would be "thrown out of a wine show". When it comes to selling wine however, controversy is good.

In 1994, influential U.S. writer Robert Parker Jr discovered *Astralis*, quickly putting the cat amongst the pigeons. The wine immediately captured the attention of a generation of fine wine lovers, catapulting Clarendon Hills to fame and leaving the industry gob-smacked. Asian collectors claimed it as one of their 'first growths' in the same way they did *Le Pin* and *Valandraud*. By the 1998 vintage, Clarendon Hills had found a place in the ultra-fine wine firmament.

Plush, exotic, and massively structured, *Astralis* is yet to prove itself in the secondary market, although it is highly prized by a number of collectors. No doubt much of the small production is headed for the U.S. and Asia.

Clarendon Hills has expanded its portfolio of single vineyard wines – all derived from 30 to 75 year old dry grown vines from the Clarendon, Blewitt Springs, and Kangarilla sub-regions. Clarendon Hills makes a point of highlighting the soil types of each vineyard. *Astralis* and the astonishingly good *Piggott Range Shirazes* derive from a mixture of clay, ironstone, and gravelly soils; *Brookman Shiraz* from a complex soil profile of sand, gravel ironstone, and clay; *Hickinbotham* from hard clay and ironstone in the Onkaparinga Valley; and the *Piggott Range* on solid rock.

*Liandra Shiraz* is interesting, particularly the 1998. It is too early to judge its potential. The Grenache-based wines are highly alcoholic, but have heaps of fruit definition and flavour. The *Sandown Cabernet Sauvignon* is promising.

Roman Bratasiuk, once seen as a marauder, should more fairly be seen as a pathfinder. He's taken the idea of a distinguished vineyard site to the *nth* degree, enhancing the reputation of McLaren Vale in the process, and inspired a whole generation of young winemakers to follow their hearts rather than be constricted by the contemporary winemaking paradigm.

## CORIOLE, McLAREN VALE

*Langton's selections – Coriole Lloyd Reserve Shiraz, Coriole Mary Kathleen Cabernet Sauvignon, Coriole Shiraz*

The 1990s brought renewed prosperity to Coriole, one of the leading producers in McLaren Vale. The vineyard, with its contoured plantings, is reminiscent of a plantation. The winery is a family concern run by brothers Mark and Paul Lloyd, established in 1969 and about 6km north of McLaren Vale township, at an elevation of 100 metres.

The *Coriole Lloyd Reserve* is a *tete de cuvee* wine reflecting the best parcels of fruit from the vineyard resources. Curiously, almost the entire fruit component comes from a vineyard planted in 1919. On deep clay soils, the east-facing site is located in the curvaceous landscape known by locals as the 'Seaview area'.

*Coriole Lloyd Reserve Shiraz*, a traditional but modern classic, is a robust but beautifully balanced style. The wines have intense, ripe, blackberry/black olive aromas and meaty complexity with plenty of palate richness, fruit sweetness, and texture. They are deceptively forward when young, but should cellar and develop for the medium to long term. Certainly, it is an excellent market performer with growing interest. *Coriole Shiraz* is always good value but not really an investment wine, although good vintages can do well. It is sourced from vines at least 25 years old, the majority Coriole's own, and is matured in French and American oak hogsheads and *barriques* for 12 months.

The wines show ripe, berry-fruit aromas, with pepper and spice characters, and excellent extract, fruit sweetness, and flavour. Coriole is also experimenting with Sangiovese, though it is still early days, and is also involved successfully in olive oil production. The *Mary Kathleen Cabernet Sauvignon* is always worth seeking out.

- *CORIOLE Lloyd Reserve Shiraz*
  *McLaren Vale S.A. – Excellent*

The 80 year old vines are rod and cane pruned, and trellised on a traditional two foliage wire trellis. Fruit is hand-picked, usually around mid-March, at optimum flavour development and usually at around 13.5-14.5° Baume. Fermentation takes place in concrete and steel open fermenters, regularly plunged to extract colour and flavour. Towards the end of fermentation – about one degree Baume – the wine is drained and pressed into a combination of new and old American and French oak. Fermentation is completed in barrel, a technique that meshes oak and wine flavours. The wine is then matured for 16 to 18 months before bottling.

## d'ARENBERG, McLAREN VALE

*Langton's selections – d'Arenberg Dead Arm Shiraz, d'Arenberg Old Vines Shiraz, d'Arenberg Footbolt Shiraz*

In 1912 Joseph Osborn, a teetotaller and director of Thomas Hardy and Sons (now BRL Hardy), purchased some well established vineyards, planted the previous century. Cellars were built in 1928 and the wine sold throughout the Empire.

In the late 1950s, d'Arry Osborn assumed control of the winery. His tremendous flair and focus on quality brought considerable fame to the d'Arenberg winery, producing the first cult wines in the Australian market. Its livery, distinctive with its a red diagonal stripe, gave the brand considerable impetus in the market.

Success in the Australian wine show system (winning the Jimmy Watson Trophy) helped d'Arenberg become an important wine producer. By the 1980s, d'Arenberg was considered a little old fashioned and on the edge of innovation. In truth, what happened was a shift in sentiment to cool climate wines. Chester Osborn, a Roseworthy trained winemaker, took over the reigns in 1984.

By 1990, the market again embraced the opulence of McLaren Vale Shiraz. During the 1990s, d'Arenberg was a hive of imagination, eccentricity, and fine winemaking. With significant vineyard holdings in McLaren Vale, d'Arenberg owns approximately 340 acres on various elevations, trellising systems, and soil types, ranging from red/brown loamy sands to hard clay, ironstone, and gravels. It has some of the oldest Shiraz, Grenache, and Mourvedre in the region.

The seriously good *Dead Arm Shiraz* takes its name from a fungal disease. 'Dead arm'-affected blocks are often considered to have one foot (arm?) in the grave, but d'Arenberg's truncated, gap-toothed old vines have been producing small bunches of highly flavoured grapes for more than 100 years. *Dead Arm Shiraz* has ripe, plummy, blackberry/liquorice aromas, superb fruit sweetness, concentration, and length with toasty American oak. This wine has tremendous potential on the auction market. The wines are very consistent across vintage. d'Arenberg has a fair swag of individual wines – *Old Vine Shiraz*, *Footbolt Shiraz*, and *Ironstone Pressings*, that are also well regarded but yet to make a firm impact on the market.

## ELDERTON, BAROSSA VALLEY

*Langton's selections – Elderton Command Shiraz, Elderton Shiraz*

Under leadership of the late Neil Ashmead, Elderton gained a reputation for big vinous statements and brash self-promotion. The critics were silenced however, when Elderton won Australia's prestigious Jimmy Watson Trophy, a victory that must have been very sweet. Neil's wife, Lorraine Ashmead, has since taken over running the vineyard. The wines are made by winemaker Richard Sheedy and assistant winemaker Allister Ashmead (Lorraine and Neil's son), with consulting help from Jim Irvine, a Barossa winemaker.

*Elderton Command Shiraz*, a classic old vine Barossa Shiraz style, is so-named because the best fruit commanded special treatment. About 2,000 cases are made each year. *Elderton Command* has attracted quite a following. The wines are neither as strong or overt as the traditional Barossa style, but are extremely well-balanced, having benefited from an extra 18 months of maturation. They are of medium to high intensity with raspberry/blackberry meaty fruit and some dark chocolate, pronounced tannin structure and integrated oak. The *Elderton Shiraz* is also a well-crafted wine. *Elderton Command* is an emerging secondary market staple with plenty of buyer interest.

- *ELDERTON Command Shiraz*
  *Barossa Valley S.A. – Excellent*

The fruit is entirely estate-grown on three vineyards – 78, 90, and 95 years old respectively. The vineyards are located on the banks of the Para River at Nuriootpa at the centre of the Barossa Valley. Soils here are alluvial, deep, underlaid by limestone and overlaid by silts deposited when the river (really a creek) breaks its banks. This occurs on average every 10 years, bringing fresh nutrients and rejuvenating soil fertility. Vines are trellised on a single wire and the fruit is picked on flavour development.

There is a saying in the Barossa that winemakers 'pick on shrinkle not shrivel', referring to the condition and ripeness of the fruit. Vintage takes place in late March/early April. The wine is made in a traditional manner – open fermented at approximately 30° C for eight to 10 days, regularly plunged and pumped over to maximise colour and flavour. The fermenting must is also headed down – waxed wooden boards keeping the cap (mass of grape skins) submerged.

Towards dryness, the wine is racked into a combination of new French (35%) and American oak to complete fermentation – a technique used extensively in Barossa Shiraz. It is then matured for approximately 12 to 18 months in new oak, depending on vintage. The wine is then assembled and further aged in two and three year old oak for a further 18 months before bottling.

## DUTSCHKE WINES, BAROSSA VALLEY

*Langton's selections – Oskar Semmler Shiraz, St Jakobi Shiraz, Willow Bend Merlot-Shiraz-Cabernet Sauvignon*

Dutschke Wines, at the southern end of the Barossa, is a relatively new entrant to the Barossa scene. Dutschke illustrates how vineyard provenance, high-quality winemaking, and recognition from Robert Parker Jr can immediately thrust a relatively obscure name into the marketplace in such a convincing way. Wayne Dutschke's family established the vineyard on their land in the 1930s, supplying fruit to local co-operatives. By 1975, the vineyard had been re-established with Shiraz and Cabernet varieties, with most of the fruit going to Krondorf and Mildara Blass. The vineyard, on darker loams over clay, is approximately 43 acres, mostly trellised on a single wire, open canopy system. The fruit is usually picked at 14° Baume on flavour development. The wines are vinified in static fermenters with regular pumping over. At dryness, the *Oskar Semmler* is drained and pressed off into 80 to 100 per cent new French oak; the *St Jakobi* sees 20 per cent new, predominantly French with some American oak. *Willow Bend Merlot-Shiraz-Cabernet Sauvignon* is matured in 20 per cent new, predominantly American and some French oak.

*Oscar Semmler Shiraz* is a ripe, blackberry fruit-spangled wine with plenty of liquorice and cedar, smoky oak, a richly flavoured palate with high-pitched fruit, and refined French oak characters. It has plenty of opulence but also a naturally textured palate. Easy to see why this wine has attracted so much enthusiasm. The wine is classically proportioned and shows strong regional definition.

*St Jakobi Shiraz* is also an incredibly well-made wine, with intense ground-coffee liquorice aromas and flavours with underlying oak, and sinewy tannin structure.

While Dutschke has almost no presence on the market, it has the hallmarks of a star performer. The quality of its debut wines is simply breathtaking. Simply one of the most exciting new wines on the market.

## FOX CREEK, McLAREN VALE

*Langton's selections – Fox Creek Reserve Shiraz*

In 1984, Jim and Helen Watts bought their 100 acre Malpas Road property. Between McLaren Vale and Willunga, the land was previously used for barley crops and sheep grazing. A vineyard was established in 1985 and planted to a Scott-Henry or vertical shoot position trellis system. In 1995, a partnership, the Fox Creek Wine Company, was formed to process fruit from three vineyards, including Malpas Road.

Fox Creek made an immediate impact with its *Shiraz* – the winemakers, Sarah (nee Watts) and Sparky Marquis, winning the local Bushing King and Queen trophy for the best wine made from McLaren Vale fruit. A swag of great reviews, wine show trophies, and high praise from Robert Parker Jr for the 1996 and 1997 *Reserve Shiraz* and 1997 *JSM Shiraz Cabernet Sauvignon*, fast-tracked Fox Creek onto the international stage – bringing substantial interest from wine geeks the world over. By 1999, Fox Creek invested in a new barrel store and 1,000 tonne winery.

The fairytale start appeared to end with the departure of Sarah and Sparky Marquis. The official line is that they remain as consultants.

So far, the wines still look extremely good. The 1998 and 1999 *Reserve Shirazes* are excellent, illustrating a philosophy of low-cropping viticulture and focused winemaking. The *Reserve Shiraz* is a highly concentrated, well made McLaren Vale style that has managed to capture the imagination of wine investors, despite its relatively new presence in the marketplace. Although the froth has come off the market for cult wines, Fox Creek – on the back of realistic values – attracts good levels of support.

## GLAETZER, BAROSSA VALLEY

*Langton's selections – Glaetzer Shiraz, Glaetzer The Bishop Shiraz*

Glaetzer is one of the emerging stars of the Barossa. Although this family venture was established only in 1995, philosophically, and by heritage, Glaetzer is Barossa down to its boot-straps. A Roseworthy-trained father and son team, Colin and Ben Glaetzer, makes the wines. Colin is the man behind the spectacularly successful *Barossa Valley Estates E&E Black Pepper Shiraz.*

*Glaetzer Shiraz* – first vintage 1996 – epitomises the strong sense of place emerging in the Barossa. This is a wine that goes further than expressing Barossa floor Shiraz. The fruit is sourced entirely from low yielding unirrigated vines (mostly around 60 to 80 years old) around the village of Ebenezer. Here, soils are sandy clay loams and the climate is distinctly hotter and drier than Barossa south. Glaetzer believes the Shiraz fruit in Ebenezer is softer and rounder. *Glaetzer Shiraz* is open fermented and regularly pumped over to optimise flavour. Towards dryness, it is racked into new American puncheons to complete fermentation and malo-lactic fermentation. Maturation takes approximately 12 to 18 months, depending on vintage, prior to bottling.

*Glaetzer Shiraz* is very open-knit with intense, plummy, mulberry aromas and touches of meaty complexity. The fruit is rich and supple, with underlying fine lacy tannins, but beautifully balanced oak and plenty of length. Although only four vintages have been released, *Glaetzer Shiraz* already shows strong regional provenance with all the class one would expect from a top Barossa Shiraz.

The *Bishop Shiraz*, seemingly with religious connotations, is actually named after Colin's wife's family. The fruit is sourced from younger Ebenezer vineyards, mostly around 30 years old. After fermentation, the wine is matured in six year old American and French oak hogsheads. The style is quite similar to Penfolds *St Henri*.

## GRANT BURGE, BAROSSA VALLEY

*Langton's selections – Grant Burge Meshach Shiraz, Grant Burge Filsell Shiraz, Grant Burge Holy Trinity Grenache-Shiraz-Mourvedre*

Grant Burge has earned an extraordinary reputation for quality and consistency. A fifth generation Barossa winemaker, he named *Meshach Shiraz* after his great grandfather, who arrived in South Australia in 1855 at age 11, later established the Wilsford Winery at Lyndoch, and lived to the ripe old age of 98.

Grant Burge has one of the largest vineyard holdings in Barossa, mainly the Central and Southern parts of the Barossa Valley, and in the Eden Valley. Dovetailing superb viticultural resources, a family history, and a bit of show business, Grant Burge has become a highly successful commercial wine producer, making wines at several price points. Its *Meshach* is a *tete-de-cuvee* wine from the 80 year old Filsell vineyard, near Lyndoch. The vineyard, planted on deep alluvial soils, is triaged for optimum ripeness and flavour development – often around 14° Baume. The wine is vinified in open headed down fermenters at warm temperatures. Towards dryness, the wine is drained and pressed, completing fermentation in mostly new American oak hogsheads.

*Meshach* is a highly concentrated and generous Barossa style with a ripe, dense palate packed with fruit, pronounced tannins, and supported by American oak. *Meshach* is already highly regarded for its potential longevity and structure. It attracts moderate interest on the market but occasional spikes suggest strong potential. It is certainly a convincing style and important to the rising fortunes of the Barossa. *Filsell Shiraz* is also very good and at realistic prices. *Shadrach Cabernet Sauvignon* is an evolving style and attracts a mixed response.

## GREENOCK CREEK, BAROSSA VALLEY

*Langton's selections – Greenock Creek Roennfeldt Road Shiraz, Greenock Creek Block Shiraz, Greenock Creek Seven Acre Shiraz, Greenock Creek Apricot Block Shiraz, Greenock Creek Roennfeldt Road Shiraz, Greenock Creek Cabernet Sauvignon*

Tucked away behind Seppeltsfield, on the western edge of the Barossa, is Greenock Creek, established by Michael and Annabelle Waugh in 1975. The scattered vineyards lie in a pocket cut by a creek that is now a dry bed of varying earths, ranging from red loamy material to alluvial, bordering on clay soils. The original homestead was built in the 1850s with a small never used underground cellar, but built presumably to make wine.

Greenock Creek is now a red wine specialist, having grafted over its Chardonnay vines. There are now 45 acres of vines – all dry grown and cropped at an impossibly low one-and-a-half to two tonnes per acre. A new winery, beautifully sited on the Roennfeldt Road, shows the leaps and bounds Greenock Creek has made in recent years. The wines are vinified in open sunk slate fermenters and regularly plunged over. The free-run wine and pressings are kept separate to increase blending options. The wines are drained and pressed in Hypac basket presses, then into a combination of new and used oak, depending on the vineyard parcel. The *Roennfeldt Road Cabernet Sauvignon* and *Roennfeldt Road Shiraz*, both off vines planted during the early 1950s, are matured for 36 months in new French oak. Production is limited to just a few barrels. The *Creek Block Shiraz* is matured for 26 to 27 months in a combination of 10 per cent new and old French oak.

The Waughs have a fairly *laissez faire* attitude to maturation, leaving the barrels bunged at 'one o'clock' and no topping up. Michael Waugh is totally self-trained and has little time for techno-crap. In a former life, he was a builder and stonemason. Indeed, he rebuilt the beautiful Rockford Winery and extended the Henschke Cellars. His winemaker friends drop by offering tidbits of technical advice. The whole Greenock Creek experience is one of great charm. Here is an example where intuitive and creative winemaking, together with a smattering of technical inexperience and confident enthusiasm, have combined to bring something new and unique to the Barossa.

The sudden success of Greenock Creek, generated by the enthusiasm of Robert Parker Jr, has left the Waughs completely flummoxed. The wines are incredibly opulent with a silken palate structure and plenty of fruit richness. A new *Alice's Block Shiraz* will bring the Greenock Creek portfolio to five Shirazes, two Cabernet Sauvignons, and a Grenache.

## GROSSET, CLARE VALLEY

*Langton's selections – Grosset Polish Hill Riesling, Grosset Watervale Riesling, Grosset Gaia Cabernet Sauvignon*

Jeffrey Grosset established Grosset Wines in 1981, in the southern end of Clare Valley, at historic Auburn. Grosset's exquisite *Polish Hill* and *Watervale* Rieslings led the Clare Valley Riesling renaissance. *Polish Hill*, an exclusive trademark, was named after the nearby Hill River settlement, established by Polish migrants in the 1840s. The wine contributes greatly to the acceptance that Clare Valley Riesling is from one of the premier Riesling regions of the world. The *Watervale Riesling* is a classic Clare style. If *Polish Hill* is power and intensity, *Watervale* is restraint and pure fruit, reflecting the red loam over limestone soils. It evokes the expectation of a mouth-watering palate and delivers it.

"Making Riesling is the purest form of winemaking," says Jeff Grosset, "because the winemaker is very restricted in what can be done. No oak, no malo-lactic, and usually no extended lees contact or grape-skin contact is employed. A disciplined approach is needed to retain the inherent fruit characters and expression of individual vineyard site". Recently Grosset, like many Clare producers, has been bottling its wine with Stelvin cap – a brilliant move ensuring freshness and typicity for the consumer.

Although Jeffrey Grosset has been canonised by Riesling fanatics, he's not half bad at Chardonnay either. He makes a fine wine from Piccadilly (Adelaide Hills) fruit, showing grapefruit and tropical fruit aromas, a creamy palate, and well-integrated new oak. To round out the offering, *Grosset Gaia* is an extremely fine Cabernet blend – the most recent vintage also available under Stelvin cap.

Grosset Rieslings, with long term cellaring potential and a strong track record, are star performers on the secondary wine market.

Recently Grosset and Yalumba announced a joint-'adventure' to make an ultra-fine *Eden Valley Riesling*. More philosophical than profit driven, this project will do much to show the class of this undervalued sub-region of the Barossa. The wine 'Mesh' from its 2002 vintage has received positive response.

- *GROSSET Polish Hill Riesling*
  *Clare Valley S.A. – Outstanding*

The Grosset Polish Hill vineyard is located in a U-shaped ridge formation, with Mount Horrocks (close to the centre of the region) at its base. Soils here are low in fertility, mostly poor shaley, slightly acid soil, with underlying slate and a topsoil crust of clay interspersed with shale. The vineyard, at an elevation of 460 metres, was planted between 1966 and 1978 and is fully mature. The vines are trellised to double foliage wire vertical trellis. Vine vigour is low, with yields averaging 3.1 tonnes per acre. Berries are smaller and more concentrated than Watervale. Vintage takes place in early April, normally a few weeks later than Watervale. Each parcel of fruit is hand-picked, de-stemmed and crushed, then drained immediately. Pressings are never used in Polish Hill. The free-run juice is cold-settled for four days before being yeasted and fermented in closed stainless steel fermenters. In July, each parcel of wine is tasted, then assembled ready for bottling.

This is the most successful Australian Riesling. Grosset is a perfectionist and the wines have incredible perfume and fruit purity, the lime/floral fruit profile balanced by an indelible acidity that cuts across the palate. This wine does much to define the distinctive character of Clare Valley Riesling.

- *GROSSET Watervale Riesling*
  *Clare Valley S.A. – Excellent*

Grosset sources fruit from a hilltop site with a very thin crust of topsoil. Vines are deeply rooted into slate/shale bedrock. Vertical shoot position trellis systems are used extensively to increase exposure to sunlight. *Watervale* enjoys plenty of sunshine but nights are usually very cool, so the natural acidity of the Riesling grape tends to be restrained. Fruit is picked late March/early April with cropping levels around three to four tonnes per acre. Vinification is almost identical to *Polish Hill*.

Grosset's *Watervale Riesling* is as impressive a wine as the same maker's *Polish Hill Riesling*, although not quite as tightly structured or delicate.

**HENSCHKE, KEYNETON (EDEN VALLEY/ BAROSSA)**

*Langton's selections – Henschke Hill of Grace Shiraz, Henschke Mount Edelstone Shiraz, Henschke Cyril Henschke Cabernet Sauvignon, Henschke Abbott's Prayer Merlot-Cabernet Sauvignon, Henschke Keyneton Estate Shiraz-Cabernet Sauvignon-Malbec, Henschke Julius Riesling*

During the 1950s, Cyril Henschke established the *Hill of Grace* label in 1956. However, it is Stephen Henschke and his viticulturist partner Prue Henschke, who have painstakingly developed the vineyard and wine since 1978. Both the *Hill of Grace* and *Mount Edelstone* vineyards, established in 1862 and the 1920s respectively, are producing Shiraz of immense purity, intensity, and flavour. These old vines, Prue Henschke believes, provide a critical edge to the concept of 'distinguished vineyard site'. Each wine style differs, illustrating that each vineyard has its own character.

*Hill of Grace* has intense blackberry and spice aromas balanced by meaty barrel ferment characters. The palate is richly concentrated, with complex, gamy, blackberry/ chocolate flavours, ripe tannins, and integrated oak.

*Mount Edelstone* is looser knit, with opulent, blackberry/vanillin aromas and a fleshy palate, underpinned by structured tannins. Both wines age beautifully and are considered quintessential Barossa wines.

*Cyril Henschke Cabernet Sauvignon* (hard to believe it was once the most expensive of the trio) is also a superb wine. Affectionately known by the wine trade, as 'The Squirrel', this wine has marvellous fruit definition, with blackcurrants and meaty, barrel ferment nuances.

Stephen and Prue Henschke's attention to detail and commitment are exemplary. Indicative is the rise and rise of the brand since they took over the family business in the late 1970s. *Keyneton Estate*, for instance, is a more commercial Henschke red, but such a good one that it attracts investors. *Abbott's Prayer* is a Merlot-Cabernet Sauvignon from the Adelaide Hills. It may not have the concentration or opulence of *Hill of Grace*, but does show enormous fruit purity and structure. *Julius Riesling* is a fine, definitive example of the Eden Valley style – less perfumed than Clare Riesling, but with highly defined fruit and linear acidity. The *Adelaide Hills Croft Chardonnay* is in evolution.

Henschke enjoys a strong cornerstone presence on the secondary market especially for its *Hill of Grace Shiraz* and *Mount Edelstone Shiraz*. Its overall market performance – like *Grange* – can be linked to general economic sentiment.

- *HENSCHKE Hill of Grace Shiraz*
  *Keyneton S.A. – Exceptional*

Henschke *Hill of Grace* is regarded as something of a national treasure. Nicolaus Stanitski, a Henschke ancestor, planted the original *Hill of Grace* vineyard in the 1860s. The Barossa Valley Shiraz vines, many now over 140 years old, are amongst the world's oldest genetic Shiraz plant material. It is remarkable that the vineyard survived intact, considering the economic uncertainty and the social conditions at the time. There are several blocks: Grandfather's Post Office Blocks One and Two; Young, which comprises younger, selected material from vines near the old Post Office; Church Block; House Block; and Windmill Block.

Vintage takes place mid to late April – each parcel vinified separately, to maximise blending options. Vinification takes place in open headed down fermenters with regular pumping over. Towards dryness, the wine is drained and pressed. Partial barrel fermentation follows, in a combination of new American and French oak , to integrate oak and create complexity. The wine is then matured in the same oak for about 18 months, before bottling and further maturation.

Vintages before 1978 are hit and miss and not worth seeking out, unless for reference purposes. Today the vineyard speaks for itself. Older vintages show gamy/earthy complexity and superb structure. Production is usually about 1,500-2,000 cases, although it can be quite a lot smaller.

- *HENSCHKE Cyril Henschke Cabernet Sauvignon*
  *Keyneton S.A. – Outstanding*

This now entirely single vineyard wine, is named after the late Cyril Henschke, who bought the Eden Valley property in the 1970s when Cabernet Sauvignon was all the rage. The first vintage in 1978, comprised 100 per cent Cabernet Sauvignon, but the style has evolved to include small elements of Merlot and Cabernet Franc. On a north-easterly slope, about 450 metres above sea-level, the vineyard has generally well drained sandy loams over gravel, and patches of clay. Vines are vertical shoot positioned, using four foliage wires and mostly cane pruned to 50-60 buds. Harvest is normally at the end of April.

Fermentation takes place in headed down open fermenters, pumping over to maximise colour; flavour extraction occurs at least twice a day. The ferment is temperature controlled to maximise fruit expression and minimise harsh tannin structures. The wine is transferred to French oak, mainly Vosges, Alliers, and Berce, to complete fermentation. At the end of primary fermentation, malolactic fermentation is also encouraged. The wine matures in oak for 18 months before blending and bottling.

Since 1986, the wine has shown extraordinary quality consistency. Even lesser vintages should not be overlooked.

- *HENSCHKE Mount Edelstone Shiraz Keyneton S.A. – Outstanding*

From the German *Edelstein* meaning gemstone, Mount Edelstone is a single, dry-grown Shiraz vineyard planted by Ronald Angas in the 1920s. Henschke made wines from Mount Edelstone as early as 1952, although Cyril Henschke did not buy the vineyard until 1974. By then, it was already recognised as an important vineyard site. On the eastern slopes of Mount Edelstone, this 40 acre vineyard comprises low-yielding, gnarled vines, many well into their 80s, planted on deep red, sandy loams, over laminated silt stones. This low input vineyard is being gradually re-trellised to the Scott Henry system, where shoots are trained upwards and downwards to maximise sunlight exposure to leaves and fruit. The oldest vines are trained on a traditional two wire trellis.

Prue Henschke constantly seeks improvement in the vineyard, her aim, best colour and flavour development. The site is cooler and higher than the Barossa floor, although the climate is essentially Mediterranean. Vintage is mid to late April. The wine is fermented in open top slate headed down fermenters. Fermentation completes in a combination of new American and French oak.

Although *Hill of Grace* is lionised by the cognoscenti, *Mount Edelstone* is, in many respects, the ultimate in Australian Shiraz, with wonderful opulence of both fruit and structure. I have always felt the wine to be undervalued.

## HOLLICK, COONAWARRA

*Langton's selections – Hollick Cabernet Sauvignon-Merlot, Hollick Ravenswood Cabernet Sauvignon*

In 1975, Ian Hollick, formerly Mildara's national vineyard manager, established the Hollick vineyard on 40 acres of prime Coonawarra *terra rossa* soils. A winery was built in 1984 and Hollick quickly gained a heightened presence in the market by winning the coveted Jimmy Watson trophy in 1985. The cellar door is the former childhood home of John Shaw Nielson, a prominent, late 19th century Australian lyric poet. The vineyards now comprise 160 acres all within the Coonawarra boundary.

The *Hollick Ravenswood Cabernet Sauvignon*, a special selection verging on an essence-of-Coonawarra style, is sourced from the oldest vines, growing in the shallowest *terra rossa* soils and trellised on a single wire and bilateral cordon. Meticulous vineyard management, including cover crops and individual row drip irrigation, ensures high-quality, low-yielding fruit with optimum skin to juice ratios. The wine is vinified in static fermenters with regular pumping over. Towards dryness, it is pressed, drained, then completes fermentation in 100 per cent new French oak *barriques*. The wine is then racked off lees and matured in the same oak for 18 months. *Hollick Cabernet Sauvignon-Merlot*, also comprising some Cabernet Franc and Petit Verdot, is vinified in similar fashion, but matures in approximately 30 per cent new French oak hogsheads.

Hollick is making classic Coonawarra Cabernet Sauvignon-Merlot with highly defined blackcurrant aromas, fine-grained tannins and balance. *Hollick Wilgha Shiraz* sees 100 per cent American oak, but has a low profile in the market. The wines have plenty of cassis, cedar aromas, and a grainy textured palate, underpinned by oak. Rather unexposed on the secondary market, the *Ravenswood* label has been around for some time. It is seriously undervalued.

## IRVINE, EDEN VALLEY

*Langton's selections – Irvine Grand Merlot*

Irvine sources its fruit entirely from its elevated (390-430 metres) Springhill Vineyard in the Eden Valley, a sub-region of the Barossa geographical indication. Irvine was established by winemaking consultant and all-rounder James Irvine. The vineyard provides fruit for his *Eden Crest* label, yet he has become known as a specialist Merlot producer, sold under the *Irvine* label. He even makes a sparkling Merlot, a variation on the classic Australian style.

*Irvine Grand Merlot*, the first Australian Merlot to be included in *Langton's Classification*, is something of an aberration. The name derives from Jim Irvine's grand introduction to Merlot – a glass of *Chateau Petrus*. Don't expect an elegant, plummy style. This wine is a massive, almost abrasive style, with plenty of fruit, oak and tannin.

Jim Irvine explains that oak plays a supporting role to extremely dense, concentrated fruit. These multi-layered wines are very much an experience. He recommends that these wines be decanted at least three hours prior to drinking. They are powerful, tightly structured wines with plush plummy fruit, plenty of oak,and firm tannins.

Quite a controversial style, the wine is just so massively structured that it polarises opinion. However, it performs well against some of the world's most recognised Merlots in wine competitions. *Irvine Merlot* has a strong, loyal following with solid results on the secondary market.

- *IRVINE Grand Merlot, Eden Valley S.A. – Excellent*

Fruit for this wine is sourced from Irvine's Spring Hill vineyard in the cool Eden Valley, on grey-brown podzolic loams interspersed with schistic gravels. The 3.6 hectare vineyard,

390-410 metres above sea-level, is increasingly being trellised to a Smart Dyson system to allow better fruit exposure with corresponding ripeness and flavour benefits. Vintage takes place late April/early May. Wines are vinified in open fermenters at around 30° C, regularly plunged and pumped over to increase colour and flavour. At dryness, they are drained and pressed, then macerated in stainless steel tanks for about three weeks. The wine is then matured in one-third new high toast Alliers Oak, one-third used, and one-third older oak – all barrels coopered by Seguin Moreau. Jim Irvine explains that oak plays a supporting role to the extremely dense, concentrated fruit. Maturation takes place for a staggering 33-42 months, depending on vintage!

### JIM BARRY, CLARE VALLEY

*Langton's selections – Jim Barry The Armagh Shiraz, Jim Barry McRae Wood Shiraz*

In 1959, Jim Barry bought land near the township of Clare, replanting much of it to vineyard. Highly influential in the Australian wine scene, he worked for the Clarevale Co-operative for two decades and established Taylor's for the Sydney-based Taylor family. He also formed a strong relationship with Roly Birks at Wendouree, making his own wines there in the late 1960s. In 1973, Barry built his own winery, quickly earning a fine reputation for his wines, mostly in the 'excellent value for money' category. The *Armagh* vineyard was planted by Jim Barry in 1968 with Shiraz clones originally sourced from Israel.

Towards the end of the 1980s, the fortunes of Jim Barry Wines changed dramatically. Peter and Mark Barry have shown incredible marketing and winemaking intuition. The *Armagh* has achieved outstanding success and is regarded as one of the finest Shirazes in the country.

The *Armagh*, made by Mark Barry, is a powerfully compressed Australian Shiraz style, a wine of monumental proportions that explodes with aroma and flavour. The oak, particularly in classic years, is hidden behind curtains of deep, ripe, intense fruit and extraordinarily fine, structured tannins.

The *Armagh* has attracted attention as a paradigm for the current enthusiasm for highly-concentrated, massively proportioned Australian Shirazes. Fashion aside, this wine is surely a beacon of quality, showing extraordinary consistency across vintages. The quality is excellent.

The *McRae Wood Shiraz* is a loose-knit style showing plenty of regional definition and complexity.

- *JIM BARRY The Armagh Shiraz Clare Valley S.A. – Outstanding*

Named after the nearby settlement of Armagh, which was settled by Irish in about 1859. The vineyard, elevated at 400 metres, is planted on its own roots, on black alluvial soils over sandy gravel. Vines are trellised on vertical twin wires and rod and spur pruned. A full canopy, running north-south, is used without hedging. Fruit is typically hand-picked in mid-April. The grapes are crushed into an open top fermenter and warmed to approximately 25° C, before yeast (Bordeaux Red) inoculation. Fermentation lasts approximately 10 days – extended maceration happening only rarely. Auto plunging occurs every 90 minutes. Pressings are blended back. A naturally induced malo-lactic fermentation follows. The wine is racked off lees at least twice before transfer to a combination of heavily-toasted new American and French oak. A light, egg-white fining and coarse filtration takes place after 12 to 14 months' barrel maturation.

## JOSEPH, ADELAIDE PLAINS

*Langton's selections – Joseph Moda Amarone Cabernet Sauvignon-Merlot*

Joe Grilli, the enthusiastic, inquisitive, and highly innovative winemaker behind the *Joseph* label, has taken a small winery from the backwaters of the Australian wine industry to the forefront of the niche wine market. His father Primo, an Italian immigrant, established Primo Estate in prime market gardening country north of Adelaide. Its stock in trade wines were simple easy-drinking styles and a fruity Colombard. Experimentation in double pruning, induced botrytis affected, Amarone, and sparkling red wines, led to new and very successful wines being launched. The exquisitely packaged *Joseph* label reflects the utmost attention to detail. Olive oil and vinegar are also produced under this label.

*Joseph Moda Amarone Cabernet Sauvignon-Merlot* is an emerging modern classic, reflecting the multi-culturalism and multi-viticulturism of the Australian wine industry. Using fruit from McLaren Vale and Coonawarra, this blend's philosophy is that McLaren Cabernet Sauvignon provides richness and power, and Coonawarra Cabernet Sauvignon provides perfume and structure. The McLaren Vale Merlot component softens out the palate. In recent vintages, fruit is also sourced from Wrattonbully and Currency Creek. The philosophy, however, remains the same!

*Joseph Moda Amarone* shows gamy, chocolaty fruit aromas with well-integrated oak and well-defined, grainy tannins. The overall style transcends the vagaries of vintage, making it a very reliable wine. It's not overtly varietal; rather a house style with excellent ageing potential. It is a solid market performer with an excellent volume of interest at reasonable price levels.

- *JOSEPH Moda Amarone Cabernet Sauvignon-Merlot Coonawarra-McLaren Vale S.A. – Excellent*

This wine style harks back to the Amarone method of production that originated in Valpolicella in Northern Italy. After picking, the fruit is allowed to dry out on racks to increase the skin to juice ratio. The wine is made in a traditional way, using open fermenters, followed by maturation in a combination of French, German, and American oak for 14 to 20 months, depending on the vintage.

## KATNOOK ESTATE, COONAWARRA

*Langton's selections – Katnook Estate Cabernet Sauvignon, Katnook Odyssey Cabernet Sauvignon*

Katnook (Aboriginal word meaning 'fat land') is the second largest vigneron in Coonawarra. It is owned by the Spanish conglomerate Freixenet and the Yunghanns family. The estate was named by Coonawarra pioneer, John Riddoch, who owned this property in the 1890s and made his first vintage in 1895. Riddoch, an entrepreneur by all accounts, is considered the father of Coonawarra. He bought a vast tract of land and, recognising the potential of this region, created the Coonawarra Fruit Colony and sub-divided the land into 10 acre blocks. It wasn't a great success. Riddoch was clearly 50 years ahead of his time.

In 1970, the vineyards were replanted. In 1980, in the historic woodsheds, under Wayne Stehben's watchful eyes, the first vintage for 83 years started the modern era of winemaking at Katnook. The vineyards comprise more than 1,000 acres planted on *terra rossa* soils over limestone, with mainly traditional open sprawling canopies. The best parcels are used in Katnook wines, the remainder for the *Riddoch* label, or contract grown.

*Katnook Cabernet Sauvignon* reflects the unique Coonawarra vineyard site, attracting considerable support in recent years. The wine shows plenty of intense blackcurrant/mulberry fruit definition, mid-palate richness, fine-grained tannins, and excellent length. It is a medium to long term prospect, although buyers should keep a weather eye on vintage reputation.

The *Odyssey*, which is Katnook's essence of Coonawarra Cabernet Sauvignon style, is matured for 38 months in French oak. The *Prodigy* is an essence of Coonawarra Shiraz style, vinified in open fermenters and matured in 50/50 new American and French oak for 24 months.

Katnook enjoys a strengthening presence on the secondary market. The *Odyssey* is impressive and could do well – the overall resources and commitment to quality are there. However, rapid expansion in production of its ultra-fine portfolio, against a background of large acreage, will need tremendous imagination in the marketing and distribution departments. In the meantime, Katnook has solid support.

- *KATNOOK ESTATE Cabernet Sauvignon Coonawarra S.A. – Distinguished*

Vines are mainly with traditional open, sprawling canopies. Recent plantings are vertically shoot positioned to emphasise fruit exposure. Grapes are picked around mid-April at optimum ripeness and flavour development. Vinification takes place in closed static fermenters with regular pumping over of the floating cap. The wine macerates on skins for approximately 14 days before transfer to approximately 50-60 per cent new French oak – predominantly medium grained Nevers – for around 24 months before bottling.

## KNAPPSTEIN, CLARE VALLEY

*Langton's selections – Knappstein Handpicked Riesling, Knappstein Enterprise Cabernet Sauvignon, Knappstein Enterprise Shiraz*

Tim Knappstein established Knappstein in the mid 1970s, in the old Enterprise Brewery in Clare. In 1992, Petaluma acquired the business. A management change followed in 1995, with Andrew Hardy brought in as winemaker, Tim Knappstein leaving to set up his Lenswood vineyards in the Adelaide Hills.

The *Knappstein Handpicked Riesling* is one of the region's classic wines. It is classically vinified – the juice being cold settled for a couple of weeks, before seeding with R2 yeast, and cold-fermenting for up to six weeks. The re-emergence of selected parcels of fruit under the *Knappstein Enterprise* label is a positive move.

The *Enterprise Cabernet Sauvignon* (with a portion of Malbec) is sourced from low-yielding vines on *terra rossa* soils, and vinified in Potter and open fermenters, before maturation in French oak *barriques* for up to 28 months. The *Enterprise Shiraz* is matured in used French oak for 24 months. Knappstein wines have only a moderate profile on the secondary market.

## LEASINGHAM, CLARE VALLEY

*Langton's selections – Leasingham Classic Clare Shiraz, Leasingham Classic Clare Cabernet Sauvignon*

Leasingham winery was purchased in 1893 when a partnership including the merchant J. Knappstein, bought the Clare

Jam Factory. Known initially as the Stanley Wine Company and owned through various entities, this winery has followed the ebb and flow of economic fortune in the Clare Valley, playing host to a litany of bright winemakers including Tim Knappstein and Tim Adams. BRL Hardy acquired the winery in 1988.

Leasingham's reputation as a great Clare name, declined during the 1980s due to its focus on commercial brands, including cask wine. Its reputation as a quality producer however, has been rejuvenated by the *Classic Clare* label, and the winery has earned accolades for its *Leasingham Classic Clare Shiraz*. The 1994 vintage established its pedigree by winning the highly coveted Jimmy Watson Trophy at the Melbourne Wine Show.

*Leasingham Classic Clare Shiraz* fruit is sourced from the windswept Shrober's Vineyard, just north of Auburn. The vines, on variable soils of *terra rossa* and slate, are in a constant rain shadow and yield extremely concentrated Shiraz fruit. The resulting wines are no shrinking violets. Richly flavoured, they have highly defined plum/berry fruit characters and integrated oak. The *Classic Clare Cabernet Sauvignon* is a similarly structured wine. These wines perform extremely well on the secondary market, and represent value at moderate price levels.

## LECONFIELD, COONAWARRA

*Langton's selections – Leconfield Cabernet Sauvignon, Leconfield Shiraz*

At the southern end of Coonawarra, Leconfield is one of the region's leading small winemakers. Leconfield was established in 1974 by Sydney Hamilton, at age 76. He named the vineyard after his predecessor Lord Leconfield. Making light of political correctness, the original labels stated "the grapes are hand-picked by experienced young girls". Sydney Hamilton's nephew, Dr Richard Hamilton, now owns the winery.

The *Cabernet Sauvignon* is by far its most important wine and has a strong following, although some critics not do like the style. There is also a good *Cabernet Franc*, *Shiraz*, and *Merlot*, and a rare and interesting *Petit Verdot*.

The 70 acre vineyard is planted on famed Coonawarra *terra rossa* clay-based loam soils, over a free draining limestone crust. The majority of vines are over 20 years old. Most are direct producing, although a proportion of the Sauvignon is planted on rootstocks. Trellising systems are varied – the winemaker exploring every flavour nuance.

The wines reflect the vineyard site, typically with extravagant, ultra-defined fruit flavours of cassis and anise, the palate tightly structured and compact, with underlying new oak characters. The *Shiraz* is an elegant style with raspberry/pepper aromas and excellent palate richness. Leconfield has a moderate profile on the secondary market, however the *Cabernet Sauvignon* has a solid following. Vintage reputation is important.

- *LECONFIELD Cabernet Sauvignon*
  *Coonawarra S.A. – Distinguished*

The wine is fermented in closed stainless steel fermenters. After fermentation, it is left on skins for a period determined by flavour development. The wine is matured in a combination of new and one-year old French oak for 12 to 18 months before bottling. At Leconfield, low intervention, low input winemaking is a feature, so the wines reflect vineyard site. Quite a controversial wine.

## LEO BURING, CLARE VALLEY

*Langton's selections – Leo Buring Riesling, Leo Buring Leonay Riesling, Leo Buring Watervale Riesling*

Hermann Paul Leopold Buring, better known as Leo Buring, was born in 1876 in South Australia to German parents. In 1902, he joined Minchinbury Cellars near Mt Druitt in N.S.W. In 1931, with Reginald Mowat of Great Western, Buring formed a business partnership, Leo Buring & Co. His first wine was made in the early 1930s, from grapes grown at his property in Emu Plains, N.S.W. In 1945, Buring moved the major part of his wine operations to South Australia's Barossa Valley. Now, the old Barossa-based Leonay winery is owned by Orlando and Southcorp owns the brand. The Leonay name comes from Leo's Emu Plains home and vineyard, and derives from his name and his wife's nickname 'Nay'.

If circumstances had been more kind, the name Leo Buring would still have enormous cachet – the best Buring Rieslings from the Eden and Clare Valleys are certainly close to perfection. However, the defection of Riesling master John Vickery to Orlando, label changes, a bin numbering system that would confuse a NASA scientist, plus a decade or so of visionless brand management, have muddied what should have been bright waters.

Leo Buring Rieslings are always worth seeking out. The *Leonay* Rieslings – from the best parcels of fruit – have been revamped and now show, once again, the confusing bin number system. Nevertheless, these wines have superb cellaring powers. Enjoy the delicate floral aromas, fruit purity, and searing acidity right away, or wait a while as they complete their legendary metamorphosis. These wines are becoming increasingly rare on the secondary market. Values have risen markedly in the last few years, a reflection of their scarcity. Leo Buring is now part of the Southcorp umbrella. Interestingly the label design is returning to the classical Leo Buring designs of the 1970s.

### LINDEMANS, COONAWARRA

*Langton's selections – Lindemans St George Vineyard Cabernet Sauvignon, Lindemans Limestone Ridge Vineyard Shiraz-Cabernet Sauvignon, Lindemans Pyrus Cabernet Sauvignon-Merlot-Malbec*

Lindemans is an important wine brand. Its highly successful *Bin 65 Chardonnay* has seduced the tastebuds of millions. At the other end of the spectrum, Lindemans remains a significant Coonawarra producer of high quality Cabernet and Shiraz blends such as *St George Vineyard Cabernet Sauvignon*, *Limestone Ridge Vineyard Cabernet Sauvignon-Shiraz*, and *Pyrus Cabernet Sauvignon-Merlot-Malbec*. These wines enjoyed considerable fame but time, fashion, and a degree of complacency have diminished their reputations. Happily they seem to be coming back into form and look to have excellent potential.

Lindemans' *Limestone Ridge* vineyard sits on the main north-south ridge in Coonawarra, and is named after the limestone cap that passes just below the surface. Lindemans *Pyrus* is named after the original orchard and Nursery vineyard, established in the 1890s. The inaugural 1985 vintage won the prestigious Jimmy Watson Trophy in 1986, making up what is known as the Lindemans Trio.

Made from Cabernet Sauvignon, Merlot, Cabernet Franc, and Malbec, blended in varying proportions depending on the season, Lindemans *Pyrus* (unlike *St George Vineyard* and *Limestone Ridge Vineyard*) is a multi-vineyard blend with premium fruit from a variety of vineyard blocks. The *St George* vineyard is named after Hinton St George, who bought portion of the original Coonawarra Fruit Colony subdivision from John Riddoch in the early 1900s. This 12 hectare vineyard, on the western side of the Riddoch Highway, is arguably Australia's most famous Cabernet Sauvignon vineyard.

The *St George Vineyard* is a restrained, brooding style of wine with some excellent Cabernet Sauvignon definition and smoky cedary oak, which, in a lighter year, can seem to sit on the wine rather than integrate. From a comparative point of view, *St George* is elegance, *Pyrus* is fruit, and *Limestone Ridge* is richness. These wines are enjoying something of a renaissance in the secondary market, especially recognised vintages.

• *LINDEMANS Limestone Ridge Shiraz-Cabernet Sauvignon Coonawarra S.A. – Distinguished*

*Limestone Ridge* vineyard, planted in 1967, comprises 22 hectares – about two-thirds Shiraz, the remaining to Cabernet Sauvignon, recent grafting increasing the latter component. Vines are planted north-south on unusually shallow *terra rossa* soils over limestone. The vines, on a two-wire trellis system, are pruned and harvested mechanically. Harvesting takes place early to mid-April. This naturally low-yielding vineyard, 2.5km south of Lindemans St George, is cropped at around 3 tonnes per acre. After vinification, the wine usually matures for 14 months in new American oak, then for nearly two years in the bottle, before release. The combination of Shiraz and American oak works extremely well.

• *LINDEMANS Pyrus Cabernet Blend Coonawarra S.A.*

Lindemans *Pyrus* is named after the original orchard and nursery vineyard established in the 1890s. It is made from classic Bordeaux varieties – Cabernet Sauvignon, Merlot, Cabernet Franc, and Malbec – blended in varying proportions, depending on vintage. The make-up is generally Cabernet Sauvignon- and Merlot-driven. Typically, after vinification, the wine is matured in a combination of 85 per cent new, and one year old French oak, for approximately 16 to18 months. *Pyrus* is really a fruit-driven wine, exemplifying the modern Australian Cabernet Blend, with plenty of plum/cherry flavours, fine velvety tannins and savoury oak.

• *LINDEMANS St. George Cabernet Sauvignon Coonawarra S.A. – Distinguished*

This 12 hectare vineyard is arguably Australia's most famous Cabernet Sauvignon vineyard. Certainly it is one of Coonawarra's choicest sites. The vineyard is planted east-west, on a two-wire vertical shoot position trellis system that allows mechanical pruning and machine harvesting. As with all Lindemans Coonawarra vineyard holdings, particular attention is paid to soil moisture and vine stress management. A sprinkling system is used during frost alerts – a major threat in spring. This is a low-yielding vineyard, cropped at around three tonnes per acre. Harvest takes place early to mid-April. After vinification, the wine matures for 16 months in a mix of new French oak *barriques* and hogsheads.

## MAJELLA, COONAWARRA

*Langton's selections – Majella Malleea Cabernet Sauvignon-Shiraz, Majella Cabernet Sauvignon, Majella Shiraz*

Majella, established by the energetic and hugely popular 'Prof' Brian Lynn, is a relatively small producer, bringing much lustre to the Coonawarra name. The winery was built in 1995, although a six acre vineyard was planted to Shiraz in 1968. The first Cabernet Sauvignon vines were planted in 1970. Over the next 30 years, the vineyard expanded to now include more than 160 acres, most of it planted to Cabernet Sauvignon, Shiraz, and Merlot. Some of the fruit is contract grown for Wynns Coonawarra Estate. Majella's first vintage was in 1991.

Vines, generally grown on a single fruiting wire, are machine-pruned and harvested. The wines are made at Brand's Laira, under the weather eye of winemaker Bruce Gregory. In 1996, Majella produced an ultra-fine wine called *Malleea*, an Aboriginal word meaning 'green field'. The wines are vinified in a combination of static, headed down static, and rotary fermenters, to maximise blending options. Towards dryness, the wines are all barrel fermented. The *Malleea Cabernet Sauvignon* (55%), *Shiraz* (45%), is matured in 100 per cent French oak. The *Cabernet Sauvignon* is matured in 50/50 new and used French oak. The *Shiraz* matures in 80 per cent new American oak. All three, for approximately 18 months.

Majella wines are extremely well made, drawing excellent reviews. This is Robert Parker Jr's favourite Coonawarra winery. His rave reviews have tapped an international market. Majella is yet to make an impact on the secondary market, but a strong primary following suggests this label has excellent potential. Its success is much needed.

## MITCHELL, CLARE VALLEY

*Langton's selections – Mitchell Watervale Riesling, Mitchell Shiraz, Mitchell Cabernet Sauvignon*

Mitchell has substantial vineyard holdings in Watervale, Sevenhill, and Auburn, elevated at 300 to 400 metres. The *Mitchell Watervale Riesling* vineyard was planted in 1962, on exposed eastern slopes, and is dry-grown on red, loamy soils over limestone. Pruning the steep slopes has resulted in the vineyard being nicknamed Alcatraz. Fruit is hand-picked on flavour development and optimum ripeness, then crushed, drained, and cold settled, before a 10 day fermentation period.

Mitchell is arguably one of the top five Riesling producers in Australia. Its *Watervale Riesling* is extraordinary, as much for its superb fruit definition and minerality, as its value. In recent vintages, this wine has become as good as Grosset's *Watervale Riesling*, but at half the price.

*Mitchell Peppertree Shiraz* takes its name from a pepper tree in the unirrigated Shiraz vineyard at Watervale. The grapes are cold-macerated prior to vinification in open fermenters. The wine then matures in small (20% new) French and American oak *barriques* for 18 months. The result is always reliable – high-pitched anise/liquorice and black-berry aromas, ripe tannins and flavours. Another seriously undervalued wine.

The *Sevenhill Cabernet Sauvignon* has a strikingly pure fruit profile and underlying new French oak. Andrew and Jane Mitchell run Mitchell as a partnership with a deep commitment to the Clare Valley and its prosperity. The wines are not particularly strong market performers and appear only occasionally. However, they are beautifully made with all the hallmarks of their origin – an important concept when it comes to wine investment. A sleeper perhaps?

### MOUNTADAM, EDEN VALLEY

*Langton's selections – Mountadam Chardonnay, Mountadam The Red Cabernet Sauvignon-Merlot*

Mountadam was established in the mid-1970s by Adam Wynn and father David, who founded the highly successful Wynns Coonawarra Estate winery in the 1950s. Built in 1984, the Mountadam winery included the latest winemaking toys and technology.

Fruit is sourced entirely from its Eden Valley vineyards. Superb resources and technical skills should make Mountadam one of Australia's leading small winemakers. Indeed, by the early 1990s, it was one of Australia's leading boutique wineries. However in recent years, the overall quality of its *Chardonnay* has inexplicably slumped, after many years of outstanding consistency (a low point, 1995 to 1997).

It is something of a relief to find that the 1998, vinified in classic Burgundian fashion, is back to form. It is excellent, with all the creamy complexity and savoury oak characters for which it was once famous. These are medium term wines, with only the best vintages lasting the distance.

The red wines are improving. The *Cabernet Sauvignon* is well made and structured. The *Red* is a Cabernet Sauvignon-Merlot-Cabernet Franc blend, with excellent cellaring potential. The *Patriarch* (under Mountadam label since 1999) is an evolving style, yet to make an impact.

In 2000, Mountadam joined Cape Mentelle and Cloudy Bay as part of the French LVMH luxury goods group. This is clearly a move for the better. The *Chardonnay* is on its way back, but the reds are yet to make an impact on the secondary market. Mountadam's renewed quality focus could quickly turn things around.

- *MOUNTADAM Chardonnay*
  *Eden Valley S.A. – Distinguished*

The search for an ideal vineyard site ended on a rocky spine of land on the High Eden Ridge about 550 metres above sea-level, and conveniently close to the Barossa and Adelaide. Soils here are shallow sands over rock with excellent drainage. In this relatively cool, dry climate, the fruit ripens slowly, with vintage taking place in late April. The fruit is picked at optimum ripeness and flavour development. *Mountadam Chardonnay* is made in typical Burgundian fashion – the wine is whole-bunch pressed, cold-settled in stainless steel, before 100 per cent cold fermentation in fine-grained French oak Troncais barrels, then kept on lees for approximately 11 months with regular less stirring (*battonage*) to achieve complexity.

## MOUNT HORROCKS, CLARE VALLEY

*Langton's selections – Mount Horrocks Watervale Riesling, Mount Horrocks Shiraz*

Mount Horrocks is located in the old railway station at Auburn, a one pub town and birthplace of Australian poet C.J. Dennis. The rails have since been pulled up, but the platform and station buildings make a fine cellar door. The Ackland brothers established the Mount Horrocks label in 1981 to process fruit from their substantial vineyards, first planted in 1967. For many years, Jeffrey Grosset acted as a consultant winemaker. The wine business was eventually acquired by the independent and competitive Stephanie Toole, who makes the wine herself, combining production of high quality wine with her intuitive flair for marketing. A relative newcomer to Clare, she is a forceful proponent for the region and has done much to entice fine wine lovers and critics to embrace the wines of the Clare. Competitiveness with her partner Jeffrey Grosset is legendary. They will race each other to find the best fruit, yet they delight in each other's successes.

The *Mount Horrock's Watervale Riesling* is a classic, minerally Clare Riesling, with plenty of clear fruit definition and flavour. The *Shiraz* could well be a rising star. It has plenty of varietal definition and perfume, yet excellent richness and suppleness on the palate. Mount Horrocks has a minimal presence on the market, but has a strong chance of becoming a real performer as it has all the elements of an investment wine.

## NOON, McLAREN VALE

*Langton's selections – Noon Reserve Shiraz, Noon Eclipse (Grenache-Shiraz), Noon Reserve Cabernet Sauvignon*

Noon is a micro-winery producing the superb *Reserve Shiraz*, *Reserve Cabernet Sauvignon*, *Eclipse Grenache-Shiraz*, and the knockout *Solaire Grenache*. Drew Noon returned to his childhood home and family property in 1996 to take over the reigns of winemaking. The 10 acre vineyard was entirely planted to Grenache in 1934 and 1945, on chocolaty, sandy loams over red clay. Fruit is also sourced from Langhorne Creek, from mature vineyards planted in the early 1960s and 1970s. Overall production is minuscule. Roseworthy-trained, Drew Noon was Victoria's State Oenologist, before a winemaking stint in New South Wales. He is also one of Australia's few Masters of Wine. Drew and his wife Rae (the labels' designer and assistant winemaker) have quickly taken the winery from fringe dweller to the centre of winemaking refinement and magic. With limited financial resources, they have managed to show the superiority of the vineyard sites.

The grapes are vinified in open fermenters and hand-plunged to maximise extraction of colour and flavour. The *Cabernet Sauvignon* receives some extended maceration. Wines are matured for 18 months in a combination of new (25-50%) and used American oak, supplied to Noon by the same cooper, Schahinger, for the last 25 years.

These wines speak with volumes of fruit and perfume, and have captured the imagination of the local and American market. Noon is under enormous pressure to raise prices, currently locked in at well below their apparent real value. With Torbreck and Three Rivers attracting high values for similar quality wines, it is a conundrum for Drew Noon. He has no wish to disenfranchise his loyal band of followers and absolutely no intention to raise prices on the back of powerful endorsements. But Robert Parker Jr has made his pronouncement that life is too short not to be drinking the wine of Drew Noon. Consequently the consumer will take advantage rather than the winemaker, illustrating how contemptible speculative markets can be.

## ORLANDO, BAROSSA VALLEY

*Langton's selections – Orlando Steingarten Riesling, Orlando St Hugo Cabernet Sauvignon, Orlando Lawson's Shiraz, Orlando Jacaranda Ridge Cabernet Sauvignon*

Orlando owns the most successful wine brand in the world, yet the notion that a quality image trickles down, makes the huge success of *Jacobs Creek* a double-edged sword for Orlando. This may be one of the reasons for the release of the *Jacob's Creek Reserve* label! In recent years, after many years of sluggish interest, some of Orlando's high quality brands are finally making an impression on the market.

*Lawson's Padthaway Shiraz* has really performed well over the last few years. Here is a wine that can claim regional definition and consistency of quality. *Orlando Lawson's Shiraz* is named after Robert Lawson, one of the pioneers of the cool climate Padthaway region. These are rich, flavoursome wines with plenty of rich Shiraz fruit definition, a touch of menthol, ripe, mouth-filling tannin structures, and good length. *Orlando St Hugo* has long been one of Coonawarra's leading Cabernets with an enviable track record of quality. The wine is a made from select parcels of Cabernet Sauvignon, mostly older plantings, all grown on the iron rich *terra rossa* soils over limestone. While positioned in quality and price point under *Jacaranda Ridge*, *St Hugo* is a far more consistent wine, showing refined varietal intensity and flavours, fine tannin structure, and good length.

*St Helga Eden Valley Riesling* can be good, but never seems to excel. *St Hilary Padthaway Chardonnay* regularly disappoints. *Orlando Steingarten Riesling* is a Barossa Ranges 'super-brand' in waiting. Lack of vision has caused style problems for *Jacaranda Ridge Coonawarra Cabernet Sauvignon*, which was launched with the same marketing 'bang' as Wynns *John Riddoch*.

Orlando does suffer a little from being seen as a distinctly commercial enterprise. Consumers however do recognise the inherent quality and potential of *Lawson's Shiraz* and *St Hugo Cabernet Sauvignon* which draw moderate, even strengthening interest in the secondary market. The relatively new *Centenary Hill Shiraz* is yet to make its mark.

- *ORLANDO Lawsons Shiraz*
  *Padthaway S.A. – Distinguished*

Fruit is sourced from a single vineyard planted in 1968 on deep sandy soils on gentle eastern slopes. Surrounded by eucalypt trees, the vines are all cane-pruned and trellised on a narrow tee system. Harvest is usually mid to late April, depending on vintage conditions. The grapes are de-stemmed and crushed into wide-based static fermenters. At dryness, the wines receive extended maceration on skins to achieve optimum extraction of colour, flavour, and tannins structure. Fermentation is completed in barrel with some wine racked off to increase blending options and complexity. It is then matured for up to 25 months, depending on vintage conditions, in new American oak hogsheads. It then sees almost two and a half years of bottle age, prior to release. Orlando *Lawson's* has really come of age in the last five years and enjoys strengthening buyer interest. Overall consistency of quality is impressive and the wines have a regional menthol edge that is constant, regardless of vintage.

- *ORLANDO St. Hugo Cabernet Sauvignon*
  *Coonawarra S.A.*

Vintage takes place early to late April; the fruit picked to optimum Baume levels and flavour development. Each vineyard parcel is kept separate during fermentation and maturation to increase blending options. Fermentation takes place in static fermenters at 20-26° C. Ferments are pumped over regularly to irrigate the skin cap and enhance extraction and polymerisation of tannins. Some parcels are racked off towards dryness, to complete fermentation in French oak hogsheads. The wine matures in mainly French oak (some American oak) for 18 to 21 months, before final blending and bottling. It then matures in bottle for another 14 months prior to release.

Orlando *St Hugo* is a classic Coonawarra Cabernet Sauvignon showing refined varietal intensity and flavours, fine tannins structure, and good length. It shows plenty of regional definition – a much valued character in wine.

## PARKER COONAWARRA ESTATE, COONAWARRA

*Langton's selections – Parker Coonawarra Estate Terra Rossa First Growth Cabernet Blend, Parker Coonawarra Estate Terra Rossa Cabernet Sauvignon, Parker Coonawarra Estate Terra Rossa Merlot*

In 1985, the late John Parker established Parker Coonawarra Estate, culminating in the release of the 1988 *First Growth Cabernet Blend* in 1991. The 50 acre vineyard at the southern end of Coonawarra, is planted on classic *terra rossa* over limestone soils – with minor plantings of Merlot, Petit Verdot, and Cabernet Franc, but predominantly Cabernet Sauvignon. The vines are trellised on a single wire and bilateral cordon. The fruit is batch-vinified.

The *Terra Rossa First Growth* is made along traditional Bordelais lines, with extended maceration and maturation for 20 to 24 months in a combination of tightly-grained new and used French oak. A little American oak is used for the Merlot component. The name *First Growth* – based on an old world philosophy – seems less absurd now as winemakers throughout Australia hone in on their best parcels of fruit. If the grapes fail to reach optimum standard in any given vintage, the fruit is declassified and used for the standard Cabernet Sauvignon. No *Terra Rossa First Growth* was made in 1992, 1995, or 1997.

*First Growth*, a brilliantly seductive wine, has unbelievable depth of fruit, balance, and structure. Another consistent decade or so may see *Terra Rossa First Growth* become something of a legend. The more staid *Cabernet Sauvignon* missed out on the magic. A newly built winery at Coonawarra, reflects the growing importance of Parker Coonawarra Estate. The highly sought after *First Growth* is recognised as one of the region's finest wines, narrowly missing inclusion in *Langton's Classification* due to its limited number of vintages.

## PENFOLDS, SOUTH AUSTRALIA

*Langton's selections – Penfolds Bin 95 Grange Shiraz, Penfolds Bin 707 Cabernet Sauvignon, Penfolds St Henri Shiraz-Cabernet Sauvignon, Penfolds Bin 389 Cabernet Sauvignon-Shiraz, Penfolds Magill Estate Shiraz, Penfolds RWT Shiraz, Penfolds Bin 90A Cabernet Sauvignon-Shiraz, Penfolds Bin 920 Cabernet Sauvignon-Shiraz, Penfolds Bin 80A Cabernet Sauvignon-Shiraz, Penfolds Bin 820 Cabernet Sauvignon-Shiraz, Penfolds Bin 407 Cabernet Sauvignon, Penfolds Bin 144 Yattarna Chardonnay, Penfolds Bin 28 Kalimna Shiraz, Penfolds Koonunga Hill Shiraz-Cabernet Sauvignon*

Penfolds is probably the most exceptional of the world's wine brands, with an enviable reputation for quality at every price level. The original Penfold was an English doctor who, in 1844, planted grapes at Magill, now a suburb of Adelaide. It is really only since the late 1940s, that Penfolds forged a reputation for red wine. Penfolds traditional reds are mostly multi-regional blends. The result is a litany of consistently high-quality wine. Overall, the style is about highly-defined fruit aromas, fruit sweetness, ripe tannins, richness, power, and concentration.

Penfolds *Grange*, *Bin 707 Cabernet Sauvignon*, *St Henri*, *Magill Estate*, and *Bin 389 Cabernet Sauvignon-Shiraz* are all strongly sought after on the investment market. Even a recent wine such as *Bin 407 Cabernet Sauvignon* (poor man's *Bin 707* perhaps?) is brilliantly made and already showing impressive ageing ability. *Penfolds RWT Barossa Shiraz* is an excellent wine, but is yet to prove itself on the secondary market. Both *Bin 28 Kalimna Shiraz* and *Bin128 Coonawarra Shiraz*, despite being at the lower end of the Penfolds hierarchy, can hardly be described as little wines. *Koonunga Hill*, a wine of modest ambitions, has been so successful that the price had to go up. In its wake are *Rawson's Retreat* and the newly launched *Thomas Hyland*.

Winemakers have also been allowed to experiment. It is this quasi-commercial research and development program that has enabled Penfolds to achieve such awesome levels of quality and reliability. *Penfolds Bin 60A*, a 1962 blend of Coonawarra Cabernet Sauvignon and Kalimna Shiraz, is often been described as the greatest red wine ever made in Australia. *Bin 620 Coonawarra Cabernet Sauvignon* 1966 and *Bin 7* of 1967 were also well sought. The most famous recent experimental wines are *Bin 80A* – 1980, *Bin 820* – 1982, *Bin 90A* – 1990, and *Bin 920* – 1990, each reflecting the original styles of the 1960s. The 1996 *Block 42 Cabernet Sauvignon* is also an impressive one-off wine.

There have also been releases of white wines of varying quality. The much-hyped *Yattarna Chardonnay* is a delicious wine with nutty complexity and creaminess, but overvalued. Penfolds is the most reliable wine on the secondary market, although vintage specificity has become increasingly important. John Duval, Penfolds long-time chief winemaker, recently handed the reigns to Peter Gago.

• *PENFOLDS Bin 95 Grange Shiraz S.A. – Exceptional*

Penfolds *Grange* is the most sought after and best known Australian wine on the international market, recently being designated a heritage icon by the National Trust of S.A. Max Schubert, who died in 1994, made the first vintage in 1951 (*Bin 1*). Vintages of the 1950s are extremely rare and valuable (although many are now past their best). The 1955 vintage was a show wine, produced in larger quantities. *Bin 95* became standard in 1960. Originally made from Shiraz fruit grown at Magill in Adelaide, the core source is now the Kalimna vineyard in the Barossa. Fruit, if good enough, can also be sourced from as far afield as Coonawarra. Penfolds has a 'Shiraz Club' and a 'Grange Club' that ensure long term relationships with high-quality grape growers.

*Grange* usually comprises a small component of Cabernet Sauvignon. Temperature controlled vinification takes place in headed down stainless steel fermenters with occasional draining and pumping of free run wine. Towards dryness, the wine is drained and pressed, then transferred to American oak hogsheads to complete fermentation with about 18 months of further maturation. The wine is superbly opulent, with massive concentration and flavour. It is typically quite appealing when young, with lots of bright fruit, though drinkers committing vinous infanticide will miss the extraordinary, meaty complexity and richness of aged vintages.

So far, there is no such thing as a bad *Grange*, although some vintages are beginning to fade. Collectors and investors are aware of the best vintages and tend to pay a premium for them. About 10,000 dozen are produced.

• *PENFOLDS Bin 707 Cabernet Sauvignon S.A. – Exceptional*

Penfolds *Bin 707 Cabernet Sauvignon* was introduced in 1964 (by an ex-Qantas marketing man) and was one of Australia's first varietal Cabernet Sauvignons. It was discontinued in 1969 because of inconsistency in fruit quality and supply. The wine was re-introduced in 1976, the core fruit component coming from Coonawarra, renowned for its quality of Cabernet Sauvignon. Fruit is also sourced from the Barossa and Clare Valleys and further afield.

The wine is made in exactly the same manner as *Grange*. Partial barrel fermentation and 18 months maturation in new American oak hogsheads (300 litre barrels) are central to the style. Varietal expression is often hidden by the strong thumbprint of house style. Immensely concentrated, with deep-set plum and cassis aromas, and coconutty American oak, the wines are plush and packed with fruit sweetness and flavour. There is so much stuffing in these wines that they age superbly. The 1981, 1995,and 2000 vintages were not made, illustrating Penfolds commitment to quality.

- *PENFOLDS Bin 389 Cabernet Sauvignon-Shiraz S.A. – Excellent*

Penfolds *Bin 389 Cabernet Sauvignon-Shiraz* is an absolute Australian classic. In earlier years it was called 'poor mans' *Grange*. Fruit for the original *Bin 389* was sourced from the old Auldana Vineyard near Magill Estate – now swallowed up by urban development. The wine was predominantly a Barossa wine at one point, but is now a multi-district wine sourced from the premium wine districts of the Barossa Valley, Coonawarra, Padthaway, McLaren Vale, Langhorne Creek, and Clare Valley. The proportion of Cabernet Sauvignon is usually around 60 per cent, but it can vary according to vintage. The wine is made in a traditional manner. The must is fermented in stainless steel tanks – headed down – to keep the cap submerged. Some components of the blend complete fermentation in barrel. The wine is matured in a combination of new (20-30%) and one and two year old (70-80%) American hogsheads for 18 months, prior to bottling. Many of the barrels have been used for the previous vintage of *Grange*.

*Bin 389* epitomises the superb marriage of Cabernet Sauvignon and Shiraz. In a good vintage, these wines are absolutely magical, eclipsing some of the greatest Australian wines. This is a highly reliable wine style with intense blackberry/gamy aromas, immense concentration of fruit, ripe tannins, well-seasoned oak and generosity of flavour. A wine investment staple, although vintage reputation is important. For instance, the 1996 and 1998s are excellent, but keep well clear of the 1997.

- *PENFOLDS St Henri Shiraz-Cabernet Sauvignon S.A. – Excellent*

Penfolds *St Henri* is the original fruit-driven Australian wine style. The first official vintage was in 1956, an experimental wine that is exceedingly rare, yet does not command quite the same rarefied collectors' appeal as 1951 *Grange*. At the 2002 Penfolds Clinic, a bottle of 1955 *St Henri* appeared, but without the Penfolds brand name. Reportedly, a half bottle of 1953 exists in Adelaide.

The creator John Davoren, was overshadowed by the success of *Grange*. The original Penfolds *St Henri* sourced fruit from Paracombe and Auldana, now suburbs of Adelaide. The wine has now evolved in style, combining traditional winemaking techniques and today's technology. Fruit is sourced from throughout South Australia including the Barossa Valley, McLaren Vale, Clare Valley, Langhorne Creek, and Eden Valley. While predominantly a Shiraz-based wine, it includes a proportion of Cabernet Sauvignon from Coonawarra and the Barossa.

The wine is fermented in open stainless steel tanks with headed down cap. After fermentation, it is matured in large 2,000 litre old oak casks – the wine relying on maturation effect, rather than new oak influence. During the 1980s the style was tweaked, bringing much clearer fruit definition and flavour. Once criticised for being too traditional, this wine really illustrates the complexities of the market.

*St Henri*, in a good year, is one of the most desirable wines on the market. Ageing potential is relative to the quality of the vintage. Hence wines with direct, perfectly ripened fruit, good concentration, fine but ripe tannins, and plenty of fruit sweetness (essence of the style) will age beautifully. Lesser vintages, such as 1997, are best drunk young. Here youthful fruit can hide blemishes.

- *PENFOLDS Magill Estate Shiraz*
  *Adelaide S.A. – Distinguished*

Magill Estate was Penfolds winemaking headquarters until 1973. The site is now regarded as the home of the Penfolds brand. Indeed *Grange* is once again being matured in these cellars. The Penfold family settled here in 1844, just eight years after the founding of Adelaide. Indeed the original 'Grange' Cottage still stands. Much of the extensive vineyards around Magill Estate have been lost to urban development. Only 5.2 hectares of old vine Shiraz remain.

As Penfolds *Magill Estate* is a single vineyard wine from one of the few city vineyards in the world, it is outside the traditional Penfolds' style. Originally, the fruit was picked early, making the wines quite lean and tight. Not all of the wines made in the 1980s have been great cellaring successes. The 1984 should be avoided.

During the 1990s, the style was refocused with brighter fruit definition and greater palate vitality. Fruit is picked on flavour development. The wine is made in a traditional manner – open fermented in wax lined concrete tanks with a headed down cap at cool temperatures. Towards the end of fermentation, the wine is drained and basket pressed. Fermentation is completed, then matured for 12 to 14 months in a combination of French and American oak barrels of roughly equal proportions.

This has been an evolving style. In truth, it is a wine that has lived on the shirt-tails of the Penfolds name. Until recently, it has been a flawed style, punctuated by the occasional surprise. Since 1990, the wine has gradually built a strong thread of quality. Certainly the 1996 and 1998 vintages are wines to impress. As it matures in the bottle, its chocolate, spice and plum aromas and taut structure, give way to more complex, earthy, liquorice-like characters. These can be wines of richness and finesse.

## PENLEY ESTATE, COONAWARRA

*Langton's selections – Penley Estate Reserve Cabernet Sauvignon, Penley Estate Phoenix Cabernet Sauvignon, Penley Estate Hyland Shiraz*

Kym Tolley established Penley Estate in 1988, following a tradition of winemaking from both sides of the family. Penley is a synthesis of Penfold and Tolley. The winery has around 200 acres of vines planted predominantly to Cabernet Sauvignon and Shiraz with a smattering of Cabernet Franc, Merlot, Pinot Noir, Pinot Meunier, and Chardonnay. Vineyards are planted on classic *terra rossa* over limestone soils, on various trellis systems, mostly single wire. Recent yields have been reduced to optimise quality and flavour. The reds were released in 1991 with the 1989 vintage, winning immediate show acclaim but struggling through economic recession, finally returning to focus in the late 1990s.

The *Cabernet Sauvignon*, now bottled under the *Reserve* label to avoid confusion, is batch-vinified using traditional heading down tanks, open pot and rotary fermenters. Towards dryness, the wine is drained and pressed, then barrel fermented. Maturation takes place in a combination of new French (70%) and American oak for up to 30 months – each aspect of winemaking adjusted to suit the vagaries of vintage.

Penley Estate with Tim Abegg (Penley's Swiss wine marketer) makes a joint venture wine called *Ausvetia*, a Shiraz-based wine. The fruit is sourced from McLaren Vale, Barossa Valley, and Coonawarra. It is matured for two years in 100 per cent American oak. This wine is rare in the Australian market, although it has been marketed and lionised by critics in Europe and the U.S.

The *Reserve Cabernet Sauvignon* is a classic Cabernet-style with cedary, blackcurrant aromas, ripe, fine-grained tannins, fruit sweetness, concentration, and length. Always at the riper end of the spectrum, it has the structure to age. *Phoenix Cabernet Sauvignon*, named after an old family enterprise, is the standard Cabernet Sauvignon and matures in new and old, fine-grained Troncais French and American oak. The *Hyland Shiraz* is matured in new and old 50/50 American and French oak.

Penley Estate is well thought of, and is just breaking into the wine investment scene.

**PETALUMA, ADELAIDE HILLS**

*Langton's selections – Petaluma Riesling, Petaluma Chardonnay, Petaluma Tiers Chardonnay, Petaluma Coonawarra Cabernet Sauvignon-Merlot, Petaluma Merlot*

Established by Brian Croser in the late 1970s, Petaluma is among Australia's most important winemakers. Croser captured the imagination of the wine world with his exquisitely proportioned Chardonnay, derived from South Australia's cool climate Adelaide Hills. In defining this wine, Croser introduced the idea of distinguished vineyard site, a variation of the French concept of *terroir*.

*Petaluma Chardonnay* has terrific definition, with tropical fruit, particularly grapefruit aromas, new oak, and a creamy palate balanced by cutting acidity. Petaluma recently released a single vineyard Chardonnay named *Tiers* – from a slightly warmer vineyard adjacent to the winery.

*Petaluma Coonawarra Cabernet-Merlot* reflects the remarkable shift in winemaking and consumer sentiment over the last 20 years. The *Petaluma Coonawarra* is a refined style reflecting the uniqueness of its vineyard site. It is elegantly structured with restrained blackcurrant pastille aromas, fine-grained tannins, subtle, savoury oak, and excellent length.

Croser describes his *Petaluma Riesling* as a dry, late-picked style, sourced from Petaluma's Hanlin Hill vineyard. It displays superb fruit purity, flavour, and indelible acidity.

Petaluma's limited release *Merlot* shows ripe, plummy fruit, underpinned by classy French oak. Invariably elegantly structured, with an emphasis on finesse, this wine is one of the few in Australia offered *en primeur* by the single case.

Petaluma and its affiliated wineries were recently swallowed up by the Lion Nathan Group.

- *PETALUMA Coonawarra Cabernet Sauvignon-MerlotCoonawarra S.A – Excellent*

*Petaluma Coonawarra Cabernet Sauvignon-Merlot* is a wine that pre-empted 'regionality' – the idea of regional definition in wine. The wine is labelled simply as Coonawarra and its fruit is derived from the Evans vineyard, purchased by Petaluma in 1978 from The Evans Wine Company. The vines were planted in 1969 to Cabernet Sauvignon and Shiraz. Early Petaluma's were Cabernet Shiraz blends (first vintage 1979). In what seemed a fit of madness, Croser bulldozed, or grafted, the Shiraz to Merlot – sticking his fingers up at the great traditional Australian combo – and showing the future for Cabernet Sauvignon was with Merlot.

"The vineyard is hand-pruned, canopy-trained, crop-moderated, hand-picked and dry land vineyard-managed, among a sea of mechanised convenience-managed vineyards", says Croser. Fruit is usually picked early, cropped at around two to three tonnes per acre. The wines are made in closed headed down fermenters and roto-fermenters to allow gentle extraction, then matured in French oak.

- *PETALUMA Chardonnay*
  *Piccadilly Valley S.A. – Excellent*

*Petaluma Chardonnay* is sourced from six distinguished sites in the Piccadilly Valley, each bringing specific aromas, flavours and structural elements.

Brian Croser describes the various fruit characteristics as ranging "from the most exotic grapefruit to more subtle tropical fruit, pear, peach and nectarine".

Curiously Petaluma is seen as the quintessential high-tech winery, yet this wine reflects an almost *laissez faire* philosophy. Vintage takes place in early to mid April – the fruit picked on flavour development. The wine is crushed and transferred to stainless steel where the wine is cold-settled (naturally clarified). Vinification kicks off in stainless steel, although the fermenting juice is soon racked into 100 per cent new fine grained Dargaud and Jaegle Vosges oak, to complete barrel fermentation. This takes place in cold storage, ensuring an extended and slow fermentation. The wine is left on its lees with occasional *battonage* (lees stirring) for approximately 12 months before final assemblage, a light bentonite fining, and bottling.

*Petaluma Chardonnay* is one of the leading Australian Chardonnays. Its place in the secondary market is more a function of supply and demand. These are medium term wines. Avoid the earliest vintages, pre-1987.

Petaluma recently released a single vineyard Chardonnay named *Tiers* – the vineyard adjacent to the winery, considered a slightly warmer site. While the wine reflects Petaluma's high standards of winemaking, it is, in my opinion, no more superior to its modestly-priced stable mate.

- *PETALUMA Riesling, Clare Valley S.A.- Excellent*

Petaluma's Hanlin Hill vineyard, on the western face of the Clare Hills, is one of the highest vineyards in the region at an elevation of 500 metres. Soils here are mostly red brown soils interspersed with gravelly shales. Vintage takes place late March to early April. Fruit is hand-picked at optimum flavour development. It is crushed and allowed to cold-settle in stainless steel, before draining and light pressing into stainless steel fermenters. The clear juice, inoculated with Petaluma's own yeast strains, is cool fermented, after which the wine is cold-settled, racked, then bottled in July.

This is a quintessential Clare Valley Riesling with proven cellaring potential. Older vintages can show incredible complexity. Even the 1997, which did not appear top notch at release, looks outstanding now, showing that fruit quality always wins out in the end. *Petaluma Riesling* does not have the same cult following as Grosset now, but the wine is a worthy sparring partner!

### PETER LEHMANN, BAROSSA VALLEY

*Langton's selections – Peter Lehmann Stonewell Shiraz, Peter Lehmann Eight Songs Shiraz, Peter Lehmann Mentor Cabernet Blend*

As a young man, Peter Lehmann worked at Yalumba during the 1940s, beginning a lifetime of achievement in the Barossa Valley. He is one of the most important characters in the Barossa. The son of a Lutheran pastor, Lehmann kept the spirit alive during periods of severe economic downturn. His reward is access to some of the very best fruit in the Barossa Valley. Lehmann's reputable winemaker is Andrew Wigan, who has been making quality Shiraz since the 1950s. In winemaking terms, Wigan blends traditional thought and modern practice.

*Stonewell Shiraz* reflects a fundamental truth of the wine industry – that vineyards, if left alone, are the only constant. Superb, immensely concentrated, low-yield fruit, combined with skilled winemaking, are the basis of this great Australian Shiraz. These wines show plenty of Christmas cake/plum/chocolate aromas, sweet fruit, structured tannins, well-seasoned oak flavours, and tremendous length. This wine is hugely undervalued when compared to other Barossa classics.

The *Mentor Cabernet Blend* also has a good following. The beautifully packaged *Eight Songs Barossa Valley Shiraz*, matured in French oak and produced in minute quantities, could well inspire wine investors with its strong regional quality. *Seven Surveys*, a Shiraz-Mouvedre-Grenache blend, has only moderate potential because of its medium term cellaring prospects. Peter Lehmann has a strong emerging presence on the market.

- *PETER LEHMANN Stonewell Shiraz*
  *Barossa Valley S.A. – Excellent*

Andrew Wigan has had a tumultuous career orchestrating vintages in both good and bad times. Accustomed to scarce resources in the past, including no oak, he has used inventiveness and imagination to make good wine. With renewed confidence from the commercial success of 1989 vintage, Wigan was finally given the resources he needed. And in *Stonewell*, Peter Lehmann's ultra-fine Barossa Shiraz, he is making one of the great contemporary Barossa Shirazes. The wine is derived from 14 Shiraz vineyards located in the drier sub-districts of the Barossa, such as Stonewell (hence the name), Marananga, Greenock, Kalimna, and Ebenezer. The wine is made using traditional methods including partial barrel fermentation and maturation in American oak and French oak hogsheads. This wine is hugely undervalued when compared to other Barossa classics.

## PIKES, CLARE VALLEY

*Langton's selections – Pikes Reserve Riesling, Pikes Riesling, Pikes Reserve Shiraz*

Like Mitchell, this small Clare Valley producer deserves better recognition for its beautifully defined Rieslings and fruit-driven Shirazes. Pikes Wines was established in 1984 by Neil Pike, and now comprises 90 acres of south-east facing vineyard, planted on red/brown earth over yellow clay subsoil and slate, in the cool Polish Hill River sub-region of the Clare Valley. The vines are trellised to a single wire, with movable foliage wires for vertical shoot positioning. Supplementary irrigation is used only as necessary and fruit is all picked by hand at optimum ripeness.

Pikes' crisply structured *Riesling* is cold-settled prior to fermentation in stainless steel tanks. The *Reserve Shiraz* comes from the Kelly Vineyard at Polish Hill River – planted in the early 1900s (even the growers are unsure of the actual vine age). Pikes crops the two-and-a-half acres of gnarled old vines at under two tonnes per acre.

The *Reserve* is produced only in exceptional vintages and is now matured in French oak *barriques* for up to 24 months. Also produced are a Cabernet Sauvignon and a Reserve Merlot. Pikes has only a small presence on the secondary market however, it is making quintessential Rieslings and deserves mention.

## REYNELL, McLAREN VALE

*Langton's selections – Reynell Basket Press Shiraz*

John Reynell was one of the pioneers of Australian wine and is credited with establishing the first vineyard in South Australia. The fate of the Reynells, however, is sad. Like so many other Australian families, they were decimated by war. Carew Reynell lost his life at Gallipoli, in the Dardanelles in 1915. His son Richard was a Hawker Hurricane test pilot who perished in the Battle of Britain in 1941. A succession of family tragedies saw the end of a family winemaking dynasty in 1971. BRL Hardy now owns Chateau Reynella. The grounds are fully restored, including the National Trust-registered Old Cave Cellar.

BRL Hardy has kept the Reynell name alive with its *Reynell Basket Press Shiraz*, an opulent, deep-set, choc-berry flavoured style with plenty of supporting oak. *Chateau*

*Reynella Vintage Port*, like Hardy's, exemplifies a traditional fortified style. Waning interest, however, has seen both removed from *Langton's Classification*. A pity, as these are lovely wines that are well worth seeking out and are often great bargains.

## ROCKFORD, BAROSSA VALLEY

*Langton's selections – Rockford Basket Press Shiraz, Rockford Black Shiraz (sparkling red), Rockford Home Block Cabernet, Rockford Moppa Springs Grenache*

During the early 1980s, the technocrats and style merchants said the future was cool climate viticulture, literally causing widespread uprooting of old vines – known as the 'vine pull scheme'. Robert O'Callaghan's deep sense of history and belief in traditional Barossa values began a vinous counter-reformation. He has inspired a generation of Barossa wine-makers. Rockford embraces the inherent qualities of old vine Shiraz – the physicality of winemaking, where muscle and personal touch transform process into an art-form; the traditional tools of trade (basket press, open fermenter); and the complementary nuances of American and French oak maturation, without smothering fruit. O'Callaghan's commitment to labour-intensive techniques for the sake of going the extra mile in quality, makes *Rockford Basket Press* the quintessential hand-made wine. It encapsulates traditional and contemporary winemaking practice and philosophy.

*Rockford Basket Press Shiraz*, now presented in the most lovely brown '50s style bottle, is made in the classic mould with strong, ripe, blackberry and fine chocolate fruit characters, underscored by excellent palate richness, well-seasoned American and French oak, and ripe tannins. This is a very approachable wine style suited to both relatively early drinking and medium to long term cellaring. It is curious that many people think of this wine as being massively structured, as it is so clearly not!

O'Callaghan also makes a mean but idiosyncratic *Black* (sparkling) *Shiraz*, a style that is highly sought. Although the date of *triage* is on the back label, it is a non-vintage wine, produced in minute quantities, that is absolutely delicious (the 'crave factor' can override all logic). The *Home Block* is a cellar door-only release. Rockford recently released a special selection of single vineyard Shirazes: *Flaxman's* (Eden Ridge), *Moorooroo* (near Kalimna), and *Hoffmann* (Ebenezer). These are 'one-offs' specially made for Robert O'Callaghan's loyal, long term customers. They are completely different to his *Basket Press*, embracing the fascination of single vineyards, sub-regional provenance, and fruit power.

O'Callaghan wants to keep Rockford away from the trophy hunters and to maintain affordable prices for his customers. His long term supporters are a major priority. It is ironic therefore that quality, reputation, and scarcity make such a double-edged sword. Rockford also makes a very good Grenache-based red called *Moppa Springs*, and a very fine Semillon and Riesling.

- *ROCKFORD Basket Press Shiraz*
  *Barossa Valley S.A. – Outstanding*

Fruit, from local growers, is sourced from many of the best dry-grown old vine Shiraz vineyards in the Barossa, including around Kalimna, Ebenezer, Moppa Springs, the Eden Valley, and Central Barossa. The vines – 60 to 136 years old – give fruit of tremendous colour, power and richness. Vintage takes place in mid April. The fruit is hand-forked into an old Bagshaw crusher, then into open slate or open half vat fermenters – each parcel of fruit kept separate to maximise blending options. Fermentation takes around five days, after which the wine is basket pressed and transferred to stainless steel where fermentation and malo-lactic fermentation completes. At dryness, the wine is racked into a combination of used and new American and French oak for 24 to 30 months, depending on vintage. The final wine comprises no more than 15 per cent new oak – the wine reflecting the superb fruit definition of Barossa Old Vine Shiraz. A great wine style.

## ROSEMOUNT, McLAREN VALE

*Langton's selections – Rosemount Balmoral Syrah*

Rosemount's *Balmoral McLaren Vale Syrah* is fast becoming an Australian 'super-Shiraz'. Named after the Oatley family homestead, this wine fits nicely with Rosemount's *Roxburgh Hunter Valley Chardonnay*.

*Balmoral* is made from dry-grown, low-yielding vineyards, the vines 40 to 100 years old. It is able to combine perfume, structure, and density, from three distinctive soil types: the sandy loams of Blewitt Springs, the darker soils of McLaren Flat, and the *terra rossa* over limestone near Chapel Hill.

Phillip Shaw explains, "The juice is cold soaked between McLaren Vale and the Upper Hunter Valley. The travelling and rolling about in a tanker through the Hay plains and up the back road to Rosemount, extracts soft edged tannins and flavours."

Although a proportion of the wine is barrel fermented, the oak plays a supporting role to the fruit. These are deeply coloured wines, with powerful, plummy, black fruits and dark chocolate aromas, underpinned by American oak – hugely concentrated, velvety, with soft-edged tannins, plush fruit, and a firm finish.

Made for the long haul, *Balmoral Syrah* narrowly missed inclusion in *Langton's Classification* because of the number of vintages made. It is well thought of and has strengthening market presence. Rosemount recently folded itself into Southcorp, Australia's most prominent wine company, which includes Penfolds, Seppelt, Lindemans, and Wynns brands.

## RYMILL, COONAWARRA

*Langton's selections – Rymill Cabernet Sauvignon, Rymill Riddoch Run*

Peter Riddoch Rymill's family has been inextricably linked to Coonawarra for more than a century. John Riddoch, the 'father of Coonawarra' and founder of the Penola Fruit Colony, is Peter Rymill's great grandfather. His father, John Rymill, was a distinguished polar explorer who led the British Graham Land Expedition from 1934 to 1937. In 1974, Peter and Judy Rymill, local graziers and horse breeders, became grape growers, planting 100 hectares of vines on what is now known as the Riddoch Run vineyard, at the northern end of Coonawarra. Initially providing fruit for local vignerons, they established their own label in 1987, moving towards full-scale production in 1989. John Innes, winemaker/general manager, has overseen considerable change over the last decade.

Rymill, with its new landmark winery, is now a prominent feature on the Coonawarra landscape. *Rymill Coonawarra Cabernet* is partially barrel fermented and sees maturation in French oak. An evolving style, it is the strongest card in the Rymill pack, with plenty of cellaring potential. *Rymill Riddoch Run Shiraz* is also worth seeking out.

## SEPPELT, BAROSSA VALLEY

*Langton's selections – Seppelt Dorrien Cabernet Sauvignon*

Seppeltsfield in the Barossa, is an extraordinary folly, with its Seppelt family mausoleum, palm tree-lined roads, and beautifully preserved buildings. The fortified wines are some of the best in Australia. The *DP 117 Show Fino*, a style pioneered by John Fornachon, is as good as the best from Spain. The *DP 116 Show Amontillado* is also brilliant and Seppelt *Para Liqueur* Ports are lovely, absolutely definitive Tawnies. From the 1920s, wines were not always made entirely from one vintage, and numbers (beginning with 101) were used to comply with labelling laws, with vintage-dated *Para Liqueur* beginning again in 1976. *Centenary Ports*, dating back to 1978, are fabulous – immense concentration – but cost an arm and a leg. These wines are generally sluggish at auction, so bargains can be picked up.

- *SEPPELT Dorrien Cabernet Sauvignon Barossa Valley S.A. – Distinguished*

The Dorrien vineyard, located in the heart of the Barossa Valley, comprises vines, averaging 55 years of age, planted on red brown earth and trellised on a single wire. Harvest is around late March, based on fruit flavour. Grape bunches are de-stemmed and crushed before fermentation in stainless steel fermenters, where the must is allowed to ferment to approximately 28° C, then taken down to 20-22° C. After about five days, and towards the end of fermentation, the wine is pressed off using a Miller Press. Pressings are added back and wine completes fermentation in (unusually) new French hogsheads. After malo-lactic fermentation, it is racked and matured in a combination of new French and American oak hogsheads for around 15 months.

*Dorrien* is a classic, ripe, Barossa Cabernet Sauvignon style with excellent oak handling. Blackcurrant and liquorice aromas combine with cedary oak and fine-grained tannins. These can be extremely impressive wines, especially those from recognised great Barossa vintages. Amazingly this wine is being discontinued due to brand re-organisation. The fruit will no doubt find its way into *Penfolds Bin 707* – another highly regarded Southcorp wine!

## ST HALLETT, BAROSSA VALLEY

*Langton's selections – St Hallett Old Block Shiraz*

The Lindner family established St Hallett in the heart of the Barossa Valley near Tanunda, with wines going back to 1944. After a relatively sleepy beginning producing fortified wines, the winery restructured its ownership, introducing new ideas, winemaking skills and capital. The metamorphosis has been remarkable.

St Hallett is one of the Barossa's great commercial success stories, a tribute to the rambunctious energy of Bob McLean, one of the great characters of the Barossa. This success however, may have swamped the lustre and image of its extremely fine *Old Block Shiraz*, a quintessential Barossa Valley style. In the early 1980s, demand was so poor, the original Old Block vineyard was nearly uprooted.

*Old Block Shiraz* is one of the leading wines of the district – a Shiraz reflecting the traditional Barossa Valley style. The style is warm, rich, and full-bodied, with complex, plum, mulberry and dark chocolate aromas, soft tannins, and vanillin oak. It has excellent cellaring potential. *Faith Shiraz* and *Blackwell Shiraz* are both variations on a theme, although they have only moderate potential on the market.

St Hallett is now owned by brewer Lion Nathan.

- *ST HALLETT Old Block Shiraz*
  *Barossa Valley S.A. – Excellent*

St Hallett *Old Block* sources fruit from a rich palette of 28 low-yielding old vine vineyards in the Barossa. The vineyards are in the higher elevated areas around Eden Valley and Springton on the Barossa Floor, especially around Ebenezer and Lyndoch. Soil types, aspects and mesoclimates vary, although most of the vines are between 70 and 100 years old. The vines, mostly trellised to a single wire, are all hand-pruned and hand-picked. Vintage takes place on the valley floor in March, continues right through until late April, with the Eden Valley vineyards ripening significantly later. Each vineyard parcel is fermented separately in open headed down fermenters, ensuring a submerged skin cap. Towards dryness, the wine is racked into barrel – a range of new and one year old American and French oak. Maturation takes place for approximately 22 to 24 months before final assemblage and bottling. It is then given a further 12 months bottle maturation before release.

*St Hallett Old Block* is a benchmark Barossa Shiraz delivering typical, rich, opulent, spicy, Christmas pudding-like aromas with oodles of new oak, ripe tannins and deep-set fruit on the palate.

## TIM ADAMS, CLARE VALLEY

*Langton's selections – The Aberfeldy Shiraz*

Tim Adams is not unlike his wine – robust and blunt. He appears abrupt, if not distant… until you start talking. Then the richness and generosity appears. The son of a local bank manager who fell into winemaking, Adams is a classic self-reliant Australian, with excellent bush engineering skills, and could run a car on the smell of an oily rag. He has achieved rapid success by concentrating on developing his winemaking enterprise, rather than investing in vineyards. Adams is making extremely fine Shiraz – a variety he is passionate about – and good Cabernet Sauvignon. His oak regime is also fundamental to his style.

"I use exclusively American oak from eight different coopers from Australia, the United States, and France," says Adams, claiming that this combination gives strong vanillin characters with subtle nuances of cloves and cinnamon.

Adams established his winery in 1986 after an early career with Stanley Leasingham, first as a cellar hand and eventually as a winemaker. His winery is located near Wendouree, towards the northern edge of Clare. It crushes around 500 tonnes of grapes, sourced from 11 established growers, as well as its own vineyards. It also provides contract winemaking services to smaller vignerons in the area.

His top wine, *Tim Adams Aberfeldy Shiraz*, is a traditional style owing much to the vineyard site as to the gentleness of his basket press. Although highly regarded, it has had an erratic presence on the market. Fruit is principally sourced from the low-cropping Aberfeldy vineyard, once owned by Wendouree. The fruit is always picked on optimum ripeness and flavour. The wine is open fermented with extended skin maceration, before being drained and basket pressed. Pressing is integral to the blend. The wine then spends 12 months in one year old oak, mostly American, before transfer to new American oak from the Nadalie, A.P. John, and Kelvin cooperages, for a further eight months. The wine is a deeply concentrated style with blackberry aromas, malty/cedary oak, and a textured but firm tannin structure.

*Tim Adams Shiraz* is also high quality and worth seeking out. The *Cabernet Sauvignon*, a high-pitched but firm style, is matured for 12 months in French oak. The Tim Adams style is certainly leaning towards the firm adroit style – a bit like Tim's handshake. The *Aberfeldy* has plenty of potential.

## THREE RIVERS, BAROSSA VALLEY

*Langton's selections – Three Rivers Shiraz, Randall's Hill Shiraz (declassified Three Rivers)*

Astonishing reviews from Robert Parker Jr of this obscure tin-shack wine, have catapulted it from minor cult wine to super-star status. It has made Chris Ringland (Rockford's co-winemaker) the vinous equivalent of a movie star, fêted from one side of the planet to the other. It was never planned. It just happened.

Ringland is a passionate proponent of Barossa Shiraz. *Three Rivers* is an impossibly small vinification, ranging from two to three hogsheads, producing approximately 100 cases at the very most. Fruit is sourced from Ringland's dry-grown vineyard on the edge of the Barossa Valley (technically in Eden Valley) along Flaxman's Valley near Randall's Hill. The shallow soils are skeletal granitic sandy loams, but underlying clay podzols allow excellent water-retention. Cropping levels are extremely low at less than one tonne per acre, meaning highly concentrated fruit. Ringland believes his century-old vines yield Shiraz of unique lushness, tremendous concentration, and unusually thick skins. The vines will ripen up to 17° Baume yet retain excellent acid balance and flavour.

Ringland describes *Three Rivers* as a celebration of tiny parcels of true vineyard selected fruit. The wines are "painstakingly hand-made" in open fermenters, regularly plunged to extract colour, flavour and tannins. Towards dryness, the wines are drained and pressed through a traditional wooden basket press. Fermentation is completed in 100 per cent new French oak hogsheads, and matured in them for up to 40 months.

*Three Rivers* is opulence, richness, and sheer concentration. The U.S. market sucks up the wines almost exclusively. Retail values jumped from $60 to $600 in a single year, illustrating the demand... and price insensitivity. Its short supply and mythical status now makes it Australia's most expensive Shiraz. Is this wine a lasting sensation, or a flash in the pan? As far as Chris Ringland is concerned, he's more interested in making a wine that leaves an indelible mark on the Barossa landscape.

## TORBRECK, BAROSSA VALLEY

*Langton's selections – Torbreck The Steading Grenache-Mourvedre-Shiraz, Torbreck Juveniles Grenache-Mourvedre-Shiraz, Torbreck Descendant Shiraz, Torbreck Run Rig Shiraz*

Torbreck is a revelation. Its very existence challenges the Barossa paradigm (about 30 years of conventional winemaking assumptions). David Powell, former lumberjack turned winemaker, established Torbreck in 1994, and the world is already smitten with his highly opulent and perfumed wines. The winery is the absolute reverse of the Barossa vernacular. It is astonishing to find the open concrete fermenters and basket presses lying in the middle of a paddock, open to the elements. Completing this early 20th century back-to-basics picture are old dairy vats out the back, behind a tiny little pillbox office and a lean-to apricot cutting shed. Torbreck sources from five different dry-grown, low-yield vineyards located on the western ridge of the Barossa Valley, and as far south as the Jacob's Creek area. It either share-farms or has full vineyard management control, ensuring optimum fruit quality, ripeness, and flavour development. Wines are batch-vinified in open fermenters, with a palette of winemaking options including pre-fermentation cold-soak, extended maceration, partial whole bunch fermentation, warm and cooler ferment regimes, and regular pumping over.

*Run Rig* is Torbreck's ultra-cuvee Shiraz-Viognier (3%). The Viognier is free run into barrel to complete fermentation. The name derives from a Scottish method of property distribution. The wine is matured in 40 per cent new French oak – coopered exclusively in France – for up to two-and-a-half years. The pressings are matured in American oak.

The wine is incredibly opulent with super ripe fruit expressions and dense velveteen, tannin structures. The *Descendant* Shiraz-Viognier (8%) goes into older wood – the fruit sourced from the young Descendant Block vineyard, adjacent to the winery. The vines here are from cuttings from the Run Rig vineyard, hence the name.

*Factor Shiraz* is matured in older French oak with a touch of American oak-aged pressings to create further complexity. The *Steading*, an old Scottish term used for a group of homes on a ridge, and *Juveniles*, named after a Parisian winebar known for its penchant for Rhone Reds, are both classic Grenache-Mourvedre (Mataro)-Shiraz blends. These are aged in older oak and stainless steel respectively.

The winemaking philosophy is suitably offbeat, with strong ideas about the effects of ultra-violet and polymerising of tannins, gravitational pull, phases of the moon and their effects on fermentation, and Baume levels. This is a marvellously eccentric little place doing its own thing. And it's all paying off. From a secondary market perspective, Torbreck has gone from zero to 600kmh in 60 seconds. Not bad for a knock-about bloke in search of his own nirvana.

## TURKEY FLAT, BAROSSA VALLEY

*Langton's selections – Turkey Flat Shiraz*

Turkey Flat, named after the bush turkeys that used to roam freely here, was established by fourth generation grape growers Peter and Christie Schulz, at their property on the banks of Tanunda Creek. Johann Friedrich Fiedler, one of the Silesian pioneers brought out by William Angas, planted the first Shiraz vines in 1843. Gottlieb Ernst Schulz, a butcher whose family later ventured into dairy farming, purchased the property in 1865. A modern, Italian-designed state-of-the-art winery was recently built adjacent to the historic bluestone butcher's shop.

The *Turkey Flat Shiraz* is a classic Barossa style with fruit sourced from various vineyards of varying ages. Vintage takes place typically in late March/April. Fermentation is allowed to run between 18 and 24° C. The wine is generally macerated on skins for about seven days before being drained and pressed off. This is followed by maturation for 22 months in a combination of new and seasoned French and American oak hogsheads.

*Turkey Flat Shiraz* is becoming increasingly popular on the secondary market. In the context of Barossa Shiraz, it offers strong regional provenance at a more affordable level. The wines often show dark cherry, chocolaty aromas and flavours, ripe textured tannins, and plenty of fruit sweetness, concentration, and length.

## VERITAS, BAROSSA VALLEY

*Langton's selections – Veritas Hanisch Shiraz, Veritas Heysen Shiraz, Magpie Estate The Malcolm Shiraz*

The new Veritas winery on Seppelt Road is a monument to the spectacular recent success of the highly amusing but politically incorrect, Rolf Binder. Rarely offered on the Australian secondary market, most of his top wines find their way directly onto the U.S. and European markets. It is also a reflection of taste – Australian critics are known for deriding over-lavish and massively proportioned wines.

The *Hanisch* and *Heysen* Shirazes are at the ultra-ripe end of the Barossa Shiraz spectrum, with deep-set blackberry/aniseed fruit, and a rich multi-pixillated tannin structure. Sourced from mature vineyards planted in the early 1970s, fruit is batch-vinified in open and open headed down fermenters, and partially barrel fermented in American and French oak, of which about 30-50 per cent is new. Maturation takes place over two years.

This producer has become a new rising star by totally reinventing itself in recent years. The wines are super. And with a new winery, the innovative winemaking of Rolf Binder, and plenty of energy and enthusiasm, Veritas will attract significant interest in the future.

Newly released, Magpie Estate *The Malcolm* – highly alcoholic, richly concentrated, and in need of cellaring – is the result of a joint venture with Noel Young, a small independent Cambridge (U.K.) wine merchant. Not produced every vintage, and sourced from a vineyard near Marananga, it has created a storm in the U.S. and will polarise critics. Limited production will not satisfy initial demand, either from the curious, or from those who genuinely like the style. *Christa Rolf Shiraz-Grenache* and the retro-labelled Shiraz-Mourvedre pressings, are also worth seeking out. Rolf Binder has also made the *Killibinbin* wines from Langhorne Creek, an almost unheard of label in Australia, but the object of Robert Parker Jr's enthusiasms. He also makes the J.J. Hahn range of wines.

## WENDOUREE, CLARE VALLEY

*Langton's selections – Wendouree Shiraz, Wendouree Cabernet Malbec, Wendouree Cabernet Sauvignon, Wendouree Shiraz Malbec, Wendouree Shiraz Mataro*

Wendouree is a great Australian small producer with an important cultural and historical identity. The Wendouree vineyards were first planted in 1893 on an easterly ridge towards the northern end of Clare. A small winery was built in the early 1900s, replaced by a stone winery and cellars in 1914. Virtually the entire production of Wendouree was sold in bulk during the 1950s. In 1917, A.P. Birk's son, Roly took over winemaking and spent 60 consecutive vintages at Wendouree. Roly Birks used to travel around South Australia selling hogsheads off the back of a truck. It is, to all intents and purposes, a living museum making old fashioned wondrous wines. The wines are still made in the original cellars today, using much of the same equipment. The press, purchased in 1920, is still used.

Roly Birks put up his winemaking boots at Wendouree finally in 1983. However, after three years of commercial freefall Lita and Tony Brady assumed management control in 1974. In the ensuing years, the vineyards and winery were spruced up. Tony, with almost 30 years' winemaking experience, makes the wine. Lita completed wine science studies at Wagga in the late 1980s, and became involved in the vineyard and winery. Since 1981, Stephen George, one of Australia's most independent-thinking winemakers, has been their sounding board on viticultural and vinicultural matters. This has become an enduring friendship, resulting in profoundly individual wines. The Wendouree style is strongly focused, with emphasis on fruit power and weight.

If *Wendouree Shiraz* is considered one of Australia's greatest, Tony Brady is a reluctant star. The vineyard is tiny, with low-yielding, beautifully formed old vines, many from the original 1893 plantings. Wendouree is recognised as producing great wines, and herein lies the dilemma – great wine attracts followers and, by the law of supply and demand, Brady's wines should attract higher cellar door values. Tony wishes, however, to sell at what he believes are fair prices. Hence, the wines have achieved local cult status for both enthusiasts and investors.

The current enthusiasms from the U.S. have not yet reached these wines, making them relatively affordable in the scheme of things. Wendouree also produces spellbindingly good, but idiosyncratic, *Shiraz-Malbec*, *Shiraz-Mataro*, *Cabernet Sauvignon-Malbec*, and *Cabernet Sauvignon*. They are very muscular, powerful wines with vice-like tannins and require long term ageing. They perform very well on the secondary market.

• *WENDOUREE Shiraz Clare Valley S.A. – Exceptional*

*Wendouree Shiraz* is made from old Shiraz vines, mostly planted in 1893. These are dense, strongly flavoured and tannic wines. In many respects, it is an idiosyncratic style – largely because it harks back to traditional winemaking ideas rather than contemporary practices. It has beautifully intense varietal fruit, massive concentration, and a muscular sinewy tannin template, very much a hallmark of Wendouree. In *Wendouree Shiraz*, the mass of fruit sweetness complements the overall toughness of the wine. These wines benefit from the cellar – while the tannins hardly soften, the wines do become more complex. The wine will age for a long period of time, maintaining prominent tannin structures. One of the great Australian wine experiences.

- *WENDOUREE Cabernet Sauvignon-Malbec*
  *Clare Valley S.A. – Outstanding*

The *Cabernet Sauvignon-Malbec* reflects the spirit of this remarkable place. This profound wine style has intense bright fruit, underlying oak and firm, but pronounced, vice-like tannin structures. The generosity of fruit and austerity of the tannins, provide an interesting juxtaposition.

- *WENDOUREE Cabernet Sauvignon*
  *Clare Valley S.A. – Outstanding*

*Wendouree Cabernet Sauvignon* – the oldest plantings go back to 1970 – reflects its unique vineyard site and is one of the country's most individual and characterful Cabernets. The wines are incredibly complex with high-pitched fruit, massive concentration and jaw-locking, iron-like tannins. These wines have intrinsic ageing potential, although the tannins will hardly soften out. Regardless, this is one of Australia's great wine experiences.

- *WENDOUREE Shiraz-Malbec*
  *Clare Valley S.A. – Outstanding*

*Wendouree Shiraz-Malbec* is a highly individual style with plenty of blackberry/plum/mulberry and menthol-like fruit and fine, rusty, almost unyielding, tannins.

- *WENDOUREE Shiraz-Mataro*
  *Clare Valley S.A. – Outstanding*

As expected, these wines are highly individual, showing the stamp of both vineyard site and traditional values. *Wendouree Shiraz-Mataro* is a toughly structured wine with a central core of blackberry liquorice fruit and pronounced iron-fisted tannins. These are strong, gripping wines that demand cellaring.

**WIRRA WIRRA, McLAREN VALE**

*Langton's selections – Wirra Wirra The Angelus Cabernet Blend, Wirra Wirra R.S.W. Shiraz, Wirra Wirra Church Block*

Wirra Wirra is a distinguished McLaren Vale winery. Robert Strangeways Wigley, a noted cricketer, founded it in 1893, and exported his wines in barrel to P.B. Burgoyne in the U.K., mostly as tonic wines. In 1969, Gregg and Roger Trott purchased the derelict property and deep alluvial river flat vineyards.

The *Angelus* is a McLaren Vale Coonawarra Cabernet Blend, sourced from the winery block and from Kym Tolley, in a fruit swap arrangement. The wines are vinified in open fermenters, regularly plunged down. Towards dryness, they are drained and basket- or airbag-pressed into mostly French oak to complete fermentation. Maturation takes place for around 22 months in approximately 50 per cent new and 50 per cent used French oak. A few parcels are matured in French coopered American oak.

The *Angelus* is named after a three-quarter tonne bell from an old Adelaide Church. *RSW Shiraz* is named after stencils used by the original owner. This wine is vinified in static and open fermenters, partially barrel fermented, and matured in a combination of new (40-50%), American (20%), and French (80%) oak *barriques*. The *Church Block* is named after an old vineyard at nearby Bethany (not to be confused with Bethany in the Barossa). This savoury maturation style sees no more than 10 per cent new oak.

On the secondary market, Wirra Wirra has not been a big achiever. Its entire production however, is on allocation, and the wines are highly regarded. It's really a question of 'watch this space'.

## WOLF BLASS, BAROSSA VALLEY

*Langton's selections – Wolf Blass Black Label Cabernet Blend*

Wolf Blass Bilyara (meaning 'Eaglehawk') was established in 1973 by Wolf Blass, a German winemaker brought out by Kaiser Stuhl to run its sparkling wine production. Starting out with an old shed winery on two and a half acres and a $2,000 overdraft, growth has been rapid and attributable to premium winemaking, ostentatious marketing, and sheer guile.

Wolf Blass was one of the early masters of wine marketing. His considerable winemaking, blending, and wood-handling skills, ensured consistency and reliability across all quality levels. Wolf Blass is now a brand name within the global entity Beringer Blass, a multi-billion dollar subsidiary of Foster's Brewing.

At the top of the heap is *Wolf Blass Black Label Dry Red* – essentially a Cabernet Sauvignon-driven blend, and the only Wolf Blass wine with investment potential. The individual parcels of fruit are vinified separately in open fermentation tanks, then allowed to complete fermentation in French and American hogsheads. The wine spends up to three years in new American and French oak, prior to bottling.

Wolf Blass invented the term, "No wood – no good". If Max Schubert started the idea of partial barrel fermentation in red winemaking, arguably Wolf Blass spread the news. Certainly, the *Hill of Grace* style originated from a discussion between Blass and Cyril Henschke. This technique is used extensively in the Australian wine industry.

*Wolf Blass Black Label* is substantially propped up by oak. In a high quality vintage, the fruit sucks up and integrates well, making wines of superb richness and flavour. An example is the 1991 vintage, which is simply exquisite. In a year like 1995, the oak sits on top of the wine and doesn't impress. The newly released, and unimaginatively named, *Platinum Label*, illustrates the lazy and greed-focused culture of corporate marketing.

- *WOLF BLASS Black Label Cabernet Blend S.A. – Excellent*

Wolf Blass *Black Label*, essentially a traditional Australian Cabernet Sauvignon-Shiraz, is based on the best parcels of fruit available. It can sometimes comprise 100 per cent Cabernet. The fruit source is multi-regional, including the Barossa Valley, Langhorne Creek, McLaren Vale, and the Clare Valley. Wolf Blass initiated the *Black Label* in 1974, which went on to win the highly prestigious Jimmy Watson Trophy. He did it again the following year, entrenching this wine as one of Australia's emerging great wines. In 1999, the *Black Label* won the same trophy for the fourth time, illustrating its universal appeal and astonishing quality.

The fruit is harvested at optimum ripeness and flavour development, usually around 13° Baume. Wolf Blass *Black Label* is substantially propped up by oak, as the wine spends up to three years in new American and French oak, prior to bottling. A highly important Australian wine.

## WYNNS COONAWARRA ESTATE, COONAWARRA

*Langton's selections – Wynns Coonawarra Estate John Riddoch Cabernet Sauvignon, Wynns Coonawarra Estate Cabernet Sauvignon, Wynns Coonawarra Estate Michael Shiraz, Wynns Coonawarra Estate Shiraz*

Wynns Coonawarra Estate is the largest single vigneron in Coonawarra with almost 2,200 acres of classic *terra rossa*. The distinct gabled winery was built in 1896 by John Riddoch, founder of the Coonawarra Fruit Colony. It was once known as Chateau Comaum, briefly home to the rare and wonderful *Woodleys Treasure Chest Series* wines, produced during the late 1940s and very early 1950s.

Noted Melbourne wine merchants Samuel and David Wynn, purchased the winery and land in 1951. Winemaking leviathan Southcorp now owns it.

Top of the range is the *John Riddoch Cabernet Sauvignon* – not a single vineyard wine, rather a single varietal ultra-Cabernet Sauvignon using fruit from Wynns' extensive Cabernet Sauvignon vineyards. After years of strong support, this wine now attracts a modest but important following. The relatively new *Michael Shiraz*, named after the superb but one-off 1955 *Michael Hermitage*, has attracted significant interest, particularly the 1990 and 1991 vintages. *Wynns Coonawarra Estate Cabernet Sauvignon* is referred to as Black Label. This wine, more than any other, has helped define Coonawarra. In a super vintage, this wine can appear alarmingly like a second or third growth Bordeaux, with its pure cassis aromas and cedary complexity.

The *Shiraz* is blindingly good value, almost repeating the Cabernet Sauvignon irony. A *Riesling*, *Chardonnay*, and *Cabernet Sauvignon-Shiraz-Merlot* are also made, providing great drinking at competitive prices. Wynns enjoys a moderate volume of interest, which spikes on recognised vintage form.

- *WYNNS COONAWARRA ESTATE John Riddoch Cabernet Sauvignon Coonawarra S.A. – Excellent*

Most of the fruit for Wynns *John Riddoch* is derived from older blocks planted on their own roots in the 1960s and 1970s. Although varied, the trellises are generally pruned to a narrow and relatively tall hedge, with open canopies and good fruit exposure. Cropping levels are low for Coonawarra, at around one-and-a-half to two-and-a-half tonnes per acre. Harvest is in late April. Fermentation takes place immediately after crushing, at relatively warm temperatures for five to eight days, after which it is pressed off at dryness. The philosophy is that ripe tannins and flavours are extracted while "retaining fruit sweetness and structure". Maturation takes place in new French oak hogsheads for 18 to 26 months, depending on vintage conditions.

While Wynns *John Riddoch* is invariably a well made wine, does it reflect the unique *terra rossa* soils of Coonawarra? Or is it really a 'house style'? The wine is jam-packed with fruit and tannins and immersed in new oak, needing several years to integrate. I suspect that medium to long term ageing is the way to go. There are a few convincing examples – namely the 1982 and 1986 vintages – in which the spirit of Coonawarra emerges through this densely proportioned wine. After many years of strong support, this wine now attracts a modest but important following. This wine style may well prove its detractors resoundingly wrong.

- *WYNNS COONAWARRA ESTATE Cabernet SauvignonCoonawarra S.A. – Distinguished*

Referred to as Black Label – *Wynns Coonawarra Estate Cabernet Sauvignon*, more than any other, has helped define Coonawarra. Its history dates back to 1954, and it was one of the early Australian wine brands. Fruit is sourced from Wynns' extensive holdings of Cabernet Sauvignon vineyards – of varying vine age – on highly desirable *terra rossa* over limestone soils. Trellis systems are varied, but generally pruned to a narrow and relatively tall hedge with open canopies and good fruit exposure. Cropping levels are around three to four tonnes per acre – harvested in late April. Fermentation takes place immediately after crushing, at relatively warm temperatures for five to eight days, after which it is pressed off at dryness. The wines are matured in a combination of new and old American and French oak for 12 to 18 months, depending on vintage.

This value-for-money wine is highly prized for its incremental return in both quality and outlay. A classic Coonawarra Cabernet Sauvignon with bright blackcurrant/cedar fruit that develops into a rich chocolaty wine with age. The American oak component is subtle and attractive, usually underpinning the wine.

## YALUMBA, BAROSSA VALLEY

*Langton's selections – Yalumba Octavius Shiraz, Yalumba Reserve Shiraz, Yalumba Signature Cabernet Sauvignon-Shiraz, Yalumba Menzies Cabernet Sauvignon*

Samuel Smith established the Yalumba winery in 1849. The company has vineyards primarily in Barossa and Coonawarra. Robert Hill-Smith now presides over the family enterprise, combining conservatism and tradition with up-to-date winemaking technology and thinking.

*Yalumba Octavius* is made from dry-grown Shiraz with an average age of 82 years, the oldest from a vineyard planted in 1908. The wines are matured for two years in small American oak Octaves (80 litre barrels) coopered at Yalumba winery. To leach undesirable flavours from the oak, the Missouri timbers are left in the elements for eight years. With a higher than normal surface-area-to-wine ratio, *Octavius* is a wine of great richness, intensity and power. Its pronounced vanillin, black berry/liquorice aromas, ripe tannins, sweet fruit, and extract, suggest longevity. The *Yalumba Reserve Shiraz* is made only in special vintages from prime parcels of Barossa and smaller tranches of Coonawarra and Langhorne Creek fruit. The *Menzies* is a Coonawarra Cabernet Sauvignon, vinified along typical Bordelais lines and matured in 33 per cent new French oak hogsheads for up to 24 months. The *Signature* (first vintage, 1962) is a Cabernet Sauvignon-Shiraz blend partially barrel fermented and matured in a combination of new and old American and French oak hogsheads.

A lineage of three decades, proven cellaring potential, immense resources, and a good winemaking team, are all hallmarks for potential success. *Yalumba Octavius* is emerging as a very strong performer with quality runs on the board. Yalumba's investment in the sublime grape variety, Viognier, has resulted in the super-fine *Virgilius*. It challenges the notion that great wine needs to be a cellaring proposition. Yalumba is an exciting producer with a clear eye on the cult and fine wine market.

### ZEMA ESTATE, COONAWARRA

*Langton's selections – Zema Estate Family Selection Cabernet Sauvignon, Zema Estate Cabernet Sauvignon, Zema Estate Cluny Cabernet Blend, Zema Estate Shiraz*

Established in 1982, Zema Estate comprises approximately 150 acres of vineyard on prime *terra rossa* soils over limestone, predominately planted to Cabernet Sauvignon. It is a small family company making classic Coonawarra Shiraz and Cabernet Sauvignon. Vines are planted on their own roots on two-wire vertical trellis system and single wire trellis, with typically low yields to optimise flavour development. The vines are machine harvested. Vinification is in potter fermenters and vinimatics, sometimes with extended skin maceration depending on vintage conditions.

The *Family Selection Cabernet Sauvignon*, only released in an excellent vintage, is matured in a high proportion of new tightly-grained French oak. The standard Cabernet Sauvignon is matured in a combination of new and old French and American oak for 16 to 24 months. *Zema Estate Shiraz* is partly barrel fermented and is one of the better Coonawarra Shirazes, with plenty of pure fruit and mid-palate richness. Zema Estate has a moderate profile in the marketplace and commands a small but loyal following.

## VICTORIA

### BAILEY'S, GLENROWAN (NEAR RUTHERGLEN)

*Langton's selections – Bailey's 1904 Block Shiraz, Bailey's 1920s Block Shiraz*

Bailey's at Glenrowan, is located in classic bushranger country – known as Kelly Country, after Ned Kelly and his gang, who once roamed the area around Glenrowan. Richard Bailey, a merchant who supplied goods to gold miners, purchased the property in 1853. The first wine was made in 1870. The family eventually sold its business in 1972 and Beringer Blass acquired Bailey's in 1986. The low-yielding vineyards, replanted in the early 1900s because of phylloxera, are located on red granitic soils in what is a relatively hot and continental climate.

The district is best known for its fortified wines, how-ever, Bailey's produces robust, well-focused, single vineyard *1904* and *1920s Block* Shirazes. These are limited release wines. Only six tonnes comes off the *1904* Block. The wines are made in traditional open fermenters and matured in a combination of American and French oak. The overall profiles of these wines make them ideal secondary market staples, though they have yet to perform.

*Winemaker's Selection Liqueur Muscat* and *Tokay* are, in every respect, brilliant wines. The *Muscat* has that beautiful, burnished bronze colour with slightly green edges. Strong rancio characters pervade the wine, bringing utter joy. The *Tokay* suggests more tea-leafy aromas and is decadent in flavour. Made using a solera system, these wines are not vintage dated. Sadly, undated fortifieds lack value in the secondary market. They are beacons of quality nonetheless.

## BANNOCKBURN, GEELONG

*Langton's selections – Bannockburn Pinot Noir, Bannockburn Chardonnay*

The late Stuart Hooper established Bannockburn in 1973. The winery, just north-west of Geelong, is one of Australia's leading Pinot Noir and Chardonnay producers. Winemaker Gary Farr, is notoriously fastidious and has a deep understanding of his material.

Bannockburn's *Pinot Noir* clone was brought out as part of the James Busby collection, originally planted in Sydney's Botanical Gardens, and sourced from Clos Vougeot. Indeed the vines look remarkably similar to their Burgundian antecedents.

With more than 20 Australian vintages under his belt and the equivalent in Burgundy, Farr believes in vineyard individuality and vintage personality. Hence, *Bannockburn Pinot Noir* reflects the character of the vintage and never appears contrived. *Bannockburn Pinot Noir* is a highly defined wine with black cherry aromas and meaty complexity, a silky palate, and deep-set flavours.

When it comes to *Chardonnay*, as with his Pinot, Farr holds to the tried and tested older clones. His winemaking philosophy is low input/maximum flavour, preserving the inherent qualities of fruit and site. This is an immensely complex Chardonnay, showing all the winemaker's art. Tropical fruit aromas, nutty, vanillin complexity, ripe fruit, a creamy palate and fruit sweetness, make it one of the best Chardonnays in the country. It is also one of the longest-lived. Move over *Puligny* !

*SRH Chardonnay* – named after Stuart Hooper, founder of Bannockburn – and *Serre Pinot Noir*, are examples of the burgeoning new breed of ultra-fine, selected-parcel wines. It is only a matter of time before they begin to make an impression on the market. The *Bannockburn Shiraz* is a classic cool-climate wine.

Bannockburn is well regarded on the secondary wine market but because its star wines are medium term cellaring propositions, they perform erratically. The quality, however, is outstanding.

- *BANNOCKBURN Pinot Noir*
  *Geelong Vic. – Outstanding*

The Serre Vineyard, a closely-spaced, metre-by-metre vineyard, plays an essential role in the wine. Gary Farr's own vineyard provides other material. Farr prefers the vineyard to do the talking. No hedging, shoot, or crop thinning is employed. He prefers the technique of *saignee* or juice run off, if necessary, to achieve optimum flavour. Vintage occurs normally in mid-March but can extend to early April.

The grapes are 75 per cent de-stemmed and gravity fed into five tonne open fermenters, where fermentation takes approximately 15 days or so. The cap is punched down regularly by automatic *pigeageurs*, which encourages extraction of colour and tannin. Residual stems give more backbone and perfume to the wine.

The wine is drained and pressed, then transferred to 100 per cent new French oak occasionally racked using an American 'Bulldog' – a means of pushing wine by nitrogen (or air) without ripping apart the inherent texture of the wine. The wine is matured in oak for approximately 14-16 months before final assemblage and bottling.

Gary Farr had a long association with Domaine Dujac in Burgundy, which has given him a worldly view of Pinot Noir. "If you can't make good Pinot Noir from some of the older clones in Australia," he says, "it is highly unlikely you can make good wine from the newer clones."

- *BANNOCKBURN Chardonnay*
  *Geelong Vic. – Excellent*

The first vineyards were planted in 1978, with vines spaced at approximately two-and-a-half metres. *Bannockburn Chardonnay* uses five different clones, although the backbone of the wine is the Penfolds 58 clone, originally sourced from the Hunter Valley. The low vigour vertical shoot positioned vineyards are on a range of volcanic over limestone soils, in what is essentially a cool maritime climate. Blustery weather during spring can effect flowering and fruit set. The wine is whole bunch pressed and drained into barrels where it awaits ferment. Fermentation takes place generally over a six week period, although it is not unusual for some barrels to take several months. The wine is stirred on its lees for three months until completion of malo-lactic fermentation. Maturation takes place in a combination of oak from the previous year, and one-third new French oak, for approximately nine to 11 months. Farr believes that oak should play a supporting role in the overall Chardonnay style. The overall winemaking philosophy is low input – maximum flavour – preserving the inherent qualities of fruit and site.

### BASS PHILLIP, GIPPSLAND

*Langton's selections – Bass Phillip Premium Pinot Noir, Bass Phillip Reserve Pinot Noir, Bass Phillip Old Cellar Pinot Noir, Bass Phillip Crown Prince Pinot Noir, Bass Phillip Village Pinot Noir*

Bass Phillip is located in prime dairy country near Leongatha in South Gippsland, in an area known for its regular rainfall pattern. The vineyards have a north-easterly aspect and are planted on deep silty loams with a high iron content – a factor that gives tremendous colour to the fruit. Phillip Jones is a perfectionist who crops his fruit at incredibly low levels to achieve his flavour development objectives. Jones calls his Pinot Noir 'precocious'. He firmly believes in a gentle hand. Racking is kept to a minimum and no pumps are used in the winery.

"Wine flows through a pipe like a fast running stream – at speed in the centre, slow on the sides," says Jones, "The sheer force created by the pump just tears the wine apart. The difference between good and great Pinot Noir is texture."

Bass Phillip uses a philosophy of low input viticulture and winemaking. Phillip Jones is increasingly employing biodynamic principles in his vineyard. Ultimately, his priority is to produce a wine that is completely natural and that expresses vineyard site. This may sound simple, but such a high standard requires relentless pursuit of perfection… and a degree of madness. Rigorous triaging of fruit, together with an almost insane passion and attention to detail, has resulted in the most exquisite of Australian Pinot Noirs. The wines have beautiful, black cherry, floral and gamy aromas, supple, velvety tannins, underlying smoky oak, and plenty of length.

In recent years, Jones has developed new vineyards to become commercially more comfortable without compromising quality. The market is already embracing the *Old Cellar Pinot Noir* and *Crown Prince Pinot Noir* – off relatively young vines. The *Reserve Pinot Noir* is almost impossible to get, but is arguably the greatest Pinot Noir produced in Australia. These wines are on the fringe of the cult scene and can perform spectacularly well.

- *BASS PHILLIP Premium Pinot Noir*
  *Gippsland Vic. – Outstanding*

The vineyard is closely spaced with 3,200-4,000 vines per acre. Although Phillip Jones crops at approximately one to one-and-a-half tonnes per acre, the yield per vine is a third to a quarter of what would normally be considered a low-cropping level. Fruit is picked on flavour and natural acidity. Hand harvesting takes place in mid-April. A *laissez faire* approach is used in the winery. The Pinot Noir is completely de-stemmed and crushed (through a modified crusher to allow a proportion of whole berries in the ferment) into a closed stainless steel fermenter. The ferment is regularly plunged, day and night. At dryness, the wine is transferred by gravity to 100 per cent lightly toasted new oak – mostly Alliers – where the wine is allowed to mature for between 18 and 20 months, depending on vintage.

## BEST'S, GREAT WESTERN

*Langton's selections – Best's Centenary Shiraz,*
*Best's Thomson Family Shiraz, Best's FHT Shiraz,*
*Best's Bin O Shiraz*

The history of Best's goes back to 1893, when William Thomson purchased the vineyard (first vines planted in 1868) and winery at Rhymney. This property was subsequently renamed St Andrew's, to acknowledge the Thomson Family's Scottish origins. Frederick Thomson acquired the property from his father in 1911, and in 1920, purchased Best's Concongella Vineyard at Great Western (originally planted in 1866). The Great Depression forced the Thomsons off their land, but by the early 1930s, the family was back in control again through both dogged persistence and luck. The Thomson family are inextricably linked to Great Western, the fourth generation's Viv Thomson now running the family business. This producer has always been highly regarded.

The release of the 1992 *Thomson Centenary Shiraz* – to commemorate a century of winemaking – illustrates the cellaring potential of Great Western Shiraz. The wine, rebadged *Thomson Family Shiraz*, is only released in exceptional vintages – 1992, 1994, 1995, 1996, 1997, and 1998. It was not produced in 1993, 1999, and 2000. The wine is made entirely off the 15 rows of vines planted by Henry Best in the 1860s. The Concongella vineyard, elevated at 234 metres, and planted on powdery sandy loams over deep clay, is cropped at levels of up to three tonnes per acre. *Thomson Family Shiraz* is now open-fermented in small 'tubs'. At dryness, the wine is pressed off and matured in a 50/50 combination new and old American oak for approximately 24 months.

The wines show bright raspberry, mulberry fruit aromas and flavours, with silken tannins and underlying smoky oak. Severe frosts in October 1998 reduced the 1999 crop dramatically, making it impossible to make a *Thomson Family Shiraz*. However the wine, blended with a component of *Best's Bin O Shiraz*, and matured in American oak puncheons, was isolated and bottled as *Best's FHT Shiraz*. In 2000, the old vines 'simply ran out of steam' and failed to yield the quality needed for Thomson Family designation.

*Best's Bin O Shiraz*, made from Concongella Shiraz fruit, is a classic Great Western Style with emphasis on fruit quality. Best's convincingly affirms the key concern of regional provenance, illustrating that history and sense of place are important elements of fine wine.

## BINDI, MACEDON

*Langton's selections – Bindi Block 5 Pinot Noir, Bindi Original Vineyard Pinot Noir, Bindi Quartz Chardonnay*

The minuscule Bindi vineyard is located on a parcel of elevated grazing land, on the slopes of Mount Gisborne, at the heel of the Great Dividing Range. Although a vineyard was proposed in the 1970s, inappropriate advice delayed planting until the mid 1980s, when the local Gisborne Shire began to encourage alternative agriculture. Michael Dhillon helped his father Bill, an engineer and great wine enthusiast, to plant their 11 acre vineyard in 1988. While studying economics at Monash University in Melbourne, he developed his own passion for wine, and rather than take the standard technical trail through wine university, he became a travelling cellar rat. Michael however regards visiting winemaker consultant Stuart Anderson (the founder of Balgownie) as his most profound influence. This rounded vocational start – through both experience and hands-on mentoring – is highly unusual from an Australian perspective. Michael Dhillon is fluent in contemporary wine philosophy. He talks of making wines that are "ethereal and seductive" rather than just "satisfying and chunky" and that Bindi's soils "have the strength of character to talk through the wine." This all relates, of course, to the idea of vineyard site and sense of place (*terroir*). Dhillon is convinced that flavour profiles are inextricably linked to soil type.

The Bindi vineyard, now 15 acres and growing the classic Burgundian varieties of Pinot Noir and Chardonnay, are planted on predominately two soil profiles – shattered quartz over alluvial silts, and top soil (mostly sandy grey loams over clay). The vineyards, elevated at approximately 500 metres, are on gentle north facing slopes. Block 5 is the most naturally protected vineyard, while a windbreak of trees guards the more exposed original vineyard. The vines are all vertically shoot positioned to optimise exposure to sunlight. Yields are typically as low as one-and-a-half tonnes per acre. Wine making is strictly "non-interference, but not uncontrolled". Dhillon believes strongly in natural wines showing "perfume, harmony and elegance".

The *Block 5 Pinot Noir* sees about 25 to 40 per cent new French oak. The *Quartz Chardonnay* and *Original Vineyard Pinot Noir* see between 20 and 30 per cent new oak, depending on vintage. Wild yeast fermentation and minimal filtration are also employed.

The commitment to quality at Bindi goes beyond wine-making. An afforestation program (through natural seeding) is another project being under-taken. The wines of Bindi are dedicated to the late mathematician and professor, Kostas Rind (1909-1983), whom Bill Dhillon describes as a "Lithuanian sage who epitomised wisdom and humility and introduced me to wine." Bindi also makes a non-vineyard designated Chardonnay, and *Bindi Cuvee* – a sparkling (*methode champenoise*) wine.

## COLDSTREAM HILLS, YARRA VALLEY

*Langton's selections – Coldstream Hills Reserve Chardonnay, Coldstream Hills Reserve Pinot Noir*

The *Reserve Chardonnay* and the *Reserve Pinot Noir* have played an important role in the genesis of fine Australian expressions of these varieties. Noted Australian wine writer James Halliday and his wife Suzanne established Coldstream Hills in 1985. Halliday juggled his career as a lawyer in the early days. He could often be seen tending his vines at god-forsaken hours to squeeze in his workload. He finally lost financial control of Coldstream Hills in 1996 to Southcorp (Australia's largest wine company), but maintains a consultant winemaker's role.

Vintage usually takes place in mid-April with extremely low cropping levels. The *Coldstream Hills Chardonnays* are made in traditional Burgundian fashion from fruit mainly sourced from estate-grown grapes. Richness and potential longevity are philosophical elements of the style, particularly for the *Reserve*, although these wines seem, at most, medium term wines.

The *Reserve Pinot Noir* is, in every respect, one of Australia's leading Pinot Noirs, although in recent years its reputation (but not its quality) has been eclipsed by the advent of the cult wine scene. The wines have plenty of fruit definition and complexity, and are fleshy and ripely textured on the palate. These wines have medium cellaring potential only; the best vintages going for any distance. They are erratic performers on the secondary market.

- *COLDSTREAM HILLS Reserve Chardonnay Yarra Valley Vic.*

The *Reserve Chardonnay* is made from fruit mainly sourced from estate-grown grapes. The fruit is whole bunched pressed and cold-settled prior to initiation of fermentation in barrel. Fermentation takes place in cold storage – in a mix of new and used French oak *barriques* (mainly Vosges but some Troncais) which moderates oak pick up and lengthens fermentation time. About six months of lees contact follows, with occasional *battonage*. Only about 20 per cent of the wine goes through malo-lactic fermentation.

- *COLDSTREAM HILLS Reserve Pinot Noir Yarra Valley Vic. – Distinguished*

Fruit is almost entirely sourced from the extraordinary and dramatic Amphitheatre Block, originally planted in 1985. Constant experimentation with new clones and winemaking techniques – notably cold-soaking (essentially a pre-ferment cold maceration) – shows that when it comes to Pinot Noir, winemaking is a philosophical (and physical) effort. At dryness, the wine is drained and lightly pressed, which breaks unbroken berries, and increases Baume levels to about three degres. The wine is then racked into a combination of new and used Troncais (French) oak, from mainly Dargaud and Jaegle, to complete primary fermentation and malo-lactic fermentation. The wine is made in Burgundian fashion with substantial use of whole bunch fermentation and *pigeage* (foot stamping). These wines have medium cellaring potential, only the best vintages going for any distance.

## CRAIGLEE, SUNBURY

*Langton's selections – Craiglee Shiraz*

*Craiglee Shiraz* is regarded as one of Victoria's top Shirazes. Located west of Melbourne, at Sunbury, Craiglee's historic bluestone winery was built by J.S. Johnston in 1865, and is set on grounds among beautiful Moreton Bay Fig trees. The winery went out of production in the 1920s. In the 1950s, a cache of 1872 *Craiglee Sunbury Shiraz* was found buried at the winery. After tasting the wine, John Brown of Milawa fame, encouraged the Carmody family to re-establish the vineyard and winery. He said, "Any site, anywhere in the world, that can produce a wine that lasts for 100 years is worth being replanted".

The re-planted 10 hectare vineyard is now more than 25 years old. Sited on alluvial river flats close to Jackson Creek, a tributary of the Maribyrnong River, the soils comprise sands over river stones.

Since the 1985 vintage, the wines have shown extraordinary consistency of quality. Reflecting its site uniqueness, these wines are quite different to any other, with earthy, pepper, raspberry, and black olive aromas, tightly structured palates, and iron-like tannins. They age well as they become more earthy and complex, with softer tannins and length. Regardless, opinion is quite divided over the style. Consequently, the market can fluctuate markedly – the strongest demand being generated by Victorian buyers.

- *CRAIGLEE Shiraz Sunbury Vic. – Excellent*

Vintage takes place around mid-April/early May with primary fermentation in open cement fermenters. A small portion is partially barrel fermented. Maturation is in a combination of new one and two year old French and American oak for 12 to 18 months. In recent times, the proportion of French oak has increased markedly. Since the 1985 vintage, the wines have shown extraordinary consistency of quality. The most recent vintages have shown a further lift in quality.

**DALWHINNIE, MOONAMBEL (PYRENEES)**

*Langton's selections – Dalwhinnie Shiraz, Dalwhinnie Cabernet Sauvignon, Dalwhinnie Eagle Shiraz, Dalwhinnie Chardonnay*

Purchased in 1973 by Ewan Jones, now managed by his son David, the Dalwhinnie vineyard was first planted in 1976. Initial design and layout was provided by David Hohnen of Cape Mentelle fame, and Australian tenor David Hobson helped plant vines. First vintage was in 1979. There is now a contemporary tilt-slab 50 tonne winery, designed by Ewan Jones (an architect), and a new 300 tonne capacity winery is in the pipeline.

This is classic gold-mining country, with quartz and decomposed slatey soils over friable clays. The vineyards, at an altitude between 360-595 metres, are set in a natural amphitheatre, accentuated by contour-planted vines. The prevailing philosophy is one of low input and low yields.

The *Shiraz* has great purity of fruit, with sweet, cracked pepper and blackberry aromas, a fleshy palate, with concentrated anise, blackberry, and pepper fruit, underlying oak, and sublime power. The *Cabernet Sauvignon* is also a leader, but has fairly pronounced tannin structures and needs time to soften.

The *Eagle Shiraz* is the supposed *ne plus ultra*, produced in 1986, 1992, 1997,1998, 2000, 2001, and 2002. This wine is sourced from a select two-and-a-half acre Shiraz block planted in 1977. Cropping level is approximately one-and-a-half tonnes per acre. The wine is vinified in small open fermenters and matured for two years in French oak *barriques*. Production is limited to about 200-300 tonnes.

Dalwhinnie would do well to concentrate on its outstanding *Shiraz*, already one of the best in the country. The *Eagle*, only produced in exceptional vintages, shows plenty of secondary market promise. The *Chardonnay* is also worth a look.

- *DALWHINNIE Shiraz Moonambel Vic. – Outstanding*

*Dalwhinnie Shiraz* is 100 per cent estate grown. The vines are trained on a vertical shoot positioned trellis, allowing maximum exposure to sunlight. While not totally organic, a low input philosophy is applied in the vineyard with minimal spray programs. Vintage takes place mid-March through to mid-April, with cropping levels at below two-and-a-half tonnes per acre. David Jones believes the fruit is best when picked around 13° Baume, although the vineyard is triaged at varying levels of ripeness to achieve a broader flavour spectrum. Usually the ideal flavour development happens when the grapes begin to 'shrinkle'. The fruit is hand-picked, lightly crushed and de-stemmed. The must is fermented in Potter fermenters using natural yeast strains. Dalwhinnie is experimenting with extended maceration to increase complexity and the use of open fermenters. Towards dryness, the wine is drained and pressed using a traditional basket press. The wine is then matured in a combination of new and used American oak and Nevers/Alliers *barriques* for up to 16 months. The overall level of new oak is about 10 per cent American and 30 per cent French. The wine becomes more complex as it evolves, developing a pruney, earthy bouquet, and softening out on the palate.

- *DALWHINNIE Cabernet Sauvignon Moonambel Vic. – Excellent*

*Dalwhinnie Cabernet* is 100 per cent estate grown. Vintage takes place mid-March to mid-April, although picking is staggered to take advantage of a broad spectrum of flavours. Fruit is fermented in Potter fermenters with regular pumping over. Vinification includes extended skin maceration to polymerise and soften tannins. The wine matures in a combination of new and used French oak, with a touch of American, for 16 months. About 30-40 per cent is new oak.

*Dalwhinnie Cabernet Sauvignon* is elegantly structured, with earthy, cassis-like aromas and underlying oak, ripe tannins and a fruit sweetness balanced by marked acidity.

## DE BORTOLI, YARRA VALLEY

*Langton's selections – De Bortoli Pinot Noir, De Bortoli GS Reserve Shiraz, De Bortoli Melba Barrel Select Cabernet Blend*

De Bortoli purchased the Chateau Yarrinya winery in the Yarra Valley in 1987, and over the last seven years, has completely reinvented itself. It has increased plantings to 130 hectares and also brings in fruit. Total crush is around 3,500 tonnes. In 1997, De Bortoli won the prestigious Jimmy Watson Memorial Trophy for its 1996 *GS Reserve Shiraz*, firming its position as one of the Valley's emerging stars. The '96 however, is as rare as hen's teeth. Interestingly, Chateau Yarrinya won the same trophy for its 1977 *Cabernet*, perhaps illustrating the quality of site. The *Pinot Noir* is one of the country's best. The 1997 and 1998 vintages are superb.

Outstanding wines are being made right across the varietal board. The *Melba Barrel Select* blend (now predominantly Cabernet) is named after Australian opera great, Dame Nellie Melba, and the Melba Highway that passes through De Bortoli's vineyards. The *Chardonnay* has potential. De Bortoli is an undervalued producer and, although it has been making impressive Pinot Noir, its Shiraz could well perform better. Refer also to De Bortoli's N.S.W listing.

## GIACONDA, BEECHWORTH

*Langton's selections – Giaconda Chardonnay, Giaconda Pinot Noir*

Rick Kinzbrunner spent 10 years making wine in Europe, New Zealand, and California, before settling in Australia. He established the Giaconda vineyard near Brown Brother's old Everton Hills vineyard. Kinzbrunner's wines are sublime, reflecting the fastidiousnous of the wine-maker.

*Giaconda Chardonnay*, first released in 1987 (the 1986 vintage) is enjoying fame among the cognoscenti. It is also something of an enigma. It is a classic style with excellent fruit definition and creamy flavours, all balanced by deft oak handling, and fine acid cut.

The wines appear to benefit from cellaring, which puts them in the elite league of Australian Chardonnays. An exciting wine with so much complexity and interest. The *Pinot Noir* is made in a typically Burgundian manner and is highly sought on the secondary market. Giaconda also produces a lesser known, but well made, Cabernet Sauvignon and a Shiraz. Recently Giaconda released a 100 per cent Roussanne named *Aeolia*, and a Chardonnay Roussanne blend called *Nantua Les Deux*. Rick Kinzbrunner has experimented greatly with Rousanne. If he can produce a wine similar in quality to his Chardonnay, he could attract new enthusiasm for this scarce variety.

- *GIACONDA Chardonnay*
  *Beechworth Vic. – Outstanding*

Located in a small valley, and planted at an altitude of 400 metres, the vineyard is minute, unusual also in that it is on south-facing slopes, following a theory that the vines do not need the sun's full impact. Soils are granitic loams over decomposed gravels and clays. Irrigation is minimal, used only to prevent stress. Rainfall occurs mostly in winter. Vintage is typically between mid-March/early-April with fruit hand-picked in the early morning. Vinification follows traditional Burgundian lines, including barrel fermentation in new and used French oak. Overall, the wine sees approximately 40 per cent new Alliers and Vosges oak for maturation over approximately 18 months.

- *GIACONDA Pinot Noir, Beechworth Vic.- Outstanding*

Vinification follows the lines of traditional Burgundian techniques. Not as remarkable as Giaconda's *Chardonnay*, the *Pinot Noir* still has plenty of varietal definition and flavour with good oak support. It can certainly claim to be one of Australia's better Pinot Noirs. The wine is highly sought on the secondary market.

## JASPER HILL, HEATHCOTE

*Langton's selections – Jasper Hill Georgia's Paddock Shiraz, Jasper Hill Emily's Paddock Shiraz-Cabernet Franc*

Jasper Hill, at Heathcote, is largely responsible for bringing fame to what many believe will become one of Australia's classic wine regions. Jasper Hill's Shiraz-based wines – *Emily's Paddock* and *Georgia's Paddock,* named after Ron and Elva Laughton's daughters – are simply superb.

The vineyards are elevated at around 320 metres on the slopes of the Great Dividing Range, on Cambrian-derived soils of friable red-brown gravelly loams, that run north-south along a non-continuous strip between two parallel fault lines.

In 1987, Jasper Hill experienced a devastating bushfire – its *Georgia's Paddock* vineyard was severely burned. The vineyard has since been re-developed. *Georgia's* Paddock's red label commemorates this event.

Jasper Hill practises a low-input philosophy. The vineyards are all unirrigated and totally organic. A *laissez faire* winemaking approach is central to each wine style. Production is small with the small brick winery producing only around 3,000 cases a year. Jasper Hill recently entered a joint venture with Chapoutier, a notable Rhone Valley vigneron, although this is separate from the Jasper Hill enterprise. The winery is also experimenting with Nebbiolo.

"Our production is as finite as any other producer and may suffer the vagaries of Nature," says Ron Laughton. "Severe drought in 1983 and 1995, and a bushfire in 1987 are extreme examples. But as farmers, we philosophically accept that Nature is far more powerful than mere mortal vignerons."

Jasper Hill is a very strong market performer. Consistency of style across vintage shows attention to detail and the superiority of this vineyard site. Extremely beautiful wines.

- *JASPER HILL Emily's Paddock Shiraz-Cabernet Franc Heathcote Vic. – Outstanding*

Emily's Paddock is planted to 3.2 acres of Shiraz and some Cabernet-Franc. At an altitude of 320 metres and on steeper slopes than Georgia's Paddock, this is an unirrigated, low-vigour vineyard, yielding approximately one tonne per acre. Pruning and harvesting are done by hand.

Central to the style is a *laissez faire* winemaking approach. Fermentation typically takes three to four weeks – Ron Laughton wishing to achieve supple tannin structures. Pumping over and hand plunging is used extensively during this period. Increasingly, natural yeasts are being used. After fermentation, the wine is gravity transferred to a mix of new and old French oak – mostly Alliers oak. Malo-lactic occurs during the following late spring/early summer. After 14 months' maturation, the wine is finally bottled, ready for market.

The winemaker's theory is to preserve maximum flavour by minimising input damage – a belief that is becoming widespread in ultra-fine Australian wine.

When young, *Emily's Paddock* shows power and refinement, with ripe fruit matching well-handled oak. Tannins are a feature, but they appear to soften over time. These are multi-textured wines that deserve cellaring.

- *JASPER HILL Georgia's Paddock Shiraz Heathcote Vic. – Outstanding*

Georgia's Paddock is elevated at 320 metres, and planted to 12 hectares of Shiraz. It's an unirrigated low-vigour vineyard on gentler slopes than Emily's Paddock and, like Emily's, relies only on natural rainfall. Yields are approximately two tonnes per acre – almost twice that of Emily's Paddock.
Fermentation typically takes three to four weeks – Ron Laughton wishing to achieve supple tannins structures. Pumping over and hand plunging is used extensively during this period. Increasingly natural yeasts are being used. After fermentation the wine is gravity transferred to a mixture of new and old French and American oak – never more than 20 per cent new oak. Malo-lactic occurs during the following late spring/early summer. After 14 months' maturation, the wine is finally bottled, ready for market.

Plush, exotic fruit, underlying oak, richness on the palate, pronounced tannin and fruit sweetness, make this an obvious cellaring style. An excellent foil to *Emily's Paddock*, with equal consistency.

## MITCHELTON, NAGAMBIE LAKES

*Langton's selections – Mitchelton Print Shiraz, Mitchelton Blackwood Park Riesling*

Mitchelton was established in 1969 at Blackwood Park, an old grazing station on the edge of Nagambie Lakes near Tahbilk, by Melburnian entrepreneur, Ross Shelmardine. The vineyard site is adjacent to an important early river crossing that was discovered in 1836 by Major Mitchell, who opened the route between Sydney and Melbourne. Colin Preece (of Seppelt Great Western fame) steered this venture through the early years. Since 1974, Don Lewis (himself a significant industry stalwart) has been the principal winemaker. The building, with its almost bizarre looking control tower, is reminiscent of Dulles International Airport in Washington DC. However it somehow works and is an excellent foil to that other pagoda-style folly at Tahbilk, just across the river.

Mitchelton is best known for its high quality *Print Shiraz*. The 1990 vintage won the prestigious Jimmy Watson Trophy in 1991. It hasn't exactly fired on the secondary market but the quality consistency is there. The wine, made from the best parcels of fruit, is partially barrel fermented and aged in a combination of new and second year oak.

The *Mitchelton Blackwood Park Riesling* is highly regarded, but often shows botrytis – something that can be attractive in young wines, but not always successful when the wine ages. Brewer, Lion Nathan, now owns Mitchelton.

**MOUNT LANGI GHIRAN, GREAT WESTERN**

*Langton's selections – Mount Langi Ghiran Langi Shiraz, Mount Langi Ghiran Langi Cabernet Sauvignon Merlot*

Langi Ghiran means 'home of the yellow tailed black cockatoo'. The Fratin brothers planted the vineyards in the late 1960s. Trevor Mast, Best's Great Western winemaker at the time, was the winemaking consultant for many years, before purchasing the property in 1987. Significant capital investment has allowed expansion of vineyards and a new winery. His *Langi Shiraz* is now considered one of the top five Shirazes from Victoria.

The wines are elegant, fruit-driven styles, underpinned by a combination of American and French oak of varying ages and sizes. They have intense raspberry, blackberry, and cracked pepper aromas, and ripe but elegantly structured, palates. Restrained but complex, with long term ageing potential, they make excellent foils to the Barossa Valley style. *Mount Langi Ghiran's Langi Cabernet Sauvignon-Merlot* is also highly regarded, but has a sluggish presence on the market. The *Langi Shiraz* is a strong market performer especially for recognised vintages. Its smart *Cliff Edge Shiraz* was launched recently to underpin its reputation as a fine Australian Shiraz producer.

- *MOUNT LANGI GHIRAN Langi Shiraz Grampians Vic. Excellent*

The original Shiraz vineyard was planted in 1969, using cuttings from Great Western, on sandy and red clay loams punctuated by ironstone nodules. The well-ventilated vineyard is trellised to an arched cane system that promotes a more even budburst. The canopy is vertically shoot positioned with one pair of foliage wires. Overall vineyard management is designed to limit the occurrence of fungal disease and to promote even ripening and flavour development. A sophisticated netting system is used in the vineyard. The wines are picked on flavour profile, usually in mid-April. The grapes are de-stemmed and crushed, and the must is allowed to cold-macerate for about three days before being transferred to shallow open fermenters, with regular hand plunging of a lightly wetted cap. When fermentation is complete, the wine is free drained into a combination of *barriques* and puncheons, mostly lightly charred. No pressings are added to the wine. *Mount Langi Ghiran Langi Shiraz* is aged in a combination of American and French oak for approximately 12 months before bottling. In a great vintage, it can outclass almost anything.

## MOUNT MARY, YARRA VALLEY

*Langton's selections – Mount Mary Quintet Cabernets, Mount Mary Pinot Noir, Mount Mary Chardonnay*

Mount Mary, one of the great small wineries of Australia, was established by Dr John Middleton in 1972. Production is tiny. Mount Mary is noted for its character and the high quality and individuality of its wines. The winery is open to pilgrims only two weekends a year.

Since the first (commercial) vintage in 1976, Mount Mary has established itself as one of Australia's most highly regarded producers. Using 42 vintages of experience, as well as analysis and 'feel' to achieve optimum fruit quality, Middleton is fanatical.

The *Quintet Cabernets* is based on five classic Bordeaux varieties – Cabernet Sauvignon, Cabernet Franc, Malbec, Merlot, and Petit Verdot. Production is around 1,000-1,500 cases, although the 1997, 1998, and 1999 vintages were unusually small. This wine is sought with almost religious zeal. Quality is usually outstandingly good, although as a single vineyard wine, the vagaries of vintage can come into play. Classically proportioned with cedar and blackcurrant aromas, and fine-grained tannins, it exhibits a purity of fruit found in few Australian Cabernets.

The *Chardonnay* is outside the Australian paradigm, displaying a waxy, lanolin-like complexity that is at once highly idiosyncratic, yet appealing. It is one of the few Australian Chardonnays that really improves with age. Interestingly, it can look incredibly Burgundian.

Mount Mary has long been known for its excellent *Pinot Noir*, although these days, it is equalled or bettered by other producers. Mount Mary is one of the vanguard producers of Australian Pinot Noir. Critics occasionally pooh-pooh the wine, but generally the quality is superb, with strong, varietal, strawberry/cherry aromas and a supple, evenly proportioned palate. These wines are very delicate (rarely performing well when tasted blind) but inevitably, always delicious to drink – illustrating that wine is an experience.

Mount Mary is a strong performer across the board with a reputation for quality and longevity. The *Quintet* is the most successful wine, although *Pinot Noir* and *Chardonnay* both achieve strong interest.

- *MOUNT MARY Quintet Cabernet Blend*
  *Yarra Valley Vic. – Exceptional*

The vineyard is planted on essentially grey soils – sandy clay loams overlying degenerating Silurian shales. Vintage takes place in early to mid-April – the fruit picked on optimum ripeness and flavour development. Vinification is respectful of Mount Mary's overall fruit quality and character. The wines are not given extended maceration on skins, and only a small proportion of the wine sees new oak.

The wines became richer and more complex during the 1990s, more due to vine age than winery practice. Oak plays an underlying role in the wine – Middleton prefers lightly-toasted French (Nevers) oak from Maison Tonnellerie de Bourgogne and Nadalie.

Classically proportioned with cedar and blackcurrant aromas and fine-grained tannins, it exhibits a purity of fruit found in few Australian Cabernets. *Quintet* is an elegant style with wonderful poise and structure. It requires medium to long term cellaring, although young vintages can be very appealing. In Australia, Mount Mary commands an almost mythical status. The *Quintet* is over-subscribed, although limited quantities are regularly traded through the secondary market. And it rarely does well in blind tastings!

- *MOUNT MARY Pinot Noir*
  *Yarra Valley Vic. – Outstanding*

Only 10 per cent of the Mount Mary vineyard is devoted to Pinot Noir. Vine trunk disease is an ongoing problem. However, it positively impacts on yield levels and overall quality by putting the brakes on vigour. This means the vineyard is low yielding, producing fruit of intense varietal definition. Middleton tries to preserve the inherent quality of the fruit. The grapes are de-stalked prior to fermentation and the wines see very little new French oak – rarely above 10 per cent. The wines are essentially fruit-driven with soft tannins. Curiously they seem to build complexity and interest over time.

- *MOUNT MARY Chardonnay*
  *Yarra Valley Vic. – Excellent*

This wine will become increasingly rare, as many of the vines have now been replaced. This style has polarised opinion. It is not a fruit-driven wine, although it sees only a modicum of new oak. I have often thought of these wines as Chablis-like – in that they show quite strong lanolin-like aromas and plenty of minerality – not the peachy melon and oak of Australian Chardonnays that seem to keep winning wine shows. These wines have plenty of integrity and purity and really seem to develop well with age. This is one of the top 10 Chardonnays being produced in Australia, and one of the few with proven cellaring potential.

## NICHOLSON RIVER WINERY, GIPPSLAND

*Langton's selections – Nicholson River Reserve Chardonnay*

Beginning in 1978 as a hobby for Ken and Juliet Eckersley, Nicholson River Winery is located in the emerging wine region of East Gippsland, about three-and-a-half hours' drive east of Melbourne. Ken Eckersley's early career in science gave way to social work, along the way travelling Europe and Israel, where he picked up an interest in winemaking that included a few 'quickie courses' in Bordeaux and Burgundy.

Scientific inquisitiveness, perception, enthusiasm, and a 'sense of place' brought about Nicholson River Winery. The Eckersleys quickly realised that their vineyard, on a Scott Henry trellis system, offered something unique.

The combination of gravelly loam soils and limestone clays, a mild maritime climate, appropriate grape varieties, and personal commitment to quality, has eventuated in the micro production of 12 wines (including three Chardonnays and three Pinot Noirs) – usually between 50 and 300 cases. Vintage normally takes place from mid-March to mid-April.

The highly regarded *Nicholson River Reserve Chardonnay* (150-220 cases) has an oscillating presence on the secondary market. However the combination of quality and short supply always ensures strong interest. This wine matures in 40 per cent new French oak for approximately 12 months before bottling.

"I like to make the wine as complex and multi-layered as possible using various techniques including malo-lactic fermentation," says Ken Eckersley. "Our wine style has developed over the years. Learning science helped me appreciate the importance of fundamentals, but also the need for an open mind."

The *Nicholson River Reserve Chardonnay* is a highly individual style – richly flavoured with plenty of creamy complexity. Apparently East Gippsland Chardonnay has the longest ripening period for a dry style wine in the world (160-180 days). *Nicholson River Reserve Pinot Noir* (approximately 100 cases) is only made in good vintages.

## OAKRIDGE ESTATE, YARRA VALLEY

*Langton's selections – Oakridge Estate Reserve Cabernet Sauvignon, Oakridge Estate Reserve Merlot*

Michael Zitzlaff established Oakridge Estate in 1978. The original winery was on the southern side of the Yarra Valley at Seville. After significant capital raising, it relocated in 1997, near to Coldstream along the Maroondah Highway.

The winery crushes about 1,100 tonnes, sourcing fruit from its own 27 acre vineyard, and through contract growers. The *Reserve* wines are almost entirely single vineyard wines, sourced from at least 10 year old vines.

The *Reserve Merlot* and *Reserve Cabernet Sauvignon* are vinified in open fermenters and hand plunged, before maturation in a combination of 40 per cent new and 60 per cent used Sirugue French oak.

Oakridge has been very successful on the international wine circuit with its *Reserve* wines. In reality, there has been tremendous empire building based on production based values. The vineyards are all relatively young and the best is probably yet to come. From a secondary market perspective, these are erratic performers but they do deserve a mention. The *Reserve Merlot* and *Reserve Cabernet Sauvignon* lurch from elegant to opulent, vintage being very important. Oakridge recently merged with Margaret River based winery, Evans and Tate.

## PARINGA ESTATE, MORNINGTON PENINSULA

*Langton's selections – Paringa Estate Pinot Noir, Paringa Estate Shiraz*

Paringa Estate at Red Hill, was established by schoolteacher Lindsay McCall. With limited capital and resources, Paringa specialised in red grapes because "red wine could be made in the garage, and you didn't need refrigeration".

Paringa has about 10 acres of vines and a further 18 acres under contract, mostly on a Lyre (or U) trellis system, the purpose of which is to divide the canopy and maximise light penetration and fruit quality. Vineyard management is all about achieving optimum ripeness in what is often regarded as a marginal wine-growing region.

Paringa is best known for its extraordinary Shiraz and high quality Pinot Noir. These are hard-to-find wines, and attract a loyal following. The *Estate Shiraz* is a strongly flavoured wine with plenty of peppery, blackberry aromas, and richness on the palate. The *Pinot Noir* shows plenty of meaty complexity, fruit sweetness, and a silken palate.

These wines have a relatively low presence on the secondary market, but always attract a good volume of interest. The *Shiraz* is probably the longer-term prospect, but it is Paringa's *Estate Pinot Noir* that has shown the most amazing consistency, with a swag of show awards and critical acclaim. Paringa also makes a Chardonnay and a Pinot Gris.

## REDBANK, AVOCA (PYRENEES)

*Langton's selections – Redbank Sally's Paddock Cabernet Sauvignon-Shiraz-Cabernet Franc-Merlot*

The four hectare *Sally's Paddock* vineyard, in the cool/mild climate of Victoria's Pyrenees district, was planted by Neil Robb and his wife Sally in 1973 to an assortment of grape varieties – Cabernet Sauvignon, Shiraz, Cabernet Franc, Malbec, and Merlot. The unirrigated vines are in alluvial gravels over rich, friable red clay soils at an altitude of 420 metres.

Redbank's flagship wine, the Cabernet Sauvignon-based *Sally's Paddock*, is sourced from the original vineyard and has become a modern Victorian classic – elegantly structured, and a long term cellaring style that can show plenty of richness in a good vintage. They show plenty of blackcurrant pastille and cedar wood aromas, with underlying oak, and fine grippy tannins.

Redbank also produces a *Long Paddock* range of wines, named after the Australian drover's saying, "Driving the long paddock", which refers to sheep and cattle being pastured far-afield during times of drought. These wines are really pitched at a more commercial level but illustrate the winery's philosophy of not compromising the quality of its top wine, even in periods of drought when yields are pitifully low. *Sally's Paddock* achieves moderate support in the secondary market. Vintage is an important factor.

- *REDBANK Sally's Paddock Cabernet Shiraz-Cabernet Franc-Merlot, Redbank Vic. – Excellent*

The vineyard has a southerly aspect with vines running north-south to maximise exposure to sunlight. Yields are generally low and vintage takes place in mid-April. The ripening time of each grape variety varies, which means that the vineyard is triaged – each batch picked according to flavour development. The fruit is vinified in approximately 13 tranches, giving the winemaker plenty of blending options. The wines are open-fermented with continual hand punching of the cap (skins and seeds). Towards dryness, the wine is racked into oak to complete fermentation. The wine is matured in a combination of new and old American and French oak for approximately 15 months.

**SEPPELT, GREAT WESTERN**

*Langton's selections – Seppelt Shiraz, Seppelt Show Sparkling Shiraz*

Seppelt at Great Western was built at the end of the Gold Rush, its extensive drives and cellars built by scores of out-of-work prospectors. Originally established by Joseph Best, it passed to Hans Irvine, then in 1918, to Seppelt, which was renowned for its sparkling wines and its house speciality, Sparkling 'Burgundies' (Shiraz).

These wines command great interest whenever they come up for auction, sadly an increasingly rare event. They are something of an acquired taste – a bit like English beer. However, no self-respecting wine enthusiast would pass up the experience. Seppelt Great Western is where one of the fathers of the modern day wine industry, Colin Preece, also plied his craft. Ian Mackenzie, recently retired, steered Seppelts during the 1980s and 1990s as its chief winemaker and architect. This venerable winery, now a Victorian icon, represents a connection with the past, but also illustrates the possibilities of the future.

*Seppelt Great Western Shiraz* has made a remarkable dent in the secondary market, especially in good vintages. The wines of the late 1990s are more concentrated styles, with plenty of colour, richness, and flavour. It is interesting to note that the white pepper associated with cool climate Victorian Shiraz is no longer a feature of the style.

- *SEPPELT Great Western Shiraz*
  *Grampians Vic. – Distinguished*

Fruit is sourced from three vineyards, of various trellis configurations, all planted on weathered volcanic soils and all typically low yielding – cropped at around two tonnes per acre. Spring frosts are a major concern, with most vineyards at relatively high elevation to reduce the risk of damage. Harvest is mid-March to mid-April, depending on vintage conditions. Sugar levels of at least 13° Baume are sought for optimum flavour development. Fruit is vinified in batches to increase blending options. The wine is fermented in static fermenters for about five days until dryness, with a standard pump over regime to extract colour, flavours and tannins. A small portion is allowed to go through partial barrel fermentation. After draining and pressing, the wine is typically matured in French oak for a period of 16 months.

Seppelt *Great Western Shiraz* is an immensely complex wine with raspberry/blackberry/liquorice/meaty aromas balanced by vanilla. The palate is packed with fruit, ripe, pronounced tannins, and intensity.

Since 2000, this wine has been renamed *Seppelt St Peters Vineyard Great Western Shiraz*.

## SEVILLE ESTATE, YARRA VALLEY

*Langton's selections – Seville Estate Shiraz*

Seville Estate was established by Dr Peter McMahon, who shared a medical practice with Dr John Middleton of Mount Mary fame. McMahon sold Seville Estate to Brokenwood in 1997. The vineyards, at the southern end of Yarra Valley, are on red volcanic soils over clay. Vines are quite vigorous, although viticultural management encourages low yields.

*Seville Estate Shiraz*, the only wine here with any secondary market presence, is a more restrained style, with a highly defined fruit profile, texture and balance, underscored by the vanillin flavours of American oak.

It is likely the *Shiraz* will improve as Iain Riggs (of Brokenwood) and winemaker Alistair Butt get a handle on the fruit quality and winemaking practice. In the meantime, the wine attracts erratic support, with only recognised vintages achieving any semblance of buoyant market values.

## STONIERS, MORNINGTON PENINSULA

*Langton's selections – Stoniers Reserve Chardonnay, Stoniers Reserve Pinot Noir*

Brian Stonier established Stoniers in 1977, at Merricks, a seaside town at the mouth of Western Port Bay on the Mornington Peninsula. The winery specialises in Pinot Noir and Chardonnay. The mostly 12 to 20 year old vineyards are on elevated north, north-west, and north-east facing slopes, and are protected from prevailing on-shore southerly winds. The soils are mostly rich, red clay, and sandy loams and the vines are grown on Scott Henry, VSP, or Lyre trellis systems, depending on the site. Stoniers manages 155 acres of vineyard (including 50 acres of its own) in Merricks, Merricks North, Moorooduc, Balnarring, Cape Schanck, and Red Hill. Todd Dexter, who's had a strong impact on quality, makes Stoniers wines.

Both the *Reserve Chardonnay* and *Pinot Noir* are sourced from three established vineyards, all with very low cropping levels and proven quality. The fruit is all triaged and handpicked, to achieve optimum fruit quality. Each parcel is handled separately throughout vinification and maturation. Stoniers uses a full spectrum of winemaking technology – whole-bunch pressing, barrel fermentation, *battonage*, then maturation for about 11 months in approximately 40 per cent new, and 60 per cent one and two year old tightly-grained French Vosges oak.

The *Reserve Pinot Noir*, arguably one of Australia's best, is also batch-vinified in open fermenters. Parcels are cold-soaked, whole-bunch fermented, or given extended maceration to maximise fruit impact. The wines mature in a combination of about 35 per cent new, one, and three year old Troncais oak for a period of around 11 months. These superior wines currently attract only moderate support on the secondary market, a reflection on the erratic fortunes of Australian Pinot Noir generally.

## TAHBILK, NAGAMBIE LAKES (GOULBURN VALLEY)

*Langton's selections – Tahbilk 1860 Vines Shiraz, Tahbilk 1933 Vines Reserve Shiraz, Tahbilk Reserve Cabernet Sauvignon*

Near Nagambie, lies Tabilk Tabilk ('place of many water holes'), an important early river crossing. Tahbilk ('h'-enhanced), known until recently as Chateau Tahbilk, is Victoria's oldest family-owned winery, celebrating almost 140 years of continuous wine production. Also dating back to that time, is the pagoda-style weatherboard tower that looks over the winery complex.

The fabulous new cellar was excavated in 1875. This place reeks of history. Indeed a National Trust plaque near the cellar door recognises the property as being "among highly significant examples of early rural architecture worthy of preservation".

The Purbrick family bought the property in 1925. Alister Purbrick, a third generation winemaker, has modernised Tahbilk without abandoning the past. Upholding views about Australia's place in the world, it recently dropped the word 'Chateau'.

Tahbilk makes a wide range of wines and is particularly known for its high quality Cabernet Sauvignons and Shirazes. It is also Australia's most famous producer of Marsanne.

Its 1860s *Vines Shiraz*, made from fruit grown on a small patch of pre-phylloxera vines, is a rarity, and attracts significant interest on the wine auction market. Of immense proportions, it has earthy, plum and mulberry aromas, pronounced tannins, and structure. It becomes softer, fleshier, and more complex with bottle age. Although the 1979 vintage was the first of this Shiraz release, the label design harks back to an original Tahbilk wine label used during the 1870s. Produced in minuscule quantities, this wine is made very much in the traditional fashion, with an emphasis on fruit flavours and the maturation effect, rather than oak. This is an excellent cellaring style, with vintage an important factor.

The *Reserve Shiraz*, from 1933 vines, has been simply astonishing in recent years. Tahbilk is a Victorian icon and is always worth a visit. The *Reserve Shiraz* and *Cabernet Sauvignon*, excellent as they are, are yet to perform on the secondary market.

- *TAHBILK 1860 Vines Shiraz*
  *Nagambie Lakes Vic. – Outstanding*

The *1860s Vines Shiraz* derives from a small half-hectare patch of ungrafted pre-phylloxera, original estate-planted vines. These are some of the oldest direct-producing Shiraz vines in the world. The wine is both a curio and an experience. Fruit is hand-picked and fermented in century-old oak vats before maturation in French oak for 18 months prior to bottling. The wine is further aged in bottle for four years before release – making it six years after vintage, before it reaches market. An excellent cellaring style.

**TALTARNI, MOONAMBEL (PYRENEES)**

*Langton's selections – Taltarni Cabernet Sauvignon*

Taltarni has experienced major changes in recent years. Wealthy American John Goelet, who owns the Clos de Val winery in the Napa Valley, established the vineyard. Taltarni captured the imagination of the wine consumer in the early 1980s, but did not capitalise on the changing and burgeoning market for ultra-fine Australian wine. As Taltarni's star dimmed, next-door neighbour Dalwhinnie began attracting the interest of wine enthusiasts.

Clearly, the Taltarni vineyard site is capable of producing superior wines. David Hohnen, who went on to establish Cape Mentelle in Margaret River, laid it out. The 700 hectare property, 420m above sea-level, was selected because of its cool continental climate and for its red clay, quartz, and sandy loam soils. The vineyards are all contour planted and vertically shoot positioned to maximise exposure to sunlight.

One U.K. wine writer was moved to describe this site as "one of the most beautiful vineyards on the planet".

As it redefines its style, Taltarni is going through a period of experimentation at all levels. Fruit is being picked at riper levels of sugar and flavour, vinification is being refined, and attention is now being given to oak treatment.

Older vintages have been restrained and elegant, with earthy tones and plenty of interesting complexity. I've often described Taltarni' s *Cabernet* as one of the most undervalued ultra-fine wines on the market, yet in recent times, I feel the potential is not materialising. The *Shiraz*, matured in a combination of French and American oak, is an elegant style, but is frankly disappointing.

- *TALTARNI Cabernet Sauvignon Moonambel Vic. – Distinguished*

Each of the vineyard blocks is picked separately at vintage. The vinification starts cool, building to a warm fermentation with regular pumping over. At dryness, the wine is allowed to macerate on skins for approximately 30 days, to break down tannins. Some batches are partially barrel fermented to achieve complexity and to increase blending options. The wine then matures in a combination of 30 per cent new and 30 per cent one year old French oak for up to 18 months. The best is probably yet to come.

## TARRAWARRA, YARRA VALLEY

*Langton's selections – Tarrawarra Chardonnay, Tarrawarra Pinot Noir*

Tarrawarra is at the eastern end of the Yarra Valley near Healesville. Established in 1983 by Marc and Eva Besen, this winery has emerged as one of the region's important producers. The vineyards, on grey/brown clay loams, with relatively (and ideal) low fertility, have north-east to north-west aspects, and are in relatively sheltered and warm sites. Fruit is triaged and handled separately. The *Chardonnay* is batch-vinified in the classic Burgundian manner, with whole-bunch pressing, barrel fermentation, *battonage*, and maturation in French oak. The *Pinot Noir* is a blend of the finest fruit from different blocks, the vines between nine and 16 years old. The wine is open-fermented in three tonne pot fermenters, and matured in small French oak *barriques* comprising 25 per cent new, the others one and two year old.

Tarrawarra is making some excellent wines and is an emerging producer of good Pinot Noir that exhibits a cherry/strawberry aroma and a fleshy, nicely concentrated palate. A string of good vintages will almost certainly help draw attention to this winery and consolidate its presence. The *Chardonnay* is also extremely good, but has minimal presence on the secondary market.

Tarrawarra produces a range of wines under the *Tin Cows* label, named after a herd of tin cow sculptures loitering under a stand of trees on the driveway up to the winery. It also produces a kosher wine under the Kidron label.

## T'GALLANT, MORNINGTON PENINSULA

*Langton's selections – T'Gallant Tribute Pinot Gris*

T'Gallant was established by husband and wife team Kevin McArthy and Katherine Quealy both trained winemakers. Both show exceptional flair. This small Mornington

Peninsula winery has been at the vanguard of innovation, particularly in the development of Pinot Gris, a variety until recently, not widely known in Australia. However their ideas have gone beyond quality winemaking into marketing and packaging (often mimicked by larger organisations).

This is a nest of creativity and deserves recognition even though its wines perform erratically in the secondary market. The emphasis is on white wine making – particularly Pinot Gris and Chardonnay. The best vineyards are on deep red volcanic soils, and sheltered from prevailing winds.

Katherine Quealy says, "We find our wines have flavours evocative of red soil and autumnal air, with generous acid backbone and finesse that defies their impressive alcohol."

An old 1950s apple coldstore has been converted into a modern winery, especially designed for minimal handling. The fruit is whole-bunch pressed before vinification. There is no crushing or pumping of grape must. The *Tribute Pinot Gris* is the strongest card in its pack. In a good vintage, it can be quite high in alcohol, yet show beautifully perfumed aromas and plenty of flesh and viscosity on the palate.

T'Gallant is sailor's slang for 'Topgallant', the top sail of a square-rigger ship. It is also an obscure term used by Shakespeare to mean the best.

**VIRGIN HILLS, MACEDON RANGES**

*Langton's selections – Virgin Hills Cabernet-Shiraz-Merlot-Malbec*

Virgin Hills vineyard, at Lauriston, 15km west of Kyneton, Victoria, is 600 metres up on north-facing slopes of the Macedon Ranges. The climate here is cool with mostly winter rainfall and a dry growing season. The vineyard is planted to Cabernet Sauvignon, Shiraz, Merlot, and Malbec on friable red/brown soils over moisture-holding red clay. Planted in 1968, the vines are all dry-grown – the site's steepness allowing air drainage to reduce spring frost exposure. Each grape variety is picked, vinified, and matured separately to maximise final blending options. The Malbec and Cabernet Sauvignon see partial barrel fermentation to increase complexity and to mesh new oak characters. After fermentation, the wine matures in new French oak for about a year, before further maturation in one year old French oak.

Virgin Hills has a low input philosophy claiming to "investigate and implement the use of quality tools to reduce the need for chemical intervention". This wine captured the imagination of wine drinkers in the 1980s. Its marginal vineyard site offers wines of varying quality but, in a good vintage, they can be excellent, restrained styles with blackcurrant/cedar aromas and compact palate structures.

After a disastrous period of ownership under failed public company Vincorp, Virgin Hills was bought by Michael Hope, a Lower Hunter Valley vigneron. He says that his team are "working tirelessly to maintain the reputation that was bestowed on Virgin Hills". The secondary market still looks favourably on Virgin Hills, although there is much to do before it can achieve its former glory.

- *VIRGIN HILLS Cabernet Sauvignon-Shiraz-Merlot-Malbec Kyneton Vic. – Distinguished*

The Cabernet and Malbec see partial barrel fermentation to increase complexity and to mesh new oak characters into the wine. After fermentation, the wine is matured in New French oak for about a year before further maturation in one year old French oak.

**WILD DUCK CREEK, HEATHCOTE**

*Langton's selections – Wild Duck Creek Spring Flat Shiraz, Wild Duck Creek Duck Muck Shiraz, Wild Duck Creek Alan's Cabernets*

Wild Duck Creek Estate, located in voluptuous countryside around Heathcote, was established in 1980 when, at the age of 18, David Anderson used his first pay packet to get a bank loan and buy his first block of land there. Anderson is the quintessential Australian bush engineer whose career as a fencing contractor and vineyard developer has given him an insight into the best sites in the area. Wild Duck Creek Estate now comprises nine acres of vineyard, located on mudstones and shales, interspersed with quartz – 'classic broken up gold country'. Fruit is also sourced from another seven vineyards in the area, planted on varying soils, including Heathcote's red loams. Vineyard management is definitely low input.

The vines are vertically shoot positioned and grown on a protected easterly aspect to take advantage of the morning sun. Vintage takes place over six to eight weeks, every vine triaged for optimum ripeness and flavour development. The fruit comes in with naturally high acids and a staggeringly high 17-plus degrees Baume. The wines are vinified in a jumble of different-sized open fermenters, and regularly hand plunged. At dryness, the wines are drained and pressed in a home-made hydraulic press, then transferred to 100 per cent new French and American oak.

The *Duck Muck Shiraz* – about 200 cases produced – is made only in exceptional vintages. Interestingly, and almost impossibly, some of Anderson's wines are made without any sulphur addition whatsoever.

The *Duck Muck Shiraz*, first produced in 1994, has quickly become a cult wine, attracting bewildering values.

The 1995, released at AUD$25, and the 1997, at AUD$50, have attracted bids over AUD$1,000, although the market in 2002, has ebbed to more realistic values.

The *Springflat Shiraz* is a larger vinification, but follows similar lines. The wine is matured in 60 per cent new American oak. For the *Alan's Cabernets*, approximately 30 per cent new oak is used, of which 90 per cent is French.

Here is a winery with all the elements of a star performer. While it's great to see enthusiasm rewarded with enthusiasm, there are plenty of mean-spirited 'wine flippers' out there who could threaten this relaxed and charming place.

### YARRA YERING, YARRA VALLEY

*Langton's selections – Yarra Yering Dry Red No.1, Yarra Yering Dry Red No.2, Yarra Yering Pinot Noir, Yarra Yering Underhill Shiraz*

Dr Bailey Carrodus is one of the great characters of the Yarra Valley, producing highly individual wines that owe as much to his high quality vineyards as to his winemaking theories. They are wines literally out of the box. Hundreds of enthusiasts throng to his cellar door to pick up a few precious bottles of *No. 1* or *No. 2* each year. Carrodus established Yarra Yering in 1969, purchasing prime vineyard land at Gruyere, near Coldstream in Victoria's Yarra Valley, a thriving wine community during the late 1800s. His search for suitable vineyard land was based on a simple premise – that it should be where vines had thrived before without succumbing to damage from the spring frosts. Armed with a contour map, he eventually chose what is now regarded as one of the choicest vineyard sites in the region. Planted on a north-facing midriff of hillside, on deep, broken-up, secondary gravelly soils with excellent drainage, the vineyard is now about 70 acres. The cellar was originally set up so a single person could run it. The system remains more or less intact, although the winery is making more wine than in the early days.

Carrodus's objective is to make wines of complexity, palate evenness and after-taste. He likes to ferment his wines at warm temperatures in small open fermenters. He has 92 of them – all designed to fill a single hogshead with free-run wine, and a third of a single hogshead with pressings. Carrodus believes he should keep in the background and allow the wines to speak for themselves, but admits that the wines do have some of the winemaker's thumbprint.

All of Yarra Yering's wines attract a strong following, particularly the *Yarra Yering Dry Red No 1*. His Merlot, produced in tiny quantities, was once among the most expensive Australian wines, but now looks more reasonably valued. Yarra Yering also released a *Dry Red No 3*, a Sangiovese-based wine, although it is yet to have a presence on the secondary market. The *Underhill Shiraz* is also highly prized. The Chardonnay however, is very individual, and is the weakest card in his pack. The Yarra Yering reds have a house look, showing an exotic complexity, and perhaps revealing a combination of unique vineyard site and winemaker philosophy.

- *YARRA YERING Dry Red Wine No.1 Cabernets Yarra Valley Vic. – Outstanding*

Dr Bailey Carrodus may be an academic by nature, but he is also a pragmatist. His vines were originally planted widely to allow a standard tractor through the rows, but in recent years, he has planted his vines more closely, believing this to be more suitable. Carrodus prefers a sprawling canopy for his Cabernet. Vintage takes place around mid April. The fruit is picked on ripeness and flavour development. The fermenting wine is regularly pumped and is finished with an extended maceration to increase complexity and tannin balance. At dryness, the wine is drained and pressed, then transferred to 'closely textured' new Seguin Moreau French oak for up to 22 months' maturation.

Carrodus likens seasoning of oak in wine to salt in porridge. "If it is pronounced, it makes it taste terrible," he says.

The *Yarra Yering Dry Red No 1* is a Cabernet Sauvignon-dominant Bordeaux blend – with Merlot, Cabernet Franc, Malbec, and Petit Verdot. It has plenty of bright blackcurrant fruit characters and savoury complexity. The palate is plump and massively structured, with plenty of fruit sweetness, ripe fine tannins, balanced by savoury/bacony oak. The wines can easily age for 10 to 15 years, developing extraordinary exotic and gamy nuances over time.

- *YARRA YERING Dry Red Wine No.2 Shiraz Yarra Valley Vic. – Excellent*

Dr Carrodus prefers a vertically positioned canopy for his Shiraz, to increase exposure to sunlight. Vintage takes place around mid-April. The fermenting wine is regularly pumped and finished with an extended maceration to increase complexity and tannin balance. At dryness, the wine is drained and pressed, then transferred to 30 per cent new, and previously used 'closely textured' Seguin Moreau French oak, to mature for up to 22 months.

It is hard to pinpoint this style, as it is quite individual and subject to vintage variation. The best vintages show intense raspberry/choco-berry aromas with touches of white pepper, and ripe tannin structures with plenty of complexity.

- *YARRA YERING Pinot Noir*
  *Yarra Valley Vic. – Distinguished*

The *Yarra Yering Pinot Noir* vines are trellised on a vertically shoot positioned system to maximise fruit exposure. Vintage takes place around mid-April, cropping at no more than two-and-a-half tonnes per acre. Carrodus likes to ferment his wines at warm temperatures in small open fermenters – he has 92 of them. He does not like the meaty characters derived from whole bunch fermentation (comprising some carbonic maceration), believing the process compromises longevity. However he does like stems in the ferment to achieve more complexity.

The fermenters have been designed so the volume of free run wine can be drained into a single hogshead (300 litres), with the pressings and residual free run making up a third of a hogshead. He likes to drain and press the wine when it is still gassy, to protect it from oxidation. The *Pinot Noir* spends about 18 months in new tightly grained French oak, coopered by Seguin Moreau. A few barrels are highly toasted to achieve darkness in the fruit. It is left on yeast lees for anywhere between six months and 12 months, depending on the vintage and the degree of complexity required.

*Yarra Yering Pinot Noir* is a very individual style, perhaps showing the unique properties of vineyard site. The wines are indeed complex and my notes on some of the wines do suggest a level of meatiness amongst the dark cherry, strawberry fruit characters, and strong sinewy palate. But this may just be semantics and I like that type of complexity anyway.

## YERINGBERG, YARRA VALLEY

*Langton's selections – Yeringberg Cabernet Sauvignon*

Guillaume de Pury, grandfather of current owner Guil de Pury, established the historically important Yeringberg in 1862. The original wine business flourished during the boom times from the late 1860s until the turn of the century. A superb weatherboard winery, again in use, was built in 1885, with substantial underground cellars. At the height of its production, Yeringberg, a mixed farming enterprise, had 30 hectares under vine. The wine business fell into decline through insufficient demand, caused by a dwindling export market and a consumer shift to fortified wines. The winery closed in 1921 – a victim of the boom and bust cycle of the fledgling Australian economy.

In 1969, Guil de Pury planted a small one acre vineyard on the grubbed-out old Yeringberg vineyard site. It has expanded over the years, to approximately five acres. This site is arguably one of the very best in the Yarra Valley. The property, still mostly given over to grazing, has seen an expansion of plantings, most of which is contract grown.

The fruit structure of the *Yeringberg Cabernet Sauvignon* can be strikingly similar to Mount Mary. The wines show lovely pure blackcurrant fruit and cedary oak. Ripe, fine-grained tannins, high-pitched acid, and a palate packed with fruit, give it excellent dimension and ageing potential. Although vintage specific, production from a two acre patch of vines is limited – only about 400 dozen bottles. In a recognised vintage, these sublime, utterly seductive wines can seriously challenge a great Bordeaux Chateau.

- *YERINGBERG Cabernet Blend*
  *Yarra Valley VIC Outstanding*

This low fertility, potassium poor, vineyard site is north-east facing on silty clay loams, interspersed with buckshot gravels. The mature vines, all cane pruned, are from 15 to more than 30 years of age. Vintage takes place early to late April. "If we haven't picked by ANZAC Day, the 26th of April, we start to worry," says Guil. This vineyard is relatively low cropping at around three tonnes per acre, with fruit of excellent natural balance. Essentially the "wine makes itself". The must is fermented in open steel fermenters to dryness, pressed and transferred to stainless steel to complete malo-lactic fermentation, then to a combination of 30 per cent Alliers, Troncais, and Nevers French oak – all Tarancaud. Gravity racking takes place a few times over, until the wine is bottled, prior to vintage in the second year.

## YERING STATION, YARRA VALLEY

*Langton's selections – Yering Station Reserve Pinot Noir*

Yering Station was the first vineyard in Victoria. It was planted in 1838 by William Ryrie and acquired in 1850 by Paul de Castella, a Swiss immigrant who enjoyed considerable acclaim for his wines. He expanded the vineyard using cuttings from *Chateau Lafite*, which survived the arduous passage to Australia by being packed in moss. Paul's brother-in-law, a sea captain, brought the latest winemaking equipment back from the Bordeaux exhibition of 1859.

Yering Station's wines drew considerable international and local interest, but the end of a strong economic cycle, underpinned by gold and wool and the fashion of the time, led to a depressed market for wine. By the early 1920s, the entire fledgling Yarra Valley wine industry had been lost, most of the land returning to general agricultural use. Yering Station primarily farmed cattle until 1988, when a 20 acre vineyard was planted.

In 1996, the Rathbone family – the current owners – acquired Yering Station and immediately expanded The

Estate vineyard to 120 acres. Other sites have also been leased or acquired, taking total vineyard holdings to 252 acres. The scale of this venture verges on Napa Valley proportions – the whole vertically integrated wine dream on one site. Yering Station formed a partnership with Champagne Devaux that produces *Yarrabank*, a sparkling wine based on Chardonnay and Pinot Noir.

What makes Yering Station so interesting is its *Reserve Pinot Noir*. Tom Carson employs typical Burgundian winemaking practices, including cold soak pre-fermentation maceration, partial barrel fermentation and *pigeage*. The wines mature in a combination of new and one year old French oak. The *Reserve Pinot Noir* has no track record on the secondary market but clearly shows a strong commitment to quality and regional expression. Yering Station also produces highly impressive Reserve Cabernet and Reserve Chardonnay.

## NEW SOUTH WALES

### BROKENWOOD, HUNTER VALLEY

*Langton's selections – Brokenwood Graveyard Vineyard Shiraz*

Brokenwood was established in the early 1970s by a group of wine enthusiasts including James Halliday, John Beeston, and the late Tony Albert. The winery is known for its legendary parties and spirit of place.

Over the years, ownership has changed, but consistency has been retained under the strong leadership of chief winemaker, partner, and industry mentor, Iain Riggs.

The winery is located at Pokolbin, in the heart of the lower Hunter Valley, within sight of the Brokenback Ranges. Its vineyards take their names from a 19th century Pokolbin town-planning map. The famous 40 hectare Graveyard vineyard, for instance, is planted on the site where the Pokolbin Graveyard was to be established. Cricket Pitch is another a well-known brand named in similar fashion.

Brokenwood has been an innovative force in the Hunter Valley, known for its abundance of boutique/hobby wineries. It pioneered the concept of multi-regional wines, and was one of the first to embrace the concept of distinguished vineyard site by acknowledging vineyard source. The overall quality of its wines is excellent. Originally, it was a champion of Cabernet Sauvignon and, at one stage, had a *Graveyard Cabernet Sauvignon*, although it was discontinued due to a lack of suitable red wine grape sites and the growing pre-eminence of Shiraz. However Brokenwood's *Graveyard Vineyard Shiraz* has been a major success and is considered one of Australia's quintessential wines.

The winemaking philosophy harks back to traditional Barossa techniques, including partial barrel fermentation, but has been refined to include pre-fermentation, cold-soak, and maturation in increasing proportions of French oak. The relaxed warm atmosphere, but clearly focused winemaking, has made Brokenwood winery a popular destination for young up-and-coming winemakers. Some of Australia's most talented winemakers have held positions as winemaker, or graduated a vintage 'university' at Brokenwood.

- *BROKENWOOD Graveyard Vineyard Shiraz Hunter Valley N.S.W. – Outstanding*

The *Graveyard* vineyard is sited where Pokolbin's cemetery was to be, but neither the township or the graveyard ever eventuated. The vineyard was planted in 1970 on heavy red clay over loam soils. The topsoil is very shallow which has made the vines struggle and resulted in very low yields, averaging about one tonne per acre. The wine is hand-picked, hand-sorted, de-stemmed, and crushed, before fermentation in headed down stainless steel. At 2-3° Baume, about two-thirds of the wine is transferred to barrels – a combination of American and French *barriques* – where fermentation is completed. Maturation in barrel takes 14 months before the wine is bottled.

The *Graveyard Vineyard Shiraz* was introduced in 1984 and has quickly evolved into a modern classic, showing liquorice aromas and, when aged, a polished-leather complexity. The 1986, 1991, 1998, and 2000 vintages are the most impressive and sit quite comfortably alongside *Grange* and *Hill of Grace* in terms of quality and sheer enjoyment. Interestingly, the winemaking is strikingly similar. The 1992 was not made – the rain must have washed away the body.

## CLONAKILLA, SOUTHERN N.S.W. (CANBERRA DISTRICT)

*Langton's selections – Clonakilla Shiraz Viognier*

Established by CSIRO Chief Research Scientist John Kirk in 1971, Clonakilla illustrates how Australia's wine industry aspirations are limited only by the imagination. This enterprise reflects shared enthusiasms and a generosity of spirit based on strong family values.

John's son, Tim Kirk is a theologian turned winemaker, learning his craft from his father and mentors, Bailey Carrodus of Yarra Yering, and Phillip Jones of Bass Phillip. The Schools of Hard Knocks and Bruised Egos have also played their part.

The Clonakilla vineyard, now approximately 12 acres, was first planted to Riesling and Cabernet. Shiraz was added in 1972. The site is south-facing and planted on sandy clay loams over friable, moisture retentive clays. Sunshine is plentiful and de-vigourating (Swartzman) root-stocks are used. The vines are trellised on both VSP and split canopy Smart Dyson systems. Tim Kirk's north/north-east facing vineyard, planted on similar soil, will create more options in the future.

From the mid 1970s, through the 1980s, Cabernet and Shiraz were always blended together. During the boutique winery boom of the 1980s, the need to be different moved Clonakilla away from the mainstream in 1986, and into the unproven but tantalising possibilities of Viognier. A visit to the Rhone in 1991, and a barrel tasting of Marcel Guigal's single vineyard *Cote Roties* from the 1988 vintage, was a cathartic experience for Tim Kirk who discovered the astounding nuances of Viognier as a co-factor in the vinification of Shiraz.

In 1990, Clonakilla made its first single vineyard Shiraz, matured in American oak. Spurred on by wine show success, positive critical reviews, and with a new outlook on the communion between Viognier and Shiraz, Tim Kirk and family beared away into unchartered waters. Unblinkered by the constraints of a technical background, Kirk began to experiment with pre-fermentation macerations, varietal blending options, running fermentations to relatively high temperatures (often as high as 34° C in small open stainless steel tub fermenters), and experimenting with whole bunch fermentation, extended post-fermentation soaking, partial barrel fermentation, and new oak maturation philosophy.
While the style is constantly being assessed and fine tuned, *Clonakilla Shiraz Viognier* is now an approximately plus-or-minus 93 per cent/7 per cent blend, seeing about one third new oak.

"The Clonakilla style is about the fruit leading the wood," says Kirk. "We now prefer French coopered oak (Serugue and Francois Freres) because of its restrained power. It compliments the cool-climate profile of our Shiraz."

*Clonakilla Shiraz Viognier* is the first wine from the emerging Canberra District to draw serious enthusiasm from wine collectors and commentators. Its potential is phenomenal.

## DE BORTOLI, RIVERINA

*Langton's selections – De Bortoli Noble One Botrytis Semillon*

Originally a commercial winemaker, this producer has become an innovator at the top end – first through the creation of *Noble One Botrytis Semillon*, a richly exotic, sweet, dessert wine that has set the pace for well over 15 years; and second, through investment in Victoria's Yarra Valley. In 1924, Vittorio de Bortoli arrived in Griffith, the centre of the Riverina region and part of the Murrumbidgee Irrigation Area. Returning soldiers from WW1 and Italian immigrants are largely responsible for the growth of this important wine-growing region.

De Bortoli established a mixed farming business and hobby winery in 1927, purchasing a 55 acre fruit farm. Itinerant Italian labourers, who arrived in the Riverina during the fruit-picking season, encouraged Vittorio to start making wine commercially.

The venture has thrived through the second and third generation with Deen de Bortoli, his son Darren, son-in-law Steve Webber, and other family members, improving quality, and expanding markets and production. In 2000, this winery crushed approximately 47,000 tonnes. Although the focus has been on commercial wine, it has achieved an astonishing reputation for dessert wine.

*De Bortoli Noble One Botrytis Semillon* first released with the 1982 vintage, stormed the wine world by showing that Australia is capable of making a sweet wine of classic proportions. Certainly this wine has captured more trophies and medals at wine shows than any other single wine. De Bortoli remains a family venture. The *De Bortoli Noble One* is the only dessert wine in *Langton's Classification*. These are beautifully made wines with intense, honeyed apricot aromas, and a luscious sweet, highly viscous, but beautifully balanced and uncloying palate.

- *DE BORTOLI Noble One Botrytis Semillon*
  *Riverina N.S.W. – Excellent*

The consistency of quality in this wine is unbelievable. *Botrytis cinerea* is also known as noble rot – a mould that, given the right conditions, will grow on grapes. As the mould grows, hyphae (filaments) shrivel the fruit, concentrating the juice, increasing viscosity and imparting new flavour characteristics. The Semillon grapes are entirely sourced from De Bortoli's own vineyards near Yenda and Bilbul. The vines are planted on medium to heavy clay loams and the vineyards are managed to ensure a high level of humidity between the vines, to promote botrytis. The fruit is crushed and pressed to release the highly viscous and sweet juice. Each parcel is kept separate. After settling, the wine is fermented with specially selected yeasts. Fermentation is stopped at a desirable level of sweetness and alcohol balance. The wine is then matured in French oak *barriques* for approximately 12 months to add further dimension to style.

## LAKE'S FOLLY, HUNTER VALLEY

*Langton's selections – Lake's Folly White Label Cabernets, Lake's Folly Yellow Label Chardonnay*

Dr Max Lake, a Sydney surgeon in a previous life, established Lake's Folly in the 1960s. The original 'A-frame' winery is remembered on Lake's Folly labels. The operation has grown haphazardly over the years, as the extraordinary winery edifice attests, and "all wine is grown, vintaged, and bottled on the Estate". In 1963, the first Cabernet Sauvignon vines were planted, much to the consternation of local growers, many believing the variety was totally unsuited to the Hunter Valley. Chardonnay vines were planted in 1969.

Located in the lower Hunter Valley, the vineyard has a south-easterly aspect and a combination of volcanic and alluvial soils. In the 1970s Lake's Folly rose to prominence as one of Australia's most famous boutique wineries, drawing considerable attention from the international media.

By the early 1980s, Stephen Lake, almost entirely trained by his father, became winemaker. By the late 1980s, the wines were trading strongly on the secondary market although there were critical concerns about quality control. However, by the mid-1990s the wines had improved markedly. In 2000, the Lake family decided to sell the property to someone who would continue to share their winemaking philosophy. Peter Foggarty, a West Australian businessman, now owns the winery and intends to keep the operation small.

In some respects, it is make or break time for this winery. If it can continue its recent form, it will no doubt enjoy the continued support of its loyal followers. Lake's Folly dropped its *Reserve* label in favour of retaining a strong focus on its *White Label Cabernets*.

- *LAKE'S FOLLY White Label Cabernet Blend Hunter Valley N.S.W. Excellent*

The first vintage of Lake's Folly *Cabernet* was released in 1966. The vines are heavily pruned to reduce vigour and promote high quality fruit. The vineyard is trellised with vertical shoot positioning, allowing more consistency in fruit quality in more difficult years. The fruit is picked in early March by hand, and immediately crushed in the winery.

The *Cabernet* is open fermented with gentle cap management and temperature controlled, if necessary. After completion, the wine is racked into oak casks for malo-lactic fermentation and natural settling. After a year, the wine is transferred to a combination of new, one and two year old French oak barriques, the proportion of new oak ranging from a third to a half, depending on vintage. Maturation takes place for approximately 12 months. Increasingly the blend has incorporated Shiraz, Merlot, and Petit Verdot.

The wines have polarised opinion from wine critics over recent years. Controversially included in Langton's *Classification*, this wine has had a very strong following with wine investors for many years but is now beginning to lose ground. An elegant style with earthy, blackcurrant-like fruit, fine-grained tannins and a restrained palate.

- *LAKE'S FOLLY Yellow Label Chardonnay*
  *Hunter Valley N.S.W. – Distinguished*

Yields are typically about two to three tonnes per acre. Fruit is picked early to mid-March by hand, and immediately crushed in the winery. The *Chardonnay* is barrel fermented and aged on its yeast lees for several months in new, one and two year old French oak *barriques*, regularly stirred (*battonage*) to achieve complexity. There is no malolactic fermentation – the winemaker preferring the pure fruit characters of Chardonnay. The wine matures for seven months and sees about one-third new oak. A restrained Chardonnay style with citrus and melon aromas, a well integrated, balanced palate with plenty of flavour and underlying oak. The quality control problems of the 1980s, particularly cork taint, appear to be resolved.

## LINDEMANS, HUNTER VALLEY

*Langton's selections – Lindemans Hunter River Bin (various) Semillon, Lindemans Hunter River Bin (various) Shiraz, Lindemans Hunter River Reserve Bin (various) Shiraz*

Lindemans was established in 1843 by Royal Navy surgeon Dr Henry John Lindeman, who planted vines at Cawarra in the Hunter Valley. Business thrived and in 1870, Lindeman purchased land at Ben Ean in the lower Hunter Valley. *Ben Ean* continues to be Lindemans 'brand home'.

Although Lindemans experienced difficulties, takeovers, and restructures throughout the 20th century, its reputation for table wine remained unsullied. Today, Australia's largest wine company, Southcorp, owns the Lindemans brand.

During the late 1950s and 1960s, Lindemans was renowned for its Shirazes. Witness the catalogue of brilliant wines, particularly the 1959 *Bin 1590*, 1965 *Bin 3100*, and *Bin 3110 Hunter River Burgundy*, arguably the greatest wines ever produced in the Hunter.

Despite the growing reputation of its benchmark Semillons, Lindemans' image faded during the 1970s. Fashion and poor brand marketing largely caused this hiatus (positive wine show results attest to this). Notwithstanding, the Hunter Valley can produce some of the most beautifully complex wines.

Lindemans *Hunter River* Shiraz wines, particularly *Steven Vineyard*, can be excellent, but are probably not investment wines. They simply don't have a track record on the secondary market. Similarly, the Semillons (once called *White Burgundy*, *Hunter River Riesling*, and *Chablis*!) suffer the same problem. The wines are nonetheless reliable, although the reds can lack concentration.

Although no longer considered the pinnacle of quality, Lindemans is trying to redress that. Most of Lindemans' vineyards lie on classic red clay soils around the foothills of the Brokenback ranges, or on the sandy alluvial soils of the creek flat below. The seven hectare Stephen Vineyard planted in 1968, was recently sold off.

## McWILLIAM'S, GRIFFITH

*Langton's selections – McWilliam's 1877 Cabernet Sauvignon Shiraz, McWilliam's Barwang Cabernet, McWilliam's Barwang Shiraz, McWilliam's Limited Release Barwang Merlot*

McWilliam's is one of Australia's oldest family wine companies – established in 1877 by Irish immigrant Samuel McWilliam, who planted its first vines at Corowa in the Murray Basin in N.S.W. His son John James, planted vines in Griffith in 1913. The success of McWilliam's, inextricably linked to fortified wine and the very commercial end of wine production, has over-shadowed its premium wine production. In 1941, it bought the Mount Pleasant Winery, the cradle of the modern Australian wine industry. And in 1989, it purchased the Barwang vineyard, in the Hilltops region on the south-west slopes of the Great Dividing Range, near Young in New South Wales. This vineyard, planted in 1969 from cuttings sourced from McWilliam's, is now mature.

The exemplary *Barwang Cabernet Sauvignon*, *Barwang Shiraz*, and *Barwang Limited Release Merlot*, are all grossly undervalued, considering their overall quality. It is difficult to see these wines performing strongly on the secondary market for some time, but they are worth seeking out… after all, we can't all afford to drink investment wines every day.

McWilliam's new *1877 Cabernet Sauvignon Shiraz* commemorates the company's 125th anniversary, and attempts to become something of a 'flagship wine'. This Cabernet Shiraz Merlot blend is a cross-regional wine made from selected parcels of fruit from McWilliam's vineyard holdings in Coonawarra (S.A.), Hilltops (N.S.W.), and the Yarra Valley (Vic.). The *1877* rather flies in the face of the current penchant for single vineyard provenance. The emphasis is on winemaking. The wine is bolstered by highly concentrated and flavoured wine 'drainings' and double-oaking, a technique used widely by some of the larger resource-rich wine companies. "This is a style which really highlights the strength and diversity of our vineyard resources," Jim Brayne, chief winemaker at McWilliam's since 1986.

The Hilltops vineyard however, is where I think McWilliam's will probably find its fine winemaking soul. McWilliam's also owns Brand's of Coonawarra and Lilydale Vineyards in the Yarra Valley.

## MOUNT PLEASANT, HUNTER VALLEY

*Langton's selections – Mount Pleasant Lovedale Semillon, Mount Pleasant Elizabeth Semillon, Mount Pleasant OP&OH Shiraz, Mount Pleasant Maurice O'Shea Shiraz*

In the past, McWilliam's has been a lily in a mud pond – its greatest wines hidden below a portfolio of fortified and commercial wines. Its incredible Hunter Valley Semillons, beautifully made and aged before release, are among the most consistent and attractive wines one could come across.

The Mount Pleasant winery was established in 1880 by Charles King, then purchased by Maurice O'Shea, considered one of the fathers of the modern day wine industry. Current owner, McWilliam's, purchased a half-share in the winery in 1932, eventually securing full ownership.

McWilliam's reds have not compared favourably with early Mount Pleasant wines. *Mount Pleasant Elizabeth Semillon* (once called *Hunter River Riesling*), is a perennial favourite amongst wine enthusiasts. These wines, always released with bottle age, represent some of the best value on the market. Honeyed, straw-like aromas, profound fruit and vitality, are all hallmarks of the style.

McWilliam's *Lovedale* is a 'super-Semillon' from one of the most famous vineyards in the Hunter, produced only in exceptional vintages. Although the Shirazes have an impressive heritage – based on 1880 vines and having once been made by Maurice O'Shea – the overall style is blurred. The *OP & OH* (*Old Paddock and Old Hill*) *Shiraz*, *Rosehill Shiraz*, and *Maurice O'Shea Shiraz*, are the top reds.

It may take some years for Mount Pleasant to move beyond a nominal presence and become a secondary market performer. Nevertheless the potential is certainly there.

## ROSEMOUNT, HUNTER VALLEY & MUDGEE

*Langton's selections – Rosemount Show Reserve Hunter Valley Chardonnay, Rosemount Roxburgh Hunter Valley Chardonnay, Rosemount Mountain Blue Mudgee Shiraz-Cabernet Sauvignon*

Rosemount, in the hills of the Upper Hunter Valley is one of the most successful producers in Australia, driven by a well-managed combination of business acumen, charm, and sheer talent. Recently it snared Southcorp in what could be considered a reverse take-over. Rosemount has been successful with its upper Hunter Valley Chardonnays.

Its *Roxburgh Chardonnay*, perhaps unfairly considered a 'badge' wine, is either rarely cellared or clients are hiding it. The wine rarely comes up for auction. It is immensely complex and idiosyncratic, with ripe, tropical fruit aroma and flavour, high-toned new oak, and a wondrously fleshy palate. While it deserves recognition for sheer drinking pleasure, it is unlikely the wine will become a secondary market performer.

The *Show Reserve Chardonnay* is now in a similar class. Investment markets are not convinced as to the long term cellaring potential of Chardonnay, and Hunter Valley Chardonnay particularly. This should not bother Rosemount, as it has had extraordinary success with its white wines in Australian and in export markets.

Forays into the ultra-fine red wine market have proved successful – *McLaren Vale Balmoral Shiraz* is already a Shiraz icon. Rosemount's move into Mudgee has quickly reaped success and brought attention the region. *Mountain Blue Mudgee Shiraz-Cabernet Sauvignon* is almost certain to break into the market – the quality is simply outstanding. Considerable capital investment and the talent of Philip Shaw, now Southcorp's chief winemaker, will no doubt bring attention to *Mountain Blue* in the future.

## TYRRELL'S, HUNTER VALLEY

*Langton's selections – Tyrrell's Vat 1 Semillon, Tyrrell's Vat 47 Chardonnay, Tyrrell's Vat 9 Shiraz*

In 1850, Edward Tyrrell arrived in Sydney. He was granted 330 acres of prime Hunter Valley, planting his first vines in 1858. Tyrrell's first vintage in 1864, began a family tradition of winemaking in the Hunter Valley. His original slab hut still stands today. Tyrrell's continues to harvest Shiraz fruit from blocks planted in 1879 and 1892, on bright red clay, the core provenance of Tyrrell's *Vat 9*. Tyrrell's vineyards are known to be some of the best in the Hunter.

The economic slump in the 1930s, saw a decline in production as demand waned. Tyrrell's managed to survive. Indeed 'Dan' Tyrrell supervised 75 vintages before his death at the age of 86. During his years as winemaker, most of the wine was sold to Maurice O'Shea, a highly skilled winemaker regarded as one of the pioneers of the modern-day Australian wine industry.

The *Vat 47 Chardonnay* is credited with being the first commercial Chardonnay produced in Australia. The late Murray Tyrrell used to stop by the old HVD vineyard as a child and help himself to a few bunches of Chardonnay grapes. In those days, the wine was sold as white Pineau. In 1967, he hopped the fence and got enough cuttings to plant his first one-and-a-half acres on the Short Flat vineyard.

The first *Vat 1 Semillon* was made in 1963, in the days when Semillon was called Hunter River Riesling. The vines are grown on heavy, rich volcanic clay soils at the Short Flat vineyard, most vines being 30 to 70 years old. Tyrrell's *Vat 9 Shiraz* is a traditional maturation style of Hunter Shiraz. The emphasis is on elegance, softness, and 'somewhereness'.

- *TYRRELL'S Vat 47 Pinot Chardonnay*
  *Hunter Valley N.S.W. – Excellent*

Interestingly the HVD vineyard, now over 80 years old, was purchased by Tyrrell's in 1982 and now contributes about 30 per cent to the *Vat 47* blend. Newer blocks of the NVC vineyard, planted in 1980, are also an important fruit source. The mother vineyard, known as the Short Flat, contributes 60 per cent. All fruit is hand-picked on flavour. The grapes are brought in, pressed, then cold-settled for 24 hours before fermentation is "kicked off" in stainless steel. Just past the peak of fermentation, the fermenting must is transferred to new French oak. At Tyrrell's, the name of the cooper rather than forest is valued. Hence Bruce Tyrrell refers to Seguin Moreau, Francois Freres, Demptos, and Remond. After completion of barrel fermentation, the wine is left on its lees to add further complexity. The length of time depends on the character of the vintage. The wine sees no malo-lactic fermentation. Apparently the level of tartaric acid in Hunter Valley Chardonnay is very high – almost double its equivalent in some of the cooler districts of Victoria, so *Vat 47* – named after the original cask number – has excellent levels of natural acidity. The wine is matured in oak for three-and-a-half to seven months.

Tyrrell's *Vat 47* is an aberrant wine with its incredibly fresh style, plenty of bright fine Chardonnay fruit, a soupçon of oak, and incredible concentration and length. These wines age beautifully, outperforming almost every other Hunter Valley Chardonnay by a country mile.

- *TYRRELL'S Vat 1 Semillon*
  *Hunter Valley N.S.W. – Excellent*

The Semillon fruit is picked usually mid to late February, at relatively low sweetness levels (making some of the lowest alcohol wines produced in Australia), and are crushed immediately after picking. The juice is cold-settled prior to cold fermentation in closed fermenters. Depending on vintage, the wine receives between one and eight weeks yeast lees contact to increase overall complexity. The wine never sees new oak. During the 1960s and 1970s, the wine was made in 60-100 year old French and German vats, but since the 1980s, *Vat 1* has been made in stainless steel. The result is plenty of pure, delicate fruit characters, and a clean steely backbone. This is the only Australian Semillon with a proven track record in the secondary market. An extraordinary wine that, when young, shows fresh, lemony, citrus aromas and a lively palate. Over time it becomes extremely complex, with a golden colour, honeyed, straw-like aromas and a soft, immensely complex and flavoursome palate. A real wine lover's wine.

- *TYRRELL'S Vat 9 Shiraz*
  *Hunter Valley N.S.W. – Distinguished*

Tyrrell's *Vat 9 Shiraz*, originally called *Hermitage*, was first released in 1962. The Shiraz grapes are sourced primarily from the estate's four acre block (planted 1879) and eight acre block (planted turn of the 20th century). Over 70 per cent of the vineyard comprises original plantings of Busby collection cuttings, brought to Australia in the 1830s. Much of this collection was planted at Camden, just south of Sydney, Adelaide Botanical Gardens in South Australia, and at Kirkton in the Hunter Valley. During the 1960s, every second row was removed to allow tractor cultivation – horses worked the original vineyard.

Tyrrell's *Vat 9* follows a tradition of winemaking created by legendary Hunter winemakers, Dan Tyrrell and Maurice O'Shea. Wines are open fermented for four to five days in original concrete vats at temperatures not exceeding 26° C. The cap is regularly plunged to extract colour and flavour. Malo-lactic fermentation is encouraged at the end of primary fermentation. The wine is then transferred to large French oak casks, racked of its lees between four and six weeks later. It then matures for around 12 months until bottling. In more recent years, a small proportion of the wine is matured in 2,250 litre new French oak casks.

Tyrrell's *Vat 9 Shiraz* is typically a more elegant style with plenty of maturation characteristics. It has lovely earthy, raspberry aromas, with hints of polished leather – all of which are regional characteristics. The palate is full of fruit sweetness, ripe but underlying tannins and excellent length. Oak plays a secondary, or supplementary role, but gives freshness to the wine.

## TASMANIA

### DOMAINE 'A', COAL RIVER VALLEY, SOUTHERN TASMANIA

*Langton's selections – Domaine A Cabernet, Domaine A Pinot Noir*

Domaine A is a 20 hectare property in Coal River Valley. Originally established in 1973, the vineyards now comprise approximately 11 hectares of close-planted vines – mostly red varieties – on gentle north west facing slopes. The overall winemaking philosophy is as uncompromising as it is simple: "Let the fruit talk". The search for fruit quality has resulted in meticulous, almost fanatical, vineyard management. Yields are carefully controlled.

Swiss born Peter Althaus, has applied intensive viticultural practices, with a density of 6,000 vines per hectare and a foliage height of 1.4 metres. He believes that ripeness can be achieved every year – especially for Cabernet – because of the prevailing warm, dry, northern winds which funnel up the valley during the growing season. Fermentation takes place in open stainless steel vats. Maceration takes approximately 10 days. At dryness, the wine is pressed off in a pneumatic press, prior to maturation in 100 per cent new Seguin Moreau barriques (225 litre) for 18 months.

Domaine A wines are only produced in exceptional vintages. The property also markets wine under the Stoney Vineyard Label.

## FREYCINET, EASTERN TASMANIA

*Langton's selections – Freycinet Pinot Noir*

Beautifully situated on the picturesque east coast of Tasmania, Freycinet Winery is located near the fishing port of Bicheno (famous for abalone) and the early penal colony of Maria Island. Geoff Bull bought the 450 acre bushland property in 1978. Originally called Cosgrove, it was one of the earliest land grants in the colony. The vineyard – now 20 acres, elevated at 100 metres – was planted intuitively on protected slopes, reminiscent of an amphitheatre. The site is unique. Whilst the land faces east, the slopes have a northerly and sheltered aspect. The meso-climate is moderated by the nearby Moulting Lagoon and a row of small hills which buffers prevailing cold south and south-east winds. Frost is non-existent during the growing season – a rarity in Tasmania – though rainfall is erratic. The soils are generally granitic with high iron content. A split canopy trellising system is used to maximise fruit exposure to sunlight. The vines are cane pruned, with vintage taking place in April. The *Pinot Noir* is picked according to flavour development and optimum ripeness, then vinified in a roto-fermenter (unusual for this variety). During fermentation, the vat is rotated at regular intervals to extract colour and flavour. At dryness, the wine is drained, pressed, then matured in a combination of new and used French oak.

Clearly it is vineyard practice, combined with inherent qualities of site, that bring unique quality fruit. The wines are richly coloured and flavoured with excellent fruit definition and a slippery complexity. This is a seriously impressive wine, with remarkable consistency of quality. It should be considered one of the country's top Pinot Noirs. Freycinet is found irregularly on the market, although it has a keen following. Freycinet also produces other wines including Riesling, Chardonnay, Cabernet Sauvignon-Merlot and a sparkling wine called *Radenti*, named after winemaker Claudio and Lyndey Radenti. Its *Pinot Noir*, however, is its strongest card.

## PIPERS BROOK, NORTHERN TASMANIA

*Langton's selections – Pipers Brook Riesling, Pipers Brook Chardonnay*

Originally a boutique winery founded by Dr Andrew Pirie, Pipers Brook followed a path of rapid expansion during the 1990s. Its need to generate profits for shareholders blurred its goals. In 2001, after down-sizing its operation to once again concentrate on smaller scale winemaking, Pipers Brook became a takeover target. Kreglinger (Australia) Pty Ltd, a Belgian owned company primarily concerned with wool and sheep exports since 1893, is now the majority shareholder. It also owns a new winery in the emerging Mount Benson region on South Australia's Limestone Coast.

*Pipers Brook Riesling*, its fruit sourced primarily from the original A13 Block, near Pipers River, is one of the best performing Rieslings outside the Clare and Eden Valleys. Established in 1974, the Chardonnay vineyard is one of the oldest Chardonnay plantings in Australia. The vineyards are close-planted (an unusual practice in Australia) on well-drained gravelly soils. Vintage is generally in late April, with cropping levels around two-and-a-half tonnes per acre.

Pipers Brook also specialises in Pinot Noir and recently released a Pinot Gris. So far, it's the only Tasmanian winery to have made an impact on the secondary market, however its presence has been on the wane. Its vineyards are in marginal sites and weather can have a massive impact on quality.

The *Riesling* is by far the best wine and should be counted as one of Australia's best. Its *Gewürztraminer* and, more recently, *Pinot Gris*, are good. The Chardonnays are less impressive. *Pipers Brook Chardonnay* was once one of Australia's leading wines, but is now lost in a sea of Australian Chardonnays. The *Summit Chardonnay* is disappointing and has not fired at auction.

The challenge for Pipers Brook is to produce consistent wines at the top end. Its sparkling wine, *Pirie*, has received excellent reviews. Renewed focus and the growing interest in regional difference may allow Pipers Brook to reclaim its status as a Australia's pre-eminent Chardonnay producer. In the meantime it has released a new portfolio of convincing single site Pinot Noirs, Reserve, and Estate wines.

- *PIPERS BROOK VINEYARD Riesling*
  *Pipers Brook Tas. – Distinguished*

*Pipers Brook Riesling* is picked on ripeness and flavour development, normally in the early morning so that the juice is naturally chilled, preventing loss of delicate flavours. After cold-settling and pressing, the juice is cold fermented in stainless steel and bottled immediately after the settling of yeast lees. A cool maritime climate ensures that this is a vintage-by-vintage proposition. Botrytis in the vineyard is not uncommon, giving these wines marmalade fruit character. In good vintages, these wines have strong, lemon curd, lime-like aromas, deep-set fruit and natural mineral acidity.

**MOORILLA ESTATE, SOUTHERN TASMANIA**

*Langton's selections – Moorilla Estate Reserve Pinot Noir, Moorilla Estate Winter Collection Reserve Cabernet Sauvignon-Merlot, Moorilla Estate Winter Collection Reserve Merlot*

"One kilometre long and almost as wide, its shape is not round, the isthmus is broad, and the land rises up gently and then drops towards the river in steep banks covered by native casuarinas, the beautiful green-grey she-oaks which, in that area, have a round canopy instead of the more common pine-like shape." So wrote Claudio Alcorso, something of a renaissance man, who founded Moorilla Estate in the 1950s.

After early success, the winery imploded due to financial difficulties. Its current owners have revamped the winery spectacularly, making it an important tourist destination and, at the same time, enhancing the reputation of its wines. It has been a somewhat tragic journey. Jason Winter, Moorilla's bright young winemaker, is remembered by his friends and colleagues through the *Winter Collection*. They are really the best, and show the great potential of Merlot. These wines are vinified in the traditional manner, with about 18 months in French oak. Also worth seeking is the *Reserve Pinot Noir*.

Moorilla is an Aboriginal word meaning 'a rock by the water', as the winery is located on the edge of the Derwent River. The Moorilla Estate logo is derived from a Chinese symbol – the unbroken lines and icons depict the constant change and influence of the four seasons.

Certainly, the climate in Tasmania is variable, though Moorilla has a wide range of resources with vineyards also located in the Tamar Valley. Moorilla has had little impact on the secondary market, but is an important and long established Tasmanian winery.

# VINTAGE REPORTS

*A comprehensive set of vintage reports can be found at www.langtons.com.au.*

## PENFOLDS GRANGE, SOUTH AUSTRALIA

**1951** A hot and dry growing season.
**1952** Average to normal rainfall and weather conditions.
**1953** Dry, mild to warm weather followed a cool, but even, growing season. *Grange* has an alcohol level of 12.8 per cent. Regarded as a great *Grange* vintage.
**1954** A cool to mild growing season followed by a warm vintage. To meet internal criticism, the *Grange* style – still in evolution – was lightened, receiving only nine months in oak.
**1955** Mild to warm growing season, with intermittent, but well above average, rainfall. A warm, dry vintage. The least rare, but most successful, of the 1950s *Granges*. It won 12 trophies and 51 gold medals on the show circuit. Regarded as a great *Grange* vintage.
**1956** A moderate vintage with cooler than average growing season and vintage.
**1957** A mild, dry growing season with very low rainfall. A dry, mild to warm vintage. The first of the so-called 'hidden *Granges*'. Matured in one-year old oak. Penfolds management had ordered Max Schubert to cease production – so resources now scarce.
**1958** An even growing season followed by a mild to warm vintage. The second 'hidden *Grange*'.
**1959** Cool to mild growing season followed by a warm vintage. This is known by Penfolds as the third 'hidden *Grange*'. However, there are three bin numbers: 46, 49, and 95. The latter with the familiar *Grange* label design is, in Langton's opinion, a fully-fledged commercial release.
**1960** A hot and moderately dry vintage. Penfolds recognises this vintage as the officially resumed commercial production of *Grange*.
**1961** A hot, dry vintage. The first *Grange* to be made with grapes sourced from Coonawarra.
**1962** A warm, moderately dry and even growing season, followed by a dry vintage. The Kalimna vineyard, purchased by Penfolds in 1945, is now the mother vineyard of *Grange*. Regarded as a great *Grange* vintage.
**1963** A warm and dry growing season and vintage. Although only moderately successful on the Australian wine show circuit, the 1963 *Grange* is now regarded by many as the great vintage of the 1960s.

**1964** A wet growing season, then a dry, but cool vintage.
**1965** A warm, dry growing season and vintage. The 1965 *Grange* won the Jimmy Watson Trophy, but is only regarded as a moderate vintage.
**1966** A dryish vintage, with intermittent rain during the growing season. Vintage was warm and dry. Considered by many as a great *Grange* vintage.
**1967** A relatively dry growing season followed by a warm vintage. The Clare Valley is now a source of grapes. Won the Jimmy Watson Trophy, but is only regarded as a moderate vintage.
**1968** A hot, dry vintage, but with an alcohol level of only 12.1 per cent.
**1969** A very wet growing season followed by a mild, wet vintage. Did well on the show circuit, but probably a 'lily in a mud pond'.
**1970** A dry, mild growing season and vintage. While most bottles have been bottled under *Bin 95* since 1959, this vintage marked the standardisation of *Bin 95*.
**1971** An ideal warm, dry growing season and vintage. Often regarded as the greatest of all *Granges* until the arrival of the 1990 vintage. A definitive *Grange*. Only 12.3 per cent alcohol.
**1972** A dry growing season followed by a mild vintage. Bottling problems turned a good follow-up vintage into a variable experience. Some bottles are simply outstanding. Others – unintentionally oxidised during bottling – vary considerably in quality.
**1973** A dry growing season followed by a cool vintage. Last *Grange* to be made at Magill Winery in Adelaide.
**1974** Difficult wet vintage and growing season. Downy mildew outbreak just before vintage created new challenges. The grapes were rigorously triaged ensuring a good, but low, volume *Grange* (only 2,300 dozen).
**1975** A cool summer followed by a mild, dry vintage. This very tannic year polarised opinion. Year that Max Schubert retired.
**1976** A warm/hot, dry vintage producing wines of immense power and richness. Not a particularly successful wine show performer, but regarded by many as a great vintage. Cork problems plague the 1976 *Grange* with variable levels.
**1977** A moderately cool vintage followed by a mild vintage. The last *Grange* to be entered into the Australian Wine Show System.
**1978** A warm, dry season followed by a mild/warm vintage. The 1978, whilst not considered a great *Grange*, has grown in stature over the years.

**1979** An unusually wet and hot, almost sub-tropical, growing season followed by a mild, wet vintage. Unlike the 1969 and 1973 vintage, this *Grange* is curiously well regarded on the secondary market.
**1980** Ideal growing season followed by a cool vintage. Not regarded by the market as a great *Grange*, although many believe this wine is a classic.
**1981** A warm to hot, drought-affected growing season, followed by ideal vintage conditions. A very big, tannic vintage.
**1982** A mild growing season followed by a hot vintage. An odd vintage for Penfolds and *Grange*. Initially hailed as a great vintage, many now believe this to be only a moderate year.
**1983** Known as the 'bushfire year'. Desiccating northerly winds over a tinder-dry landscape created an ideal canvas for the devastating Ash Wednesday bushfire. Bizarrely, this was followed by March flooding. A monumental wine, and a great *Grange* vintage.
**1984** A cool summer followed by a cool, dry, late vintage. Regarded as an early-drinking year, but has surprised many for its complexity.
**1985** A cool to mild growing season and vintage, although intermittent rains delayed picking.
**1986** A warm, dry high-quality vintage. A great *Grange*.
**1987** A cool season with crop levels moderated by hailstorms in October 1986.
**1988** A warm high-quality vintage with below-average rainfall. Described as an unhurried vintage.
**1989** An odd growing season. Generally quite cool to start with, but a burst of very hot weather in February shrivelled grapes. Heavy rains then set in, making it a difficult vintage. Despite all this, not a bad *Grange*..
**1990** A dry and even growing season produced Shiraz of incredible opulence. Regarded by many as the quintessential *Grange* vintage.
**1991** A warm, dry growing season punctuated by hot weather in late summer, produced an early vintage. A brilliant follow up to 1990. Considered a great *Grange* year.
**1992** A cool growing season followed by a late vintage, with intermittent rains.
**1993** A difficult growing season with very high rainfall. A very late dry, but relatively low-yielding, vintage.
**1994** A dry, slow growing season, followed by a late vintage in the Barossa. Other areas experienced a wet vintage. Add the components together and this vintage represents a classic *Grange* year.

**1995** The driest growing season in 10 years. Yields were low due to September 1994 frosts and a continuing drought. The vintage looked very promising until late March when temperatures fell and drizzle set in.
**1996** A good soak in autumn and winter (the wettest July at Magill in 10 years) preceded a generally dry and even growing season. The hot summer was followed by a damp March. A cool vintage. A great *Grange* year.
**1997** Good winter and early spring rains replenished dams and soil moisture. The growing season started damp, becoming dry and cool. By December, temperatures ebbed and flowed with a burst of extreme heat in February. A cool, dry late vintage.
**1998** A dry, and increasingly hot, growing season. With drought conditions prevailing, dam water was all but exhausted. In spite of the very hot weather over vintage, Shiraz was spectacular. Expect a great *Grange* Vintage.
**1999** An each-way bet. Drought conditions prevailed because of low winter rainfall. Autumn and spring rains pushed the growing season along, although conditions were still described as dry. A deluge in March slowed vintage in the Barossa. In other areas, the vintage was dry. Expect a very good vintage.
**2000** Dry, cool growing conditions with a hot spell in late January. Rain in late February/early March slowed ripening and vintage. Expect a good vintage.

## HUNTER VALLEY SEMILLON

**1986** Brilliant year for Hunter Semillon. A cool spring followed by a hot summer allowed fruit to reach optimum maturity. Intermittent light rain during the final stages of the growing season kept vines in balance. The wines will be long-lived.
**1987** Cool, dry growing conditions prevailed, allowing fruit to ripen evenly. The Semillons are generous and full-flavoured, but have excellent concentration and structure. Medium-term cellaring prospects.
**1988** A vintage that most would prefer to forget. Heavy downpours ruined any chance of making high-quality wine.
**1989** A hot spring followed by a cool summer allowed even ripening. The Semillons have good depth of flavour, naturally high acidity, and excellent cellaring potential.
**1990** Almost perfect growing conditions prevailed until the first week of February, when more than 300mm of rain dropped. Those who picked before the deluge, made wines of great finesse and structure. A very muddy vintage, but nevertheless a good year for Semillon.

**1991** Ideal weather conditions during the growing season resulted in wines of good quality. Those who picked early, made elegant Semillons of classic proportions with naturally high acidity levels.

**1992** Drought conditions throughout 1991 resulted in yields reduced by as much as 50 per cent. Picking began in the third week of January, which was fortunate as February was a cool, wet month. The wines have excellent flavour and structure.

**1993** One of the Hunter Valley's coolest-ever vintages, after an extended ripening period. Semillons were picked at relatively low sugar levels and naturally high acidity, producing wines of restraint but excellent structure.

**1994** A near-perfect growing season was marred by 17 consecutive days of 40-plus degrees Centigrade, and strong westerly winds. Stressed vines slowed, resulting in an extended ripening period. The wines have very intense aroma and colour.

**1995** Drought during 1994 ensured lower-than-average crops. Extreme conditions prevailed until the crucial ripening period between mid-December and February. Unseasonably cool conditions allowed the vines to accumulate excellent flavours. Not a great year, but certainly a good one.

**1996** High-quality vintage. A cool summer allowed vines to ripen evenly, and rain at the right time ensured their good health. Vintage began in late January or early February, with warm-to-hot and dry conditions and cool nights. The wines have tremendous concentration and good acidity.

**1997** An almost perfect growing season hampered by intermittent rain during vintage, and extreme heat. Although many growers experienced Botrytis in the vineyard, those who picked selectively were able to make extremely good wines with naturally high acidity and good flavours.

**1998** Brilliant vintage in which all the elements came together at the right time. Rain can come at the most inopportune time in this region. Luckily dry, hot weather during the critical ripening period led to ideal berry composition. The Semillons are excellent.

**1999** Very good year with spring rains, a hot summer, and a relatively even growing season. Early rains during vintage worried winemakers – some picking early to avoid crop damage. The wines are very lean but will age into classic Semillons.

**2000** A hot vintage marked by extreme heat in February. A light sprinkling of rain over vintage did nothing to reduce quality. Fruit was clean with excellent flavour profiles. Acidity levels were brilliant, so expect some long-lived Semillons.

## HEATHCOTE SHIRAZ

**1984** A drought-breaking year with ample rainfalls during winter and spring. A protracted growing season because of a cool summer. An elegant vintage.

**1985** After a cold winter, this region experienced a mild growing season with a dry, but cool, summer. Vintage was two weeks late.

**1986** A miracle year. Despite a wet spring and early summer rainfall, random hailstorms on December 4, and occasional outbreaks of downy mildew, summer was dry and cool, extending the ripening period. The Shiraz quality is exceptional.

**1987** A cool, dry season marked by some late spring frosts. Vintage was later than normal. Moderate vintage.

**1988** A good quality year. Following good spring rains, this region experienced mild growing conditions and intermittent, but useful light rains. Summer was very warm.

**1989** Cool to mild growing season, followed by a hot summer. Mid-vintage rains reduced quality of harvest. An odd vintage.

**1990** Beneficial rains in winter and early spring, were followed by a perfect growing season with mild to warm conditions. Summer was warm, but never scorching, allowing even ripening. A great Shiraz vintage.

**1991** A mild to hot, dry growing season followed by a very hot vintage. Fruit quality was excellent with no disease or rain damage. Continual hot weather reduced the crop size by 10-15 per cent.

**1992** A cool to mild growing season, extended ripening, which resulted in a late vintage. Although the wines have excellent colour and flavour, the overall structure of the wine is quite sinewy and firm.

**1993** A particularly difficult vintage season – unseasonable periods of rain from budburst through flowering, continuing until just before harvest, created fungal problems. Although vintage conditions were dry, the Shirazes show very 'cool spectrum' characters. An ordinary year.

**1994** A mild to warm growing season, interrupted by thunderstorms and heavy rainfall in February. A delayed, but warm to hot vintage ensured excellent quality fruit. The Shirazes have excellent concentration and flavour, with ripe tannins.

**1995** After the driest winter in years, vineyards struggled and relied heavily on irrigation (if they could get it). Although warm and dry, this vintage is regarded as a moderate one.
**1996** An early spring frost scare, followed by a cool, but very favourable, growing season.
**1997** Frost damage hit some vineyards early in the season. A warm, dry growing season, punctuated by a hot summer, ensured excellent flavour development. An outstanding season, with some very rich and powerful Shirazes.
**1998** An excellent follow up to the 1997 vintage. A mild, relatively dry spring, followed by a warm to hot and dry summer, producing fruit of tremendous flavour and concentration. An exceptional vintage.
**1999** A good quality vintage. Severe frosts in some vineyards created problems early in the growing season. This was followed by warm, dry conditions. Vintage was marginally late, and marred by bird problems as well as random hailstorms.
**2000** A good spring soaking was followed by dry conditions. Hot weather, mid to late summer, stressed vines already suffering after near-drought conditions for almost three years. The result is a very low-cropping but intensely flavoured vintage.

## YARRA VALLEY CABERNETS

**1981** A hot vintage, producing wines of excellent quality.
**1982** A hot, dry summer and near drought conditions. Excellent Cabernets.
**1983** A difficult season marked by severe water stress and defoliation. An average vintage.
**1984** Interestingly, local vignerons regard the fruit quality as being the best since 1977. The market, always trying to simplify things, does not regard this as a great vintage. Spring was very wet and a cool, sometimes humid, summer and autumn followed.
**1985** Cool, wet weather over spring, affected flowering and fruit set. Some areas suffered hail damage in November. Warm weather and intermittent, but beneficial rains, followed a cool, early summer. A wet vintage for Cabernet.
**1986** A wet and cool start to the growing season was followed by a dry and cool summer. Some vineyards experienced powdery mildew. A burst of warm weather, before a very late vintage, improved the situation, producing fruit of good flavour and intensity. Vineyard specific vintage. The best sites produced some wonderful Cabernets.

**1987** Beneficial rains over winter and spring were followed by a cool, dry growing season. Regarded as a moderate to good year in the Yarra Valley. Lighter year for Cabernet Sauvignon.
**1988** A wet spring was followed by a hot summer, with intermittent but beneficial rains. February cooled down, but a burst of warm weather before vintage began early picking. Regarded as a better than average year for Cabernets.
**1989** A topsy-turvy year. The wrong combination of weather patterns: a dry winter, a windy and dry period during flowering, then a deluge and a heat wave in February, followed by more cool weather. did not allow even ripening. A lighter early drinking vintage.,.
**1990** A perfect growing season. Plentiful rain over winter and early spring restored dam levels and soil moistures. A warm, late spring and dry, warm summer ensured perfect ripening conditions. A great Cabernet vintage. Mount Mary and Yeringberg made some truly outstanding wines.
**1991** Early spring rains were followed by a warm, dry summer, although vintage was early. Some vines struggled towards vintage. A rich, ripe Cabernet year.
**1992** A good soak over spring affected fruit set and potential cropping levels. A cool but bright summer allowed slow ripening conditions. A burst of warm weather in April allowed the fruit to reach optimum maturity. A very good Cabernet vintage.
**1993** A wet winter followed by a cool, wet spring and summer extended the growing season and caused some concerns. Some vineyards experienced downy mildew. By March, a change to warm, dry weather allowing rapid development of fruit. An elegant drinking Cabernet vintage. Mount Mary describes theirs as magical.
**1994** A mild growing season beset by severe hailstorm damage in early summer. Botrytis was a problem, although the best managed sites escaped difficulty. A burst of warm, dry weather before and during vintage, allowed some excellent Cabernets to be made.
**1995** An unusual growing season, marked by a very dry spring and summer, brought on a very early vintage. Temperatures fell and rain set in, extending the harvest season. A moderate to good Cabernet year. Some excellent wines from the best vineyard sites.
**1996** Intermittent rains followed a short, mild spring and a very cool summer. It was the coldest December in 140 years. A hot, dry February desiccated vineyards and began to stress vines. By April, the weather had cooled down. A very moderate Cabernet year.

**1997** Describedby the locals as the vintage of the century. After a wet spring, generally mild, dry weather culminated in hot vintage conditions. A good Cabernet year.
**1998** The second excellent vintage in a row. After some early spring frosts in some corners of the Yarra, growing conditions were generally mild and fine. Most vineyards enjoyed almost perfect ripening conditions. An exceptional year for Mount Mary, Yarra Yering, and Yeringberg.
**1999** A very dry winter was followed by early budburst. The early growing season experienced variable temperatures. Rainfall over the New Year was welcomed, but a deluge and above-average heat brought on near tropical conditions. This is very much a site-specific vintage. Low-cropping vineyards fared the best. A moderate Cabernet year.
**2000** Mild growing conditions were followed by a warm to hot February, a mild, dry April, and rain in early May. Some vineyards suffered water stress. The best sites were able to make some very good wines, although probably not top notch.

## COONAWARRA CABERNET SAUVIGNON

**1980** A rather famous vintage in Coonawarra, marked by extremely favourable and warm weather conditions. Some beneficial and intermittent rains over late summer/early autumn ensured an excellent season. At the time, everyone described this vintage as a classic. However the test of time suggests this was a rather hyped-up, though better than average, season.
**1981** A 'dark horse' vintage. A warm summer was followed by hot conditions over vintage. Some light rains fell during March. Not regarded as a very good vintage at the time, but more recently, many have reassessed its quality. Better than good!.
**1982** An above average year for many, although a high-cropping vintage. The growing season was warm and hot with some good top-up rains in late spring. A producer-specific vintage.
**1983** A very wet growing season with huge Botrytis problems in the vineyards. Low-cropping vineyards made the best wines. It was a year that many vignerons would prefer to forget.
**1984** A forgotten vintage. Mild summer conditions and intermittent rains marked an ideal growing season in March. Regarded by the locals as excellent.
**1985** Mild growing conditions with little rain. A heatwave in March rumpled vines, but overall fruit quality was excellent.

**1986** Classic Coonawarra vintage. A warm, dry growing season combined with very low cropping levels ensured wines of immense power and richness. Highly defined fruit, ripe but pronounced tannins. Wonderful balance and fruit sweetness.
**1987** A cool, dry vintage of moderate quality with medium term cellaring potential. Hard autumn frosts in mid-March. Optimum ripeness was achieved through desiccation. Tannins are therefore slightly bitter.
**1988** Moderately good vintage with quality varying from producer to producer. The elegant styles are far more successful than the soupy, essence-of-Cabernet wines. Medium term cellaring potential for Coonawarra Cabernet Sauvignon. A year marked by severe spring frosts.
**1989** A below-average vintage. Mostly early-drinking styles without the structure to age. A hot summer followed by autumn rains, led to wines of only moderate concentration.
**1990** Certainly a great vintage. An early harvest after a dry and warm autumn. Yields were above average, but with extraordinary ripeness and definition. The wines are extremely rich and opulent, with immense fruit concentration and depth of flavour. Remarkable.
**1991** Classic vintage, arguably better than 1990, although overshadowed by the hyperbole. Brilliantly defined wines with direct, blackcurrant/mulberry aromas, ripe tannins and fruit sweetness. A hot summer followed by an extended, mild autumn brought low yields and highly concentrated fruit.
**1992** Average year. Spring frosts and cool, windy weather resulted in moderate to poor yields. Fruit proved difficult to ripen. Consequently the wines are quite restrained and at the cooler end of the spectrum of Cabernet aroma and flavour.
**1993** Average, if not good, year. A wet spring followed by a mild, dry autumn brought on a very late vintage. The wines are generously structured with medium-term cellaring prospects.
**1994** Winemakers are more reserved about this vintage than critics are. A very hot, dry summer and continuing drought conditions saw excellent fruit development. Rain towards the end of vintage however brought mixed quality. There are nevertheless many wines of outstanding quality with superb concentration and structure.
**1995** Worst year since 1983 for Coonawarra, but showing how regions within one state can have vastly different vintages (see Barossa Shiraz). Drought and spring frosts substantially reduced yields. Rains during vintage

hampered winemakers. Wines are moderate in concentration and lack the superb varietal definition of a good year. Neither Wynns *John Riddoch* nor Penfolds *Bin 707* was made this year.

**1996** One of the coolest growing seasons on record, with average yields. Vintage was later than usual. The extended ripening season will see wines of wonderful concentration and balance.

**1997** A cool spring followed by a hot, dry summer will see some good quality Coonawarra Cabernet Sauvignon. Strong varietal characters with pronounced cassis-like aromas and concentration are expected. Tannins are quite sinewy. A moderate year.

**1998** A great vintage that will rival or better the outstanding 1990 and 1991 pair. Coonawarra winemakers themselves place 1998 somewhere between "the best of the 1990s" and "the best for 20 years". The harvest was a few weeks early, after a dry summer. Expect some great Cabernet Sauvignon.

**1999** Early vintage brought on by a warm, dry summer. Although rain threatened during March, dry weather persisted and the vintage provided excellent fruit. In the shadow of the hyped-up 1998 vintage – actually a very fine, possibly great vintage.

**2000** The 2000 vintage was the earliest on record in Coonawarra, but produced Cabernet Sauvignon fruit of exquisite quality. The long, cool ripening conditions, together with below-average rainfall during the growing season, ensured small berry sizes and low bunch numbers, producing wines of excellent flavour development and balance. A vintage of tremendous potential.

## BAROSSA VALLEY SHIRAZ

**1986** Brilliant vintage. A cool, dry summer allowed prolonged, but even, ripening. These conditions produced full-bodied, big-flavoured wines with extraordinary dimension and flavour.

**1987** One of the coolest summers on record. Grapes continued to ripen until the third week of April when frost and cold weather set in. An average year.

**1988** During October 1987, a severe hailstorm passed through sections of the Barossa ranges, wreaking a path of destruction. A cool, mild growing season. Producers employing a judicious oak regime made wines that have aged extremely well.

**1989** A mild winter, then a dry summer and extreme heat in March. Acidity levels were extremely low. Wines are generally of average quality, many already past their best.

**1990** The so-called 'vintage of the century' and certainly a brilliant year. After a warm start, summer was generally mild, with maximum temperatures for most of January, February and March, between 22 and 28 degrees Centigrade. Ideal conditions allowed flavour accumulation without loss of natural acidity. The wines have immense power and richness.

**1991** Superb, but early vintage. A long, hot, dry summer ensured phenolic ripeness. Although yields were down on 1990 by as much as 30 per cent, the wines are extraordinarily seductive and opulent. Many critics believe 1991 to be slightly better than the over-hyped, but extremely fine, 1990 vintage.

**1992** Intermittent rain during vintage followed a cool, mild growing season. Some vineyards experienced powdery mildew. Generally, average quality wines.

**1993** Difficult growing season characterised by a wet spring and an early summer. Some vineyards experienced outbreaks of downy mildew. Warm, dry weather towards the end of the growing season and during vintage, saved what could have been a disaster. Many of the wines are excellent, especially from old, dry-grown vines.

**1994** Above-average, but late vintage for many producers. A dry, mild growing season allowed slow but even ripening. Classically proportioned wines with ripe tannins and fruit sweetness.

**1995** Driest growing season for 10 years, with many vineyards experiencing extreme water stress. A vintage characterised by reduced yields, but good quality fruit. Average for most producers.

**1996** An early start to the growing season followed a mild winter. The Barossa was fortunate to escape frosts that hit inland areas in early spring. Spring rainfall was below average, but growing conditions were almost perfect. The wines are generally of excellent quality, particularly from low-yielding, old vines.

**1997** Outstanding vintage characterised by a hot, dry summer with cool evening temperatures. The wines have massive concentration and high alcohols, but ripe tannins and good fruit definition.

**1998** A superb vintage, arguably the best in 30 years. Warm to hot, dry ripening period over summer followed spring rains, allowing an even ripening period and a high-quality, but low-yielding harvest. Expect great wine.

**1999** After a dry, parched summer and a promising growing season, March rains settled in, making this a difficult vintage. Overall quality varies, with vineyard and producer reputation being an important factor.

**2000** A succession of dry winters finally caught up with Barossa Shiraz, producing some very low yields. Hot weather during summer was followed by damp, cool conditions necessitating considerable vineyard attention. Despite this, a moderately good year.

### CLARE VALLEY RIESLING

**1986** Warm, even ripening season. Generously flavoured wines with superb structure and ageing potential. Wonderful vintage.

**1987** Cool growing season produced wines with naturally high acid levels. Generally above-average wines with lovely fruit definition and flavour.

**1988** Hotter season. Generally, quite prematurely developed wines, but retaining flavour and balance. Drink up.

**1989** A dull vintage marred by damaging rains and Botrytis infections. Many wines lack definition and flavour. Drink up.

**1990** Brilliant year for Clare Riesling. A mild growing season, unhampered by inclement weather, resulted in wines of immense fruit purity and natural acidity. The best wines will age long into the future.

**1991** Warm, benign growing season saw wines of average-to-good quality. Not quite as good as 1990, with many wines lacking finesse and flavour.

**1992** Below-average to good vintage, with uneven ripening conditions. Many wines lack power and concentration. Producer is very important.

**1993** A vintage characterised by delayed ripening. Very heavy rains in December and early January, promoted outbreaks of downy mildew. Producers who picked early, made relatively lean wines. Those who picked in April were rewarded with richly flavoured wines.

**1994** Fine vintage – relatively dry, cool conditions. Wines are quite restrained, with good flavours and structure.

**1995** Mild, dry growing season ensured good flavours and naturally high acid levels. The wines have excellent fruit intensity. Will age beautifully.

**1996** Early harvest with relatively high yields. Dry conditions ensured generally high-quality fruit, although many wines are lean and austere.

**1997** Exceptional vintage, considered the best in memory. Essentially dry conditions prevailed except for a brief spell of rain during early February. A burst of hot weather late in February caused vines to stall for a few weeks. This resulted in delayed ripening during cooler conditions. The wines are beautifully structured and have great fruit purity.

**1998** One of the driest winters in 20 years, followed by spring rains that restored soil moistures and dams to normal levels. A warm, even growing season saw an excellent Riesling vintage, with some outstanding wines and only an occasional disappointment.
**1999** Miracle year. A dry summer punctuated by much-needed rainfall, produced wines with excellent varietal definition and flavour. While the Clare Valley did not suffer the problematic March rains, quality of vineyard site was an important factor. Those with an intimate knowledge of their vineyards, produced the best wines. A leaner year.
**2000** Awkward year in which vineyard site was a critical factor. Sunburned grapes were quite prevalent in Watervale. Handpicking around damaged fruit (triaging) ensured good varietal definition and flavour. Rieslings vary from powerful, fine and limey, to leaner styles. A stronger line-up than expected.
**2001** A paradox year. An early but very good quality vintage despite a difficult growing season. After excellent rains in winter and spring, conditions became drier with extended periods of excessively hot weather during January and February.
**2002** Vintage of the Century year! Very good winter rains replenished soil moistures and dams. This was followed by a cool spring with intermittent rainfall, a cool summer and dry, warm autumn. Ripening was slow but even, resulting in a late but compressed vintage. The Rieslings are stunningly beautiful.

## MARGARET RIVER CABERNET SAUVIGNON

**1980** A very hot, dry summer with good winter rains. Good crop levels.
**1981** Another hot and dry vintage.
**1982** Excellent rains during the growing season in December. Long and cool ripening period gave another great season for Cabernet Sauvignon.
**1983** Poor winter rains, then very hot and dry, with many bushfires. Low acid levels and high tannins resulted in a moderate to good quality vintage.
**1984** A long ripening season, no birds, and good crop levels. A better than average year.
**1985** A hot and dry vintage with rain in March. A moderate Cabernet vintage.
**1986** A relatively cool summer and growing season produced wines with classic cedar and blackcurrant aromas, fine-grained tannins, and good structure. In hindsight, an outstanding cellaring vintage.

**1987** One of the coolest and driest vintages on record, resulting in wines that are restrained and with excellent structure and balance.

**1988** Yields were down by as much as 30 per cent in some vineyards. An Indian Summer followed a mild January. Hailed as another great year by some producers, it is at least a very good one. Margaret River's benign climate does it again!.

**1989** A vintage heading for greatness. A cool, dry summer followed by difficult spring conditions. Silver-eyes, parrots, and wattlebirds plundered some vineyards. The aromas and flavours are at the cooler end of the Cabernet spectrum. Probably ready, or near ready, to drink.

**1990** A mild, dry summer saw grapes ripen at a gentle pace. Rain, particularly Cyclone Vincent, threatened the vintage. But despite downpours during harvest, the fruit was extremely fine, with excellent flavour development and concentration. The beginning of an outstanding decade of vintages.

**1991** Some believe this to be a great vintage. Certainly it is a fine one... like something out of the textbook, with an almost perfect ripening season. A brief hot spell during January was followed by mild weather conditions.

**1992** An extremely fine vintage. Heavy rains during winter and early spring, caused considerable concern. The growing season, however, was mocked by a hot, dry conditions in January and February. Cool conditions with intermittent but light rain, prevailed during March, ensuring even flavour development. The wines are extremely well balanced.

**1993** Hail during flowering in November meant some producers saw a 20 per cent decline in their yields. A dry but relatively cool summer, allowed fruit to achieve good ripeness and varietal flavours.

**1994** Great vintage with perfect ripening conditions. A very dry, hot summer, followed by a cooler autumn, giving fruit of lovely intensity and definition, ripe tannins and structure.

**1995** A long and exceptionally hot, dry summer resulted in wines of immense concentration and power. Drought conditions saw the need for supplementary irrigation. Yields, however, were moderate, if not low. Considered a great year.

**1996** Warm to hot and dry vintage, with almost perfect ripening conditions during late summer and early autumn. The wines have great intensity of colour, brightness of fruit, and ripe tannins. Cabernet from older vines was of especially good quality.

**1997** Good vintage, potentially great, for some producers. After a nerve-wracking start with a heat wave and heavy rains, an enormous high-pressure system to the south staved off the threat of a deluge at vintage time. Lower than average yields from mature vines have delivered wines of great concentration and flavour.

**1998** Late summer rains dashed many hopes. Un-netted vineyards were dive-bombed by squadrons of silver-eyes. It turned out to be quite a difficult vintage. Those who waited out the unseasonable rains before picking, saw good batches of fruit and some exceptional wines were made, despite the vicissitudes of grape growing.

**1999** Miracle year. A late growing season and a long warm spell over January, February, were followed by intermittent cloud and scattered showers in March caused by Elaine, Vance, and Gwenda – three tropical cyclones to the north of Western Australia. After a worrying few weeks, the skies cleared, producing even ripening conditions. Expect some very good wines.

**2000** An early vintage marked by heavy rains and severe anti-cyclonic weather. This was very much a vineyard management year – the best wines made off low cropping, well-sited vineyards. Downy mildew – newly discovered in Margaret River – caused little damage. Some relatively good wines were made despite difficult conditions. Cabernet was often picked earlier than Shiraz.

# VINTAGE CHART

| | 1980 | 1981 | 1982 | 1983 | 1984 | 1985 | 1986 |
|---|---|---|---|---|---|---|---|
| Henschke Hill of Grace | 9 | 9 | 9 | 9 | 8 | 7 | 10 |
| Penfolds Grange | 9 | 9 | 9 | 10 | 7 | 6 | 10 |
| **NSW** | | | | | | | |
| Hunter Valley Cabernet | 8 | 7 | 7 | 9 | 5 | 9 | 8 |
| Hunter Valley Chardonnay | 8 | 8 | 7 | 8 | 5 | 7 | 8 |
| Hunter Valley Semillon | - | - | - | - | - | - | 10 |
| Hunter Valley Shiraz | 8 | 7 | 6 | 9 | 5 | 6 | 8 |
| Mudgee Chardonnay | - | - | - | - | - | - | - |
| Mudgee Shiraz | - | - | - | - | - | - | - |
| Orange Cabernet Sauvignon | - | - | - | - | - | - | - |
| Orange Chardonnay | - | - | - | - | - | - | - |
| Orange Shiraz | - | - | - | - | - | - | - |
| Riverina (Murrumbidgee) Botrytis Semillon | - | - | 9 | 6 | 10 | 5 | 5 |
| Southern NSW Cabernet Sauvignon (Canberra District, Hilltops) | - | - | - | - | - | - | - |
| Southern NSW Chardonnay (Canberra District, Hilltops) | - | - | - | - | - | - | - |
| Southern NSW Shiraz (Canberra District, Hilltops) | - | - | - | - | - | - | - |
| **VIC** | | | | | | | |
| Beechworth Chardonnay | - | - | - | - | - | - | 9 |
| Beechworth Pinot Noir | - | - | - | - | - | - | 9 |
| Geelong Chardonnay | - | - | - | - | - | - | - |
| Geelong Pinot Noir | - | - | - | - | - | - | - |
| Gippsland Pinot Noir | - | - | - | - | - | - | - |
| Goulburn Valley & Ngambie Lakes Shiraz | - | - | - | - | 7 | 7 | 10 |
| Grampians Shiraz | - | - | - | - | 7 | 7 | 8 |
| Heathcote Valley Shiraz | - | - | - | - | 7 | 7 | 10 |
| Macedon Ranges Chardonnay | - | - | - | - | - | - | - |
| Macedon Ranges Pinot Noir | - | - | - | - | - | - | - |
| Mornington Peninsula Chardonnay | - | - | - | - | - | - | - |
| Mornington Peninsula Pinot Noir | - | - | - | - | - | - | - |
| Pyrenees Cabernet | - | - | - | - | 6 | 7 | 9 |
| Pyrenees Shiraz | - | - | - | - | 5 | 7 | 10 |
| Sunbury Shiraz | 8 | 6 | 7 | 7 | 6 | 7 | 8 |
| Yarra Valley Cabernet | - | 8 | 9 | 6 | 7 | 5 | 9 |
| Yarra Valley Chardonnay | - | - | - | - | 8 | 8 | 7 |
| Yarra Valley Pinot Noir | - | - | - | - | 7 | 7 | 8 |
| **SA** | | | | | | | |
| Adelaide Hills Chardonnay | - | - | - | - | - | - | - |
| Barossa Valley Shiraz | - | - | - | - | - | - | 10 |
| Clare Valley Riesling | - | - | - | - | - | - | 10 |
| Clare Valley Shiraz | - | - | - | - | - | - | 10 |
| Coonawarra Cabernet | 8 | 7 | 8 | 5 | 7 | 7 | 10 |
| Coonawarra Shiraz | 8 | 7 | 8 | 4 | 7 | 7 | 9 |
| Eden Valley Cabernet | 9 | 7 | 9 | 9 | 8 | 7 | 10 |
| Eden Valley Riesling | 10 | 8 | 9 | 7 | 8 | 7 | 8 |
| Eden Valley Shiraz | 9 | 7 | 9 | 9 | 8 | 7 | 10 |
| McLaren Vale Shiraz | - | - | - | - | 6 | 6 | 7 |
| Padthaway Chardonnay | - | - | - | - | - | - | - |
| Padthaway Shiraz | - | - | - | - | - | - | - |
| **WA** | | | | | | | |
| Great Southern Cabernet | - | - | - | - | - | - | - |
| Great Southern Shiraz | - | - | - | - | - | - | - |
| Margaret River Cabernet | 7 | 7 | 8 | 7 | 7 | 6 | 9 |
| Margaret River Chardonnay | - | - | - | - | - | - | - |
| Margaret River Shiraz | 8 | 8 | 9 | 7 | 8 | 6 | 10 |
| Pemberton Pinot Noir | - | - | - | - | - | - | - |
| **TAS** | | | | | | | |
| Eastern Tasmania | - | - | - | - | - | - | - |
| Northern Tasmania | - | - | - | - | - | - | - |
| Southern Tasmania | - | - | - | - | - | - | - |

*Wines listed here have been rated out of 10.*
*Refer www.langtons.com.au for a comprehensive Vintage Chart.*

| 1987 | 1988 | 1989 | 1990 | 1991 | 1992 | 1993 | 1994 | 1995 | 1996 | 1997 | 1998 | 1999 | 2000 | 2001 | 2002 |
|---|---|---|---|---|---|---|---|---|---|---|---|---|---|---|---|
| 6 | 8 | 7 | 10 | 10 | 6 | 9 | 8 | 7 | 9 | 7 | 10 | 7 | - | - | - |
| 7 | 9 | 7 | 10 | 10 | 7 | 6 | 9 | 6 | 10 | 6 | 10 | 8 | - | - | - |
| | | | | | | | | | | | | | | | |
| 8 | 4 | 6 | 7 | 9 | 7 | 6 | 9 | 7 | 9 | 7 | 10 | 8 | 9 | - | - |
| 7 | 4 | 6 | 6 | 8 | 7 | 6 | 9 | 7 | 8 | 7 | 10 | 7 | 9 | 7 | - |
| 8 | 4 | 8 | 8 | 8 | 7 | 7 | 8 | 7 | 9 | 8 | 10 | 8 | 9 | 8 | - |
| 7 | 4 | 6 | 7 | 10 | 7 | 6 | 7 | 6 | 9 | 6 | 10 | 8 | 9 | 7 | - |
| - | - | - | 6 | 6 | 5 | 6 | 8 | 8 | 8 | 5 | 9 | 6 | 5 | 4 | - |
| - | - | - | 7 | 7 | 5 | 5 | 8 | 9 | 8 | 5 | 9 | 8 | 5 | 4 | - |
| - | - | - | - | - | - | - | - | - | - | 7 | 8 | 7 | 6 | 8 | - |
| - | - | - | - | - | - | - | - | - | - | 7 | 8 | 7 | 6 | 8 | - |
| - | - | - | - | - | - | - | - | - | - | 7 | 8 | 7 | 6 | 8 | - |
| 8 | 8 | 3 | 8 | 6 | 6 | 9 | 10 | 9 | 9 | 8 | 8 | 9 | 9 | - | - |
| - | - | - | - | - | - | - | - | - | - | 6 | 9 | 7 | 7 | 9 | - |
| - | - | - | - | - | - | - | - | - | - | 6 | 9 | 7 | 7 | 9 | - |
| - | - | - | - | - | - | - | - | - | - | 6 | 9 | 7 | 7 | 9 | - |
| | | | | | | | | | | | | | | | |
| 7 | 8 | 8 | 9 | 10 | 8 | 8 | 7 | 7 | 8 | 7 | 10 | 7 | 9 | 8 | 10 |
| 6 | 8 | 7 | 9 | 10 | 8 | 8 | 7 | 8 | 9 | 6 | 9 | 9 | 9 | 8 | 10 |
| - | - | - | 7 | 10 | 8 | 8 | 8 | 8 | 8 | 8 | 7 | 9 | 7 | 9 | - |
| - | 8 | 7 | 9 | 9 | 8 | 6 | 8 | 9 | 8 | 9 | 7 | 8 | 8 | 9 | - |
| - | - | - | - | - | - | - | - | - | - | 8 | 9 | 8 | 10 | 7 | - |
| 6 | 9 | 6 | 10 | 9 | 7 | 5 | 8 | 6 | 9 | 8 | 10 | 8 | 8 | 10 | - |
| 6 | 7 | 5 | 9 | 9 | 8 | 5 | 8 | 8 | 9 | 8 | 9 | 8 | 6 | 9 | - |
| 6 | 8 | 6 | 10 | 9 | 7 | 5 | 8 | 6 | 8 | 9 | 10 | 7 | 8 | 10 | - |
| - | - | - | - | - | - | - | - | - | - | - | - | 7 | 7 | 7 | - |
| - | - | - | - | - | - | - | - | - | - | - | - | 7 | 8 | 7 | - |
| - | - | - | 9 | 8 | 5 | 7 | 7 | 7 | 6 | 7 | 8 | 7 | 9 | 8 | - |
| - | - | - | 9 | 8 | 6 | 7 | 6 | 8 | 6 | 8 | 7 | 7 | 9 | 8 | - |
| 5 | 8 | 6 | 10 | 8 | 6 | 4 | 8 | 6 | 9 | 7 | 10 | 7 | 6 | 10 | - |
| 5 | 8 | 6 | 10 | 9 | 7 | 4 | 8 | 6 | 10 | 8 | 10 | 7 | 7 | 10 | - |
| 6 | 8 | 5 | 10 | 9 | 7 | 7 | 8 | 5 | 8 | 8 | 8 | 7 | 8 | 9 | - |
| 5 | 8 | 4 | 10 | 9 | 8 | 8 | 8 | 7 | 7 | 8 | 10 | 7 | 8 | 10 | - |
| 7 | 7 | 4 | 9 | 8 | 7 | 8 | 7 | 6 | 7 | 9 | 9 | 7 | 8 | 9 | - |
| 7 | 8 | 5 | 8 | 9 | 7 | 6 | 8 | 6 | 7 | 10 | 9 | 7 | 10 | 9 | - |
| | | | | | | | | | | | | | | | |
| - | - | - | - | 9 | 8 | 7 | 7 | 9 | 9 | 8 | 10 | 7 | 7 | - | - |
| 6 | 8 | 5 | 10 | 10 | 6 | 8 | 8 | 7 | 10 | 7 | 10 | 8 | 7 | 9 | - |
| 8 | 7 | 6 | 10 | 7 | 7 | 7 | 8 | 9 | 8 | 10 | 8 | 9 | 6 | 8 | - |
| 7 | 8 | 5 | 10 | 10 | 7 | 8 | 9 | 6 | 9 | 7 | 10 | 8 | 7 | 9 | - |
| 6 | 7 | 5 | 10 | 10 | 6 | 7 | 8 | 4 | 9 | 7 | 10 | 8 | 9 | 7 | - |
| 6 | 7 | 6 | 10 | 10 | 7 | 7 | 9 | 5 | 9 | 7 | 10 | 8 | 9 | 7 | - |
| 6 | 8 | 7 | 10 | 10 | 6 | 9 | 8 | 7 | 9 | 7 | 10 | 7 | 7 | 10 | - |
| 8 | 7 | 8 | 10 | 9 | 8 | 8 | 8 | 7 | 10 | 10 | 8 | 7 | 7 | 10 | - |
| 6 | 8 | 7 | 10 | 10 | 6 | 9 | 8 | 7 | 9 | 7 | 10 | 7 | 7 | - | - |
| 6 | 8 | 5 | 10 | 10 | 7 | 7 | 8 | 6 | 10 | 7 | 10 | 5 | 7 | 10 | - |
| - | - | - | - | - | - | - | - | - | - | 9 | 10 | 8 | 8 | 9 | - |
| - | - | - | 9 | 9 | 5 | 6 | 7 | 5 | 10 | 8 | 10 | 9 | 8 | 9 | - |
| | | | | | | | | | | | | | | | |
| - | - | - | - | 8 | 8 | 6 | 8 | 9 | 9 | 8 | 7 | 6 | 6 | 10 | - |
| - | - | - | - | 7 | 8 | 6 | 9 | 9 | 9 | 8 | 7 | 6 | 6 | 10 | - |
| 8 | 8 | 6 | 10 | 9 | 9 | 7 | 10 | 10 | 9 | 8 | 7 | 8 | 7 | 10 | - |
| 9 | 8 | 7 | 8 | 9 | 10 | 6 | 9 | 10 | 8 | 9 | 6 | 7 | 7 | 10 | - |
| 8 | 9 | 6 | 9 | 9 | 8 | 6 | 8 | 9 | 8 | 8 | 7 | 8 | 7 | 10 | - |
| - | - | - | - | - | - | - | - | - | - | 6 | 6 | 8 | 6 | 8 | - |
| | | | | | | | | | | | | | | | |
| - | - | - | - | - | - | - | - | - | - | 8 | 9 | 7 | 9 | 7 | - |
| - | - | - | - | - | - | - | - | - | - | 8 | 9 | 7 | 8 | 7 | - |
| - | - | - | - | - | - | - | - | - | - | 8 | 9 | 6 | 8 | 6 | - |

## LANGTON'S FINE WINE INDEX

*Endorsed by Australia's leading independent economic forecaster and analyst, Access Economics,* Langton's Fine Wine Index *is a response to the demand for a reliable and accurate means to gauge the investment potential of fine Australian wine (updated regularly at* www.langtons.com.au*).*

*Langton's Fine Wine Index* is an 'easy to follow' guide to price changes in the Australian fine wine auction market. With a similar format to the All Ordinaries Index, it shows the investment performance of Australian fine wine compared to other traditional investments.

This *Fine Wine Index* tracks the performance of 28 'Classified' Australian wines from three "rolling' vintages. The wines and vintages that comprise the Index are not fixed

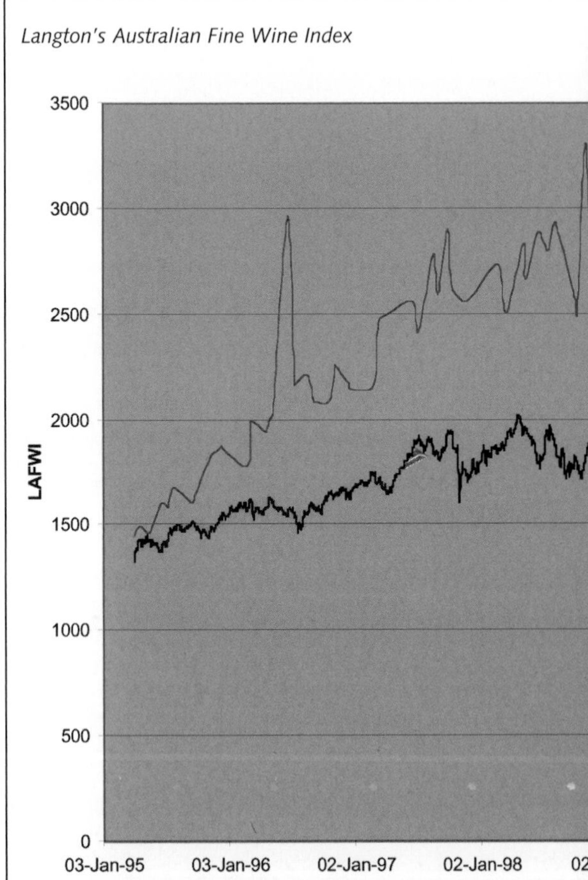

– new vintages will be added and old vintages deleted, just as companies are added and deleted from global share indices. Wine is after all a 'consumption good' and the stock of each wine is destined to fall over time.

While the Index in no way represents a guarantee that investing in wine will provide financial returns, the fundamentals in the fine wine market remain unchanged. Demand for very high quality wine continues to increase while supply is severely restricted. Accompanied by the inevitable hiccup or two along the way, such conditions have, in the past, sent prices in only one direction.

*Langton's Fine Wine Index* reveals that wine investment throughout the 1990s has been an extremely attractive option. In comparing the performance of *Langton's Fine Wine Index* against the All Ordinaries, it would appear that fine wine has been an attractive investment over the past decade and will most likely continue to be so in the future.

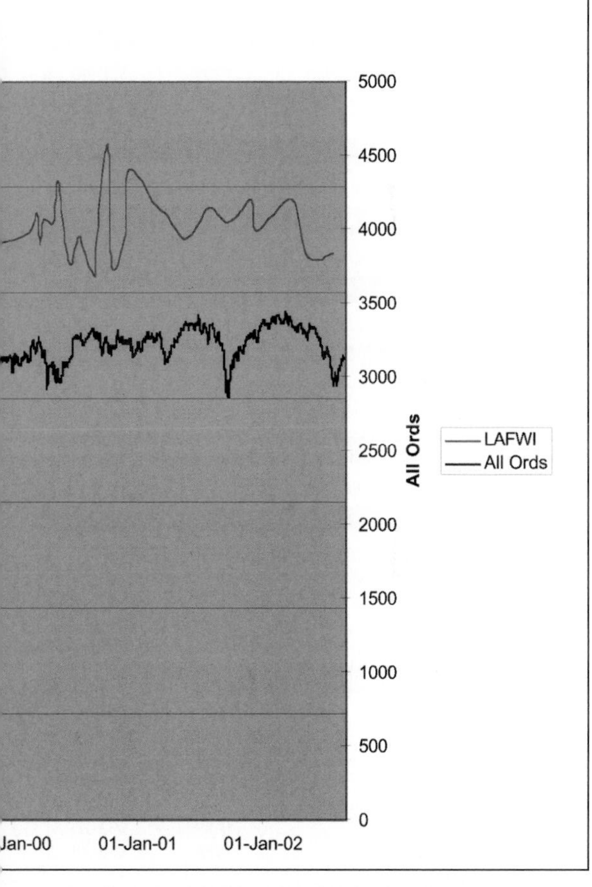

# SECONDARY MARKET PRICES

*The following secondary wine market prices (shown in Australian dollars) are based on wine auction price realisations at Langton's.*

*These values are effectively estimates and have been manipulated, in some instances, to reflect the current market sentiment. The prices assume bottles are in good condition and do not include buyer's premium.*

*A comprehensive database of prices can also be found at www.langtons.com.au*

## ADAMS & CO.

| Wine | Vintage | Price | Size |
|---|---|---|---|
| *Tawny Port, Victoria* | 1919 | $85-120 | *B* |

## ALKOOMI VINEYARD

| Wine | Vintage | Price | Size |
|---|---|---|---|
| *Blackbutt Cabernet Malbec Merlot, Frankland River* | 1994 | $30-40 | *B* |
| | 1995 | $36-45 | *B* |

## ALL SAINTS

| Wine | Vintage | Price | Size |
|---|---|---|---|
| *Centenary Vintage Port, Rutherglen* | 1965 | $33-40 | *B* |
| *Museum Release 1932-58-63 Blend Liqueur Muscat, Rutherglen* | | $86-120 | *B* |

## ANDRAOS BROS.

| Wine | Vintage | Price | Size |
|---|---|---|---|
| *Winilba Grandfathers Reserve Shiraz, Sunbury* | 1998 | $30-40 | *B* |

## ANDREW HARRIS VINEYARDS

| Wine | Vintage | Price | Size |
|---|---|---|---|
| *The Vision Shiraz Cabernet, Orange/Mudgee* | 1995 | $28-36 | *B* |

## ARMSTRONG

| Wine | Vintage | Price | Size |
|---|---|---|---|
| *Shiraz, Heathcote* | 1998 | $28-35 | *B* |

## ASHTON HILLS VINEYARD

| Wine | Vintage | Price | Size |
|---|---|---|---|
| *Pinot Noir, Adelaide Hills* | 1993 | $28-36 | *B* |
| | 1999 | $28-40 | *B* |

## BAILEYS OF GLENROWAN

| Wine | Vintage | Price | Size |
|---|---|---|---|
| *1904 Block Shiraz, Glenrowan* | 1992 | $28-40 | *B* |

## BALGOWNIE ESTATE

| Wine | Vintage | Price | Size |
|---|---|---|---|
| *Cabernet Sauvignon, Bendigo* | 1978 | $56-70 | *M* |
| | 1979 | $50-65 | *M* |
| | 1980 | $30-40 | *B* |
| | 1980 | $80-110 | *M* |
| | 1982 | $56-70 | *M* |

## BANNOCKBURN VINEYARDS

| Wine | Vintage | Price | Size |
|---|---|---|---|
| *Cabernet Merlot, Geelong* | 1988 | $80-90 | *M* |
| | 1991 | $35-45 | *B* |
| | 1991 | $76-85 | *M* |
| | 1992 | $70-90 | *M* |
| *Cabernet Sauvignon, Geelong* | 1986 | $28-35 | *B* |
| | 1987 | $50-70 | *M* |
| | 1988 | $26-35 | *B* |

| Wine | Vintage | Price | Size |
|---|---|---|---|
| | 1988 | $85-120 | M |
| | 1989 | $28-35 | B |
| | 1991 | $75-100 | M |
| *Chardonnay, Geelong* | 1988 | $26-35 | B |
| | 1989 | $30-40 | B |
| | 1989 | $80-95 | M |
| | 1990 | $40-50 | B |
| | 1990 | $85-120 | M |
| | 1991 | $40-48 | B |
| | 1992 | $36-50 | B |
| | 1992 | $80-95 | M |
| | 1993 | $40-55 | B |
| | 1993 | $86-110 | M |
| | 1994 | $35-45 | B |
| | 1995 | $40-48 | B |
| | 1996 | $35-45 | B |
| | 1996 | $85-100 | M |
| | 1997 | $26-35 | B |
| | 1998 | $35-45 | B |
| | 1999 | $28-35 | B |
| *Pinot Noir, Geelong* | 1984 | $30-40 | B |
| | 1988 | $55-75 | B |
| | 1988 | $75-100 | M |
| | 1989 | $50-65 | B |
| | 1989 | $80-95 | M |
| | 1990 | $45-56 | B |
| | 1991 | $50-65 | B |
| | 1991 | $80-110 | M |
| | 1992 | $46-65 | B |
| | 1992 | $90-110 | M |
| | 1993 | $46-60 | B |
| | 1994 | $45-56 | B |
| | 1994 | $90-120 | M |
| | 1995 | $46-60 | B |
| | 1995 | $90-120 | M |
| | 1996 | $45-60 | B |
| | 1996 | $90-120 | M |
| | 1997 | $50-70 | B |
| | 1998 | $45-55 | B |
| | 1999 | $45-60 | B |
| *S.R.H Chardonnay, Geelong* | 1993 | $66-86 | B |
| | 1995 | $70-95 | B |
| *Serre Pinot Noir, Geelong* | 1990 | $86-120 | B |
| | 1991 | $85-120 | B |
| | 1996 | $110-150 | B |
| *Shiraz, Geelong* | 1985 | $33-40 | B |
| | 1988 | $36-50 | B |
| | 1988 | $80-100 | M |
| | 1990 | $40-46 | B |
| | 1990 | $80-100 | M |
| | 1991 | $33-40 | B |
| | 1992 | $28-36 | B |
| | 1993 | $33-40 | B |
| | 1993 | $80-100 | M |
| | 1994 | $30-45 | B |
| | 1994 | $66-90 | M |
| | 1995 | $30-40 | B |
| | 1995 | $76-90 | M |
| | 1996 | $40-50 | B |
| | 1997 | $30-40 | B |
| | 1998 | $30-40 | B |

## BAROSSA VALLEY ESTATE

| Wine | Vintage | Price | Size |
|---|---|---|---|
| *E & E Black Pepper Shiraz, Barossa Valley* | 1988 | $66-80 | *B* |
| | 1989 | $55-70 | *B* |
| | 1990 | $56-80 | *B* |
| | 1990 | $120-160 | *M* |
| | 1991 | $46-60 | *B* |
| | 1991 | $160-220 | *M* |
| | 1992 | $40-55 | *B* |
| | 1993 | $45-65 | *B* |
| | 1994 | $46-60 | *B* |
| | 1995 | $40-55 | *B* |
| | 1996 | $55-80 | *B* |
| | 1997 | $45-65 | *B* |
| | 1998 | $50-65 | *B* |
| | 1999 | $45-55 | *B* |
| *E & E Sparkling Shiraz, Barossa Valley* | 1990 | $40-50 | *B* |
| | 1991 | $45-55 | *B* |
| | 1992 | $30-45 | *B* |
| | 1993 | $40-55 | *B* |
| | 1994 | $30-40 | *B* |
| | 1995 | $28-40 | *B* |
| | 1996 | $30-40 | *B* |

## BASEDOW WINES

| Wine | Vintage | Price | Size |
|---|---|---|---|
| *Johannes Shiraz, Barossa Valley* | 1996 | $32-40 | *B* |

## BASS PHILLIP WINES

| Wine | Vintage | Price | Size |
|---|---|---|---|
| *4 KM Pinot Noir, Gippsland* | 1997 | $50-66 | *B* |
| | 1998 | $55-70 | *B* |
| *Belrose Vineyard Pinot Noir, Gippsland* | 1997 | $55-66 | *B* |
| | 1998 | $70-95 | *B* |
| *Chardonnay, Gippsland* | 1995 | $35-46 | *B* |
| | 1997 | $40-50 | *B* |
| | 1998 | $40-50 | *B* |
| *Crown Prince Pinot Noir, Gippsland* | 1999 | $150-210 | *M* |
| *Old Cellar Chardonnay, Gippsland* | 1998 | $50-65 | *B* |
| *Old Cellar Pinot Noir, Gippsland* | 1993 | $50-70 | *B* |
| | 1998 | $50-60 | *B* |
| | 1999 | $50-60 | *B* |
| *Pinot Blend Pinot Noir Gamay, Gippsland* | 1992 | $36-45 | *B* |
| *Pinot Noir, Gippsland* | 1985 | $240-280 | *M* |
| | 1990 | $70-85 | *B* |
| | 1991 | $56-70 | *B* |
| | 1992 | $60-76 | *B* |
| | 1993 | $55-75 | *B* |
| | 1994 | $65-76 | *B* |
| | 1995 | $56-75 | *B* |
| | 1996 | $65-80 | *B* |
| | 1997 | $60-80 | *B* |
| | 1998 | $55-70 | *B* |
| | 1998 | $55-65 | *H* |
| *Premium Pinot Noir, Gippsland* | 1985 | $380-440 | *M* |
| | 1990 | $110-140 | *B* |
| | 1991 | $160-210 | *B* |
| | 1991 | $380-440 | *M* |
| | 1992 | $130-180 | *B* |
| | 1993 | $280-350 | *M* |
| | 1994 | $120-170 | *B* |
| | 1994 | $280-350 | *M* |
| | 1995 | $110-150 | *B* |
| | 1995 | $330-400 | *M* |

| Wine | Vintage | Price | Size |
|---|---|---|---|
| | 1996 | $110-150 | B |
| | 1996 | $280-350 | M |
| | 1997 | $120-170 | B |
| | 1997 | $760-950 | D |
| | 1997 | $280-350 | M |
| | 1998 | $120-160 | B |
| | 1999 | $140-190 | B |
| *Reserve Chardonnay, Gippsland* | 1998 | $55-70 | B |
| *Reserve Pinot Noir, Gippsland* | 1994 | $180-220 | B |
| | 1994 | $370-440 | M |
| | 1995 | $160-210 | B |
| | 1996 | $190-250 | B |
| | 1997 | $220-290 | B |
| | 1997 | $500-600 | M |
| | 1998 | $160-200 | B |
| | 1998 | $75-90 | H |
| | 1999 | $170-230 | B |
| *Village Pinot Noir, Gippsland* | 1997 | $50-65 | B |
| | 1999 | $45-65 | B |

## BEST'S WINES

| Wine | Vintage | Price | Size |
|---|---|---|---|
| *Bin 0 Shiraz, Grampians* | *1977* | *$30-40* | *B* |
| | *1990* | *$30-40* | *B* |
| | *1991* | *$30-40* | *B* |
| | *1992* | *$30-40* | *B* |
| | *1993* | *$28-35* | *B* |
| | *1996* | *$28-40* | *B* |
| | *1997* | *$26-35* | *B* |
| | *1998* | *$26-35* | *B* |
| *Thomson Family Centenary Shiraz, Grampians* | 1992 | $66-80 | B |
| | 1992 | $140-190 | M |
| *Thomson Family Shiraz, Grampians* | 1994 | $56-75 | B |
| | 1994 | $140-180 | M |
| | 1995 | $56-75 | B |
| | 1995 | $130-160 | M |
| | 1996 | $65-85 | B |
| | 1996 | $160-220 | M |
| | 1997 | $60-85 | B |
| | 1997 | $130-160 | M |
| | 1998 | $75-90 | B |

## BINDI

| Wine | Vintage | Price | Size |
|---|---|---|---|
| *Chardonnay, Macedon* | 1994 | $36-45 | B |
| | 1995 | $30-40 | B |
| | 1996 | $28-35 | B |
| | 1997 | $30-45 | B |
| | 1998 | $33-45 | B |
| | 1999 | $30-35 | B |
| *Original Vineyard Chardonnay, Macedon* | 1999 | $36-45 | B |
| *Original Vineyard Pinot Noir, Macedon* | 1995 | $66-85 | B |
| | 1996 | $55-75 | B |
| | 1997 | $55-75 | B |
| | 1998 | $50-70 | B |
| | 1999 | $40-55 | B |
| *Wine Growers Quartz Chardonnay, Macedon* | 1995 | $36-45 | B |
| | 1998 | $35-50 | B |
| | 1999 | $30-45 | B |

## BLACKJACK VINEYARDS

| Wine | Vintage | Price | Size |
|---|---|---|---|
| *Cabernet Merlot, Bendigo* | 1995 | $60-76 | M |
| | 1999 | $26-35 | B |
| *Shiraz, Bendigo* | 1995 | $60-80 | M |

## BLACKJACK VINEYARDS

| Wine | Vintage | Price | Size |
|---|---|---|---|
| | 1996 | $30-40 | *B* |
| | 1996 | $76-100 | *M* |
| | 1997 | $26-35 | *B* |
| | 1998 | $30-40 | *B* |

## BLUE PYRENEES ESTATE

| Wine | Vintage | Price | Size |
|---|---|---|---|
| *Dry Red, Pyrenees* | 1986 | $56-75 | *M* |
| | 1990 | $65-86 | *M* |
| | 1992 | $66-85 | *M* |
| | 1995 | $70-95 | *M* |

## BOWEN ESTATE

| Wine | Vintage | Price | Size |
|---|---|---|---|
| *Cabernet Sauvignon, Coonawarra* | 1982 | $36-45 | *B* |
| | 1984 | $28-40 | *B* |
| | 1986 | $36-45 | *B* |
| | 1990 | $36-50 | *B* |
| | 1991 | $28-38 | *B* |
| | 1992 | $26-35 | *B* |
| | 1996 | $28-35 | *B* |
| | 1998 | $26-35 | *B* |
| *Shiraz, Coonawarra* | 1990 | $33-45 | *B* |
| | 1991 | $26-35 | *B* |
| | 1992 | $70-86 | *M* |
| | 1996 | $28-35 | *B* |
| | 1998 | $26-35 | *B* |

## BRAND'S OF COONAWARRA

| Wine | Vintage | Price | Size |
|---|---|---|---|
| *Laira Cabernet Sauvignon, Coonawarra* | 1977 | $50-65 | *M* |
| | 1978 | $56-65 | *M* |
| | 1988 | $75-90 | *M* |
| *Laira Original Vineyard Shiraz, Coonawarra* | 1982 | $30-40 | *B* |
| | 1990 | $28-35 | *B* |

## BRIAR RIDGE VINEYARD

| Wine | Vintage | Price | Size |
|---|---|---|---|
| *Stockhausen Shiraz, Hunter Valley* | 1993 | $156-290 | *D* |

## BROKENWOOD WINES

| Wine | Vintage | Price | Size |
|---|---|---|---|
| *Graveyard Vineyard Shiraz, Hunter Valley* | 1986 | $80-110 | *B* |
| | 1988 | $66-80 | *B* |
| | 1989 | $56-70 | *B* |
| | 1990 | $76-100 | *B* |
| | 1991 | $86-110 | *B* |
| | 1991 | $270-340 | *M* |
| | 1993 | $70-86 | *B* |
| | 1994 | $70-90 | *B* |
| | 1995 | $60-80 | *B* |
| | 1996 | $85-120 | *B* |
| | 1996 | $200-260 | *M* |
| | 1997 | $60-85 | *B* |
| | 1998 | $70-90 | *B* |
| | 1998 | $210-290 | *M* |
| *Cabernet Sauvignon, Hunter Valley* | 1986 | $66-86 | *B* |
| | 1989 | $33-40 | *B* |
| | 1991 | $35-46 | *B* |
| *Rayner Vineyard Shiraz, McLaren Vale* | 1997 | $26-35 | *B* |
| | 1998 | $30-40 | *B* |
| *The Mistress Block Shiraz, Hunter Valley* | 1996 | $26-35 | *B* |

## BURGE FAMILY WINEMAKERS

| Wine | Vintage | Price | Size |
|---|---|---|---|
| *Draycott Reserve Shiraz, Barossa Valley* | 1996 | $70-140 | *B* |
| *Draycott Shiraz, Barossa Valley* | 1998 | $30-40 | *B* |
| | 1999 | $35-50 | *B* |

## CAMPBELLS WINES

|  |  |  |
|---|---|---|
| *The Barkly, Durif, Rutherglen* | 1995 | $36-45...*B* |

## CAPE JAFFA ROBE

|  |  |  |
|---|---|---|
| *Shiraz, Limestone Coast* | 1997 | $46-60 .*M* |

## CAPE MENTELLE

|  |  |  |
|---|---|---|
| *(Hermitage) Shiraz, Margaret River* | 1981 | $30-40...*B* |
| | 1983 | $26-35...*B* |
| | 1986 | $35-46...*B* |
| *Cabernet Sauvignon, Margaret River* | 1978 | $70-95...*B* |
| | 1980 | $35-50...*B* |
| | 1982 | $60-80...*B* |
| | 1983 | $76-100...*B* |
| | 1984 | $55-70...*B* |
| | 1985 | $56-75...*B* |
| | 1986 | $50-66...*B* |
| | 1987 | $60-85...*B* |
| | 1988 | $50-66...*B* |
| | 1989 | $55-80...*B* |
| | 1990 | $75-90...*B* |
| | 1991 | $60-85...*B* |
| | 1991 | $170-230 .*M* |
| | 1992 | $50-65...*B* |
| | 1992 | $150-200 .*M* |
| | 1993 | $56-80...*B* |
| | 1993 | $120-170 .*M* |
| | 1994 | $50-70...*B* |
| | 1995 | $50-65...*B* |
| | 1996 | $50-70...*B* |
| *Chardonnay, Margaret River* | 1996 | $30-45...*B* |
| | 2000 | $30-40...*B* |
| *Shiraz, Margaret River* | 1984 | $55-75...*B* |
| | 1988 | $50-65...*B* |
| | 1990 | $40-50...*B* |
| | 1991 | $45-60...*B* |
| | 1992 | $40-50...*B* |
| | 1993 | $28-40...*B* |
| | 1994 | $30-40...*B* |
| | 1995 | $30-35...*B* |
| | 1996 | $30-40...*B* |
| | 1998 | $26-35...*B* |
| *Zinfandel, Margaret River* | 1984 | $40-50...*B* |
| | 1988 | $30-40...*B* |
| | 1990 | $28-36...*B* |
| | 1993 | $28-35...*B* |
| | 1995 | $28-35...*B* |
| | 1996 | $30-40...*B* |
| | 1997 | $28-40...*B* |

## CHAPEL HILL

|  |  |  |
|---|---|---|
| *Cabernet Sauvignon, McLaren Vale* | 1990 | $28-38...*B* |
| *Reserve Cabernet Sauvignon, McLaren Vale* | 1992 | $26-35...*B* |
| | 1992 | $75-96 .*M* |
| *Reserve Cabernet Shiraz, McLaren Vale-Coonawarra* | | |
| | 1992 | $33-45...*B* |
| | 1992 | $66-85 .*M* |
| *Reserve Shiraz, McLaren Vale* | 1990 | $45-56...*B* |
| *Shiraz, McLaren Vale* | 1990 | $30-40...*B* |
| | 1991 | $28-40...*B* |
| | 1993 | $26-35...*B* |

## CHAPEL HILL

| Wine | Vintage | Price | Size |
|---|---|---|---|
| *The Vicar Cabernet Shiraz, McLaren Vale* | 1994 | $80-110 | *M* |

## CHARLES CIMICKY

| Wine | Vintage | Price | Size |
|---|---|---|---|
| *Cabernet Cabernet Franc, Barossa Valley* | 1995 | $28-35 | *B* |
| *Signature Shiraz, Barossa Valley* | 1989 | $26-35 | *B* |
| | 1990 | $35-46 | *B* |
| | 1992 | $28-35 | *B* |
| | 1993 | $30-40 | *B* |
| | 1994 | $28-35 | *B* |
| | 1995 | $26-35 | *B* |
| | 1996 | $30-40 | *B* |

## CHARLES MELTON WINES

| Wine | Vintage | Price | Size |
|---|---|---|---|
| *Nine Popes Shiraz Grenache Mourvedre, Barossa Valley* | | | |
| | 1992 | $30-40 | *B* |
| | 1993 | $36-45 | *B* |
| | 1993 | $95-130 | *M* |
| | 1994 | $36-45 | *B* |
| | 1994 | $95-130 | *M* |
| | 1995 | $28-36 | *B* |
| | 1995 | $80-110 | *M* |
| | 1996 | $35-45 | *B* |
| | 1996 | $280-350 | *D* |
| | 1996 | $100-140 | *M* |
| | 1997 | $30-40 | *B* |
| | 1997 | $85-110 | *M* |
| | 1998 | $35-45 | *B* |
| | 1998 | $95-130 | *M* |
| | 1999 | $30-40 | *B* |
| *Pressings, Barossa Valley* | 1992 | $55-75 | *M* |
| *Shiraz, Barossa Valley* | 1996 | $28-35 | *B* |
| | 1997 | $28-35 | *B* |
| | 1998 | $28-35 | *B* |
| | 1998 | $55-75 | *M* |

## CLARENDON HILLS

| Wine | Vintage | Price | Size |
|---|---|---|---|
| *Astralis Shiraz, McLaren Vale* | 1994 | $140-180 | *B* |
| | 1995 | $130-170 | *B* |
| | 1996 | $120-170 | *B* |
| | 1998 | $140-190 | *B* |
| *Blewitt Springs Cabernet Sauvignon, McLaren Vale* | | | |
| | 1992 | $30-40 | *B* |
| | 1994 | $30-40 | *B* |
| | 1994 | $70-90 | *M* |
| *Blewitt Springs Merlot, McLaren Vale* | 1990 | $30-40 | *B* |
| | 1991 | $28-38 | *B* |
| | 1992 | $30-40 | *B* |
| | 1993 | $30-35 | *B* |
| | 1993 | $76-95 | *M* |
| | 1994 | $70-95 | *M* |
| | 1996 | $30-40 | *B* |
| | 1997 | $26-35 | *B* |
| *Blewitt Springs Old Vine Grenache, McLaren Vale* | | | |
| | 1992 | $36-50 | *B* |
| | 1993 | $30-40 | *B* |
| | 1994 | $30-40 | *B* |
| | 1994 | $70-90 | *M* |
| | 1995 | $30-40 | *B* |
| | 1996 | $35-45 | *B* |
| | 1997 | $30-40 | *B* |
| *Blewitt Springs Shiraz, McLaren Vale* | 1993 | $30-40 | *B* |
| | 1993 | $66-86 | *M* |

|  |  |  | |
|---|---|---|---|
| | 1994 | $36-45 | *B* |
| | 1995 | $35-45 | *B* |
| *Brookman Shiraz, McLaren Vale* | 1997 | $28-35 | *B* |
| *Clarendon Vineyard Old Vine Grenache, McLaren Vale* | 1994 | $30-35 | *B* |
| | 1996 | $30-40 | *B* |
| | 1997 | $26-35 | *B* |
| *Clarendon Vineyard Shiraz, McLaren Vale* | 1991 | $35-46 | *B* |
| | 1992 | $46-60 | *B* |
| | 1992 | $100-140 | *M* |
| | 1995 | $30-40 | *B* |
| *Liandra Shiraz, McLaren Vale* | 1997 | $30-40 | *B* |
| *Piggott Ranges Shiraz, McLaren Vale* | 1997 | $75-100 | *B* |

## CLONAKILLA

|  |  |  | |
|---|---|---|---|
| *Shiraz Viognier, Canberra District* | 1995 | $30-40 | *B* |

## COLDSTREAM HILLS

|  |  |  | |
|---|---|---|---|
| *Reserve Cabernet, Yarra Valley* | 1992 | $36-45 | *B* |
| | 1993 | $28-36 | B |
| | 1994 | $28-36 | *B* |
| *Reserve Chardonnay, Yarra Valley* | 1990 | $26-33 | *B* |
| | 1991 | $28-40 | *B* |
| | 1992 | $28-36 | *B* |
| | 1993 | $28-36 | *B* |
| | 1994 | $36-45 | *B* |
| | 1995 | $30-45 | *B* |
| | 1996 | $30-38 | *B* |
| | 1997 | $26-35 | *B* |
| | 1998 | $35-45 | *B* |
| *Reserve Pinot Noir, Yarra Valley* | 1990 | $30-36 | *B* |
| | 1992 | $35-46 | *B* |
| | 1993 | $35-46 | *B* |
| | 1994 | $36-45 | *B* |
| | 1995 | $33-40 | *B* |
| | 1996 | $35-45 | *B* |
| | 1997 | $35-45 | *B* |
| | 1998 | $30-40 | *B* |

## CORIOLE

|  |  |  | |
|---|---|---|---|
| *Lloyd Reserve Shiraz, McLaren Vale* | 1989 | $45-60 | *B* |
| | 1990 | $50-65 | *B* |
| | 1991 | $50-65 | *B* |
| | 1992 | $45-56 | *B* |
| | 1992 | $86-110 | *M* |
| | 1993 | $40-50 | *B* |
| | 1994 | $50-60 | *B* |
| | 1994 | $100-140 | *M* |
| | 1995 | $46-55 | *B* |
| | 1996 | $50-60 | *B* |
| | 1996 | $110-150 | *M* |
| | 1997 | $35-50 | *B* |
| *Mary Kathleen Cabernet Merlot Cabernet Franc, McLaren Vale* | 1994 | $26-33 | *B* |
| *Mary Kathleen Cabernet Merlot Cabernet Franc, McLaren Vale* | 1995 | $28-35 | *B* |

## CRAIGLEE

|  |  |  | |
|---|---|---|---|
| *Cabernet Sauvignon, Sunbury* | 1984 | $28-40 | *B* |
| | 1992 | $28-35 | *B* |
| | 1998 | $28-35 | *B* |
| *Shiraz, Sunbury* | 1980 | $30-45 | *B* |

| Wine | Year | Price | Size |
|---|---|---|---|
| | 1984 | $35-45 | *B* |
| | 1986 | $44-55 | *B* |
| | 1987 | $45-55 | *B* |
| | 1988 | $36-50 | *B* |
| | 1989 | $30-40 | *B* |
| | 1990 | $50-65 | *B* |
| | 1991 | $45-56 | *B* |
| | 1992 | $40-50 | *B* |
| | 1992 | $100-130 | *M* |
| | 1993 | $38-48 | *B* |
| | 1993 | $100-140 | *M* |
| | 1994 | $40-50 | *B* |
| | 1995 | $30-38 | *B* |
| | 1995 | $76-100 | *M* |
| | 1996 | $35-50 | *B* |
| | 1997 | $35-50 | *B* |
| | 1998 | $35-45 | *B* |

## CULLEN WINES

| Wine | Year | Price | Size |
|---|---|---|---|
| *Cabernet Merlot, Margaret River* | 1979 | $75-95 | *B* |
| | 1982 | $65-80 | *B* |
| | 1984 | $75-100 | *B* |
| | 1986 | $76-90 | *B* |
| | 1987 | $75-86 | *B* |
| | 1988 | $70-90 | *B* |
| | 1989 | $55-70 | *B* |
| | 1990 | $80-110 | *B* |
| | 1991 | $75-90 | *B* |
| | 1992 | $70-96 | *B* |
| | 1992 | $210-290 | *M* |
| | 1993 | $70-90 | *B* |
| | 1993 | $40-48 | *H* |
| | 1993 | $170-230 | *M* |
| | 1994 | $75-90 | *B* |
| | 1994 | $30-36 | *H* |
| | 1994 | $1600-2200 | *I* |
| | 1994 | $140-190 | *M* |
| | 1995 | $75-96 | *B* |
| | 1995 | $38-45 | *H* |
| | 1995 | $230-300 | *M* |
| | 1996 | $76-95 | *B* |
| | 1996 | $160-210 | *M* |
| | 1997 | $75-90 | *B* |
| | 1997 | $160-220 | *M* |
| | 1998 | $70-95 | *B* |
| | 1998 | $170-230 | *M* |
| | 1999 | $66-85 | *B* |
| *Cabernet Sauvignon, Margaret River* | 1980 | $40-55 | *B* |
| *Chardonnay, Margaret River* | 1993 | $28-36 | *B* |
| | 1995 | $26-35 | *B* |
| | 1996 | $45-55 | *B* |
| | 1997 | $110-140 | *M* |
| | 1998 | $30-40 | *B* |
| | 1999 | $30-40 | *B* |
| *Pinot Noir, Margaret River* | 1995 | $28-36 | *B* |
| | 1997 | $26-35 | *B* |
| | 1998 | $30-35 | *B* |
| *Reserve Cabernet Merlot, Margaret River* | 1988 | $76-95 | *B* |
| | 1989 | $70-90 | *B* |
| | 1990 | $90-120 | *B* |
| | 1991 | $76-100 | *B* |
| | 1991 | $210-290 | *M* |

| | | | |
|---|---|---|---|
| | 1992 | $80-110 | B |
| | 1992 | $190-240 | M |
| | 1993 | $70-95 | B |
| | 1993 | $190-250 | M |
| | 1994 | $80-110 | B |
| | 1994 | $180-240 | M |

## DALWHINNIE

| | | | |
|---|---|---|---|
| *Cabernet Sauvignon, Pyrenees* | 1980 | $45-60 | B |
| | 1982 | $50-70 | B |
| | 1986 | $50-65 | B |
| | 1989 | $45-60 | B |
| | 1990 | $45-55 | B |
| | 1991 | $45-56 | B |
| | 1992 | $36-50 | B |
| | 1993 | $36-50 | B |
| | 1994 | $40-50 | B |
| | 1995 | $36-45 | B |
| | 1996 | $35-45 | B |
| | 1997 | $30-45 | B |
| | 1998 | $35-45 | B |
| | 1999 | $35-45 | B |
| *Chardonnay, Pyrenees* | 1990 | $35-50 | B |
| | 1992 | $35-46 | B |
| | 1993 | $26-35 | B |
| | 1994 | $26-35 | B |
| | 1996 | $28-35 | B |
| | 1998 | $28-35 | B |
| | 1999 | $30-40 | B |
| | 2000 | $26-35 | B |
| *Eagle Shiraz, Pyrenees* | 1986 | $110-140 | B |
| | 1992 | $140-180 | B |
| | 1997 | $90-120 | B |
| *Pinot Noir, Pyrenees* | 1998 | $30-45 | B |
| *Shiraz, Pyrenees* | 1980 | $65-85 | B |
| | 1988 | $55-70 | B |
| | 1990 | $56-70 | B |
| | 1991 | $56-70 | B |
| | 1992 | $55-70 | B |
| | 1993 | $50-66 | B |
| | 1994 | $50-65 | B |
| | 1995 | $40-55 | B |
| | 1996 | $55-70 | B |
| | 1997 | $46-65 | B |
| | 1998 | $50-65 | B |
| | 1999 | $45-65 | B |

## D'ARENBERG WINES

| | | | |
|---|---|---|---|
| *Ironstone Pressings Grenache Shiraz Mourvedre, McLaren Vale* | | | |
| | 1988 | $40-50 | B |
| | 1996 | $35-50 | B |
| | 1997 | $28-40 | B |
| | 1998 | $26-35 | B |
| *The Coppermine Road Cabernet Sauvignon, McLaren Vale* | | | |
| | 1996 | $40-50 | B |
| *The Dead Arm Shiraz, McLaren Vale* | 1994 | $50-68 | B |
| | 1995 | $46-65 | B |
| | 1996 | $50-70 | B |
| | 1997 | $50-65 | B |
| | 1998 | $45-60 | B |

## DE BORTOLI WINES

| Wine | Vintage | Price | Size |
|---|---|---|---|
| *GS Reserve Shiraz, Yarra Valley* | 1996 | $75-96 | *B* |
| *Melba Vineyard Cabernet, Yarra Valley* | 1994 | $30-40 | *B* |
| | 1995 | $28-35 | *B* |
| *Noble One Botrytis Semillon, Riverina* | 1982 | $50-65 | *B* |
| | 1982 | $40-55 | *H* |
| | 1983 | $46-60 | *B* |
| | 1983 | $30-45 | *H* |
| | 1984 | $35-45 | *H* |
| | 1985 | $30-40 | *B* |
| | 1985 | $38-46 | *H* |
| | 1986 | $56-70 | *B* |
| | 1987 | $45-60 | *B* |
| | 1987 | $33-40 | *H* |
| | 1988 | $46-55 | *B* |
| | 1988 | $30-40 | *H* |
| | 1990 | $46-60 | *B* |
| | 1990 | $35-46 | *H* |
| | 1991 | $46-65 | *B* |
| | 1991 | $30-38 | *H* |
| | 1992 | $46-60 | *B* |
| | 1992 | $30-38 | *H* |
| | 1993 | $40-48 | *B* |
| | 1993 | $28-36 | *H* |
| | 1994 | $50-66 | *B* |
| | 1994 | $30-38 | *H* |
| | 1995 | $28-36 | *H* |
| | 1996 | $45-60 | *B* |
| | 1996 | $28-35 | *H* |
| | 1997 | $30-45 | *B* |
| | 1998 | $40-50 | *B* |
| | 1998 | $28-35 | *H* |

## DEVIL'S LAIR WINES

| Wine | Vintage | Price | Size |
|---|---|---|---|
| *Cabernets, Margaret River* | 1993 | $33-40 | *B* |
| | 1993 | $130-180 | *M* |
| | 1994 | $30-44 | *B* |
| | 1995 | $40-48 | *B* |
| | 1995 | $110-140 | *M* |
| | 1996 | $35-45 | *B* |
| | 1996 | $110-140 | *M* |
| | 1997 | $110-140 | *M* |
| *Chardonnay, Margaret River* | 1995 | $30-36 | *B* |
| | 1996 | $30-40 | *B* |
| | 1997 | $26-35 | *B* |
| | 1998 | $28-35 | *B* |
| | 1999 | $26-35 | *B* |

## DIAMOND VALLEY VINEYARDS

| Wine | Vintage | Price | Size |
|---|---|---|---|
| *Black Label Close Planted Pinot Noir, Yarra Valley* | | | |
| | 1993 | $33-45 | *B* |
| | 1994 | $35-46 | *B* |
| | 1995 | $36-50 | *B* |
| | 1996 | $44-55 | *B* |
| *Estate Pinot Noir, Yarra Valley* | 1994 | $30-36 | *B* |
| | 1995 | $28-38 | *B* |
| | 1996 | $28-35 | *B* |
| | 1997 | $30-40 | *B* |

## DOMAINE A

|  |  |  |
|---|---|---|
| *Stoney Vineyard Pinot Noir, Southern Tasmania* | 1997 | $45-58...*B* |
| *Stoney Vineyard Unfiltered Pinot Noir, Southern Tasmania* | 1998 | $48-60...*B* |

## DRAYTONS FAMILY WINES

|  |  |  |
|---|---|---|
| *William Old Vines Shiraz, Hunter Valley* | 1995 | $30-38...*B* |

## DROMANA ESTATE VINEYARDS

|  |  |  |
|---|---|---|
| *Reserve Pinot Noir, Mornington Peninsula* | 1996 | $28-35...*B* |

## ELDERTON

|  |  |  |
|---|---|---|
| *Cabernet Sauvignon, Barossa Valley* | 1992 | $80-100 .*M* |
| *Command Shiraz, Barossa Valley* | 1987 | $40-50...*B* |
| | 1988 | $44-55...*B* |
| | 1990 | $50-60...*B* |
| | 1992 | $46-55...*B* |
| | 1993 | $36-45...*B* |
| | 1994 | $45-55...*B* |
| | 1995 | $36-50...*B* |
| | 1996 | $50-60...*B* |
| | 1996 | $180-230 .*M* |
| | 1997 | $45-60...*B* |
| *Shiraz, Barossa Valley* | 1991 | $28-35...*B* |
| | 1992 | $66-80 .*M* |

## FLYNN & WILLIAMS

|  |  |  |
|---|---|---|
| *Cabernet Sauvignon, Heathcote* | 1991 | $76-96 .*M* |

## FOX CREEK

|  |  |  |
|---|---|---|
| *Reserve Cabernet Sauvignon, McLaren Vale* | 1995 | $30-38...*B* |
| | 1996 | $35-45...*B* |
| | 1997 | $30-40...*B* |
| | 1998 | $45-60...*B* |
| *Reserve Shiraz, McLaren Vale* | 1995 | $60-85...*B* |
| | 1996 | $60-75...*B* |
| | 1997 | $65-85...*B* |
| | 1997 | $140-180 .*M* |
| | 1998 | $75-100...*B* |
| | 1998 | $180-230 .*M* |
| | 1999 | $55-75...*B* |
| *J.S. M. Shiraz Cabernet, McLaren Vale* | 1999 | $56-70 .*M* |

## FREYCINET VINEYARDS

|  |  |  |
|---|---|---|
| *Pinot Noir, Southern Tasmania* | 1998 | $86-120 .*M* |

## GALAH WINE

|  |  |  |
|---|---|---|
| *Cabernet Sauvignon, Clare Valley* | 1994 | $35-50...*B* |
| | 1995 | $30-40...*B* |
| | 1996 | $35-45...*B* |

## GIACONDA

|  |  |  |
|---|---|---|
| *Buffalo River Shiraz, Beechworth* | 1998 | $50-70...*B* |
| *Cabernet Sauvignon, Beechworth* | 1987 | $75-90...*B* |
| | 1990 | $60-76...*B* |
| | 1992 | $66-90...*B* |
| | 1993 | $60-76...*B* |
| | 1994 | $50-70...*B* |
| | 1995 | $60-78...*B* |
| | 1996 | $55-75...*B* |

| Wine | Vintage | Price | Size |
|---|---|---|---|
| | 1997 | $50-70 | B |
| | 1998 | $55-80 | B |
| | 1999 | $50-70 | B |
| *Chardonnay, Beechworth* | 1987 | $110-140 | B |
| | 1991 | $86-95 | B |
| | 1992 | $100-140 | B |
| | 1993 | $100-130 | B |
| | 1994 | $120-160 | B |
| | 1995 | $120-170 | B |
| | 1996 | $130-180 | B |
| | 1997 | $110-150 | B |
| | 1998 | $110-150 | B |
| | 1999 | $120-160 | B |
| | 2000 | $110-140 | B |
| *Pinot Noir, Beechworth* | 1989 | $76-90 | B |
| | 1990 | $76-95 | B |
| | 1991 | $65-90 | B |
| | 1992 | $96-130 | B |
| | 1993 | $80-110 | B |
| | 1994 | $75-90 | B |
| | 1995 | $70-90 | B |
| | 1996 | $90-120 | B |
| | 1997 | $80-110 | B |
| | 1998 | $75-100 | B |
| | 1999 | $70-100 | B |
| *Reserve Cabernet Blend, Beechworth* | 1986 | $75-86 | B |
| *Reserve Chardonnay, Beechworth* | 1987 | $66-85 | B |
| *Shiraz, Beechworth* | 1999 | $66-80 | B |
| *Warner Vineyard Shiraz, Beechworth* | 1999 | $50-65 | B |

## GLAETZER

| Wine | Vintage | Price | Size |
|---|---|---|---|
| *John's Blend 23 Cabernet Sauvignon, Langhorne Creek* | 1996 | $30-40 | B |
| *Shiraz, Barossa Valley* | 1997 | $26-35 | B |
| | 1997 | $95-130 | M |
| | 1998 | $30-40 | B |

## GOUNDREY

| Wine | Vintage | Price | Size |
|---|---|---|---|
| *Reserve Selection Cabernet Sauvignon, Mount Barker* | 1996 | $28-35 | B |

## GRANT BURGE

| Wine | Vintage | Price | Size |
|---|---|---|---|
| *Meshach Shiraz, Barossa Valley* | 1988 | $75-100 | B |
| | 1990 | $130-160 | B |
| | 1990 | $230-300 | M |
| | 1991 | $70-86 | B |
| | 1991 | $180-240 | M |
| | 1992 | $56-75 | B |
| | 1992 | $160-190 | M |
| | 1993 | $60-76 | B |
| | 1993 | $150-190 | M |
| | 1994 | $60-80 | B |
| | 1994 | $130-170 | M |
| | 1995 | $56-70 | B |
| | 1995 | $560-700 | I |
| | 1995 | $150-180 | M |
| | 1996 | $55-75 | B |
| | 1998 | $65-85 | B |
| *MSJ Shiraz Cabernet, Barossa-Coonawarra* | 1996 | $40-50 | B |
| *Shadrach Cabernet Sauvignon, Barossa Valley* | 1993 | $60-85 | M |

## GREENOCK CREEK

|  |  |  |
|---|---|---|
| *Apricot Block Shiraz, Barossa Valley* | 1998 | $70-100...*B* |
| | 1999 | $50-70...*B* |
| *Cabernet Sauvignon, Barossa Valley* | 1996 | $75-100...*B* |
| | 1997 | $45-60...*B* |
| | 1998 | $40-50...*B* |
| | 1999 | $30-40...*B* |
| *Cornerstone Grenache, Barossa Valley* | 1998 | $30-40...*B* |
| *Creek Block Shiraz, Barossa Valley* | 1995 | $45-60...*B* |
| | 1996 | $100-140...*B* |
| | 1998 | $160-220...*B* |
| *Roennfeldt Road Cabernet Sauvignon, Barossa Valley* | 1995 | $330-650...*B* |
| *Roennfeldt Road Shiraz, Barossa Valley* | 1995 | $340-660...*B* |
| | 1996 | $350-500...*B* |
| *Seven Acre Shiraz, Barossa Valley* | 1994 | $70-100...*B* |
| | 1995 | $70-90...*B* |
| | 1996 | $60-80...*B* |
| | 1997 | $60-80...*B* |
| | 1998 | $70-90...*B* |
| *Shiraz, Barossa Valley* | 1988 | $46-55...*B* |
| | 1990 | $380-450..*D* |
| | 1991 | $46-55...*B* |

## GROSSET

|  |  |  |
|---|---|---|
| *Gaia Cabernet Cabernet Franc Merlot, Clare Valley* | 1993 | $36-45...*B* |
| | 1994 | $35-45...*B* |
| | 1995 | $30-40...*B* |
| | 1996 | $35-45...*B* |
| | 1997 | $35-45...*B* |
| | 1998 | $26-35...*B* |
| | 1999 | $30-40...*B* |
| *Piccadilly Chardonnay, Adelaide Hills* | 1995 | $28-35...*B* |
| | 1999 | $30-40...*B* |
| *Pinot Noir, Clare Valley* | 1994 | $26-35...*B* |
| | 1998 | $28-35...*B* |
| *Polish Hill Riesling, Clare Valley* | 1988 | $36-50...*B* |
| | 1990 | $45-56...*B* |
| | 1994 | $40-48...*B* |
| | 1995 | $45-58...*B* |
| | 1996 | $35-45...*B* |
| | 1997 | $35-45...*B* |
| | 1998 | $28-40...*B* |
| | 1999 | $30-40...*B* |
| | 2000 | $28-35...*B* |
| | 2001 | $26-35...*B* |
| *Reserve Pinot Noir, Clare Valley* | 1994 | $33-45...*B* |
| *Watervale Riesling, Clare Valley* | 1997 | $28-40...*B* |
| | 1999 | $26-35...*B* |
| | 2000 | $26-33...*B* |

## HAAN

|  |  |  |
|---|---|---|
| *Bin 38 Prestige Estate Merlot, Barossa Valley* | 1996 | $36-45...*B* |

## HANGING ROCK WINERY

|  |  |  |
|---|---|---|
| *Shiraz, Heathcote* | 1989 | $26-35...*B* |
| | 1990 | $40-50...*B* |
| | 1991 | $30-40...*B* |
| | 1992 | $86-110.*M* |
| | 1997 | $26-35...*B* |

|  |  |  |
|---|---|---|
| | 1998 | $40-50...*B* |
| | 1999 | $35-45...*B* |
| | 2000 | $35-45...*B* |

## HARDY'S

|  |  |  |
|---|---|---|
| *Bin M177 Show Aged Tawny Port, Barossa Valley* | 1954 | $56-70...*B* |
| *Eileen Hardy Cabernet Malbec, S.A.* | 1980 | $28-40...*B* |
| *Eileen Hardy Cabernet Sauvignon, Keppoch* | 1979 | $30-40...*B* |
| *Eileen Hardy Cabernet Sauvignon, McLaren Vale* | 1973 | $26-35...*B* |
| | 1976 | $28-40...*B* |
| *Eileen Hardy Malbec Cabernet, Keppoch* | 1981 | $28-40...*B* |
| *Eileen Hardy Shiraz, S.A.* | 1970 | $76-95...*B* |
| | 1977 | $30-38...*B* |
| | 1987 | $46-55...*B* |
| | 1988 | $46-60...*B* |
| | 1989 | $45-56...*B* |
| | 1990 | $50-65...*B* |
| | 1990 | $190-260.*M* |
| | 1991 | $55-66...*B* |
| | 1991 | $130-170.*M* |
| | 1992 | $46-60...*B* |
| | 1992 | $96-130.*M* |
| | 1993 | $46-60...*B* |
| | 1994 | $50-65...*B* |
| | 1995 | $45-60...*B* |
| | 1996 | $45-60...*B* |
| | 1997 | $45-60...*B* |
| | 1998 | $60-76...*B* |
| *Hardy's Old Brandy, S.A.* | 1946 | $56-75...*B* |
| *Private Bin Hermitage, McLaren Vale* | 1965 | $30-45...*B* |
| *Reserve Bin Cabernet Sauvignon, Coonawarra* | | |
| | 1961 | $55-75...*B* |
| | 1962 | $46-60...*B* |
| | 1963 | $44-55...*B* |
| *Reserve Bin Cabernet Sauvignon, Coonawarra-McLaren Vale* | | |
| | 1962 | $70-95...*B* |
| *Shiraz Mataro, Barossa Valley-McLaren Vale* | 1966 | $46-60...*B* |
| *Show Aged Tawny Port, S.A.* | 1943 | $50-65...*B* |
| | 1947 | $45-60...*B* |
| | 1951 | $40-55...*B* |
| | 1954 | $40-55...*B* |
| *St.Thomas Burgundy* | 1955 | $56-75...*B* |
| | 1959 | $70-96...*B* |
| *Thomas Hardy Cabernet Sauvignon, Coonawarra* | | |
| | 1990 | $36-50...*B* |
| | 1991 | $33-45...*B* |
| | 1992 | $28-36...*B* |
| | 1993 | $30-38...*B* |
| | 1994 | $30-38...*B* |
| *Vintage Port, McLaren Vale* | 1951 | $110-150...*B* |
| | 1954 | $100-140...*B* |
| | 1958 | $80-110...*B* |
| | 1966 | $46-55...*B* |
| | 1967 | $45-60...*B* |
| | 1968 | $35-50...*B* |
| | 1971 | $36-50...*B* |
| | 1973 | $35-45...*B* |
| | 1975 | $38-46...*B* |
| | 1977 | $30-40...*B* |

## HASELGROVE WINES

|  |  |  |
|---|---|---|
| *H Reserve Shiraz, McLaren Vale* | 1996 | $180-230..*D* |

| Wine | Vintage | Price | Size |
|---|---|---|---|
| | 1998 | $80-110 | *M* |

## HENRY'S DRIVE

| Wine | Vintage | Price | Size |
|---|---|---|---|
| *Reserve Shiraz, Padthaway* | 1999 | $50-65 | *B* |

## HENSCHKE

| Wine | Vintage | Price | Size |
|---|---|---|---|
| *Abbotts Prayer Merlot Cabernet, Lenswood* | 1989 | $35-45 | *B* |
| | 1990 | $56-75 | *B* |
| | 1990 | $170-230 | *M* |
| | 1991 | $50-60 | *B* |
| | 1992 | $46-60 | *B* |
| | 1993 | $46-55 | *B* |
| | 1994 | $50-60 | *B* |
| | 1995 | $40-50 | *B* |
| | 1996 | $45-60 | *B* |
| | 1997 | $40-50 | *B* |
| | 1998 | $45-55 | *B* |
| *Cyril Cabernet Sauvignon, Eden Valley* | 1978 | $80-100 | *B* |
| | 1979 | $90-120 | *B* |
| | 1981 | $70-90 | *B* |
| | 1982 | $100-140 | *B* |
| | 1983 | $75-100 | *B* |
| | 1984 | $70-96 | *B* |
| | 1985 | $85-110 | *B* |
| | 1986 | $85-120 | *B* |
| | 1987 | $65-85 | *B* |
| | 1988 | $95-130 | *B* |
| | 1989 | $70-90 | *B* |
| | 1990 | $80-110 | *B* |
| | 1990 | $420-520 | *M* |
| | 1991 | $85-120 | *B* |
| | 1991 | $260-330 | *M* |
| | 1992 | $66-85 | *B* |
| | 1993 | $66-80 | *B* |
| | 1994 | $70-86 | *B* |
| | 1995 | $66-90 | *B* |
| | 1996 | $75-100 | *B* |
| | 1997 | $65-90 | *B* |
| *Giles Pinot Noir, Lenswood* | 1998 | $32-40 | *B* |
| *Hill Of Grace Shiraz, Eden Valley* | 1959 | $750-900 | *B* |
| | 1966 | $240-300 | *B* |
| | 1968 | $140-200 | *B* |
| | 1970 | $166-200 | *B* |
| | 1971 | $120-160 | *B* |
| | 1972 | $110-150 | *B* |
| | 1973 | $130-160 | *B* |
| | 1975 | $96-136 | *B* |
| | 1976 | $140-170 | *B* |
| | 1977 | $130-180 | *B* |
| | 1978 | $170-230 | *B* |
| | 1979 | $140-200 | *B* |
| | 1979 | $500-600 | *M* |
| | 1980 | $160-210 | *B* |
| | 1981 | $140-180 | *B* |
| | 1982 | $160-220 | *B* |
| | 1982 | $510-600 | *M* |
| | 1983 | $210-260 | *B* |
| | 1983 | $430-500 | *M* |
| | 1984 | $190-260 | *B* |
| | 1984 | $470-530 | *M* |
| | 1985 | $160-210 | *B* |
| | 1986 | $320-400 | *B* |

| Wine | Vintage | Price | Size |
|---|---|---|---|
| | 1986 | $560-690 | *M* |
| | 1987 | $200-260 | *B* |
| | 1987 | $510-600 | *M* |
| | 1988 | $210-260 | *B* |
| | 1989 | $170-220 | *B* |
| | 1989 | $360-440 | *M* |
| | 1990 | $360-440 | *B* |
| | 1990 | $730-1,000 | *M* |
| | 1991 | $210-260 | *B* |
| | 1991 | $1,000-1,400 | *D* |
| | 1991 | $3,250-4,350 | *I* |
| | 1992 | $180-240 | *B* |
| | 1993 | $190-260 | *B* |
| | 1994 | $200-260 | *B* |
| | 1995 | $190-250 | *B* |
| | 1996 | $230-300 | *B* |
| *Keyneton Estate Shiraz Cabernet Malbec, Eden Valley* | | | |
| | 1980 | $36-45 | *B* |
| | 1982 | $30-40 | *B* |
| | 1983 | $28-35 | *B* |
| | 1984 | $28-40 | *B* |
| | 1985 | $30-40 | *B* |
| | 1986 | $40-55 | *B* |
| | 1987 | $28-35 | *B* |
| | 1988 | $30-36 | *B* |
| | 1990 | $28-40 | *B* |
| | 1991 | $28-35 | *B* |
| | 1993 | $26-35 | *B* |
| | 1996 | $26-35 | *B* |
| *Malbec, Eden Valley* | 1975 | $36-45 | *B* |
| *Mount Edelstone Shiraz, Eden Valley* | 1963 | $66-85 | *B* |
| | 1967 | $76-100 | *B* |
| | 1969 | $50-70 | *B* |
| | 1970 | $56-75 | *B* |
| | 1972 | $55-76 | *B* |
| | 1975 | $50-70 | *B* |
| | 1980 | $56-75 | *B* |
| | 1982 | $100-140 | *B* |
| | 1983 | $56-76 | *B* |
| | 1984 | $50-70 | *B* |
| | 1985 | $60-80 | *B* |
| | 1986 | $90-120 | *B* |
| | 1987 | $55-75 | *B* |
| | 1988 | $66-85 | *B* |
| | 1989 | $50-66 | *B* |
| | 1990 | $86-110 | *B* |
| | 1990 | $260-330 | *M* |
| | 1991 | $70-95 | *B* |
| | 1991 | $190-250 | *M* |
| | 1992 | $46-66 | *B* |
| | 1993 | $55-66 | *B* |
| | 1994 | $50-66 | *B* |
| | 1995 | $50-60 | *B* |
| | 1996 | $55-70 | *B* |
| | 1997 | $40-55 | *B* |
| | 1998 | $50-70 | *B* |
| *Old Liqueur Tawny Port, Eden Valley* | 1942 | $100-130 | *B* |
| *Vintage Port, Eden Valley* | 1983 | $28-35 | *B* |

## HEWITSON

| Wine | Vintage | Price | Size |
|---|---|---|---|
| *L'Oizeau Shiraz, McLaren Vale* | 1998 | $30-40 | *B* |
| | 1998 | $86-120 | *M* |

| Wine | Vintage | Price | Size |
|---|---|---|---|
| *Shiraz, Barossa Valley* | 1998 | $28-40 | *B* |

## HICKINBOTHAM

| Wine | Vintage | Price | Size |
|---|---|---|---|
| *'Paul' Mornington Peninsula, Chardonnay* | 1998 | $45-60 | *M* |

## HIGHBANK VINEYARDS

| Wine | Vintage | Price | Size |
|---|---|---|---|
| *Basket Press Cabernets, Coonawarra* | 1994 | $26-35 | *B* |

## HOLLICK

| Wine | Vintage | Price | Size |
|---|---|---|---|
| *Cabernet Sauvignon, Coonawarra* | 1984 | $40-55 | *B* |
| *Ravenswood Cabernet Sauvignon, Coonawarra* | | | |
| | 1988 | $35-45 | *B* |
| | 1989 | $35-45 | *B* |
| | 1990 | $40-50 | *B* |
| | 1991 | $30-45 | *B* |
| | 1991 | $80-110 | *M* |
| | 1992 | $33-45 | *B* |
| | 1992 | $86-120 | *M* |
| | 1993 | $30-38 | *B* |
| | 1993 | $76-100 | *M* |
| | 1994 | $30-38 | *B* |
| | 1996 | $30-40 | *B* |

## HOUGHTON

| Wine | Vintage | Price | Size |
|---|---|---|---|
| *Jack Mann Cabernet Shiraz Malbec, Great Southern* | | | |
| | 1994 | $46-60 | *B* |
| | 1994 | $76-100 | *M* |
| | 1995 | $36-45 | *B* |
| | 1995 | $95-130 | *M* |
| | 1996 | $40-50 | *B* |
| | 1996 | $85-120 | *M* |
| *Malbec* | 1958 | $46-55 | *B* |

## HOWARD PARK

| Wine | Vintage | Price | Size |
|---|---|---|---|
| *Cabernets, Western Australia* | 1986 | $75-100 | *B* |
| | 1987 | $70-86 | *B* |
| | 1988 | $70-90 | *B* |
| | 1989 | $56-76 | *B* |
| | 1990 | $80-110 | *B* |
| | 1990 | $270-350 | *M* |
| | 1991 | $66-80 | *B* |
| | 1991 | $190-240 | *M* |
| | 1992 | $56-76 | *B* |
| | 1992 | $180-220 | *M* |
| | 1993 | $60-76 | *B* |
| | 1993 | $140-190 | *M* |
| | 1994 | $50-66 | *B* |
| | 1994 | $170-240 | *M* |
| | 1995 | $45-66 | *B* |
| | 1995 | $140-180 | *M* |
| | 1996 | $55-66 | *B* |
| | 1996 | $150-210 | *M* |
| | 1997 | $50-70 | *B* |
| | 1997 | $130-170 | *M* |
| | 1998 | $55-70 | *B* |
| *Chardonnay, Western Australia* | 1994 | $26-33 | *B* |
| | 1995 | $28-38 | *B* |
| | 1996 | $28-35 | *B* |
| | 1997 | $30-40 | *B* |
| | 1998 | $28-35 | *B* |
| | 1998 | $50-70 | *M* |

## IRVINE GRAND

| Wine | Vintage | Price | Size |
|---|---|---|---|
| *Merlot, Eden Valley* | 1985 | $70-95 | *B* |
| | 1987 | $70-88 | *B* |
| | 1987 | $330-400 | *D* |
| | 1987 | $160-210 | *M* |
| | 1988 | $65-80 | *B* |
| | 1989 | $60-76 | *B* |
| | 1989 | $130-170 | *M* |
| | 1990 | $70-95 | *B* |
| | 1990 | $460-550 | *D* |
| | 1990 | $180-230 | *M* |
| | 1991 | $70-86 | *B* |
| | 1992 | $65-85 | *B* |
| | 1992 | $150-190 | *M* |
| | 1993 | $60-76 | *B* |
| | 1993 | $140-190 | *M* |
| | 1994 | $60-85 | *B* |
| | 1994 | $350-430 | *D* |
| | 1994 | $150-180 | *M* |
| | 1995 | $60-76 | *B* |
| | 1996 | $55-75 | *B* |
| | 1997 | $50-70 | *B* |

## JAMES HASELGROVE

| Wine | Vintage | Price | Size |
|---|---|---|---|
| *Reserve Shiraz, McLaren Vale* | 1996 | $66-85 | *M* |

## JASPER HILL

| Wine | Vintage | Price | Size |
|---|---|---|---|
| *Emilys Paddock Shiraz Cabernet Franc, Heathcote* | | | |
| | 1984 | $80-110 | *B* |
| | 1987 | $100-140 | *B* |
| | 1989 | $70-90 | *B* |
| | 1990 | $100-140 | *B* |
| | 1991 | $85-120 | *B* |
| | 1992 | $85-120 | *B* |
| | 1992 | $260-330 | *M* |
| | 1993 | $75-100 | *B* |
| | 1994 | $90-120 | *B* |
| | 1995 | $220-290 | *M* |
| | 1996 | $75-100 | *B* |
| | 1997 | $100-130 | *B* |
| | 1998 | $110-150 | *B* |
| | 1999 | $100-130 | *B* |
| | 2000 | $80-100 | *B* |
| *Georgia And Friends Dry Red, Heathcote* | 1986 | $46-60 | *B* |
| | 1988 | $50-66 | *B* |
| *Georgia's Paddock Shiraz, Heathcote* | 1982 | $55-75 | *B* |
| | 1984 | $66-86 | *B* |
| | 1985 | $86-120 | *B* |
| | 1986 | $70-90 | *B* |
| | 1989 | $60-76 | *B* |
| | 1990 | $86-110 | *B* |
| | 1990 | $190-250 | *M* |
| | 1991 | $75-100 | *B* |
| | 1991 | $180-250 | *M* |
| | 1992 | $70-95 | *B* |
| | 1992 | $160-200 | *M* |
| | 1993 | $75-96 | *B* |
| | 1994 | $70-96 | *B* |
| | 1995 | $66-85 | *B* |
| | 1995 | $160-210 | *M* |
| | 1996 | $70-90 | *B* |

| | | | |
|---|---|---|---|
| | 1996 | $40-55 | H |
| | 1997 | $70-95 | B |
| | 1997 | $170-240 | M |
| | 1998 | $75-100 | B |
| | 1998 | $40-50 | H |
| | 1998 | $200-240 | M |
| | 1999 | $65-85 | B |
| | 1999 | $30-40 | H |
| | 1999 | $160-210 | M |
| | 2000 | $70-90 | B |
| | 2000 | $160-210 | M |

## JIM BARRY WINES

| | | | |
|---|---|---|---|
| *The Armagh Shiraz, Clare Valley* | 1985 | $120-170 | B |
| | 1987 | $110-140 | B |
| | 1988 | $110-150 | B |
| | 1989 | $110-140 | B |
| | 1990 | $130-170 | B |
| | 1991 | $100-140 | B |
| | 1991 | $240-390 | M |
| | 1992 | $100-140 | B |
| | 1993 | $100-140 | B |
| | 1994 | $110-140 | B |
| | 1995 | $100-140 | B |
| | 1995 | $220-300 | M |
| | 1996 | $110-150 | B |
| | 1997 | $100-140 | B |
| | 1998 | $100-140 | B |

## JOSEPH

*Moda Amarone Cabernet Merlot, McLaren Vale-Coonawarra*

| | | | |
|---|---|---|---|
| | 1987 | $45-56 | B |
| | 1990 | $45-60 | B |
| | 1993 | $36-48 | B |
| | 1994 | $40-55 | B |
| | 1995 | $33-45 | B |
| | 1996 | $36-45 | B |
| | 1997 | $33-44 | B |
| | 1998 | $35-45 | B |
| | 1998 | $80-100 | M |

## KATNOOK ESTATE

| | | | |
|---|---|---|---|
| *Cabernet Sauvignon, Coonawarra* | 1981 | $50-60 | M |
| | 1982 | $60-85 | M |
| | 1984 | $230-280 | I |
| | 1985 | $240-300 | I |
| | 1986 | $36-50 | B |
| | 1986 | $85-120 | M |
| | 1988 | $30-40 | B |
| | 1990 | $40-50 | B |
| | 1990 | $100-140 | M |
| | 1991 | $50-65 | B |
| | 1992 | $40-46 | B |
| | 1993 | $30-45 | B |
| | 1994 | $33-45 | B |
| | 1994 | $380-440 | I |
| | 1994 | $76-100 | M |
| | 1995 | $26-35 | B |
| | 1996 | $30-40 | B |
| | 1996 | $70-90 | M |
| | 1998 | $30-40 | B |
| *Odyssey Cabernet Sauvignon, Coonawarra* | 1991 | $46-60 | B |

| Wine | Year | Price | Size |
|---|---|---|---|
| | 1992 | $46-56 | B |
| | 1994 | $45-58 | B |
| | 1996 | $46-60 | B |
| *Prodigy Shiraz, Coonawarra* | 1997 | $46-60 | B |

## KAY BROS

| Wine | Year | Price | Size |
|---|---|---|---|
| *Amery Block 6 Old Vine Shiraz, McLaren Vale* | 1989 | $56-70 | B |
| | 1992 | $30-56 | B |
| | 1993 | $40-56 | B |
| | 1994 | $46-60 | B |
| | 1995 | $40-56 | B |
| | 1996 | $65-90 | B |
| | 1997 | $26-35 | B |
| | 1998 | $110-150 | B |
| | 1999 | $56-70 | B |

## LAKE'S FOLLY

| Wine | Year | Price | Size |
|---|---|---|---|
| *Reserve Cabernet, Hunter Valley* | 1993 | $44-50 | B |
| | 1993 | $76-100 | M |
| | 1994 | $44-55 | B |
| | 1994 | $86-120 | M |
| *White Label Cabernets, Hunter Valley* | 1967 | $55-75 | B |
| | 1970 | $30-35 | B |
| | 1971 | $30-38 | B |
| | 1972 | $30-45 | B |
| | 1974 | $30-36 | B |
| | 1975 | $28-35 | B |
| | 1976 | $30-40 | B |
| | 1977 | $30-40 | B |
| | 1978 | $35-50 | B |
| | 1979 | $35-45 | B |
| | 1980 | $35-45 | B |
| | 1980 | $440-480 | I |
| | 1980 | $70-100 | M |
| | 1981 | $40-50 | B |
| | 1982 | $35-45 | B |
| | 1983 | $30-40 | B |
| | 1983 | $90-120 | M |
| | 1984 | $30-40 | B |
| | 1985 | $45-60 | B |
| | 1985 | $380-440 | I |
| | 1985 | $86-120 | M |
| | 1986 | $33-40 | B |
| | 1986 | $95-130 | M |
| | 1987 | $30-40 | B |
| | 1987 | $220-280 | D |
| | 1987 | $70-95 | M |
| | 1988 | $40-50 | B |
| | 1988 | $75-100 | M |
| | 1989 | $35-46 | B |
| | 1989 | $140-180 | D |
| | 1989 | $80-110 | M |
| | 1990 | $45-60 | B |
| | 1991 | $35-45 | B |
| | 1991 | $85-120 | M |
| | 1992 | $35-45 | B |
| | 1993 | $35-48 | B |
| | 1994 | $36-50 | B |
| | 1995 | $35-50 | B |
| | 1996 | $35-45 | B |
| | 1996 | $200-280 | D |
| | 1996 | $95-130 | M |

| Wine | Vintage | Price | Size |
|---|---|---|---|
| | 1997 | $35-45 | B |
| | 1997 | $80-110 | M |
| | 1998 | $30-45 | B |
| | 1998 | $160-210 | D |
| | 1998 | $75-100 | M |
| *Yellow Label Chardonnay, Hunter Valley* | 1982 | $30-40 | B |
| | 1983 | $30-40 | B |
| | 1984 | $28-35 | B |
| | 1985 | $30-40 | B |
| | 1986 | $30-40 | B |
| | 1988 | $30-40 | B |
| | 1989 | $28-40 | B |
| | 1990 | $28-40 | B |
| | 1991 | $26-35 | B |
| | 1992 | $28-35 | B |
| | 1993 | $26-35 | B |
| | 1994 | $26-35 | B |
| | 1995 | $28-40 | B |
| | 1996 | $35-45 | B |
| | 1997 | $35-45 | B |
| | 1998 | $35-45 | B |

## LEASINGHAM

| Wine | Vintage | Price | Size |
|---|---|---|---|
| *Bin 56 Cabernet Malbec, Clare Valley* | 1978 | $190-260 | I |
| *Classic Clare Cabernet Sauvignon, Clare Valley* | | | |
| | 1994 | $76-96 | M |
| | 1991 | $28-36 | B |
| | 1993 | $46-65 | M |
| | 1994 | $40-50 | B |
| | 1994 | $76-90 | M |
| | 1995 | $46-65 | M |
| | 1996 | $28-35 | B |
| | 1996 | $75-100 | M |
| | 1998 | $30-40 | B |

## LECONFIELD

| Wine | Vintage | Price | Size |
|---|---|---|---|
| *Cabernet Sauvignon, Coonawarra* | 1986 | $35-46 | B |
| | 1990 | $35-45 | B |
| | 1991 | $60-85 | M |
| | 1992 | $28-35 | B |
| | 1992 | $190-250 | I |
| | 1992 | $70-95 | M |
| | 1993 | $26-35 | B |
| | 1993 | $70-95 | M |
| | 1994 | $26-35 | B |
| | 1994 | $65-85 | M |
| | 1995 | $60-75 | M |
| | 1996 | $28-36 | B |
| | 1996 | $60-80 | M |
| *Reserve Cabernet Sauvignon, Coonawarra* | 1990 | $33-45 | B |
| | 1990 | $86-110 | M |

## LEEUWIN ESTATE

| Wine | Vintage | Price | Size |
|---|---|---|---|
| *Art Series Cabernet Sauvignon, Margaret River* | | | |
| | 1981 | $44-55 | B |
| | 1982 | $56-70 | B |
| | 1982 | $120-160 | M |
| | 1984 | $44-50 | B |
| | 1985 | $44-55 | B |
| | 1985 | $86-110 | M |
| | 1986 | $45-55 | B |
| | 1987 | $45-60 | B |

| Wine | Year | Price | Size |
|---|---|---|---|
| | 1988 | $45-60 | B |
| | 1988 | $110-140 | M |
| | 1989 | $40-55 | B |
| | 1990 | $50-65 | B |
| | 1990 | $120-160 | M |
| | 1991 | $45-65 | B |
| | 1991 | $110-140 | M |
| | 1992 | $40-50 | B |
| | 1992 | $100-140 | M |
| | 1993 | $40-50 | B |
| | 1993 | $110-140 | M |
| | 1994 | $45-58 | B |
| | 1994 | $80-110 | M |
| | 1995 | $45-58 | B |
| | 1996 | $40-50 | B |
| *Art Series Chardonnay, Margaret River* | 1980 | $75-100 | B |
| | 1983 | $70-95 | B |
| | 1983 | $160-220 | M |
| | 1984 | $80-110 | B |
| | 1985 | $70-90 | B |
| | 1986 | $66-90 | B |
| | 1987 | $110-170 | B |
| | 1987 | $260-310 | M |
| | 1988 | $66-85 | B |
| | 1989 | $60-85 | B |
| | 1990 | $66-86 | B |
| | 1991 | $70-86 | B |
| | 1992 | $66-85 | B |
| | 1992 | $150-210 | M |
| | 1993 | $70-90 | B |
| | 1993 | $170-230 | M |
| | 1994 | $70-86 | B |
| | 1995 | $85-110 | B |
| | 1995 | $220-300 | M |
| | 1996 | $60-75 | B |
| | 1996 | $150-200 | M |
| | 1997 | $60-80 | B |
| | 1997 | $150-200 | M |
| | 1998 | $55-75 | B |
| *Art Series Pinot Noir, Margaret River* | 1989 | $26-35 | B |
| | 1993 | $26-35 | B |
| *Cabernet Sauvignon, Margaret River* | 1978 | $46-60 | B |

## LENGS & COOTER

| Wine | Year | Price | Size |
|---|---|---|---|
| *Old Vine Shiraz, Clare Valley* | 1998 | $30-38 | B |

## LENSWOOD VINEYARDS

| Wine | Year | Price | Size |
|---|---|---|---|
| *Lenswood Chardonnay, Adelaide Hills* | 1998 | $26-35 | B |
| *Lenswood Pinot Noir, Adelaide Hills* | 1995 | $28-35 | B |
| | 1996 | $30-45 | B |
| | 1997 | $33-40 | B |
| | 1998 | $30-46 | B |

## LEO BURING

| Wine | Year | Price | Size |
|---|---|---|---|
| *DW 115 Spatlese Riesling, Eden Valley* | 1979 | $28-35 | B |
| *DW318 Show Reserve Auslese Rhine Riesling, Barossa Valley* | 1982 | $28-40 | B |
| *DWC 11 Show Reserve Riesling, Barossa Valley* | 1973 | $46-56 | B |
| *DWC 14 Show Reserve Watervale Spätlese Riesling, Clare Valley* | 1973 | $36-50 | B |
| *DWC 17 Riesling, Eden Valley* | 1973 | $50-66 | B |

*DWE 18 Show Reserve Watervale Spätlese Riesling, Clare Valley* ........ 1975 ........ $30-38...B
*DWF 25 Riesling, Eden Valley* ........ 1976 ........ $35-45...B
*DWG 45 Spätlese Riesling, Barossa Valley* .... 1977 ........ $26-35...B
*DWH 23 Show Reserve Riesling, Eden Valley* 1978 ........ $35-45...B
*DWR 13 Watervale Riesling, Clare Valley* ..... 1988 ........ $26-35...B
*DWS 18 Riesling, Eden Valley* ........ 1989 ........ $28-35...B
*DWT 13 Watervale Riesling, Clare Valley* ...... 1990 ........ $30-44...B
*DWT 17 Riesling, Eden Valley* ........ 1990 ........ $26-35...B
*DWU 17 Riesling, Eden Valley* ........ 1991 ........ $28-36...B
*DWZ 13 Watervale Riesling, Clare Valley* ...... 1970 ........ $33-40...B
*Leonay Watervale Riesling, Clare Valley* ....... 1988 ........ $28-40...B
........ 1991 ........ $26-36...B

## LINDEMANS

*150th Anniversary Cabernet Sauvignon, Coonawarra* ........ 1990 ........ $110-140 .M
*Bin 1270 Porphry Semillon, Hunter Valley* .... 1956 ........ $110-140...B
*Bin 1275 Classic Release Vintage Port, S.A.* .. 1957 ........ $66-80...B
*Bin 1280 Vintage Port, S.A.* ........ 1957 ........ $56-70...B
*Bin 1320 Burgundy Shiraz, Hunter Valley* ..... 1958 ........ $96-120...B
*Bin 1590 (Burgundy) Shiraz, Hunter Valley* ... 1959 ........ $480-570...B
*Bin 2011 (Burgundy) Shiraz, Hunter Valley* ... 1961 ........ $35-45...B
*Bin 3100 (Burgundy) Shiraz, Hunter Valley* ... 1965 ........ $240-300...B
*Bin 3110 (Burgundy) Shiraz, Hunter Valley* ... 1965 ........ $260-350...B
*Bin 3140 Vintage Port, Barossa Valley* ........ 1962 ........ $30-40...B
*Bin 3303 (Burgundy) Shiraz, Hunter Valley* ... 1966 ........ $46-60...B
*Bin 3310 (Burgundy) Shiraz, Hunter Valley* ... 1966 ........ $38-45...B
*Bin 3455 (Riesling) Semillon, Hunter Valley* . 1968 ........ $30-40...B
*Bin 3470 (Burgundy) Semillon, Hunter Valley* 1968 ........ $30-45...B
*Bin 3603 (Burgundy) Shiraz, Hunter Valley* ... 1967 ........ $35-50...B
*Bin 3642 Vintage Port, Rutherglen* ........ 1967 ........ $35-45...B
*Bin 3690 Riesling-Spätlese, Watervale* ........ 1969 ........ $33-45...B
*Bin 3703 (Burgundy) Shiraz, Hunter Valley* ... 1968 ........ $26-35...B
*Bin 3803 (Burgundy) Shiraz, Hunter Valley* ... 1969 ........ $36-50...B
*Bin 3804 (Burgundy) Shiraz, Hunter Valley* ... 1968 ........ $35-45...B
*Bin 3855 Riesling, Hunter Valley* ........ 1970 ........ $66-80...B
*Bin 3875 (Chablis) Semillon, Hunter Valley* .. 1970 ........ $96-130...B
*Bin 3910 (Burgundy) Shiraz, Hunter Valley* ... 1969 ........ $26-35...B
*Bin 4000 (Burgundy) Shiraz, Hunter Valley* ... 1970 ........ $35-45...B
*Bin 4090 Riesling, Watervale* ........ 1971 ........ $28-40...B
*Bin 4103 (Burgundy) Shiraz, Hunter Valley* ... 1970 ........ $28-35...B
*Bin 4103 (Burgundy) Shiraz, Hunter Valley* ... 1970 ........ $65-85 .M
*Bin 4110 (Burgundy) Shiraz, Hunter Valley* ... 1970 ........ $30-40...B
*Bin 4180 Porphyry Sauternes, Hunter Valley* 1967 ........ $45-60...B
*Bin 4215 Shiraz Cabernet, Watervale* ........ 1970 ........ $26-35...B
*Bin 4810 (Burgundy) Shiraz, Hunter Valley* ... 1973 ........ $46-60...B
*Bin 504 Vintage Port, S.A.* ........ 1954 ........ $76-90...B
*Bin 5100 (Burgundy) Shiraz, Hunter Valley* ... 1975 ........ $56-70 .M
*Bin 5103 (Burgundy) Shiraz, Hunter Valley* ... 1975 ........ $26-35...B
*Bin 5104 (Burgundy) Shiraz, Hunter Valley* ... 1975 ........ $50-56 .M
*Bin 5180 Porphyry Sauternes, Hunter Valley* 1975 ........ $28-35...B
*Bin 5181 Porphyry Sauternes, Hunter Valley* 1975 ........ $28-36...B
*Bin 5182 Porphyry Sauternes, Hunter Valley* 1975 ........ $30-40...B
*Bin 5889 Reserve Porphyry Sauternes, Hunter Valley* ........ 1978 ........ $28-35...B
*Bin 6600 (Burgundy) Shiraz, Hunter Valley* ... 1983 ........ $45-60...B
*Bin 6600 (Burgundy) Shiraz, Hunter Valley* ... 1983 ........ $90-120 .M
*Bin 6610 Stevens VineyardHermitage, Hunter River* ........ 1983 ........ $30-40...B
*Bin 7071 Classic Semillon, Hunter Valley* ...... 1987 ........ $28-36...B
*Bin 7400 (Burgundy) Shiraz, Hunter Valley* ... 1987 ........ $26-35...B

*Bin 7600 (Burgundy) Shiraz, Hunter Valley*...1988..............$30-36...*B*
*Bin 7625 Steven Vineyard Shiraz, Hunter Valley*
.............1988..............$28-35...*B*
*Bin 7855 Semillon, Hunter Valley*..............1991..............$26-35...*B*
*Bin 7870 (White Burgundy) Semillon, Hunter Valley*
.............1991..............$28-35...*B*
*Bin 8025 Steven Vineyard Shiraz, Hunter Valley*
.............1990..............$28-35...*B*
*Bin 8200 Reserve Shiraz, Hunter Valley*........1991..............$30-40...*B*
*Bin 8203 (Burgundy) Shiraz, Hunter Valley*...1991..............$26-35...*B*
*Bin 8225 Steven Vineyard Reserve Shiraz, Hunter Valley*
.............1991..............$30-40...*B*
*Bin 8803 Shiraz, Hunter Valley*..............1994..............$26-33...*B*
*Bin 9025 Steven Vineyard Reserve Shiraz, Hunter Valley*
.............1995..............$26-35...*B*
*Limestone Ridge Vineyard Shiraz Cabernet, Coonawarra*
.............1971..............$36-45...*B*
.............1976..............$56-75...*B*
.............1976..........$120-160 .*M*
.............1978..............$30-40...*B*
.............1979..............$46-60...*B*
.............1980..............$36-45...*B*
.............1981..............$36-45...*B*
.............1982..............$40-50...*B*
.............1984..............$40-55...*B*
.............1985..............$35-45...*B*
.............1986..............$46-60...*B*
.............1987..............$28-40...*B*
.............1988..............$35-45...*B*
.............1989..............$26-33...*B*
.............1990..............$36-45...*B*
.............1991..............$40-55...*B*
.............1991............$90-120 .*M*
.............1992..............$28-40...*B*
.............1993..............$28-35...*B*
.............1994..............$28-38...*B*
.............1994..............$76-95 .*M*
.............1996..............$36-45...*B*
.............1996............$80-100 .*M*
.............1997..............$30-40...*B*
.............1998..............$30-40...*B*
*Pyrus Cabernets, Coonawarra*..............1985..............$35-45...*B*
.............1986..............$40-50...*B*
.............1987..............$35-45...*B*
.............1988..............$30-40...*B*
.............1990..............$40-55...*B*
.............1991..............$35-50...*B*
.............1991............$86-120 .*M*
.............1992..............$28-36...*B*
.............1993..............$30-38...*B*
.............1994..............$30-40...*B*
.............1994..............$76-90 .*M*
.............1996..............$28-40...*B*
.............1996..............$60-80 .*M*
*'Special Reserve' Porphyry Semillon Sauternes*
.............1930 .........$410-496...*B*
.............1978..............$28-40...*B*
.............1979..............$28-40...*B*
.............1980..............$46-60...*B*
.............1980............$90-120 .*M*
.............1981..............$28-35...*B*
.............1982..............$35-50...*B*

| | | |
|---|---|---|
| | 1984 | $35-45...B |
| | 1985 | $30-40...B |
| | 1986 | $40-55...B |
| | 1987 | $28-35...B |
| | 1988 | $35-45...B |
| | 1989 | $30-40...B |
| | 1990 | $35-45...B |
| | 1991 | $35-50...B |
| | 1991 | $85-120.M |
| | 1992 | $30-40...B |
| | 1993 | $28-40...B |
| | 1993 | $80-95.M |
| | 1994 | $28-35...B |
| | 1996 | $28-35...B |
| | 1997 | $50-70.M |
| *Long Gully Estate Irma's Cabernet, Yarra Valley* | 1994 | $110-150..D |

## MAGLIERI

| | | |
|---|---|---|
| *Family Reserve Shiraz, McLaren Vale* | 1990 | $30-36...B |
| *Steve MaglieriShiraz, McLaren Vale* | 1994 | $30-38...B |
| | 1995 | $30-40...B |
| | 1998 | $40-50...B |

## MAIN RIDGE ESTATE

| | | |
|---|---|---|
| *Half Acre Pinot Noir, Mornington Peninsula* | 1993 | $33-40...B |
| | 1994 | $33-45...B |
| | 1997 | $36-45...B |
| | 1998 | $30-40...B |

## MAJELLA

| | | |
|---|---|---|
| *Cabernet Sauvignon, Coonawarra* | 1996 | $45-65...B |
| | 1998 | $40-50...B |
| *Riesling, Coonawarra* | 1999 | $46-55.M |
| *Shiraz, Coonawarra* | 1993 | $28-38...B |
| | 1996 | $36-50...B |
| | 1997 | $33-45...B |
| | 1998 | $40-50...B |
| *The Malleea Shiraz Cabernet, Coonawarra* | 1997 | $46-60...B |
| | 1999 | $45-56...B |

## McWILLIAM'S

| | | |
|---|---|---|
| *Mount Pleasant (Hermitage) Shiraz, Hunter Valley* | 1964 | $35-45...B |
| *Mount Pleasant Anne Riesling, Hunter Valley* | 1979 | $33-45...B |
| *Mount Pleasant Cabernet Shiraz, Hunter Valley* | 1967 | $46-60...B |
| *Mount Pleasant Charles Shiraz, Hunter Valley* | 1959 | $76-95...B |
| *Mount Pleasant Elizabeth Semillon, Hunter Valley* | 1979 | $26-35...B |
| *Mount Pleasant Lovedale Semillon, Hunter Valley* | 1984 | $36-45...B |
| | 1986 | $44-50...B |
| *Mount Pleasant Maurice O'shea Shiraz, Hunter Valley* | 1993 | $28-38...B |
| | 1994 | $36-45...B |
| | 1996 | $30-40...B |
| *Mount Pleasant O.H. & O.H. (Hermitage) Shiraz, Hunter Valley* | 1967 | $66-85...B |
| | 1968 | $46-55...B |
| *Mount Pleasant P. & O.P. (Hermitage) Shiraz, Hunter Valley* | 1958 | $86-120...B |

## McWILLIAM'S

|  |  |  |
|---|---|---|
| *Mount Pleasant Philip (Hermitage) Shiraz, Hunter Valley* | 1966 | $28-35...B |
| *Mount Pleasant Pinot Noir Shiraz, Hunter Valley* | 1952 | $96-130...B |
| *Mount Pleasant Richard (Hermitage) Shiraz, Hunter Valley* | 1959 | $66-80...B |
| *Mount Pleasant T.Y. Shiraz, Hunter Valley* | 1942 | $460-580...B |

## MILDARA

|  |  |  |
|---|---|---|
| *Alexanders Dry Red, Coonawarra* | 1990 | $33-40...B |
| | 1963 | $160-220...B |
| | 1966 | $28-35...B |
| *Peppermint Patty Cabernet Sauvignon, Coonawarra* | 1963 | $240-300...B |
| *Yellow Label Cabernet Shiraz, S.A.* | 1963 | $28-40...B |

## MITCHELL WINERY

|  |  |  |
|---|---|---|
| *Cabernet Sauvignon, Clare Valley* | 1991 | $70-96.M |
| | 1993 | $46-65.M |
| *Peppertree Vineyard Shiraz, Clare Valley* | 1990 | $26-35...B |

## MITCHELTON WINES

|  |  |  |
|---|---|---|
| *Preece Cabernet Sauvignon, Goulburn Valley* | 1991 | $220-290....I |
| | 1995 | $56-70..D |
| | 1995 | $150-200....I |
| | 1995 | $35-45.M |
| *Preece Chardonnay, Goulburn Valley* | 1996 | $45-60..D |
| *Print Label Cabernet Sauvignon, Goulburn Valley* | 1993 | $30-40...B |
| *Print Label Shiraz, Goulburn Valley* | 1990 | $40-46...B |
| | 1991 | $30-40...B |
| | 1995 | $30-36...B |
| | 1996 | $30-40...B |
| | 1996 | $66-85.M |

## MOORILLA ESTATE

|  |  |  |
|---|---|---|
| *Reserve Pinot Noir, Southern Tasmania* | 1997 | $26-35...B |

## MORRIS WINES

|  |  |  |
|---|---|---|
| *Aged Tawny Port, Rutherglen* | 1954 | $44-55...B |
| *Bin 241 Aged Tawny Port, Rutherglen* | 1961 | $26-35...B |
| *Durif, Rutherglen* | 1986 | $70-95.M |
| | 1987 | $66-80.M |
| *Mick Morris Premium Selection Durif, Rutherglen* | 1990 | $26-35...B |

## MOSS WOOD

|  |  |  |
|---|---|---|
| *Cabernet Sauvignon, Margaret River* | 1974 | $160-190...B |
| | 1975 | $160-180...B |
| | 1976 | $140-180...B |
| | 1977 | $110-160...B |
| | 1979 | $85-120...B |
| | 1980 | $110-160...B |
| | 1981 | $100-140...B |
| | 1982 | $100-140...B |
| | 1983 | $86-110...B |
| | 1984 | $100-140...B |
| | 1985 | $100-140...B |
| | 1986 | $110-140...B |
| | 1987 | $80-110...B |
| | 1988 | $100-130...B |

| | | |
|---|---|---|
| | 1989 | $110-160...B |
| | 1990 | $120-170...B |
| | 1991 | $100-140...B |
| | 1992 | $95-130...B |
| | 1993 | $90-110...B |
| | 1993 | $280-390.M |
| | 1994 | $80-110...B |
| | 1994 | $260-330.M |
| | 1995 | $100-130...B |
| | 1995 | $300-390.M |
| | 1996 | $90-120...B |
| | 1996 | $180-240.M |
| | 1997 | $80-110...B |
| | 1997 | $200-280.M |
| | 1998 | $80-110...B |
| *Chardonnay, Margaret River* | 1986 | $28-35...B |
| | 1990 | $30-40...B |
| | 1991 | $26-35...B |
| | 1995 | $28-35...B |
| | 1996 | $40-50...B |
| | 1997 | $28-40...B |
| | 1998 | $40-50...B |
| *Chardonnay, Pemberton* | 1997 | $26-35...B |
| | 1998 | $28-40...B |
| *Glenmore Vineyard Cabernet Sauvignon, Margaret River* | | |
| | 1997 | $30-40...B |
| | 1998 | $33-40...B |
| | 1999 | $26-36...B |
| *Pinot Noir, Margaret River* | 1989 | $26-35...B |
| | 1990 | $40-50...B |
| | 1993 | $28-36...B |
| | 1995 | $35-45...B |
| | 1996 | $26-35...B |
| | 1997 | $28-35...B |
| | 1998 | $28-35...B |
| *Pinot Noir, Pemberton* | 1995 | $28-40...B |
| *Semillon, Margaret River* | 1981 | $30-40...B |
| | 1995 | $26-35...B |
| | 1997 | $30-40...B |
| *Special Reserve Cabernet Sauvignon, Margaret River* | | |
| | 1983 | $130-180...B |
| | 1987 | $140-180...B |
| | 1990 | $120-160...B |
| | 1991 | $130-170...B |
| | 1994 | $100-130...B |

## MOUNT LANGI GHIRAN VINEYARDS

| | | |
|---|---|---|
| *Langi Cabernets, Grampians* | 1989 | $95-130.M |
| | 1990 | $45-60...B |
| | 1991 | $70-95.M |
| | 1993 | $28-36...B |
| | 1994 | $28-35...B |
| *Langi Shiraz, Grampians* | 1985 | $46-65...B |
| | 1986 | $66-90...B |
| | 1988 | $45-65...B |
| | 1989 | $40-50...B |
| | 1990 | $55-70...B |
| | 1991 | $44-55...B |
| | 1991 | $110-140.M |
| | 1992 | $38-50...B |
| | 1992 | $110-150.M |
| | 1993 | $35-50...B |

| Wine | Vintage | Price | Size |
|---|---|---|---|
| | 1994 | $40-48 | *B* |
| | 1995 | $45-58 | *B* |
| | 1996 | $45-60 | *B* |
| | 1996 | $100-130 | *M* |
| | 1997 | $35-45 | *B* |
| | 1998 | $40-50 | *B* |

## MOUNT MARY

| Wine | Vintage | Price | Size |
|---|---|---|---|
| *Chardonnay, Yarra Valley* | 1977 | $30-40 | *B* |
| | 1978 | $50-70 | *B* |
| | 1979 | $35-45 | *B* |
| | 1981 | $40-55 | *B* |
| | 1982 | $35-45 | *B* |
| | 1986 | $35-50 | *B* |
| | 1987 | $28-35 | *B* |
| | 1988 | $28-40 | *B* |
| | 1989 | $30-45 | *B* |
| | 1990 | $45-60 | *B* |
| | 1991 | $30-45 | *B* |
| | 1992 | $36-50 | *B* |
| | 1993 | $35-46 | *B* |
| | 1994 | $36-50 | *B* |
| | 1995 | $40-55 | *B* |
| | 1996 | $40-50 | *B* |
| | 1997 | $30-40 | *B* |
| | 1998 | $45-60 | *B* |
| | 2000 | $40-50 | *B* |
| *Pinot Noir, Yarra Valley* | 1977 | $55-75 | *B* |
| | 1978 | $55-75 | *B* |
| | 1979 | $45-60 | *B* |
| | 1980 | $56-65 | *B* |
| | 1981 | $35-45 | *B* |
| | 1982 | $60-75 | *B* |
| | 1983 | $56-75 | *B* |
| | 1984 | $50-65 | *B* |
| | 1985 | $66-90 | *B* |
| | 1986 | $65-86 | *B* |
| | 1987 | $66-90 | *B* |
| | 1987 | $130-180 | *M* |
| | 1988 | $60-80 | *B* |
| | 1989 | $60-80 | *B* |
| | 1990 | $75-96 | *B* |
| | 1990 | $44-55 | *H* |
| | 1990 | $180-240 | *M* |
| | 1991 | $85-100 | *B* |
| | 1991 | $160-190 | *M* |
| | 1992 | $65-80 | *B* |
| | 1993 | $66-80 | *B* |
| | 1993 | $140-190 | *M* |
| | 1994 | $60-85 | *B* |
| | 1994 | $140-190 | *M* |
| | 1995 | $60-85 | *B* |
| | 1995 | $140-180 | *M* |
| | 1996 | $70-95 | *B* |
| | 1997 | $75-100 | *B* |
| | 1997 | $30-40 | *H* |
| | 1998 | $70-90 | *B* |
| *Quintet Cabernets, Yarra Valley* | 1976 | $260-350 | *B* |
| | 1977 | $170-220 | *B* |
| | 1978 | $160-220 | *B* |
| | 1979 | $140-190 | *B* |
| | 1980 | $95-130 | *B* |

| Wine | Vintage | Price | Size |
|---|---|---|---|
| | 1980 | $40-50 | *H* |
| | 1980 | $360-480 | *M* |
| | 1981 | $86-110 | *B* |
| | 1981 | $300-400 | *M* |
| | 1982 | $140-190 | *B* |
| | 1982 | $370-440 | *M* |
| | 1983 | $85-120 | *B* |
| | 1983 | $320-440 | *M* |
| | 1984 | $95-130 | *B* |
| | 1984 | $460-540 | *M* |
| | 1985 | $100-130 | *B* |
| | 1985 | $360-480 | *M* |
| | 1986 | $160-200 | *B* |
| | 1986 | $460-580 | *M* |
| | 1987 | $75-110 | *B* |
| | 1987 | $290-400 | *M* |
| | 1988 | $120-160 | *B* |
| | 1989 | $80-110 | *B* |
| | 1990 | $200-260 | *B* |
| | 1990 | $65-85 | *H* |
| | 1990 | $660-800 | *M* |
| | 1991 | $140-180 | *B* |
| | 1991 | $50-56 | *H* |
| | 1991 | $290-380 | *M* |
| | 1992 | $100-140 | *B* |
| | 1992 | $66-80 | *H* |
| | 1992 | $360-440 | *M* |
| | 1993 | $100-140 | *B* |
| | 1993 | $950-1,250 | *D* |
| | 1993 | $310-400 | *M* |
| | 1994 | $100-130 | *B* |
| | 1994 | $750-1,050 | *D* |
| | 1994 | $350-430 | *M* |
| | 1995 | $90-120 | *B* |
| | 1995 | $46-65 | *H* |
| | 1996 | $100-130 | *B* |
| | 1996 | $350-500 | *M* |
| | 1997 | $110-150 | *B* |
| | 1997 | $36-45 | *H* |
| | 1998 | $95-130 | *B* |
| | 1999 | $90-120 | *B* |
| *Triolet Semillon Sauvignon Blanc Muscadelle, Yarra Valley* | | | |
| | 1991 | $30-36 | *B* |
| | 1992 | $28-36 | *B* |
| | 1993 | $26-36 | *B* |
| | 1994 | $26-35 | *B* |
| | 1995 | $35-45 | *B* |
| | 1996 | $26-35 | *B* |
| | 1997 | $26-35 | *B* |
| *Mount Pleasant Hunter Valley Dry Red* | 1947 | $96-140 | *B* |

## MOUNTADAM

| Wine | Vintage | Price | Size |
|---|---|---|---|
| *Chardonnay, Eden Valley* | 1994 | $30-40 | *B* |
| | 1996 | $30-40 | *B* |
| | 1997 | $30-45 | *B* |
| *The Red Cabernet Merlot, Eden Valley* | 1991 | $75-96 | *M* |
| | 1994 | $30-40 | *B* |
| | 1996 | $33-40 | *B* |

## NICHOLSON RIVER WINERY

| Wine | Vintage | Price | Size |
|---|---|---|---|
| *Cabernets, Gippsland* | 1994 | $28-40 | *B* |
| *Chardonnay, Gippsland* | 1994 | $36-45 | *B* |

| Wine | Vintage | Price | Size |
|---|---|---|---|
| | 1995 | $28-36 | B |
| | 1995 | $50-70 | M |
| *Pinot Noir, Gippsland* | 1996 | $26-35 | B |

## NOON WINERY

| Wine | Vintage | Price | Size |
|---|---|---|---|
| *Eclipse Blend Grenache Shiraz, McLaren Vale* | 1997 | $75-100 | B |
| | 1998 | $65-85 | B |
| | 1999 | $90-120 | B |
| | 2000 | $65-85 | B |
| *Grenache Shiraz, McLaren Vale* | 1996 | $46-60 | B |
| *Reserve Cabernet Sauvignon, Langhorne Creek* | 1996 | $160-200 | B |
| | 1997 | $85-120 | B |
| | 1998 | $110-140 | B |
| | 1999 | $75-100 | B |
| *Reserve Shiraz, Langhorne Creek* | 1997 | $110-140 | B |
| | 1998 | $110-140 | B |
| | 1999 | $110-150 | B |
| *Shiraz Pressings, McLaren Vale* | 1992 | $33-55 | B |
| *Solaire Reserve Grenache, McLaren Vale* | 1996 | $36-45 | B |
| *Traditional Red Shiraz, Langhorne Creek* | 1991 | $33-46 | B |
| | 1993 | $40-56 | B |
| *Vintage Port, McLaren Vale* | 1985 | $30-40 | B |

## ORLANDO

| Wine | Vintage | Price | Size |
|---|---|---|---|
| *Cabernet Sauvignon, Barossa Valley* | 1970 | $75-96 | B |
| *Centenary Hills Shiraz, Barossa Valley* | 1995 | $26-36 | B |
| *Jacaranda Ridge Cabernet Sauvignon, Coonawarra* | 1982 | $36-50 | B |
| | 1986 | $36-45 | B |
| | 1987 | $28-35 | B |
| | 1988 | $30-40 | B |
| | 1989 | $26-35 | B |
| | 1991 | $30-40 | B |
| | 1991 | $96-130 | M |
| | 1992 | $30-40 | B |
| | 1994 | $28-35 | B |
| | 1996 | $38-50 | B |
| *Lawson's Shiraz, Padthaway* | 1984 | $33-40 | B |
| | 1985 | $36-46 | B |
| | 1986 | $38-45 | B |
| | 1987 | $26-36 | B |
| | 1988 | $35-45 | B |
| | 1989 | $26-33 | B |
| | 1990 | $36-50 | B |
| | 1991 | $36-50 | B |
| | 1992 | $28-36 | B |
| | 1992 | $85-120 | M |
| | 1993 | $28-38 | B |
| | 1994 | $33-40 | B |
| | 1996 | $35-50 | B |
| *St. Hugo Cabernet Sauvignon, Coonawarra* | 1981 | $30-40 | B |
| | 1982 | $26-35 | B |
| | 1984 | $30-38 | B |
| | 1985 | $35-45 | B |
| | 1986 | $35-45 | B |
| | 1988 | $30-40 | B |
| | 1988 | $76-100 | M |
| | 1989 | $28-36 | B |
| | 1990 | $45-65 | B |
| | 1991 | $40-50 | B |
| | 1991 | $66-85 | M |

| | | | |
|---|---|---|---|
| | 1992 | $30-40 | *B* |
| | 1992 | $80-110 | *M* |
| | 1993 | $28-36 | *B* |
| | 1994 | $33-45 | *B* |
| | 1996 | $30-40 | *B* |
| | 1997 | $26-35 | *B* |
| | 1998 | $26-35 | *B* |
| *Steingarten Classic Maturation Release Riesling, Eden Valley* | 1980 | $33-45 | *B* |
| *Steingarten Riesling, Eden Valley* | 1970 | $26-35 | *B* |
| *Tawny Port, Barossa Valley* | 1935 | $60-85 | *B* |
| | 1940 | $55-70 | *B* |
| | 1947 | $40-55 | *B* |
| | 1948 | $50-65 | *B* |
| | 1951 | $40-55 | *B* |
| | 1955 | $40-55 | *B* |
| | 1957 | $45-60 | *B* |
| | 1959 | $30-45 | *B* |
| | 1963 | $33-45 | *B* |

## PARINGA ESTATE

| | | | |
|---|---|---|---|
| *Pinot Noir, Mornington Peninsula* | 1995 | $28-35 | *B* |
| | 1996 | $30-40 | *B* |
| | 1997 | $50-70 | *B* |
| | 1998 | $30-40 | *B* |
| *Shiraz, Mornington Peninsula* | 1992 | $30-40 | *B* |
| | 1993 | $30-38 | *B* |

## PARKER COONAWARRA ESTATE

| | | | |
|---|---|---|---|
| *Terra Rossa 1st Growth Cabernet Merlot Cabernet Franc, Coonawarra* | 1988 | $70-86 | *B* |
| | 1989 | $50-66 | *B* |
| | 1990 | $76-90 | *B* |
| | 1991 | $70-96 | *B* |
| | 1993 | $66-80 | *B* |
| | 1994 | $66-85 | *B* |
| | 1995 | $46-60 | *B* |
| | 1996 | $65-85 | *B* |
| | 1998 | $65-80 | *B* |
| *Terra Rossa Cabernet Sauvignon, Coonawarra* | 1997 | $26-35 | *B* |

## PENFOLDS

| | | | |
|---|---|---|---|
| *5 Star Club Tawny Port, S.A.* | 1945 | $50-70 | *B* |
| | 1950 | $75-96 | *B* |
| | 1953 | $50-65 | *B* |
| | 1956 | $36-45 | *B* |
| *Bin 1 Grange Shiraz, S.A.* | 1951 | $41,000-46,000 | *B* |
| *Bin 10 Grange Shiraz, S.A.* | 1953 | $11,000-13,800 | *B* |
| | 1953 | $3,850-5,200 | *H* |
| *Bin 11 Grange Shiraz, S.A.* | 1954 | $9,100-12,600 | *B* |
| *Bin 12 Grange Shiraz, S.A.* | 1954 | $12,100-15,550 | *B* |
| *Bin 128 Shiraz, Coonawarra* | 1962 | $44-50 | *B* |
| | 1966 | $40-50 | *B* |
| | 1968 | $30-40 | *B* |
| | 1969 | $38-45 | *B* |
| | 1970 | $28-35 | *B* |
| | 1980 | $26-35 | *B* |
| | 1982 | $26-35 | *B* |
| | 1986 | $28-40 | *B* |
| | 1990 | $28-35 | *B* |

| Wine | Vintage | Price | Size |
|---|---|---|---|
| *Bin 13 Grange Shiraz, S.A.* | 1955 | $1,700-2,450 | *B* |
| *Bin 14 Grange Shiraz, S.A.* | 1955 | $1,850-2,300 | *B* |
| | 1956 | $11,000-13,600 | *B* |
| *Bin 21 Shiraz, Coonawarra* | 1982 | $35-45 | *B* |
| *Bin 28 Shiraz, Kalimna* | 1966 | $35-50 | *B* |
| | 1968 | $40-55 | *B* |
| | 1969 | $30-40 | *B* |
| | 1971 | $30-40 | *B* |
| | 1975 | $26-35 | *B* |
| | 1976 | $30-40 | *B* |
| | 1980 | $26-35 | *B* |
| | 1982 | $28-35 | *B* |
| | 1986 | $30-40 | *B* |
| | 1990 | $26-35 | *B* |
| *Bin 389 Cabernet Shiraz, S.A.* | 1961 | $66-85 | *B* |
| | 1964 | $50-60 | *B* |
| | 1966 | $76-90 | *B* |
| | 1967 | $76-90 | *B* |
| | 1969 | $46-60 | *B* |
| | 1970 | $50-65 | *B* |
| | 1971 | $66-80 | *B* |
| | 1972 | $30-40 | *B* |
| | 1973 | $36-40 | *B* |
| | 1974 | $30-40 | *B* |
| | 1975 | $36-50 | *B* |
| | 1976 | $56-75 | *B* |
| | 1977 | $30-40 | *B* |
| | 1979 | $28-35 | *B* |
| | 1980 | $36-48 | *B* |
| | 1981 | $28-40 | *B* |
| | 1982 | $40-55 | *B* |
| | 1983 | $40-55 | *B* |
| | 1984 | $30-36 | *B* |
| | 1985 | $30-35 | *B* |
| | 1986 | $50-66 | *B* |
| | 1987 | $28-35 | *B* |
| | 1988 | $30-38 | *B* |
| | 1990 | $50-70 | *B* |
| | 1991 | $38-50 | *B* |
| | 1992 | $28-35 | *B* |
| | 1993 | $28-35 | *B* |
| | 1994 | $30-35 | *B* |
| | 1994 | $80-110 | *M* |
| | 1995 | $60-80 | *M* |
| | 1996 | $36-45 | *B* |
| | 1996 | $110-150 | *M* |
| | 1997 | $60-76 | *M* |
| | 1998 | $26-35 | *B* |
| *Bin 4 Grange Shiraz, S.A.* | 1952 | $15,100-18,400 | *B* |
| | 1952 | $3,160-4,200 | *H* |
| *Bin 407 Cabernet Sauvignon, S.A.* | 1990 | $35-46 | *B* |
| | 1991 | $30-45 | *B* |
| | 1996 | $26-32 | *B* |
| *Bin 414 Special Show Sauternes, S.A.* | 1962 | $70-95 | *B* |
| *Bin 46 Grange Shiraz, S.A.* | 1958 | $12,300-16,100 | *B* |
| | 1959 | $1,250-1,600 | *B* |
| | 1960 | $800-1,050 | *B* |
| *Bin 465 Shiraz Cabernet, Magill* | 1959 | $270-350 | *B* |
| *Bin 480 Vintage Port, Barossa Valley* | 1958 | $85-120 | *B* |
| *Bin 49 Grange Shiraz, S.A.* | 1958 | $9,800-13,500 | *B* |
| | 1960 | $760-1,050 | *B* |
| *Bin 50 Grange Shiraz, S.A.* | 1957 | $12,000-16,100 | *B* |

| Wine | Vintage | Price | Size |
|---|---|---|---|
| *Bin 51 Shiraz Mataro, Magill* | 1960 | $110-150 | *B* |
| *Bin 53 Grange Shiraz, S.A.* | 1956 | $12,000-13,600 | *B* |
| *Bin 556 Burgundy Shiraz, Magill* | 1956 | $140-200 | *B* |
| *Bin 58 Cabernet Shiraz, Kalimna* | 1961 | $96-130 | *B* |
| *Bin 60A Cabernet Shiraz, Kalimna-Coonawarra* | 1962 | $540-660 | *B* |
| *Bin 61 Shiraz, Kalimna-Eden Valley* | 1963 | $76-100 | *B* |
| *Bin 620 Cabernet Shiraz, Coonawarra* | 1966 | $180-250 | *B* |
| *Bin 621 Vintage Port, Barossa Valley* | 1962 | $50-65 | *B* |
| *Bin 63 Cabernet Shiraz, Magill-Eden Valley* | 1963 | $100-130 | *B* |
| *Bin 630 Vintage Port, Barossa Valley* | 1964 | $55-70 | *B* |
| *Bin 7 Cabernet Shiraz, Coonawarra-Kalimna* | 1967 | $260-500 | *B* |
| *Bin 707 Cabernet Sauvignon, S.A.* | 1965 | $100-140 | *B* |
| | 1966 | $190-260 | *B* |
| | 1967 | $95-130 | *B* |
| | 1968 | $40-55 | *B* |
| | 1969 | $70-95 | *B* |
| | 1976 | $110-150 | *B* |
| | 1977 | $85-110 | *B* |
| | 1978 | $80-110 | *B* |
| | 1979 | $76-100 | *B* |
| | 1980 | $75-100 | *B* |
| | 1980 | $80-110 | *M* |
| | 1982 | $95-130 | *B* |
| | 1982 | $180-240 | *M* |
| | 1983 | $86-110 | *B* |
| | 1983 | $140-180 | *M* |
| | 1984 | $80-96 | *B* |
| | 1984 | $120-170 | *M* |
| | 1985 | $75-100 | *B* |
| | 1985 | $160-220 | *M* |
| | 1986 | $100-136 | *B* |
| | 1986 | $210-290 | *M* |
| | 1987 | $70-90 | *B* |
| | 1987 | $170-230 | *M* |
| | 1988 | $80-90 | *B* |
| | 1988 | $160-200 | *M* |
| | 1989 | $75-90 | *B* |
| | 1989 | $160-200 | *M* |
| | 1990 | $110-146 | *B* |
| | 1990 | $220-280 | *M* |
| | 1991 | $80-100 | *B* |
| | 1991 | $200-270 | *M* |
| | 1992 | $70-90 | *B* |
| | 1992 | $130-180 | *M* |
| | 1993 | $75-90 | *B* |
| | 1993 | $150-200 | *M* |
| | 1994 | $76-100 | *B* |
| | 1994 | $180-250 | *M* |
| | 1996 | $75-100 | *B* |
| | 1996 | $190-260 | *M* |
| | 1997 | $60-80 | *B* |
| | 1997 | $120-170 | *M* |
| | 1998 | $75-100 | *B* |
| | 1998 | $170-230 | *M* |
| *Bin 80A Cabernet Shiraz, Coonawarra-Kalimna* | 1980 | $150-180 | *B* |
| *Bin 820 Cabernet Shiraz, Coonawarra* | 1982 | $140-180 | *B* |
| *Bin 868 Sauternes, S.A.* | 1967 | $80-110 | *B* |
| *Bin 9 Grange Cabernet, S.A.* | 1953 | $6,600-11,400 | *B* |
| *Bin 90A Cabernet Shiraz, Coonawarra-Barossa Valley* | 1990 | $176-240 | *B* |

| Wine | Vintage | Price | Size |
|---|---|---|---|
| *Bin 920 Cabernet Shiraz, Coonawarra* | 1990 | $156-210 | *B* |
| *Bin 95 Grange Shiraz, S.A.* | 1955 | $1,800-2,200 | *B* |
| | 1959 | $1,300-1,750 | *B* |
| | 1960 | $960-1,310 | *B* |
| | 1961 | $800-1,050 | *B* |
| | 1962 | $600-800 | *B* |
| | 1963 | $600-750 | *B* |
| | 1964 | $540-650 | *B* |
| | 1965 | $360-450 | *B* |
| | 1966 | $420-500 | *B* |
| | 1967 | $270-350 | *B* |
| | 1968 | $200-250 | *B* |
| | 1969 | $220-290 | *B* |
| | 1970 | $220-290 | *B* |
| | 1971 | $510-650 | *B* |
| | 1972 | $220-290 | *B* |
| | 1973 | $220-290 | *B* |
| | 1974 | $230-300 | *B* |
| | 1975 | $200-280 | *B* |
| | 1976 | $360-450 | *B* |
| | 1977 | $220-290 | *B* |
| | 1978 | $220-290 | *B* |
| | 1979 | $220-290 | *B* |
| | 1979 | $960-1700 | *M* |
| | 1980 | $230-300 | *B* |
| | 1980 | $900-1,350 | *M* |
| | 1981 | $230-300 | *B* |
| | 1981 | $900-1,200 | *M* |
| | 1982 | $220-290 | *B* |
| | 1982 | $900-1200 | *M* |
| | 1983 | $290-350 | *B* |
| | 1983 | $900-1200 | *M* |
| | 1984 | $230-300 | *B* |
| | 1984 | $900-1100 | *M* |
| | 1985 | $220-300 | *B* |
| | 1985 | $14,900-20,150 | *I* |
| | 1985 | $850-1,050 | *M* |
| | 1986 | $400-500 | *B* |
| | 1986 | $1,000-1,250 | *M* |
| | 1987 | $220-290 | *B* |
| | 1987 | $800-950 | *M* |
| | 1988 | $220-290 | *B* |
| | 1988 | $900-1,100 | *M* |
| | 1989 | $220-280 | *B* |
| | 1989 | $850-1,050 | *M* |
| | 1990 | $440-530 | *B* |
| | 1990 | $1,000-1,400 | *M* |
| | 1991 | $280-350 | *B* |
| | 1991 | $900-1,250 | *M* |
| | 1992 | $230-290 | *B* |
| | 1992 | $950-1,250 | *M* |
| | 1993 | $230-290 | *B* |
| | 1993 | $900-1,100 | *M* |
| | 1994 | $220-290 | *B* |
| | 1994 | $900-1,200 | *M* |
| | 1995 | $210-260 | *B* |
| | 1995 | $900-1,200 | *M* |
| | 1996 | $260-350 | *B* |
| | 1996 | $21,250 | *I* |
| | 1996 | $1,000-1,450 | *M* |
| *Bin 95a Reserve Chardonnay, Adelaide Hills* | 1995 | $46-65 | *B* |

| Wine | Vintage | Price | Size |
|---|---|---|---|
| *Block 42 Kalimna Cabernet Sauvignon, Barossa Valley* | 1996 | $190-260 | *B* |
| *Club Port, Barossa Valley* | 1956 | $28-40 | *B* |
| *Dalwood Claret Cabernet Shiraz, S.A.* | 1965 | $46-60 | *B* |
| | 1966 | $26-35 | *B* |
| *Grandfather Aged Tawny Port, S.A.* | 1940 | $85-120 | *B* |
| | 1945 | $85-110 | *B* |
| *Old Tawny Port, S.A.* | 1940 | $56-75 | *B* |
| *Rwt Shiraz, Barossa Valley* | 1997 | $70-90 | *B* |
| | 1998 | $80-100 | *B* |
| | 1998 | $260-330 | *M* |
| *Shiraz Ouillade, S.A.* | 1969 | $28-35 | *B* |
| *St. Henri Shiraz Cabernet, S.A.* | 1955 | $230-300 | *B* |
| | 1961 | $90-120 | *B* |
| | 1962 | $76-85 | *B* |
| | 1963 | $66-85 | *B* |
| | 1964 | $76-100 | *B* |
| | 1965 | $60-80 | *B* |
| | 1966 | $75-100 | *B* |
| | 1967 | $76-95 | *B* |
| | 1968 | $50-65 | *B* |
| | 1969 | $46-55 | *B* |
| | 1970 | $40-50 | *B* |
| | 1971 | $66-85 | *B* |
| | 1972 | $40-50 | *B* |
| | 1973 | $30-40 | *B* |
| | 1974 | $30-40 | *B* |
| | 1975 | $50-65 | *B* |
| | 1976 | $70-95 | *B* |
| | 1977 | $35-45 | *B* |
| | 1978 | $40-55 | *B* |
| | 1979 | $36-45 | *B* |
| | 1980 | $46-55 | *B* |
| | 1980 | $140-180 | *M* |
| | 1981 | $40-50 | *B* |
| | 1982 | $45-55 | *B* |
| | 1982 | $100-130 | *M* |
| | 1983 | $35-45 | *B* |
| | 1983 | $110-150 | *M* |
| | 1984 | $40-50 | *B* |
| | 1985 | $36-45 | *B* |
| | 1985 | $95-130 | *M* |
| | 1986 | $60-75 | *B* |
| | 1986 | $110-140 | *M* |
| | 1987 | $30-40 | *B* |
| | 1987 | $90-120 | *M* |
| | 1988 | $40-50 | *B* |
| | 1988 | $100-140 | *M* |
| | 1989 | $30-40 | *B* |
| | 1989 | $85-120 | *M* |
| | 1990 | $50-66 | *B* |
| | 1990 | $140-190 | *M* |
| | 1991 | $40-50 | *B* |
| | 1991 | $100-140 | *M* |
| | 1992 | $35-45 | *B* |
| | 1992 | $85-110 | *M* |
| | 1993 | $40-50 | *B* |
| | 1993 | $76-100 | *M* |
| | 1994 | $35-45 | *B* |
| | 1994 | $90-120 | *M* |
| | 1995 | $30-40 | *B* |
| | 1995 | $80-110 | *M* |

| Wine | Vintage | Price | Size |
|---|---|---|---|
| | 1996 | $50-65 | *B* |
| | 1996 | $100-130 | *M* |
| | 1997 | $30-40 | *B* |
| | 1997 | $80-100 | *M* |
| *The Magill Estate Shiraz, Magill* | 1983 | $45-60 | *B* |
| | 1985 | $36-45 | *B* |
| | 1986 | $40-55 | *B* |
| | 1987 | $35-45 | *B* |
| | 1988 | $40-50 | *B* |
| | 1989 | $35-45 | *B* |
| | 1990 | $46-60 | *B* |
| | 1991 | $46-60 | *B* |
| | 1992 | $35-45 | *B* |
| | 1993 | $33-45 | *B* |
| | 1994 | $35-46 | *B* |
| | 1995 | $35-45 | *B* |
| | 1996 | $40-50 | *B* |
| | 1997 | $38-45 | *B* |
| *Trial Bin Chardonnay, Adelaide Hills* | 1996 | $26-35 | *B* |
| *Yattarna Chardonnay, S.A.* | 1995 | $70-90 | *B* |
| | 1996 | $70-95 | *B* |
| | 1997 | $70-90 | *B* |
| | 1998 | $70-90 | *B* |

## PENLEY ESTATE

| Wine | Vintage | Price | Size |
|---|---|---|---|
| *Ausvietia Shiraz, Coonawarra* | 1995 | $30-40 | *B* |
| *Cabernet Sauvignon, Coonawarra* | 1989 | $30-40 | *B* |
| | 1990 | $33-45 | *B* |
| | 1993 | $28-40 | *B* |
| | 1994 | $30-40 | *B* |
| | 1995 | $26-35 | *B* |
| | 1996 | $26-35 | *B* |
| | 1997 | $26-35 | *B* |

## PEPPER TREE WINES

| Wine | Vintage | Price | Size |
|---|---|---|---|
| *Reserve Merlot, Coonawarra* | 1996 | $44-55 | *B* |

## PETALUMA

| Wine | Vintage | Price | Size |
|---|---|---|---|
| *Chardonnay, Piccadilly Valley* | 1979 | $30-40 | *B* |
| | 1987 | $30-40 | *B* |
| | 1988 | $33-40 | *B* |
| | 1989 | $28-36 | *B* |
| | 1990 | $30-40 | *B* |
| | 1991 | $33-40 | *B* |
| | 1992 | $30-40 | *B* |
| | 1992 | $60-80 | *M* |
| | 1993 | $26-36 | *B* |
| | 1994 | $28-38 | *B* |
| | 1995 | $26-35 | *B* |
| | 1996 | $30-45 | *B* |
| | 1997 | $30-40 | *B* |
| | 1997 | $70-90 | *M* |
| | 1998 | $28-40 | *B* |
| | 1999 | $26-35 | *B* |
| *Petaluma Coonawarra Cabernet Merlot, Coonawarra* | | | |
| | 1979 | $56-75 | *B* |
| | 1980 | $46-60 | *B* |
| | 1982 | $45-60 | *B* |
| | 1982 | $80-110 | *M* |
| | 1984 | $33-40 | *B* |
| | 1986 | $45-60 | *B* |

| Wine | Vintage | Price | Size |
|---|---|---|---|
| | 1986 | $90-120 | *M* |
| | 1987 | $38-45 | *B* |
| | 1987 | $150-210 | *D* |
| | 1987 | $270-350 | *I* |
| | 1987 | $75-100 | *M* |
| | 1988 | $40-50 | *B* |
| | 1988 | $240-290 | *D* |
| | 1988 | $85-120 | *M* |
| | 1990 | $46-54 | *B* |
| | 1990 | $256-290 | *D* |
| | 1990 | $450-540 | *I* |
| | 1991 | $46-60 | *B* |
| | 1991 | $260-380 | *D* |
| | 1991 | $370-440 | *I* |
| | 1992 | $40-55 | *B* |
| | 1992 | $160-210 | *D* |
| | 1992 | $350-440 | *I* |
| | 1993 | $30-40 | *B* |
| | 1993 | $240-300 | *D* |
| | 1993 | $360-440 | *I* |
| | 1994 | $36-45 | *B* |
| | 1995 | $35-45 | *B* |
| | 1995 | $150-210 | *D* |
| | 1996 | $35-45 | *B* |
| | 1997 | $35-45 | *B* |
| | 1997 | $150-210 | *D* |
| | 1997 | $95-130 | *M* |
| | 1998 | $35-45 | *B* |
| *Croser Brut, Adelaide Hills* | 1988 | $55-75 | *M* |
| *Merlot, Coonawarra* | 1987 | $35-45 | *B* |
| | 1990 | $36-45 | *B* |
| | 1991 | $30-38 | *B* |
| | 1992 | $28-36 | *B* |
| | 1993 | $30-38 | *B* |
| | 1994 | $30-38 | *B* |
| | 1995 | $30-40 | *B* |
| | 1996 | $30-40 | *B* |
| | 1997 | $35-45 | *B* |
| | 1998 | $28-40 | *B* |
| *Riesling, Clare Valley* | 1980 | $36-45 | *B* |
| | 1983 | $44-55 | *B* |
| | 1990 | $33-45 | *B* |
| | 1994 | $26-33 | *B* |
| *Shiraz, Adelaide Hills* | 1998 | $30-40 | *B* |
| *Tiers Chardonnay, Piccadilly Valley* | 1996 | $85-120 | *B* |
| | 1997 | $80-110 | *B* |
| | 1998 | $70-90 | *B* |

## PETER LEHMANN

| Wine | Vintage | Price | Size |
|---|---|---|---|
| *Eight Songs Shiraz, Barossa Valley* | 1996 | $30-40 | *B* |
| | 1997 | $30-40 | *B* |
| *Mentor Cabernet Malbec Shiraz Merlot, Barossa Valley* | 1991 | $26-35 | *B* |
| *Shiraz, Barossa Valley* | 1988 | $28-35 | *B* |
| *Stonewell Shiraz, Barossa Valley* | 1987 | $50-65 | *B* |
| | 1988 | $50-65 | *B* |
| | 1989 | $130-170 | *M* |
| | 1990 | $66-85 | *B* |
| | 1991 | $56-70 | *B* |
| | 1992 | $46-60 | *B* |
| | 1993 | $44-56 | *B* |

| Wine | Vintage | Price | Size |
|---|---|---|---|
| | 1994 | $50-65 | *B* |
| | 1995 | $50-65 | *B* |
| | 1996 | $55-75 | *B* |
| | 1996 | $520-610 | *I* |
| | 1998 | $45-60 | *B* |
| *The Barossa Shiraz, Barossa Valley* | 1995 | $46-60 | *M* |

## PICARDY

| Wine | Vintage | Price | Size |
|---|---|---|---|
| *Cabernet Merlot, Pemberton* | 1997 | $26-33 | *B* |

## PICCADILLY

| Wine | Vintage | Price | Size |
|---|---|---|---|
| *Piccadilly Port15 Year Old Tawny, Reynella District* | 1995 | $65-75 | *M* |

## PIERRO

| Wine | Vintage | Price | Size |
|---|---|---|---|
| *Cabernet Merlot, Margaret River* | 1994 | $30-45 | *B* |
| | 1995 | $45-65 | *B* |
| | 1996 | $45-60 | *B* |
| | 1997 | $45-60 | *B* |
| | 1998 | $45-60 | *B* |
| *Chardonnay, Margaret River* | 1989 | $50-66 | *B* |
| | 1990 | $55-70 | *B* |
| | 1991 | $46-60 | *B* |
| | 1992 | $50-66 | *B* |
| | 1993 | $46-60 | *B* |
| | 1994 | $50-70 | *B* |
| | 1995 | $45-65 | *B* |
| | 1996 | $50-60 | *B* |
| | 1997 | $45-60 | *B* |
| | 1998 | $45-65 | *B* |
| | 1999 | $45-65 | *B* |
| | 2000 | $40-50 | *B* |
| *Pinot Noir, Margaret River* | 1994 | $30-40 | *B* |
| | 1996 | $33-40 | *B* |
| | 1999 | $30-40 | *B* |

## PIKES

| Wine | Vintage | Price | Size |
|---|---|---|---|
| *Cabernet Sauvignon, Clare Valley* | 1996 | $60-76 | *M* |
| *Reserve Shiraz, Clare Valley* | 1992 | $30-38 | *B* |
| | 1994 | $33-40 | *B* |
| *Shiraz, Clare Valley* | 1994 | $60-70 | *M* |
| | 1995 | $45-60 | *M* |
| | 1998 | $100-130 | *D* |

## PIPERS BROOK VINEYARD

| Wine | Vintage | Price | Size |
|---|---|---|---|
| *Cabernet Sauvignon, Northern Tasmania* | 1982 | $76-100 | *M* |
| *Opimian Cabernet Blend, Northern Tasmania* | 1990 | $50-70 | *M* |
| | 1994 | $66-80 | *M* |
| | 1998 | $45-60 | *M* |
| *Pellion Pinot Noir, Northern Tasmania* | 1992 | $35-50 | *M* |
| | 1988 | $28-40 | *B* |
| | 1990 | $50-65 | *M* |
| *Reserve Pinot Noir, Northern Tasmania* | 1998 | $46-65 | *M* |

## PLANTAGENET

| Wine | Vintage | Price | Size |
|---|---|---|---|
| *Cabernet Sauvignon, Great Southern* | 1985 | $36-50 | *B* |
| | 1990 | $40-50 | *B* |
| | 1991 | $36-50 | *B* |
| | 1994 | $40-48 | *B* |
| | 1994 | $86-120 | *M* |
| | 1995 | $30-40 | *B* |
| | 1996 | $35-45 | *B* |

|  |  |  |
|---|---|---|
| *Shiraz, Great Southern* | 1990 | $33-40...*B* |
| | 1991 | $33-45...*B* |
| | 1993 | $28-35...*B* |
| | 1994 | $36-45...*B* |
| | 1995 | $26-35...*B* |
| | 1996 | $35-45...*B* |
| | 1996 | $76-90 .*M* |
| | 1998 | $35-45...*B* |
| | 1998 | $76-90 .*M* |
| | 1999 | $35-45...*B* |

## PORT PHILLIP ESTATE

|  |  |  |
|---|---|---|
| *Reserve Pinot Noir, Mornington Peninsula* | 1996 | $28-40...*B* |
| | 1997 | $26-35...*B* |
| | 1998 | $28-35...*B* |

## PRINCE ALBERT VINEYARD

|  |  |  |
|---|---|---|
| *Pinot Noir, Geelong* | 1990 | $30-40...*B* |
| | 1992 | $33-44...*B* |
| | 1995 | $26-35...*B* |
| | 1998 | $30-45...*B* |

## PUNTERS CORNER

|  |  |  |
|---|---|---|
| *Spartacus Reserve Shiraz, Coonawarra* | 1998 | $38-50...*B* |
| | 1999 | $36-45...*B* |

## R.L. BULLER & SONS

|  |  |  |
|---|---|---|
| *25th Anniversary Tawny Port, Rutherglen* | 1952 | $46-55...*B* |
| *Vintage Port, Rutherglen* | 1972 | $56-70 .*M* |

## REDBANK

*Sally's Paddock Cabernet Shiraz Cabernet Franc Merlot, Pyrenees*

|  |  |  |
|---|---|---|
| | 1980 | $35-45...*B* |
| | 1981 | $80-110 .*M* |
| | 1982 | $100-140 .*M* |
| | 1984 | $30-35...*B* |
| | 1985 | $28-40...*B* |
| | 1986 | $40-55...*B* |
| | 1987 | $28-40...*B* |
| | 1988 | $35-45...*B* |
| | 1988 | $95-130 .*M* |
| | 1989 | $28-40...*B* |
| | 1990 | $30-45...*B* |
| | 1991 | $35-46...*B* |
| | 1992 | $30-40...*B* |
| | 1992 | $76-90 .*M* |
| | 1993 | $30-40...*B* |
| | 1994 | $30-40...*B* |
| | 1994 | $70-95 .*M* |
| | 1995 | $30-40...*B* |
| | 1996 | $30-40...*B* |
| | 1997 | $30-40...*B* |
| | 1997 | $60-80 .*M* |
| | 1998 | $30-40...*B* |

## REDMAN

|  |  |  |
|---|---|---|
| *Cabernet Sauvignon, Coonawarra* | 1971 | $85-96 .*M* |
| | 1972 | $44-55 .*M* |
| | 1973 | $46-60 .*M* |
| | 1974 | $160-220....*I* |
| | 1974 | $36-45 .*M* |
| | 1975 | $140-180....*I* |

| | | | |
|---|---|---|---|
| | 1975 | $35-50 | M |
| | 1976 | $170-240 | I |
| | 1976 | $50-70 | M |
| | 1977 | $140-190 | I |
| | 1977 | $36-50 | M |
| | 1978 | $130-170 | I |
| | 1978 | $35-50 | M |
| | 1979 | $100-140 | I |
| | 1979 | $26-35 | M |
| | 1980 | $170-230 | I |
| | 1980 | $40-50 | M |
| | 1981 | $140-190 | I |
| | 1981 | $40-50 | M |
| | 1982 | $120-160 | I |
| | 1982 | $36-45 | M |
| | 1983 | $140-180 | I |
| | 1983 | $36-45 | M |
| | 1984 | $160-220 | I |
| | 1984 | $46-60 | M |
| | 1986 | $40-55 | M |
| | 1987 | $40-55 | M |
| | 1990 | $150-210 | I |
| | 1990 | $56-70 | M |
| | 1991 | $170-220 | I |
| | 1991 | $50-65 | M |
| | 1992 | $45-60 | M |
| | 1996 | $220-280 | I |

## REYNELL

| | | | |
|---|---|---|---|
| *Basket Pressed Shiraz, McLaren Vale* | 1993 | $26-33 | B |
| | 1995 | $26-35 | B |
| *Stony Hill Cabernet Sauvignon, McLaren Vale* | 1990 | $66-80 | M |
| *Vintage Port, McLaren Vale* | 1964 | $55-70 | B |
| | 1967 | $45-60 | B |
| | 1968 | $40-55 | B |
| | 1970 | $35-45 | B |
| | 1971 | $40-55 | B |
| | 1972 | $30-40 | B |
| | 1973 | $26-35 | B |
| | 1974 | $28-35 | B |
| | 1975 | $30-40 | B |
| | 1978 | $28-35 | B |

## ROCKFORD

| | | | |
|---|---|---|---|
| *Basket Press Shiraz, Barossa Valley* | 1988 | $70-86 | B |
| | 1989 | $55-70 | B |
| | 1990 | $86-120 | B |
| | 1990 | $190-260 | M |
| | 1991 | $75-95 | B |
| | 1991 | $190-240 | M |
| | 1992 | $55-76 | B |
| | 1992 | $160-220 | M |
| | 1993 | $46-60 | B |
| | 1994 | $56-75 | B |
| | 1994 | $160-220 | M |
| | 1995 | $50-65 | B |
| | 1995 | $160-200 | M |
| | 1996 | $85-100 | B |
| | 1996 | $200-270 | M |
| | 1997 | $60-80 | B |
| | 1997 | $166-230 | M |
| | 1998 | $75-100 | B |

| Wine | Vintage | Price | Size |
|---|---|---|---|
| | 1999 | $60-85 | B |
| *Cabernet Sauvignon, Barossa Valley* | 1986 | $30-40 | B |
| | 1987 | $26-35 | B |
| | 1988 | $30-40 | B |
| | 1990 | $33-40 | B |
| | 1993 | $28-33 | B |
| | 1995 | $26-35 | B |
| *Home Block Cabernet, Barossa Valley* | 1992 | $55-76 | M |
| | 1993 | $56-75 | M |
| | 1994 | $66-80 | M |
| | 1996 | $55-70 | M |

## ROSEMOUNT ESTATE

| Wine | Vintage | Price | Size |
|---|---|---|---|
| *Balmoral Syrah, McLaren Vale* | 1992 | $45-56 | B |
| | 1993 | $46-56 | B |
| | 1994 | $45-56 | B |
| | 1995 | $40-65 | B |
| | 1996 | $46-60 | B |
| | 1997 | $35-50 | B |
| | 1998 | $45-60 | B |
| *Mountain Blue Shiraz Cabernet, Mudgee* | 1994 | $35-44 | B |
| | 1995 | $30-40 | B |
| | 1996 | $35-45 | B |
| | 1997 | $30-40 | B |
| | 1998 | $35-50 | B |
| *Show Reserve Cabernet Sauvignon, Coonawarra* | 1990 | $36-45 | B |

## ROUGE HOMME WINERY

| Wine | Vintage | Price | Size |
|---|---|---|---|
| *Winery Cabernet Sauvignon, Coonawarra* | 1982 | $28-40 | B |
| *Winery Richardson Red Block Cabernet Blend, Coonawarra* | 1993 | $30-38 | B |

## SALTRAM

| Wine | Vintage | Price | Size |
|---|---|---|---|
| *Claret, Barossa Valley* | 1971 | $26-35 | B |
| *Vintage Port, Barossa Valley* | 1958 | $46-60 | B |
| | 1959 | $30-40 | B |
| | 1961 | $60-80 | B |
| *Mamre Brook Cabernet Sauvignon, Barossa Valley* | 1996 | $46-55 | M |
| | 1978 | $230-270 | I |
| *Metala Original Plantings Old Vine Shiraz, Langhorne Creek* | 1996 | $26-35 | B |
| *Metala Shiraz Cabernet, Langhorne Creek* | 1986 | $56-75 | M |
| *No.1 Shiraz, Barossa Valley* | 1994 | $26-33 | B |
| *Pinnacle Selection Amontillado Sherry, Barossa Valley* | 1951 | $50-70 | B |
| *Pinnacle Selection Show White Port, Barossa Valley* | 1949 | $45-60 | B |

## SCARBOROUGH

| Wine | Vintage | Price | Size |
|---|---|---|---|
| *Chardonnay, Hunter Valley* | 1996 | $30-45 | M |

## SCARPANTONI ESTATE

| Wine | Vintage | Price | Size |
|---|---|---|---|
| *Block 3 Shiraz, McLaren Vale* | 1998 | $26-35 | B |

## SEAVIEW

| Wine | Vintage | Price | Size |
|---|---|---|---|
| *Cabernet Sauvignon, McLaren Vale* | 1961 | $33-45 | B |
| *Tawny Port, S.A.* | 1955 | $35-46 | B |

## SEPPELT

| Wine | Vintage | Price | Size |
|---|---|---|---|
| *Bin EC 4 Barossa Valley, Cabernet-Hermitage* | 1968 | $45-60 | M |

## SEPPELT

|  |  |  | |
|---|---|---|---|
| *CH 21 Great Western Burgundy Shiraz, Grampian* | 1963 | $56-65 | *B* |
| *Chalambar Shiraz, Grampians* | 1998 | $26-35 | *B* |
| *Colin Preece Memorial Shiraz, Grampians* | 1967 | $60-80 | *B* |
| *'Dorrien' Cabernet Sauvignon, Barossa Valley - Distinguished* | 1971 | $70-95 | *B* |
| | 1980 | $30-36 | *B* |
| | 1986 | $30-36 | *B* |
| | 1988 | $28-40 | *B* |
| | 1990 | $40-50 | *B* |
| | 1991 | $33-40 | *B* |
| | 1992 | $28-40 | *B* |
| | 1993 | $28-35 | *B* |
| | 1994 | $28-38 | *B* |
| | 1996 | $26-35 | *B* |
| *DP 13 Vintage Port, Rutherglen* | 1965 | $30-45 | *B* |
| *DP 136 Seppeltsfield Vintage Port, Barossa Valley* | 1948 | $110-140 | *B* |
| *DP 151 Seppeltsfield Vintage Port, Barossa Valley* | 1951 | $76-100 | *B* |
| *DP 32 Seppeltsfield Vintage Port, Barossa Valley* | 1965 | $30-40 | *B* |
| *Great Western Show Sparkling Burgundy, Grampians* | 1946 | $440-510 | *B* |
| | 1961 | $360-470 | *B* |
| | 1984 | $50-66 | *B* |
| | 1985 | $56-70 | *B* |
| *Great Western Show Sparkling Shiraz, Grampian* | 1986 | $60-76 | *B* |
| | 1987 | $56-70 | *B* |
| | 1994 | $33-40 | *B* |
| *Great Western Sparkling Shiraz, Grampians* | 1993 | $46-65 | *B* |
| *Harpers Range Cabernet Sauvignon, S.A.* | 1991 | $36-45 | *B* |
| *M 56-59 Shiraz, Grampians* | 1956 | $56-75 | *B* |
| *MY 22 Shiraz, Grampians* | 1966 | $46-65 | *B* |
| *Para Liqueur Port, Barossa Valley* | 1878 | $760-1100 | *B* |
| | 1889 | $660-800 | *B* |
| | 1893 | $740-1050 | *B* |
| | 1899 | $660-870 | *B* |
| | 1922 | $600-800 | *B* |
| | 1925 | $410-560 | *B* |
| | 1927 | $130-170 | *B* |
| | 1930 | $66-85 | *B* |
| | 1933 | $56-65 | *B* |
| | 1939 | $55-70 | *B* |
| | 1944 | $45-60 | *B* |
| | 1947 | $45-60 | *B* |
| | 1976 | $30-40 | *B* |
| *Seppeltsfield DP 108 Tawny Port, Barossa Valley* | 1927 | $96-130 | *B* |
| *Seppeltsfield Vintage Port, Barossa Valley* | 1948 | $75-100 | *B* |
| | 1952 | $55-70 | *B* |
| *Show Sparkling Red, Grampians* | 1983 | $50-70 | *B* |
| *Vintage Port, Barossa Valley* | 1951 | $60-85 | *B* |

## SETTLEMENT WINE CO.

|  |  |  | |
|---|---|---|---|
| *Vintage Port, McLaren Vale* | 1933 | $66-85 | *B* |

## SEVILLE ESTATE

|  |  |  | |
|---|---|---|---|
| *Cabernet Sauvignon, Yarra Valley* | 1994 | $30-38 | *B* |
| *Shiraz, Yarra Valley* | 1990 | $38-46 | *B* |
| | 1991 | $26-35 | *B* |

| | | |
|---|---|---|
| | 1997 | $26-35...B |

## ST. HALLETT

| | | |
|---|---|---|
| *Old Block Shiraz, Barossa Valley* | 1980 | $46-60...B |
| | 1986 | $45-65...B |
| | 1987 | $46-60...B |
| | 1988 | $45-56...B |
| | 1988 | $80-110.M |
| | 1989 | $45-60...B |
| | 1989 | $110-160.M |
| | 1990 | $60-80...B |
| | 1990 | $120-170.M |
| | 1991 | $46-60...B |
| | 1992 | $35-48...B |
| | 1992 | $75-96.M |
| | 1993 | $36-45...B |
| | 1993 | $100-140.M |
| | 1994 | $36-48...B |
| | 1994 | $96-120.M |
| | 1995 | $35-45...B |
| | 1996 | $40-55...B |
| | 1996 | $100-140.M |
| | 1997 | $35-45...B |
| | 1998 | $35-45...B |

## STANTON & KILLEEN WINES

| | | |
|---|---|---|
| *Shiraz Vintage Port, Rutherglen* | 1976 | $28-40...B |
| *Vintage Muscat, Rutherglen* | 1977 | $45-60...B |

## STONIER WINES

| | | |
|---|---|---|
| *Stonier Pinot Noir, Mornington Peninsula* | 1997 | $95-130.M |
| *Stonier Reserve Chardonnay, Mornington Peninsula* | 1994 | $28-40...B |
| *Stonier Reserve Pinot Noir, Mornington Peninsula* | 1993 | $36-45...B |
| | 1994 | $28-36...B |
| | 1997 | $26-35...B |

## STONYFELL

| | | |
|---|---|---|
| *Metala Shiraz Cabernet, Barossa Valley* | 1986 | $50-70.M |
| | 1992 | $45-56.M |
| *Original Plantings Centenary Release Cabernet Shiraz, Barossa Valley* | 1991 | $60-76.M |
| *Vintage Port, Barossa Valley* | 1945 | $100-140...B |
| | 1950 | $50-65...B |
| | 1954 | $36-48...B |
| | 1958 | $45-65...B |

## SUMMERFIELD WINES

| | | |
|---|---|---|
| *Reserve Shiraz, Pyrenees* | 1997 | $30-40...B |
| | 1999 | $30-36...B |
| *Shiraz, Pyrenees* | 1988 | $28-35...B |

## TAHBILK WINES

| | | |
|---|---|---|
| *1860 Vines Shiraz, Nagambie Lakes* | 1979 | $66-80...B |
| | 1982 | $75-100...B |
| | 1984 | $66-85...B |
| | 1985 | $50-66...B |
| | 1986 | $76-100...B |
| | 1987 | $66-80...B |
| | 1989 | $50-66...B |

| Wine | Vintage | Price | Size |
|---|---|---|---|
| | 1990 | $66-85 | *B* |
| | 1991 | $66-80 | *B* |
| | 1991 | $180-240 | *M* |
| | 1992 | $56-75 | *B* |
| | 1992 | $160-210 | *M* |
| | 1994 | $60-80 | *B* |
| | 1994 | $150-180 | *M* |
| *Cabernet Sauvignon, Nagambie Lakes* | 1965 | $46-65 | *B* |
| | 1971 | $30-40 | *B* |
| | 1978 | $26-35 | *B* |
| | 1980 | $28-35 | *B* |
| | 1986 | $30-40 | *B* |
| | 1987 | $55-75 | *M* |
| | 1990 | $70-86 | *M* |
| | 1997 | $44-55 | *M* |
| *Private Bin 28 Cabernet Sauvignon, Nagambie Lakes* | 1960 | $56-75 | *B* |
| *Private Bin 65 Cabernet Sauvignon, Nagambie Lakes* | 1978 | $33-40 | *B* |
| *Private Bin 68 Cabernet Sauvignon, Nagambie Lakes* | 1981 | $30-40 | *B* |
| *Private Bin Cabernet Sauvignon, Nagambie Lake* | 1981 | $45-60 | *B* |
| | 1983 | $36-45 | *B* |
| | 1984 | $35-45 | *B* |
| | 1988 | $35-50 | *B* |
| *Reserve Cabernet Sauvignon, Nagambie Lakes* | 1985 | $33-45 | *B* |
| *Shiraz, Nagambie Lakes* | 1964 | $28-40 | *B* |
| | 1965 | $30-40 | *B* |
| | 1966 | $36-50 | *B* |
| | 1971 | $30-45 | *B* |
| | 1979 | $28-35 | *B* |
| | 1980 | $26-35 | *B* |
| | 1981 | $30-45 | *B* |
| | 1986 | $30-45 | *B* |
| | 1987 | $30-40 | *B* |

## TALTARNI

| Wine | Vintage | Price | Size |
|---|---|---|---|
| *Cabernet Sauvignon, Pyrenees* | 1977 | $30-36 | *B* |
| | 1979 | $26-35 | *B* |
| | 1979 | $76-95 | *M* |
| | 1982 | $40-50 | *M* |
| | 1983 | $45-60 | *M* |
| | 1986 | $28-35 | *B* |
| | 1986 | $60-80 | *M* |
| | 1987 | $28-35 | *B* |
| | 1987 | $60-85 | *M* |
| | 1988 | $26-35 | *B* |
| | 1988 | $65-90 | *M* |
| | 1989 | $170-210 | *I* |
| | 1989 | $76-90 | *M* |
| | 1990 | $130-170 | *D* |
| | 1990 | $210-290 | *I* |
| | 1990 | $80-110 | *M* |
| | 1991 | $160-190 | *D* |
| | 1991 | $210-280 | *I* |
| | 1991 | $66-80 | *M* |
| | 1992 | $26-33 | *B* |
| | 1992 | $66-80 | *M* |
| | 1993 | $120-170 | *D* |
| | 1993 | $260-330 | *I* |
| | 1993 | $65-90 | *M* |

|  |  |  |
|---|---|---|
| | 1994 | $110-150..*D* |
| | 1994 | $260-330....*I* |
| | 1994 | $70-95 .*M* |
| *Shiraz, Pyrenees* | 1981 | $28-40...*B* |
| *Special Reserve Cabernet Sauvignon, Pyrenees* | | |
| | 1984 | $76-95 .*M* |
| | 1988 | $28-35...*B* |
| | 1992 | $35-50...*B* |

## TARRAWARRA ESTATE

|  |  |  |
|---|---|---|
| *Pinot Noir, Yarra Valley* | 1993 | $28-36...*B* |
| | 1994 | $36-45...*B* |
| | 1996 | $35-45...*B* |
| | 1997 | $28-35...*B* |
| | 1998 | $30-40...*B* |
| | 1998 | $55-75 .*M* |

## TATACHILLA WINERY

|  |  |  |
|---|---|---|
| *Winery Foundation Shiraz, McLaren Vale* | 1996 | $30-40...*B* |
| | 1998 | $30-40...*B* |
| *Winery Keystone Grenache Shiraz, McLaren Vale* | | |
| | 1997 | $26-35 .*M* |

## THE McALISTER

|  |  |  |
|---|---|---|
| *Cabernet-Cabernet Franc-Merlot, Gippsland* | 1984 | $36-50...*B* |
| | 1986 | $30-40...*B* |
| | 1987 | $33-45...*B* |
| | 1990 | $36-45...*B* |
| | 1991 | $35-46...*B* |
| | 1992 | $33-40...*B* |
| | 1994 | $36-45...*B* |
| | 1995 | $26-33...*B* |
| | 1996 | $30-38...*B* |

## THE RIDDOCH RUN

|  |  |  |
|---|---|---|
| *Shiraz, Coonawarra* | 1992 | $56-65 .*M* |

## THREE RIVERS

|  |  |  |
|---|---|---|
| *Shiraz, Barossa Valley* | 1989 | $500-660...*B* |
| | 1989 | $800-1000 .*M* |
| | 1990 | $660-1100...*B* |
| | 1991 | $560-770...*B* |
| | 1992 | $500-660...*B* |
| | 1993 | $500-650...*B* |
| | 1994 | $600-1,150...*B* |
| | 1995 | $500-650...*B* |

## TIM ADAMS

|  |  |  |
|---|---|---|
| *Shiraz, Clare Valley* | 1997 | $40-55 .*M* |
| | 1998 | $160-200....*I* |
| *The Aberfeldy Shiraz, Clare Valley* | 1990 | $44-50...*B* |
| | 1990 | $76-95 .*M* |
| | 1991 | $33-45...*B* |
| | 1991 | $76-95 .*M* |
| | 1992 | $70-85 .*M* |
| | 1993 | $28-35...*B* |
| | 1993 | $66-90 .*M* |
| | 1994 | $35-45...*B* |
| | 1994 | $70-90 .*M* |
| | 1995 | $30-45...*B* |
| | 1995 | $75-100 .*M* |
| | 1996 | $35-45...*B* |

|  |  |  |
|---|---|---|
| | 1996 | $70-90 .M |
| | 1997 | $30-40...B |
| | 1998 | $30-40...B |
| | 1998 | $70-95 .M |

## TORBRECK

|  |  |  |
|---|---|---|
| *Descendant Shiraz Viognier, Barossa Valley* | 1998 | $76-100...B |
| | 1999 | $76-90...B |
| *Runrig Shiraz, Barossa Valley* | 1995 | $300-400...B |
| | 1996 | $280-360...B |
| | 1997 | $260-350...B |
| | 1998 | $290-400...B |
| | 1999 | $250-350...B |
| *The Factor Shiraz, Barossa Valley* | 1998 | $90-120...B |
| *The Steading Grenache Mataro Shiraz, Barossa Valley* | | |
| | 1996 | $45-65...B |
| | 1997 | $50-70...B |
| | 1998 | $50-66...B |
| | 1999 | $45-65...B |
| | 2000 | $44-50...B |

## TULLOCH

|  |  |  |
|---|---|---|
| *'Private Bin' Dry Red, Hunter Valley* | 1965 | $90-120...B |
| *'Private Bin' Dry Red, Pokolbin* | 1959 | $76-90...B |
| | 1963 | $56-75...B |

## TURKEY FLAT

|  |  |  |
|---|---|---|
| *Cabernet Sauvignon, Barossa Valley* | 1997 | $50-66 .M |
| *Shiraz, Barossa Valley* | 1992 | $35-50...B |
| | 1993 | $33-40...B |
| | 1994 | $30-40...B |
| | 1995 | $30-40...B |
| | 1996 | $35-45...B |
| | 1997 | $30-40...B |
| | 1997 | $70-90 .M |
| | 1998 | $35-45...B |
| | 1998 | $95-130 .M |
| | 1999 | $30-40...B |

## TYRRELL'S

|  |  |  |
|---|---|---|
| *Vat 1 Semillon, Hunter Valley* | 1978 | $30-40...B |
| | 1979 | $28-35...B |
| | 1984 | $26-35...B |
| | 1986 | $45-60...B |
| | 1987 | $40-50...B |
| | 1988 | $26-35...B |
| | 1990 | $30-40...B |
| | 1991 | $30-40...B |
| | 1992 | $28-35...B |
| | 1993 | $76-90 .M |
| | 1994 | $30-40...B |
| | 1995 | $66-80 .M |
| *Vat 47 Chardonnay, Hunter Valley* | 1976 | $35-50...B |
| | 1982 | $26-35...B |
| | 1983 | $30-40...B |
| | 1984 | $26-35...B |
| | 1985 | $28-40...B |
| | 1986 | $35-45...B |
| | 1986 | $70-95 .M |
| | 1987 | $30-40...B |
| | 1988 | $33-40...B |
| | 1990 | $36-45...B |

| Wine | Vintage | Price | Size |
|---|---|---|---|
| | 1991 | $35-44 | B |
| | 1992 | $30-40 | B |
| | 1992 | $76-100 | M |
| | 1993 | $30-40 | B |
| | 1994 | $26-35 | B |
| | 1994 | $66-85 | M |
| | 1995 | $30-40 | B |
| | 1995 | $70-95 | M |
| | 1996 | $26-35 | B |
| | 1996 | $66-80 | M |
| | 1997 | $30-40 | B |
| | 1998 | $30-40 | B |
| | 1999 | $56-70 | M |
| | 2000 | $30-38 | B |
| | 2001 | $30-36 | B |
| *Vat 61 Shiraz, Hunter Valley* | 1968 | $30-40 | B |
| *Vat 70 Cabernet Sauvignon, Hunter Valley* | 1977 | $26-35 | M |
| *Vat 8 Shiraz, Hunter Valley* | 1995 | $30-40 | B |
| *Vat 80 Dry Red, Hunter Valley* | 1966 | $33-40 | B |
| *Vat 9 Shiraz, Hunter Valley* | 1980 | $36-45 | B |
| | 1981 | $28-40 | B |
| | 1991 | $36-45 | B |
| | 1992 | $28-36 | B |
| | 1993 | $28-36 | B |
| | 1994 | $30-38 | B |
| | 1995 | $30-40 | B |
| | 1998 | $30-40 | B |
| | 2000 | $26-35 | B |

## VASSE FELIX

| Wine | Vintage | Price | Size |
|---|---|---|---|
| *Cabernet Sauvignon, Margaret River* | 1977 | $45-60 | B |
| | 1978 | $30-40 | B |
| | 1979 | $45-60 | B |
| | 1980 | $30-45 | B |
| | 1982 | $35-45 | B |
| | 1983 | $30-45 | B |
| | 1984 | $30-40 | B |
| | 1985 | $45-60 | B |
| | 1986 | $45-60 | B |
| | 1987 | $30-45 | B |
| | 1988 | $35-45 | B |
| | 1990 | $28-40 | B |
| | 1991 | $50-65 | B |
| | 1992 | $30-40 | B |
| | 1993 | $30-40 | B |
| | 1994 | $30-36 | B |
| | 1995 | $45-60 | B |
| | 1996 | $30-40 | B |
| | 1997 | $30-40 | B |
| | 1998 | $40-50 | B |
| *Heytesbury Cabernets, Margaret River* | 1995 | $45-60 | B |
| | 1996 | $50-60 | B |
| | 1997 | $45-60 | B |
| | 1998 | $36-45 | B |
| *Heytesbury Chardonnay, Margaret River* | 1997 | $30-35 | B |
| | 1998 | $26-35 | B |
| | 1999 | $30-40 | B |
| *Shiraz, Margaret River* | 1993 | $26-35 | B |
| | 1997 | $26-35 | B |
| | 1998 | $26-35 | B |

## VERITAS WINES

|  |  |  |
|---|---|---|
| *Binder's Bulls Blood Shiraz Mouvedre Pressings, Barossa Valley* | 1996 | $44-55...*B* |
| | 1997 | $36-44...*B* |
| *Cabernet Sauvignon, Barossa Valley* | 1996 | $36-45...*B* |
| *Hanisch Vineyard Shiraz, Barossa Valley* | 1995 | $190-270...*B* |
| | 1996 | $130-180...*B* |
| | 1997 | $110-160...*B* |
| | 1998 | $230-300...*B* |
| | 1999 | $140-200...*B* |

## VIRGIN HILLS

|  |  |  |
|---|---|---|
| *Cabernet Shiraz Merlot Malbec, Macedon* | 1974 | $36-50...*B* |
| | 1979 | $26-35...*B* |
| | 1980 | $26-35...*B* |
| | 1982 | $30-45...*B* |
| | 1985 | $30-40...*B* |
| | 1990 | $28-35...*B* |
| | 1995 | $60-70.*M* |
| *'Reserve' Dry Red, Kyneton* | 1990 | $28-36...*B* |
| | 1990 | $66-80.*M* |

## WANTIRNA ESTATE

|  |  |  |
|---|---|---|
| *Cabernet Merlot, Yarra Valley* | 1982 | $36-45...*B* |
| | 1985 | $44-55...*B* |
| | 1992 | $40-50...*B* |
| | 1994 | $40-55...*B* |
| *Isabella Chardonnay, Yarra Valley* | 1995 | $45-56...*B* |
| *Lily Pinot Noir, Yarra Valley* | 1996 | $26-35...*B* |

## WARRENMANG

|  |  |  |
|---|---|---|
| *Grand Pyrenees Dry Red, Pyrenees* | 1994 | $26-33...*B* |

## WENDOUREE

|  |  |  |
|---|---|---|
| *Cabernet Malbec, Clare Valley* | 1976 | $80-110...*B* |
| | 1987 | $60-80...*B* |
| | 1989 | $50-65...*B* |
| | 1990 | $75-100...*B* |
| | 1991 | $65-85...*B* |
| | 1992 | $46-65...*B* |
| | 1993 | $45-65...*B* |
| | 1994 | $50-66...*B* |
| | 1995 | $50-65...*B* |
| | 1996 | $50-70...*B* |
| | 1997 | $45-60...*B* |
| | 1998 | $55-70...*B* |
| | 1999 | $50-65...*B* |
| *Cabernet Sauvignon, Clare Valley* | 1985 | $76-100...*B* |
| | 1986 | $85-110...*B* |
| | 1987 | $66-85...*B* |
| | 1988 | $65-85...*B* |
| | 1990 | $75-100...*B* |
| | 1991 | $65-90...*B* |
| | 1992 | $56-70...*B* |
| | 1994 | $60-76...*B* |
| | 1995 | $50-65...*B* |
| | 1996 | $50-65...*B* |
| | 1997 | $45-60...*B* |
| | 1998 | $65-90...*B* |
| *Pressings, Clare Valley* | 1980 | $76-95...*B* |
| | 1985 | $50-65...*B* |

| Wine | Vintage | Price | Size |
|---|---|---|---|
| | 1987 | $56-75 | *B* |
| | 1988 | $55-75 | *B* |
| | 1997 | $45-60 | *B* |
| *Shiraz Malbec, Clare Valley* | 1990 | $70-95 | *B* |
| | 1991 | $65-90 | *B* |
| | 1992 | $50-65 | *B* |
| | 1993 | $50-70 | *B* |
| | 1994 | $46-65 | *B* |
| | 1996 | $60-80 | *B* |
| | 1998 | $50-65 | *B* |
| | 1999 | $45-60 | *B* |
| *Shiraz Mataro, Clare Valley* | 1987 | $70-95 | *B* |
| | 1990 | $65-90 | *B* |
| | 1991 | $50-65 | *B* |
| | 1993 | $50-65 | *B* |
| | 1995 | $50-65 | *B* |
| | 1996 | $50-65 | *B* |
| | 1997 | $45-60 | *B* |
| | 1998 | $50-65 | *B* |
| | 1999 | $45-60 | *B* |
| *Shiraz, Clare Valley* | 1975 | $110-140 | *B* |
| | 1986 | $110-150 | *B* |
| | 1988 | $90-120 | *B* |
| | 1989 | $66-85 | *B* |
| | 1990 | $100-130 | *B* |
| | 1990 | $300-430 | *M* |
| | 1991 | $86-110 | *B* |
| | 1992 | $65-90 | *B* |
| | 1993 | $80-100 | *B* |
| | 1994 | $80-110 | *B* |
| | 1995 | $75-100 | *B* |
| | 1996 | $100-130 | *B* |
| | 1997 | $65-85 | *B* |
| | 1998 | $95-130 | *B* |
| | 1999 | $70-95 | *B* |
| *Vintage Port, Clare Valley* | 1985 | $35-45 | *B* |

## WIGNALLS WINES

| Wine | Vintage | Price | Size |
|---|---|---|---|
| *King River Albany Pinot Noir, Great Southern* | 1995 | $30-40 | *M* |
| | 1996 | $26-35 | *B* |

## WILD DUCK CREEK ESTATE

| Wine | Vintage | Price | Size |
|---|---|---|---|
| *Alan's Cabernets, Heathcote* | 1992 | $95-130 | *M* |
| *Alan's Vat 1 Cabernets, Heathcote* | 1994 | $28-36 | *B* |
| | 1995 | $35-45 | *B* |
| | 1996 | $26-35 | *B* |
| | 1996 | $70-95 | *M* |
| | 1997 | $30-45 | *B* |
| *Black Label Reserve Shiraz, Heathcote* | 1994 | $60-76 | *B* |
| *Duck Muck Shiraz Cabernet, Heathcote* | 1994 | $300-500 | *B* |
| | 1995 | $560-1150 | *B* |
| | 1997 | $600-800 | *B* |
| *Reserve Cabernet Sauvignon, Heathcote* | 1994 | $40-55 | *B* |
| | 1996 | $44-55 | *B* |
| *Reserve Merlot, Heathcote* | 1996 | $35-50 | *B* |
| *Springflat Shiraz, Heathcote* | 1994 | $35-45 | *B* |
| | 1995 | $40-55 | *B* |
| | 1996 | $33-46 | *B* |
| | 1997 | $35-50 | *B* |
| | 1998 | $28-35 | *B* |
| *The Blend Shiraz Cabernet, Heathcote* | 1998 | $40-55 | *B* |

## WINE BY FARR

*Shiraz, Geelong* ........ 1999 ........ $33-40...*B*

## WIRRA WIRRA

*Church Block Cabernet Shiraz Merlot, McLaren Vale*
........ 1991 ........ $190-250....*I*
........ 1994 ........ $130-170..*D*
........ 1995 ........ $100-140..*D*
*R.S.W. Shiraz, McLaren Vale* ........ 1990 ........ $28-38...*B*
........ 1991 ........ $26-35...*B*
........ 1995 ........ $28-36...*B*
........ 1996 ........ $26-35...*B*
*The Angelus Cabernet Sauvignon, McLaren Vale*
........ 1991 ........ $30-40...*B*
........ 1992 ........ $26-35...*B*

## WOLF BLASS WINES

*Black Label Cabernet Blend, S.A.* ........ 1973 ........ $55-70...*B*
........ 1974 ........ $50-66...*B*
........ 1975 ........ $50-70...*B*
........ 1976 ........ $50-65...*B*
........ 1977 ........ $50-65...*B*
........ 1978 ........ $40-55...*B*
........ 1979 ........ $50-65...*B*
........ 1980 ........ $46-65...*B*
........ 1980 ........ $140-190.*M*
........ 1981 ........ $50-70...*B*
........ 1982 ........ $60-80...*B*
........ 1983 ........ $55-70...*B*
........ 1984 ........ $56-75...*B*
........ 1984 ........ $86-110.*M*
........ 1985 ........ $56-70...*B*
........ 1985 ........ $100-130.*M*
........ 1986 ........ $60-85...*B*
........ 1986 ........ $110-150.*M*
........ 1987 ........ $50-65...*B*
........ 1988 ........ $50-70...*B*
........ 1989 ........ $50-60...*B*
........ 1990 ........ $55-75...*B*
........ 1991 ........ $56-70...*B*
........ 1992 ........ $46-60...*B*
........ 1993 ........ $50-70...*B*
........ 1994 ........ $50-65...*B*
........ 1995 ........ $50-65...*B*
........ 1996 ........ $50-70...*B*
*Edition One Cabernet Sauvignon, S.A.* ........ 1994 ........ $66-90.*M*
*John's Blend Selected Dry Red, S.A.* ........ 1992 ........ $26-35...*B*
*Museum Reserve Cabernet Sauvignon, Langhorne Creek*
........ 1983 ........ $28-35...*B*
*XXX Years Cabernets, Clare Valley* ........ 1988 ........ $120-160.*M*

## WOODLEY'S

*Queen Adelaide Treasure Chest Series Dry Red, Coonawarra*
........ 1953 ........ $380-500...*B*
*Skeleton Treasure Chest Series Dry Red, Coonawarra*
........ 1956 ........ $350-500...*B*

## WYNNS COONAWARRA ESTATE

*Cabernet Sauvignon, Coonawarra* ........ 1957 ........ $75-100...*B*
........ 1960 ........ $60-80...*B*
........ 1962 ........ $76-95...*B*

| Wine | Vintage | Price | Size |
|---|---|---|---|
| | 1965 | $44-55 | *B* |
| | 1965 | $100-140 | *M* |
| | 1966 | $56-70 | *B* |
| | 1966 | $160-220 | *M* |
| | 1967 | $35-45 | *B* |
| | 1968 | $26-35 | *B* |
| | 1970 | $36-45 | *B* |
| | 1971 | $36-50 | *B* |
| | 1971 | $76-100 | *M* |
| | 1973 | $76-95 | *M* |
| | 1974 | $50-65 | *M* |
| | 1975 | $65-85 | *M* |
| | 1976 | $45-60 | *B* |
| | 1976 | $86-120 | *M* |
| | 1980 | $26-35 | *B* |
| | 1982 | $40-50 | *B* |
| | 1986 | $36-50 | *B* |
| | 1988 | $28-40 | *B* |
| | 1990 | $36-45 | *B* |
| | 1991 | $30-40 | *B* |
| | 1997 | $56-65 | *M* |
| *Cabernet, Coonawarra* | 1957 | $56-75 | *B* |
| | 1959 | $56-70 | *B* |
| | 1962 | $36-45 | *B* |
| *Centenary Shiraz Cabernet, Coonawarra* | 1991 | $40-50 | *B* |
| *Centenary Shiraz Cabernet, Coonawarra* | 1991 | $95-136 | *M* |
| *Claret, Coonawarra* | 1953 | $50-65 | *B* |
| | 1954 | $65-85 | *B* |
| | 1956 | $45-60 | *B* |
| | 1960 | $40-56 | *B* |
| *John Riddoch Cabernet Sauvignon, Coonawarra* | | | |
| | 1982 | $70-86 | *B* |
| | 1984 | $50-70 | *B* |
| | 1985 | $40-50 | *B* |
| | 1986 | $60-85 | *B* |
| | 1987 | $40-50 | *B* |
| | 1988 | $40-55 | *B* |
| | 1988 | $90-120 | *M* |
| | 1990 | $66-90 | *B* |
| | 1990 | $96-140 | *M* |
| | 1991 | $50-66 | *B* |
| | 1991 | $120-160 | *M* |
| | 1992 | $40-50 | *B* |
| | 1992 | $70-96 | *M* |
| | 1993 | $40-50 | *B* |
| | 1993 | $85-120 | *M* |
| | 1994 | $45-60 | *B* |
| | 1994 | $90-120 | *M* |
| | 1996 | $45-60 | *B* |
| | 1996 | $110-150 | *M* |
| | 1997 | $40-50 | *B* |
| *Michael Shiraz, Coonawarra* | 1955 | $410-540 | *B* |
| | 1990 | $65-76 | *B* |
| | 1991 | $50-65 | *B* |
| | 1993 | $40-50 | *B* |
| | 1993 | $100-140 | *M* |
| | 1994 | $40-50 | *B* |
| | 1994 | $100-140 | *M* |
| | 1996 | $40-50 | *B* |
| | 1996 | $80-110 | *M* |
| | 1997 | $35-45 | *B* |

## XANADU

| | | |
|---|---|---|
| *Cabernet Reserve, Margaret River* | 1989 | $30-40...*B* |
| | 1990 | $56-65...*B* |
| | 1991 | $40-50...*B* |
| | 1992 | $30-40...*B* |
| | 1993 | $30-40...*B* |
| | 1994 | $30-36...*B* |
| | 1995 | $30-40...*B* |
| | 1996 | $28-40...*B* |
| *Cabernet Sauvignon, Margaret River* | 1991 | $30-40...*B* |
| | 1991 | $80-110.*M* |
| | 1992 | $55-75.*M* |
| | 1994 | $76-90.*M* |
| | 1996 | $26-35...*B* |
| | 1997 | $26-35...*B* |

## YALUMBA

| | | |
|---|---|---|
| *Octavius Old Vine Shiraz, Barossa Valley* | 1988 | $50-65...*B* |
| | 1990 | $60-76...*B* |
| | 1992 | $50-66...*B* |
| | 1993 | $50-65...*B* |
| | 1994 | $50-66...*B* |
| | 1995 | $45-60...*B* |
| | 1996 | $50-65...*B* |
| | 1997 | $46-65...*B* |
| *The Menzies Cabernet Sauvignon, Coonawarra* | | |
| | 1988 | $70-90.*M* |
| | 1989 | $170-220....*I* |
| | 1990 | $130-180..*D* |
| | 1990 | $260-330....*I* |
| | 1990 | $65-85.*M* |
| | 1991 | $150-200..*D* |
| | 1991 | $210-260....*I* |
| | 1991 | $66-90.*M* |
| | 1992 | $120-160..*D* |
| | 1992 | $150-210....*I* |
| | 1992 | $60-75.*M* |
| | 1994 | $60-80.*M* |
| *The Reserve Shiraz, Barossa Valley* | 1990 | $60-75...*B* |
| | 1992 | $46-60...*B* |
| *The Signature Cabernet Shiraz, Barossa Valley* | | |
| | 1968 | $40-50...*B* |
| | 1977 | $35-50...*B* |
| | 1988 | $30-40...*B* |
| | 1988 | $66-85.*M* |
| | 1990 | $30-38...*B* |
| | 1990 | $86-120.*M* |
| | 1991 | $26-33...*B* |
| | 1991 | $120-160..*D* |
| | 1991 | $60-75.*M* |
| | 1992 | $30-38...*B* |
| | 1992 | $140-180..*D* |
| | 1992 | $66-85.*M* |
| | 1993 | $26-35...*B* |
| | 1993 | $240-290....*I* |
| | 1996 | $26-35...*B* |
| | 1996 | $50-70.*M* |
| *The Virgilius Viognier, Eden Valley* | 1999 | $26-35...*B* |

## YARRA BURN

| | | |
|---|---|---|
| *Bastard Hill Chardonnay, Yarra Valley* | 1996 | $26-36...*B* |

| | | | |
|---|---|---|---|
| | 1994 | $28-38 | B |
| | 1996 | $28-35 | B |
| | 1997 | $30-40 | B |

## YARRA RIDGE

| | | | |
|---|---|---|---|
| *Shiraz, Yarra Valley* | 1990 | $45-56 | B |
| *Single Barrel Unfiltered Pinot Noir, Yarra Valley* | 1996 | $76-95 | M |

## YARRA YARRA VINEYARD

| | | | |
|---|---|---|---|
| *Vineyard Cabernet Blend, Yarra Valley* | 1983 | $76-95 | M |
| | 1984 | $76-100 | M |
| | 1990 | $50-66 | B |
| | 1990 | $86-110 | M |
| | 1991 | $44-55 | B |
| | 1993 | $36-50 | B |
| | 1994 | $36-45 | B |
| | 1994 | $76-95 | M |
| *Vineyard Reserve Cabernet Sauvignon, Yarra Valley* | 1993 | $46-60 | B |
| | 1994 | $50-66 | B |
| | 1997 | $66-85 | B |

## YARRA YERING

| | | | |
|---|---|---|---|
| *Dry Red Wine No.1 Cabernet Blend, Yarra Valley* | 1974 | $50-65 | B |
| | 1976 | $55-75 | B |
| | 1977 | $60-85 | B |
| | 1980 | $60-80 | B |
| | 1981 | $65-90 | B |
| | 1982 | $56-75 | B |
| | 1983 | $55-70 | B |
| | 1984 | $60-76 | B |
| | 1985 | $50-70 | B |
| | 1986 | $55-66 | B |
| | 1987 | $60-80 | B |
| | 1988 | $55-70 | B |
| | 1988 | $115-146 | M |
| | 1989 | $45-60 | B |
| | 1990 | $75-95 | B |
| | 1990 | $140-180 | M |
| | 1991 | $70-88 | B |
| | 1991 | $120-160 | M |
| | 1992 | $50-70 | B |
| | 1992 | $96-125 | M |
| | 1993 | $50-70 | B |
| | 1993 | $100-130 | M |
| | 1994 | $55-70 | B |
| | 1994 | $100-136 | M |
| | 1995 | $50-60 | B |
| | 1995 | $95-126 | M |
| | 1996 | $45-65 | B |
| | 1996 | $100-140 | M |
| | 1997 | $50-70 | B |
| | 1998 | $60-80 | B |
| | 1998 | $100-140 | M |
| *Dry Red Wine No.2 Shiraz, Yarra Valley* | 1980 | $45-60 | B |
| | 1981 | $36-45 | B |
| | 1982 | $40-50 | B |
| | 1984 | $45-60 | B |
| | 1985 | $45-60 | B |
| | 1986 | $46-60 | B |

| Wine | Year | Price | Size |
|---|---|---|---|
| | 1987 | $47-60 | B |
| | 1987 | $90-120 | M |
| | 1989 | $36-45 | B |
| | 1990 | $65-86 | B |
| | 1990 | $100-140 | M |
| | 1991 | $60-76 | B |
| | 1991 | $110-150 | M |
| | 1992 | $50-70 | B |
| | 1992 | $100-140 | M |
| | 1993 | $36-48 | B |
| | 1993 | $95-130 | M |
| | 1994 | $50-70 | B |
| | 1994 | $80-110 | M |
| | 1995 | $100-140 | M |
| | 1996 | $40-55 | B |
| | 1996 | $95-120 | M |
| | 1997 | $46-55 | B |
| | 1998 | $50-70 | B |
| | 1998 | $90-110 | M |
| *Malbec, Yarra Valley* | 1995 | $160-190 | M |
| *Merlot, Yarra Valley* | 1990 | $76-100 | B |
| | 1992 | $86-110 | B |
| | 1993 | $70-90 | B |
| *Pinot Noir, Yarra Valley* | 1983 | $28-40 | B |
| | 1990 | $36-50 | B |
| | 1991 | $45-56 | B |
| | 1992 | $46-65 | B |
| | 1992 | $86-120 | M |
| | 1993 | $40-48 | B |
| | 1994 | $36-48 | B |
| | 1995 | $35-50 | B |
| | 1996 | $40-55 | B |
| | 1996 | $80-110 | M |
| | 1997 | $35-45 | B |
| | 1998 | $110-150 | M |
| *Underhill Shiraz, Yarra Valley* | 1989 | $35-45 | B |
| | 1990 | $38-50 | B |
| | 1991 | $40-50 | B |
| | 1991 | $96-130 | M |
| | 1992 | $40-55 | B |
| | 1993 | $44-55 | B |
| | 1994 | $40-50 | B |
| | 1994 | $100-140 | M |
| | 1995 | $30-45 | B |
| | 1995 | $85-120 | M |
| | 1996 | $35-50 | B |
| | 1996 | $85-110 | M |
| | 1998 | $38-50 | B |
| | 1998 | $130-166 | M |
| *Yering Station Reserve Pinot Noir, Yarra Valley* | 1997 | $26-35 | B |
| | 1998 | $28-36 | B |

## YERINGBERG

| Wine | Year | Price | Size |
|---|---|---|---|
| *Cabernet Blend, Yarra Valley* | 1978 | $46-60 | B |
| | 1979 | $50-70 | B |
| | 1980 | $45-60 | B |
| | 1982 | $66-80 | B |
| | 1983 | $35-45 | B |
| | 1984 | $50-65 | B |
| | 1985 | $46-60 | B |
| | 1986 | $50-65 | B |

|  |  |  |
|---|---|---|
| | 1987 | $36-48...*B* |
| | 1988 | $60-80...*B* |
| | 1989 | $35-46...*B* |
| | 1990 | $65-80...*B* |
| | 1991 | $56-70...*B* |
| | 1992 | $45-65...*B* |
| | 1993 | $50-65...*B* |
| | 1994 | $55-66...*B* |
| | 1995 | $45-55...*B* |
| | 1996 | $50-60...*B* |
| | 1997 | $66-85...*B* |
| | 1998 | $45-65...*B* |
| *Pinot Noir, Yarra Valley* | 1990 | $36-45...*B* |
| | 1992 | $36-45...*B* |
| | 1993 | $28-38...*B* |
| | 1994 | $30-38...*B* |
| | 1996 | $30-40...*B* |
| | 1998 | $26-35...*B* |

## ZEMA ESTATE

|  |  |  |
|---|---|---|
| *Cabernet Sauvignon, Coonawarra* | 1986 | $28-40...*B* |
| | 1990 | $30-40...*B* |
| | 1994 | $28-35...*B* |
| *Family Selection Cabernet Sauvignon, Coonawarra* | | |
| | 1988 | $35-45...*B* |
| | 1990 | $36-44...*B* |
| | 1991 | $32-45...*B* |
| | 1992 | $30-40...*B* |
| | 1993 | $33-40...*B* |
| | 1994 | $33-40...*B* |
| | 1996 | $36-45...*B* |
| | 1998 | $32-44...*B* |
| *Shiraz, Coonawarra* | 1990 | $28-36...*B* |
| | 1991 | $26-35...*B* |

# TASTING WITH A MARKET PERSPECTIVE

*An overview and interpretation of the ultra-fine Australian wine scene, based on extensive tastings and the unique perspective of secondary market observer.*

My view of Australian Wine benefits from my perspective as a specialist wine auctioneer. Being in tune with factors that drive sentiment in the auction market is, for me, a necessity. I cannot imagine a world without chatting with wine-makers and tasting their wines.

Over the years I've realised how terribly important it is to keep an open mind. Even so, I doubt that I could have ever predicted the emergence of Three Rivers, Torbreck, or Noon. Shifts such as these have largely been caused by the infectious enthusiasm of sommeliers and wine columnists!

I am certainly aware of the bizarre relationship between the price of wine and its quality. Recently I tasted a vertical of *Three Rivers Shiraz* – wines of extraordinary perfume and shape. The price of this vintage leapt tenfold in a single year. Yet for all its wonder and complexity, I know of so many other wines that are as interesting and as beautiful – some yet to be discovered by collectors and wine enthusiasts.

It is not possible for anyone to taste – meaningfully – all wines produced in Australia each year. My focus is on wines that I am likely to see through the wine auction market – a small number of white, but mostly red wines. These include emerging wines and the occasional 'outside chances' – usually stumbled upon in various tastings.

Ultimately, the following Tasting Notes section of this book, is a collection of personal tasting notes and opinions. My tastes are eclectic and I have no axe to grind. I am constantly aware that for many people, winemaking is their life. A wine that scores 80 points can be as enjoyable as a wine that scores 100 points. The crucial component of company, good or bad, is not entered in the equation. Indeed, like many of us, I've sometimes found myself in the presence of great wine but unsympathetic company. On these occasions the mind can wander off completely!

## VINTAGE REPUTATION

Vintage reputation has become an increasingly important factor in wine investment and collecting. The PR engines of major commercial wineries are largely responsible for market impressions of vintage. The 1990s, particularly, are riddled with marketing-driven misinformation.

While developing Langton's website, I spent hours reviewing, researching, and interviewing winemakers, about the issue of vintage. Polarisation of opinion is extraordinary. Complete rejection of one camp by another is not uncommon. Reports compiled within the Industry, while improving, are often inadequate and require much "reading between the lines".

I have found that atypical vintages are often hailed as great vintages. Euphoria for the 1990 vintage rippled throughout Eastern Australia, yet it was hardly a classic vintage in some regions. The over-hyped 1998 vintage, with its wines of extraordinary concentration and power, is certainly a very fine vintage. However, I am convinced that the 1999 Barossa Shirazes and the 1999 Coonawarra Cabernets, are both generally superior. Indeed they are classics. The 2000 Coonawarra vintage, which completely escaped the inclement weather to the north, is also an extremely fine year. It could well eclipse the 1999 vintage.

Also it should be remembered that wineries are capable of pulling a hare out of the hat. The most palpable example is the 1995 *Petaluma Coonawarra* – a wine that is beautifully refined and balanced.

**Riesling**

The Clare Valley is regarded as Australia's quintessential Riesling region. Grosset leads a pack of impressive producers, but interestingly, only Petaluma and Mitchell seem to have any real presence on the market. Leo Buring, once the leader of the pack – now lost in ineffective branding – is a superlative example of Clare Riesling. Mount Horrocks and Knappstein Hand Picked are making terrific examples. O'Reilly too, though hardly known, is excellent. Clare Riesling generally has superb aging potential.

The Eden Valley is likely to make a comeback in forthcoming years. Leo Buring Riesling selections come from this sub region of the Barossa. 'Mesh', the new Yalumba/Grosset joint venture wine, illustrates the overall confidence in the future of this region. Heggies and Henschke are probably the most prominent successes in the Eden Valley, although, at present, their Rieslings don't seem to perform particularly well on the auction market. The Eden Valley has huge potential – surprising that it has not materialised sooner.

Outside these two classic Riesling areas it comes down to producer. In Victoria, I am most impressed by the exquisite Crawford River and the mouthwatering *Delatite Rieslings*. Mitchelton *Blackwood Park* has a strong following. Piper's Brook in Tasmania lurches in quality, but when it's good, it can be very good. Howard Park and Frankland Estate in Western Australia are also making some very fine Rieslings. In truth, there are several very fine Rieslings on the market. Ultimately Grosset and Petaluma will continue to dominate this category. In the short term, Clare Valley producers will be the winners.

The increasing use of Stelvin screw-top caps will have a positive impact on the market. Asides from nullifying the issue of cork taint, Rieslings seem to develop more slowly under screw cap. Older vintages are much fresher and livelier. We can all look forward to a wonderful treasure trove of aged, fault free Rieslings in the future!

**Chardonnay**

Margaret River and the Adelaide Hills have been very successful in the production of Chardonnay. Leeuwin Estate, Pierro, Cape Mentelle and Cullen are well regarded and established market performers. Brookland Valley, Voyager Estate, and Devil's Lair are also making convincing Chardonnays. *Petaluma Chardonnay* and its ultra-cuvee *Tiers Chardonnay* are stand out Adelaide Hills Chardonnays. *Petaluma Yattarna*, which draws a large proportion of its fruit from this part of the world, is very good but was caught in the updraught of over-pricing. This has compromised its integrity. Geoff Weaver, Shaw and Smith, Nepenthe, and Chain of Ponds are making some excellent wines but these are yet to spark the secondary market.

I've noticed in recent years that some winemakers from both these classic Chardonnay areas are drifting towards restrained, almost under-fruited, Chardonnay styles. These wines may develop in the bottle – but the quest for delicacy and exquisite fruit seems to come at the expense of an enjoyable drink.

Hardy's *Eileen Hardy*, a multi-regional blend, is always a reliable Chardonnay but has limited potential on the secondary market. Clarendon Hills Chardonnays are totally off-centre but are very interesting wines to drink.

*Giaconda Chardonnay* from Beechworth Victoria, is a profoundly beautiful wine and is today regarded alongside Leeuwin Estate *Art Series*, as Australia's best Chardonnay. It is very difficult to find, but the experience is worth it.

In the Yarra Valley, *Mount Mary Chardonnay*, a minuscule make, is a superbly eccentric style with plenty of lanolin complexity and flavour length. *Yering Station Reserve Chardonnay* is a newcomer with potential. Rich in resources and with an outstanding winemaker at its helm, it's difficult not to see this wine becoming an important benchmark. Tarrawarra, always on the fringe of the secondary market, is a lovely wine and worth seeking out. *Stoniers Reserve Chardonnay*, from Mornington Peninsula, is another highly impressive wine with superb fruit definition and structure. *Main Ridge Chardonnay*, from a tiny winemaker, is also very highly regarded by the market place, but almost impossible to find.

The Hunter's *Lake's Folly Chardonnay* and *Tyrrell's Vat 47* are both very reliable, well made wines with surprising but excellent, medium term ageing potential.

**Semillon**

On the secondary market, Semillon – once called 'Hunter River Riesling' – is a disaster. Yet the wines are so highly individual and distinctive. *Tyrrell's Vat 1 Semillon*, and certain vintages of *Mount Pleasant Lovedale*, are the only wines with strong auction credentials. *McWilliam's Elizabeth* is a superb wine style with proven cellaring potential, but makes only a small impression in the secondary market, largely because the make is almost 40,000 cases. *Lindeman's Hunter River Semillon* (some older bottlings called Chablis) has lost its lustre but the wines are good.

There are countless Semillon producers in the Hunter. Only a famed wine has any chance of performing on the secondary market. Aged Semillion has sadly become something of an Australian Secondary Market Curio despite the enthusiasms of wine drinkers.

**Other whites**

Viognier is one of the more interesting new varieties. *Yalumba's Virgilius* is a highly successful style, already with a presence on the secondary market. Clonakilla is also making a superb example. Petaluma is making a restrained style.

Pinot Gris, another highly aromatic variety, is also making headway. T'Gallant probably makes the best example.

It is unlikely these highly perfumed varieties will be anything more than a small feature on the secondary market, mainly because they are just so lovely to drink when young.

**Shiraz**

Most secondary market excitement centres on Shiraz – a variety highly valued only in the last 10 years. In the early 1980s, valuable vineyards were pulled out because of lack of interest. It has to be said though, that the vine-pull scheme helped fund new vineyard plantings, many of which are providing extremely high quality fruit.

The movement to cool climate viticulture and cool climate wine made the Barossa, of all places, look rather irrelevant. This trend however, dramatically reversed with the

internationalisation of Australia's wine market and renewed enthusiasm from local buyers.
Use of the word Hermitage, an Australian synonym for Shiraz but also a French wine region, was also discontinued by producers in the early 1990s.

From today's perspective, Shiraz is the strongest bow in Australia's wine armoury. The extraordinary diversity of quality and the universal enjoyment of Australian Shiraz, has propelled a significant number of wines onto the market.

As early as 1830, pioneer James Busby observed that "had New South Wales been settled by the French, the inhabitants would have regaled their palates and invigorated their bodies, with this first of the blessings which nature bestows."

It was in fact James Busby who, after travelling around France and Spain, gave his collection of 678 varieties to the British Authorities. This collection was planted in Sydney's Royal Botanic Gardens. Extensive sections were propagated and sent to the Botanic Gardens in Adelaide and to Busby's parents' property in the Hunter Valley.

This material is probably the original genetic source of many Australian vineyards – although some believe Shiraz was brought out earlier. Indeed historians think it may have been Gregory Blaxland who identified Shiraz as early as 1816. It is difficult to pinpoint when it came into Australia. It was common practice in the early days, for settlers to bring cuttings to Australia, from South Africa etc.

What is certain is that Australia can boast some of the oldest plantings of Shiraz in the world, largely because of the cataclysmic disaster – phylloxera – in Europe.

A single patch of Tyrrell's vines was planted in 1879 in the Hunter Valley. Henschke's Hill of Grace Vineyard was planted in the 1860s, and is some of the oldest genetic Shiraz material known to Man. Indeed most Shiraz plantings in Australia relate to the extraordinary material brought out by our forefathers. And these have been improved upon over the years through selection.

Curiously, not many clones are used – the main ones are 1654, PT23, 1125. Because there just isn't a body of information, Southcorp recently planted a new vineyard in the Barossa to trial their own clone.

In 2001, Penfolds celebrated 50 vintages of *Grange* – in many respects a celebration of half a century of the Modern Australian Wine industry. While there are other winemakers who made important contributions – Maurice O'Shea, Colin Preece, etc – it is Max Schubert's legacy that is so palpable. His wine-making philosophies and innovations percolate throughout the industry. Not all were his own ideas – some were borrowed and improved upon.

The techniques employed in the research and development of *Grange* are astonishing. Max Schubert and his team pioneered major advances in yeast technology and, with Ray Beckwith, paper chromatography. They developed the understanding and use of pH in controlling bacterial spoilage; the use of headed down/submerged cap fermentation, and the technique of rack and return; cold fermentation practices; the use of American oak as a maturation vessel; and perhaps most critically, the use of partial barrel fermentation.

These techniques – once kept under strict wraps – are now employed extensively within the Australian wine industry.

Other great Australian wines can also trace their winemaking origins to *Grange*. *Brokenwood Graveyard Shiraz*, *Henschke Hill of Grace*, and *Wolf Blass Black Label*, are all examples. Even regional style – specifically the Barossa Valley Shirazes – has been highly influenced by the work of Max Schubert and his team.

Today, the diversity of Shiraz in Australia is quite extraordinary, comprising traditional styles such as *Tyrrell's Vat 9* to more radical, innovative wines, such as *Torbreck Descendants Shiraz Viognier*.

The most important Australian Shiraz on the secondary market is *Penfolds Bin 95 Grange*. It accounts for a large percentage of turnover through its established market presence and overall bottle values. The occasional sale of a *Grange* Collection – now around $160,000-200,000 – also helps. Its reputation, however, is built on quality. The wines are incredibly opulent, with immense concentration and power. They develop beautifully in the bottle, although the most memorable experiences are of well-cellared vintages with at least 15 years' bottle age.

The 1955 is very difficult now to find and justify opening. The 1963 and 1966 are drinking well but becoming scarce. The 1971 is also very expensive. Even the value of the 1986 vintage has increased by 25 per cent in the last 18 months.

Anyone wishing to enjoy an old *Grange* need go no further than to buy less recognised vintages or bottles that may be in less than mint condition. Bottles with poor label condition but good levels, often suggests a damp cellar. The market discounts these wines by as much as 50 per cent!

I am very excited about the integrity and diversity of Barossa Shiraz, which embraces the Eden Valley and the Barossa Valley. These wines spearhead Australia's international reputation. The region has a wonderful and unique heritage that adds further appeal to the wines. The extraordinary generosity of spirit found in the Barossa somehow envelops the aromas and flavours.

The most important Barossa Shirazes are the beautifully

perfumed and symmetrical *Henschke Hill of Grace*; the opulently structured *Peter Lehmann Stonewell Shiraz*, and the ethereal classic *Rockford Basket Press Shiraz*. This triptych encapsulates the pure fruit definition of the Eden Valley, the woven richness and texture of fruit and oak, and the intrinsic fruit qualities of Barossa Valley shiraz.

The impossibly small Three Rivers is in a league of its own. Perched on the edge of the Eden Valley and the Barossa it seems to combine all those elements into one. *Barossa Valley Estates - Grant Burge Meshach E&E Black Pepper*, *Henschke Mount Edelstone*, *Yalumba Octavius* and *Elderton Command* make up a very strong second row. Bethany *GR Reserve*, Charles Melton, St Hallett *Old Block*. Turkey Flat, and the very convincing Glaetzer, follow.

The immensely concentrated and impressive *Veritas Hanisch Vineyard* and *Heyson Vineyard* are so compressed with fruit they are almost like essence. In the same mould, *Torbreck Run Rig* – lionised by U.S. critics – has leapt into the collective heart and mind of wine enthusiasts. The extraordinarily decadent and supple *Torbreck Descendant Shiraz-Viognier* is so extravagantly exotic and sublime it could blow your mind... the more sensitive souls may need to avoid this one. *Greenock Creek's Roennfeldt Road* and *Apricot Block* are highly individual and have a strong following of devotees.

Recently I've become extremely impressed with *Dutschke Oscar Semmler* and *St Jakobi Shiraz* – both of which show strong regional provenance and deft winemaking. *Penfolds RWT Shiraz*, with only a few vintages under its belt, is a classic Penfolds wine that will no doubt find its eventual way into the firmament – it's a pity the marketers only came up with an acronym for Red Wine Trial. This newcomer could perhaps have instead been named in honour of Max Schubert, who had such a profound influence on Penfolds and the Barossa. Finally *Kaesler Old Bastard* and *Langmeil Freedom* – based on prime fruit – are up and coming labels worth noting.

McLaren Vale Shiraz, despite being overshadowed by the Barossa's rise to prominence, has through the 1990s, captured the hearts and minds of collectors throughout the world. Auction staples have been *Coriole Lloyd Reserve* and *Hardy's Eileen Hardy* – both of which draw fruit from this area.

*D'Arenberg's Dead Arm* and *Rosemount Balmoral* have fared extremely well over recent years. Both are convincing styles. Clarendon Hills, an outsider for a long time, has brought enormous kudos to the region through the success of its *Astralis* and *Piggott Range Shiraz*. These wines are

of its *Astralis* and *Piggott Range Shiraz*. These wines are still not mainstream but they do show the tantalising prospect of sub-regional definition. Noon Winery has also enhanced McLaren Vale's reputation, although it's *Reserve Shiraz* is a Langhorne Creek wine. This wine has performed outstandingly at auction (many of Noon's clientele have taken advantage of the low cellar door prices).

Fox Creek, which took the market by storm on the back of positive U.S. reviews, attracts strong market support. To retain its status, its forthcoming vintages need to continue to impress this faction. Chapel Hill makes a fairly classic McLaren Vale Shiraz style, but is an erratic performer. Pirramimma is an old label but has failed to attract serious interest on the auction market, although I've always enjoyed these honest wines. Pertaringa, an unfamiliar name on the secondary market, is also making interesting wine.

The Clare Valley is making muscular and solid Shirazes. The tannins are quite strong, sometimes extremely firm, as typified by the wondrously individual *Wendouree Shiraz* and Shiraz blends. With similar tannin structures, but a more opulent curtain of fruit, *Tim Adams Aberfeldy* is gaining auction support for this very intensely flavoured Shiraz. *Leasingham Classic Clare* – a crowd pleaser with softer and fleshier flavours, is very well regarded for its good value.

*Jim Barry's The Armagh* is an extraordinarily plush style, drenched in fruit and massively concentrated. It is a highly successful auction performer. Lengs and Cooter – really on the fringe of the cult wine scene – is also making a very convincing regional *Reserve Shiraz*. The elegantly structured and highly convincing *Mitchell Peppertree Shiraz*, is a ludicrously undervalued wine and a perennial under-achiever at auction. *Mount Horrocks Shiraz* is yet to fire on the market but certainly has plenty of potential.

Coonawarra is also a major Shiraz region. *Woodley's Treasure Chest Series,* produced during the late 1940s and 1950s, began a tradition of Australian wine collecting. I am amazed that no one has resurrected these wonderful labels. Most of the *Treasure Chest* wines are curios these days, although occasionally there are reports of life. Cabernet Sauvignon has really taken a pre-eminent position in the Coonawarra region, for very good reason. Nevertheless, the Shirazes are excellent too and can be a welcome change to the strongly flavoured and opulent wines further to the north. One of the most famous wines produced in Coonawarra is the 1955 *Wynns Coonawarra Michael Hermitage* (Shiraz) – a wine with an illustrious Australian Wine Show record.

Wynn's revived the name in 1990 as a foil to its *John Riddoch* label. The first few vintages were successes at

oriented but over-wrought wine style. The 1998 vintage is a great improvement and could bring this wine back into focus once again.

Katnook Estate has also recently produced an essence of Coonawarra Shiraz called *Prodigy*. However when compared to its excellent standard Shiraz, it's difficult to convince oneself that extra stuffing equals extra quality. Bowen Estate, Penley Estate, Punters Corner, Majella, and Zema Estate all produce well-rounded, flavoursome Shirazes.

Padthaway has become a very important source of Shiraz, especially for larger wine companies. Hardy's *Eileen Hardy Shiraz* uses material from this region. Orlando *Lawson's Shiraz*, with its strong choc-mint aromas and palate richness, is a very convincing style.

Victoria adds further diversity to Australia's rich gene pool of Shiraz. The most enlightening Shirazes come from around Central Victoria. The combination of vineyard site and producer is very important. Jasper Hill, Dalwhinnie Mount Langi Ghiran, and Seppelt Great Western, are the most impressively reliable wines – each offering highly individual, often superb Shirazes.

Jasper Hill's wonderfully evocative *Emily's Paddock Shiraz Cabernet Franc* and *Georgia's Paddock Shiraz* have a strong following at auction. The wines are superbly concentrated and beautifully balanced. *Mount Langi Ghiran Langi Shiraz* is a more elegant style, but delivers a very strong punch in better vintages. Indeed it can be one of Victoria's greatest wines. Dalwhinnie and *Seppelt Great Western* are fabulously consistent, combining both cooler regional expression and opulence.

Recently I have been incredibly impressed by the fabulous palate structure and flavours of *Mitchelton Print Shiraz*. Across the river Tahbilk is making very interesting Shirazes – the *1860 Vines* has long been an auction staple and has an awesome heritage. The wines are frankly up and down, but the 1999 is simply wonderful. The *Reserve 1933 Vines Shiraz* is also worth seeking out. *Craiglee Shiraz* from Sunbury, is a cool expression of Shiraz with plenty of white pepper characters. It has much support from punters – especially in Victoria.

The 1997 *Wild Duck Creek's Duck Muck Shiraz* – a production of just a few barrels – drew acclamations from Robert Parker Jr that propelled Wild Duck Creek onto the cult wine market. It is incredible that a wine of this calibre could demand over $1,400 a bottle at the height of the cult wine boom. Is it the blind leading the blind? Or the enlightened leading the blind, into the garden of Eden?

Other producers making an impact on the secondary

market are Bannockburn in Geelong and Mornington Peninsula's Paringa Estate.

It is more difficult to pin down regional style in Western Australia. There are plenty of well made wines in this State, but in the end the producer's name is most important. Heading the list is Vasse Felix, based in Margaret River. The Shiraz style is plump and savoury with plenty of flavour length. Cape Mentelle's *Shiraz* is a disappointment when compared to its brilliant Cabernet. It does have a good secondary market following, but the style is not convincing. Graylyn Estate in the Margaret River has potential. Howard Park is making forays with this variety, especially with its new Scotsdale label. However a single vintage does not make a lasting impression. Plantagenet Shiraz in the Lower Great Southern has now been around for many years and has a very loyal following.

In New South Wales, Brokenwood *Graveyard Vineyard Shiraz* is by far the most important Shiraz on the market. The wine has really shown its spurs in the last decade. The 1986 vintage – like the 1965 *Lindemans Bin 3100 Hermitage* – shows what the Hunter can do in a good year. Over the years, the consistency has been remarkable. It takes little convincing to recognise *Graveyard Vineyard* as one of the top 10 Shirazes in Australia.

With so much heritage and early promise, it is incredible that the Hunter has been incapable of exciting the contemporary secondary market. *Tyrrell's Vat 9* is a perfectly good fruit-driven and maturation style that draws a moderate level of support. But what other Hunter Shiraz is worth shouting about? Mudgee's Huntington Estate makes a Reserve Shiraz that is very traditional in style, but could perform well in the future. The most exciting new entrant on the secondary market is Clonakilla *Shiraz-Viognier* from the Canberra District – an entirely convincing wine style with plenty of perfume and fruit richness.

### Cabernet Sauvignon and Cabernet Blends

Australian Shiraz has somewhat overshadowed Australian Cabernet. The most impressive Cabernet Sauvignon or Cabernet blends come from Margaret River and Coonawarra. Margaret River's reputation has probably eclipsed Coonawarra's in the last decade, although Coonawarra is well and truly on the come-back trail.

The great *Moss Wood Cabernet Sauvignon* and the svelte and beautifully balanced *Cullen Cabernet-Merlot* lead the list of Margaret River Cabernets. Recently Cape Mentelle has lifted its game completely, making superlative Cabernet with brilliantly rounded tannin structures. Pierro – better known for its Chardonnay – is making a very fine claret style. Vasse Felix, which now draws fruit from a wider field, is incredibly under-valued. I have so enjoyed these wines with their excellent fruit definition, wonderful texture, and flavour length. The use of micro-oxygenation is a means of softening the tannin structures. Clive Otto has used this technique to great effect.

Howard Park produces a sublime *Western Australian Cabernet Merlot* – sourced from both lower Great Southern and Margaret River fruit. Michael Kerrigan's deft handling takes craftsmanship into the realms of wizardry. Leeuwin Estate *Art Series Cabernet* has also improved greatly over recent years although, like Xanadu, it presents with very strong tannins. *Voyager Estate's Cabernet Merlot* is another emerging secondary market wine.

Clare Valley's *Wendouree Cabernet Sauvignon* – renowned for its very strong tannin structures is better than ever, with sensational fruit definition and flavour length. The *Cabernet Malbec* is similar in nature with wiry tannins. Knappstein – an old Clare Valley name – is making a more approachable, softer style, and could rise to prominence in the future. *Leasingham Classic Clare* is a very good, with excellent fruit definition, some grippy tannins, but plenty of stuffing. This is a very well priced wine that ultimately ensures early drinking. But the quality is certainly there. Henschke's *Cyril Henschke* – an Eden Valley wine – is still hitting the mark, but has not inspired the market recently – probably a reflection of the Shiraz versus Cabernet battle. Henschke's *Abbott's Prayer Merlot Cabernet*, on the other hand, is coming of age and is a brilliantly seductive wine.

Barossa Cabernet Sauvignons are generally quite chocolaty and opulent. *Wolf Blass Black Label Dry Red*, which teeters from partial to one hundred per cent Barossa provenance, probably has the strongest track record.

*Penfolds Bin 707* – a multi regional blend – also comprises fruit from the Barossa. *Penfolds Bin 42 Kalimna Cabernet Sauvignon* is produced in relatively small quantities. It's an experimental bin that comes off the historical Kalimna vineyard – one of the oldest Cabernet vineyards in Australia.

Rockford *Home Block Cabernet* is highly regarded although quite scarce. Inexplicably, the highly regarded and classified Seppelt *Dorrien Cabernet Sauvignon* is to be discontinued – the fruit no doubt finding its way into *Penfolds Bin 707* or other Southcorp labels. The marketing will spin a new story for this vineyard's important heritage.

Coriole's *Mary Kathleen Cabernet-Merlot* is one of the more important McLaren Vale Cabernets, with plenty of blackcurrant pastille aromas and quite grippy tannins.

Clarendon Hills *Sandown* and *Hickinbotham Cabernets,* sometimes exciting, are high-priced and extremely hedonistic. *Noon Reserve Cabernet*, sourced from Langhorne Creek, is superbly concentrated and continues to interest the market.

The big Cabernet news item however, is South Australia's Coonawarra – long regarded one of Australia's top wine producing regions. The 1963 *Mildara Cabernet Sauvignon* has earned national applause and the nickname 'Peppermint Patty' (patty is an Australian term for a sweet/lolly). The 1980 *Lindemans St George* also won considerable fame.

During the 1980s Coonawarra Cabernet was hot property and Wynns Coonawarra Estate and Lindemans dominated the scene for years. Both are still making very high quality wines. The standard Wynns 'black label' Cabernet, with its blackcurrant cedar aromas and flavours, has been a staple for many years, rarely disappointing the buyer. Wynns *John Riddoch*, re-priced in the primary markets in 2002, has improved greatly. The wine has far more impact with its generously proportioned fruit, intertwined with strong integrated tannins, and well-seasoned new oak. Suddenly this wine looks relevant in the market again.

Lindemans 'trio' – the highly regarded but waning star *St George,* plus *Limestone Ridge* and *Pyrus* – has drawn auction interest for many years. A rather prolonged dull period has prevailed, but I have been impressed by the clear differences and overall quality of the wines.

*Penfolds Bin 707 Cabernet* also draws fruit from Coonawarra (and other regions). This is a wine made in the reflected winemaking glory of *Grange*. But it has struggled to maintain prominence in the market place, largely because of the Coonawarra Cabernet revival and the strength of Margaret River.

The most impressive emerging producers are Katnook, which is making almost flawless Cabernet at the moment; Hollick (particularly the Ravenswood); Majella, which has taken the wine market by storm for its well-poised, beautifully defined Cabernet; Balnaves – still under-performing on the secondary market but making ravishingly good Cabernet; the superbly concentrated and decadent *Parker Coonawarra Estate*; Balnaves Penley Estate, Petaluma, and Zema Estate.

Bowen Estate, once the darling of the Coonawarra scene, is still very well regarded. Orlando *St Hugo* retains a solid following and in recent years has become an important market staple. Joseph *Moda Amarone*, which draws fruit from Coonawarra and McLaren Vale, is an impressive individual style that I greatly admire.

The Yarra Valley's beautifully sited Mount Mary, Yarra

Yering, and Yeringberg have dominated the scene for many years and continue to command enormous respect from the market. These are profoundly important wines with a strong and loyal primary market.

The remarkable *Mount Mary Quintet* is an elegantly structured style with plenty of cedar blackcurrant aromas, fine grained tannins and underlying oak. In a fine vintage, this wine can be highly desirable. The richer and exotic *Yarra Yering Dry Red No 1* is also a very high calibre and individual wine. *Yeringberg Cabernet* – produced in minuscule qualtities – is a highly perfumed and delicate style that becomes rich and complex in the cellar.

Yering Station is the most interesting new addition in many a year. A very convincing regional style results from outstanding resources and Tom Carson's winemaking skills. However much of the success must relate to vineyard site.

Elsewhere in Victoria I have been impressed by *Tahbilk Reserve Cabernet*. Dalwhinnie, already well regarded, is also making very fine Cabernet, although the secondary market looks more favourably on its *Shiraz*. Across the road, Taltarni, which promises so much, continues to disappoint. The wines are perfectly decent, but they just don't quite deliver the promise of their vineyards. Redbank *Sally's Paddock* can, in a good year, reach a sublime level. This is the antithesis of the monster Cabernet, with pure, almost flowery Cabernet and underlying, sinewy tannin structures. The style only seems to work in a fine vintage.

### Merlot

With an increasingly important role in Cabernet blends, Merlot, as a single variety, is yet to show promise on the secondary wine market. The ultra-fine Merlot revolution in Australia, without convincing leaders, is really a merry-go-round. *Irvine Grand Merlot* has certainly made an impression, however the style is influenced more by winemaking philosophy than variety. Petaluma's *Coonawarra Merlot* has a reasonable following at auction, but is hardly a benchmark style. Considering the fanaticism of the winemaker, it is rather disappointing. Katnook Estate and Brand's are making interesting Coonawarra Merlot, although the style is yet to prove itself. Clarendon Hills *Brookman* and Coldstream Hills have also made some good examples.

### Cabernet Shiraz Blends

Cabernet Shiraz and Shiraz Cabernet are classic Australian blends. The mouth-filling qualities of Shiraz are well known – McLaren Vale Shiraz was often described as the middle palate of Australia. Cabernet, on the other hand, is known for its flavour impact on the front palate and finish. The aim is to intertwine the two varieties perfectly to make a wine of greater complexity and even proportions. While there may be plenty of merit to the theory, the concept – bandied around by every wine educator in the country – is something of a cliché.

Penfolds *Bin 389 Cabernet Shiraz*, and Lindemans *Limestone Ridge*, both leading examples, are worth seeking out. Wolf Blass *Black Label* sometimes comprises Cabernet and Shiraz. Majella's *Mallea* is a newish label that has aroused interest from the American market. Rosemount *Mountain Blue Cabernet Shiraz*, from Mudgee and showing the region's potential, is becoming a minor classic.

### Pinot Noir

The profoundly capricious Pinot Noir is something Australia is becoming better known for. This variety seems to encapsulate the romance and mythology of wine. Capturing the heady perfume and exotic elixir of Pinot Noir is a quest rewarding only an esoteric few. The search for quality has driven many winemakers to the brink of insanity. The best of these wines are rare potions, enjoyed and exhalted by a strong, almost fanatical following of Pinot Noir tragics.

Bass Philip, in Gippsland, is the greatest Australian Pinot Noir producer, making freakish wine – so incredibly sublime and unworldly that it can virtually create a stampede at auction... especially for its *Reserve* and *Premium* Pinot Noirs.

Mount Mary and Yarra Yering were important pioneers, but these days, the quality is less impressive. The contemporary market is keen on Bannockburn *Serre* and its standard *Pinot Noir*, Bindi, Freycinet, Giaconda, and Paringa *Estate Reserve*. Stoniers *Reserve*, Main Ridge (when found), Coldstream Hills, and de Bortoli are all well regarded.

In my own tastings this year, I have found wonderful Pinot Noirs from Panorama, Tasmania, and Yering Station Reserve, Yarra Valley. It would appear that the most successful Pinot Noirs on the secondary market come from the Melbourne 'Dress Circle' and in Tasmania. Adelaide Hills in South Australia and Pemberton in Western Australia show plenty of promise.

### Other Reds

Many producers are experimenting with grape varieties that are new to Australia. Italian varieties are beginning to make a small impact on the primary markets. Jasper Hill has released a Nebbiolo. And both Coriole and Penfolds make a very good Sangiovese.

# TASTING NOTES

*By Andrew Caillard MW*

*These tasting notes are my own personal opinions and may not correspond to investment potential.*

*One of the curious aspects of the fine wine market is that great tasting wine can attract little or no interest from investors. Indeed many – in my opinion – ordinary wines can bring remarkable results.*

*Investment potential is based on market perception and experience. One of the five investment maxims is to read more than one wine critic. James Halliday, Huon Hooke, Jeremy Oliver, Tim White, Philip White, and Max Allen are highly regarded wine writers. American, Robert Parker Jr, is hugely influential.*

Langton's Fine Wine Investment Guide *uses the 100 point score system – now considered an international standard.*

## SCORE

93-100 Outstanding to Perfection
85-92 Well Made to Very Good
78-84 Fair to Moderate

## INVESTMENT POTENTIAL

*The challenge for the investor is to recognise wines that will withstand the test of time. This relates to both cellaring potential, perceptions of quality, and fashion. As an example, 1980 Lindemans St George was considered a great investment wine in its early life. It is now considered a disappointment.*

*The secondary market is the principal source of mature Australian wine, although some retail wine stockists do specialise in back vintages.*

*Growing interest in wine investment will almost certainly see a larger volume of mature Australian wine released into the market place. In the first instance, refer to* www.langtons.com.au

*Investment potential takes into account the current market, vintage and producer reputation, a certain amount of crystal ball gazing, and my own opinion. Use these Tasting Notes as a guide only.*

▼ = Weak; ■ = Moderate; ▲ = Strong; ☆ = Rare; ❍ = Not Saleable.

## ASHTON HILLS

**1999** *Adelaide Hills – Pinot Noir* **S.A.**
Medium crimson. Vanilla/strawberry/nettle/stalk aromas. Palate is hard with cherry/strawberry fruit, green edged tannins finishing firm. Core of fruit sweetness but really not a long lasting proposition.
▼ *81* *Now*

**2000** *Adelaide Hills – Pinot Noir* **S.A.**
Medium crimson. Straw/slight barnyard/mushroom/strawberry apricot aromas. Well structured palate with strawberry/cherry/apricot/game/plum flavours. Fruit-drenched, silky tannins with slightly smoky/spicy oak. Finishing long and flavoursome. Lovely fruit intensity.
▼ *93* *Now-2005*

## BAILEY'S

**1999 '1904 Block'** *Glenrowan – Shiraz* **Vic.**
Deep crimson. Choc-berry/rum and raisin aromas. Plenty of barrel work here. Choc-berry/rum and raisin/vanillin flavours and some briar/earthy characters. Pronounced tannins. Plenty of concentration and length.
■ *86* *2004-2014*

**1994 '1920s Block'** *Glenrowan – Shiraz* **Vic.**
Deep crimson. Meaty/gamy, raspberry-like fruit with some underlying oak. Rich, loose-knit, meaty, raspberry-flavoured wine. Almost a meal in itself, with ripe tannins, and lovely concentration and length.
■ *91* *Now-2008*

**1995 '1920s Block'** *Glenrowan – Shiraz* **Vic.**
Medium crimson. Earthy/mushroom/leather aromas with some raspberry. Already quite developed, with oak coming to the fore and drying, almost austere tannins. Can't see this improving.
▼ *78* *Now*

**1996 '1920s Block'** *Glenrowan – Shiraz* **Vic.**
Deep crimson. Concentrated, prune/plum fruit with some cedary, earthy nuances. Ripe, deep, cedary, plum-like flavours, with grainy tannins and good length.
■ *84* *Now-2006*

**1997 '1920s Block'** *Glenrowan – Shiraz* **Vic.**
Deep crimson/purple. Well made but chunky wine with raspberry fruit and spicy, vanillin oak characters. Fresh, ripe, raspberry/blackberry fruit flavours, classy savoury/malty oak, gravelly tannins and good length.
▼ *92* *2002-2008*

**1999 '1920s Block'** *Glenrowan – Shiraz* **Vic.**
Medium deep crimson. Prominent menthol/tropical oak over elegant raspberry fruit. Rich succulent palate with squashy raspberry/mulberry fruit and smoky/tropical oak, fine very drying tannins finishing firm but with good flavour length. Oak at the fore. Needs to settle down.
■ *87* *2004-2014*

## BALNAVES

**1998 The Tally Reserve** *Coonawarra – Cabernet Sauvignon* **S.A.**
Deep crimson. Perfumed black cherry/mocha slightly savoury/nutty aromas. Well balanced wine with black cherry flavours and plenty of mocha/vanilla oak. Lovely fine grained drying tannins with some cedar/mocha nuances on the finish.
■ *93* *2004-2012*

**2000 The Tally Reserve** *Coonawarra – Cabernet Sauvignon* **S.A.**
Deep crimson. Intense black olive/lead pencil aromas with some juicy fruit/cassis notes. Well concentrated but tightly-knit palate. Black olive/blackcurrant/mint flavours, fine sinewy tannins, underlying cedar oak, touch of meaty complexity, finishing dry and firm. Still quite elemental.
■ *89* *2004-2012*

**1998** *Coonawarra – Cabernet Sauvignon* **S.A.**
Deep crimson. Generous chocolate/cassis aromas with plenty of vanilla/cedar. Monumental style. Richly flavoured wine with chocolate/game/blackcurrant flavours, plenty of malty oak, strong slightly gritty tannins, finishing firm and dry.
■ *90* *2002-2008*

**1999** *Coonawarra – Cabernet Sauvignon* **S.A.**
Deep crimson. Intense choc-berry/malt/liquorice aromas. Deep-set choc-berry flavours with strong dense/gravelly/dry tannins, under-lying malty oak, plenty of fruit-sweetness but finishing quite firm. Needs more time.
■ *91* *2002-2010*

**2000** *Coonawarra – Cabernet Sauvignon* **S.A.**
Deep crimson. Chocolate/cedar/menthol aromas with some smoky bacon oak complexity. Rich chocolate/blackberry flavours, with strong underlying cedar/grainy oak. Loose-knit tannins and plenty of flavour length. This will definitely improve as elements intertwine.
■ *90* *2004-2012*

## BANNOCKBURN VINEYARDS

**1997 Serre** *Geelong – Pinot Noir* **Vic.**
Medium crimson. Menthol/gamy/cherry/bramble aromas. Complex brambly/dark cherry/gamy flavours, fine slightly sinewy tannins, but plenty of fruit and flavour length.
■ *91* *Now-2008*

**1993** *Geelong – Shiraz* **Vic.**
Medium crimson. Light raspberry/tomato leaf aromas with touch of stalkiness. Light bodied, under-fruited wine with tomato leaf flavours, touch of white pepper, fine tannins and medium length.
▼ *76* *Now*

**1999** *Geelong – Shiraz* **Vic.**
Deep crimson. Medium concentrated wine with peppery/menthol/raspberry/earthy aromas and flavours, fine grained tannins, medium concentration and length.
▼-■ *78* *Now-2006*

**1998** *Geelong – Chardonnay* **Vic.**
Pale yellow. Delicate but lovely and complex tropical fruit/melon aromas with hints of roasted nuts and smoky oak – superb definition. Tightly structured, but complex balanced palate. Tropical fruit and smoky oak flavours and nutty barrel ferment nuances. Excellent concentration and length.
■ *93* *Now-2005* *Excellent*

**1999** *Geelong – Chardonnay* **Vic.**
Pale yellow. Guava/passionfruit/pineapple aromas and some nectarine notes which follow on to the palate, some oil skin nuances, but plenty of creamy complexity, concentration and flavour length.
■ *87* *Now-2007* *Excellent*

**2000** *Geelong – Chardonnay* **Vic.**
Pale yellow. Intense honey dew melon/nectarine aromas with some vanilla/toasty oak nuances. Quite classical. Palate is quite tightly structured and minerally, with melon/nectarine/quartz flavours, fine long mouth-watering acidity, some underlying oak, finishing with plenty of length.
■ *93* *Now-2007* *Excellent*

**1997** *Geelong – Pinot Noir* **Vic.**
Medium crimson. Meaty, gamy, dark cherry aromas. Lovely intensity. Slight leafiness. Silky palate with deep set dark cherry stone flavours, and underlying spicy oak flavours, plenty of richness across the mid-palate with a touch of leafiness. Finishing medium length.
■ *94* *Now-2005* *Outstanding*

**1998** *Geelong – Pinot Noir* **Vic.**
Medium crimson. Intense, slightly sappy black cherry aromas. Complex palate with sappy, earthy, black cherry, cherry stone and rhubarb-like flavours. Fine, slightly grainy tannins but good concentration and length. Hail damage year.
▼-■ *80* *Now-2005* *Outstanding*

**1999** *Geelong – Pinot Noir* **Vic.**
Medium crimson. Intense dark cherry/mulberry/menthol aromas with some gumleaf, smoky nuances. Fruit-sweet palate with rhubarb/menthol/dark cherry and flinty flavours, fine tannins with good flavour length.
■ *86* *Now-2006* *Outstanding*

**2000** *Geelong – Pinot Noir* **Vic.**
Medium crimson. Dark cherry/rhubarb aromas with some smoky oak characters. Well balanced wine with deep-set cherry/rhubarb flavours and spicy oak – some gamy complexity – fine, slightly grippy tannins and plenty of flavour length.
■ *94* *Now-2008* *Outstanding*

## BAROSSA VALLEY ESTATES

**1988 E & E Black Pepper Barossa Valley** -*Shiraz* **S.A.**
Medium crimson. Choc-berry/menthol/citrus rind aromas but immensely complex. Richly flavoured palate with choc-orange/sweet mocha fruit, sinewy tannins and malt oak. Finishes firm and grippy.
▲ *91* *Now-2006* *Excellent*

**1990 E & E Black Pepper** *Barossa Valley – Shiraz* **S.A.**
Deep crimson. Developed, earthy, hazelnut-like aromas with touches of polished leather. Richly flavoured palate with ripe, even tannin structure, and medium concentration and length. Drink soon.
▲ *91* *Now-2005* *Excellent*

**1992 E & E Black Pepper** *Barossa Valley – Shiraz* **S.A.**
Crimson. Very classical but complex Barossa Shiraz with dried fruits/chocolate/berry aromas and vanilla/cinnamon/vanilla nuances. The palate is quite oak driven with well seasoned cinnamon/malt/menthol oak intertwined with plump chocolate/berry fruit characters and fine ripe lacy tannins. Finishes long and sweet fruited.
▲ *89* *Now-2010* *Excellent*

**1994 E & E Black Pepper** *Barossa Valley – Shiraz* **S.A.**
Deep crimson. Loose-knit, with meaty, somewhat cordial-like aromas and hints of allspice. Sweet, cedary and earthy on the palate, with raspberry and allspice flavours, seasoned American oak and grainy, slightly chunky tannins. Medium length.
▲ *90* *Now-2012* *Excellent*

**1995 E & E Black Pepper** *Barossa Valley – Shiraz* **S.A.**
Deep crimson/purple. Lifted blackberry and tar-like aromas with touches of truffles and aniseed. Medium concentration yet with excellent blackberry/tar fruit definition, ripe, textured tannins and well-seasoned vanillin oak. A medium-powered wine with moderate potential.
■ *89* *Now-2012* *Excellent*

**1996 E & E Black Pepper** *Barossa Valley – Shiraz* **S.A.**
Crimson. Intense, incredibly barrel worked wine with some meaty, gamy nuances and plenty of spicy/cinnamon/malty oak. A very rich and full flavoured wine with ripe deep-set, blackberry/liquorice/Christmas cake fruit and cinnamon/coconutty oak. Finishes firm but plenty of flavour length. Quintessential in-your-face Barossa Shiraz.
▲ *94* *Now-2010* *Excellent*

**1997 E & E Black Pepper** *Barossa Valley – Shiraz* **S.A.**
Crimson/purple. Aromas of beetroot, blackberry, roasted meat and prosciutto, with plenty of savoury oak. Palate is ripe and sweet-fruited with savoury, meat and bacon-like flavours, ripe, evenly proportioned tannins and excellent concentration and length.
■ *91* *2005-2015* *Excellent*

**1998 E & E Black Pepper** *Barossa Valley – Shiraz* **S.A.**
Crimson. Beautifully defined wine with ripe musky/mulberry/chocberry fruit aromas and spicy cinnamon/malty oak. The palate is deeply set with rich, ripe exotic musky/prune/mulberry fruit, fine grainy tannins, plenty of concentration, finishing firm and tight. This wine has bucket loads of fruit-sweetness.
▲ *95* *2005-2012* *Excellent*

## BASS PHILLIP

**1992 Premium** *Gippsland – Pinot Noir* **Vic.**
Earthy medium crimson. Meaty/gamy, strawberry/black cherry aromas. Richly flavoured, well-textured palate with meaty/spicy/spicy black cherry fruit and supple, slightly gripping tannins, underlying oak and good length. Beautifully balanced, but drink soon.
▲ *94* *Now-2006* *Outstanding*

**1994 Premium** *Gippsland – Pinot Noir* **Vic.**
Medium crimson. Meaty/gamy, strawberry-like aromas with underlying savoury oak. Beautifully concentrated palate with fleshy, meaty/meaty, strawberry-like fruit and a hint of the smoke from a struck match. Fine, slightly gripping tannins and excellent length.
▲ *90* *Now-2006* *Outstanding*

**1997 Premium** *East Gippsland – Pinot Noir* **Vic.**
Medium deep crimson. Intensely perfumed mocha/spice/clove aromas. Richly flavoured, insanely concentrated exotic wine with plenty of viscosity, mocha/spice/deep plummy musk flavours, fine tannins and excellent length. Fabulous.
▲ *98* *Now-2008* *Outstanding*

**1998 Premium** *East Gippsland – Pinot Noir* **Vic.**
Medium deep crimson. Meaty/brothy/cherry/musky aromas with touches of savoury/malty oak. Palate is complex and sweet-fruited with

meaty/brothy/mushroom flavours, touches of demi-glace/apricot, fine pixilated but lacy tannins, finishing quite firm and dry.
▲ 93 Now-2005 *Outstanding*

**1996 Reserve** *East Gippsland – Pinot Noir* **Vic.**
Medium deep crimson. Intense game/meaty aromas with plenty of liquorice/vegemite and cherry characters. The palate is immensely deep, stuffed with musky/plum/apricot flavours, and balanced by superb slinky tannins, marvellous concentration and length. Finishes firm but long. Marvellously eccentric.
▲ 94 Now-2006

**1998 Reserve** *East Gippsland – Pinot Noir* **Vic.**
Medium deep crimson. Very perfumed exotic apricot/dark cherry/strawberry/musky aromas with malty, spicy oak. Immensely complex and superbly concentrated palate. Lovely meaty/strawberry/Turkish Delight flavours. Fine supple/lacy tannins, finishing almost without end.
▲ 94 Now-2008

## BEST'S

**1993 Thompson Family Reserve** *Grampians – Shiraz* **Vic.**
Medium crimson. Bright raspberry mulberry fruit. Ripe, silken palate. Beautifully balanced with pure berry fruit flavours, with supporting oak. Quite lovely.
■ 93 Now-2008

**1996 Thompson Family Reserve** *Grampians – Shiraz* **Vic.**
Deep crimson. Rich, ripe prune/blackberry aromas, balanced with plenty of new vanillin/coconut/cedar oak. Rich, ripe generously proportioned palate with ripe blackberry/prune/meaty flavours. Tannins are quite pronounced and thick but may soften out. This is a monumental wine with plenty of richness and texture.
■ 90 2004-2012

**1997 Thompson Family Reserve** *Grampians – Shiraz* **Vic.**
Deep crimson. Very intense, mocha/coffee aromas with touch of caramel and plenty of meaty complexity. Richly flavoured fruit-sweet wine with fleshy blackberry/mocha fruit and smoky/vanillin oak. Fine tannins, finishing dry and long.
■ 86 Now-2010

## BETHANY

**1996 'GR'** *Barossa Valley – Shiraz* **S.A.**
Deep crimson. Dark chocolate/malty/savoury/mulberry aromas. The palate is very sweet-fruited with plenty of plum/mulberry fruit and savoury/malty oak, lovely concentration, supple tannins finishing long and flavoursome.
■ 93 2003-2010

**1994** *Barossa Valley – Shiraz* **S.A.**
Deep crimson. Restrained earthy/prune-like leafy aromas with touches of aniseed. Richly flavoured cedary earth/prune flavours, fine, grippy, slightly leafy tannins, medium concentration and length.
■ 85 Now-2006

**1995** *Barossa Valley – Shiraz* **S.A.**
Deep crimson. Brambly briar/chocolate aromas. Brambly, briar fruit flavours, tightly knit palate with sinewy fine tannins, hard cedar oak. Fine firm finish.
■ 85 Now

**1996** *Barossa Valley – Shiraz* **S.A.**
Crimson/purple. Sweet prune/plum/liquorice/earthy aromas. Compact palate with earthy developing prune/chocolaty flavours, grainy savoury oak, fine velvety tannins, medium concentration and length.
■ 90 Now-2006

**1997** *Barossa Valley – Shiraz* **S.A.**
Crimson/purple. Intense raspberry mocha aromas with touches of vanilla and chocolate. Ripe, loose-knit wine with sweet-fruited raspberry/mocha aromas with touches of vanilla/chocolate, ripe tannins, underlying slightly sappy oak. Medium to high concentration. Finishing long.
■ 86 Now-2006

**1998** *Barossa Valley – Shiraz* **S.A.**
Purple/crimson. Bright plummy mint/menthol/chocolate aromas. Menthol/sappy oak over pruney/chocolaty fruit, sinewy tannins. Medium concentration and length. Oak at the fore needs to settle down.
■ *89* *Now-2008*

**1999** *Barossa Valley – Shiraz* **S.A.**
Medium deep crimson. Intense chocolaty/savoury cedar/smoky aromas with some leafy nuances. Ripe, choc-berry/mulberry flavours, plenty of savoury oak characters. Fine sinewy tannins. Finishes with good length.
■ *87* *Now-2010*

**2000** *Barossa Valley – Shiraz* **S.A.**
Medium deep crimson. Lovely perfumed plum nectarine aromas with hints of white pepper and cinnamon. Ripe, delicious wine with plummy/chocolate flavours, ripe supple tannins and underlying oak. Finishes grippy but long. Excellent wine.
■ *93* *2004-2012*

## BINDI WINE GROWERS

**1998 Block 5** *Macedon – Pinot Noir* **Vic.**
Medium crimson. Intense lifted plummy/red berry/musk aromas. Palate is squashy and medium concentrated with plenty of plummy/strawberry flavours, fine tannins, finishing firm and tight.
▲ *89* *Now-2005*

**2000 Original Vineyard** *Macedon – Pinot Noir* **Vic.**
Medium crimson. Intense dark cherry/ginger aromas with touch of aniseed. Ripe high pitched palate with dark cherry fruit flavours, fine slightly grippy tannins, quite hot on the finish. Plenty of flavour. Firm.
▲ *86* *Now-2006*

## BOWEN ESTATE

**1998 Ampelon** *Coonawarra – Shiraz* **S.A.**
Deep colour. Intense ripe blueberry/mulberry aromas with some smoky/gamy/ savoury nuances. Ripe, velvety wine with blueberry/ mulberry fruit flavours and touches of smoky bacon/bitumen, leafy/granular tannins, plenty of fruit-sweetness and length.
■ *92* *2004-2012*

**1996** *Coonawarra – Cabernet Sauvignon* **S.A.**
Crimson/purple. Gamy, plummy, chocolate and liquorice-like aromas with some cedar. Dark cherry/chocolate flavours with firm tannins and cedary oak. Moderate concentration and length.
■ *88* *Now-2008* *Distinguished*

**1997** *Coonawarra – Cabernet Sauvignon* **S.A.**
Deep crimson/purple. Aromatic blackcurrant/mulberry fruit and slightly savoury, smoky, vanillin oak. Moderately concentrated palate with cassis and cigar box flavours, pronounced oak and fine, gripping tannins. Good length. Still showing its baby fat. Reasonable potential.
▼-■ *90* *Now-2008* *Distinguished*

**1998** *Coonawarra – Cabernet Sauvignon* **S.A.**
Deep crimson. Leafy choc-berry fruit aromas with some cedary notes. Sweet leafy/ red berry fruits, fine sinewy cedar tannins, underlying oak, finishing with a tannin slick. Very restrained wine.
■-▲ *91* *2004-2010* *Distinguished*

**1999** *Coonawarra – Cabernet Sauvignon* **S.A.**
Deep crimson. Intense dark chocolate/liquorice aromas with malty/ mocha oak. Dense wine with chocolate savoury nuances, iodine/seaweed touches. Fine pronounced tannins. Finishes quite grippy and tight.
■ *88* *2004-2010* *Distinguished*

**1996** *Coonawarra – Shiraz* **S.A.**
Crimson. Ripe blackberry and liquorice aromas with some ground coffee and pepper. Palate is quite tight with some blackberry/pepper fruit and firm, almost green tannins. Lacks generosity of flavour.
■ *85* *Now-2010* *Distinguished*

**1997** *Coonawarra – Shiraz* **S.A.**
Crimson/purple. Blackberry and fruit pastille aromas with some leafiness. Blackberry and leafy flavours on the palate too, with touches of pepper, leafy tannins. Medium concentration and length. A little hard.
▼ *77* *Now-2006* *Distinguished*

## BOWEN ESTATE

**1998** *Coonawarra – Shiraz* **S.A.**
Deep crimson/purple. Aromas of pepper, blackberries and blackcurrant pastilles. Plenty of pure fruit characters on the palate with blackberries and underlying, spicy American oak. Lovely concentration, ripe, textured, slightly gripping tannins and a firm finish. Excellent structure but still elemental. Needs time to evolve.
▼-■ *94* *Now-2008* *Distinguished*

**1999** *Coonawarra – Shiraz* **S.A.**
Deep crimson. Very aromatic white pepper/aniseed/camphor aromas over pure blackberry. Cool flavoured wine with white pepper/aniseed and some blackberry, verging on medicinal, fruit characters. Pronounced almost green tannins but good overall length.
▼-■ *79* *Now-2006* *Distinguished*

## BRAND'S OF COONAWARRA

**1999** *Coonawarra – Shiraz* **S.A.**
Medium crimson. Intense juicy fruit/plum/blackberry aromas. Well concentrated juicy fruit/plum flavours with supple tannins, medium concentration and length.
▼ *84* *Now-2010*

**1996 Patron's Reserve** *Coonawarra – Cabernet Shiraz Merlot* **S.A.**
Deep crimson. Intense black cherry/blackcurrant/mint aromas with smoky/savoury oak. Sweet fruited palate with black cherry flavours, underlying savoury oak. Fine sinewy tannins, finishing long and sweet.
▼ *88* *Now-2010*

**1997 Patron's Reserve** *Coonawarra – Cabernet Shiraz Merlot* **S.A.**
Deep crimson. Dark blackcurrant, juicy fruit aromas with savoury/nutty/cedar/spice nuances. Rich succulent wine with savoury/nutty/cedary flavours and touches of chocolate, fine grained – quite pronounced – tannins, finishing long and sweet.
▼ *87* *Now-2008*

**1998 Patron's Reserve** *Coonawarra – Cabernet Shiraz Merlot* **S.A.**
Deep crimson. Intense deep dark chocolate/blackcurrant/mocha/spicy aromas. Richly flavoured concentrated wine with deep choc-berry/mocha flavours and savoury spicy oak, lovely concentration, pronounced slightly leafy tannins but plenty of length.
▼-■ *90* *2004-2012*

**1999 Patron's Reserve** *Coonawarra – Cabernet Shiraz Merlot* **S.A.**
Deep crimson. Intense Parma violet cassis/chocolate aromas. Lovely definition. Restrained violet/cassis/chocolate flavoured palate with underlying savoury oak, fine Loose-knit velveteen tannins, finishing long and sweet.
▼ *93* *2004-2012*

**1998 Special Release** *Coonawarra – Merlot* **S.A.**
Crimson purple. Intense quince paste/plum/frangipani aromas tropical oak. Elegant style with quince plum fruit, fine grained tannins and savoury barrel flavours, finishing quite firm.
▼-■ *89* *2003-2010*

**1999 Special Release** *Coonawarra – Merlot* **S.A.**
Crimson purple. Rich cedar/spice, Turkish Delight and cassis aromas. Quite exotic. Richly flavoured cedar/cassis/plum flavours with loose-knit, fine grained tannins. Finishes quite grippy and firm. Well made wine.
▼ *91* *2003-2010*

**1996 Stentiford's Reserve Old Vines** *Coonawarra – Shiraz* **S.A.**
Deep crimson. Intense mulberry aromas with malty/vanilla oak and meaty/gamy nuances. Sweet demi glace/consomme/meaty complexity on the palate with silky tannins and savoury oak flavours, finishing long and sweet.
■ *93* *Now-2008*

**1997 Stentiford's Reserve Old Vines** *Coonawarra – Shiraz* **S.A.**
Deep crimson. Intense cassis/nutmeg aromas with savoury/malty oak and flavours. Fine drying/chalky tannins, good concentration, with some cedary complexity. Finishing long and flavoursome.
▼ *86* *Now-2006*

**1998 Stentiford's Reserve Old Vines** *Coonawarra – Shiraz* **S.A.**
Deep crimson. Deep blackberry/briar/curranty/gamy aromas with touches of aniseed/cigar box. Immensely deep-set wine with blackberry/chocolate/briary flavours, bristling tannins, and plenty of

new oak. Still very elemental, blocked out wine. Plenty of concentration and flavour length. Will come around.
■ *88* *2005-2012*

**1999 Stentiford's Reserve Old Vines** *Coonawarra – Shiraz* **S.A.**
Deep crimson. Intense liquorice/black cherry/mulberry aromas with underlying cedary oak and some aniseed/ginger. Richly flavoured wine. Black cherry/mulberry flavours, underlying savoury oak, pronounced chewy tannins but good length of flavour. Tannins a bit drying.
▼-■ *90* *2004-2010*

**1999** *Coonawarra – Cabernet Sauvignon* **S.A.**
Deep crimson. Lovely cedar/spice/leafy aromas with some blackcurrant. Medium concentrated wine with cedar/spice/walnut flavours, long pronounced sinewy tannins finishing quite firm.
▼-■ *83* *2004-2010*

**2000** *Coonawarra – Cabernet Sauvignon* **S.A.**
Deep crimson. Classic restrained leafy/cedary style with some cassis/mint characters. Cedar/leafy/cassis flavours. Medium concentration. Fine grippy/grainy tannins building up firm and tight. Very nice core of fruit-sweetness.
▼-■ *84* *2004-2010*

## BROKENWOOD

**1989 Graveyard Vineyard** *Hunter Valley – Shiraz* **N.S.W.**
Deep crimson. Complex raspberry/coffee aromas with some hazelnut/sweet fruit/demi-glace complexity. Delicious drinking wine with hazelnut/demi glace/soy fruit characters. Lovely concentration. Fine, lacy tannin structure. Underlying oak. Plenty of length. A lovely wine.
▲ *96* *Now-2006* *Outstanding*

**1990 Graveyard Vineyard** *Hunter Valley – Shiraz* **N.S.W.**
Deep crimson. Perfumed, meaty, tobacco-like aromas with touches of polished leather. Meaty/gamy fruit with a sweet, slightly herbal, leathery edge, but plenty of concentration. Tannins are firm and gripping, even slightly tough, and the finish is also firm.
■-▲ *84* *Now-2008* *Outstanding*

**1993 Graveyard Vineyard** *Hunter Valley – Shiraz* **N.S.W.**
Crimson/purple. Intense, almost Cabernet-like wine with cassis/black cherry aromas and savoury, meaty oak nuances. Palate has blackcurrant, cedar and meaty flavours, thick, soupy tannins and good length. Already developing.
■-▲ *88* *Now-2010* *Outstanding*

**1994 Graveyard Vineyard** *Hunter Valley – Shiraz* **N.S.W.**
Deep crimson. Complex and savoury mushroom/demi-glace/soy aromas with plenty of underlying sweet fruit. Richly flavoured palate with demi-glace/soupy/meaty flavours, fine velveteen tannins and plenty of length and texture. Wonderfully balanced wine.
▲ *93* *Now-2008* *Outstanding*

**1996 Graveyard Vineyard** *Hunter Valley – Shiraz* **N.S.W.**
Deep crimson. Very complex mushroom/earthy/cherry/cherry stone aromas with some liquorice/leather. Beginning to show some bottle age. Earthy/mushroom flavours with some cherry stone/plummy fruit, fine sinewy tannins and plenty of length. Well structured wine with plenty of balance and complexity.
▲ *89* *2003-2010* *Outstanding*

**1997 Graveyard Vineyard** *Hunter Valley – Shiraz* **N.S.W.**
Deep crimson/purple. Ripe berry, complex iodine-like aromas with hints of pepper and menthol. Blackberry pastille-like fruit flavours with slight earthy, menthol/pepper characters, moderate to high concentration, fine-grained tannins and good length. Well balanced wine.
■-▲ *89* *Now-2008* *Outstanding*

**1998 Graveyard Vineyard** *Hunter Valley – Shiraz* **N.S.W.**
Deep crimson/purple. Intense and generous, with strong, deep aromas of blackberry, raspberry, liquorice and aniseed, balanced by savoury, beautifully seasoned oak. Palate is highly concentrated with warm, squashy, blackberry jam and liquorice-like fruit, pronounced but fine, smoky, savoury oak, Loose-knit, ripe tannins and excellent length. A classic in the making.
▲ *94* *2005-2012* *Outstanding*

**1999 Graveyard Vineyard** *Hunter Valley – Shiraz* **N.S.W.**
Deep crimson colour. Very deep intense choc-mulberry/plum aromas with some vanilla/tropical oak. Very elemental wine with plenty of choc-plum fruit and savoury gamy nuances, fine grainy tannins, underlying tropical/vanilla oak, finishing firm and flavoursome.
▲ *93* *2004-2012* *Outstanding*

**2000 Graveyard Vineyard** *Hunter Valley – Shiraz* **N.S.W.**
Deep crimson colour. Intense black cherry/choc-berry aromas with cedar/savoury/ smoky bacon oak. Rich ripe palate with black cherry/ choc-berry fruit and meaty gamy nuances. Fine ripe tannins, plenty of concentration and length. Lovely fruit-sweetness. Lovely wine for long term ageing.
▲ *98* *2005-2014* *Outstanding*

## CAPE MENTELLE

**1992** *Margaret River – Cabernet* **W.A.**
Crimson/purple. Leafy cassis aromas with touches of earth and iodine. Leafy cassis flavours with some cedary oak, mineral acidity, fine grained slightly green tannins, medium concentration finishing firm.
■ *89* *Now-2008* *Outstanding*

**1993** *Margaret River – Cabernet* **W.A.**
Purple/crimson. Leafy mulberry/dark chocolate aromas. Leafy/ chocolaty flavours with underlying oak. Pronounced, almost green tannins. Medium to high concentration and a firm finish.
■ *85* *Now-2008* *Outstanding*

**1994** *Margaret River – Cabernet* **W.A.**
Black/purple. Restrained but powerful, with black olive, blackcurrant aromas and cedar oil oak characters. Palate is deep and concentrated, with sweet, cedar wood/black olive/blackcurrant fruit, fine grained, Loose-knit, gravelly tannins, savoury oak and a firm finish.
■ *93* *Now-2010* *Outstanding*

**1995** *Margaret River – Cabernet* **W.A.**
Crimson/purple. Earthy, grainy, leathery, menthol-like aromas. Finely structured palate with restrained, earthy, liquorice-like fruit flavours, fine, grainy tannins, underlying but barely noticeable oak and a firm finish. A quiet wine.
■ *88* *Now-2010* *Outstanding*

**1996** *Margaret River – Cabernet* **W.A.**
Crimson/purple. Classic blackcurrant/cedar/black olive/iodine aromas. Ripe-flavoured wine with plenty of blackcurrant fruit, fine-grained, slightly gravelly tannins, savoury oak and a firm finish.
■-▲ *94* *Now-2010* *Outstanding*

**1998** *Margaret River – Cabernet* **W.A.**
Deep crimson. Intense sweet dark chocolate/mocha aromas with beautiful cedary undertones. Super complexity with dark chocolate/ mocha flavours and plenty of cedar/leafy/undergrowth nuances. Lovely underlying oak, fine grained textured tannins finishing long and cedary. Perfectly balanced wine.
■-▲ *95* *2005-2015* *Outstanding*

**1999** *Margaret River – Cabernet* **W.A.**
Deep crimson. Intense mocha/savoury vanillin aromas some cedary tones. Rich savoury wine with choc-berry fruit flavours and some blackcurrant/black olive nuances, fine grainy Loose-knit tannins, finishing very long and cedary. Very nice wine.
■ *91* *2005-2012* *Outstanding*

**1996** *Margaret River – Chardonnay* **W.A.**
Pale yellow. Peachy/melon aromas with roasted nuts, leesy complexity and oak. The palate is showing a touch of bottle age complexity with plenty of sweet fruit, savoury new oak, lovely concentration and length.
■ *92* *Now* *Distinguished*

**1997** *Margaret River – Chardonnay* **W.A.**
Pale yellow. Aromas of peach, melon, honey, roasted nuts and savoury oak. Palate is creamy and squashy, with peaches, melon, savoury oak, lanolin complexity, fine, rapier-like acidity and excellent length.
■ *95* *Now-2005* *Distinguished*

**1998** *Margaret River – Chardonnay* **W.A.**
Pale gold. Pear drop/roasted nut/melon aromas, very pure and tight with a touch of malty oak. Lovely deep-set but tangy palate with

fleshy, creamy pear/grapefruit/melon flavours, lovely toasty oak and fine acid cut. Excellent length of flavours.
■ 94 Now-2005 *Distinguished*

**1999** *Margaret River – Chardonnay* **W.A.**
Pale yellow. Restrained lemony lanolin/pear-skin aromas with touches of peach and spicy oak. Just a touch herbal. Pear-skin/apple/peach flavours with plenty of roasted nut complexity, some malty savoury oak flavours, but with tight acidity and good length. Elegant style with plenty of concentration. Falling just short of top notch.
■ 90 Now-2005 *Distinguished*

**2000** *Margaret River – Chardonnay* **W.A.**
Pale yellow. Creamy lovely honeysuckle/melon aromas with touch of malt and roasted nuts. Excellent fruit definition. Interesting palate with squashy melon/malt/roasted nut flavours, pronounced acidity but balanced by creamy fruit-sweetness. Finishes long but a touch grippy.
■ 88 Now-2006 *Distinguished*

**1994** *Margaret River – Shiraz* **W.A.**
Crimson. Menthol/pepper/leafy raspberry aromas. Lightly concentrated early drinking style. Peppery/raspberry fruit characters. Angular tannins. Pronounced acidity but good length. Not a long term proposition.
▼-■ 78 Now-2005 *Distinguished*

**1995** *Margaret River – Shiraz* **W.A.**
Deep crimson. Complex and medium concentrated wine with raspberry/coffee/bramble/menthol aromas. The palate is quite restrained with raspberry/leathery/menthol flavours, drying tannins, underlying oak, finishing very dry and tight.
▼-■ 80 Now-2008 *Distinguished*

**1996** *Margaret River – Shiraz* **W.A.**
Deep crimson/purple. Black cherry/tar aromas with touches of raspberry. The palate is concentrated and rich with black cherry/tar flavours, grainy tannins and slightly sappy oak. Finishes firm.
▼-■ 86 Now-2006 *Distinguished*

**1997** *Margaret River – Shiraz* **W.A.**
Crimson/purple. Leafy, tarry, slightly green-edged aromas with touches of liquorice. Moderately concentrated, soupy palate with leafy, liquorice-like flavours, gripping tannins and a firm finish.
▼-■ 83 Now-2005 *Distinguished*

**1998** *Margaret River – Shiraz* **W.A.**
Deep crimson/purple. Leafy, peppery, aniseed-like aromas. Smoky, leafy flavours with some cedary notes, pronounced, gripping tannins, and moderate concentration. Quite an elegant wine that should build up in the cellar.
▼-■ 88 Now-2008 *Distinguished*

**1999** *Margaret River – Shiraz* **W.A.**
Deep crimson. Smoky bacon/lanolin/mineral/plum aromas. Plenty of plum/seaweed/lanolin fruit flavours, fine Loose-knit, well-resolved, tannins, finishing long and flavoursome. Very complex wine.
▼-■ 87 Now-2008 *Distinguished*

**2000** *Margaret River – Shiraz* **W.A.**
Deep crimson. Cool/high pitched blackberry/aniseed/white pepper aromas. Sweet blackberry/peppery flavours with fine tannins, medium concentration and length. Very clear fruited wine. Great now but medium term prospect.
▼-■ 88 Now-2008 *Distinguished*

## CHARLES MELTON WINES

**1995** *Barossa Valley – Shiraz* **S.A.**
Crimson. Classical Barossa Shiraz with Loose-knit choc-mulberry/soy aromas and beautifully seasoned malty oak. Rich multi-layered palate with choc-berry fruit-sweetness. Fine lacy tannins and malty, slightly cedary oak. Very textured wine with excellent length.
■ 93 Now-2006

**1996** *Barossa Valley – Shiraz* **S.A.**
Deep crimson. Menthol, almost spearmint aromas with raspberry/blackberry tones. Palate is rich with ripe penetrating tannins, lovely concentration and length. Oak is slightly over the top, but could meld.
■ 90 Now-2008

**1997** *Barossa Valley – Shiraz* **S.A.**
Medium crimson. Lifted juicy fruit/mulberry/plum aromas. Medium concentrated wine with juicy mulberry fruit, lacy but slightly grippy tannins, some underlying oak, finishing chalky firm but with good flavour length.
■ *85* *Now-2008*

**1998** *Barossa Valley – Shiraz* **S.A.**
Deep crimson. Pure blackberry pastille/gamy aromas. Touch of white pepper. Pure blackberry/mulberry fruit flavours, marked gravelly tannins. Excellent mid-palate richness and length. Slightly grippy at the finish.
■ *90* *2004-2012*

**1999** *Barossa Valley – Shiraz* **S.A.**
Medium deep crimson. Raspberry/blackberry/meaty aromas with touch of tropical /vanilla complexity. Restrained but fruit-sweet palate with raspberry/mulberry/rhubarb flavours, fine sinewy tannins. Finishing tight and firm but excellent flavour length.
■ *88* *2004-2012*

**1993 Nine Popes** *Barossa Valley – Shiraz Grenache Mourvedre* **S.A.**
Crimson/purple. Gamy, earthy, slightly weedy wine. Developed palate with gamy, weedy flavours, quite lean and mean on the mid-palate with green-edged tannins and a firm finish.
■ *75* *Now* *Excellent*

**1996 Nine Popes** *Barossa Valley – Shiraz Grenache Mourvedre* **S.A.**
Crimson/purple. Sappy, cedary, prune/plum/liquorice/musk aromas with plenty of fresh oak character. Palate is sappy and cedary with plum and liquorice flavours, immense concentration, fine, ripe tannins, savoury oak, and great length.
■ *94* *Now-2008* *Excellent*

**1997 Nine Popes** *Barossa Valley – Shiraz Grenache Mourvedre* **S.A.**
Deep crimson. Exotic plum/prune and mulberry, almost frankincense aromas with new oak background. Rich, ripe, squashy plum/mulberry fruit characters. Pronounced, structured, firm tannins. Some oak accents.
■ *93* *Now-2008* *Excellent*

**1998 Nine Popes** *Barossa Valley – Shiraz Grenache Mourvedre* **S.A.**
Medium crimson. Almond/walnutty/leathery aromas – plenty of maturation characters. Developing wine with almond/walnutty/leathery/ polish flavours, fine sinewy tannins finishing long and sweet. Has developed quite dramatically.
■ *86* *Now-2006* *Excellent*

**1999 Nine Popes** *Barossa Valley – Shiraz Grenache Mourvedre* **S.A.**
Medium crimson. Aromatic raspberry/leafy/plum/pear aromas with violet nuances. Medium concentrated wine with squashy pear/raspberry/ musky/violet flavours, fine slightly grippy tannins and moderate length. Finishes with an alcoholic kick.
■ *88* *Now-2008* *Excellent*

## CLARENDON HILLS

**1994 Astralis** *McLaren Vale – Shiraz* **S.A.**
Deep crimson. Slightly over ripe/developed roasted coffee/herb garden/ Christmas cake aromas and flavours. Fine mocha/tawny port flavours, with fine slightly gritty tannins.
▼-■ *84* *Now-2010*

**1996 Astralis** *McLaren Vale – Shiraz* **S.A.**
Deep crimson. Perfumed raspberry/apricot/blackberry aromas with some malt /roasted nut complexity. Beautifully concentrated wine with deep-set blackberry/liquorice spice flavours, fine long slinky tannins, restrained oak, excellent balance and length.
■ *97* *2004-2012*

**1997 Astralis** *McLaren Vale – Shiraz* **S.A.**
Deep crimson. Complex liquorice/red cherry/meaty/game/mineral aromas with some vanilla nuances. Ripe plummy/apricot flavours. Firm, fine, slightly aggressive tannins. Finishing tight and firm. Sweet and sour impression.
▼-■ *86* *2004-2010*

**1998 Astralis** *McLaren Vale – Shiraz* **S.A.**
Deep crimson.. Blackberry/meaty/rhubarb aromas with some touch of straw apricot. Immensely concentrated palate with plenty of blackberry

pastille/meaty flavours and malty oak. Ripe tannins, building up firm and tight. Excellent length.

▼-■ *94* *Now-2010*

**1999 Astralis** *McLaren Vale – Shiraz* **S.A.**
Deep crimson. Densely packed wine with ripe, pure blackberry aromas and savoury/smoky oak. Savoury blackberry/meaty flavours. Fine sinewy, long tannins, intertwined with beautifully seasoned oak. Plenty of flavour length.

▼-■ *93* *2005-2012*

**2001 Astralis** *McLaren Vale – Shiraz* **S.A.**
Deep crimson. Very floral apricot/jasmine/Earl Grey tea aromas over underlying blackberry *confit*. Superb definition. Incredibly deep, almost essence, wine with apricot/ prune/*paneforte* and bramble/ blackberry flavours. Slinky tannins building up to a fine net at the back. Superb savoury/mocha oak and excellent flavour length. Incredibly seductive wine.

▼-■ *97* *2006-2015*

**1998 Brookman Vineyard** *McLaren Vale – Merlot* **S.A.**
Deep crimson. Intense complex dark chocolate/meaty/menthol aromas. Rich viscous palate with choc-berry/slight herb garden flavours, fine sinewy tannins, finishing long and sweet fruited.

▼-■ *89* *2004-2008*

**1999 Brookman Vineyard** *McLaren Vale – Merlot* **S.A.**
Deep crimson. Highly perfumed vanilla, choc-berry meaty aromas. Soft supple wine with choc-berry fruit, fine silky ripe tannins, underlying oak, and plenty of flavour length.

▼-■ *92* *2003-2010*

**1998 Brookman Vineyard** *McLaren Vale – Shiraz* **S.A.**
Deep crimson. Perfumed lanolin/gun-flint/tomato-leaf aromas and flavours. Palate has plenty of concentration. Fine, silty tannins building up firm and tight. Sweet and sour wine.

▼-■ *82* *2004-2008*

**1999 Brookman Vineyard** *McLaren Vale – Shiraz* **S.A.**
Deep crimson. Earthy/plum/menthol/smoky bacon oak. Touch jammy. Ripe squashy plum-berry flavours, fine long silken tannins, underlying but beautifully seasoned savoury oak. Plenty of flavour length.

▼-■ *90* *2004-2012*

**1998 Hickinbotham** *McLaren Vale – Cabernet Sauvignon* **S.A.**
Deep crimson. Roasted coffee/choc-cassis/nutmeg aromas. Very tight unyielding wine with choc-berry/cassis/tomato leaf flavours, very fine grippy tannins, plenty of fruit-sweetness, finishing firm.

▼-■ *87* *2004-2010*

**1999 Hickinbotham** *McLaren Vale – Cabernet Sauvignon* **S.A.**
Deep crimson. Intense menthol/chocolate/coffee/blackberry pastille aromas. Massive palate with strong choc-berry menthol flavours. Pronounced, dense, grippy tannins and underlying malty oak. Finishes firm.

▼-■ *87* *2004-2008*

**1998 Hickinbotham** *McLaren Vale – Chardonnay* **S.A.**
Medium pale colour. Lemon scented aromas with some gardenia/ cashew nut/tropical characters. Tighter than expected on the palate with lemony tropical fruit flavours. Touch of cashew nuts. Lovely balance and length.

▼-■ *91* *Now*

**1999 Hickinbotham** *McLaren Vale – Chardonnay* **S.A.**
Medium pale colour. Intense lemon/lanolin aromas with wheat/malty undertones. Richly flavoured fleshy wine with deep-set lemon curd flavours, fine linear acidity, underlying oak and plenty of length.

▼-■ *93* *Now*

**1999 Hickinbotham** *McLaren Vale – Pinot Noir* **S.A.**
Medium crimson.. Complex and evolved earthy/leather/menthol/floral aromas. Textured wine with earthy/sweet truffley/tomato leaf/herbal flavours. Fine grainy but supple tannins, finishing firm but with plenty of flavour length.

▼-■ *84* *Now*

**1998 Liandra** *McLaren Vale – Shiraz* **S.A.**
Deep crimson. Elegant blackberry pastille/tomato leaf aromas with touches of vanilla. Loose-knit silky palate with blackberry pastille

flavours and fine grainy tannin structures, underlying malty/cedary oak finishing long and flavoursome.

▼-■ 92 2004-2012

**1999 Liandra** *McLaren Vale – Shiraz* **S.A.**

Deep crimson. Scented plum/smoky/gunflint/red cherry/earthy aromas. Very plummy fruit-sweet palate, with smoky undertones, fine ripe tannins, plenty of concentration and flavour length. Really nice tension to the wine.

▼-■ 94 2005-2015

**1998 Piggott Range** *McLaren Vale – Shiraz* **S.A.**

Deep crimson. Profound raspberry/blackberry aromas with plenty of ultra-ripe liquorice/ aniseed nuances. Opulently flavoured deep blackberry/mulberry/liquorice flavours, with fine sinewy tannins, immense concentration and power. Long lasting cellaring style.

▼-■ 95 2006-2016

**1999 Piggott Range** *McLaren Vale – Shiraz* **S.A.**

Deep crimson. Immensely complex wine with liquorice/game/black cherry/chocolate aromas with some smoky oak immensely concentrated wine with chocolate/game/dark fruit/mocha flavours, fine pronounced tannins and superb flavour length. Beautiful.

▼-■ 98 2004-2012

**1998 Sandown Vineyard** *McLaren Vale – Cabernet Sauvignon* **S.A.**

Deep crimson. Highly aromatic chocolate/liquorice/prune/ malt aromas. Immensely concentrated wine with deep-set chocolate/apricot/meaty flavours, some vanilla oak, fine strong sinewy tannins with plenty of flavour length and tannin slick.

▼-■ 95 2004-2012

**1999 Sandown Vineyard** *McLaren Vale – Cabernet Sauvignon* **S.A.**

Deep crimson. Intense perfumed raspberry/cassis/choc-berry apricot aromas with touch of vanilla. Well focused supple palate with apricot/ smoky blackberry flavours, fine quite sinewy tannins and some malty vanillin oak. Plenty of length. Delicious.

▼-■ 93 2004-2012

## CLONAKILLA

**1997** *Canberra District – Shiraz Viognier* **N.S.W.**

Deep crimson. Intense cracked pepper/malty/blackberry aromas with touches of menthol. Lean, cool flavoured wine with menthol/peppery flavours and some blackberry pastille characters. Medium concentration, grippy tannins, finishing firm and tight.

▼-■ 80 Now-2008

**1998** *Canberra District – Shiraz Viognier* **N.S.W.**

Deep crimson. This is a real fruit bomb with deep aromatic blackberry/ chocolate/aniseed aromas and smoky bacon oak. The palate is plush with blackberry/fruit pastille/chocolate/ginger flavours, plenty of underlying oak, pronounced tightly knit but fine grippy tannins and flavour length. Still looking very young and promising.

▲ 89 2004-2010

**1999** *Canberra District – Shiraz Viognier* **N.S.W.**

Medium deep crimson. Saddle leather/iodine/white pepper aromas. Cool flavoured wine with saddle-leather/iodine flavours and sinewy tannin structures.

▼-■ 83 Now-2008

**2000** *Canberra District – Shiraz Viognier* **N.S.W.**

Deep crimson. Intense perfumed lanolin/blackberry/pepper aromas with plenty of savoury/meaty complexity. The palate is richly concentrated with deep-set blackberry/pepper/meaty flavours and underlying savoury oak, fine ripe grainy tannins finishing firm but flavoursome. Excellent wine.

▲ 94 2005-2012

**2001** *Canberra District – Shiraz Viognier* **N.S.W.**

Medium crimson. Very cool, but fruit direct, raspberry pastille, white pepper aromas. Medium concentrated wine with raspberry/white pepper/apricot flavours, fine sinewy slightly bitter tannins finishing peppery/dry. Cool flavoured wine.

▲ 92 2004-2008

## COLDSTREAM HILLS

**1998 Reserve** *Yarra Valley – Cabernet Sauvignon* **Vic.**
Deep crimson. Very attractive sweet mocha/earthy/liquorice aromas with some cassis/vanilla oak. Sweet fruit flavours with coffee/demi glace nuances. Fine grained, classic tannin structures. Plenty of fruit-sweetness and length. Showing a touch of development but an excellent wine.
▼-■ *91* *Now-2008*

**2000 Reserve** *Yarra Valley – Cabernet Sauvignon* **Vic.**
Deep crimson. Aromatic meaty/red cherry/bayleaf aromas – touch of cedar spice notes. Red cherry/gamy flavours. Fine grainy tannins with nice core of fruit-sweetness and malty, cedary oak. Plenty of fruit-sweetness and length.
▼-■ *87* *Now-2006*

**1998 Reserve** *Yarra Valley – Chardonnay* **Vic.**
Pale yellow. Melon/peach/apricot aromas with background oak and nutty, nougat-like barrel ferment complexity. Palate is ripe and fleshy with melon/peach/apricot fruit, toasty, nutty oak, and lovely concentration and length.
▼-■ *94* *Now* *Distinguished*

**1999 Reserve** *Yarra Valley – Chardonnay* **Vic.**
Pale yellow. White peach/melon/grapefruit aromas with some cinnamon oak and roasted nut/yeasty/butterscotch aromas. Excellent palate with melon/grapefruit flavours. Cinnamon nuances, savoury oak. Plenty of mid-palate richness. Finishing clean and long. Very minerally.
▼-■ *93* *Now* *Distinguished*

**2000 Reserve** *Yarra Valley – Chardonnay* **Vic.**
Pale yellow. Intense fresh melon/lime/peach and roasted nut aromas. Restrained melon/ lime flavours with fine attenuated acidity, underpinned by biscuity oak, finishing long and flavoursome.
▼-■ *86* *Now* *Distinguished*

**1998** *Yarra Valley – Merlot* **Vic.**
Crimson purple. Perfumed raspberry/chocolate aromas. Plenty of richness on the palate with sweet fruited plummy/choc-berry/earthy flavours, ripe tannins and underlying oak building up quite firm and tight at the finish. Good flavour length.
▼-■ *92* *2004-2012*

**1998 Reserve** *Yarra Valley – Pinot Noir* **Vic.**
Crimson. Restrained cherry stone, slightly musky/smoky oak aromas and touches of meat. Palate has some good fruit-sweetness with cherry stone flavours, slightly hot but fleshy middle, with good overall length. Youthful, but has medium-term cellaring potential.
▼-■ *88* *Now* *Distinguished*

**2000 Reserve** *Yarra Valley – Pinot Noir* **Vic.**
Medium crimson. Intense red cherry/ginger/meaty aromas touch of malt. Smooth flavoured wine with red cherry flavours/touches of ginger and gunflint/smoke, fine grippy tannins building up firm at the finish. Nice wine.
▼-■ *86* *Now-2006* *Distinguished*

## CORIOLE

**1992 Lloyd Reserve** *McLaren Vale – Shiraz* **S.A.**
Deep crimson/purple. Intense, earthy/rusty and blackberry aromas with some tar and underlying oak. Palate has a core of sweet, earthy, blackberry-like fruit, with fine but pronounced tannins, and excellent concentration and length.
■-▲ *90* *Now-2010* *Excellent*

**1993 Lloyd Reserve** *McLaren Vale – Shiraz* **S.A.**
Deep crimson. Blackberry/chestnut aromas with a lavish dollop of American oak. Very barrel-driven wine with plenty of new oak plastered over shy, meaty, blackberry fruit. Tannins are slightly aggressive. Needs a bit more time but suspect that the underlying structure is a touch green.
■-▲ *84* *Now-2008* *Excellent*

**1994 Lloyd Reserve** *McLaren Vale – Shiraz* **S.A.**
Deep crimson. Ultra-ripe choc-berry/prune/liquorice aromas. Really ripe and sweet fruit wine with choc-berry/soy fruit, fine, grainy

tannins, underlying oak, pronounced but velveteen tannins, finishing quite dry and tight. Flavour fades towards the end.

■-▲ 86 Now-2010. *Excellent*

**1995 Lloyd Reserve** *McLaren Vale – Shiraz* **S.A.**

Medium crimson. Pronounced liquorice/cedar/tropical/menthol/oak aromas. Deeply concentrated, brooding wine. Black cherry/chocolate/ liquorice flavours. Slightly angular almost bitter tannins, but good length. Medium term tannins will come to the fore as fruit evolves.

■ 90 Now-2006 *Excellent*

**1996 Lloyd Reserve** *McLaren Vale – Shiraz* **S.A.**

Deep crimson/purple. Intense liquorice deep-set almost tarry aromas with some blackberry/ black olive nuances and new oak in background. Palate is rich and thick with blackberry/olive/savoury oak flavours – oak slightly dominant. Gravelly tannins finishing firm.

■-▲ 92 Now-2010 *Excellent*

**1997 Lloyd Reserve** *McLaren Vale – Shiraz* **S.A.**

Deep crimson. Lanolin/dark cherry aromas with plush sweet fruit characters and meaty complexity. Well structured wine with cherry lanolin gamy flavours, underlying savoury oak, fine long grainy tannins and plenty of length.

■ 88 2004-2012 *Excellent*

**1998 Lloyd Reserve** *McLaren Vale – Shiraz* **S.A.**

Deep crimson. Very savoury wine plenty of new oak characters. Intense cedar/blackberry fruit with touches of nougat. Blackberry/ mocha flavours. Lovely, fine grained tannins. Oak slightly to the fore but has plenty of length and savouriness to age well. Plenty of mouth-feel.

▲ 92 2004-2012 *Excellent*

**1999 Lloyd Reserve** *McLaren Vale – Shiraz* **S.A.**

Deep crimson. Profoundly deep blackberry/dark olive/dark chocolate and malt/tropical aromas. Still elemental with deep-set blackberry/black olive/ cedar/chocolate and tropical flavours, immense concentration, ripe gravelly tannins, finishing very long and flavoursome.

■-▲ 92 2005-2012 *Excellent*

**1996 Mary Kathleen Reserve McLaren Vale –** *Cabernet Merlot* **S.A.**

Deep crimson. Intense ripe blackcurrant/aniseed aromas with some toasty oak characters. Rich, ripe blackcurrant flavours. Soft, fine tannins, high concentration and firm finish.

▼-■ 86 Now-2008

**1997 Mary Kathleen Reserve McLaren Vale –** *Cabernet Merlot* **S.A.**

Deep crimson. Very cedary but sweet-fruited aromas with some leafy complexity. Classical palate with cedary/blackcurrant flavours and underlying savoury oak. Fine grainy tannins. Plenty of flavour length.

▼ 85 2004-2010

**1998 Mary Kathleen Reserve McLaren Vale –** *Cabernet Merlot* **S.A.**

Deep crimson. Restrained but perfumed plum-berry/minty aromas. Deep-set sweet plum/berry fruit flavours balanced by very strong pronounced grippy tannins finishing quite grippy but long.

▼-■ 88 2004-2012

**1999 Mary Kathleen Reserve McLaren Vale –** *Cabernet Merlot* **S.A.**

Deep crimson. Gunpowdery/flint and pure blackcurrant pastille aromas with some complex bracken/undergrowth characters. Richly flavoured wine with blackcurrant/smoky/gunflint flavours, pronounced tannins plenty of mocha and malty oak. Nice looking wine.

▼-■ 87 2004-2012

**1996** *Shiraz McLaren Vale – Shiraz* **S.A.**

Crimson/purple. Ripe blackberry liquorice aromas with slight earthiness. Extremely fine wine with ripe blackberry fruit, gripping tannins and plenty of fruit-sweetness. Lovely purity of fruit and underlying but barely noticeable oak.

■ 94 Now-2005

**1998** *Shiraz McLaren Vale – Shiraz* **S.A.**

Deep crimson. Well pitched chocolaty blackberry aromas. Loose-knit wine with choc-berry fruit flavours. Fine but slightly grippy net of tannins. Finishing long and sweet. Easy drinking wine.

■ 84 Now-2006

**1999** *Shiraz McLaren Vale – Shiraz* **S.A.**
Medium deep crimson. Intense pure blackberry/mulberry aromas with touches of mocha. Succulent mulberry/blackberry flavours, with fine gritty tannins, building up firm and tight.
■ *86* *Now-2008*

**2000** *Shiraz McLaren Vale – Shiraz* **S.A.**
Medium crimson. Leafy/blackberry pastille/red cherry aromas. Blackberry/rhubarb flavours, fine ripe tannins, with plenty of mid palate flesh. Finishing long and sweet. Medium weighted Shiraz.
■ *85* *Now-2008*

## CRAIGLEE

**1990** *Sunbury – Shiraz* **Vic.**
Deep crimson. Rhone-like pepper/spice characters with some meaty characters. Quite perfumed and attractive. Blackberry and pepper/spice flavours with soupy tannins, high concentration, lovely underlying oak and great length.
■ *93* *Now-2008* *Excellent*

**1994** *Sunbury – Shiraz* **Vic.**
Medium crimson. Gamy, red cherry, touch of menthol aromas, with some chocolate/cedar characters. Well balanced palate with gamy/red cherry flavours, gravelly/grippy tannins but good flavour length.
■ *91* *Now-2008* *Excellent*

**1995** *Sunbury – Shiraz* **Vic.**
Medium crimson. Milk chocolate/earthy aromas with some mint. The palate is quite underpowered, with soft tannins and acidity poking through. Drink up.
■ *81* *Now* *Excellent*

**1996** *Sunbury – Shiraz* **Vic.**
Medium crimson. Pepper/crushed leaf aromas, with some red cherry nuances. Strongly flavoured palate with red cherry/pepper characters and pronounced, bristling tannins. Finishes firm and tight but good fruit-sweetness.
■ *88* *Now-2008* *Excellent*

**1997** *Sunbury – Shiraz* **Vic.**
Deep crimson. Deep-set liquorice/prune/plum/prune aromas. Rich, ripe, sweet fruited prune/blackberry flavours. Plenty of chocolaty richness. Lovely loose-knit, lacy tannins and superb length. Delicious wine.
■ *93* *Now-2008* *Excellent*

**1998** *Sunbury – Shiraz* **Vic.**
Deep purple. Blackcurrant and dark cherry aromas. Whiffs of pepper and spice. Lightly structured palate with raspberry, cherry and white pepper flavours, grainy tannins and good length. A medium term wine.
■ *83* *2002-2010* *Excellent*

**1999** *Sunbury – Shiraz* **Vic.**
Deep crimson. Restrained white pepper/pure blackberry aromas. White pepper, pure blackberry flavours, lovely core of fruit-sweetness balanced by sinewy long tannins. Finishing firm but plenty of flavour length.
■ *90* *Now-2008* *Excellent*

**2000** *Sunbury – Shiraz* **Vic.**
Medium colour. Red cherry/cranberry aromas with savoury/nutty oak complexity. The palate is well structured with red cherry/cranberry flavours and savoury new oak. Fine, grainy tannins finishing firm and tight. The restrained use of new French oak bolsters the wine style in a convincing way.
■ *92* *Now-2010* *Excellent*

## CRAWFORD RIVER

**1995** *Crawford River – Riesling* **Vic.**
Pale yellow. Bright melon/lanolin/straw aromas with a touch of kero. Lively fresh palate with lanolin/melon flavours and some chalkiness, pronounced linear acidity, finishing clean and tight.
■ *93* *Now-2008*

**1996** *Crawford River – Riesling* **Vic.**
Pale yellow. Lifted sweet-fruited/lime/floral aromas. Slightly sweet/limey/jasmine flavours with a touch of herbaceousness; quite concentrated and slightly grippy, but good overall length.
■ *90* *Now-2005*

## CRAWFORD RIVER

**1997** *Crawford River – Riesling* **Vic.**
Pale yellow. Bright lemon-peel/clear-fruited aromas. Sweet lemon-peel/mandarin flavours with pronounced acidity balanced by plenty of sweet fruit with a long, dry finish.
■ 86 Now-2004

**1998** *Crawford River – Riesling* **Vic.**
Pale yellow. Lemony lime/fruit glace aromas with touches of apricot. Lemon curd/limey flavours, with racy acidity right across the palate, finishing dry and tight.
■ 93 Now-2007

**1999** *Crawford River – Riesling* **Vic.**
Pale yellow. Intense lemon curd/tropical fruit aromas. The palate is ripe with melon/sweet lemon curd flavours. Fine cutting acidity. Plenty of concentration and length. Very nice, but medium term wine.
■ 94 Now-2005

## CULLEN

**1995** *Margaret River – Cabernet Merlot* **W.A.**
Deep crimson. Developed malt/blackcurrant/cedar aromas with some sweet liquorice earthy undertones. Richly flavoured concentrated blackcurrant/cedar flavours with meaty liquorice complexity, fine strong tannins, with plenty of flavour length.
▲ 95 2004-2012 *Outstanding*

**1996** *Margaret River – Cabernet Merlot* **W.A.**
Medium crimson. Glorious wine. Rich deep-set blackcurrant aromas and beautifully balanced savoury mocha oak. Touch of gamy complexity. Succulent fruit-sweet palate with plenty of ripe blackcurrant coffee flavours, supple grainy/gravelly tannins underlying malty oak, finishing quite firm. Shockingly good wine.
▲ 100 2005-2014 *Outstanding*

**1997** *Margaret River – Cabernet Merlot* **W.A.**
Deep crimson. Ripe Intense mocha/chocolate/blackcurrant aromas with plenty of vanillin undertones. Well-structured palate with choc-berry fruit flavours. Fine, loose-knit, slightly gravelly tannins, underlying savoury vanillin oak. Plenty of concentration and length. Extremely well balanced wine.
▲ 94 2004-2012 *Outstanding*

**1998** *Margaret River – Cabernet Merlot* **W.A.**
Deep crimson. Ultra ripe cassis aromas with chocolate/nut crackle/malty complexity. Quite structured palate with choc-berry fruit flavours. Fine, loose-knit slightly grippy tannins, underlying malty oak. Finishing very firm.
▲ 92 2004-2012 *Outstanding*

**1999** *Margaret River – Cabernet Merlot* **W.A.**
Deep crimson. Intense deep-set choc-berry fruit aromas with savoury vanillin oak. Well balanced wine with concentrated bitter-sweet chocolate/mulberry/blackcurrant fruit flavours, fine slightly grippy tannins but excellent flavour length. Tannin slick at the finish.
▲ 94 2006-2014 *Outstanding*

**2000** *Margaret River – Cabernet Merlot* **W.A.**
Deep crimson. Cedar/vanillin/cassis aromas with touches of coffee/spice/herb garden. Richly flavoured and concentrated wine with deep-set blackcurrant/blueberry flavours, cedary oak. Strong, fine tannins structures. Finishing firm and tight. Could develop into something.
▲ 90 2005-2012 *Outstanding*

**1995** *Margaret River – Chardonnay* **W.A.**
Pale gold. Intense apple/honey dew melon/leesy/roasted nut aromas with some vanilla. Richly concentrated slippery palate with honeydew melon/lemon curd flavours all kept together by fine marked acidity. Plenty of length.
■ 93 Now-2005 *Excellent*

**1996** *Margaret River – Chardonnay* **W.A.**
Pale gold. Perfumed pear/vanilla aromas with some ripe melon/lanolin complexity. Showing some development with pear/vanilla flavours and yeasty complexity, pronounced long acidity, excellent concentration and length.
■ 90 Now-2005 *Excellent*

**1997** *Margaret River – Chardonnay* **W.A.**
Pale yellow. Highly individual but well focused lime/pear/lanolin aromas with some leesy/ yeasty/savoury undertones. Restrained complex flavours with ripe pear/peach flavours, penetrating quartz acidity and some leesy/lanolin complexity. Finishes long. Really interesting wine. Illustrates how this style builds up with age.
■ *94* *Now-2005* *Excellent*

**1998** *Margaret River – Chardonnay* **W.A.**
Pale yellow. Very complex and intense mineral/lanolin/ripe pear aromas with some apricot nuances. Developing apricot/pear flavours, with underlying oak, fine long acidity finishing minerally and flavoursome.
■ *86* *2003-2006* *Excellent*

**1999** *Margaret River – Chardonnay* **W.A.**
Pale yellow. Floral/jasmine/ripe apple aromas with hint of peach/fig. Palate is complex but tight with apple/peach/lanolin flavours, chalky mouth-feel, indelible acidity but finishing long.
■ *88* *2003-2007* *Excellent*

**2000** *Margaret River – Chardonnay* **W.A.**
Pale yellow. Pale yellow. Very restrained wine with chalky/lanolin nuances and some vanilla. Seems quite closed. Restrained palate with white peach/pear flavours, fine clear penetrating acidity, underlying oak, plenty of concentration and length, underlying oak. A racehorse. Will certainly improve.
■ *92* *2004-2008* *Excellent*

## DALWHINNIE

**1990** *Pyrenees – Cabernet Sauvignon* **Vic.**
Deep crimson. Intense, rusty, blackcurrant-like aromas with some menthol notes. Leafy, curranty flavours, moderate-to-high concentration and fine-grained tannins. Quite classically structured but a little hollow/lean in the middle.
■ *88* *Now – 2010* *Excellent*

**1993** *Pyrenees – Cabernet Sauvignon* **Vic.**
Deep crimson. Menthol, almost medicinal, eucalypt/minty/cassis aromas. Sweet-fruited/chocolaty/cassis flavours and fine, loose, gravelly tannins and plenty of oak support. Plenty of mouth-feel and texture. Firm finish.
■ *90* *Now-2010* *Excellent*

**1994** *Pyrenees – Cabernet Sauvignon* **Vic.**
Deep crimson/purple. Blackberry/allspice aromas with some cedary oak. Finely structured wine with chocolaty berry flavours, Loose-knit, lacy but slightly leafy tannin structure, some cedary oak. Firm finish.
■ *92* *2002-2008* *Excellent*

**1995** *Pyrenees – Cabernet Sauvignon* **Vic.**
Crimson/purple. Liquorice/cherry/rhubarb/cassis aromas with touches of vanillin. Rich, ripe and plush cherry/rhubarb/exotic fruits, with ripe, textured, velvety tannins, plenty of new oak and length.
■ *92* *Now-2010* *Excellent*

**1996** *Pyrenees – Cabernet Sauvignon* **Vic.**
Medium crimson. Menthol/herbaceous/cassis aromas with some liquorice. Menthol/herbal/cassis flavours with underlying oak, but quite aggressive furry tannins. Finishes and hard. Might not soften out.
■ *84* *2002-2008* *Excellent*

**1997** *Pyrenees – Cabernet Sauvignon* **Vic.**
Crimson/purple. Leafy iodine/cheesy/cassis/menthol aromas. Loose-knit palate with soupy *bouillabaisse* flavours. Some cassis characters. Fine, rasping, green tannins. Firm finish. Tannins may not soften out.
■ *80* *2002-2008* *Excellent*

**1998** *Pyrenees – Cabernet Sauvignon* **Vic.**
Purple/crimson. Strong menthol/chocolate/orange/clove aromas. Plenty of sweet fruit and chocolate/menthol fruit flavours on the palate, with immense, grainy tannins and medium length.
■ *81* *2002-2010* *Excellent*

**2000** *Pyrenees – Cabernet Sauvignon* **Vic.**
Deep crimson. Very young, elemental wine with ethereal menthol/ gingersnap/brothy/ plum aromas with touches of lanolin. Youthful

plum/ginger/aniseed flavours. Plenty of savoury oak in the background. Pronounced tannins. Finishes with plenty of length. Very impressive wine.
■ 94 2004-2012 *Excellent*

**2000** *Pyrenees – Chardonnay* **Vic.**
Pale yellow. Intense passion fruit/ripe pear aromas with underlying oak. Simple passionfruit/pear flavours – almost smells like Sauvignon. Some tropical characters. Medium concentration. Fine indelible acidity with good length. Early drinking style.
▼-■ 82 Now-2006

**1998** *Pyrenees – Pinot Noir* **Vic.**
Medium crimson. Menthol/dark cherry/mint/chocolate/ginger aromas. Very complex and interesting. Complex menthol/gingersnap/savoury oak and dark cherries, slight velvety tannins, finishing firm and tight. Idiosyncratic wine.
▼-■ 90 Now-2005

**2000** *Pyrenees – Pinot Noir* **Vic.**
Medium deep crimson. Ginger/dark cherry/rhubarb, slight citrus peel aromas. Deep-set, ripe, dark cherry/plum fruit, new savoury/vanillin oak. Long, fine granular tannins, finishing firm and tight. Oak dominates wine.
▼-■ 84 Now-2007

**1990** *Pyrenees – Shiraz* **Vic.**
Deep crimson. Earthy/chocolaty/brambly/liquorice-like aromas with a touch of green pepper/capsicum. Earthy/chocolaty fruit on the palate, with pronounced tannins and a firm finish. Quite lean-structured and lacking in generosity of fruit.
■-▲ 84 Now-2008 *Outstanding*

**1993** *Pyrenees – Shiraz* **Vic.**
Medium crimson. Matchstick/tropical/menthol aromas with raspberry/jammy characters. The palate has plenty of raspberry essence fruit and touches of leafiness, grainy, slightly bitter tannins, medium concentration and length. Drinking nicely now but probably not a long-term prospect.
■-▲ 89 Now-2005 *Outstanding*

**1994** *Pyrenees – Shiraz* **Vic.**
Medium crimson. Sweet brambly/chocolate/blackberry aromas with lifted savoury oak. Deeply concentrated wine with ripe chocolate/blackberry fruit and malty/savoury oak, fine gravelly tannins and a firm tight finish. A bit of a racehorse.
■-▲ 94 2003-2010 *Outstanding*

**1995** *Pyrenees – Shiraz* **Vic.**
Medium crimson. Peppery clove/slightly creosote aromas. Sweet peppery raspberry fruit, marked, slightly bitter tannins and moderate concentration and length. Some earthy notes.
■-▲ 85 Now-2007 *Outstanding*

**1996** *Pyrenees – Shiraz* **Vic.**
Deep crimson/purple. Lifted cherry/raspberry/blackberry aromas with savoury oak character. The palate is tangy and tight with cherry/blackberry fruit and some underlying oak, finely grained tannins, high concentration and medium length. Needs time.
■-▲ 90 2002-2010 *Outstanding*

**1997** *Pyrenees – Shiraz* **Vic.**
Deep crimson/purple. Strong vanillin, blackberry/plum fruit. Well-meshed aromas with touches of liquorice. Palate is sweet and pithy with blackberry/plum/quince-like fruit, underlying oak, pronounced grainy textured tannins, lovely concentration and length. Needs a little time.
■ 91 2002-2010 *Outstanding*

**1998** *Pyrenees – Shiraz* **Vic.**
Deep crimson/purple. Rich, ripe, youthful, blackberry/rhubarb aromas with some chocolate and ginger nuances. Richly flavoured, with deep, blackfruit/rhubarb/liquorice flavours, ripe, thick tannins and underlying oak. Finishes firm. Still in evolution, with tremendous power and fruit purity. Something of a fruit bomb. Will develop.
■-▲ 93 2005-2012 *Outstanding*

**1999** *Pyrenees – Shiraz* **Vic.**
Deep crimson. Raspberry cordial aromas with touches of pepper and aniseed. Elegant raspberry flavours with plenty of fruit-sweetness and

peppery/aniseed nuances, fine grained tannins and underlying oak. Finishing firm.
■-▲ 83 Now-2006 *Outstanding*

**2000** *Pyrenees – Shiraz* **Vic.**
Deep crimson. Intense almost creamy blackberry smoky/white pepper aromas. Deep-set pure blackberry/mulberry flavours, with fine ripe lacy tannins finishing firm and sweet. Delicious wine – still youthful, needing age to become more complex.
■-▲ 94 2005-2012 *Outstanding*

**1997 Eagle** *Pyrenees – Shiraz* **Vic.**
Crimson/purple. Bright blackberry/raspberry/smoky aromas – quite Rhone-ish. Fresh blackberry/raspberry/smoky flavoured wine with touches of liquorice, pronounced grainy tannins, plenty of fruit-sweetness and a grippy finish.
■-▲ 93 2002-2008

**1998 Eagle** *Pyrenees – Shiraz* **Vic.**
Medium crimson. Pure blackberry/raspberry aromas with some aniseed/peppery nuances. Elegant style combining the elements of cool climate and warm varietal richness. Blackberry/raspberry fruit flavours with touch of cracked pepper, mid-palate richness. Fine gravelly tannins, underlying oak and plenty of length. Excellent wine.
■-▲ 94 2005-2012

## d'ARENBERG

**1999 Original** *McLaren Vale – Shiraz Grenache* **S.A.**
Medium deep crimson. Young wine with some tropical guava characters. Well concentrated wine with fruit pastille flavours, pronounced drying tannins finishing quite aggressively dry and alcoholic. Needs time to settle down.
▼ 81 2003-2005

**2000 Original** *McLaren Vale – Shiraz Grenache* **S.A.**
Deep crimson. Gamy plum berry aromas touch of liquorice. Well structured wine with plum berry gamy fruit flavours, fine sinewy tannins which build up dry and chalky, but good flavour length.
▼ 88 Now-2005

**1998 Coppermine Road** *McLaren Vale – Cabernet Sauvignon* **S.A.**
Deep crimson. Plush dark chocolate/cassis aromas with some liquorice/savoury notes. Massively concentrated wine with deep-set dark chocolate/black olive flavours. Pronounced vice-like tannins that build up to being very firm – but excellent flavour length. Very youthful.
▼ 89 2003-2008

**1999 Coppermine Road** *McLaren Vale – Cabernet Sauvignon* **S.A.**
Deep crimson. Chocolate/tomato/leafy blackcurrant aromas with some smoky cedar nuances. Classically proportioned wine with blackcurrant/cedar flavours with some savoury notes, Loose-knit but fine grained tannins, medium concentration but plenty of fruit-sweetness and length. Moderate potential.
▼ 85 2004-2010

**1995 The Dead Arm** *McLaren Vale – Shiraz* **S.A.**
Deep crimson. Very attractive Christmas cake/prune/plum aromas with touches of coconut. Prune/plum/*paneforte* flavours with ripe tannins and plenty of new, seasoned coconut/vanillin oak – slightly tarry. Medium drinking prospect but well balanced wine.
■ 91 2002-2008

**1996 The Dead Arm** *McLaren Vale – Shiraz* **S.A.**
Deep crimson/purple. Beautifully focused wine with berry/grilled bacon/meaty aromas, and pronounced oak. Rich ripe plump fruit, classy oak handling, superb tannin structure, concentration, balance and length. This is a convincing wine.
■ 94 2002-2010

**1997 The Dead Arm** *McLaren Vale – Shiraz* **S.A.**
Deep crimson. Rich, ripe, blackberry fruit with beautiful savoury grilled bacon oak definition. Rich, ripe sweet fruited wine with deep-set choc-berry/liquorice fruit, fine slightly grippy tannins but excellent length of flavour. Refined style with plenty of underlying fruit-sweetness and flavour.
■ 94 2003-2008

**1998 The Dead Arm** *McLaren Vale – Shiraz* **S.A.**
Deep crimson. Pure blackberry pastille aromas with touches of chocolate and cedar. Very generous silky palate with superb blackberry/mocha flavours and plenty of mid palate richness. Oak is well seasoned with some cedary/tropical characters. Finishing firm but flavoursome.
■-▲ *93* *2004-2012*

**1999 The Dead Arm** *McLaren Vale – Shiraz* **S.A.**
Deep crimson. Intense mulberry/blackberry/dark chocolate/smoky aromas. Ripe, sweet fruit flavours. Lacy but gravelly tannins with some tropical malty/savoury oak and walnut nuances. Finishes quite grippy and tight.
■ *91* *2004-2010*

**1996 The Footbolt Old Vines** *McLaren Vale – Shiraz* **S.A.**
Deep crimson/purple. Raspberry/matchstick/blackcurrant aromas. Lightly concentrated wine with raspberry/blackberry fruit, fine tannins and some leathery/brambly undertones. Well made but short-term wine.
▼-■ *88* *Now-2005*

**1997 The Footbolt Old Vines** *McLaren Vale – Shiraz* **S.A.**
Deep crimson/purple. Abundant, youthful menthol/pepper/raspberry fruit. Lively palate with plenty of peppery raspberry fruit, textured tannins, good balance and length. Youthful wine.
▼-■ *89* *Now*

**1998 The Footbolt Old Vines** *McLaren Vale – Shiraz* **S.A.**
Deep crimson. Perfumed leafy/raspberry aromas with some choc-menthol notes. Leafy dark chocolate/raspberry flavours, long sinewy tannins, with nice core of fruit-sweetness. Finishes musky and firm.
▼-■ *90* *2003-2008*

**1999 The Footbolt Old Vines** *McLaren Vale – Shiraz* **S.A.**
Medium crimson. Sweet raspberry/tomato leaf liquorice aromas. Loose-knit but fruit-sweet tomato leaf/cherry plum flavours, fine tannins and plenty of length.
▼-■ *80* *Now-2006*

**2000 The Footbolt Old Vines** *McLaren Vale – Shiraz* **S.A.**
Medium crimson. Red cherry/raspberry aromas with some vanilla. Medium crimson. Loose-knit raspberry/damson flavours with vanilla characters, fine loose-knit, slightly grippy tannins finishing quite long and flavoursome.
▼-■ *83* *Now-2006*

## DE BORTOLI

**1996 'GS' Reserve** *Yarra Valley – Shiraz* **Vic.**
Medium deep crimson. Jimmy Watson Trophy winner. Intense chocolate/mocha aromas with touches of leafy/mint complexity. Richly flavoured wine with chocolaty/leafy flavours and mocha complexity and sinewy slightly bitter tannins, building up firm and tight.
▼-■ *84* *Now-2006*

**1997 GS Reserve** *Yarra Valley – Shiraz* **Vic.**
Medium deep crimson. Intense choc-berry/plum aromas with savoury/malt oak characters. Rich, well-flavoured wine with choc-berry/plum flavours, underscored by smoky spice, savoury oak, fine ripe tannins and plenty of length.
▼-■ *91* *Now-2008*

**2000 GS Reserve** *Yarra Valley – Shiraz* **Vic.**
Medium crimson. Raspberry/mulberry/white pepper aromas with touch of leafy complexity. Raspberry pastille/pepper flavours with some smoky/vanillin nuances and fine long slightly grippy tannins.
▼-■ *90* *2004-2010*

**1992 Melba Vineyard** *Yarra Valley – Cabernet* **Vic.**
Medium crimson. Rich, ripe chocolate/plum/menthol fruit aromas. Loose-knit palate with chocolate/plum/minty flavours, lacy tannins, medium concentration and length. Drink soon.
▼-■ *84* *Now*

**1993 Melba Vineyard** *Yarra Valley – Cabernet* **Vic.**
Crimson. Minty menthol/earthy/savoury aromas. Very restrained style with minty almost weedy fruit characters, bitter tannins, medium concentration and length.
▼-■ *75* *Now*

**1994 Melba Vineyard** *Yarra Valley – Cabernet* **Vic.**
Deep crimson. Intense cedar-oil/minty blackcurrant aromas. Highly concentrated wine with minty cedar/earthy/mocha flavours, pronounced tannins and oak. Needs time to come around.
▼-■ *88* *Now-2010*

**1995 Melba Vineyard** *Yarra Valley – Cabernet* **Vic.**
Deep crimson. Cedar/nutmeg/all-spice aromas over cassis fruit. Tight concentrated wine with plenty of cedary/smoky oak and blackcurrant fruit, fine-grained tannins and excellent length. Terrific wine.
▼-■ *94* *Now-2006*

**1995 Noble One** *Riverina (Murrumbidgee) – Botrytis Semillon* **N.S.W.**
Gold/yellow. Unctuous apricot/nectarine-like aromas with nuances of honey and gingersnap. Palate is sweet and luscious with apricot/honeyed fruit flavours, lovely concentration, good acidity and a drying finish.
■ *93* *Now-2008* *Excellent*

**1996 Noble One** *Riverina (Murrumbidgee) – Botrytis Semillon* **N.S.W.**
Brassy yellow. Intense, apricot/peach/honey aromas. Complex, rich, sweet and unctuous, with honeyed, apricot-like, nutty fruit; plenty of viscosity, mineral acidity and a dry finish.
■ *93* *Now-2010* *Excellent*

**1997 Noble One** *Riverina (Murrumbidgee) – Botrytis Semillon* **N.S.W.**
Brassy yellow. Intense, lifted, creamy, apricot and citrus-like aromas with a touch of apple. Palate is tight and slightly coarse with pithy, citrus-peel/apricot/marmalade flavours and good length.
■ *85* *Now-2010* *Excellent*

**1998 Noble One** *Riverina (Murrumbidgee) – Botrytis Semillon* **N.S.W.**
Yellow. Complex, apricot/almond/baked apple aromas. Almost treacle-like fruit on the palate. Touches of baked apple and almonds, background oak and vivid acidity. Still very youthful, but should evolve.
■ *94* *Now-2012* *Excellent*

**1999 Noble One** *Riverina (Murrumbidgee) – Botrytis Semillon* **N.S.W.**
Yellow. Developed honey/lemon/marmalade aromas. Richly flavoured and powerful wine with deep-set honey/marmalade and dried apricot/plum fruit flavours intertwined with tangy/lively acidity finishing long and drying.
■ *94* *Now-2010* *Excellent*

**2000 Noble One** *Riverina (Murrumbidgee) – Botrytis Semillon* **N.S.W.**
Yellow. Intense and fresh honey/apricot/panetone aromas. Fleshy sweet honey/apricot flavours, very viscous, but balanced by lovely bright acidity and plenty of flavour length.
■ *91* *Now-2012* *Excellent*

**2001** *Yarra Valley – Chardonnay* **Vic.**
Pale yellow. Lovely white peach/honeydew/melon aromas with some vanillin/savoury oak characters. Ripe honeydew/melon/toasty/bran like flavours with underlying vanillin oak, fine minerally acidity and plenty of length.
▼ *91* *Now*

**1998** *Yarra Valley – Pinot Noir* **Vic.**
Medium crimson. Charry, smoky, sweet strawberry/mulberry aromas. Plenty of sweet succulent strawberry/dark cherry fruit flavours. Charry oak, slightly grippy tannins, medium concentration but excellent length.
▼-■ *89* *Now*

**1999** *Yarra Valley – Pinot Noir* **Vic.**
Medium crimson. Complex smoky/gunflint/toasty aromas (oak) with underlying cherry fruit. Plenty of sweet mushroom/cherry flavours, fine ripe tannins building up firm, finishing tight and clean.
▼-■ *80* *Now*

**2000** *Yarra Valley – Pinot Noir* **Vic.**
Medium crimson. Ginger bread/dark cherry aromas with slight stalky/smoked meat background. Sweet supple palate with dark cherry/smoky bacon flavours, fine grain tannins, plenty of fruit-sweetness and good length.
▼-■ *88* *Now-2006*

## DEVIL'S LAIR

**1998** *Margaret River – Chardonnay* **W.A.**
Pale yellow. Melon/tropical fruit/passion fruit aromas – slightly contrived? Melon/tropical fruit flavours with natural tangy acidity,

underlying savoury oak, medium length. Well-balanced wine but fruit seems just a little simple. Good extract and depth.

▼-■ *84* *Now*

**1999** *Margaret River – Chardonnay* **W.A.**
Pale yellow. Intense banana/peach/juicy pear aromas. Minerally peachy/pear/ ripe apple flavours, fine minerally acidity but underlying creamy flavours and long cashew nut/malty finish.

▼-■ *87* *Now-2005*

**2000** *Margaret River – Chardonnay* **W.A.**
Pale yellow. Leafy/honey dew aromas with roasted nut/malty/nougat characters. Restrained melon/leafy flavours and some cashew nut complexity, touch grippy, but with plenty of fruit-sweetness, underlying oak and flavour length.

▼-■ *84* *Now-2005*

**1995** *Margaret River – Cabernet Merlot Cabernet Franc* **W.A.**
Deep crimson. Interestingly complex wine with cherry/earthy aromas and smoky/meaty/gamy characters. Lovely deep-set cassis/meaty flavours, ripe fine-grained tannins, moderate to high concentration and good length. Will improve in cellar.

■ *93* *Now*

**1998** *Margaret River – Cabernet Merlot Cabernet Franc* **W.A.**
Deep crimson. Intense savoury/malty aromas with liquorice fruit pastille characters. Smooth elegant wine with blackberry pastille/cedary/ malty flavours. Tannins are loose-knit but build up quite firm and tight at the finish.

■ *89* *2005-2014*

**1999** *Margaret River – Cabernet Merlot Cabernet Franc* **W.A.**
Deep crimson. Intense mulberry/blackcurrant *confit*/malty aromas with touches of mint. Well concentrated palate with blackcurrant malty/ minty flavours, fine grained/bitter tannins finishing long and flavoursome. Some briary notes at the finish.

■ *86* *2004-2010*

## DIAMOND VALLEY

**1999 Close Planted** *Yarra Valley – Pinot Noir* **Vic.**
Medium crimson. Red cherry/strawberry/smoky – slight matchstick aromas. Supple red cherry/strawberry flavours with some new oak complexity, fine slinky tannins and good length.

■ *87* *Now-2008*

**2000 Close Planted** *Yarra Valley – Pinot Noir* **Vic.**
Medium crimson. Loose-knit wine with red cherry/strawberry aromas and touch of smokiness. Complex wine with stalky cherry/strawberry flavours, fine tannins and slightly oily/tangy flavours.

■ *84* *Now-2006*

**1998 White Label** *Yarra Valley – Pinot Noir* **Vic.**
Medium crimson. Complex malty/juicy fruit/meaty/game aromas. Well structured wine with sweet dark cherry flavours, balanced by malty oak characters, supple almost lacy tannins with plenty of concentration and flavour length. Lovely wine.

■ *95* *Now-2008*

**1999 White Label** *Yarra Valley – Pinot Noir* **Vic.**
Medium crimson. Classic aromatic wine. Strawberry/cherry/chamomile aromas with some charry undertones. Concentrated strawberry/meaty/ nutty flavours, fine grainy long tannins, plenty of fruit-sweetness and length. Lovely wine.

■ *94* *Now-2006*

**2000 White Label** *Yarra Valley – Pinot Noir* **Vic.**
Medium crimson. Complex plum/dark cherry aromas with some vanilla spicy notes. Well concentrated wine with plum/dark cherry flavours, some spicy new oak. Fine slightly drying tannins but good overall length.

■ *90* *Now-2006*

## DOMAINE A

**1998** *Coal River – Cabernet Sauvignon* *Tas.*
Medium deep crimson. Very intense deep-set wine with black olive/ blackcurrant aromas and touches of mint. Very clean pure wine with

black olive/blackcurrant flavours, fine grainy – almost velvety tannins, underlying cedar oak. Finishing firm but with excellent flavour length.
▼ *94* *2004-2010*

**1999** *Coal River – Cabernet Sauvignon* *Tas.*
Deep crimson. Beautifully scented wine with lovely cedar spice cassis and herb garden aromas. Classically proportioned wine with cedar/spice/lead pencil/blackcurrant and musky/herb garden flavours, lacy fine tannins finishing almost without a vanishing point. Incredibly perfumed complex and restrained wine. This is a wine which sits on the cusp of ripeness bringing the most extraordinary complexity and vibrancy. Domaine A is not particularly well known on the Australian secondary market (much of its wine is exported). However it is clearly a top Tasmanian estate.
▼ *95* *2004-2010*

**1997***Coal River – Cabernet Sauvignon* *Tas.*
Deep crimson. Classical and attractive cedar/blackcurrant aromas with touch of violet. Rich chocolaty wine with plenty of herb garden/violet complexity, strong gravelly tannins building up firm and tight. Plenty of flavour length.
▼ *89* *Now-2006*

## DUTSCHKE

**1998 Oscar Semmler** *Barossa Valley – Shiraz* **S.A.**
Crimson black. Deep-set blackberry/liquorice aromas with tar/rose nuances. The palate is very concentrated with ripe blackberry/mulberry/juicy fruit flavours and meaty complexity, dense chalky tannins, finishing firm but with plenty of flavour length.
▼-■ *91* *2004-2008*

**1999 Oscar Semmler** *Barossa Valley – Shiraz* **S.A.**
Deep crimson. Very savoury refined wine with pure blackberry fruit/liquorice/aniseed aromas and cedary/smoky oak. Intensely flavoured and powerful wine with ripe blackberry/aniseed fruit, tremendously strong gravel tannins, lovely savoury oak and plenty of flavour length. Super wine.
▼-■ *94* *2005-2013*

**2000 Oscar Semmler** *Barossa Valley – Shiraz* **S.A.**
Medium crimson. Pure raspberry/blackberry pastille aromas. Medium concentrated wine with raspberry/blackberry pastille flavours. Very fine tannins, and underlying but very subtle oak, finishing long. Elegant style.
▼-■ *86* *2004-2008*

**1998 St Jakobi** *Barossa Valley – Shiraz* **S.A.**
Crimson black. Very intense and complex ground coffee/mocha/liquorice aromas. Immensely sweet fruited palate with plenty of liquorice/coffee/meaty characters, chewy almost sinewy tannins, lovely underlying oak and superb length of flavour. Terrific wine.
▼-■ *94* *2004-2010*

**2000 St Jakobi** *Barossa Valley – Shiraz* **S.A.**
Medium crimson. Perfumed mulberry/raspberry aromas with some underlying savoury oak. Savoury wine with mulberry/raspberry fruit flavours, well-seasoned/refined oak, fine but grippy tannins, marked acidity, finishing long and flavoursome. Well balanced wine which should improve with age.
▼-■ *89* *2004-2010*

**2000 Willow Bend** *Barossa Valley – Merlot Cabernet* **S.A.**
Medium deep crimson. Ethereal vanilla/cedar/mocha/berry aromas with some smoky undertones. Loose-knit slightly underpowered wine with malty/berry flavours, fine long sinewy tannins, some underlying oak, finishing quite firm and tight.
▼ *83* *Now-2006*

## ELDERTON

**1988 Command** *Barossa Valley – Shiraz* **S.A.**
Full crimson. Intense, chocolaty, gamy, sweet-fruit aromas. Powerful palate with chocolaty/marzipan-like fruit, high concentration, pronounced, hard tannins – but all in balance.
■ *94* *Now-2008*

**1992 Command** *Barossa Valley – Shiraz* **S.A.**
Crimson. Very fine dark chocolate mocha aniseed aromas. The palate is richly concentrated with dark chocolate/prune flavours, fine slightly grippy tannins, plenty of fruit-sweetness and length.
■ *86* *Now-2006*

**1994 Command** *Barossa Valley – Shiraz* **S.A.**
Crimson/purple. Restrained but clear, blackberry/mulberry-like aromas. Rich, ripe vanillin, deep-set fruit, sweet, ripe tannins with cutting acid and good length.
■ *93* *Now-2008*

**1996 Command** *Barossa Valley – Shiraz* **S.A.**
Crimson. Very intense and attractive blackberry/mocha aromas with faint whiff of white pepper. Well concentrated and very complex fruit-sweet palate with blackberry/lanolin flavours and touches of cedar oak. Finishes firm and tight.
■ *88* *Now-2008*

**1998 Command** *Barossa Valley – Shiraz* **S.A.**
Deep crimson. Intense liquorice/aniseed/blackberry intensity with some savoury/coconut nuances. Ripe generous but quite oak-driven wine with liquorice/mulberry flavours and plenty of smoky/savoury/malty oak. Very pronounced tannins but plenty of concentration – almost amontillado complexity – and good length.
■ *90* *2004-2012*

**1999 Command** *Barossa Valley – Shiraz* **S.A.**
Medium deep crimson. Mulberry/cranberry aromas with some savoury notes. Refined mulberry/cranberry flavours, ripe velvet tannins, lovely savoury oak, building up quite chalky and ethereal. Surprising wine.
■ *93* *2004-2012*

## ELSEWHERE

**2000 Bay of Eight** *Southern Tasmania – Pinot Noir* **Tas.**
Medium crimson. Quite classical rich plum strawberry aromas with spicy/malt oak Richly flavoured wine with plum/cherry fruit flavours, touches of spice and herb. Ripe fine tannins. Plenty of underlying oak.
▼ *93* *Now-2005*

## FOX CREEK

**1994** *McLaren Vale – Shiraz* **S.A.**
Deep crimson. Developed vegetal/meaty aromas with some sweet fruit characters/liquorice notes. Ripe palate with developed meaty/vegetal flavours, very fine pixilated tannins, finishing dry and meaty.
■ *88* *Now-2008*

**1995 Reserve** *McLaren Vale – Shiraz* **S.A.**
Deep crimson. Intense sweet mulberry/mocha/tar aromas with some minerally notes and slight tropical characters. Ripe mulberry/tar flavours, fine dry gravel tannins, with underlying oak, finishing firm but with good flavour length.
■ *86* *Now-2006*

**1996 Reserve** *McLaren Vale – Shiraz* **S.A.**
Medium deep crimson. Dry cherry stone/liquorice/plum aromas, with some mulberry notes. Well balanced sweet fruited wine with dark cherry/liquorice flavours, almond nuances. Fine, slightly tough tannins, finishing almondy and tight. Has lost its robe of fruit-sweetness.
▲ *85* *Now-2006*

**1997 Reserve** *McLaren Vale – Shiraz* **S.A.**
Deep crimson. Intense vanilla/blackberry aromas with lovely seasoned mocha oak. Plenty of fruit-sweetness. Developed squashy wine with blackberry/meaty/prune/ fruit-sweet wine, underlying savoury oak complexity, fine long but lacy/grippy tannins finishing long and sweet.
■ *93* *2004-2010*

**1998 Reserve** *McLaren Vale – Shiraz* **S.A.**
Deep crimson. Ripe liquorice/blackberry/fruit pure wine with touch of demi-glace. Massively flavoured wine with grilled bacon/blackberry flavours, fine grained tannins supported by smoky new oak. Plenty of concentration and length. Finishes quite firm but flavoursome.
▲ *92* *2005-2012*

## FREYCINET

**1998** *Southern Tasmania – Pinot Noir* **Tas.**
Medium crimson. Intense dark cherry/meaty cherry aromas. The palate is quite hard with sour cherry/meaty flavours, pronounced acidity, finishing quite grippy. Very big and chewy.
■ *78* *Now*

**2000** *Southern Tasmania – Pinot Noir* **Tas.**
Medium light crimson. Aromatic meaty/spicy/black cherry/herb aromas and flavours, with elegantly proportioned palate with fine long tannins, underlying fruit-sweetness and plenty of length.
■ *88* *Now-2006*

## GIACONDA

**1995** *Beechworth – Chardonnay* **Vic.**
Pale yellow/gold. Restrained mineral, grapefruit and vanillin aromas. Fresh, quite delicate palate with grapefruit-like tropical fruit flavours, savoury, grainy oak, fine, mineral acidity, lovely creaminess across the mid-palate and good length.
▲ *93* *Now-2010* *Outstanding*

**1996** *Beechworth – Chardonnay* **Vic.**
Pale yellow/gold. Complex lanolin and lemon aromas with touches of passionfruit, plus really lovely, savoury, nutty, smoky oak. Complex and flavoursome palate with lanolin, passionfruit, smoky oak and appealing creaminess across the middle. Fine acid cut and great length. A super wine.
▲ *95* *Now-2008* *Outstanding*

**1997** *Beechworth – Chardonnay* **Vic.**
Medium yellow. Developed complex butterscotch, chalky/mineral lanolin aromas with some ripe melon nuances. Richly complex wine with lanolin/butterscotch/peach flavours, fine quartz acidity but excellent creamy mouth-feel. Finishes long and minerally.
▲ *91* *Now-2006* *Outstanding*

**1998** *Beechworth – Chardonnay* **Vic.**
Pale yellow. Lemon grass/sea salt aromas with some lanolin/flinty characters and some savoury oak. Restrained and tight lemony palate with deep-set lemon curd grapefruit flavours, some toasty, savoury oak, lovely acid cut and good length.
▲ *92* *Now-2008* *Outstanding*

**2000** *Beechworth – Chardonnay* **Vic.**
Pale yellow. Very complex lanolin/mineral and lemon/grapefruit aromas. Very interesting wine with complex lanolin//slatey/lemon/grapefruit flavours, fine minerally acidity, intertwined with superb new savoury oak, building up creamy and long. Can almost taste the earth.
▲ *95* *Now-2006* *Outstanding*

**1992** *Beechworth – Pinot Noir* **Vic.**
Medium crimson brown. Intense brown onion/meaty/mushroom aromas. Very complex sweet fruited wine with mushroom/demi-glace flavours. Very grippy almost velveteen tannins. Plenty of mid-palate richness and length.
▲ *91* *Now-2006* *Outstanding*

**1995** *Beechworth – Pinot Noir* **Vic.**
Medium red. Vegetal/iodine-like/tarry/slightly over-sweet strawberry aromas. Earthy, vegetal fruit characters with some strawberry fruit, fine but attenuated tannins and good overall concentration and length. Sits on the fence a bit.
▲ *80* *Now-2005* *Outstanding*

**1996** *Beechworth – Pinot Noir* **Vic.**
Medium crimson. Meaty and slightly varnishy, with some gamy, aromatic fruit. Lightly structured wine with gamy, spicy flavours and some fruit-sweetness, but slightly green tannins.
▲ *82* *Now-2005* *Outstanding*

**1998** *Beechworth – Pinot Noir* **Vic.**
Crimson. Intense, fresh, lifted strawberry/meaty aromas with touches of cherry stone and new oak. Sweet-fruited wine with deep, fleshy strawberry/meaty flavours, fine-grained tannins with underlying new oak and good overall length.
▲ *91* *Now-2008* *Outstanding*

**1999** *Beechworth – Pinot Noir* **Vic.**
Medium light crimson. Complex cheesy/dark cherry/ choc-mint aromas. Sweet fruit choc-minty/cherry flavours, ultra-fine tannins, finishing long and sweet.
▲ *85* *Now-2007* *Outstanding*

**2000** *Beechworth – Pinot Noir* **Vic.**
Medium crimson. Intense dark cherry/smoky/lanolin aromas. Some floral notes. Well structured wine with dark cherry/smoky, fine silky tannins and underlying new oak. Finishes long and fruit-sweet. Lovely wine.
▲ *94* *Now-2008* *Outstanding*

## GLAETZER

**1996** *Barossa Valley – Malbec Cabernet* **S.A.**
Deep crimson. Choc-cassis/meaty/herb garden/liquorice aromas. Palate is silky and plump with plenty of fruit-sweetness, chocolaty tannins and well-seasoned malty oak. Finishes long.
▼ *86* *Now-2006*

**1997** *Barossa Valley – Cabernet Malbec* **S.A.**
Deep crimson. Developed herbal/earthy, blueberry aromas. Palate has earthy/ chocolate flavours, fine slightly grippy tannins, finishing tight.
▼ *80* *Now-2008*

**1996** *Barossa Valley – Shiraz* **S.A.**
Deep crimson. Intense plum/chocolate/tropical/malt aromas. Classic, developed Barossa chocolate/mocha fruit, fine lacy tannins, some underlying cedar and excellent flavour length.
▼ *91* *Now-2008*

**1997** *Barossa Valley – Shiraz* **S.A.**
Deep crimson. Intense complex liquorice/leafy/chocolate/leafy fruit. Well concentrated wine with plenty of liquorice/cedary/mulberry fruit, fine long grainy tannins, finishing fruit-sweet. Very successful for vintage.
▼ *92* *Now-2006*

**1998** *Barossa Valley – Shiraz* **S.A.**
Deep crimson. Intense Plum/smoky bacon/meaty/game aromas and flavours with some tropical oak nuances. Rich, supple, classically proportioned palate with lovely fine grainy tannins, plenty of fruit-sweetness and length.
▼ *94* *2004-2010*

**1999** *Barossa Valley – Shiraz* **S.A.**
Deep crimson. Dark chocolate/mocha/plummy/mulberry aromas. Lovely chocolate/ mocha/rich plum/spice flavours, fine ripe tannins which build up firm, subtle oak and plenty of flavour length.
▼ *93* *2004-2012*

**2000** *Barossa Valley – Shiraz* **S.A.**
Deep crimson. Contrived black cherry/meaty aromas and flavours with slight tomato leaf characters, moderate concentration, gritty tannins, finishing firm and tight.
▼ *83* *2004-2008*

## GRANT BURGE

**1998 Filsell Shiraz Barossa Valley –** Shiraz **S.A.**
Medium crimson. Red cherry aromas and strong malt/tropical oak. Overpowered malty/tropical oak dominates palate. Underlying raspberry/mulberry mocha characters, fine tannins, finishing long.
▼ *83* *Now-2004*

**1999 Filsell Shiraz** *Barossa Valley – Shiraz* **S.A.**
Medium crimson. Chocolate/rum and raisin aromas with some mulberry/meaty characters. Ripe chocolate/mulberry flavours, plenty of tropical oak flavours, fine ripe tannins finishing long and sweet/hot.
▼ *85* *Now-2006*

**2000 Filsell Shiraz** *Barossa Valley – Shiraz* **S.A.**
Deep crimson. Intense blackberry/vanilla aromas with a touch of ginger. Ripe creamy blackberry/plum flavours with underlying malt/ vanilla oak flavours, fine ripe tannins and plenty of length. Extremely well balanced wine.
▼ *90* *Now-2006*

**1988 Meshach** *Barossa Valley – Shiraz* **S.A.**
Crimson. Earthy prune aromas with hints of polished leather and aniseed. Earthy prune flavours – quite lean, with slightly green and hard, bitter tannins.
■ *82* *Now-2005*

**1990 Meshach** *Barossa Valley – Shiraz* **S.A.**
Deep crimson. Immensely concentrated wine with high-pitched plummy blackberry/pitch/tar/compost aromas. Rich ripe sweet fruited palate with prune/tarry flavours, fine sweet tannins and plenty of length.
■ *92* *Now-2006*

**1991 Meshach** *Barossa Valley – Shiraz* **S.A.**
Crimson. Loose-knit raspberry/earthy aromas with some liquorice characters. Juicy fruit – amazingly fresh. Very deep-set fruit, plenty of succulent choc-berry flavours, fine grained even tannins with plenty of concentration and flavour. Oak beautifully integrated. Brilliant wine.
■ *95* *Now-2010*

**1992 Meshach** *Barossa Valley – Shiraz* **S.A.**
Crimson. Pronounced coconut/cedar/oaky aromas dominating raspberry essence fruit – clear Barossa style. Oak-driven palate with underlying raspberry/blackberry fruit flavours, strong seasoned oak, moderate concentration, grippy tannins and finishing firm. Will develop into a tough old bird.
■ *82* *Now-2006*

**1993 Meshach** *Barossa Valley – Shiraz* **S.A.**
Medium deep crimson. Coffee/green bean/herbal edged wine. Well concentrated but soupy wine with vegetal green bean flavours, firm tannins and medium length. Has probably gone its distance, although will hold for some years to come.
■ *80* *Now-2006*

**1994 Meshach** *Barossa Valley – Shiraz* **S.A.**
Deep crimson. Very deep, still youthful wine, with dark chocolate, plum fruits, and malt oak. Touch of game. Very direct. Rich chocolaty wine with deep-set choc-berry fruit flavours, ripe tannins, and plenty of malt savoury oak. Finishes long with plenty of malty, grainy flavours. Has come around really well.
■ *93* *2003-2010*

**1995 Meshach** *Barossa Valley – Shiraz* **S.A.**
Medium deep crimson. Barrel-driven wine with a strong dose of vanilla/malt aromas over underlying blackberry/coffee characters. The palate is well concentrated with choc-berry/malty/vanilla flavours, sinewy loose-knit tannins, building up grippy and tight. Still plenty of fruit weight, but oak-dominant wine.
■ *85* *Now-2005*

**1996 Meshach** *Barossa Valley – Shiraz* **S.A.**
Medium deep crimson. Lifted, choc-mint aromas with some coffee/ liquorice nuances. Underlying savoury oak. Deep-set liquorice/ chocolaty fruit, pronounced blanket of drying/pixelated tannins, finishing with a bitter tannin slick. Fruit-sweetness holds up the wine.
■ *89* *Now-2008*

**1998 Meshach** *Barossa Valley – Shiraz* **S.A.**
Medium deep crimson. Intense deep rum chocolate/bramble aromas and tropical nuances. Deep-set choc-berry flavours with chocolate/ mocha/tropical characters, plentiful concentration, ripe tannins and length.
■ *93* *2005-2012*

**1999 Meshach** *Barossa Valley – Shiraz* **S.A.**
Medium deep crimson. Intense sweet cherry/mulberry/plum aromas with plenty of savoury/malty/vanillin new oak. Ripe sweet dark cherry/plum flavours matched with savoury/Smoky oak flavours, fine ripe tannins and plenty of length.
■ *91* *2005-2012*

## GROSSET

**1989 Gaia** *Clare Valley – Cabernet* **S.A.**
Deep crimson. Cedar/malty aromas with some raspberry/cherry nuances. Raspberry/cherry fruit flavours wrapped up by prominent cedary, tarry oak, gravelly tannins, good concentration and length.
■ *85* *Now-2006*

**1994 Gaia** *Clare Valley – Gaia Cabernet Blend* **S.A.**
Medium deep crimson. Intense blackcurrant pastille/menthol aromas with touch of herb. Blackcurrant earthy flavours, fine grippy tannins finishing quite chalky and firm. Plenty of bones but not much flesh.
■ *87* *Now-2008*

**1995 Gaia** *Clare Valley – Gaia Cabernet Blend* **S.A.**
Medium crimson. Intense blackcurrant pastille/mocha aromas with touch of cedar. Plenty of sweet fruit. Well balanced wine with deep-set cassis/mocha fruit, underlying savoury oak, fine slightly bitter/grippy tannins, building up firm and tight.
■ *86* *Now-2007*

**1996 Gaia** *Clare Valley – Gaia Cabernet Blend* **S.A.**
Medium deep crimson. Developing wine with a intense mocha/vanilla/earthy aromas and plenty of sweet/cassis fruit characters. Flavoursome palate with mocha/cedar – slight iodine flavours – but plenty of squashy fruit, fine grippy tannins building up firm/grippy.
■ *91* *Now -2010*

**1997 Gaia** *Clare Valley – Gaia Cabernet Blend* **S.A.**
Medium crimson. Aromatic black cherry/meaty/violet/mocha aromas. Lovely restrained palate with black cherry/meaty/redcurrant fruit – some mocha nuances, fine lacy tannins, finishing long and sweet. Excellent wine.
■ *93* *2004-2012*

**1998 Gaia** *Clare Valley – Gaia Cabernet Blend* **S.A.**
Deep crimson. Intense dark chocolaty/malty/mocha aromas with touches of Turkish Delight. Well balanced wine with lovely choc-cassis flavours, fine lacy/loose-knit tannins structure, plenty of concentration and flavour length. Tannins are firm and chalky dry at the finish. Nice wine.
■ *94* *2004-2012*

**1999 Gaia** *Clare Valley – Gaia Cabernet Blend* **S.A.**
Medium deep crimson. Perfectly ripe cassis/choc-berry aromas with touch of orange peel. Fruit pure wine with clear cassis/plummy flavours, plenty of sweet fruit with fine sinewy tannins and good flavour length.
■ *91* *2004-2016*

**2000 Gaia** *Clare Valley – Gaia Cabernet Blend* **S.A.**
Deep crimson. Intense perfumed aromas with mulberry/liquorice aromas, herb garden/menthol/violet nuances and underlying savoury oak. Well balanced restrained wine with mulberry/liquorice flavours. Fine slinky, slightly grippy, tannins. Immense concentration. Good flavour length. Finishes quite firm. Some bottles are bottled under Stelvin closures.
■ *89* *2005-2014*

**1981 Polish Hill** *Clare Valley – Riesling* **S.A.**
Gold/yellow. Classic Clare toasted, limey aromas with hints of honey and chestnuts. Very complex. The palate is complex and developed with lovely, toasted limey grapefruit, honey/nutty flavours. Wonderful concentration, plenty of fruit-sweetness and good acidity. A slightly off dry finish. A wondrous wine.
▲ *96* *Now-2010* *Outstanding*

**1985 Polish Hill** *Clare Valley – Riesling* **S.A.**
Yellow/gold. Very developed but sprightly wine with candied lemon-peel fruit and touches of toast. Plenty of development with candied lime/toasty flavours. Lots of fruit-sweetness and depth. Fine long finish. Drink now.
▲ *88* *Now-2010* *Outstanding*

**1990 Polish Hill** *Clare Valley – Riesling* **S.A.**
Yellow/gold. Developed liquorice/limey/slightly earthy aromas. Sweet developed limey/earthy fruit flavours with some liquorice and earthy toast. Fine tight acidity and good length.
▲ *90* *Now-2005* *Outstanding*

**1992 Polish Hill** *Clare Valley – Riesling* **S.A.**
Yellow gold. Intense jasmine/sweet lime aromas with some toasty complexity. Richly flavoured wine with jasmine/floral/lime flavours and long searing acidity. Almost no vanishing point.
▲ *90* *Now-2008* *Outstanding*

**1996 Polish Hill** *Clare Valley – Riesling* **S.A.**
Pale gold. Intense pear/lime/grapefruit aromas. Fleshy almost soft palate with lime/pear-like fruit. Slightly hard acidity, but good overall length and a crisp finish.
▲ *89* *Now-2010* *Outstanding*

**1997 Polish Hill** *Clare Valley – Riesling* **S.A.**
Pale yellow/gold. Highly defined smoky lime/lemon curd aromas with a faint touch of honey. Beautifully concentrated and mouth-watering wine with fine sweet lime/lemony fruit balanced by fine indelible acidity. Superb length. Brilliant wine – could outlive us all.
▲ *98* *Now-2010* *Outstanding*

**1998 Polish Hill** *Clare Valley – Riesling* **S.A.**
Pale yellow/gold. Generous, almost blowsy yeast/bread and some sweet lime aromas, with a hint of leafiness. Palate is strong, with sweet, pure, limey fruit flavours, slightly hard acidity. Excellent concentration and length, plus that touch of leafiness. Will develop.
▲ *90* *Now-2015* *Outstanding*

**1999 Polish Hill** *Clare Valley – Riesling* **S.A.**
Pale yellow/gold. Quite delicate, with floral/citrus/lemon/grapefruit aromas. Lemon and grapefruit on the palate too, with lovely concentration, pronounced, cutting acidity and excellent length.
▲ *93* *Now-2015* *Outstanding*

**2000 Polish Hill** *Clare Valley – Riesling* **S.A.**
Pale yellow. Intense fresh lime skin/floral aromas. Tight but concentrated lime/grapefruit/wet stone/ginger flavours with pronounced but fine rapier acidity and long mouth quenching finish.
▲ *92* *Now-2010* *Outstanding*

**2001 Polish Hill** *Clare Valley – Riesling* **S.A.**
Pale colour. Minerally aromas with intense lemon/slate/floral aromas. Classically proportioned wine with lemon/slate flavours, fine long minerally acidity and plenty of flavour length. More elegant than Watervale with minerally backbone.
▲ *93* *Now-2012* *Outstanding*

**2002 Polish Hill** *Clare Valley – Riesling* **S.A.**
Pale Colour. Intense apple/pear/chamomile/apricot aromas. Immensely concentrated wine with plenty of lime/pear/cumquat/sweet fruit flavours, intertwined with fine mineral/slatey acidity. Finishing long and flavoursome. A benchmark vintage.
▲ *97* *Now-2014* *Outstanding*

**1982 Watervale** *Clare Valley – Riesling* **S.A.**
Developed yellow. Honeyed aromas – biscuity, oily, lemon peel-like. Fresh but developed palate with lemon/honey/curd flavours, lots of sweet fruit, plenty of cutting acidity and superb length. At peak but will hold.
▲ *93* *Now-2010* *Excellent*

**1989 Watervale** *Clare Valley – Riesling* **S.A.**
Gold. Lifted and fresh honeyed jasmine aromas with touches of lime. Fresh and sweet lime honeyed flavours combined with mineral slate acidity. Lovely concentration. Excellent length. Developing beautifully.
▲ *96* *Now-2015* *Excellent*

**1992 Watervale** *Clare Valley – Riesling* **S.A.**
Yellow/gold. Developed oily/lime/lemony/slight herbal aromas. Sweet candied fruit with touch of kerosene/toasty flavours, slight grip, pronounced acidity finishing quite austerely.
▲ *84* *Now* *Excellent*

**1995 Watervale** *Clare Valley – Riesling* **S.A.**
Yellow gold. Intense sweet, lime/honeyed aromas with some grassy/hazelnut complexity. Beautifully proportioned palate wine with deep honeyed/apricot flavours, lovely viscosity, fine clean acidity and superb length. Almost a rich spätlese style.
▲ *95* *Now-2010* *Excellent*

**1996 Watervale** *Clare Valley – Riesling* **S.A.**
Pale yellow. Slate/lemon aromas with a hint of toast and lime. The palate is fresh, with plenty of lemon curd/lime-like fruit flavours, slate acidity and excellent length.
▲ *90* *Now-2010* *Excellent*

## GROSSET

**1997 Watervale** *Clare Valley – Riesling* **S.A.**
Pale gold. Lovely intense sweet lemon curd and slightly honeyed peach aromas, showing signs of development. Developing richness and viscosity on the palate with fine lemon curd/slightly honeyed flavours, hints of peach, lovely indelible acidity across the mid palate and plenty of length. A classic wine with superb fruit purity.
▲ *95* *Now-2020* *Excellent*

**1998 Watervale** *Clare Valley – Riesling* **S.A.**
Pale gold/yellow. Intense, perfumed, floral/chamomile and lemon aromas with rainwater-fresh mineral nuances. Lovely, refreshing palate with floral/chamomile flavours, plenty of mineral quartz acidity, some creamy viscosity and superb length.
▲ *99* *Now-2015* *Excellent*

**1999 Watervale** *Clare Valley – Riesling* **S.A.**
Pale yellow. Intense, lime cordial-like, slightly spicy aromas, but fresh and pure. Palate is fruit-sweet with deep-set lime and spice flavours, quartz/slate acidity and good length. As fresh and crisp as a good apple.
▲ *91* *Now-2015* *Excellent*

**2000 Watervale** *Clare Valley – Riesling* **S.A.**
Pale yellow. Intense perfumed lime/apple/pear aromas with hint of violets. Very tangy, minerally wine with lemony/pear skin flavours, indelible attenuated acidity, plenty of mid-palate richness. Finishing very long and flavoursome. A real race horse.
▲ *94* *Now-2010* *Excellent*

**2001 Watervale** *Clare Valley – Riesling* **S.A.**
Pale colour. Intense lime/chamomile/apricot aromas. Well concentrated deep-set palate with sweet lime/chamomile flavours, long but pronounced almost searing acidity and plenty of flavour length.
s▲ *90* *Now-2008* *Excellent*

**2002 Watervale** *Clare Valley – Riesling* **S.A.**
Pale colour. Perfumed apple blossom/pear aromas with some mineral notes. Very minerally palate with apple/pear/violet characters, fine indelible acidity, some savoury notes, but endlessly long flavours. A classic Clare Riesling.
▲ *95* *Now-2010* *Excellent*

**1993** *Adelaide Hills – Pinot Noir* **S.A.**
Medium crimson. Intense coffee/mocha/malt/demi-glace/meaty aromas. Developed wine with plenty of leathery chocolaty flavours and fine grained tannins. A nice old red rather than a nice old Pinot Noir.
▼ *88* *Now-2006*

**2000** *Adelaide Hills – Pinot Noir* **S.A.**
Medium crimson. Intense flinty/cherry/ginger/earthy/bramble aromas with some malty oak. Plenty of richness on the palate with raspberry/cherry/brambly flavours, silky tannins and malty smoky oak. Finishes long and flavoursome. Excellent sweet fruit and balance.
▼ *93* *Now-2006*

## HAAN

**1998 Prestige** *Barossa Valley – Shiraz* **S.A.**
Crimson black. Concentrated and complex wine with blackberry pastille/peppery/herb garden/ground coffee aromas. Palate is deeply set with blackberry fruits and liquorice/white pepper nuances, thick pixilated tannins, finishing long and flavoursome, but with a firm tannins slick.
■ *91* *2004-2012*

## HAMILTON'S EWELL VINEYARDS

**1999 Fuller's Barn** *Barossa Valley – Shiraz* **S.A.**
Deep crimson. Deep-set and exotic rhubarb/apricot/mulberry aromas and underlying savoury oak. Rich, ripe, succulent wine with deep-set ripe blackberry/apricot fruit flavours, soft ripe long supple tannins, underlying savoury oak and plenty of flavour length. Super wine.
▼ *95* *2005-2012*

## HARDY'S

**1994 Eileen Hardy** *McLaren Vale – Shiraz* **S.A.**
Deep crimson. Earthy prune/hessian aromas with tar and roses. Sweet developed earthy hessian/prune flavours and slightly gripping, grainy tannins, finishing quite firm and austere.
■ *89 Now-2010 Excellent*

**1995 Eileen Hardy** *McLaren Vale – Shiraz* **S.A.**
Deep crimson. Prune/chocolate/ginger/liquorice aromas. Sweet-fruited wine with brambly briar/chocolate flavours with touches of prune, spicy oak characters, and fine tight gripping firm tannins. Jimmy Watson Trophy winner.
■ *87 Now-2006 Excellent*

**1996 Eileen Hardy** *McLaren Vale – Shiraz* **S.A.**
Crimson/purple. Very tightly structured wine with ferrous/liquorice/ blackberry aromas and touches of menthol. Immensely concentrated, with compacted blackberry/liquorice fruit, rusty tannins, underlying oak and a firm finish.
■ *94 2004-2015 Excellent*

**1997 Eileen Hardy** *South Australia – Shiraz* **S.A.**
Deep crimson. Deep-set liquorice/blackberry/mulberry aromas with some cedary nuances. Rich, voluminous, sweet fruited wine with blackberry/mulberry fruits, strong drying tannins and charry/malty oak. Finishes firm.
■ *89 2004-2012 Excellent*

**1998 Eileen Hardy** *South Australia – Shiraz* **S.A.**
Deep crimson. Deep-set choc-berry pastille fruit aromas with touches of coffee and mint. Rich, deep-set wine with plenty of fruit-sweetness, choc-berry fruit, lovely underlying oak and firm tannins. Excellent concentration and length but still very elemental.
■ *92 2005-2012 Excellent*

**1999 Eileen Hardy** *South Australia – Shiraz* **S.A.**
Medium deep crimson. Blackcurrant pastille/pencil aromas with touches of tomato leaf. Rich ripe wine with fleshy blackberry/mocha fruit flavours, fine slinky tannins, plenty of underlying savoury oak, finishing a touch grippy – but excellent flavour length.
■ *90 Now-2008 Excellent*

**1998 Tintara Limited Release** *McLaren Vale – Grenache* **S.A.**
Deep crimson. Intense plum-chocolate aromas with some herbal notes. Rich chocolaty/plum flavoured wine with lacy fine tannins building up to a firm slick. Core of fruit brightness but tapers off towards the end.
▼-■ *85 Now-2006*

**1999 Tintara Limited Release** *McLaren Vale – Grenache* **S.A.**
Deep crimson. Intense plum/raisiny/chocolate aromas. Richly flavoured wine with deep plum/chocolate/prune flavours, lacy sweet tannins, finishing long and slinky – underlying oak.
▼-■ *85 Now-2006*

**1995 Tintara Limited Release** *McLaren Vale – Shiraz* **S.A.**
Crimson/purple. Dark cherry/plum/blackberry aromas with touches of *paneforte*. Dark cherry/*paneforte* flavours with gravelly tannins and a gripping finish. Well-proportioned underlying oak.
▼-■ *86 Now-2007*

**1996 Tintara Limited Release** *McLaren Vale – Shiraz* **S.A.**
Crimson/purple. Well-integrated blackberry/dark cherry/creamy vanillin aromas. Creamy blackberry/cherry flavours, fine velvety tannins, vanillin, grainy oak characters, plenty of fruit-sweetness, finishing quite firm.
■ *92 Now-2008*

**1997 Tintara Limited Release** *McLaren Vale – Shiraz* **S.A.**
Crimson/purple. Perfumed blackberry/violet/cassis/chocolaty aromas. Sweet-fruited wine with blackberry/chocolate/spicy aniseed flavours. Dense, gravelly, gripping tannins and seasoned smoky, cedary oak. A firm finish.
▼-■ *90 Now-2008*

**1998 Tintara Limited Release** *McLaren Vale – Shiraz* **S.A.**
Deep crimson. Serious wine with blackberry/chocolate/cedar/lead pencil aromas and plenty of fruit-sweetness. Immensely concentrated palate with strong bitumen/chocolaty flavours, pronounced tannins,

savoury oak, building up to a firm, bristling, dry finish. Good underlying concentration but needs time to come around.
■ 89 2005-2012

**1999 Tintara Limited Release** *McLaren Vale – Shiraz* **S.A.**
Deep crimson. Intense blackberry/blackberry *confit*/brambly aromas with some briary notes and hints of liquorice. Richly concentrated flavours, with some choc-berry flavours, spicy oak, gravelly tannins building up quite firm but with long cedary finish.
■ 88 2004-2012

**1995 Eileen Hardy** *Padthaway – Chardonnay* **S.A.**
Yellow/gold. Ripe, peachy butterscotch aromas with malty vanillin oak and toast. Fleshy concentrated wine with peachy butterscotch flavours, malty oak, plenty of creaminess across the mid palate and medium length. Oak and age will soon dominate – need to drink soon.
■ 87 Now

**1996 Eileen Hardy** *Padthaway – Chardonnay* **S.A.**
Yellow/gold. Intense melon/peach/vanillin/slight buttery tones. A classical Australian. Well-balanced, even wine with melon/peachy flavours and vanillin malty/toasty oak, slight grip, fine tangy acidity and good length.
■ 91 Now

**1998 Eileen Hardy** *Padthaway – Chardonnay* **S.A.**
Pale yellow. Over-worked buttery style with plenty of nougat and nuts. Full of winemaker's artifice. Tight palate with melon/peach flavours, leesy, savoury, almost malty, oak characters and fine acidity, with plenty of concentration and length. Aromas don't quite suggest the palate.
■ 81 Now

**1999 Eileen Hardy** *Padthaway – Chardonnay* **S.A.**
Pale yellow. Ripe melon/nectarine/ripe peach aromas balanced with vanilla/toasted oak. Rich creamy palate with ripe peach/nectarine flavours and plenty of new oak, finishing long and oaky dry.
■ 92 Now-2005

## HENSCHKE

**1993 Abbotts Prayer** *Adelaide Hills – Merlot Cabernet* **S.A.**
Crimson/purple. Chocolate/slightly/slightly leathery aromas and some seaweed characters. Complex seaweed/gamy fruit with some meaty characters on the palate. Strong underlying oak, pronounced but bitter tannins, high concentration and a long finish. Needs to soften out.
■ 85 Now-2008

**1994 Abbotts Prayer** *Adelaide Hills – Merlot Cabernet* **S.A.**
Crimson/purple. Very intense and rich chocolate-box/berry/liquorice and hints of coffee. Richly flavoured almost soupy wine with deep-set choc-berry fruit and pronounced new oak, grainy, slightly grippy tannins and a firm finish. Still in evolution.
■ 91 Now-2008

**1995 Abbotts Prayer** *Adelaide Hills – Merlot Cabernet* **S.A.**
Medium crimson. Perfumed red-berry/cherry aromas with some earthy notes. Lightly structured, developing palate with earthy, woody, raspberry/plummy flavours, fine, velvety tannins and medium length.
■ 79 Now-2008

**1996 Abbotts Prayer** *Adelaide Hills – Merlot Cabernet* **S.A.**
Medium deep crimson. Developing bracken/chocolate aromas with touch of herb garden/floral notes. Loose-knit palate with chocolate/nutty/almond flavours, fine sinewy but lacy tannins, underlying oak, finishing firm and blackcurranty.
■ 88 Now-2008

**1997 Abbotts Prayer** *Adelaide Hills – Merlot Cabernet* **S.A.**
Medium deep crimson. Refined blackcurrant/plum/mocha aromas with some cedar/briary notes. Well concentrated wine with deep-set blackcurrant/plum/mocha fruit and plenty of malt/cedar oak. Pronounced grippy but fine tannins, finishing firm and chalky, but with long cedary flavours.
■ 91 2004-2012

**1998 Abbotts Prayer** *Adelaide Hills – Merlot Cabernet* **S.A.**
Medium crimson. Developing coffee/malt/nougat/dark choc-berry aromas. Complex palate with plenty of fruit-sweetness, coffee/malt/

dark chocolate flavours. Strong pronounced grippy/chalky but loose-knit tannins. Plenty of plummy flavour length.
■ *92* *2004-2012*

**1999 Abbotts Prayer** *Adelaide Hills – Merlot Cabernet* **S.A.**
Deep crimson. Oak dominant wine with underlying ginger/plummy/apricot fruit. Still elemental. Pronounced new oak, underlying black fruit flavours, fine strong leafy tannins finishing with good flavour length. Still quite tight. Yet to reveal itself?
■ *84* *2005-2012*

**1993 Cyril Henschke** *Eden Valley – Cabernet Sauvignon* **S.A.**
Opaque crimson/purple. Complex and intense, meaty choc-berry aromas with smoky, coconutty oak characters. Mouth-filling wine with pure blackcurrant fruit and chocolate complexity, ripe, fine gravelly tannins, integrated well-seasoned smoky oak characters, lovely concentration. Brilliant wine.
■ *96* *2002-2012* *Outstanding*

**1994 Cyril Henschke** *Eden Valley – Cabernet Sauvignon* **S.A.**
Black/purple. Sweet, complex, dark chocolate/berry/liquorice fruit aromas. Sweet, meaty/gamy fruit on the palate, with loose-knit, grainy, slightly gripping tannins, superb oak integration, plenty of fruit-sweetness and length.
■ *94* *2005-2012* *Outstanding*

**1995 Cyril Henschke** *Eden Valley – Cabernet Sauvignon* **S.A.**
Crimson/purple. Sweet-fruited mulberry/mocha aromas with coconut/American oak aromas. Ripe, chocolaty, cassis flavours with deep-set coconut, slightly tropical American oak, pronounced tannins, high concentration and length.
■ *88* *2002-2010* *Outstanding*

**1996 Cyril Henschke** *Eden Valley – Cabernet Sauvignon* **S.A.**
Medium deep crimson. Developed cherry/cedar/coffee aromas with some nutty complexity. Very harmonious beautifully weft palate. Soft silky wine with cedary/mocha flavours, very fine silty tannins, lovely concentration and length. Superb wine
■ *94* *Now-2014* *Outstanding*

**1997 Cyril Henschke** *Eden Valley – Cabernet Sauvignon* **S.A.**
Deep crimson. Blackcurrant pastille and coffee-like aromas with some savoury, cedary oak. Palate is sweet-fruited with coffee/chocolate/blackcurrant fruit, cedary oak, dense, velvety tannins and a firm finish. One for the long haul.
▼-■ *95* *2002-2010* *Outstanding*

**1998 Cyril Henschke** *Eden Valley – Cabernet Sauvignon* **S.A.**
Deep crimson. Roasted coffee/*paneforte*/dried plum aromas. Complex interesting wine with coffee/*paneforte* flavours and some seaweedy complexity, fine grainy – almost slicky – tannins finishing tangy and long at the finish.
■ *88* *2005-2012* *Outstanding*

**1958 Hill of Grace** *Eden Valley – Shiraz* **S.A.**
Brick red. Coffee/mocha/menthol aromas. Still fresh and complex. Richly flavoured palate with chocolate/coffee flavours. Ripe but grainy tannins. Plenty of sweet fruit and length. Remarkable wine but really a curio.
☆ *95* *Now* *Exceptional*

**1959 Hill of Grace** *Eden Valley – Shiraz* **S.A.**
Brick red. Faded, slightly oxidised/mader-ised. Still drinking but just hanging on with some sweet fruit and firm tannins.
☆ *78* *Now* *Exceptional*

**1961 Hill of Grace** *Eden Valley – Shiraz* **S.A.**
Brick red. Lighter, almost floral, earthy liquorice aromas. The palate is quite light but still has some developed meaty, sweet fruit, pronounced fine-grained tannins and good length.
☆ *89* *Now* *Exceptional*

**1962 Hill of Grace** *Eden Valley – Shiraz* **S.A.**
Brick red. Complex plummy liquorice aromas. Some mint. Still quite tight and fresh. The palate is beautifully balanced with plummy, earthy, liquorice flavours, finely structured tannins and plenty of length.
☆ *93* *Now* *Exceptional*

**1963 Hill of Grace** *Eden Valley – Shiraz* **S.A.**
Brick red. Earthy prune/polished leather aromas. Quite lean and austere wine with some fruit-sweetness but slightly shaded fruit characters and firm gripping tannins.
☆ *82* *Now* *Exceptional*

**1964 Hill of Grace** *Eden Valley – Shiraz* **S.A.**
Brick red. Barnyard, slightly chloride aromas. Fruit has fallen out. Past.
☆ *70* *Past* *Exceptional*

**1965 Hill of Grace** *Eden Valley – Shiraz* **S.A.**
Brick red. Faded.
☆ *No score* *Past* *Exceptional*

**1966 Hill of Grace** *Eden Valley – Shiraz* **S.A.**
Brick red. Developed herbal, minty, prune aromas. Plenty of sweet complex prune/meaty fruit on the palate with pronounced firm tannins. At the cusp of life.
☆ *87* *Now* *Exceptional*

**1967 Hill of Grace** *Eden Valley – Shiraz* **S.A.**
Brick red. Complex coffee/medicinal/slightly mader-ised aromas. Nutty coffee/prune flavours, pronounced tannins finishing firm and tight. Fruit is beginning to fade.
☆ *75* *Now* *Exceptional*

**1968 Hill of Grace** *Eden Valley – Shiraz* **S.A.**
Brick red. Creosote/tar/prune aromas – quite ethereal, yet intense. The palate is complex and Hunter-like with leathery prune/sweet fruit flavours, very fine-grained tannins and good length.
■ *85* *Now* *Exceptional*

**1969 Hill of Grace** *Eden Valley – Shiraz* **S.A.**
Brick red. Perfumed nutty, meaty, vanillin aromas, but fruit fading on the palate – medium concentration and pronounced acidity.
■ *76* *Now* *Exceptional*

**1970 Hill of Grace** *Eden Valley – Shiraz* **S.A.**
Brick red. Tightly focused wine with liquorice/menthol/earth aromas. Tightly structured palate with some cassis fruit, fine-grained tannins finishing firm.
■ *86* *Now* *Exceptional*

**1971 Hill of Grace** *Eden Valley – Shiraz* **S.A.**
Brick red. Contrived raspberry essence/plum/chocolate aromas with a touch of caramel. The palate is well-structured with plummy, chocolate flavours, soft tannins and good length.
■ *83* *Now* *Exceptional*

**1972 Hill of Grace** *Eden Valley – Shiraz* **S.A.**
Brick red. Complex prune/polished leather/tar aromas. Lovely sweet and richly flavoured pruney fruit, with touches of leather and spice, very fine tannins and excellent length.
■ *92* *Now* *Exceptional*

**1973 Hill of Grace** *Eden Valley – Shiraz* **S.A.**
Brick red. Aromatic and intense coffee/chocolate/prune aromas. The palate is loose-knit with coffee/mocha flavours, fine lacy tannins and mineral acidity. Finishes long.
■ *91* *Now* *Exceptional*

**1974 Hill of Grace** *Eden Valley – Shiraz* **S.A.**
Not made.

**1975 Hill of Grace** *Eden Valley – Shiraz* **S.A.**
Brick red. Ethereal chocolate/aniseed/slightly varnishy aromas. The palate is high-toned with some chocolate/prune flavours, with slightly bitter tannins, finishing firm.
■ *80* *Now* *Exceptional*

**1976 Hill of Grace** *Eden Valley – Shiraz* **S.A.**
Brick red. Fresh prune/cigar box/Christmas cake aromas. Very structured palate with some cedar/chocolate flavours but green-edged tannins.
■ *83* *Now* *Exceptional*

**1977 Hill of Grace** *Eden Valley – Shiraz* **S.A.**
Brick red. Surprisingly fresh and youthful looking with raspberry/ liquorice/meaty aromas. The palate is quite austere with drying fruit and chalky tannins, finishing firm.
■ *79* *Now* *Exceptional*

**1978 Hill of Grace** *Eden Valley – Shiraz* **S.A.**
Brick red. Menthol/shellac smelling wine. The palate is sweet-fruited but oak is too strong; gravelly tannins and long finish.
▲ *82* *Now* *Exceptional*

**1979 Hill of Grace** *Eden Valley – Shiraz* **S.A.**
Deep crimson. Floral/rose aromas with some liquorice nuances. Still holding up well with some sweet fruit, grainy tannins and firm finish.
▲ *84* *Now* *Exceptional*

**1980 Hill of Grace** *Eden Valley – Shiraz* **S.A.**
Deep crimson. Intense menthol/plummy/aniseed aromas with slight char characters. The palate is plummy and sweet with underlying oak, fine but firm tannins.
▲ *86* *Now* *Exceptional*

**1981 Hill of Grace** *Eden Valley – Shiraz* **S.A.**
Deep crimson. Intense coffee/menthol/plummy aromas. The palate is rich and full bodied with ripe plum/coffee/menthol flavours, sinewy tannins and excellent length.
▲ *87* *Now* *Exceptional*

**1982 Hill of Grace** *Eden Valley – Shiraz* **S.A.**
Deep crimson. Quite exotic floral/rose/plum/cedar aromas. Palate is loose-knit with plenty of succulent plummy, cherry fruit, ripe tannins finishing firm.
▲ *91* *Now-2006* *Exceptional*

**1983 Hill of Grace** *Eden Valley – Shiraz* **S.A.**
Deep crimson. Strong American oak/oily/clove-like aromas and flavours are superimposed over perfectly ripe fruit. Structured, quite gravelly palate. Too much oak – unlikely to ever integrate.
▲ *79* *Now* *Exceptional*

**1984 Hill of Grace** *Eden Valley – Shiraz* **S.A.**
Deep crimson. Perfumed and complex blackberry/briary/liquorice aromas with some meatiness. The palate is ripe with plenty of sweet pruney, briary, fruit flavours, underscored by coconut oak, medium concentration and length. Works well.
▲ *90* *Now* *Exceptional*

**1985 Hill of Grace** *Eden Valley – Shiraz* **S.A.**
Deep crimson. Perfumed chocolate/berry aromas with touches of bramble/herbaceousness. The palate is brambly with sinewy tannins but some flesh, medium concentration and length.
▲ *77* *Now* *Exceptional*

**1986 Hill of Grace** *Eden Valley – Shiraz* **S.A.**
Deep crimson. Complex matchstick/matchstick aromas with some pure blackberry/spicy fruit characters. The palate is generous with gamy blackberry fruit and earthy/leather/spice nuances, ripe slinky/velvet tannins, underlying malty/tropical oak finishing long and flavoursome.
▲ *92* *Now-2015* *Exceptional*

**1987 Hill of Grace** *Eden Valley – Shiraz* **S.A.**
Deep crimson. Complex, earthy cedar/malty aromas. Restrained cedary, savoury palate, fine-grained tannins and finishing firm. A leaner year.
▲ *84* *Now* *Exceptional*

**1988 Hill of Grace** *Eden Valley – Shiraz* **S.A.**
Deep crimson. Lovely intense blackberry/prune aromas with integrated oak. Palate is rich and succulent with fleshy blackberry/mulberry fruit, ripe fine tannins, underlying oak, finishing firm.
▲ *91* *Now-2006* *Exceptional*

**1989 Hill of Grace** *Eden Valley – Shiraz* **S.A.**
Deep crimson. Liquorice/aniseed/earthy aromas with coconut/American oak nuances. The palate is generous with earthy blackberry fruit, sweet American oak, fine-grained tannins and excellent length. Surprisingly good for vintage.
▲ *92* *Now-2007* *Exceptional*

**1990 Hill of Grace** *Eden Valley – Shiraz* **S.A.**
Deep crimson. Intense and rich, plummy prune/blackberry aromas with lovely vanillin/malty oak characters. Palate is ripe and concentrated with fine dark chocolate/prune/plummy fruit flavours underpinned by malty, subtle oak, ripe, textured tannins and excellent length. Super wine. Can drink now but will develop over the next 15 years.
▲ *96* *Now-2015* *Exceptional*

**1991 Hill of Grace** *Eden Valley – Shiraz* **S.A.**
Deep crimson. Intense blackberry/cassis aromas with plush American oak. Deeply set palate with ripe developing cassis flavours and almost bourbon like oak and good length. Oak a little to strongly at the fore.
▲ *88* *Now-2005* *Exceptional*

**1992 Hill of Grace** *Eden Valley – Shiraz* **S.A.**
Deep crimson. Scented, meaty, soupy/soupy aromas – a touch herbal. Sweet-fruited/meaty/raspberry flavours, fine tannins and sappy oak and a firm finish. Difficult wine.
▲ *85* *Now-2006* *Exceptional*

**1993 Hill of Grace** *Eden Valley – Shiraz* **S.A.**
Deep crimson. Leafy/matchstick/blackcurrant-pastille fruit with a touch of earth. Leafy blackcurrant-pastille fruit flavours, supporting oak, fine grained tannins structure and good length. Difficult early drinking wine.
▲ *83* *Now-2007* *Exceptional*

**1994 Hill of Grace** *Eden Valley – Shiraz* **S.A.**
Deep crimson. Intense chocolate/blackberry aromas with coffee/soy/meaty complexity. Very generous but powerfully structured palate with core of deep-set blackberry fruit flavours, pronounced tannins, underlying savoury oak, finishing firm but with endless flavour length.
▲ *93* *2006-2014* *Exceptional*

**1995 Hill of Grace** *Eden Valley – Shiraz* **S.A.**
Deep crimson/purple. Perfumed, brambly berry/slightly herbal/menthol aromas with some cracked pepper/anise characters. The palate is concentrated, with some fleshy berry/brambly fruit, menthol/American oak characters and fine, firm, slightly green tannins. Difficult year.
▲ *85* *Now-2005* *Exceptional*

**1996 Hill of Grace** *Eden Valley – Shiraz* **S.A.**
Crimson. Very classical Eden Valley Shiraz with perfectly pitched blackberry pastille/ aniseed aromas with hints of white pepper balanced by underlying cinnamon oak characters. The palate is rich and ripe with deep-set blackberry fruit flavours, fine evenly textured lacy tannins all intertwined with beautifully seasoned cinnamon oak. This is a very refined elegant style with plenty of complexity.
▲ *96* *2006-2012* *Exceptional*

**1997 Hill of Grace** *Eden Valley – Shiraz* **S.A.**
Medium deep colour. Elegant mocha/cedar aromas and delicate redcurrant/berry aromas. Very refined palate with mocha/cedar/cherry flavours, loose-knit powdery/leafy tannins, some hints of game/meaty complexity and malt oak, plenty of savoury flavour length. This is a very elegant *Hill of Grace*, but without a trace of menthol/mint. Very surprising for vintage.
▲ *94* *2004-2012* *Exceptional*

**1996 Julius** *Eden Valley – Riesling* **S.A.**
Pale gold. Intense apricot/honey/lime-skin aromas. Developed apricot/lime skin/'drizabone' flavours with some slatey characters. Plenty of concentration, pronounced, but long, mouth-watering acidity. Under cork, this vintage is showing far more development with more marmalade characters.
▼-■ *86* *Now-2006*

**1997 Julius** *Eden Valley – Riesling* **S.A.**
Pale yellow. Biscuity/citrus aromas with faint lanolin characters. Lovely developed wine with biscuity/lemony flavours. Lovely fruit-sweetness and slatey mineral acidity. Delicious, well balanced wine. This was tasted from bottle in Stelvin cap – the 1997 under cork is far more developed. Still holding together but looks like an octogenarian!
▼-■ *98* *Now-2008*

**1998 Julius** *Eden Valley – Riesling* **S.A.**
Medium colour. Deep-set lime/lanolin aromas. Strong gravelly nuances. Lime/lanolin flavours. Some slatey/oil skin undertones. Mouth-watering, loose-knit acidity. Finishes with plenty of flavour length.
▼-■ *89* *Now-2008*

**1999 Julius** *Eden Valley – Riesling* **S.A.**
Medium colour. Developing lime/apple aromas with some oil-skin (aged) characters. Sweet fleshy wine with lime/apple/guava flavours, fine soft acidity building quite minerally with plenty of length.
▼-■ *89* *Now-2008*

**2000 Julius** *Eden Valley – Riesling* **S.A.**
Pale yellow. Intense lime/lemon rind aromas with touches of apricot. Lime apricot/honey flavours with plenty of mid-palate richness, fine quite mineral acidity, and good length.
▼-■ 90 Now-2006

**2001 Julius** *Eden Valley – Riesling* **S.A.**
Pale yellow. Sweet pear/lemony aromas with touches of tropical fruit. Well-concentrated palate with pear/almost floral flavours, lively acidity and plenty of flavour length.
▼-■ 87 Now-2008

**1993 Mount Edelstone** *Eden Valley – Shiraz* **S.A.**
Deep crimson. Brambly, dark chocolate aromas with savoury oak undertones. The palate is rich and ripe with lovely dark chocolate flavours, and a grainy tannin structure balanced by well-seasoned oak. Showing some development but will certainly improve.
▲ 89 Now-2010 *Outstanding*

**1994 Mount Edelstone** *Eden Valley – Shiraz* **S.A.**
Crimson. Very intense and complex coffee/mocha/dried herb garden aromas. The palate shows fresh fine chocolate/liquorice/dried herb flavours, loose-knit lacy tannins, plenty of concentration and length. This is a beautifully structured wine.
▲ 94 Now-2010 *Outstanding*

**1995 Mount Edelstone** *Eden Valley – Shiraz* **S.A.**
Deep crimson. Plush blackberry jam/raspberry essence/ginger/aniseed aromas with coconutty oak and hints of meatiness. Well-balanced palate with deep-set blackberry/meaty flavours, strong American oak, fine tannin structure, and superb length. This is a lovely wine but it is a medium cellaring prospect. Plump fruit is well balanced with oak, but age may see oak coming to the fore.
▲ 95 2002-2007 *Outstanding*

**1996 Mount Edelstone** *Eden Valley – Shiraz* **S.A.**
Deep crimson. Intense minty/pure blackberry aromas with some white pepper/meaty complexity. Intensely flavoured palate with ripe blackberry pastille/peppery/aniseed characters, fine grippy/slinky tannins melded with spicy/tropical oak. Everything is in balance and elemental.
▲ 91 Now-2010 *Outstanding*

**1997 Mount Edelstone** *Eden Valley – Shiraz* **S.A.**
Crimson/purple. Rich, ripe, plum and Christmas cake aromas with some smoky vanillin oak. Palate is rich and textured, with ripe, plummy fruit and smoky vanillin oak, fine, slightly leafy tannins and a firm finish.
▲ 88 2002-2010 *Outstanding*

**1998 Mount Edelstone** *Eden Valley – Shiraz* **S.A.**
Deep crimson. Almost picture-perfect aromas with very pure blackberry fruit characters intertwined with savoury menthol notes. Beautifully focused palate with blackberry pastille/gamy flavours and underlying tropical/malty oak. Sinewy but long tannins structures. Plenty of concentration and length.
▲ 96 2006-2014 *Outstanding*

**1999 Mount Edelstone** *Eden Valley – Shiraz* **S.A.**
Deep crimson. Deep-set pure blackberry pastille aromas with hint of menthol/gamy nuances and underlying oak. The palate is rich and ripe with blackberry menthol fruit flavours, underlying savoury oak, long lacy, chocolaty tannins, finishing firm and flavoursome.
▲ 90 2004-2010 *Outstanding*

## HEWITSON

**2000 Miss Harry** *McLaren Vale – Grenache* **S.A.**
Medium deep crimson. Red cherry/smoky/rhubarb aromas with some musky notes. Richly flavoured supple wine with red cherry/smoky flavours. Plenty of flesh in the middle, chalky dry tannins and length Touch underpowered at the finish.
▼-■ 87 Now-2006

**2001 Miss Harry** *McLaren Vale – Grenache* **S.A.**
Deep crimson. Perfumed floral musky/grapey aromas. Red cherry/musky/plum flavours – almost confectionary, soft supple tannins finishing long and sweet.
▼-■ 90 Now-2005

**1999 Old Garden** *Barossa Valley – Mourvedre* **S.A.**
Medium deep crimson. Developed earthy/walnut aromas with touches of liquorice. Interesting wine with sweet demi-glace/earthy flavours, soft supple flavours, finishing bitter sweet and quite drying/grippy.
▼-■ *85* *Now-2005*

**2000 Old Garden** *Barossa Valley – Mourvedre* **S.A.**
Medium deep crimson. Intense blackberry *confit* aromas with touches of ginger/aniseed/aniseed. Succulent fleshy mouth filling wine with deep-set blackberry/ginger flavours and touches of aniseed, fine long tannins finishing dry and firm but good overall flavour length.
▼-■ *93* *Now-2006*

**2000** *Barossa Valley – Shiraz* **S.A.**
Medium crimson. Very perfumed sweet exotic floral/raspberry/apricot aromas. Medium concentrated but fruit-sweet palate with fleshy raspberry/apricot/musky flavours, silky tannins and plenty of length. Really attractive now but with short term cellaring potential.
▼-■ *88* *Now-2006*

## HOLLICK

**1992 Ravenswood** *Coonawarra – Cabernet* **S.A.**
Crimson/purple. Sweet fruit/mocha/blackcurrant aromas with some vanillin. Richly flavoured wine with deep-set blackcurrant/mocha flavours and pronounced new oak, fine rasping tannins, and excellent length. Still quite elemental.
■ *92* *2002-2010*

**1993 Ravenswood** *Coonawarra – Cabernet* **S.A.**
Crimson/purple. Lead pencil/cassis aromas with some liquorice notes. Tangy, sweet-fruited palate with cedar/cassis flavours, fine-grained slightly pronounced oak and sinewy tannins. Finishes firm.
■ *89* *Now-2008*

**1994 Ravenswood** *Coonawarra – Cabernet* **S.A.**
Crimson/purple. Intense liquorice/raspberry/blackcurrant aromas with touches of earth and barnyard. Rich, ripe fruit, with sappy oak, soft, ripe and soupy tannins, excellent concentration and length.
■ *93* *2002-2012*

**1996 Ravenswood** *Coonawarra – Cabernet* **S.A.**
Crimson/purple. Intense, leafy cassis/chocolaty aromas with plenty of savoury oak. Deep-set cassis/chocolaty flavours and chunky cedary oak. Pronounced soupy tannins, and excellent length. A bit cumbersome but should develop.
■ *90* *2002-2015*

**1998 Ravenswood** *Coonawarra – Cabernet* **S.A.**
Deep crimson. Intense blackcurrant juicy fruit aromas with some mocha nuances. Deep-set wine with plenty of fruit-sweetness. Black currant *confit*/pastille flavours, sweet ripe grainy/lacy tannins, and plenty of mocha oak, lovely concentration and length.
■ *96* *2004-2012*

**1999 Ravenswood** *Coonawarra – Cabernet* **S.A.**
Deep crimson. Intense black olive/redcurrant/savoury/nutty aromas with some gamy notes. Sweet fruited black olive/cassis/game flavours, fine ripe tannins and plenty of underlying oak. Finishes quite chalky and firm.
■ *91* *2004-2010*

**2000 Ravenswood** *Coonawarra – Cabernet* **S.A.**
Medium crimson. Intense cassis/leafy aromas with touches of mint chocolate. Rich sweet flavoursome wine with plump choc-cassis flavours and some leafy complexity, fine slightly grippy but extended tannins finishing long.
■ *88* *2004-2010*

**1995** *Coonawarra – Cabernet* **S.A.**
Crimson. Mulberry/cassis aromas with touches of vanillin. Cassis/mulberry flavours with cedary oak. Fine-grained tannins. Moderate concentration and a firm finish.
■ *88* *Now*

**1996** *Coonawarra – Cabernet* **S.A.**
Medium crimson/purple. Mulberry/cherry/cassis aromas and a slight herbal edge. Medium concentrated wine with cherry/cassis and some

tobacco flavours, slightly herbal, fine green-edged tannins and medium length. Surprisingly ordinary for the vintage.

■ *80* *Now*

**1997** *Coonawarra – Cabernet* **S.A.**

Crimson. Developed blackcurrant meaty chocolate-dark cherry aromas with some savoury oak. Richly flavoured palate with cedary oak, pronounced gravelly tannins, plenty of fruit-sweetness and length. Very elemental needing time. Yet to market.

■ *89* *Now*

**1998** *Coonawarra – Cabernet* **S.A.**

Deep crimson/purple. Leafy liquorice/blackcurrant aromas with savoury, toasty oak characters. Blackcurrant pastille/cedar/coffee flavours with well-seasoned oak, fine-grained loose-knit but slightly grippy tannins, and a firm finish. Tannins are quite aggressive.

■ *90* *2002-2008*

**1999** *Coonawarra – Cabernet* **S.A.**

Medium crimson. Creamy blackcurrant/vanilla aromas. Deep-set creamy blackcurrant pastille flavours and underlying savoury/vanillin oak, fine grained tannins building firm at the finish. Well structured classical style.

■ *93* *2004-2010*

**2000** *Coonawarra – Cabernet* **S.A.**

Medium crimson. Restrained cherry/cassis/plum aromas. Loose-knit fruit-sweet wine with dark cherry/plum flavours, firm tannins but medium concentration and length. Earlier drinking wine.

■ *85* *Now-2006*

## HOWARD PARK

**2000 Leston Vineyard** *Margaret River – Cabernet* **W.A.**

Medium deep crimson. Intense gingersnap/cherry/violet/aniseed aromas. Still very youthful. Very young ginger/dark cherry/cassis flavours, fine but pronounced almost abrasive tannins and plenty of savoury oak. Finishes quite grippy and tight. Needs time to evolve.

▼-■ *91* *2004-2010*

**1999 Leston Vineyard** *Margaret River – Shiraz* **W.A.**

Deep crimson. Intense ripe plum/dried fruit aromas with touches of vanilla. Plush wine with plum/chocolate flavours and loose-knit ripe tannins, plenty of concentration, fruit-sweetness and length. A very textural wine with plenty of aging potential. More solid than one would expect of Margaret Shiraz.

▼-■ *90* *2004-2010*

**2000 Leston Vineyard** *Margaret River – Shiraz* **W.A.**

Medium deep crimson. Lifted raspberry/lanolin aromas with some chocolate nuances. Raspberry/lanolin flavours with some nutty complexity. Medium concentration. Fine sinewy tannins, finishing firm and dry.

▼-■ *85* *2004-2012*

**2000 Scotsdale Vineyard** *Great Southern – Cabernet* **W.A.**

Medium deep crimson. Intense blackcurrant pastille aromas with some underlying malt/savoury notes. Deep-set blackcurrant flavours with some spicy/tropical oak characters, fine quite firm tannin structure but good overall length.

▼-■ *87* *2004-2010*

**2000 Scotsdale Vineyard** *Great Southern – Shiraz* **W.A.**

Deep crimson. Intense rhubarb/blackberry/cassis aromas with touches of apricot and underlying oak. Beautifully proportioned wine with deep-set blackberry/rhubarb/apricot. Slight smoky flavours, ripe granular tannins, and plenty of underlying malty oak. Finishes long and sweet.

▼-■ *94* *2004-2010*

**1998** *Great Southern – Riesling* **W.A.**

Pale yellow. Intense, pure, lime cordial/lemon-oil aromas. Classical pure lime/lemony flavours with an indelible acid cut, plenty of pure, sweet fruit and concentration, and excellent length. Will develop nicely.

▼-■ *93* *Now*

**1999** *Great Southern – Riesling* **W.A.**
Pale yellow. Perfumed, earthy, bitter-lemon aromas with a touch of lanolin. Green apple/pear/lanolin flavours with fine mineral acidity, but quite austere and a touch green. Finishes searingly dry.
▼-■ *83* *Now*

**2000** *Great Southern – Riesling* **W.A.**
Pale yellow. Aromatic white peach/honey/floral aromas. White peach honeyed flavours with slightly hard acidity and medium length.
▼-■ *83* *Now-2006*

**2001** *Great Southern – Riesling* **W.A.**
Pale yellow. Intense lemony aromas with some honeyed nuances. Honey/lemon flavours with quite austere acid backbone. Finishes dry and steely.
▼-■ *84* *Now-2006*

**1995** *Western Australia – Cabernet Merlot* **W.A.**
Deep crimson. Developed, plummy, pure cassis aromas with some charry, smoky oak nuances – slight lift. The palate is deep-set with plummy, prune fruit, underlying smoky oak, with marked, almost green, tannins finishing long. Tasted this a few times recently – but not blind. This is often accused of having a VA lift, but I think it adds complexity to the wine.
▼-■ *89* *Now-2008* *Excellent*

**1996** *Western Australia – Cabernet Merlot* **W.A.**
Deep crimson. Chocolate/aniseed aromas with plenty of deep-set oak characters. Plush sweet fruited and thick textured wine with chocolate/mocha flavours. Lovely integrated oak. Grainy, almost chewy tannins, and superb length.
■ *94* *2002-2012* *Excellent*

**1997** *Western Australia – Cabernet Merlot* **W.A.**
Dark crimson/purple. Intense, mulberry, menthol and blackcurrant aromas with some lifted liquorice characters and savoury oak. Full-flavoured mulberry/blackcurrant fruit, deep-set, slightly extractive and cedar-oily oak, but lovely fruit-sweetness and concentration. Firm finish. Needs time but oak sticking out. Could integrate.
▼-■ *89* *2002-2012* *Excellent*

**1998** *Western Australia – Cabernet Merlot* **W.A.**
Deep crimson. Pure perfectly ripened blackcurrant/plum/cedar aromas. Plenty of sweet fruit. Elegant style but well balanced wine. Cassis cedar flavours, with chocolaty ripe tannin structures, underlying but well seasoned savoury/ smoky oak characters and excellent length. Classic wine.
■ *93* *2004-2012* *Excellent*

**1999** *Western Australia – Cabernet Merlot* **W.A.**
Deep crimson. Intense, deep-set black olive/cassis aromas with touches of cedar. Richly flavoured and concentrated wine. Black olive/chocolaty flavours, underlying cedar/spice oak. Slinky, gravelly tannins and plenty of length. A core of sweet fruit runs through the palate. Good aging potential. Also shows the benefit of multi-regional blending.
■ *93* *2004-2012* *Excellent*

**2000** *Western Australia – Cabernet Merlot* **W.A.**
Medium deep crimson. Intense gingersnap/malty/cassis aromas. Still quite elemental with deep-set ginger cassis/chocolate flavours and mocha oak, fine slinky tannins, underlying oak, finishing firm. Superb definition.
■ *98* *2006-2014* *Excellent*

**1996** *Great Southern – Chardonnay* **W.A.**
Pale yellow/gold. Limey white-peach/lanolin aromas with tight underlying oak. Classically proportioned palate with fleshy, nutty, vanillin, peachy flavours, richness across the mid-palate and excellent length. Certainly at its peak.
▼-■ *91* *Now*

**1997** *Great Southern – Chardonnay* **W.A.**
Pale yellow/gold. Sweet melon/apricot/caramel aromas – already showing some development. The palate is sweet and creamy with apricot/caramel fruit flavours, underpinned by savoury oak and marked, almost searing acidity.
▼-■ *88* *Now*

**1998** *Great Southern – Chardonnay* **W.A.**
Pale yellow. Tight melon/citrus/grapefruit aromas with hints of nuts and leesy complexity. Grapefruit, slightly green, but fleshed up with some leesiness, good concentration, and creaminess. Fine acidity, well balanced with excellent length.
▼-■ *89* *Now*

**1999** *Great Southern – Chardonnay* **W.A.**
Pale colour. Sweet grapefruit/apricot aromas and some creamy complexity. Grapefruit/apricot/lime flavours, with mineral, almost slatey, acidity. Finishing hard, but good overall concentration. More impressed this time around.
▼-■ *87* *Now*

**2000** *Great Southern – Chardonnay* **W.A.**
Pale colour. Grapefruit/guava/ violet aromas with some smoky/ butterscotch undertones. Quite a worked style with grapefruit flavours, some creamy/butterscotch complexity, fine acidity but flavours taper off at the finish.
▼-■ *81* *Now*

## IRVINE

**1988 Grand Merlot** *Eden Valley – Merlot* *S.A.*
Crimson. Intense meaty/chocolate – slightly raisined – fruit aromas with some spicy notes. The palate is already showing development with raisin/meaty/polished leather aromas, fine green/grippy tannins, plenty of concentration and flavour length.
■ *80* *Now-2006* *Excellent*

**1992 Grand Merlot** *Eden Valley – Merlot* *S.A.*
Crimson. Intense chocolate/liquorice aromas with plenty of tropical/ malty oak characters. Thick, richly concentrated palate packed with fruit-sweetness. Palate has plenty of plum/prune/Christmas cake flavours. Dense, soupy tannins. Savoury/malty oak characters. Finishing a touch grippy almost bitter. Fruit sweetness carries right across the palate.
■ *88* *Now-2008* *Excellent*

**1993 Grand Merlot** *Eden Valley – Merlot* *S.A.*
Deep crimson. Slightly contrived cherry/plummy fruit with touches of earth. Cherry/plum/sticky, sweet fruit, fine tannins, medium concentration and length.
▼-■ *78* *Now* *Excellent*

**1995 Grand Merlot** *Eden Valley – Merlot* *S.A.*
Deep crimson. Scented and very complex wine with almost smoky, sappy, menthol oak characters over plummy fruit. Palate is rich and ripe with plenty of sweet fruit, marked smoky bacon, barrel characters, ripe tannins, and excellent length. Tastes great, although this suggests an earlier drinking style.
■ *91* *Now-2008* *Excellent*

**1996 Grand Merlot** *Eden Valley – Merlot* *S.A.*
Deep crimson/purple. Sweet/cedary/chocolate/chocolate fruit with intense savoury/malty oak. Palate is squashy and ripe with deep-set blackcurrant and plum flavours cloaked with fine, ripe tannins, underlying malty oak and a firm finish. Could surprise us.
■ *87* *2002-2012* *Excellent*

**1997 Grand Merlot** *Eden Valley – Merlot* *S.A.*
Crimson purple. Rich scented plum/prune aromas with touches of spicy/frankincense and meaty/demi glace opulence. Richly flavoured and concentrated wine with deep-set plum/prune fruit, plenty of savoury oak, fine grainy but grippy tannins, finishing very firm.
■ *91* *Now-2010* *Excellent*

**1998 Grand Merlot** *Eden Valley – Merlot* *S.A.*
Medium deep crimson. Intense dark chocolate/raspberry aromas with some roasted coffee/malt nuances. Quite a worked style with malty/ roasted coffee and some berry fruit, pronounced gravelly but slightly bitter sweet tannins, tropical oak, plenty of concentration and length.
■ *88* *2004-2010* *Excellent*

## JASPER HILL

**1982 Emily's Paddock** *Heathcote – Shiraz Cabernet Franc* **Vic.**
Crimson. Developed earthy, prune aromas. Palate is dry and sinewy with some prune/earthy flavours. Drink up.
▲ *82* *Now* *Outstanding*

**1983 Emily's Paddock** *Heathcote – Shiraz Cabernet Franc* **Vic.**
Medium brick red. Dark chocolate and fennel/aniseed aromas. Amazingly concentrated, with deep-set, sweet, chocolate fruit flavours, powerful, iron-like but fine-grained tannins, underlying oak and excellent length.
▲ *94* *Now-2008* *Outstanding*

**1984 Emily's Paddock** *Heathcote – Shiraz Cabernet Franc* **Vic.**
Crimson. Sweet earth/liquorice-stick aromas. Sweet, earthy fruit, fine tannins, medium concentration and length. Drink up soon.
▲ *84* *Now* *Outstanding*

**1985 Emily's Paddock** *Heathcote – Shiraz Cabernet Franc* **Vic.**
Deep crimson. Showing some maturity with intense cedar/hazelnut/chocolate aromas and plenty of meaty/vanillin complexity. Fruit sweet palate with deep cedar/hazelnut flavours, fine grainy but drying tannins and plenty of savoury oak. Excellent mouth-feel and length.
▲ *90* *Now-2008* *Outstanding*

**1986 Emily's Paddock** *Heathcote – Shiraz Cabernet Franc* **Vic.**
Crimson. Fresh blackberry essence/raspberry fruit aromas with plenty of liquorice. Fresh blackberry/liquorice flavours with touches of mulberry, of medium concentration, with fine-grained tannins and medium length.
▲ *87* *Now* *Outstanding*

**1987 Emily's Paddock** *Heathcote – Shiraz Cabernet Franc* **Vic.**
Crimson. Intensely perfumed floral/tropical/blackberry aromas with hints of vanillin. The palate is quite angular with good meaty, blackberry fruit definition but quite oily tannins.
■ *83* *Now* *Outstanding*

**1988 Emily's Paddock** *Heathcote – Shiraz Cabernet Franc* **Vic.**
Crimson. Finely structured wine with earthy, blackcurrant fruit and some meaty complexity. The palate has some good earthy, blackcurranty fruit, but has an underlying lean structure and finishes quite firmly.
▲ *85* *Now* *Outstanding*

**1989 Emily's Paddock** *Heathcote – Shiraz Cabernet Franc* **Vic.**
Crimson. Rhubarb/blackberry/cherry fruit aromas that carry onto the palate. Lightly structured wine with some plump rhubarb/blackberry flavours and firm tannins.
■ *80* *Now* *Outstanding*

**1990 Emily's Paddock** *Heathcote – Shiraz Cabernet Franc* **Vic.**
Crimson. Ripe choc-berry aromas with touches of aniseed and cassis. Finely structured wine with earthy, cassis fruit characters and firm tannins. Quite lean for the vintage.
▲ *86* *Now* *Outstanding*

**1991 Emily's Paddock** *Heathcote – Shiraz Cabernet Franc* **Vic.**
Deep crimson. Intense, earthy, blackberry/mulberry aromas with plenty of pure fruit characters. The palate is rich and ripe, with lush dark berry fruits and touches of earth, with gravelly tannins, finishing firm and tight. A nice wine.
▲ *94* *Now* *Outstanding*

**1992 Emily's Paddock** *Heathcote – Shiraz Cabernet Franc* **Vic.**
Deep crimson/purple. Complex, spicy, smoky, gamy, meaty aromas with a hint of furniture polish. Palate has polished leather and spicy/meaty fruit, immense depth and strong, vice-like tannins, but all in balance. Could become tough over time.
▲ *91* *Now-2015* *Outstanding*

**1993 Emily's Paddock** *Heathcote – Shiraz Cabernet Franc* **Vic.**
Deep crimson. Quite vegetal/meaty aromas with touches of green bean. Difficult palate with sweet and sour profile, meaty fruit flavours but green soupy tannins finishing firm. Not a bad drink but will not develop beautifully.
■ *82* *Now-2006* *Outstanding*

**1994 Emily's Paddock** *Heathcote – Shiraz Cabernet Franc* **Vic.**
Deep crimson. Intense chocolaty prune aromas with touches of liquorice and savoury oak. Deep-set choc-berry fruit flavours with some meaty, earthy complexity, underling oak, lacy tannins and plenty of length. A terrific wine.
▲ *98* *Now-2010* *Outstanding*

**1995 Emily's Paddock** *Heathcote – Shiraz Cabernet Franc* **Vic.**
Deep crimson. Intense rhubarb/prune/raspberry aromas. Palate is medium-concentrated with raspberry/mulberry-essence flavours, fine-grained tannins and good length.
■ *85* *Now* *Outstanding*

**1996 Emily's Paddock** *Heathcote – Shiraz Cabernet Franc* **Vic.**
Deep crimson. Pure fruit aromas, Blackberry/mulberry aromas with underlying oak. Ripe fruit, pronounced tannins, high concentration and elegant raspberry, earthy, aniseed fruit flavours. Good cellaring potential.
▲ *92* *Now-2010* *Outstanding*

**1997 Emily's Paddock** *Heathcote – Shiraz Cabernet Franc* **Vic.**
Deep crimson. Rich choc-berry/liquorice aromas with vanillin, slightly sappy oak. Deep, rich, choc-berry fruit flavours with pronounced new oak, but gravelly tannins and excellent length.
■ *87* *2002-2010* *Outstanding*

**1998 Emily's Paddock** *Heathcote – Shiraz Cabernet Franc* **Vic.**
Deep purple/crimson. Deep, perfumed/frankincense, meaty, blackberry-like aromas with spicy, malty, well-seasoned American oak. Immensely concentrated and exotic; packed with squashy, blackberry-and-spice fruit and savoury/malty, smoky oak. A brilliant wine with ripe, textured tannins and excellent length.
▲ *98* *2003-2012* *Outstanding*

**2000 Emily's Paddock** *Heathcote – Shiraz Cabernet Franc* **Vic.**
Medium deep crimson. Gorgeous deep-set/liquorice blackberry aromas with some quince/apricoty/ginger nuances and underlying savoury oak. Richly concentrated wine with liquorice/blackberry flavours and some apricot nuances, ginger/malty oak, strong but long ripe tannins, plenty of spicy oak. Flavour length plus.
■ *92* *2006-2016* *Outstanding*

**1982 Georgia's Paddock** *Heathcote – Shiraz* **Vic.**
Brick red. Meaty aniseed aromas with some leather/earth and coffee/roasted nut complexity. The palate is beginning to dry out, with cherry-stone/earthy flavours, loose-knit, chalky tannins and medium length.
■ *85* *Now* *Outstanding*

**1983 Georgia's Paddock** *Heathcote – Shiraz* **Vic.**
Crimson. Highly toned. Developed meaty, bacon/fruit characters, touch of liquorice. Plenty of sweet fruit, meaty, berry, liquorice fruit flavours on the palate, fine tannins and plenty of length. Certainly ready to drink.
■ *88* *Now-2004* *Outstanding*

**1984 Georgia's Paddock** *Heathcote – Shiraz* **Vic.**
Crimson. Complex sweet/earthy/prune aromas. Rich and softly textured palate with soft lacy tannins, squashy prune/earthy flavours and good length. A nice drink, but open soon.
■ *89* *Now* *Outstanding*

**1985 Georgia's Paddock** *Heathcote – Shiraz* **Vic.**
Deep crimson. Complex earthy/soy/meaty aromas with some farmyard nuances! Showing quite a lot of development touches of primary fruit. Maturation style, hint of nutty complexity and touch of. Elegant medium concentrated style with loose-knit gravelly tannins, raspberry/soy flavours, some mid-palate richness and plenty of length.
■ *84* *Now-2006* *Outstanding*

**1986 Georgia's Paddock** *Heathcote – Shiraz* **Vic.**
Crimson. Mint/spearmint aromas over some liquorice. The palate is showing quite a lot of choc-mint characters and cracked pepper, with medium tannins and length.
▲ *84* *Now* *Outstanding*

**1987 Georgia's Paddock** *Heathcote – Shiraz* **Vic.**
Crimson. Spicy roasted meats – almost Cote Rotie-like – with some complex roasted nuts and violets. The palate is delicious with meaty, roasted nut flavours, fine gravelly tannins, and a long finish.
■ *94* *Now* *Outstanding*

**1988 Georgia's Paddock** *Heathcote – Shiraz* **Vic.**
Deep crimson. Ripe liquorice/prune/earthy aromas. Very concentrated wine with liquorice/plum/sweet fruit flavours, but quite harsh tannins.
■ *90* *Now* *Outstanding*

**1989 Georgia's Paddock** *Heathcote – Shiraz* **Vic.**
Medium crimson. Aromatic, perfumed wine that lacks guts and fruit-sweetness. Very loose-knit wine. Drink now.
■ *80* *Now* *Outstanding*

**1990 Georgia's Paddock** *Heathcote – Shiraz* **Vic.**
Deep crimson. Matchstick/pruney/brambly/liquorice fruit with a touch of game. Palate is showing deep-set prune/plum flavours, high concentration, fine, even, but soupy, tannins, and plenty of length.
▲ *90* *Now-2007* *Outstanding*

**1991 Georgia's Paddock** *Heathcote – Shiraz* **Vic.**
Deep, inky crimson. Extravagant, chocolate/coffee/prune aromas. Multi-layered, with deep-set chocolate/mocha flavours, loose-knit but firm tannins, plenty of fruit-sweetness and concentration. Excellent length.
▲ *92* *Now – 2008* *Outstanding*

**1992 Georgia's Paddock** *Heathcote – Shiraz* **Vic.**
Deep crimson. Ripe aniseed/liquorice/dark cherry aromas. Plenty of new oak background. The palate is fresh, with liquorice/dark cherry/coffee flavours, moderated by plenty of new oak, and fine, firm tannins.
■ *89* *Now-2007* *Outstanding*

**1993 Georgia's Paddock** *Heathcote – Shiraz* **Vic.**
Deep crimson. Intense choc-berry fruit aromas with plenty of savoury/leathery/meaty complexity and touches of aniseed. Very ripe and pure flavoured wine with plenty of chocolate/black fruit characters, pronounced but slightly sappy tannins. Plenty of extract and length. A choc-sappy wine.
■ *85* *Now-2008* *Outstanding*

**1994 Georgia's Paddock** *Heathcote – Shiraz* **Vic.**
Deep crimson. Complex raspberry/blackberry/liquorice aromas with underlying smoky oak. Loose-knit, silky palate. Meaty, chocolate/mulberry fruit flavours. Velvety tannins. Plenty of length. A super wine.
▲ *93* *Now-2010* *Outstanding*

**1995 Georgia's Paddock** *Heathcote – Shiraz* **Vic.**
Deep crimson. Perfumed, meaty, chocolate/hazelnut/liquorice aromas. The palate is sweet-fruited and fleshy with choc-berry fruit flavours, medium concentration, drying tannins and medium length. An early drinking wine.
■ *87* *Now* *Outstanding*

**1996 Georgia's Paddock** *Heathcote – Shiraz* **Vic.**
Deep crimson. Showing some development with smoky, meaty, mushroom/mulberry aromas. The palate is richly flavoured with meaty, mushroom/liquorice fruit, gravelly tannins, hints of cracked pepper and underlying oak, finishing firm.
▲ *91* *Now-2008* *Outstanding*

**1997 Georgia's Paddock** *Heathcote – Shiraz* **Vic.**
Deep crimson/purple. Smoky bacon/meaty/blackberry/liquorice aromas. Rich, ripe, blackberry/liquorice fruit flavours with some smoky bacon/savoury oak, massive concentration and fine, firm tannins. A very thick wine with tremendous power and flavour. Quite alcoholic, but with enough guts to carry it through.
■ *100* *2002-2010* *Outstanding*

**1998 Georgia's Paddock** *Heathcote – Shiraz* **Vic.**
Deep purple/red. Intensely focused, dark chocolate/blackberry aromas. Plenty of savoury oak. Deep, penetrating, dark choc-berry fruit with sweet/savoury oak, spicy, ripe tannins and superb length. Super wine.
▲ *95* *2002-2015* *Outstanding*

**1999 Georgia's Paddock** *Heathcote – Shiraz* **Vic.**
Deep crimson. Plush aniseed/ginger/ choc-berry aromas. Deep-set palate with immense ginger/aniseed /liquorice/ ultra ripe blackberry flavours, fine velvet tannins with immense concentration, underlying malty oak, finishing with a long tannin slick and plenty of flavour.
▲ *94* *2004-2012* *Outstanding*

**2000 Georgia's Paddock** *Heathcote – Shiraz* **S.A.**
Medium deep crimson. Mulberry/menthol aromas – touch of black pepper. Mulberry/menthol aromas with some peppery nuances,

 ▼ = *Weak* ■ = *Moderate* ▲ = *Strong* ☆ = *Rare* ❍ = *not saleble*

pronounced fine almost green tannins, finishing quite aggressively. Drying finish.

■ 83 2004-2010 *Outstanding*

## JIM BARRY

**1995 McRae Wood** *Clare Valley – Shiraz* **S.A.**
Crimson. Concentrated, savoury, sweet raspberry/blackberry fruit with seasoned oak and hints of pepper. Well-balanced palate with savoury sweet raspberry/blackberry fruit flavours, ripe tannins, underlying oak and excellent length. Lovely wine.

▼-■ 95 Now-2008

**1996 McRae Wood** *Clare Valley – Shiraz* **S.A.**
Deep crimson. Menthol/eucalypt/liquorice/raspberry aromas with touches of cracked pepper. Moderately concentrated wine with pepper/raspberry/menthol flavours, a fine tannin structure, vanillin oak and a firm finish.

▼-■ 82 Now-2008

**1997 McRae Wood** *Clare Valley – Shiraz* **S.A.**
Crimson/purple. Rhubarb/matchstick/plummy/aniseed aromas. Medium concentrated palate with plenty of fruit salad flavours, underlying oak and fine tannins. Finishes long, but medium-term prospect.

▼-■ 86 Now-2006

**1998 McRae Wood** *Clare Valley – Shiraz* **S.A.**
Deep crimson/purple. Very elemental but seductive wine with raspberry/plummy/ginger/aniseed aromas and touches of menthol. Sweet plummy/raspberry/gingersnap fruit, restrained oak and fine grained tannins. Finishes firm. Quite a wine.

▼-■ 95 2002-2006

**1999 McRae Wood** *Clare Valley – Shiraz* **S.A.**
Medium crimson. Red cherry/mineral aromas with some savoury undertones. Medium concentrated wine with red cherry/mineral/slatey flavours, loose-knit tannins building up firm and tight at the finish.

▼-■ 84 2004-2012

**1992 The Armagh** *Clare Valley – Shiraz* **S.A.**
Deep crimson. Developed choc-berry/malty aromas with some rum and raisin nuances. Richly flavoured palate with rum and raisin/musky fruit flavours, tropical oak characters and ripe tannin structure. Oak is slightly at the fore.

▲ 89 Now-2006 *Outstanding*

**1993 The Armagh** *Clare Valley – Shiraz* **S.A.**
Medium deep crimson. Sweet bourbon/vanilla aromas with underlying sweet fruit. Deeply concentrated but oak dominant wine with strong menthol/bourbon oak flavours, plenty of fruit-sweetness and fine slightly grippy tannins.

▲ 82 Now-2006 *Outstanding*

**1994 The Armagh** *Clare Valley – Shiraz* **S.A.**
Medium deep crimson. Developed and complex earthy/savoury/demi-glace aromas. Unctuous palate showing some raspberry/blackberry fruit flavours and some developed demi-glace/savoury notes. Loose-knit tannins, tapering off to a dry firm finish. At the cusp of age. Needs more time to show itself.

▲ 90 2004-2012 *Outstanding*

**1995 The Armagh** *Clare Valley – Shiraz* **S.A.**
Deep crimson. Sweet and intense prune/plum/raspberry/liquorice/matchstick aromas. The palate is deep and sweet-fruited with lovely plummy, raspberry, slightly earthy fruit, underlying oak, firm tannins and length. Complex and well proportioned wine.

▲ 92 2002-2010 *Outstanding*

**1996 The Armagh** *Clare Valley – Shiraz* **S.A.**
Deep crimson. Intense peppery/raspberry/liquorice/aniseed aromas with touch of meat/game complexity. Deep-set, richly flavoured wine with strong blackberry fruit flavours and touches of pepper, underlying savoury/smoky oak. Fine, tight tannins. Plenty of length. Super wine.

▲ 93 2004-2012 *Outstanding*

**1997 The Armagh** *Clare Valley – Shiraz* **S.A.**
Deep purple/crimson. Plush and beautifully defined, with coffee grounds, liquorice and aniseed aromas plus touches of blackberry and

coal. Deep-set, coffee/liquorice/aniseed flavours with ripe, textured tannins, massive concentration, underlying oak and plenty of length.

▲ 93 2005-2012 *Outstanding*

**1998 The Armagh** *Clare Valley – Shiraz* **S.A.**

Deep purple crimson. Extraordinary wine with exotic spicy ginger/clove/cumin/sweet-raspberry aromas with touches of coconut oak. Very complex and elemental – a paradox – with rich, ripe ultra-plush raspberry/blackberry/aniseed fruit, impassively concentrated, integrated oak and superb length.

▲ 98 2005-2015 *Outstanding*

**1999 The Armagh** *Clare Valley – Shiraz* **S.A.**

Medium deep crimson. Intense blackberry/liquorice aromas with some savoury vanillin undertones. Ripe, well-focused palate with plenty of creamy blackberry/mulberry flavours, soft integrated tannins and underlying oak. Builds up to a firm finish.

▲ 92 2005-2010 *Outstanding*

**2000 The Armagh** *Clare Valley – Shiraz* **S.A.**

Medium deep crimson. Blackberry pastille/liquorice aromas and savoury/tropical nuances. Oak-dominant palate at this stage, with savoury/nutty/malt oak flavours and some mulberry notes, grippy dry tannins, but excellent flavour length. Still elemental.

▲ 88 2005-2014 *Outstanding*

**2000 Watervale** *Clare Valley – Riesling* **S.A.**

Pale yellow. Lovely perfumed, lemon cordial/pear skin aromas – touch of violet. Pure sweet fleshy lime/lemon fruit flavours with plenty of palate richness and fruit-sweetness, lovely fine long minerally acidity and flavour length. Superb wine.

▼-■ 95 Now-2008

## JOSEPH

**1987 Moda Amarone**

*Coonawarra McLaren Vale – Cabernet Merlot* **S.A.**

Crimson brick. High pitched meaty cherry aromas with hint of aniseed and polished leather. The palate is moderately concentrated with meaty cherry flavours, grainy tannins and high pitched acid. Drink up.

▼-■ 87 Now *Excellent*

**1988 Moda Amarone**

*Coonawarra McLaren Vale – Cabernet Merlot* **S.A**

Crimson brick. Lighter style with mushroomy aromas but with some sweet fruit/soy characters. Quite firm and tight with some plump meaty mushroomy flavours, fine tannins, finishing firm.

▼-■ 88 Now-2005 *Excellent*

**1989 Moda Amarone**

*Coonawarra McLaren Vale – Cabernet Merlot* **S.A.**

Crimson brick. Developed earthy slight boiled sweet aromas. Soft and light palate with some earthy fleshy flavours, pronounced acidity, finishing long.

▼-■ 90 Now-2005 *Excellent*

**1990 Moda Amarone**

*Coonawarra McLaren Vale – Cabernet Merlot* **S.A.**

Deep Crimson. Rich gamy meaty liquorice aromas with some new oak at the fore. The palate is dense with raspberry liquorice earthy notes and sappy but balanced oak, medium concentration but ripe tannins and good length.

▼-■ 92 Now-2005 *Excellent*

**1991 Moda Amarone**

*Coonawarra McLaren Vale – Cabernet Merlot* **S.A.**

Deep crimson. Intense choc-mint blackberry aromas. Palate has plenty of sweet fruit with choc-minty flavours but quite extracted slightly bitter tannins and good length.

▼-■ 86 Now-2005 *Excellent*

**1992 Moda Amarone**

*Coonawarra McLaren Vale – Cabernet Merlot* **S.A.**

Medium deep crimson. Intense cassis/fine dark chocolate aromas with touches of mint and underlying cedar oak. Richly flavoured fine dark chocolate/cassis flavours, fine grained firm tannins, unusually strong acidity, underlying cedar oak flavours finishing firm.

▼-■ 87 Now-2007 *Excellent*

**1993 Moda Amarone**
*Coonawarra McLaren Vale – Cabernet Merlot* **S.A.**
Deep crimson. Raspberry blackberry essence aromas with plenty of tropical coconut nuances – derived from oak. Palate is rich and ripe with plenty of raspberry blackberry fruit, pronounced new oak, but finely structured lacy tannins and plenty of length.
▼-■ *90* *Now-2007* *Excellent*

**1994 Moda Amarone**
*Coonawarra McLaren Vale – Cabernet Merlot* **S.A.**
Deep crimson. Very tight well focused wine with intense aniseed liquorice ultra-ripe blackberry/gamy aromas. The palate is thick and deep with intensely flavoured blackberry gamy characters, fine gravelly tannins and supporting oak, finishing dry and long. Really well structured wine.
▼-■ *93* *2004-2012* *Excellent*

**1995 Moda Amarone**
*Coonawarra McLaren Vale – Cabernet Merlot* **S.A.**
Crimson. Lighter loose-knit style with raspberry coffee aromas and flavours, medium concentration, fine grainy tannins, and medium length. Not a long term wine.
▼-■ *80* *Now-2006* *Excellent*

**1996 Moda Amarone**
*Coonawarra McLaren Vale – Cabernet Merlot* **S.A.**
Deep crimson. Very strong youthful liquorice aniseed choc-berry fruit. Deeply set wine with plenty of ripe choc-berry fruit balanced by smoky vanillin oak, ripe tannins and long finish.
▼-■ *95* *Now-2008* *Excellent*

**1997 Moda Amarone**
*Coonawarra McLaren Vale – Cabernet Merlot* **S.A.**
Deep crimson purple. Immensely concentrated wine with intense blackberry ginger bread aromas and touches of liquorice. Very structured palate with plenty of fleshy liquorice blackberry fruit, savoury oak but pronounced slightly grippy tannins.
▼-■ *90* *Now-2006* *Excellent*

**1998 Moda Amarone**
*Coonawarra McLaren Vale – Cabernet Merlot* **S.A.**
Deep crimson. Intense savoury wine with mocha/coffee and smoky plum/blackberry aromas. Superb wine with pure cassis/mocha/coffee flavours underpinned by savoury oak, finely grained – well ripened – tannins which build up firm, lovely concentration and flavour length.
▼-■ *95* *2005-2014* *Excellent*

**1999 Moda Amarone**
*Coonawarra McLaren Vale – Cabernet Merlot* **S.A.**
Medium deep crimson. Blackcurrant pastille/earthy/chocolate aromas with some touches of iodine. Deep-set choc-berry flavours and plenty of malty oak, fine grainy but dense and long tannins finishing a touch bitter/sweet. Quite a surprising wine.
▼-■ *94* *2004-2012* *Excellent*

**2000 Moda Amarone** *South Australia – Cabernet Merlot* **S.A.**
Medium deep crimson. Lovely complex plum/raspberry/aniseed aromas with lovely savoury, slightly ginger, oak characters. Beautifully structured palate with plum/raspberry flavours, fine lacy, slightly grippy, tannins, superb savoury/ginger oak , finishing long and fine. Delicious wine. *Fruit now sourced from Wrattonbully, Currency Creek and Clarendon (McLaren Vale). Very much a House Style as opposed to regional.*
▼-■ *94* *2004-2012* *Excellent*

## KAESLER

**1998 Old Bastard** *Barossa Valley – Shiraz* **S.A.**
Lovely colour. Deep crimson. Red cherry/ meaty/mulberry/plum fruit aromas with some smoky/malty oak nuances. Very classical wine with dark chocolate/dark cherry flavours, lovely ripe loose-knit tannin structures which build up firm and tight. Plenty of underlying oak and flavour length. A 20 year + wine.
▼-■ *96* *2006-2016*

**1999 Old Bastard** *Barossa Valley – Shiraz* **S.A.**
Made off 1893 vines. Intense almost raw liquorice/aniseed, slightly oily notes. The palate is immensely concentrated and elemental with

deep-set liquorice/plum flavours, savoury new oak, fine chalky tannins, finishing quite hard but with plenty of flavour length.

▼-■ 88 2006-2014

**1998 Old Vine** *Barossa Valley – Shiraz* **S.A.**

Deep crimson. Classic opulent Barossa Shiraz with volumes of choc-mulberry fruit. Succulent fruit-sweet palate with plenty of mulberry/chocolaty/malty flavours, fine ripe but slightly grainy tannins, finishing firm and malty.

▼-■ 93 2004-2010

**1999 Old Vine** *Barossa Valley – Shiraz* **S.A.**

Deep crimson. Intense concentrated mulberry/liquorice/aniseed aromas and flavours, fine ripe gravelly tannins, underscored by some new oak characters, finishing quite firm but with plenty of flavour length. Very elemental but nicely made wine.

▼-■ 88 2004-2010

## KATNOOK ESTATE

**1991 Odyssey** *Coonawarra – Cabernet* **S.A.**

Crimson. Cassis/chocolate/mocha aromas. Rich, ripe sweet-fruited wine with chocolaty mocha flavours, well-seasoned savoury, cedary oak flavours, ripe mouth-filling tannin structure, excellent concentration and a long finish.

■ 94 Now-2015

**1992 Odyssey** *Coonawarra – Cabernet* **S.A.**

Crimson/purple. Deep chocolate/menthol/slightly rusty aromas. Rich, ripe sweet-fruited wine with deep-set chocolate/blackcurrant/menthol fruit, pronounced rusty tannins, underlying oak and a firm finish. Needs time to soften out.

■ 87 Now-2008

**1994 Odyssey** *Coonawarra – Cabernet* **S.A.**

Opaque crimson. Intense cassis/liquorice/smoky bacon/toasty aromas. Richly flavoured wine with deep-set cassis/liquorice fruit and plenty of smoky, savoury oak, ripe, slightly gravelly tannins, but excellent fruit-sweetness and length. Built for the long term.

■ 92 2002-2012

**1996 Odyssey** *Coonawarra – Cabernet* **S.A.**

Deep medium crimson. Beautifully complex ground coffee/dark chocolate/plummy aromas with some malty oak characters. Quite oak dominant now but beautifully seasoned malty/cedar flavours intertwined with ripe blackcurrant fruit, ripe velvet fruit drenched tannins finishing long and sweet.

■ 93 2006-2018

**1997 Odyssey** *Coonawarra – Cabernet* **S.A.**

Deep crimson. Pronounced new malty/nutty oak and underlying sweet cassis fruit. Concentrated wine with lashings of new malty cashew nut oak. Lovely concentration but strong sinewy underlying tannins. Finishes long. Well made wine.

■ 90 2004-2010

**1998 Odyssey** *Coonawarra – Cabernet* **S.A.**

Deep crimson. Almost butter-menthol tropical oak over red berry/cherry aromas. Rich fruit-sweet wine with lashings of tropical oak and butter menthol/mocha/vanillin characters over ripe cassis fruit flavours, fine ripe tannins, plenty of concentration and length. Impressive elements but yet to meld together.

■ 86 2004-2012

**1997 Prodigy** *Coonawarra – Shiraz* **S.A.**

Deep crimson. Complex developing sausage meat/game/malty/mocha aromas. Developed meat/game flavours with ripe lacy tannins, plenty of fruit-sweetness, concentration and length.

■ 86 2004-2010

**1998 Prodigy** *Coonawarra – Shiraz* **S.A.**

Medium deep crimson. Smoky/bitumen/liquorice/blackberry aromas. Complex evolving wine with smoky/bitumen/blackberry flavours and plenty of malty/savoury oak, pronounced slightly rasping slick of tannins, finishing firm and gritty

■ 88 2004-2012

**1999 Prodigy** *Coonawarra – Shiraz* **S.A.**
Deep crimson. Barrel-driven wine with very intense whisky/bourbon malty aromas with some oily/bitumen/savoury bacon nuances – characters that follow on to the palate but blend with underlying deep-set blackberry/chocolaty/plum fruit fine ripe tannins building up firm and tight. Gawky and young but could develop into something special.
■ *89* *2005-2012*

**1992** *Coonawarra – Cabernet Sauvignon* **S.A.**
Crimson/purple. Developing. Intense, lifted aromas of squashy blackcurrant, plum and prune, with hints of coffee and spice. Palate has some lovely, sweet fruit, blackcurrant/coffee/prune flavours, fine-grained, gripping tannins, underlying oak, high concentration and a firm finish. Quite classical, a natural-feeling wine.
■ *93* *Now-2007* *Distinguished*

**1993** *Coonawarra – Cabernet Sauvignon* **S.A.**
Crimson purple. Intense, chocolaty raspberry/blackcurrant aromas with touches of vanillin. Cedarwood, almost sappy oak, flavoured wine with underlying blackcurrant/spicy fruit, fine-grained tannins and good length. A bit cumbersome.
■ *84* *Now-2008* *Distinguished*

**1994** *Coonawarra – Cabernet Sauvignon* **S.A.**
Deep crimson/purple. Savoury blackcurrant/cedar/mocha aromas. Sweet, earthy blackcurrant flavours with grainy, savoury oak and touches of lanolin, fine, slightly grippy tannins, medium concentration and a firm finish.
■ *85* *Now-2012* *Distinguished*

**1995** *Coonawarra – Cabernet Sauvignon* **S.A.**
Deep crimson. Intense blackcurrant mulberry fruit-driven aromas with underlying oak. Deep-set thick textured palate with black fruits and dark cherries, plenty of vanillin almost sappy oak, slightly hollow, soupy high-pixel tannins and excellent length. Very good wine for year.
■ *88* *Now-2010* *Distinguished*

**1996** *Coonawarra – Cabernet Sauvignon* **S.A.**
Crimson. Intense leafy, briary, chocolaty aromas. Sweet-fruited wine with developing briary, chocolaty flavours, underlying cedary oak, with slight earth/rusty characters, fine-grained, grippy tannins, high concentration and good length.
■ *88* *Now-2008* *Distinguished*

**1997** *Coonawarra – Cabernet Sauvignon* **S.A.**
Crimson. Crimson cherry/cassis/vanillin aromas with a touch of cedar. Sweet-fruited, squashy blackcurrant pastille/cherry/cedar flavours, with fine-grained lacy tannins, lovely mid palate richness and a firm finish. Quite classical. Will build up over time.
■ *90* *Now-2008* *Distinguished*

**1998** *Coonawarra – Cabernet Sauvignon* **S.A.**
Deep crimson. Intense, deep-set blackcurrant/malty aromas – beautifully fruit, and oak-integrated. Seductive blackcurrant fruits, ripe finely grained tannins, lovely seasoned malty savoury oak, finishing long and sweet.
■ *93* *Now-2012* *Distinguished*

**1999** *Coonawarra – Cabernet Sauvignon* **S.A.**
Medium deep crimson. Elegant mocha/blackcurrant aromas with some cedar/spice complexity. Well balanced wine with beautifully smooth mocha/blackcurrant fruit underpinned by cedary oak, fine grained tannins, and plenty of flavour length.
■ *91* *2004-2016* *Distinguished*

**2000** *Coonawarra – Cabernet Sauvignon* **S.A.**
Deep crimson. Intense blackcurrant, plummy aromas with touches of mint and malty oak. Richly flavoured well-concentrated wine with beautifully focused blackcurrant /plum/cherry fruit flavours and malty oak characters, fine grained almost silky ripe tannins and plenty of length. A brilliant wine.
■ *94* *2004-2012* *Distinguished*

**1996** *Coonawarra – Merlot* **S.A.**
Crimson. Developed plum/lead pencil aromas with some tropical oak. Well concentrated wine with plenty of sweet plummy squashy fruit flavours, fine tannins and tropical/vanillin oak. Finishes firm.
▼-■ *85* *Now-2008*

**1997** *Coonawarra – Merlot* **S.A.**
Deep crimson. Loose-knit biscuity, plummy, gamy aromas; a barrel driven wine. The palate is loose-knit with plummy, biscuity flavours, sweet ripe tannins and medium length. Nice but won't last the distance.
▼-■ *85* *Now*

**1998** *Coonawarra – Merlot* **S.A.**
Crimson. Intense ultra-ripe cassis aromas with meaty/spice nuances and vanilla oak. Seductively squashy palate with cassis/plum fruit and some meaty characters. Fine lacy tannins. Underlying savoury/malty oak, finishing with a firm tannin slick. A beacon of quality.
▼-■ *93* *2003-2010*

**1998** *Coonawarra – Shiraz* **S.A.**
Deep crimson. Very tense wine with pure blackberry/lanolin/slatey aromas. Some underlying new oak complexity. Complex lanolin/ blackberry/slatey/bitumen flavours, with some cedar/leafy complexity, strong sinewy tannins, finishing long.
▼-■ *85* *2004-2010*

**1999** *Coonawarra – Shiraz* **S.A.**
Deep crimson. Bright choc-plum aromas. Touches of mocha and tropical/ malt oak characters. Rich, ripe, succulent palate with plenty of sweet fruit chocolate/plum fruit. Ripe, gravelly tannins, underpinned by malty/bran oak characters. Finishes firm but flavoursome. A very seductive – well made wine.
▼-■ *93* *2004-2010*

## KNAPPSTEIN

**1998 Enterprise** *Clare Valley – Cabernet Sauvignon* **S.A.**
Deep crimson. Ginger crackle/aniseed, blackcurrant/menthol aromas. Richly concentrated wine with deep-set blackcurrant/ginger/spice flavours, fine gravelly tannins immense fruit-sweetness, finishing firm but with plenty of flavour length. Excellent wine.
▼ *93* *2004-2010*

**1998 Enterprise** *Clare Valley – Shiraz* **S.A.**
Deep crimson. Intense choc-berry/bramble aromas with lashings of new malty/tropical oak. Rich, deeply concentrated wine, with choc-mulberry/bramble flavours, plenty of new seasoned/malty oak, fine, ripe, gravelly tannins and plenty of length.
▼-■ *88* *2004-2010*

**2000 Hand Picked** *Clare Valley – Riesling* **S.A.**
Pale yellow. Delicate aromatic wine. Floral/lemon/lime aromas. Lanolin nuances. Palate is very slatey and loose-knit. Deep-set chalky/lemon/lime flavours and minerally acidity. Plenty of length. Very perfumed wine.
▼ *90* *Now-2008*

**2001 Hand Picked** *Clare Valley – Riesling* **S.A.**
Pale colour. Perfumed chamomile/white peach/lemony aromas. Palate is beautifully balanced with chamomile/white peach flavours and some pear characters, fine long indelible acidity, and plenty of flavour length.
▼ *93* *Now-2006*

**1999** *Clare Valley – Shiraz* **S.A.**
Medium deep crimson. Plum/dark cherry/blackberry aromas with touches of aniseed. Plum cherry fruit flavours, fine ripe tannins, medium concentration and length.
▼ *78* *2004-2008*

## KOOYONG

**1999** *Mornington Peninsula – Pinot Noir* **Vic.**
Medium crimson. Cherry/apricot/malt/smoky aromas. Richly flavoured wine with squashy apricot malty flavours, fine ripe tannins, lovely new oak, finishing slightly grippy.
▼ *93* *Now-2006*

**2000** *Mornington Peninsula – Pinot Noir* **Vic.**
Medium deep crimson. Powerful dark cherry/meaty aromas with touches of liquorice. Dark cherry/liquorice flavours, hard slightly planky but spicy oak, finishing grippy and firm.
▼ *89* *Now-2006*

## LAKE'S FOLLY

**1993 White Label** *Hunter Valley – Cabernet Blend* **N.S.W.**
Crimson. Developed, complex, earthy, sweet mushroomy, demi-glace fruit aromas. Meaty, mushroomy, tangy wine. Fine tannins, medium concentration and length. Drinking now, but still a pleasant drink.
▼ *88* *Now* *Excellent*

**1994 White Label** *Hunter Valley – Cabernet Blend* **N.S.W.**
Medium deep crimson. Vanillin/blue cheesy/red berry/cassis aromas with a touch of earth. Developed blue cheese/earthy/berry flavours, sinewy tannins, but good fruit-sweetness and length. Ready to drink.
▼ *83* *Now-2006* *Excellent*

**1996 White Label** *Hunter Valley – Cabernet Blend* **N.S.W.**
Light crimson/purple. Leather, mint and allspice aromas with plenty of cedary oak. Lightly structured palate with sweet/spicy/menthol-like, red cherry flavours, slightly grippy tannins and medium length.
▼ *79* *Now-2010* *Excellent*

**1997 White Label** *Hunter Valley – Cabernet Blend* **N.S.W.**
Deep crimson. Very elegant cool-spectrum wine. Violet/herb garden aromas and underlying vanillin. Palate is restrained and quite bony with violet, herb garden flavours, fine sinewy tannin structure, a core of fruit-sweetness finishing firm and chalky with medium flavour length.
▼ *84* *2004-2012* *Excellent*

**1998 White Label** *Hunter Valley – Cabernet Blend* **N.S.W.**
Deep red/purple. Smoky, vanillin, blackcurrant, and minty aromas. The palate is quite elemental and awkward. Plenty of fruit concentration but pronounced oily oak, massive tannins and good length. A bit cumbersome.
▼ *84* *2002-2012* *Excellent*

**1999 White Label** *Hunter Valley – Cabernet Blend* **N.S.W.**
Deep crimson. Sweet liquorice/spicy/savoury/blackcurrant pastille aromas. Earthy/liquorice/blackcurrant flavours with spicy/savoury, slightly planky oak. Fine sinewy tannins. Finishing long and seaweedy.
▼ *83* *2004-2010* *Excellent*

**2000 White Label** *Hunter Valley – Cabernet Blend* **N.S.W.**
Deep crimson. Intense black olive/briary/cassis aromas. Some aniseed/gun flint nuances. Savoury palate with black olive/briary/ blackcurrant/violet flavours, fine sinewy tannins, finishing quite firm and tight. Nice palate weight.
▼ *90* *2004-2010* *Excellent*

**1996 Yellow Label** *Hunter Valley – Chardonnay* **N.S.W.**
Yellow. Peaches and cream, with vanillin and slightly herbal aromas. Soft, worked creamy, peachy flavours with savoury oak, fine acidity, excellent concentration and length. Sweet-fruited and pleasant – an early drinking wine.
▼ *86* *Now* *Distinguished*

**1997 Yellow Label** *Hunter Valley – Chardonnay* **N.S.W.**
Pale yellow. Deep, peachy, melon aromas. Some cashew nut. Touches of butterscotch. Ripe, peachy, melon flavours. Plenty of creaminess across the mid-palate, balanced with toasty oak, excellent concentration and lemony acid tang. Long finish.
▼ *92* *Now* *Distinguished*

**1998 Yellow Label** *Hunter Valley – Chardonnay* **N.S.W.**
Pale yellow. Intense lime/grapefruit/melon aromas with a touch of vanillin. Grapefruit/melon fruit with plenty of toasty vanillin oak, fruit-sweetness, concentration and length. A good wine.
▼ *93* *Now* *Distinguished*

**1999 Yellow Label** *Hunter Valley – Chardonnay* **N.S.W.**
Medium yellow. Developing honey/peach aromas with faint tobacco edges and some mineral notes. Developed honey/peachy flavours balanced with savoury/nutty oak, plenty of concentration and length. Needs drinking soon, but extremely complex.
▼ *85* *Now* *Distinguished*

**2000 Yellow Label** *Hunter Valley – Chardonnay* **N.S.W.**
Pale yellow. Lifted apricot/melon aromas with hint of butterscotch and yeasty complexity. Refined apricot/peach flavours balanced with

savoury/vanillin oak, plenty of richness/creaminess on the mid-palate and excellent flavour length.

▼ *93* *Now-2005* *Distinguished*

## LANGMEIL

**1997 The Freedom** *Barossa Valley – Shiraz* **S.A.**
Crimson. Tropical/menthol/chocolate aromas with ripe blackberry/raspberry fruit but the oak is dominant. Really well-seasoned tropical/menthol/cedary, savoury, malty and chewy oak hides lovely plummy blackberry fruit, slightly grippy tannins, good concentration and length but will not develop well as the oak is far too dominant and unlikely to integrate. Drinking nicely now.

▼-■ *85* *Now*

**1998 The Freedom** *Barossa Valley – Shiraz* **S.A.**
Medium deep crimson. Intense vanilla-bean, rum and raisin/choc-berry aromas, with some liquorice nuances. Palate is strongly oak flavoured and plush, with pronounced malty/nutty characters over ripe plum/chocolate fruit. Fine grained tannins, finishing long and flavoursome.

▼-■ *88* *Now-2008*

**1999 The Freedom** *Barossa Valley – Shiraz* **S.A.**
Deep crimson. Intense currant/prune aromas with plenty of malty oak. Well structured palate with deep-set plum/prune choc-berry flavours and some malty/grainy oak, strong gravelly tannins finishing long and savoury. Still very elemental.

▼-■ *88* *2004-2012*

## LEASINGHAM

**1994 Classic Clare** *Clare Valley – Cabernet Sauvignon* **S.A.**
Crimson/purple. Tight vanillin/savoury oak with some deep-set dark choc-berry fruit aromas. Rich, ripe style with deep-set choc-berry fruit flavours, ripe, fine tannins, with pronounced but well-balanced vanillin oak. Firm finish.

■ *92* *Now-2015*

**1995 Classic Clare** *Clare Valley – Cabernet Sauvignon* **S.A.**
Crimson/purple. Beautifully defined liquorice/blackcurrant/fine chocolate/slight menthol aromas with some earthy notes. Deep-set, blackberry fruits. Menthol/savoury and almost resiny oak. Massive gravelly tannins, huge concentration and length. Needs time to soften out.

▼-■ *88* *Now-2010*

**1996 Classic Clare** *Clare Valley – Cabernet Sauvignon* **S.A.**
Crimson/purple. Youthful and intense, exotic/gamy/bacon/ripe-berry aromas. Warm and generous palate with sweet blackcurrant/gamy fruit and lovely savoury oak, lacy fine tannins and excellent length.

■ *94* *2002-2012*

**1997 Classic Clare** *Clare Valley – Cabernet Sauvignon* **S.A.**
Crimson/purple. Menthol/eucalypt aromas over leafy cassis aromas. Leafy, chocolaty flavours with touches of blackcurrant and cedary oak, fine-grained, slightly green, tannins that build up. Firm, slightly bitter finish. Could soften out.

▼-■ *83* *2002-2010*

**1998 Classic Clare** *Clare Valley – Cabernet Sauvignon* **S.A.**
Medium deep crimson. Plush coffee bean/black cherry/meaty aromas with plenty of malty, oak characters. Rich, opulently structured wine with deep-set smoky/savoury/mocha flavours and some blackcurrants. Pronounced, almost bristling tannins, finishing firm but with good flavour length.

■ *86* *Now-2008*

**1999 Classic Clare** *Clare Valley – Cabernet Sauvignon* **S.A.**
Medium deep crimson. Intense choc-berry/cassis aromas with some smoky/coffee nuances. Richly flavoured wine with malty/choc-berry fruit flavours and some smoky characters, gravelly tannins, plenty of sweet fruit and flavour length, but finishes grippy.

■ *91* *2004-2010*

**1994 Classic Clare** *Clare Valley – Shiraz* **S.A.**
Deep crimson. Intense blackberry/brambly/menthol/iodine/dark chocolate. Richly flavoured wine with brambly/blackberry/menthol and developing

earthy flavours, slightly hard, grainy oak, with fine firm tannins, high concentration, but good length. Jimmy Watson Trophy winner.

■ 89 Now-2010

**1995 Classic Clare** *Clare Valley – Shiraz* **S.A.**
Deep crimson. Tightly-knit dark chocolate/prune aromas, with pronounced, savoury, well-seasoned, mocha/spicy oak background. Deep, full flavoured wine with chocolate/prune/mocha flavours. Sweet, slightly sappy, spicy oak, fine gripping tannins, plenty of fruit-sweetness and length. Needs time, but classical Australian Shiraz. Outstanding wine for vintage.

■ 94 Now-2006

**1996 Classic Clare** *Clare Valley – Shiraz* **S.A.**
Crimson/purple. Classic sweet fruited wine with dark plum/chocolate/ Christmas cake aromas – lovely definition. Sweet-fruited wine with dark plum chocolate flavours, beautifully seasoned savoury, malty, menthol oak, sweet, ripe lacy tannins and plenty of length.

■ 94 Now-2008

**1997 Classic Clare** *Clare Valley – Shiraz* **S.A.**
Deep crimson. Sweet-fruited mulberry/chocolate/liquorice aromas. Rich,ripe and full-flavoured wine with deep-set mulberry/chocolate flavours, sweet smoky mocha oak, and fine gripping tannins. High concentration, with a firm and sweet finish.

■ 88 Now-2006

**1998 Classic Clare** *Clare Valley – Shiraz* **S.A.**
Deep crimson. Intense smoky/blackberry chocolaty aromas with some roasted coffee nuances. The palate is rich and deep with blackberry/ mocha fruit flavours and plenty of malty oak complexity. Ripe gravelly tannins, finishing oaky dry, but with plenty of flavour length.

■ 93 2004-2010

**1999 Classic Clare** *Clare Valley – Shiraz* **S.A.**
Deep crimson. Deep liquorice, blackcurrant cedary aromas. Richly flavoured wine with redcurrant/liquorice flavours, plenty of malty oak and chocolaty tannins, finishing long and sweet. Elegant style.

■ 88 2005-2012

## LECONFIELD

**1995** *Coonawarra – Cabernet Blend* **S.A.**
Crimson/purple. Coffee and cassis-like aromas with some leafy and liquorice notes. Sweet-fruited, coffee and cassis flavours with fine, leafy tannins, a touch of meaty complexity, and some underlying oak support. Good length. More than acceptable, given the poor year.

▼ 89 Now-2006 *Distinguished*

**1996** *Coonawarra – Cabernet Blend* **S.A.**
Crimson/purple. Blackcurrant pastille, roasted meat and vanillin aromas. Palate is velvety and long, with leafy, blackcurrant flavours, ripe tannins, underlying oak and good length. A little simple, but should develop complexity over time.

▼ 87 2002-2010 *Distinguished*

**1997** *Coonawarra – Cabernet Blend* **S.A.**
Deep crimson/purple. Intense, choc-berry and blackcurrant/brambly aromas with savoury oak. Richly flavoured, pure, blackcurrant/brambly fruit, with fine-grained tannins, underlying cedary oak and good length.

▼ 93 Now-2008 *Distinguished*

**1998** *Coonawarra – Cabernet Blend* **S.A.**
Deep crimson/purple. Cassis/rhubarb/mulberry aromas with a touch of menthol. Deep-set, squashy mulberry/cassis/rhubarb fruit, underlying cedar, loose-knit fine tannins and good length. Early drinking style but quite exotic and fleshy wine.

▼ 92 Now-2010 *Distinguished*

**1999** *Coonawarra – Cabernet Blend* **S.A.**
Medium deep crimson. Ethereal wine with pure blackcurrant/ginger aromas and underlying cedar oak. Lovely fruit-sweet wine. Blackcurrant/ ginger flavours. Plenty of malty oak, some meaty nuances, fine grainy tannins, plenty of sweet fruit and flavour length, but drying tannins.

▼ 88 Now-2008 *Distinguished*

**2000** *Coonawarra – Cabernet Blend* **S.A.**
Medium crimson. Perfumed/redcurrant/lanolin, smoky herb garden aromas. Meaty/gamy fruit and plenty of classy oak. Some cassis/red

cherry – almost Pinot Noir-like flavours. Chalky, fine tannins, finishing long and smoky.

▼ 86 2004-2012 *Distinguished*

**1995** *Coonawarra – Shiraz* **S.A.**

Crimson. Earthy, iodine/pepper/tomato-leaf, almost under ripe aromas and a touch of game. Very wiry wine with almost herbal/gamy fruit characters and pronounced tannins. A worked wine.

▼ 79 Now-2005

**1996** *Coonawarra – Shiraz* **S.A.**

Deep crimson/purple. Liquorice/aniseed/plum/blackcurrant aromas with a savoury oak background. Palate is rich and ripe with sweet blackcurrant fruit, a touch of leafiness, ripe high-pixel tannins, high concentration, and finishing firm.

▼ 83 Now-2005

**1997** *Coonawarra – Shiraz* **S.A.**

Deep crimson. Raspberry/blackberry/liquorice/aniseed aromas with underlying new oak. The palate is deep and fleshy with blackberry-jammy fruit, fine-grained but ripe tannins and excellent length.

▼ 91 Now-2010

**1998** *Coonawarra – Shiraz* **S.A.**

Deep crimson/purple. Black cherry/pepper aromas with hints of menthol. Sweet black cherry flavours with peppery, spiced overtones, some fine sweet oak, fine-grained tannins, vibrant acidity and medium length.

▼ 85 2002-2010

## LEEUWIN ESTATE

**1996 Art Series** *Margaret River – Cabernet* **S.A.**

Crimson/purple. Leafy, blackcurrant-like aromas with cedary, earthy notes. Palate is classically structured with earthy, blackcurrant-like fruit and cedary oak flavours, strong, gravelly tannins and a long finish. Needs more time.

■ 88 Now-2010 *Distinguished*

**1997 Art Series** *Margaret River – Cabernet* **S.A.**

Medium deep crimson. Complex malt briary aromas with some cassis/menthol. Complex and tangy briary/menthol/earthy cassis flavours, fine grainy slightly grippy tannins, finishing long and flavoursome.

■-▲ 100 2004-2010 *Distinguished*

**1998 Art Series** *Margaret River – Cabernet* **S.A.**

Medium crimson. Sweet bramble/dark chocolate/plum aromas and underlying malt/vanilla oak. Rich plum/prune/bramble flavours with ripe fine tannins and plenty of new oak. Finishes firm and oaky.

■ 87 2005-2012 *Distinguished*

**1995 Art Series** *Margaret River – Chardonnay* **S.A.**

Pale gold. Intense, sparkling, peach and apple-like aromas with fresh, savoury, grainy oak. Well-toned peach, apple and sweet apricot flavours, supported by sappy, vanillin oak and some complex lanolin characters, a fine acid cut and super length. Still looking superb.

■-▲ 100 Now-2010 *Exceptional*

**1996 Art Series** *Margaret River – Chardonnay* **S.A.**

Pale yellow. Intense peach/nectarine pure fruit aromas with savoury oak and some nutty complexity. Immensely concentrated wine with lovely roasted nut/peachy/melon fruit. Excellent fruit purity and rapier-like, almost indelible acidity. Superb underlying savoury oak.

■-▲ 98 Now *Exceptional*

**1997 Art Series** *Margaret River – Chardonnay* **S.A.**

Pale yellow/gold. Intense, beautifully perfumed tropical aromas with banana, honey, melon and peach and touches of smoky vanillin oak. Classically proportioned, creamy palate already complex with tropical fruit and honeycomb, smoky, savoury oak, roasted nuts, an indelible acid cut and a long finish. A great wine.

■-▲ 99 Now-2010 *Exceptional*

**1998 Art Series** *Margaret River – Chardonnay* **S.A.**

Pale gold. Complex, mealy, biscuity aromas with some ripe, peach/pear aromas. Beautifully intense. Immensely concentrated wine with deep-set, mealy, biscuity, peachy flavours and nutty nuances. Plenty of creaminess but fine acid cut. Superb concentration and length. Super wine.

■-▲ 96 Now-2010 *Exceptional*

**1999 Art Series** *Margaret River – Chardonnay* **S.A.**
Pale yellow. Passionfruit, guava/mango and cashew nut aromas. Well balanced creamy palate with passionfruit/guava/aniseed and complex lemon curd/roasted nut flavours. Penetrating new oak. Excellent concentration, fine indelible acidity, and long savoury finish.
■-▲ *94* *Now-2010* *Exceptional*

**2000 Art Series** *Margaret River – Chardonnay* **W.A.**
Pale colour. Very intense tropical fruit/pear aromas with lovely cashew nut/savoury complexity. The palate is well concentrated, with creamy grapefruit/pear nuances, and integrated cashew nut/malty oak. Fine, indelible mouth-quenching acidity, finishing with a long burst of aniseed/savoury oak flavours. A classic.
▲ *95* *Now-2008* *Exceptional*

## LENGS AND COOTER

**1998 Old Vines** *Clare Valley – Shiraz* **S.A.**
Medium deep crimson. Intense choc-menthol aromas with some gingersnap. Plenty of choc-menthol flavours, and vanilla nuances, fine sinewy tannins, put plenty of fruit-sweetness. Builds up extremely firm, with iron fisted tannins.
■ *89* *2004-2012*

**1999 Old Vines** *Clare Valley – Shiraz* **S.A.**
Medium deep crimson. Very complex savoury wine with meaty/gamy/black cherry/rhubarb/blackberry aromas – touch menthol. Well structured wine with black cherry/gamy/mocha flavours, lacy fine tannins, underlying oak and plenty of length.
■ *93* *2004-2010*

**2000 Old Vines** *Clare Valley – Shiraz* **S.A.**
Deep crimson. Lanolin/smoked meaty/menthol aromas with some mulberry/raspberry. Menthol/walnut/meaty flavours, with fine grained drying tannins, some savoury oak tones, finishing long and sweet.
■ *84* *2005-2010*

**1998 Reserve** *Clare Valley – Shiraz* **S.A.**
Medium crimson. Intense dark cherry/mulberry aromas with some vanilla undertones. Dark cherry/mulberry flavours, with ripe chocolaty tannins and plenty of malty oak. Finishes chalky firm but with good flavour length.
■ *87* *2004-2012*

**1999 Reserve** *Clare Valley – Shiraz* **S.A.**
Deep crimson. Intense blackberry mocha/malt aromas with some smoky nuances. Strong roasted coffee/mocha/tropical favours. The fruit is intertwined with plenty of strong oak. Fine sinewy, slightly grippy, tannins, building up firm and tight but with long mocha flavours.
■ *89* *2004-2012*

## LENSWOOD

**1998 Palatine** *Adelaide – Cabernet Merlot Malbec* **S.A.**
Deep crimson. Barnyardy/raisiny aromas with some leafy/liquorice characters. Medium concentrated palate with liquorice/leafy flavours and sinewy/leafy tannins, finishing dry and tight. Quite austere style.
▼ *78* *Now-2008*

**1999 Palatine** *Adelaide Hills – Merlot Malbec Cabernet Sauvignon* **S.A.**
Deep crimson. Fruit-driven wine with blackcurrant pastille/ripe plum aromas. Lovely intensity. Smooth, well balanced palate with blackcurrant pastille/plum flavours and touches of black olive. Fine grained, slightly sinewy, tannin structure, but good overall length. Flavour intensity drops off towards the end.
▼ *88* *2004-2010*

**1998** *Adelaide Hills – Pinot Noir* **S.A.**
Crimson. Intense, fruit-driven wine with plum/raspberry/cherry aromas and underlying smoky oak. The palate is ripe and fleshy, with raspberry/plum/cherry and smoky oak flavours, velvety tannins and plenty of length. Early drinking wine.
▼ *93* *Now*

**2000** *Adelaide Hills – Pinot Noir* **S.A.**
Medium crimson. Intense strawberry/cherry aromas with hints of demi-glace/mushroom complexity. Richly flavoured wine with burst of

strawberry/cherry fruit, followed by complex sweet fruit characters. Fine sinewy tannins. Plenty of concentration and length.

▼ 90 Now-2005

## LINDEMANS

**1991 Limestone Ridge Vineyard** *Coonawarra – Shiraz Cabernet* **S.A.**
Deep crimson. Blackberry/dark cherry/chocolate aromas that are quite lifted and developed with hints of hazelnut. The palate is quite oak-driven with a grainy, smoky, freshly hewn timber edge and some choc-berry characters, a fine tannin structure and length. Sailing close to the wind. The oak makes the wine cumbersome, whereas the underlying fruit definition is excellent. Maybe it will integrate one day.

■ 89 Now-2008 *Distinguished*

**1992 Limestone Ridge Vineyard** *Coonawarra – Shiraz Cabernet* **S.A.**
Crimson/purple. Deep-set, sappy coconut/smoky/blackcurrant aromas with touches of tar. Sweet-fruited, smoky, blackberry flavours, with some cedar, fine-grained tannins, tangy acidity. Medium concentration and good length.

■ 84 Now-2008 *Distinguished*

**1993 Limestone Ridge Vineyard** *Coonawarra – Shiraz Cabernet* **S.A.**
Medium/crimson. Dark chocolate/blackcurrant aromas with plenty of vanillin oak characters. Pronounced, savoury, cedary, malty oak flavours that envelope the developing sweet choc-berry fruit. Ripe tannins, high concentration and length.

▼-■ 92 2002-2008 *Distinguished*

**1994 Limestone Ridge Vineyard** *Coonawarra – Shiraz Cabernet* **S.A.**
Crimson/purple. Intense liquorice/ripe blackberry fruit with touches of dark chocolate. Rich, ripe, beautifully focused wine with fine dark chocolate/blackberry/currant fruit, grainy, slightly smoky oak and a firm finish.

■ 95 2002-2012 *Distinguished*

**1996 Limestone Ridge Vineyard** *Coonawarra – Shiraz Cabernet* **S.A.**
Crimson/purple. Complex chocolate/leafy/violet/mulberry aromas. Sweet choc-berry/leafy flavours with plenty of well-seasoned, slightly coconut-like oak, fine-grained, pronounced and slightly aggressive tannins. Finishes with high concentration and good length.

■ 91 2002-2010 *Distinguished*

**1997 Limestone Ridge Vineyard** *Coonawarra – Shiraz Cabernet* **S.A.**
Crimson/purple. Red cherry/leafy aromas with touches of bacon and pure blackberry fruit. Meaty, gamy, leafy, black cherry fruit. Pronounced tannins structure, bolstered with vanillin, grainy oak. A long finish. Needs time.

▼-■ 89 2002-2008 *Distinguished*

**1998 Limestone Ridge Vineyard** *Coonawarra – Shiraz Cabernet* **S.A.**
Purple Red. Intense dark chocolate/dark cherry aromas with touches of liquorice. Smells like a bag of liquorice allsorts. Deep set, richly flavoured wine with plenty of dark cherry, liquorice flavours, loose-knit, lacy tannins and plenty of sweet American oak. Finishes long. This is a classic style showing more richness than the elegant 1998 *St George*.

■ 92 2004-2014 *Distinguished*

**1999 Limestone Ridge Vineyard** *Coonawarra – Shiraz Cabernet* **S.A.**
Medium crimson. Lifted, vanilla bean/malty aromas with some blackcurrant/mint characters. Blackcurrant/briary flavours with some mint and malty oak characters. Fine tannins. Finishing chalky and firm but with good flavour length.

■ 84 2004-2010 *Distinguished*

**1991 Pyrus** *Coonawarra – Cabernet Blend* **S.A.**
Dark brick red. Well-developed earthy, meaty, liquorice aromas. Complex and well-structured palate with earthy, meaty, slightly barnyard flavours, fine soupy tannins and plenty of sweet fruit and concentration. Super length. Oak well integrated.

■ 92 Now-2008 *Distinguished*

**1993 Pyrus** *Coonawarra – Cabernet Blend* **S.A.**
Deep red/purple. Mocha/coffee/dark cherry almost liqueur-like aromas. Sweet-fruited, quite elemental wine with dark cherry/mocha fruit flavours. Pronounced cedary oak and a massively firm tannin structure. Needs time.

▼-■ 92 Now-2008 *Distinguished*

**1994 Pyrus** *Coonawarra – Cabernet Blend* **S.A.**
Deep crimson. Earthy, rusty, liquorice/blackcurrant aromas. A ripely textured wine with rich chocolate/liquorice/blackcurrant flavours and subtle smoky, cedary oak combined with loose-knit velvety tannins. Interesting and complex.
■ *93* *Now-2010* *Distinguished*

**1995 Pyrus** *Coonawarra – Cabernet Blend* **S.A.**
Deep crimson. Coffee/chocolate/cedary aromas. Plenty of vanilla. Well flavoured but slightly spicy wine with coffee/chocolaty flavours, fine grainy tannins finishing quite dry and chalky. Plenty of flavour length.
▼-■ *89* *Now-2008* *Distinguished*

**1996 Pyrus** *Coonawarra – Cabernet Blend* **S.A.**
Crimson/purple. Rich and intense choc-berry/leafy aromas. Rich, ripely textured wine with chocolate/leafy flavours, cedary oak and fine-grained, gripping tannins, finishing firm. Very concentrated.
■ *91* *Now-2010* *Distinguished*

**1997 Pyrus** *Coonawarra – Cabernet Blend* **S.A.**
Deep crimson/purple. Pronounced coconut/vanillin oak aromas over bright, red-berry fruit. This is a barrel-driven wine with sweet coconut/vanillin/smoky flavours and squashy berry fruit, fine-grained, drying tannins and a firm finish. Super oak handling but under-fruited.
▼-■ *88* *Now-2012* *Distinguished*

**1998 Pyrus** *Coonawarra – Cabernet Blend* **S.A.**
Deep crimson. Classic smelling Cabernet with pronounced blackcurrant/cedar/vanillin aromas, plenty of sweet fruit plus a touch of chocolate. Beautifully pitched wine. Rich, ripe cassis/chocolate flavours, perfectly seasoned oak flavours. Fine fruit drenched rusty tannins. Plenty of flavour length. Needs a little time to develop. Finishes chalky dry. A wine with high-pitched fruit definition and a fascinating foil to *St George* and *Limestone Ridge*.
■ *92* *2004-2010* *Distinguished*

**1999 Pyrus** *Coonawarra – Cabernet Blend* **S.A.**
Deep crimson. Blackcurrant pastille with some cedar/vanilla nuances. Well structured palate with blackcurrant pastille/chocolate flavours. Fine grainy but drying tannins. Underlying mocha/cedar oak. Finishing dry and firm.
■ *88* *2004-2012* *Distinguished*

**1976 St George Vineyard** *Coonawarra – Cabernet Sauvignon* **S.A.**
Crimson brick. Developed mushroom/demi-glace aromas with hints of truffle and soy. Fully developed wine with sweet fruited mushroom, demi-glace/capsicum flavours, soft fine tannins, plenty of concentration and length. Lovely mature wine.
■ *94* *Now* *Distinguished*

**1978 St George Vineyard** *Coonawarra – Cabernet Sauvignon* **S.A.**
Crimson brick. Freshly ground coffee aromas with touches of chocolate and cassis. Medium concentrated palate with plenty of ground coffee/sweet cherry flavours. Fine, slightly green-edged tannins, finishing firm and tight. Quite simple.
■ *84* *Now* *Distinguished*

**1980 St George Vineyard** *Coonawarra – Cabernet Sauvignon* **S.A.**
Crimson brick. Asparagus, capsicum aromas with some contrived cherry notes. Palate is fruit-sweet with asparagus/mushroom flavours. Medium concentrated, fine sweet tannins and plenty of length. Holding up. Winner of the 1981 Jimmy Watson Trophy – but illustrates how the wine quality goal posts have moved over the last 15 years.
■ *82* *Now* *Distinguished*

**1985 St George Vineyard** *Coonawarra – Cabernet Sauvignon* **S.A.**
Crimson brick. Cedar/cherry aromas with slight furniture nuances. The palate is richer than expected with cedar/dark cherry fruit, fine grained tannins, matched with savoury oak and finishing firm. A moderately concentrated wine which is a bit tense and unyielding.
▼-■ *83* *Now-2005* *Distinguished*

**1986 St George Vineyard** *Coonawarra – Cabernet Sauvignon* **S.A.**
Crimson red. Intense cassis/mocha aromas with touch cedar/vanillin. Richly flavoured with deep-set coffee/meaty flavours and underlying oak. Firm but fine grained tannins with good length. Plenty of flavour.
■ *91* *Now-2008* *Distinguished*

**1990 St George Vineyard** *Coonawarra – Cabernet Sauvignon* **S.A.**
Crimson red. Liquorice choc-cassis aromas with sweet vanillin/cedar oak. The palate is thick and soupy with deep-set cassis liquorice chocolate flavours and a pronounced slick of firm tannins finishing quite gritty. Very tight wine with strong oak nuances.
■-▲ *86* *Now-2008* *Distinguished*

**1991 St George Vineyard** *Coonawarra – Cabernet Sauvignon* **S.A.**
Crimson red. Loose-knit style with plenty of perfumed, coffee/gamy aromas and touches of sweet dark chocolate. The palate is medium concentrated with coffee/mulberry/gamy fruit flavours, fine sweet lacy tannins and plenty of length. Very supple easy to drink wine. Arguably the best ever *St George*.
■-▲ *94* *Now-2005* *Distinguished*

**1992 St George Vineyard** *Coonawarra – Cabernet Sauvignon* **S.A.**
Crimson red. Intense blackcurrant/saddle leather aromas with touches of anise. A little green edged. The palate is richly flavoured with blackcurrant/aniseed flavours, rather bitter tannins but plenty of concentration and length. Not a long term creature. As fruit develops palate structure will look greener.
■ *80* *Now-2004* *Distinguished*

**1993 St George Vineyard** *Coonawarra – Cabernet Sauvignon* **S.A.**
Red purple. Briary/blackcurrant aromas with cedar oak. Palate is evolving with plenty of blackcurrant/cedar flavours, but very hard edged tannins. Ultimately a diminishing prospect.
▼-■ *81* *Now-2006* *Distinguished*

**1994 St George Vineyard** *Coonawarra – Cabernet Sauvignon* **S.A.**
Red, purple. Intense liquorice/dark berry aromas with malty/vanillin oak. Still fresh vibrant and young with richly flavoured deep-set plum liquorice/dark berry chocolate characters, sweet chewy/grainy tannins. Good length.
■ *90* *2004-2012* *Distinguished*

**1995 St George Vineyard** *Coonawarra – Cabernet Sauvignon* **S.A.**
Medium crimson/purple. Pronounced spicy, cedary, new oak aromas dominate the nose. Moderately concentrated cedary, blackcurrant flavours on the palate, with ripe firm tannins.
▼-■ *84* *Now-2008* *Distinguished*

**1996 St George Vineyard** *Coonawarra – Cabernet Sauvignon* **S.A.**
Red, purple. Deep-set blackcurrant/dark cherry/sweet fruit aromas with underlying oak. Palate is very generous and concentrated with rich ripe choc-berry/liquorice flavours, grainy/gravelly tannins, plenty of cedar oak and flavour length. Looked terrific compared to the previous bottle.
■ *93* *2004-2012* *Distinguished*

**1997 St George Vineyard** *Coonawarra – Cabernet Sauvignon* **S.A.**
Red, purple. Intense dark cherry aromas with smoky/gunflint nuances. The palate has plenty of sweet fruit with smoky/red cherry flavours but is sinewy in structure. The tannins are a touch green edged, suggesting medium termed cellaring.
▼-■ *84* *2003-2008* *Distinguished*

**1998 St George Vineyard** *Coonawarra – Cabernet Sauvignon* **S.A.**
Purple, red. Dark chocolate/cedar box aromas with touches of savoury/nutty oak. The palate is tight but well-concentrated with plenty of ripe berry fruit and cedar nuances. Tannins are fine grained but firm, bringing a compact, hard impression. A great Coonawarra vintage – yet this wine doesn't quite reach the absolute pinnacle.
■ *90* *2004-2014* *Distinguished*

**1999 St George Vineyard** *Coonawarra – Cabernet Sauvignon* **S.A.**
Deep crimson. Perfumed floral/violet blackcurrant/mint aromas. Loose-knit wine with violet/blackcurrant/cedar flavours, chocolaty tannins building up very gritty, grippy and tight at the finish.
■ *83* *2004-2012* *Distinguished*

## MAGPIE ESTATE

**1999 The Malcolm** *Barossa Valley – Shiraz* **S.A.**
Deep crimson. Intense ripe plum/aniseed/gingersnap aromas. Richly flavoured wine with plum/blackberry/dark chocolate flavours, malty/tropical oak, grippy fine tannins and plenty of length. Massively structured wine with hot alcoholic kick at the back.
■ *88* *2004-2012*

 ▼ = *Weak* ■ = *Moderate* ▲ = *Strong* ☆ = *Rare* ❍ = *not saleble*

## MAJELLA

**1996 Malleea** *Coonawarra – Cabernet Shiraz* **S.A.**
Medium deep crimson. Developing loose-knit aromatic earthy/chocolate/plum aromas with touches of cinnamon. Loose-knit earthy/chocolate/plum flavours. Fine dense, slightly green edged, tannins and a bittersweet, chocolaty finish.
■-▲ *87* *Now-2010*

**1997 Malleea** *Coonawarra – Cabernet Shiraz* **S.A.**
Deep crimson. Intense plum/red cherry/menthol aromas with some vanillin/nutmeg nuances. Well focused wine with plum/red cherry/menthol flavours, fine supple tannins, tangy concentration. Underlying savoury oak, finishing long and flavoursome.
■ *90* *Now-2010*

**1998 Malleea** *Coonawarra – Cabernet Shiraz* **S.A.**
Deep crimson. Very youthful, elemental, blackcurrant/cherry/choc-mint aromas with plenty of savoury oak. Cool flavoured blackcurrant/cherry/slightly leafy/choc-mint flavours, fine sinewy tannins, building up firm and tight. Plenty of fruit-sweetness.
■-▲ *89* *2004-2012*

**1999 Malleea** *Coonawarra – Cabernet Shiraz* **S.A.**
Deep crimson. Intense blackcurrant/plummy aromas with some liquorice/minty nuances and vanilla/cedar oak. Densely packed wine with strong blackcurrant/cedar flavours, plush ripe tannins and plenty of malt/savoury oak and fruit-sweetness, finishing quite cedary and long.
■ *97* *2004-2014*

**1994** *Coonawarra – Cabernet Sauvignon* **S.A.**
Medium deep crimson. Complex earthy/plum/demi-glace aromas with some liquorice. Developed, earthy/chocolate flavours, some demi-glace characters. Fine grainy quite chalky tannins, finishing firm and dry.
■ *88* *2004-2010*

**1996** *Coonawarra – Cabernet Sauvignon* **S.A.**
Deep crimson. Loose-knit cassis chocolate/malty nougat aromas. Concentrated wine with choc-cassis flavours. Fine, slightly gritty, but long tannins. Strong, savoury nutmeg/cedar oak characters. Finishing with a belt of tannin slick.
■ *91* *2004-2012*

**1997** *Coonawarra – Cabernet Sauvignon* **S.A.**
Deep crimson. Dark cherry/blackcurrant pastille aromas. Lovely underlying savoury oak. Deep-set dark cherry/blackcurrant pastille flavours, with fruit drenched, fine grainy lacy tannins, finishing cedary and firm.
■ *93* *2004-2008*

**1998** *Coonawarra – Cabernet Sauvignon* **S.A.**
Deep crimson. Beautifully smooth, fine chocolate/nougat/cassis aromas with touches of gingersnap. Extremely well balanced wine with fine dark chocolate/cassis flavours. Lovely cedary oak. Fine velveteen tannins, building up firm but with plenty of flavour length. Super wine.
■ *96* *2004-2012*

**1999** *Coonawarra – Cabernet Sauvignon* **S.A.**
Deep crimson. Aromatic and perfectly ripe plum/dark cherry aromas with vanilla/malt/meaty nuances. Very classical palate with ripe plum/dark cherry/liquorice flavours, fine grained/cedary tannins, and underlying savoury oak. Finishes firm and tight.
■ *92* *2004-2012*

**2000** *Coonawarra – Cabernet Sauvignon* **S.A.**
Deep crimson. Very youthful plum/liquorice /aniseed aromas with plenty of underlying but subtle savoury oak. Very attractive, deep plum/cassis flavours, fine gravelly tannins, with plenty of concentration and fruit-sweetness. Finishing firm but with excellent flavour length. Elemental wine.
■ *93* *2005-2014*

**1996** *Coonawarra – Shiraz* **S.A.**
Medium crimson. Medium concentrated wine with leafy/undergrowth prune/blackberry/vanilla aromas. Restrained leafy/blackberry pastille flavours. Fine long sinewy tannins, but good fruit-sweetness. Finishes quite bitter.
■ *84* *Now-2008*

**1997** *Coonawarra – Shiraz* **S.A.**
Medium crimson. Paneforte/dark chocolate/prune aromas. Sweet fruited wine with *paneforte*/walnut flavours, chocolaty tannins, good concentration, finishing long and sinewy.
■ *85* *Now-2008*

**1998** *Coonawarra – Shiraz* **S.A.**
Medium deep crimson. Savoury blackcurrant/liquorice aromas with some malt/bran undertones. Well-concentrated wine with blackcurrant/liquorice flavours, grainy tannins, underlying savoury oak, quite marked tangy acidity. Needs time to settle.
■ *86* *2004-2010*

**1999** *Coonawarra – Shiraz* **S.A.**
Medium deep crimson. Well focused, blackberry/mocha aromas with some apricot/prune nuances and underlying new smoky/vanillin oak. Succulent palate with blackberry/mocha flavours, plenty of underlying savoury oak. Lacy, slightly grippy tannins, finishing dry and firm.
■ *90* *2004-2010*

**2000** *Coonawarra – Shiraz* **S.A.**
Medium deep crimson. Perfumed blackberry pastille/mint aromas with some savoury notes. Lovely balanced wine with blackberry/mint flavours. Lacy tannins, some savoury, toasty oak and plenty of flavour length. Very refined.
■ *93* *2004-2010*

## McWILLIAM'S

**1998 '1877'** *Eastern Australia (Coonawarra, Barwang, Yarra Valley) – Cabernet Shiraz* **Eastern Australia (SA, NSW & Vic)**
Deep crimson. Intense plush mulberry/dark chocolate aromas with underlying savoury oak and touches of demi-glace. Rich succulent mulberry/chocolate/mocha flavours, fine firm chocolaty tannins, intertwined with generous new oak. Plenty of fruit-sweetness and flavour length. Finishes firm. Selected fruit from McWilliam's top Barwang, Coonawarra, and Yarra Valley vineyards.
▼-■ *92* *2006-2012*

**1999 '1877'** *Eastern Australia (Coonawarra, Barwang, Yarra Valley) – Cabernet Shiraz* **Eastern Australia (SA, NSW & Vic)**
Deep crimson. Intense choc-berry/hazelnut aromas with some cedary/vanilla/spice notes. Well balanced wine with deep-set chocolate/hazelnut/coffee/berry flavours. Plenty of savoury oak. Massive pixilated tannins, fruit-sweetness and length. Still elemental. Needs time to soften out.
▼-■ *91* *2006-2014*

**1998 Barwang** *Hilltops N.S.W. – Cabernet Sauvignon* **N.S.W.**
Deep crimson. Concentrated and ripe, dark chocolate/blackcurrant aromas. Ripe, concentrated wine with dark chocolate/black currant flavours, plenty of fruit-sweetness, fine grained tannins, underlying malty oak, building up firm and tight. Needs to soften.
▼ *87* *2004-2010*

**1999 Barwang** *Hilltops N.S.W. – Cabernet Sauvignon* **N.S.W.**
Deep crimson. Choc-berry aromas with a touch of cedar. Sweet fruited palate with dark cherry/choc-berry flavours. Fine, quite aggressive, tannins. Plenty of fruit-sweetness and flavour length but builds up chalky and firm.
▼ *83* *Now-2008*

**2000 Barwang** *Hilltops N.S.W. – Cabernet Sauvignon* **N.S.W.**
Deep crimson. Dark cherry/fruit driven aromas. Well balanced wine with some dark cherry/smoky flavours and malty oak. Fine lacy tannins. Finishing quite firm. Nice core of fruit-sweetness. Not particularly complex.
▼ *87* *Now-2010*

**2000 Barwang** *Hilltops N.S.W. – Merlot* **N.S.W.**
Deep crimson. Red currant/plum/tropical oak, menthol, aromas. Deep flavoured, redcurrant/plum fruit. Furry loose-knit, slightly bitter, tannins, finishing long and sweet.
▼ *84* *Now-2010*

**1998 Barwang** *Hilltops N.S.W. – Shiraz* **N.S.W.**
Deep crimson. Intense liquorice/chocolate aromas with superb underlying oak. Richly concentrated wine with liquorice/chocolate/

mulberry flavours, pronounced, quite sinewy tannins, plenty of concentration and length. Lovely wine.

▼ 91 2004-2012

**1999 Barwang** *Hilltops N.S.W. – Shiraz* **N.S.W.**
Deep crimson. Intense choc-berry flavours with some liquorice. Richly flavoured wine with some peppermint characters, fine slinky tannins, lovely oak integration, finishing quite long and sappy/flavoursome,

▼ 90 Now-2010

**2000 Barwang** *Hilltops N.S.W. – Shiraz* **N.S.W.**
Deep crimson. Intense liquorice/slightly contrived jammy/cherry aromas and flavours with savoury oak, tangy acidity, drying tannins. Finishes firm.

▼ 79 2004-2010

## MITCHELL

**1996 Sevenhill Vineyard** *Clare Valley – Cabernet Sauvignon* **S.A.**
Deep crimson/purple. Lifted and intense blackberry/chocolate/cedar and savoury oak characters, with a slight minty edge. Tight cedary palate with black olive/cedary/savoury oak flavours. Fine-grained tannins, pronounced acidity, but good concentration and length.

▼-■ 87 2001-2005

**1997 Sevenhill Vineyard** *Clare Valley – Cabernet Sauvignon* **S.A.**
Deep crimson/purple. Elemental but strikingly fruit-pure aromas of mulberry/blackberry essence. A fruit-driven style with a rich, sweet-fruited palate of concentrated and seductive mulberry/blackberry fruit. Lacy, but slight, grippy tannins and plenty of length.

▼-■ 94 2001-2005

**1998 Sevenhill Vineyard** *Clare Valley – Cabernet Sauvignon* **S.A.**
Deep crimson/purple. Lifted aniseed/cracked pepper aromas with touches of mulberries and cedar. Plenty of youthful flesh and cedary, blackcurrant flavours with an underlying sinewy structure, grippy tannins, and a dry and firm finish.

▼-■ 89 2001-2006

**1999 Sevenhill Vineyard** *Clare Valley – Cabernet Sauvignon* **S.A.**
Medium deep crimson. Intense violet/rose garden aromas with some cassis/plum/minty nuances. Concentrated wine with deep dark chocolate/blackberry/black olive fruit flavours and plenty of malty/savoury oak. Soupy, slightly grippy, tannins, but excellent concentration and length.

▼-■ 89 2004-2012

**1992 Watervale** *Clare Valley – Riesling* **S.A.**
Yellow gold. Fresh but complex lime/apricot/custard/toast aromas. The palate has plenty of fruit-sweetness and concentration with lime/apricot flavours, fine mineral acidity, and excellent length.

▼-■ 90 Now-2006

**1998 Watervale** *Clare Valley – Riesling* **S.A.**
Yellow gold. Immensely perfumed wine with floral/violet/lime, almost slate, aromas. Classically structured wine with sweet, limey fruit and mineral-like acidity.

▼-■ 95 Now

**1999 Watervale** *Clare Valley – Riesling* **S.A.**
Medium yellow. Brioche/biscuity aromas with some marmalade nuances. Lively wine with developed biscuity/delicate lime flavours, bright acidity and excellent length.

▼-■ 91 Now-2008

**2000 Watervale** *Clare Valley – Riesling* **S.A.**
Pale yellow. Very delicate and attractive lime/apricot/stone fruit aromas. Deep-set, fleshy wine with apricot/stone fruit/lemon flavours. Fine mineral acidity and medium length. Quite a lot of viscosity and fruit-sweetness.

▼-■ 92 Now-2007

**2001 Watervale** *Clare Valley – Riesling* **S.A.**
Pale colour. Perfumed apricot/pear/honeyed aromas. Supple, almost slippery palate with sweet apricot/pear fruit flavours. Fine, long acidity that strengthens across the palate, giving a steely but flavoursome finish.

▼-■ 87 Now-2010

**1992 Peppertree Vineyard** *Clare Valley – Shiraz* **S.A.**
Crimson. Perfumed aromatic raspberry/prune/earthy/floral/tropical aromas. Bright raspberry/earthy, sappy flavours, with fine-grained tannins, fine acidity and plenty of concentration and length.
■ *88* *Now-2008*

**1993 Peppertree Vineyard** *Clare Valley – Shiraz* **S.A.**
Crimson. Dark chocolate/brambly/earthy aromas with faint cedary characters. Developed chocolaty, leafy flavours with some prune and liquorice. Mouth-filling, dense but fine tannins. Really poised between restraint and power under-ripeness/ripeness. A lovely wine.
■ *93* *Now-2006*

**1994 Peppertree Vineyard** *Clare Valley – Shiraz* **S.A.**
Crimson. Intense mocha/prune/blackberry aromas with some savoury nuances. Richly flavoured wine with prune/blackberry fruit flavours. Ripe fine-grained tannins. Underlying grainy savoury oak, finishing firm.
■ *92* *Now-2006*

**1996 Peppertree Vineyard** *Clare Valley – Shiraz* **S.A.**
Crimson. Intense, plummy, slightly musky, aromas with touches of cracked pepper and liquorice. Ripe, plummy, liquorice fruit with cedary oak in the background, under peppery nuances. Ends with fine gripping tannins and a long, flavoursome finish. Medium bodied wine.
■ *89* *Now-2006*

**1997 Peppertree Vineyard** *Clare Valley – Shiraz* **S.A.**
Crimson. Very fine perfumed aromas with leafy blackberry fruits and underlying oak. The palate is quite focused and tight with moderately concentrated blackberry/spice flavours, underlying oak, fine tannin structure and length.
▼-■ *83* *Now-2008*

**1998 Peppertree Vineyard** *Clare Valley – Shiraz* **S.A.**
Crimson. Intense blackberry/aniseed aromas with touches of dark plum and violets. Beautifully concentrated wine with rich blackberry/rhubarb flavours and chocolate characters, fine, gravelly, slightly grippy tannins and underlying oak finishing firm.
■ *95* *Now-2008*

**1999 Peppertree Vineyard** *Clare Valley – Shiraz* **S.A.**
Medium deep crimson. Very young fruit driven wine with blueberry/raspberry aromas which carry onto the palate. Fine drying tannins but plenty of fruit-sweetness and flavour length.
■ *85* *Now-2010*

**2000 Peppertree Vineyard** *Clare Valley – Shiraz* **S.A.**
Medium deep crimson. Crushed raspberry/plum /rhubarb/mulberry pepper aromas. Quite aromatic. Well made wine with mulberry/plum/peppery flavours, fine chalky tannins, with plenty of fruit-sweetness and depth. Good length.
■ *91* *Now-2008*

## MITCHELTON

**1998 Blackwood Park** *Nagambie Lakes – Riesling* **Vic.**
Pale yellow. Fresh aromas of star jasmine/gardenia with a touch of lime. Pure and tight lime/star jasmine-like fruit flavours, with plenty of succulent sweet fruit characters, fine indelible acidity, and high concentration, with tremendous length. Excellent wine.
▼ *95* *Now-2015*

**1999 Blackwood Park** *Nagambie Lakes – Riesling* **Vic.**
Pale gold. Intense lemon-zest/lime/cumquat aromas with touches of honey. Tangy, lemon/cumquat grippy flavours with pronounced fine acidity, slightly hard on the middle palate but finishing dry and tight.
▼ *85* *Now-2005*

**2000 Blackwood Park** *Goulburn Valley – Riesling* **Vic.**
Medium yellow. Lime/herb garden/pear aromas. Squashy developed palate with honey/herb flavours, strong clean acidity and plenty of flavour length. Finishes slightly grippy.
▼ *80* *Now-2006*

**2001 Blackwood Park** *Goulburn Valley – Riesling* **Vic.**
Pale yellow. Floral/lime juice/apple aromas. Supple chamomile/lime/lemony flavours. Attenuated mineral acidity. Finishes long and limey.
▼ *91* *Now-2008*

**1990 Print Label** *Goulburn Valley – Shiraz* **Vic.**
Medium crimson/purple. Vanilla/blackberry/earthy aromas with touches of aniseed. Developed blackberry/chocolate/earthy flavours, some vanillin oak, fine firm tannins and medium length.
▼ *88* *Now-2008*

**1991 Print Label** *Goulburn Valley – Shiraz* **Vic.**
Deep crimson. Blackberry/spice aromas with exotic smoky/polish nuances. The palate is ripe and sweet-fruited with immensely complex spice/blackberry/smoky flavours and some developed meaty characters, fine slightly pronounced tannins but excellent length.
▼ *94* *Now-2010*

**1992 Print Label** *Goulburn Valley – Shiraz* **Vic.**
Deep crimson. Developed aromatic cedar/spice/clove-like aromas with dark cherry/brambly undertones. The palate has plenty of developed fruit, earthy cedar/spice/dark cherry/aniseed flavours and some meatiness. Well melded wine with plenty of sweet fruit and length.
▼ *93* *Now-2008*

**1995 Print Label** *Goulburn Valley – Shiraz* **Vic.**
Deep crimson. Sweet and plush cedary, coconutty oak layered over blackcurrant plummy dried fruit. Very concentrated, developing palate with plummy fruit, slightly oily, bitter oak, fine-grained tannins and firm finish. Very textured wine.
▼ *85* *Now-2008*

**1996 Print Label** *Goulburn Valley – Shiraz* **Vic.**
Deep crimson. Very complex, intense raspberry/prune-like aromas with violets and touches of game. Deep-set and ripe prune/raspberry fruit with savoury oak, fine ripe tannins, and superb length. Brilliant wine.
▼ *97* *Now-2012*

**1998 Print Label** *Goulburn Valley – Shiraz* **Vic.**
Deep crimson. Ethereal mulberry/choc-berry aromas with beautifully integrated savoury/vanillin oak. Richly flavoured but supple wine with choc-berry flavours. Fine, ripe, almost loose-knit tannins and mocha/cinnamon oak flavours. Builds up to a very grippy/firm liquorice finish but excellent flavour length. Fruit and oak integration is brilliant. Restraint and power.
▼ *97* *2004-2014*

## MOSS WOOD

**1986** *Margaret River – Cabernet Sauvignon* **W.A.**
Brick red. Matchstick/plummy/blackcurrant fruit with touches of cedar and tar. Ripe and rich on the palate, with matchstick/plummy fruit flavours and plenty of concentration.
■-▲ *84* *Now-2005* *Exceptional*

**1987** *Margaret River – Cabernet Sauvignon* **W.A.**
Crimson. Mushroom/cedar/liquorice/blackcurrant aromas with touches of lead pencil. Structured palate with lovely opulent mushroomy, blackcurrant fruit, fine, silky tannins and plenty of length. A classic.
▲ *95* *Now-2006* *Exceptional*

**1988** *Margaret River – Cabernet Sauvignon* **W.A.**
Deep crimson/brown. Complex and developed fine dark chocolate/prune aromas with a touch of menthol lift and cedar. The palate is sweet-fruited and developed with chocolate cedary flavours. Fine gravelly tannins and good length.
■-▲ *93* *Now-2008* *Exceptional*

**1989** *Margaret River – Cabernet Sauvignon* **W.A.**
Crimson. Matchstick/cassis aromas with some aniseed and tropical fruits. Plenty of sweet fruit on the palate, fine lacy tannins, medium concentration, but a long finish.
■-▲ *85* *Now* *Exceptional*

**1990** *Margaret River – Cabernet Sauvignon* **W.A.**
Crimson. Hessian/earthy/cedar aromas with some blackcurrant. The palate has plenty of meaty, fruit pastille flavours with touches of apricots and nectarine, grainy tannins and medium length. Drink soon.
■-▲ *86* *Now-2005* *Exceptional*

**1991** *Margaret River – Cabernet Sauvignon* **W.A.**
Deep crimson. Meaty demi-glace/blackcurrant/slightly leafy aromas. Sweet-fruited squashy palate, meaty, blackcurrant fruit, finely textured silky tannins and good length.
■-▲ *94* *Now-2010* *Exceptional*

**1992** *Margaret River – Cabernet Sauvignon* **W.A.**
Brick red. Difficult wine with cool blackcurrant/black cherry/menthol and slightly salty aromas. Good core of sweet fruit with some weedy, green tannins but a good firm finish. A little gawky and unresolved.
■ *84* *Now-2008* *Exceptional*

**1993** *Margaret River – Cabernet Sauvignon* **W.A.**
Crimson. Gamy, cassis aromas with slight herbal/cheesy characters. Textured palate with complex gamy, cheesy fruit flavours, fine, gravelly tannins and finishing firm.
■ *84* *Now-2005* *Exceptional*

**1994** *Margaret River – Cabernet Sauvignon* **W.A.**
Opaque purple/crimson. Black olive/currant/fresh-timber aromas with touches of cherry. Restrained olive/cedar and slight menthol fruit, classic fine-grained tannins. Needs time.
■-▲ *88* *Now-2012* *Exceptional*

**1995** *Margaret River – Cabernet Sauvignon* **W.A.**
Crimson. Perfumed rose petal/cassis aromas with touches of violet and chocolate. The palate is classically proportioned with deep-set blackcurrant/cedar fruit, fine, gravelly tannins, and superb length. Lovely balance and texture.
▲ *96* *Now-2012* *Exceptional*

**1996** *Margaret River – Cabernet Sauvignon* **W.A.**
Deep crimson. Leafy dark chocolate aromas with touches of vanillin/spice. Rich flavoursome wine with vanilla/spice/dark chocolate/brambly fruit, fine sinewy and very drying tannins, finishing quite dry and firm.
■ *90* *2004-2016* *Exceptional*

**1997** *Margaret River – Cabernet Sauvignon* **W.A.**
Dark purple/crimson. Classic blackcurrant/cedar aromas with mulberry/vanillin characters. Beautifully structured wine with fine dark chocolate/blackcurrant-pastille fruit, fine-grained tannins, cedary oak, plenty of fruit-sweetness and length. A super wine.
■ *95* *Now-2010* *Exceptional*

**1998** *Margaret River – Cabernet Sauvignon* **W.A.**
Medium deep crimson. Perfumed blackcurrant/cedar aromas with some seabreezy/leafy characters. Violet/blackcurrant/leafy flavours, with fine grained but slightly grippy tannins, plenty of concentration, underlying cedar oak, finishing chalky but long in flavour. Super wine.
▲ *94* *2006-2018* *Exceptional*

**1999** *Margaret River – Cabernet Sauvignon* **W.A.**
Deep crimson. Intense blackcurrant/plum/cedar aromas with malty oak Very complex and interesting. Well crafted wine with cassis/mocha flavours and fine chocolaty tannin structure, plenty of malty oak, fruit-sweetness and length. Delicious wine.
▲ *94* *2006-2018* *Exceptional*

**1993** *Margaret River – Chardonnay* **W.A.**
Pale yellow/gold. Cardboard, peachy, nectarine aromas. Very developed hazelnut/brassy flavours, some toasty oak but quite simple. Has some good length and acid cut.
■ *83* *Now*

**1998** *Margaret River – Chardonnay* **W.A.**
Pale yellow. Perfumed savoury, smoky oak, over ripe tropical fruit/roasted nut. Lovely wine with plenty of sweet, squashy, tropical fruit and spicy, malty oak, fine acidity, superb concentration and length. Yet to market.
■ *93* *Now-2005*

**1999** *Margaret River – Chardonnay* **W.A.**
Pale yellow. Melon/menthol/lime aromas – quite lifted. Menthol/limey oak-derived flavours. Very tight young wine with plenty of deep-set fruit. Almost too much savoury, smoky oak character. Pronounced acid, good concentration and length. Needs time to settle down.
■ *89* *Now-2006*

**2000** *Margaret River – Chardonnay* **W.A.**
Pale yellow. Loose-knit savoury wine with tropical/grapefruit/pineapple fruit aromas and plenty of savoury/smoky oak. Richly flavoured wine with creamy grapefruit/pineapple fruit and plenty of savoury/biscuity oak. Some nougat/nutty nuances. Finishing long and fruit-sweet.
■ *90* *Now-2005*

**2001** *Margaret River – Chardonnay* **W.A.**
Pale yellow. Intense focused wine. Melon/roasted nut aromas. Touches of white peach and spice. Tightly knit wine with melon/white peach and plenty of smoky/savoury/malty oak flavours. Fine acid cut. Marvellous concentration and length. Good medium term cellaring prospect.
■ *94* *2004-2008*

## MOUNT HORROCKS

**1991 Watervale** *Clare Valley – Riesling* **S.A.**
Yellow gold. Developed sweet lime/petrol aromas. The palate is richly flavoured and fruit-sweet with deep-set lime/petrol flavours, some hazelnut complexity and fine acidity. Finishes a touch bitter.
■ *81* *Now-2005*

**2000 Watervale** *Clare Valley – Riesling* **S.A.**
Pale yellow. Fresh apple/lime-skin aromas with hint of ginger/spice. Rich mouth-filling wine with plenty of ripe apple lime flavours. Fine, almost searing acidity, but good length of flavour. Very big style.
■ *88* *Now-2008*

**2001 Watervale** *Clare Valley – Riesling* **S.A.**
Pale colour. Perfumed pure lime/pear/apricot aromas. Ripe bright lime/apricot flavours, superb concentration and crunchy mouth-watering acidity. Finishes long and flavoursome.
■ *93* *Now-2010*

**1996** *Clare Valley – Shiraz* **S.A.**
Deep crimson. Blackberry pastille/menthol aromas with some peppery/hazelnut complexity. A cool flavoured wine with blackberry pastille/menthol flavours – pronounced grippy, chocolaty. Plenty of mid-palate richness, finishing firm and tight.
■ *85* *2004-2010*

**1999** *Clare Valley – Shiraz* **S.A.**
Medium crimson. Blackberry/prune aromas with touches of pepper. Some cedary notes. Plenty of pure blackberry/peppery fruit. Fine grained, slightly bristled tannins, finishing firm and tight. May improve with age.
■ *84* *2004-2012*

**2000** *Clare Valley – Shiraz* **S.A.**
Medium crimson. High tensile blackberry/white pepper aromas with savoury malt nuances and touches of liquorice. Well concentrated palate with blackberry/white pepper flavours. Some malty/savoury/spicy oak nuances. Fine, long sinewy tannins. Finishing with plenty of length
■ *91* *2004-2010*

## MOUNT IDA

**1992** *Heathcote – Shiraz* **Vic.**
Medium crimson. Meaty, gamy, lead-pencil/blackberry/brambly aromas with some underlying oak. The palate is very complex with plenty of sweet, meaty, gamy fruit and new coconut/vanillin oak all meshed together beautifully, fine tight tannins and good length.
■ *93* *Now-2010*

**1994** *Heathcote – Shiraz* **Vic.**
Crimson. Sweet and savoury wine with liquorice/plum fruit aromas and touches of nutmeg and coconut. The palate is beautifully balanced with rich ripe plummy/blackberry/liquorice fruit, fine, ripe tannins and well integrated oak. Lovely concentration and length.
■ *95* *Now-2010*

**1995** *Heathcote – Shiraz* **Vic.**
Medium crimson. Smoky, sappy, almost oily oak over ultra-ripe raspberry essence fruit. The palate is plush and thick-set with plenty of liquorice/raspberry fruit, a touch of earth, and a forest-load of cedary, coconutty oak, excellent concentration and length. Is this wine over-oaked? I think it is.
■ *88* *Now-2008*

**1996** *Heathcote – Shiraz* **Vic.**
Deep crimson. Intense liquorice/cedar/savoury/toasty oak aromas with almost sacramental incense. Immensely concentrated but evenly proportioned wine with a fracas of nuances – liquorice, cedar and beautifully seasoned, flavoursome new oak. Still needs a little time to soften out.
■ *90* *2002-2010*

**1997** *Heathcote – Shiraz* **Vic.**
Deep crimson/purple. Cherry/tobacco/gamy/smoky oak aromas. Contrived fruit flavours and marked smoky, woody characters, chewy tannins and pronounced acidity make this wine difficult to like.
■ *77* *Now-2008*

**1999** *Heathcote – Shiraz* **Vic.**
Medium deep crimson. Classic choc-berry aromas with malt/savoury characters. Plenty of choc-berry/liquorice fruit flavours, ripe textured tannins, malty oak, finishing gravelly and with plenty of flavour length.
■ *91* *2004-2010*

## MOUNT LANGI GHIRAN

**1989 Langi** *Grampians – Shiraz* **Vic.**
Deep crimson/purple. Deep-set aniseed/plum/prune with some chocolate and pepper. A coldly flavoured wine with peppery, anise/plum fruit and high tensile, fine, but slightly green tannins and firm finish.
■ *89* *Now-2008* *Excellent*

**1993 Langi** *Grampians – Shiraz* **Vic.**
Crimson, purple. Peppery raspberry/blackberry fruit. Raspberry/pepper flavours. Long, fine tannins. Medium concentration. Plenty of sweet fruit.
■ *83* *Now-2010* *Excellent*

**1994 Langi** *Grampians – Shiraz* **Vic.**
Deep crimson/purple. Intense, bright, beautifully focused wine with sweet menthol/liquorice/cracked pepper aromas. Well balanced wine with sweet, bright mulberry/blackberry fruit with a core of intensely flavoured penetrating cracked pepper flavours. Fine tannins and plenty of length. The cool Victorian ideal.
■ *96* *Now-2010* *Excellent*

**1995 Langi** *Grampians – Shiraz* **Vic.**
Deep crimson. Intense prune/mulberry/pepper. Richly flavoured wine with deep-set, squashy, mulberry/prune/aniseed fruit, underlying savoury oak, fine drying tannins with plenty of length.
■ *90* *Now-2006* *Excellent*

**1996 Langi** *Grampians – Shiraz* **Vic.**
Crimson/purple. Liquorice/aniseed, ultra-ripe blackcurrant/cedar aromas. The palate is deeply concentrated with blackcurrant/black olive fruit flavours, ripe grainy tannins, beautiful balance, extract and length.
■ *94* *Now-2012* *Excellent*

**1997 Langi** *Grampians – Shiraz* **Vic.**
Crimson purple. Menthol, leafy, green, perfumed aromas with touches of white pepper. Leafy menthol flavours with touches of pepper, fine tannin, medium concentration and length. Elegantly structured wine.
▼-■ *84* *Now-2008* *Excellent*

**1998 Langi** *Grampians – Shiraz* **Vic.**
Deep crimson. Very intense, fine blackberry aromas with some pepper nuances. Cool flavoured wine with peppery fruit/blackberry pastille characters. Medium to high concentration. Good mid-palate richness. Fine, slightly grippy tannins. Found quite a few bottles with cork taint.
■ *89* *2004-2010* *Excellent*

## MOUNT MARY

**1992 Quintet** *Yarra Valley – Cabernets* **Vic.**
Crimson purple. Blackcurrant-pastille/leafy aromas with touches of vanillin and liquorice. Sweet-fruited, almost simple, cordial flavours, but fine tannins and underlying oak.
■ *84* *Now-2008* *Exceptional*

**1995 Quintet** *Yarra Valley – Cabernets* **Vic.**
Crimson/purple. Light, earthy, pastille, slight leafy aromas. Classically structured palate with a core of sweet, earthy, blackcurrant fruit. Fine-grained tannins, a touch of vanillin and a firm finish. Will build up.
■ *83* *Now-2012* *Exceptional*

**1996 Quintet** *Yarra Valley – Cabernets* **Vic.**
Crimson/purple. Classical blackcurrant/cedar aromas with undergrowth/mushroom complexity. Finely structured palate, with fruit-sweetness, cedary, earthy flavours, fine textured tannins and good length.
■ 88 Now-2010 *Exceptional*

**1997 Quintet** *Yarra Valley – Cabernets* **Vic.**
Deep red/purple. Blackcurrant/leafy/chocolate aromas with savoury oak. Sweet fruit, slightly cordial-like, with some chocolate/mocha characters, fine tannins, some savoury oak but medium finish. A little hollow. Early drinking wine.
■ 79 Now-2010 *Exceptional*

**1999 Quintet** *Yarra Valley – Cabernets* **Vic.**
Medium deep crimson. Intense cedar/violet cassis aromas with hints of aniseed. Long cedar/plum/blackcurrant flavours on the palate, with fine sinewy tannins which build up quite firm. Nice core of fruit brightness. Finishes tight. Still youthful and needing further ageing.
■ 88 2004-2010 *Exceptional*

**1995** *Yarra Valley – Chardonnay* **Vic.**
Pale gold. Creamy custard/lanolin with peaches and figs. Tight and lean palate with lanolin/cheesy characters, slightly abrasive acidity, but good length. In evolution. Could open up.
■ 82 Now-2010 *Excellent*

**1997** *Yarra Valley – Chardonnay* **Vic.**
Pale yellow. Grapefruit/orange-peel/lanolin aromas. Very zesty youthful aromas with some subtle oak background. Ripe nectarine/grapefruit flavours with subtle oak, fine and pronounced acidity and long finish. Doesn't quite deliver.
■ 86 Now-2006 *Excellent*

**1998** *Yarra Valley – Chardonnay* **Vic.**
Pale yellow. Intense tropical fruit/grapefruit/spicy aromas. Touches of wet quartz stone. Palate is fresh and breezy with earthy quartz/tropical fruit flavours, plenty of lanolin, indelible acidity and good length. An unusual style but should develop more richness and complexity.
■ 84 Now-2010 *Excellent*

**1999** *Yarra Valley – Chardonnay* **Vic.**
Pale yellow. Creamy/lanolin/nutty aromas with some citrus peel characters. Very minerally wine with citrus peel/crunchy pear/peach flavours, but lovely core of fruit-sweetness. Finishes dry and a touch bitter. Interesting wine.
■ 88 Now-2010 *Excellent*

**2000** *Yarra Valley – Chardonnay* **Vic.**
Pale yellow. Melon/nectarine, wet stone/gravel aromas. Restrained, but well balanced palate with nectarine/melon/peachy flavours. Some mid-palate creaminess, long quartz/mineral acidity, finishing long and flavoursome.
■ 91 Now-2012 *Excellent*

**1992** *Yarra Valley – Pinot Noir* **Vic.**
Pale crimson. Fresh cherry/earthy aromas that are quite simple, but surprisingly youthful. The palate is lightly structured with meaty, cherry fruit, fine tannins and some richness across the middle. Sweet flavoursome finish. Builds up on the palate.
■ 84 Now-2005 *Outstanding*

**1995** *Yarra Valley – Pinot Noir* **Vic.**
Medium light crimson. Bright cherry/rhubarb fruit with some development. The palate is lightly structured with cherry/rhubarb flavours, good overall fruit-sweetness, fine, slightly furry tannins and a firm finish. Short term wine.
■ 80 Now-2005 *Outstanding*

**1997** *Yarra Valley – Pinot Noir* **Vic.**
Medium crimson. Brambly choc-cherry characters, touch of herb. Quite vinous, chocolate/bramble flavours, fine grainy tannins, plenty of concentration but quite grippy at the finish.
■ 81 Now-2005 *Outstanding*

**1998** *Yarra Valley – Pinot Noir* **Vic.**
Medium light aromas. Light cherry/tobacco aromas with some leather/spice characters. Developed complex cherry tobacco flavours, fine sinewy tannins, finishing quite firm.
■ 78 Now-2005 *Outstanding*

## MOUNT PLEASANT

**1990 Elizabeth** *Hunter Valley – Semillon* **N.S.W.**
Yellow gold. Lemon curd/grassy/honey aromas. Sweet fruited palate with lemon curd – slight mocha – flavours. Fine mineral acidity with leafy finish.
▼-■ *85* *Now-2008*

**1991 Elizabeth** *Hunter Valley – Semillon* **N.S.W.**
Yellow gold. Complex menthol/herbal/leafy aromas with some sweet fruit characters. Lovely concentrated palate, with lively mouth-watering acidity.
▼-■ *91* *Now-2010*

**1992 Elizabeth** *Hunter Valley – Semillon* **N.S.W.**
Yellow gold. Fresh honeyed/*paneforte*/toasty aromas. Dry, minerally palate with tangy honey/toasty/lemony flavours Hard acidity and finish.
▼-■ *89* *Now-2008*

**1993 Elizabeth** *Hunter Valley – Semillon* **N.S.W.**
Yellow/gold. Sweet butter/honey/lemon curd aromas. Developed honeyed straw flavours, austere acidity finishing quite lean and skeletal. Needs more time to develop.
▼-■ *88* *Now-2007*

**1994 Elizabeth** *Hunter Valley – Semillon* **N.S.W.**
Medium yellow. Intense honey/straw/butter menthol aromas – touch of sweet limes. Classic Semillon. Restrained flavoured wine with honey/straw/butter menthol characters, marked lemony acidity, finishing quite lean and austere. Needs more time to become richer – and fatter!
▼-■ *92* *2006-2016*

**1995 Elizabeth** *Hunter Valley – Semillon* **N.S.W.**
Pale yellow. Fresh but complex citrus/apricot/lanolin aromas. Dry, tightly bound wine with restrained, even, lanolin/citrus/apricot flavours, fine cutting acidity and plenty of length. A real benchmark Semillon with all the class of a fine racehorse.
▼-■ *95* *Now-2015*

**1996 Elizabeth** *Hunter Valley – Semillon* **N.S.W.**
Medium yellow. Fresh, lemony, honey/straw aromas. Lightly structured wine with lemon-zest and grassy flavours and touches of straw, fine acidity and plenty of length but finishing tight and slightly grippy. Needs more time. Some marmalade characters.
▼-■ *90* *Now-2008*

**1999 Elizabeth** *Hunter Valley – Semillon* **N.S.W.**
Pale yellow. Fresh lemony/honey/lanolin aromas. Fresh lively wine with lemony/mineral flavours, marked acidity finishing long and flavoursome. Medium concentration. Tasted also under Stelvin which revealed a more intense aromatic/estery lime/lemony characters.
▼-■ *93* *2004-2012*

**2000 Elizabeth** *Hunter Valley – Semillon* **N.S.W.**
Pale yellow. Intense lemony/sweet crunchy pear aromas. Slightly under-ripe, slightly green pea pod. Sweet pea pod flavours, fine tight quite marked acidity, finishing quite tight.
▼-■ *83* *Now-2010*

**1984 Lovedale** *Hunter Valley – Semillon* **N.S.W.**
Pale yellow. Very direct but developed, toasty, lime marmalade aromas. Deep-set toasty, limey fruit flavours, balanced by fine tangy acidity, finishing dry and long. Remarkably youthful-looking wine.
▼-■ *96* *Now-2005*

**1986 Lovedale** *Hunter Valley – Semillon* **N.S.W.**
Yellow/gold. Intense straw/hay/lemon curd/honey aromas. Ginger/lime/marmalade fruit flavours, balanced by tangy acidity, high concentration and a long flavoursome finish. Really at its peak.
▼-■ *89* *Now-2005*

**1995 Lovedale** *Hunter Valley – Semillon* **N.S.W.**
Pale yellow. Limey honey/apricot aromas. Honeyed apricot/sweet lemon curd flavours carried right across the palate by fine, beautifully direct acidity, excellent concentration, and superb length. Brilliant wine.
▼-■ *97* *Now-2010*

**1996 Lovedale** *Hunter Valley – Semillon* **N.S.W.**
Pale medium colour. Intense honey/leafy/lime aromas with some toasty notes. Richly concentrated palate with limey toasty flavours, balanced

by long, slightly hard acidity. Finishes slightly grippy but has excellent flavour length.

■ *91* *Now-2010*

**1997 Lovedale** *Hunter Valley – Semillon* **N.S.W.**
Pale yellow. Complex toasty/lemon curd, slightly nettley aromas. Toasty/lemony/tangy flavours, still quite unyielding, linear acidity finishing long and dry. Still in evolution.

▼-■ *88* *2006-2016*

**1998 Lovedale** *Hunter Valley – Semillon* **N.S.W.**
Pale yellow. Very perfumed toasty/lime cordial aromas. Plenty of sweet fruit. Vibrant sweet fruit/toasty/lime cordial flavours with touch of herb, finishing quite leafy and dry.

▼-■ *91* *2004-2014*

**1999 Lovedale** *Hunter Valley – Semillon* **N.S.W.**
Pale yellow. Fresh sweet lemon/honey/apricot aromas. Richly flavoured squashy wine with apricot/tropical/lemony flavours, fine acidity, touch grippy on the finish but very nice fruit-sweetness and length. Will become a classic.

▼-■ *94* *2006-2020*

**2000 Lovedale** *Hunter Valley – Semillon* **N.S.W.**
Pale yellow. Very restrained lemon/grassy/biscuity aromas with some tropical fruit. Very dry, restrained grassy style, tangy acidity, finishing very long. Still a foetus.

▼-■ *93* *2006-2018*

**1993 Maurice O'Shea** *Hunter Valley – Shiraz* **N.S.W.**
Medium crimson. Earthy leather/tomato-leafy/soupy aromas. Earthy, leathery flavours with touches of bramble and leafiness. Fine firm tannins. A little austere.

▼ *79* *Now*

**1994 Maurice O'Shea** *Hunter Valley – Shiraz* **N.S.W.**
Medium deep crimson. Developed earthy/dark chocolate/biscuit aromas and sandalwood characters. Soupy chocolate/demi-glace/game flavours, fine chalky tannins finishing dry and firm.

▼ *84* *Now-2008*

**1995 Maurice O'Shea** *Hunter Valley – Shiraz* **N.S.W.**
Crimson. Intense raspberry/matchstick aromas with some vanillin/ savoury nuances and touches of leather. The palate is light with vibrant raspberry fruit, plenty of new oak, but slightly pronounced firm tannins. Showing strong regional Hunter definition.

▼ *86* *Now-2006*

**1996 Maurice O'Shea** *Hunter Valley – Shiraz* **N.S.W.**
Crimson. Smoky, charry oak with strawberry/raspberry essence, almost Pinot-like aromas. Lots of barrel but not much fruit on the palate, grainy tannins, medium concentration and length.

▼ *79* *Now-2005*

**1998 Maurice O'Shea** *Hunter Valley – Shiraz* **N.S.W.**
Deep crimson. Intense plum/violet/mulberry aromas with some gamy nuances. Underlying sweet American oak, mulberry/plum fruit characters. Fine drying tannins with underlying gamy characters. Very tight, good concentration and length. Nice wine. Tannins grapple with fruit.

▼ *89* *2004-2012*

**1999 Maurice O'Shea** *Hunter Valley – Shiraz* **N.S.W.**
Deep crimson. Loose-knit choc-berry fruit characters with some mulberry/ gamy/gingersnap. Intensely flavoured, juicy wine with gingersnap/ liquorice/ mulberry flavours. Fine drying tannins, finishing long and sweet.

▼ *91* *2004-2010*

**1995 Old Paddock and Old Hill** *Hunter Valley – Shiraz* **N.S.W.**
Medium crimson. Oak driven wine with pronounced coconut aromas and underlying ripe fruit. Squashy palate with ripe tannins, moderate concentration and firm finish.

▼ *85* *Now-2005*

**1996 Old Paddock and Old Hill** *Hunter Valley – Shiraz* **N.S.W.**
Medium crimson. Developed complex cedar/nougat/raspberry aromas with some floral, jasmine notes. Restrained but slinky wine with supple cedary/raspberry/walnut flavours. Fine velveteen tannins and length. Lovely wine.

▼ *93* *2003-2010*

**1997 Old Paddock and Old Hill** *Hunter Valley – Shiraz* **N.S.W.**
Medium crimson. Walnutty/earthy/raspberry/plum aromas. Walnut/sweet earthy/raspberry flavours with some leathery nuances, fine gravelly tannins, finishing with good length.
▼ *86* *2004-2010*

**1998 Old Paddock and Old Hill** *Hunter Valley – Shiraz* **N.S.W.**
Medium crimson. Savoury red cherry/liquorice aromas. The palate is medium concentrated with savoury/meaty/cherry flavours, fine sinewy but long tannins, finishing quite firm and drying.
▼ *86* *2004-2010*

**1999 Old Paddock and Old Hill** *Hunter Valley – Shiraz* **N.S.W.**
Medium crimson. Ginger snap/dark cherry/malty/earthy aromas. Loose-knit cherry/ malty flavours with lacy tannins, finishing dry and firm. Nice core of fruit-sweetness but on the restrained side.
▼ *87* *2004-2010*

**1996 Rosehill** *Hunter Valley – Shiraz* **N.S.W.**
Medium crimson. Meaty game-like aromas with pure blackberry/anise fruit. Pronounced new oak. Sweet fruit with savoury oak characters, moderate concentration, good tannin structure and length. Slightly on the restrained side. Moderate-term cellaring prospect.
▼ *89* *Now-2006*

**1998 Rosehill** *Hunter Valley – Shiraz* **N.S.W.**
Medium crimson. Dark cherry/nutty aromas with some earthy/leathery notes. Medium concentrated wine with dark cherry/nutty/leathery fruit, with lacy, slightly grippy, tannins, nice core of fruit-sweetness, finishing long and cedary.
▼ *87* *2004-2012*

## MOUNTADAM

**1996 Patriarch** *Eden Valley – Shiraz* **S.A.**
Crimson. Complex and intense toffee/blackberry fruit aromas. The palate is richly concentrated with fruit-sweet coffee/toffee characters and some smoked meat complexity. Plenty of ripe textured tannins and flavour length.
▼ *90* *Now-2008*

**1997 Patriarch** *Eden Valley – Shiraz* **S.A.**
Deep crimson. Plum/apple tart-like aromas with smoky oak. The palate is tangy, almost green, with some brambly fruit, underlying wood and medium oak. Very odd wine.
▼ *73* *Now-2005*

**1998 Patriarch** *Eden Valley – Shiraz* **S.A.**
Medium crimson. Very lightweight almost underpowered raspberry/ apricot aromas – not much complexity. Medium concentrated palate with raspberry/apricot flavours, fine tannins and medium length.
▼ *80* *Now-2005*

**1999 Patriarch** *Eden Valley – Shiraz* **S.A.**
Medium deep crimson. Intense rather simple blackberry pastille aromas – touch of leafiness. Loose-knit wine with raspberry/tomato leaf flavours, fine slightly grippy tannins finishing quite firm and tight. Should be a lot better than this.
▼ *75* *Now-2005*

**1996 The Red** *Eden Valley – Cabernet Sauvignon Merlot* **S.A.**
Deep crimson. Pure cassis/liquorice aromas with a touch of cedar and aniseed. Classify proportioned wine with cassis/liquorice flavours, cedary oak, fine-grained tannins, lovely concentration and a long finish.
▼ *93* *Now-2010*

**1998 The Red** *Eden Valley – Cabernet Sauvignon Merlot* **S.A.**
Medium crimson. Loose-knit cassis/rhubarb/ tomato leafy aromas. Slightly contrived red cherry/rhubarb/tomato leaf flavours, fine silken tannins with medium length. Early drinking style.
▼ *76* *Now-2005*

**1998** *Eden Valley – Cabernet* **S.A.**
Deep crimson. Intense blackcurrant/menthol aromas with some aniseed and dark chocolate. Sweet blackcurrant/menthol/dark chocolate flavours, underlying oak, fine grainy slightly grippy tannins but plenty of length.
▼ *87* *Now-2008*

**1996** *Eden Valley – Chardonnay* **S.A.**
Pale yellow. Fresh intense youthful passionfruit/fruit salad aromas with some creamy vanilla undertones. Developing sweet creamy tropical/passionfruit flavours, very fine acidity, underlying oak, good concentration and length. Drink soon.
▼ *85* *Now-2005* *Distinguished*

**1997** *Eden Valley – Chardonnay* **S.A.**
Pale yellow/gold. Bitter almond/apple aromas. Some nutty complexity. Almond/peach-skin flavours with touches of nuts. Slightly green edges, medium oak but building up at the end. This could develop.
▼ *85* *Now-2005* *Distinguished*

**1998** *Eden Valley – Chardonnay* **S.A.**
Pale yellow. Intense lemon curd/grapefruit aromas with touches of pear and a savoury new oak background. Classical palate with lemony, melon-like fruit, lovely oak integration, concentration and length. Good aging potential.
▼ *94* *Now* *Distinguished*

**1999** *Eden Valley – Chardonnay* **S.A.**
Pale gold. Very restrained mineral/slight leafy/white peach aromas and vanilla nuances. Restrained palate with crunchy peach/leafy flavours, fine almost searing acidity, good concentration and length.
▼ *82* *Now* *Distinguished*

**1998** *Eden Valley – Merlot* **S.A.**
Medium crimson. Plummy red cherry/gunflint aromas with hints of tobacco and cedar. Very elegant medium concentrated palate with plummy red cherry fruit, fine silky tannins, underlying oak with medium length. Already showing some development. A medium term wine although showing good varietal definition.
▼ *82* *Now-2007*

## NEPENTHE

**1997 The Fugue** *Adelaide Hills – Cabernet Sauvignon Merlot Cabernet Franc* **S.A.**
Medium deep crimson. Raspberry/redcurrant *confit*/violet aromas. Restrained, almost underpowered style. Raspberry/redcurrant flavours. Medium concentration. Fine slinky tannins. Good flavour length.
▼-■ *85* *Now-2006*

**1999 The Fugue** *Adelaide Hills – Cabernet Sauvignon Merlot Cabernet Franc* **S.A.**
Deep crimson. Dark chocolate/cassis/menthol aromas with some hints of nougat. Restrained palate with cassis/menthol flavours, fine but grippy tannins, good concentration and length.
▼-■ *84* *Now-2006*

**2000 The Fugue** *Adelaide Hills – Cabernet Sauvignon Merlot Cabernet Franc* **S.A.**
Medium crimson. Restrained wine with blackcurrant/earthy aromas with faint hint of sweet leather/iodine. Fruit sweet almost opulent wine with blackcurrant/plum favours and cedary oak. Fine, almost green edged, tannins, finishing firm and tight.
▼-■ *87* *Now – 2008*

**1998** *Adelaide Hills – Pinot Noir* **S.A.**
Medium crimson. Light cherry/strawberry/earthy aromas. Earthy/cherry flavours, sinewy tannins, building up quite grippy and tight. Structure overwhelms fruit.
▼ *77* *Now*

**2000** *Adelaide Hills – Pinot Noir* **S.A.**
Medium crimson. Intense fruit-sweet cherry/plum aromas. Medium concentrated wine with cherry/plum flavours. Supple almost silky tannins, building up firm. Good flavour length. Not a long term proposition.
▼ *87* *Now-2005*

**2001** *Adelaide Hills – Pinot Noir* **S.A.**
Medium crimson. Menthol/chocolate/cherry aromas. Sinewy lean style with menthol/milk chocolate flavours and long stringy tannins.
▼ *80* *Now*

## NICHOLSON RIVER

**1999** *East Gippsland – Chardonnay* **Vic.**
Pale gold. Intense peach/apricot/honey dew melon aromas with cashew nut/nougat/vanillin characters. Quite a worked style but richly flavoured with cashew nutty peach flavours and touches of nutmeg/ caramel. The palate is richly favoured wine with cashew nut/peach flavours, fine attenuated acidity which carries flavours right across the palate, underlying oak, finishing very malty and long. A very big Chardonnay with a complex burst of flavours.
■ *90* *Now*

**2000** *East Gippsland – Chardonnay* **Vic.**
Medium yellow. Complex almond/melon aromas with some passionfruit/ leafy aromas. Sweet fruited, creamy palate with leafy/melon/peach/ apricot flavours, hint of Botrytis, and fine clear acidity. Finishes long. Good drink but certainly not a long keeper.
■ *86* *Now*

## NOON

**1999 Reserve** *Langhorne Creek – Cabernet Sauvignon* **S.A.**
Deep crimson. Cassis/cedar/liquorice/black olive aromas. Sweet juicy and deep-set blackcurrant/chocolate/cedar characters, fine grainy tannins finishing long and sweet. Quite luscious.
▲ *88* *2004-2010*

**1999 Reserve** *Langhorne Creek – Shiraz* **S.A.**
Deep crimson. Intense and direct dark cherry/blackberry/liquorice aromas and underlying oak. Richly concentrated wine with deep-set immensely fruit-sweet blackberry/liquorice flavours, fine long grainy tannins, finishing with a slight alcoholic kick. Delicious.
▲ *95* *2004-2015*

**1997 Eclipse** *McLaren Vale – Grenache Shiraz* **S.A.**
Deep crimson. Deep-set liquorice/prune/dark chocolate flavours with touches of mocha. Rich chocolaty/mocha/prune flavours, strong bristling tannins finishing firm and dry – core of fruit-sweetness.
▲ *84* *Now-2006*

**1998 Eclipse** *McLaren Vale – Grenache Shiraz* **S.A.**
Crimson/purple. Intense, smoky, rhubarb/dark plum/blackberry aromas. Sweet-fruited, beautifully direct blackberry-essence fruit flavours with touches of aniseed and ginger, fine, gripping but loose-knit tannins, excellent concentration and length. Richly flavoured generously proportioned wine.
▲ *96* *Now-2015*

**1999 Eclipse** *McLaren Vale – Grenache Shiraz* **S.A.**
Deep crimson. Very intense and rich dark cherry/spicy/musky aromas. Richly flavoured viscous and concentrated wine with musky/dark cherry flavours, fine ripe tannins becoming sinewy towards the finish. Plenty of length.
▲ *89* *2003-2010*

**2000 Eclipse** *McLaren Vale – Grenache Shiraz* **S.A.**
Deep crimson. Scented plum/mulberry touch of violet aromas. Deep-set very concentrated, dark cherry/plum fruit flavours – some dark choc-liquorice flavours. Firm drying tannins, finishing chalky, dry but good flavour length.
▲ *85* *Now-2008*

## OLIVER'S

**1999 Tarranga Vineyard** *McLaren Vale – Shiraz* **S.A.**
Deep crimson. Deep crimson. Intense black cherry/prune and savoury/ meaty/vanillin. Rich succulent palate with black cherry/prune/meaty/ savoury flavours, fine loose-knit ripe tannins and plenty of concentration and length.
▼ *93* *Now-2010*

**2000 Tarranga Vineyard** *McLaren Vale – Shiraz* **S.A.**
Deep crimson. Very elemental choc-berry/liquorice/gamy fruit with some vanillin nuances. Deep-set choc-berry fruit flavours, fine but slightly gripping/leafy tannins, plenty of savoury oak, finishing firm and tight. Needs time to soften out.
▼ *85* *Now-2007*

## ORLANDO

**1994 Centenary Hill** *Barossa Valley – Shiraz* **S.A.**
Medium crimson. Intense juicy raspberry menthol/eucalypt aromas. Well structured palate with raspberry/menthol/ leafy flavours, fine lacy but slightly grippy tannins. Nice core of fruit brightness. Medium concentration. Finishing with good flavour length.
▼ *84* *2004-2008*

**1995 Centenary Hill** *Barossa Valley – Shiraz* **S.A.**
Crimson. Very focused blackberry/mocha/liquorice aromas. Richly flavoured sweet-fruited wine with deep-set choc-berry/liquorice flavours and lovely well-seasoned oak. Builds big and firm at the end, but a very mouth-filling satisfying drink.
▼ *92* *Now-2006*

**1996 Centenary Hill** *Barossa Valley – Shiraz* **S.A.**
Medium crimson. Raspberry *confit*/malty/vanillin/ginger aromas. Generously proportioned palate with ripe, raspberry *confit*/mulberry flavours and plenty of well-seasoned malty oak, chocolaty tannins finishing firm but with plenty of flavour length.
▼ *90* *2004-2012*

**1997 Centenary Hill** *Barossa Valley – Shiraz* **S.A.**
Medium/deep crimson. Intense choc-berry fruit aromas with plenty of new tropical/malty oak. Chocolate/berry/malty/vanillin flavours, fine grained tannins, excellent concentration and length. Good cellaring style.
▼ *88* *2004-2007*

**1998 Centenary Hill** *Barossa Valley – Shiraz* **S.A.**
Medium deep crimson. Intense dark cherry/malty oak aromas with some smoky/tropical tones. Dark cherry/malty flavours, with chocolaty tannins and plenty of mid-palate richness. Finishes chalky and long.
▼ *89* *2004-2012*

**1999 Centenary Hill Barossa Valley** *Shiraz* **S.A.**
Medium deep crimson. Malty/savoury/blueberry aromas with touch of menthol. Rich savoury wine with deep-set mocha/dark berry fruits, fine chocolaty tannins, well seasoned malty oak, finishing long and sweet.
▼ *89* *2005-2016*

**1989 Jacaranda Ridge** *Coonawarra – Cabernet Sauvignon* **S.A.**
Crimson. Restrained seaweed/liquorice/black cherry aromas with touches of menthol. Sweet cherry/menthol flavours with underlying oak, fine-grained but gripping tannins, with a nice core of sweet fruit. Good length of flavour.
▼ *89* *Now*

**1991 Jacaranda Ridge** *Coonawarra – Cabernet Sauvignon* **S.A.**
Crimson/purple. Menthol/chocolate/seaweed/slight chloride characters. Menthol/seaweed/earthy/cordial flavours with soupy, almost green, tannins, medium concentration and length.
▼ *80* *Now*

**1992 Jacaranda Ridge** *Coonawarra – Cabernet Sauvignon* **S.A.**
Deep crimson/purple. Dark chocolate/blackcurrant/vanillin aromas. Rich, ripe, dark chocolate/blackcurrant fruit, mouth filling, rasping, slightly green tannins with some cedary oak, medium to high concentration, and a firm finish.
▼ *87* *2002-2008*

**1994 Jacaranda Ridge** *Coonawarra – Cabernet Sauvignon* **S.A.**
Deep crimson. Coffee/mocha aromas with blackcurrant cordial characters and vanillin oak. Rich wine with mocha/choc-berry flavours, pronounced very strong almost searingly dry tannins, underlying malty oak, finishing quite firm and drying.
▼ *86* *Now-2008*

**1996 Jacaranda Ridge** *Coonawarra – Cabernet Sauvignon* **S.A.**
Deep crimson. Rhubarb/blackcurrant aromas with touch of rum and raisin/tropical oak. Intense blackcurrant/black olive flavours with some malty oak nuances. Very strong pronounced almost aggressive tannins finishing firm and tight. Massively chewy wine.
▼ *88* *Now-2010*

**1997 Jacaranda Ridge** *Coonawarra – Cabernet Sauvignon* **S.A.**
Deep crimson. Complex but sweet fruited cedar/seaweedy/black olive/ currant aromas. Richly flavoured silky wine with fruit inextricably

intertwined with fruit. Complex cedar/mocha flavours permeate through the wine with slinky/lacy tannins.

▼ 91 2004-2012

**1998 Jacaranda Ridge** *Coonawarra – Cabernet Sauvignon* **S.A.**
Medium crimson. Strongly scented wine with plum/berry fruit aromas and plenty of tropical oak characters. Dense plum/berry fruits with plenty of sweet tropical/vanillin oak, ripe penetrating tannins finishing firm and flavoursome.

▼ 87 2004-2012

**1999 Jacaranda Ridge** *Coonawarra – Cabernet Sauvignon* **S.A.**
Deep crimson. Redcurrant/bramble aromas with some vanilla/nutmeg nuances. Rich sweet redcurrant brambly fruit flavours, fine ripe tannins, and plenty of malty oak flavours. Finishes long, but with a belt of firm tannin slick.

▼ 88 2004-2014

**1990 Lawsons** *Padthaway – Shiraz* **S.A.**
Deep crimson. Very ripe raspberry/blackberry/slight menthol aromas with touches of leather compost. Very attractive and complex palate with ripe raspberry/blackberry/meaty/compost fruit and smoky oak, fine tannins and excellent length.

■ 95 Now-2005 *Distinguished*

**1991 Lawsons** *Padthaway – Shiraz* **S.A.**
Deep crimson. Raspberry/blackberry/menthol fruit with touches of cedar/cigar box. The palate is deeply concentrated with cedary, blackberry/menthol fruit, pronounced gripping tannin structure, underlying oak and excellent length.

■ 89 Now-2005 *Distinguished*

**1992 Lawsons** *Padthaway – Shiraz* **S.A.**
Deep crimson. Oily, almost herbal, eucalypt/raspberry aromas. Hard angular palate with very restrained fruit and furry green tannins. Firm finish. Difficult wine to like.

▼-■ 75 Now-2004 *Distinguished*

**1993 Lawsons** *Padthaway – Shiraz* **S.A.**
Deep crimson. Menthol, lifted, perfumed, dark cherry/chocolate fruit with subtle oak nuances and coffee/smoky undertones. The palate has plenty of sweet choc-menthol fruit and some smoky bacon flavours, ripe tannins, medium concentration and length. Slightly callow wine.

■ 84 Now-2008 *Distinguished*

**1994 Lawsons** *Padthaway – Shiraz* **S.A.**
Crimson purple. Intense plum/mulberry/spice/menthol aromas. Sweet menthol/mulberry fruit with underlying oak, ripe tannins and a firm finish. Very textured wine needing time to evolve.

■ 92 Now-2012 *Distinguished*

**1995 Lawsons** *Padthaway – Shiraz* **S.A.**
Deep crimson. Earthy, menthol, slightly bilgy aromas with some raspberry and pepper. The palate is medium bodied with earthy, raspberry/menthol flavours, pronounced tannins and underlying oak, that finishes firm.

▼-■ 80 Now-2007 *Distinguished*

**1996 Lawsons** *Padthaway – Shiraz* **S.A.**
Deep crimson/purple. Intense blackberry/floral/smoky aromas with sweet and savoury nuances. The palate is very corporate in style with sweet blackberry/chocolaty flavours, very dense high-pixel tannins, plenty of savoury smoky oak but good concentration and length. Still quite elemental with oak slightly at the fore.

■ 92 Now-2012 *Distinguished*

**1997 Lawsons** *Padthaway – Shiraz* **S.A.**
Crimson/purple. Surprisingly closed wine with very deep-set liquorice/blackberry/olive aromas with the savoury oak completely sucked up by fruit. The palate is still very young but highly concentrated with plenty of ripe blackberry/liquorice/ginger flavours, massively solid oak, fine-grained tannins and plenty of length. Needs time to evolve.

▼-■ 89 Now-2012 *Distinguished*

**1998 Lawsons** *Padthaway – Shiraz* **S.A.**
Purple/crimson. Very young, bright, elemental wine with plush mulberry/blackberry aromas and underlying oak. The palate is rich and

flavoursome with ripe berry/chocolate fruit flavours, pronounced tannins, high concentration and excellent length. Needs time to settle in.
■ *90* *Now-2012* *Distinguished*

**1999 Lawsons** *Padthaway – Shiraz* **S.A.**
Medium crimson. Intense menthol/ginger/chocolate/briary aromas. Concentrated palate with sweet fruited menthol/blackberry flavours and plenty of malt/tropical oak, ripe velvety tannins finishing very long.
■ *87* *Now-2012* *Distinguished*

**1991 St Hugo** *Coonawarra – Cabernet* **S.A.**
Dark crimson. Intense but deep-set perfectly ripe blackcurrant/meaty/savoury aromas. Roasted, meaty, blackcurrant flavours. Totally integrated grainy oak. Ripe, evenly proportioned tannins. Super concentration and length. Beautiful wine.
■ *95* *Now-2006* *Distinguished*

**1992 St Hugo** *Coonawarra – Cabernet* **S.A.**
Crimson/purple. Intense chocolate/blackberry/liquorice aromas. Rich ripe chocolaty wine with plenty of blackberry/liquorice fruits, integrated oak, and leafy tannins.
■ *88* *Now-2006* *Distinguished*

**1993 St Hugo** *Coonawarra – Cabernet* **S.A.**
Crimson/purple. Chocolate/*paneforte*/spicy aromas. Rich chocolate/*paneforte* flavours with cedary oak, fine-grained tannins, excellent fruit-sweetness and length.
■ *91* *2002-2012* *Distinguished*

**1994 St Hugo** *Coonawarra – Cabernet* **S.A.**
Opaque black/purple. Lifted blackcurrant/liquorice/savoury oak aromas. Flavoursome blackberry/cassis fruit, savoury oak, loose-knit tannins, moderate concentration and length. Slight painting-by-numbers feel but, could develop into something.
■ *86* *2002-2008* *Distinguished*

**1996 St Hugo** *Coonawarra – Cabernet* **S.A.**
Deep crimson. Intense blackcurrant pastille/mint aromas with some cedary tones. Leafy blackcurrant pastille flavours with some cedary oak, fine grained tannins finishing quite cedary and long.
■ *89* *2004-2012* *Distinguished*

**1997 St Hugo** *Coonawarra – Cabernet* **S.A.**
Medium deep crimson. Strong eucalypt/menthol/orange/chocolate aromas. Concentrated wine with cool eucalypt/menthol/ slightly peppery flavours, fine sinewy almost searing tannins but with a good core of fruit-sweetness. Finishes very firm – almost gritty.
▼-■ *81* *Now-2008* *Distinguished*

**1998 St Hugo** *Coonawarra – Cabernet* **S.A.**
Deep crimson. Cassis plum aromas with some smoky nuances. Richly flavoured wine with cassis/plum flavours, plenty of vanilla oak, fine grainy textured tannins with firm finish but plenty of flavour length. Very nice wine.
■ *90* *Now-2010* *Distinguished*

**1999 St Hugo** *Coonawarra – Cabernet* **S.A.**
Deep crimson. Dark cherry/plummy/mint aromas with touches of choc-berry characters. Highly concentrated richly textured palate with deep-set choc-berry fruit flavours and touches of liquorice and ginger, spicy beautifully seasoned oak, fine grained slightly gravelly tannins finishing firm but flavoursome. Excellent wine.
■ *94* *2004-2015* *Distinguished*

**2000 St Hugo** *Coonawarra – Cabernet* **S.A.**
Deep crimson. Pungent leafy/blackcurrant/gamy aromas and some ginger/spice notes. Well balanced wine with blackcurrant/leafy flavours, pronounced grippy tight tannins, cedary oak and finishing very firm and tight. Needs more time.
■ *91* *2004-2014* *Distinguished*

## PANORAMA

**2000** *Southern Tasmania – Pinot Noir* **Tas.**
Medium deep crimson. Decadently rich ripe plum/rhubarb/cherry aromas and flavours, lovely concentration and silky tannins balanced by underlying oak and finishing long. A real fruit bomb wine but with plenty of varietal definition.
▼ *95* *Now-2006*

## PANORAMA

**2001** *Southern Tasmania – Pinot Noir* **Tas.**
Medium deep crimson. Oak driven wine with malt/spicy oak over ginger/cherry/plum mulberry fruit. Very fleshy wine with red plum/ cherry flavours and malt oak, fine grained tannins, finishing grippy but long and flavoursome.
▼ *84* *Now-2004*

## PARINGA ESTATE

**1997** *Mornington Peninsula – Pinot Noir* **Vic.**
Medium deep crimson. Complex mushroom/demi-glace/game/mint/ brambly aromas. Brambly/mushroom/demi-glace flavours, but almost sweet and sour. Fine, grippy tannins finishing dry and tight.
▼ *78* *Now*

**2000** *Mornington Peninsula – Pinot Noir* **Vic.**
Medium crimson. Intense cherry/mint/game aromas with some cedar spice oak. Well flavoured wine with dark cherry/meaty flavours, some cedar spice characters and fine grained slightly grippy tannins.
▼ *90* *Now-2006*

**2000** *Mornington Peninsula – Shiraz* **Vic.**
Medium deep crimson. Medium concentrated wine with red cherry/ mulberry aromas and touches of matchstick. Game/red cherry/lanolin/ matchstick flavours, fine slightly green-edged tannins, with medium concentration and length.
▼ *85* *2004-2010*

## PARKER COONAWARRA ESTATE

**1996 Terra Rossa** *Coonawarra – Cabernet* **S.A.**
Crimson. Pure blackcurrant/cassis-like aromas with underlying oak. The palate is quite classical,if a little simple, with moderate concentration, fine-grained tannins and blackcurrant fruit characters.
▼-■ *84* *Now-2008*

**1999 Terra Rossa** *Coonawarra – Cabernet* **S.A.**
Deep crimson. Blackcurrant/liquorice/menthol aromas with some savoury notes. Highly concentrated wine with blackcurrant/liquorice, slight leafy flavours, fine gripping tannins, and strong cedary oak. Finishes firm. Will certainly evolve. Needs a bit more time.
▼-■ *90* *2004-2015*

**1996 Terra Rossa First Growth** *Coonawarra – Cabernet* **S.A.**
Deep crimson. Complex demi-glace/meaty consomme aromas. Rich savoury beautifully meshed wine with sweet consomme/demi-glace flavours, fine sweet tannins. Plenty of length. Lovely wine.
▲ *93* *Now-2012*

**1998 Terra Rossa First Growth** *Coonawarra – Cabernet* **S.A.**
Deep crimson. Intense blackcurrant/plum aromas with touches of mocha/savoury oak. Blackcurrant/plum flavours with fine grainy tannins, superb fruit-sweetness and concentration, all underpinned by plenty of savoury mocha/nutty oak. Long finish. Super wine.
▲ *94* *2006-2016*

**1999 Terra Rossa First Growth** *Coonawarra – Cabernet* **S.A.**
Deep crimson. Beautifully perfumed chocolate/blackcurrant/cedar/ mocha aromas. Seriously concentrated wine with incredibly deep blackcurrant/inky/mocha flavours. Plenty of new savoury oak. Pronounced but fine grained fruit and sweet oak tannins, immense fruit power and length. Lovely wine with plenty of cellaring potential.
▲ *100* *2006-2015*

**1998** *Coonawarra – Merlot* **S.A.**
Crimson purple. Scented plum/cassis/blackberry aromas with touches of malty oak. Ripe plummy fruit but medium concentrated wine with fine grained tannins and smoky/malty oak. Elegant style.
▼-■ *86* *2004-2012*

## PENFOLDS

**1980 Bin 128** *Coonawarra – Shiraz* **S.A.**
Brick red. Complex coconut/meaty/nutty aromas. Highly concentrated wine with rich, ripe deep-set sweet fruit, liquorice/mulberry/tar characters, ripe tannins and excellent length. At peak of development.
■ *93* *Now-2005*

**1981 Bin 128** *Coonawarra – Shiraz* **S.A.**
Brick red. Leafy earthy aromas with hints of water bag/hessian – beginning to lose fruit. Earthy, leafy, fruit, slightly bitter tannins, moderate concentration and a firm finish. Still holding together but at cusp of development.
■ *79* *Now*

**1982 Bin 128** *Coonawarra – Shiraz* **S.A.**
Brick red. Cherry/tobacco aromas with hint of game. The palate is moderately concentrated with cherry tobacco flavours, ripe-ish tannins and firm finish. Still hanging in there but a moderate cellaring prospect.
■ *81* *Now*

**1983 Bin 128** *Coonawarra – Shiraz* **S.A.**
Brick red. Green, herbal, almost under-ripe, fruit characters. Quite unyielding and fruit dry. The wine is quite hard on the palate with green herbal fruit, bitter tannins and some barnyard characters. Fruit has dropped out, but just hanging in.
■ *76* *Now*

**1984 Bin 128** *Coonawarra – Shiraz* **S.A.**
Brick red. Lightly structured wine with leafy, polished leather aromas and flavours. Well past its prime.
■ *69* *Now*

**1985 Bin 128** *Coonawarra – Shiraz* **S.A.**
Brick red. Sweet, complex earthy/tropical fruit/tobacco leaf aromas. Loose-knit, easy drinking wine with developed, raspberry/tobacco leaf flavours, fine tannins and moderate concentration. A slightly bittersweet style.
■ *85* *Now*

**1986 Bin 128** *Coonawarra – Shiraz* **S.A.**
Deep brick red. Thick, deep-set and penetrating brambly/liquorice aromas. The palate is rich and ripe with deep-set liquorice/blackberry/prune fruit, ripe fine-grained tannins and a long finish. A highly concentrated and beautifully balanced wine.
▲ *94* *Now-2010*

**1987 Bin 128** *Coonawarra – Shiraz* **S.A.**
Deep crimson. Chestnut/earthy-like fruit with touches of green pepper/menthol. The palate is well developed with slightly oily, earthy, menthol flavours, fine tannin and good length. Fading.
■ *80* *Now*

**1988 Bin 128** *Coonawarra – Shiraz* **S.A.**
Deep crimson. Meaty sweet fruit, vanillin and prune aromas. Faint varnishy notes. The palate is ripe with plenty of sweet meaty, prune-like flavours, ripe but grainy tannins and medium length. Still holding, but only a few years to go.
■ *86* *Now*

**1989 Bin 128** *Coonawarra – Shiraz* **S.A.**
Deep crimson. Hessian/polished leather aromas with hints of tar. Palate drying out with cherry/earthy/tar-like flavours, a fine-grained tannin structure, moderate concentration and firm finish. Ready to drink.
■ *80* *Now*

**1990 Bin 128** *Coonawarra – Shiraz* **S.A.**
Deep crimson. Raspberry/blackberry aromas with some aniseed and polished leather. Palate is loose-knit with raspberry/blackberry liquorice fruit, moderate to high concentration. Firm finish. Will develop further.
▲ *90* *Now-2010*

**1991 Bin 128** *Coonawarra – Shiraz* **S.A.**
Deep crimson. Brambly/prune/blackberry/gamy aromas. A touch of vanillin. Ripe, deep-set liquorice/brambly fruit. Ripe tannins, high concentration, superb length. Evenly balanced right across the palate.
▲ *93* *Now-2010*

**1992 Bin 128** *Coonawarra – Shiraz* **S.A.**
Deep crimson. Intense blackberry jam/liquorice/mulberry/earthy fruit. Palate is moderately concentrated with blackberry/earthy fruit, and drying tannins. Not a long-term wine.
■ *80* *Now*

**1993 Bin 128** *Coonawarra – Shiraz* **S.A.**
Deep crimson. Cassis/menthol/blackberry/aniseed aromas with underlying vanillin oak. Well-structured palate with leafy blackberry

flavours, fine-grained tannins and good length. Still has plenty of flesh, but a medium term prospect.
■ 92 Now

**1994 Bin 128** *Coonawarra – Shiraz* **S.A.**
Deep crimson. Ripe mulberry/rhubarb/blackberry fruit, underpinned by vanillin oak. Palate is quite succulent with plush, ripe blackberry/mulberry fruit and some earth, fine tannins, high concentration and long finish.
■ 88 Now-2006

**1995 Bin 128** *Coonawarra – Shiraz* **S.A.**
Deep crimson. Lighter wine with strawberry and blackberry fruit, hints of white pepper. Already showing bottle age development with blackberry/earthy fruit, fine tannins and medium length. An early drinking wine of little cellaring value.
■ 77 Now

**1996 Bin 128** *Coonawarra – Shiraz* **S.A.**
Deep crimson/purple. Pure raspberry/blackberry fruit with hints of liquorice and toasty oak. The palate is immensely concentrated with ripe blackberry/liquorice fruit, grainy tannins, underlying integrated oak and a firm finish. A superb wine.
▲ 95 Now-2015

**1997 Bin 128** *Coonawarra – Shiraz* **S.A.**
Deep crimson/purple. Rich, ripe and youthful blackberry/aniseed like fruit with some pepper characters. The palate has plenty of sweet blackberry fruit, fine-grained tannins and medium length. A really well made wine, but a medium term prospect.
■ 89 Now-2005

**1998 Bin 128** *Coonawarra – Shiraz* **S.A.**
Deep crimson. Quite a loose-knit style with earthy/choc-cassis/meaty aromas. Touches of black cherry. Plenty of earthy, chocolate, nectarine flavours and sweet fruit on the palate. Fine tannins and underlying oak.
■ 89 2004-2010

**1999 Bin 128** *Coonawarra – Shiraz* **S.A.**
Deep crimson. Intense blackberry pastille/mint aromas. Ripe pure blackberry fruit with some dark chocolate nuances, fine ripe tannins, plenty of fruit-sweetness, concentration and length.
■ 87 2004-2010

**1998 Bin 138 Grenache Mourvedre** *South Australia – Grenache Mourvedre* **S.A.**
Medium deep crimson. Plenty of plummy, musky aromas. Touches of gingersnap and chocolate. Palate is rich and ripe with plum/musky/ginger/mint flavours and fine-grained tannins. Certainly not a particularly good cellaring style but at the price it's excellent value.
■ 85 Now-2006

**1999 Bin 138 Grenache Mourvedre** *South Australia – Grenache Mourvedre* **S.A.**
Deep crimson. Lifted minty/musky/choc-berry fruit aromas. Richly flavoured wine with choc-berry/musky flavours. Nice core of fruit-sweetness but quite stringy tannins.
■ 84 Now-2006

**1980 Bin 28** *South Australia – Shiraz* **S.A.**
Crimson. Very complex and interesting wine. Menthol liquorice aniseed like aromas. Palate is deep and fleshy with soft ripe tannins and concentrated liquorice/prune flavours. Finishes firm.
■ 90 Now-2005

**1981 Bin 28** *South Australia – Shiraz* **S.A.**
Crimson. Odd, boot polish-like aromas with some nutty, almost aldehydic characters. Palate is highly concentrated but a little oily, with sweet meaty flavours, fine tannins and medium length. Tastes better than it smells! Only 11.3 per cent alcohol!
■ 82 Now

**1982 Bin 28** *South Australia – Shiraz* **S.A.**
Medium crimson. Deep-set cherry/chocolate aromas that seem contrived. The palate is highly concentrated with plenty of sweet fruit/chocolate/cherry flavours, squashy tannins and finishes firm. Surprisingly good for the vintage.
■ 90 Now

**1983 Bin 28** *South Australia – Shiraz* **S.A.**
Deep crimson. Tighter prune/liquorice aromas with some cedar characters. The palate is sweetly concentrated with prune/liquorice flavours, fine high-pixel tannins. Firm finish.
■ *89* *Now*

**1984 Bin 28** *South Australia – Shiraz* **S.A.**
Crimson. Rich ethereal wine with earthy, chocolate aromas. The palate is still fresh with earthy, chocolate/prune-like fruit, soft tannins, moderate concentration and good length. Still holding up well, but unlikely to improve.
■ *87* *Now*

**1985 Bin 28** *South Australia – Shiraz* **S.A.**
Crimson. Awkward, disjointed wine with apple/cedar/aniseed aromas. The palate is beginning to dry out with compact cedar fruit, fine tannins and medium length. A bit bony.
■ *77* *Now*

**1986 Bin 28** *South Australia – Shiraz* **S.A.**
Deep crimson. Lifted prune/menthol/aniseed fruit with a touch of chocolate. Rich, highly concentrated, almost soupy wine with prune/plum/chocolate flavours and good length. Slightly hot.
▲ *90* *Now-2006*

**1987 Bin 28** *South Australia – Shiraz* **S.A.**
Medium crimson. Herbal/earthy aromas with some iodine/prune characters. Lightly structured wine with pruney, earthy flavours, fine tannins and medium length. Drink now.
■ *82* *Now*

**1988 Bin 28** *South Australia – Shiraz* **S.A.**
Deep crimson. Perfumed, tarry, brambly wine with some green edges. Vegetal, pruney, brambly flavours, textured tannins, moderate concentration, good length. Fruit beginning to dry out, so drink soon.
■ *79* *Now*

**1989 Bin 28** *South Australia – Shiraz* **S.A.**
Medium crimson. Aromatic, sweet, gamy, mulberry/chocolate fruit. A ripe, concentrated wine with cherry/chocolate/mulberry fruit, chewy tannins and excellent length. Excellent for vintage.
■ *92* *Now*

**1990 Bin 28** *South Australia – Shiraz* **S.A.**
Deep crimson. Intense cedar/prune/plum/liquorice aromas with some earthy undertones. The palate is ripe and concentrated with lovely fruit-sweetness, cedar/plum/prune-like flavours, pronounced tannins and good length.
▲ *93* *Now-2007*

**1991 Bin 28** *South Australia – Shiraz* **S.A.**
Deep crimson. Brambly prune/aniseed aromas. Palate is restrained and tightly knit with brambly/aniseed flavours, fine textured tannins and a long finish. Not as generous as the 1990.
▲ *89* *Now-2005*

**1992 Bin 28** *South Australia – Shiraz* **S.A.**
Deep crimson. Menthol/eucalypt/coffee and slightly green-edged aromas. The palate is quite simple with raspberry/eucalypt fruit, slightly hard-edged, raspy tannins and a medium finish. Not one to keep for any length of time, although drinking well now.
■ *80* *Now*

**1993 Bin 28** *South Australia – Shiraz* **S.A.**
Deep crimson. Rich, ripe, prune/Christmas cake/chocolate aromas with a hint of menthol. The palate is loose-knit with prune/chocolate flavours, grainy tannins and good length.
■ *87* *Now-2005*

**1994 Bin 28** *South Australia – Shiraz* **S.A.**
Deep crimson. Youthful mulberry/blackberry aromas with hints of ginger. The palate is beautifully concentrated with ripe mulberry/blackberry fruit, softening tannins and excellent length. Good potential.
■ *93* *Now-2008*

**1995 Bin 28** *South Australia – Shiraz* **S.A.**
Crimson. Blackberry/tar/menthol aromas. Already developing. Palate is fleshy and highly concentrated. Some sweet blackberry fruit and slightly bitter tannins. Finishes a little short. Pleasant but early drinking wine.
■ *80* *Now*

**1996 Bin 28** *South Australia – Shiraz* **S.A.**
Deep crimson. Lovely perfumed blackberry/liquorice aromas. Hint of gingersnap. Ripe, deep-set blackberry/liquorice fruit. Massive concentration. Fine-grained tannins. Long finish. Beautifully balanced.
▲ *94* *Now-2010*

**1997 Bin 28** *South Australia – Shiraz* **S.A.**
Deep crimson. High-pitched aniseed/plum/choc-berry aromas. Vibrant, youthful palate with plum/aniseed/ginger fruit, fine tannin structure and good length. Exuberant and easy to like but probably not long term.
■ *92* *Now-2007*

**1998 Bin 28** *Kalimna – Shiraz* **S.A.**
Deep crimson. A lovely wine with terrific aging potential. Intense choc-berry aromas with touches of baked plum. Palate is extremely deep-set and richly flavoured, with plenty of dark chocolate/berry/prune flavours, pronounced gravelly tannins and plenty of length. As an investment, this is a great each-way bet. If it fails to meet reserve it will certainly reap great dividends in the pleasure department.
■ *94* *2004-2014*

**1999 Bin 28** *Kalimna – Shiraz* **S.A.**
Deep crimson. Perfumed plum/dark cherry aromas with some chocolate/vanillin characters. Multi-layered wine with plum/chocolate flavours, fine slightly hard tannins and underlying oak. Plenty of fruit-sweetness and length.
■ *87* *2004-2010*

**1966 Bin 389** *South Australia – Cabernet Shiraz* **S.A.**
Brick red. Classic Penfolds aged wine with sweet fruit/game-like aromas and nuances of chocolate and coffee. The palate is rich and soft with coffee/chocolate-like flavours, some nutty complexity, soft easing tannins, superb concentration and overall richness and length. Brilliant wine. Rare and eclectic.
▲ *95* *Now* *Excellent*

**1970 Bin 389** *South Australia – Cabernet Shiraz* **S.A.**
Brick red. Perfumed floral/gamy/liquorice/sweet roasted meat and hints of iodine. Beautifully structured wine with roasted, meaty, liquorice flavours, fine ripe tannins, high concentration and excellent length.
▲ *93* *Now* *Excellent*

**1971 Bin 389** *South Australia – Cabernet Shiraz* **S.A.**
Brick red. Gamy aniseed/raspberry aromas with some meaty complexity. Palate is hard, with some sweet, meaty fruit, good concentration and length. Disappointing, considering the reputation of the vintage. *Recently saw a good bottle, but this wine is really very much at its peak.*
▲ *88* *Now* *Excellent*

**1975 Bin 389** *South Australia – Cabernet Shiraz* **S.A.**
Brick red. Savoury miso-broth/liquorice aromas with some earthiness. The palate is fruit-sweet with broth/meaty flavours, underlying coconut notes, structured tannins, excellent concentration and length. Delicious.
▲ *93* *Now-2005* *Excellent*

**1976 Bin 389** *South Australia – Cabernet Shiraz* **S.A.**
Brick red. High-pitched liquorice/polished leather/aniseed aromas with meaty nuances. The palate is highly concentrated with developed leather polish/meaty flavours, slightly bitter tannins but good length. For such a good vintage a little disappointing – sweet and sour.
▲ *85* *Now* *Excellent*

**1977 Bin 389** *South Australia – Cabernet Shiraz* **S.A.**
Brick red. Menthol/Chesterfield leather/marmite and slight herbal aromas. Moderately concentrated palate with menthol/leather fruit, almost soupy flavours, hard tannins and medium length. Fruit is just hanging in there but really needs to be drunk soon.
■ *79* *Now* *Excellent*

**1978 Bin 389** *South Australia – Cabernet Shiraz* **S.A.**
Brick red. Complex floral/tropical/raspberry/warm tar aromas with touches of lanolin and coffee. Soapy, floral/tar, meaty flavours, sweet, ripe tannins and good length. Beginning to tire but better than 1977. *Herb garden/mushroom aromas and fine ripe tannins. Drink up.*
■ *84* *Now* *Excellent*

**1980 Bin 389** *South Australia – Cabernet Shiraz* **S.A.**
Brick red. Dense, tightly packed raspberry/grilled bacon/meaty/aniseed aromas. Very complex deep-set compact palate with cedary, meaty flavours, gravelly tannins and a firm finish.
■ *89* *Now* *Excellent*

**1981 Bin 389** *South Australia – Cabernet Shiraz* **S.A.**
Brick red. Fading wine with water bag/orange peel aromas. Moderately concentrated and one-dimensional wine with fruit drying out and acidity coming to the fore. Drink up.
■ *73* *Past* *Excellent*

**1982 Bin 389** *South Australia – Cabernet Shiraz* **S.A.**
Brick red. Cassis/coconut/menthol and contrived cherry aromas. Sweet cherry/cassis flavours. Fine drying tannins. Firm finish. Ready to drink.
■ *80* *Now* *Excellent*

**1983 Bin 389** *South Australia – Cabernet Shiraz* **S.A.**
Brick red. Blackcurrant/meaty/coconut/vanillin/sweet fruit aromas with some menthol. Palate is bright and highly concentrated with developed meaty, coconutty flavours, fine-grained tannins and good length.
■ *86* *Now – 2005* *Excellent*

**1984 Bin 389** *South Australia – Cabernet Shiraz* **S.A.**
Brick red. Loose-knit style with coffee/mocha aromas and leather/spice nuances. Leafy coffee/mocha flavours, moderate concentration, soupy tannins and firm finish.
■ *82* *Now* *Excellent*

**1985 Bin 389** *South Australia – Cabernet Shiraz* **S.A.**
Brick red. Complex and developing tar/coal/roasted meat aromas with liquorice and cedar. The palate still has plenty of sweet fruit and is slightly tangy with tar/meaty/cedary flavours, grainy tannins and medium length. Not a long-term prospect.
■ *83* *Now – 2005* *Excellent*

**1986 Bin 389** *South Australia – Cabernet Shiraz* **S.A.**
Deep crimson. Loose-knit, aromatic, earthy liquorice/prune-like aromas. The palate is highly concentrated with roasted meat/prune/earthy flavours ripe tannins and a firm finish. A classic year but just falls short of a classic wine. Could develop.
▲ *91* *Now-2008* *Excellent*

**1987 Bin 389** *South Australia – Cabernet Shiraz* **S.A.**
Brick red. Loose-knit, simple wine with tropical/prune/gamy fruit and vanillin aromas. Simple fruit and grainy tannins on the palate with oak coming to the fore. Compact structured wine with limited cellaring potential. Best to drink now.
■ *80* *Now* *Excellent*

**1988 Bin 389** *South Australia – Cabernet Shiraz* **S.A.**
Deep crimson. Youthful and bright blackberry/cassis aromas with some coffee and chocolate. Palate is rich and ripe with squashy blackberry/chocolate flavours, ripe tannins, lovely concentration and length.
■ *93* *Now-2010* *Excellent*

**1989 Bin 389** *South Australia – Cabernet Shiraz* **S.A.**
Deep crimson. Contrived cassis/blackcurrant fruit with some vanillin coconut. The palate is soft and fleshy, with simple cassis like flavours and moderate concentration. At peak of development.
■ *80* *Now* *Excellent*

**1990 Bin 389** *South Australia – Cabernet Shiraz* **S.A.**
Deep crimson. Lovely direct blackcurrant/chocolate fruit with hints of spice. Incredibly complex and delicious wine with concentrated choc-berry fruit, some vanillin and cedar, velvety tannins and superb length. Brilliant wine.
▲ *98* *Now-2015* *Excellent*

**1991 Bin 389** *South Australia – Cabernet Shiraz* **S.A.**
Deep crimson. Developed mocha/brambly/liquorice fruit. The palate is restrained with brambly liquorice fruit, green-edged but fine tannins and good length of flavour.
▲ *89* *Now-2008* *Excellent*

**1992 Bin 389** *South Australia – Cabernet Shiraz* **S.A.**
Deep crimson. Brambly, damson/blackberry fruit with some aniseed characters. Palate is light and simple, with blackberry fruit, moderate concentration, slightly bitter tannins but a firm finish. Not a keeper.
■ *77* *Now* *Excellent*

**1993 Bin 389** *South Australia – Cabernet Shiraz* **S.A.**
Liquorice/gingersnap-like fruit with some menthol/choc-berry characters, even a hint herbal (under ripe). The palate is quite hard-edged, almost bitter sweet, with primary fruit and slightly green tannins. Youthful exuberance is masking structure.
■ *79* *Now* *Excellent*

**1994 Bin 389** *South Australia – Cabernet Shiraz* **S.A.**
Deep crimson. Extremely deep-set, ultra-blackcurrant aromas with underlying vanillin and complex, gamy nuances. An immensely concentrated wine with volumes of blackcurrant fruit. Ripe tannins. Underlying but well-integrated coconut oak, some complex gamy/meaty characters and excellent length. A Classic year and a long haul wine.
■ *94* *Now-2010* *Excellent*

**1995 Bin 389** *South Australia – Cabernet Shiraz* **S.A.**
Crimson. Aniseed/liquorice-like fruit, blackcurrants and violets. The palate is less interesting with loose-knit, grainy, if not slightly bitter tannins and a firm finish. A little unyielding. Drink now or soon.
■ *79* *Now-2005* *Excellent*

**1996 Bin 389** *South Australia – Cabernet Shiraz* **S.A.**
Deep crimson. Developing demi-glace/meaty/choc-berry fruit aromas. Plenty of sweet fruit. Richly flavoured, smooth wine with chocolaty/meaty flavours, ripe slinky tannin structures building up firm and tight. Finishes dry and chalky. *Scored this wine 100 in our previous edition. This wine is now in evolution and is looking slightly gawky – but the fruit power and balance is there.*
▲ *94* *2004-2018* *Excellent*

**1997 Bin 389** *South Australia – Cabernet Shiraz* **S.A.**
Deep crimson/purple. Vibrant blackberry/chocolate fruit with some liquorice. Baby fat hides an underlying hard structure. The palate does present some very nice seductive fruit but as age marches on, hard, slightly oily tannins will come to the fore making it a sinewy, rather ordinary wine. At its best now, or very soon.
■ *84* *Now-2005* *Excellent*

**1998 Bin 389** *South Australia – Cabernet Shiraz* **S.A.**
An excellent follow up to the palate-shattering 1996 vintage. Beautifully perfumed wine with ripe blackberry/liquorice/violet aromas and touches of meaty complexity. The palate is very concentrated with blackberry/liquorice/meaty flavours and plenty of fruit-sweetness, complemented by underlying tropical/coconut oak and fine-grained, ripe-textured tannins. And length? Its almost as if the wine has no vanishing point – the flavours linger on forever! *I would expect the wine to go through an evolution similar to the 1996.*
■ *98* *2006-2020* *Excellent*

**1999 Bin 389** *South Australia – Cabernet Shiraz* **S.A.**
Deep crimson. Intense complex choc-berry/malty/sandalwood aromas. Well concentrated wine with choc-berry/seaweedy fruit flavours. Plenty of savoury oak and gravelly tannins. Finishing dry but with good flavour length.
■ *86* *2004-2012* *Excellent*

**2000 Bin 389** *South Australia – Cabernet Shiraz* **S.A.**
Deep crimson. Dark cherry/plum aromas with malt/tropical oak undertones. The palate is generously flavoured with plum dark cherry fruit, fine sweet tannins building up to a grippy finish. Excellent concentration and length.
■ *89* *2004-2012* *Excellent*

**1990 Bin 407** *South Australia – Cabernet Sauvignon* **S.A.**
Deep crimson. Blackcurrant/earthy/liquorice aromas with hints of mint and underlying oak. The palate is developing with highly concentrated blackcurrant/liquorice fruit, fine-grained but well ripened tannins, a slight tang and good length. A nice wine.
■ *93* *Now-2010*

**1991 Bin 407** *South Australia – Cabernet Sauvignon* **S.A.**
Deep crimson. Intense aniseed/blackcurrant/earthy aromas. Palate is quite soupy with developing blackcurrant/earthy flavours, grainy tannins. Lovely concentration. Long finish. An excellent foil to the 1990.
■ *92* *Now-2010*

**1992 Bin 407** *South Australia – Cabernet Sauvignon* **S.A.**
Deep crimson. A brooding wine with blackberry/tar/vanillin aromas with touches of under-ripe asparagus. The palate is silken with surprisingly simple cherry/blackberry flavours, fine tannins and good length. A moderately concentrated wine. Early drinker.
■ *85* *Now*

**1993 Bin 407** *South Australia – Cabernet Sauvignon* **S.A.**
Deep crimson. Fresh and vibrant wine with plenty of blackcurrants and underlying oak, perhaps a touch herbal. The palate is compact, but sweet-fruited, with direct cassis flavours, fine tannins and medium length. Another early drinking wine with plenty of youthful appeal.
■ *88* *Now-2005*

**1994 Bin 407** *South Australia – Cabernet Sauvignon* **S.A.**
Deep crimson. Intense, pure, blackcurrant fruit aromas with hints of cedary wood. Highly concentrated palate with blackcurrant/cedar flavours, underlying oak, fine-grained tannins and excellent length. Excellent definition and flavour. Long-term wine.
■ *92* *Now-2012*

**1995 Bin 407** *South Australia – Cabernet Sauvignon* **S.A.**
Crimson. Leafy blackcurrant aromas. Loose-knit, early drinking style with some good leafy blackcurrant flavours, slightly green rasping tannins and medium length. Well made but uninspiring wine.
■ *84* *Now-2005*

**1996 Bin 407** *South Australia – Cabernet Sauvignon* **S.A.**
Deep crimson. High-pitched blackcurrant/violet/cedar aromas with touches of ginger. The palate is rich and opulent with ripe blackcurrant/ginger-like fruit, structured grainy tannins and superb length. A brilliantly made wine that is sure to become a classic.
■ *95* *2005-2020*

**1997 Bin 407** *South Australia – Cabernet Sauvignon* **S.A.**
Deep crimson. Plummy, liquorice fruit with some underlying oak. The palate is full bodied with plummy, liquorice/ginger/brandy snap flavours, but underpinned by rather hard tannins. It will improve with some age, but ultimately is a short-term wine.
■ *87* *Now*

**1998 Bin 407** *South Australia – Cabernet Sauvignon* **S.A.**
Shows all the hallmarks of Cabernet Sauvignon with very direct blackcurrant/black olive aromas and some cedary oak. Very structured palate with plenty of blackcurrant fruits and black olive/cedar/iodine characters. Tannins are quite firm and rasping giving a slightly gritty mouth feel. The wine finishes firm and tight. This is a good wine but falls short of brilliance.
■ *88* *2006-2014*

**1999 Bin 407** *South Australia – Cabernet Sauvignon* **S.A.**
Deep crimson. Very direct and classical cassis aromas with touches of cedar. Clear, deep, blackcurrant/cedar flavours with fine grained tannins, underlying oak, plenty of concentration and length. The best *407* to date.
■ *94* *2006-2012*

**1995 Bin 144 Yattarna** *Multi Area Blend – Chardonnay* **S.A.**
Pale yellow/gold. Complex, rich peach/tropical fruit aromas with well-seasoned vanillin and savoury oak characters. The palate is developing with rich, ripe and creamy peach/cedary flavours, savoury almost newly carpentered oak, fresh acidity and good length. Hardly Helen of Troy – more like a Sharon Stone – fruit style. Enjoy as early as possible as this wine has very limited aging potential.
▼ *88* *Now*

**1996 Bin 144 Yattarna** *Multi Area Blend – Chardonnay* **S.A.**
Pale yellow/gold. Tight tropical fruit/grapefruit aromas with touches of pear drop. Integrated oak background. The palate is showing plenty of pear/peach fruit, pronounced acidity, restrained oak and roasted nut complexity. A real racehorse with powerful and balanced fruit.
▼ *93* *Now*

**1997 Bin 144 Yattarna** *Multi Area Blend – Chardonnay* **S.A.**
Pale yellow. Lemony, grapefruit aromas with some roasted nuts, very pure and tight. Tight, with grapefruit/melon flavours, quite subtle

savoury oak, fine linear acidity, a touch of nutty complexity, excellent concentration and length. A bit of a racehorse.

▼ 94 *Now*

**1998 Bin 144 Yattarna** *Multi Area Blend – Chardonnay* **S.A.**
Pale yellow. Intense, beautifully focused wine with melon/nectarine aromas and biscuity, roasted nut complexity, some lemon grass and plenty of grapey fruit. Very tight wine. Ripe, squashy, melon/nectarine flavours, fleshy worked wine with some grapefruit, some savoury oak. Good concentration and length.

▼ 94 *Now-2005*

**1999 Bin 144 Yattarna** *Multi Area Blend – Chardonnay* **S.A.**
Pale medium colour. Intense peach/nectarine aromas with some biscuity/malt oak and plenty of creamy complexity. Richly complex and creamy wine with peach/nectarine/melon fruit flavours balanced by savoury/toasty oak, some roasted nut nuances finishing long and flavoursome. Style does not suit long term cellaring.

▼ 92 *Now-2005*

**2000 Bin 144 Yattarna** *Multi Area Blend – Chardonnay* **S.A.**
Pale colour. Restrained and less-worked than the 1999. Well focused melon/apricot aromas with underlying savoury oak and some leesy complexity. The palate is well-concentrated and supple with creamy melon/apricot/aniseed flavours and some grainy/malt oak. Acidity comes to the fore towards the back palate. A touch under-powered at the finish. Will age further than 2000.

▼ 89 *Now-2007*

**1962 Bin 60A** *Coonawarra Cabernet* **–** *Kalimna Shiraz* **S.A.**
Brick red. Beautifully focused wine with meaty, beefy aromas, exotic fruits and hints of liquorice, which carry on to the palate. Well-balanced wine with fruit richness right across the palate with fine superbly defined tannins and marvellous length. Lovely old wine. Often referred to as being one of the greatest wines ever produced in Australia… umm. Rare and eclectic.

▲ 94 *Now*

**1966 Bin 620** *Coonawarra – Cabernet* **S.A.**
Brick red. Earthy, sweet mushroom with some beefy characters, beginning to fade. The palate is sweet and loose-knit with mushroomy, fungal, earthy flavours, fine tannins, but acidity coming to the fore. Just hanging on. Rare and eclectic.

▲ 81 *Now*

**1967 Bin 7** *Coonawarra Cabernet* **–** *Kalimna Shiraz* **S.A.**
Brick red. Chocolate/menthol aromas with hint a of green cedar. Sweet chocolate/menthol fruit, finely textured but gripping tannins and a firm finish. Still looking good. Rare.

▲ 93 *Now*

**1964 Bin 707** *South Australia – Cabernet Sauvignon* **S.A.**
Brick red. Earthy, cedar-oil/blackcurrant/tobacco aromas with some chocolate nuances. The palate is moderately concentrated with chocolate/cedar/tobacco flavours, and grainy tannins. Still holding up but fruit beginning to dry out. Rare and eclectic.

■ 87 *Now* *Exceptional*

**1965 Bin 707** *South Australia – Cabernet Sauvignon* **S.A.**
Brick red. Herbal/minty/menthol/chocolate aromas. Herbal/minty/menthol flavours with some bilgy, blue cheese characters and quite hard tannins. Just enough sweet fruit. Firm finish. *Menthol characters are becoming quite pronounced.*

■ 79 *Now* *Exceptional*

**1966 Bin 707** *South Australia – Cabernet Sauvignon* **S.A.**
Brick red. Lovely, intense, nutty sweet fruit meaty/liquorice aromas,an absolute classic. Rich, ripe, meaty, cedary flavoured wine with lots fruit-sweetness, fine-grained tannins and superb length. Great old wine. Rare and eclectic.

■ 95 *Now* *Exceptional*

**1967 Bin 707** *South Australia – Cabernet Sauvignon* **S.A.**
Brick red. Caramel/milk/chocolate/briary aromas with some menthol notes. The palate is light and soft with overdeveloped caramel flavours and fading tannins. Finishes short. *Cedary wine with some floral notes. Fine lacy tannins.*

■ 76 *Now* *Exceptional*

**1968 Bin 707** *South Australia – Cabernet Sauvignon* **S.A.**
Brick red. Mint/coffee aromas with hints of leafiness. The palate is bitter and austere with some fine chocolate flavours, but ultimately a fading wine.
■ *74* *Past* *Exceptional*

**1969 Bin 707** *South Australia – Cabernet Sauvignon* **S.A.**
Brick red. Developed meaty, gamy aromas, but some lifted aldehydic characters. Palate is silken with very fine tannins and drying out fruit.
■ *75* *Past* *Exceptional*

**1970 -1975 Bin 707** *South Australia – Cabernet Sauvignon* **S.A.**
Not made.

**1976 Bin 707** *South Australia – Cabernet Sauvignon* **S.A.**
Brick red. Ripe and surprisingly youthful blackcurrant/liquorice/cedar/aniseed aromas with coconutty oak coming through. Soft and fleshy palate with very soft-grained tannins and cedary flavours. *The deep-set liquorice characters still run through this wine quite markedly. Some excellent bottles.*
■ *89* *Now* *Exceptional*

**1977 Bin 707** *South Australia – Cabernet Sauvignon* **S.A.**
Brick red. Briary coffee/sweet/cigar box/chocolate aromas. The palate is on the leaner side with moderately concentrated briary, cedary flavours, fine tannins and high-pitched acidity. Past its best but drinking OK.
■ *86* *Now* *Exceptional*

**1978 Bin 707** *South Australia – Cabernet Sauvignon* **S.A.**
Crimson. Leafy cassis/cordial aromas with hints of coffee. The palate is sweet and fleshy with grainy tannins, cedar-wood/cassis flavours and medium length.
■ *83* *Now* *Exceptional*

**1979 Bin 707** *South Australia – Cabernet Sauvignon* **S.A.**
Crimson. Mint/chocolate aromas with herbal undertones. Palate is quite compact but of medium concentration, fine, dark chocolate/vanillin flavours but slightly bitter tannins. Firm finish.
■ *79* *Now* *Exceptional*

**1980 Bin 707** *South Australia – Cabernet Sauvignon* **S.A.**
Brick red. Herbal/eucalypt/liquorice aromas. Restrained wine with drying out fruit, bitter tannins and high-pitched acid.
■ *73* *Past* *Exceptional*

**1982 Bin 707** *South Australia – Cabernet Sauvignon* **S.A.**
Medium crimson. Cherry/strawberry/chocolate/cordial-like fruit. Sweet and fleshy on the palate, with strange sweet and sour, cordial-like flavours, grainy tannins and good length. Still holding, but not much to write home about.
■ *78* *Now* *Exceptional*

**1983 Bin 707** *South Australia – Cabernet Sauvignon* **S.A.**
Medium crimson. Complex and intense bracken/liquorice/aniseed aromas with lashings of coconut oak. The palate is rich ripe and concentrated with liquorice/coffee/chocolate flavours balanced by gripping tannins, and excellent length. A classic year.
■ *94* *Now-2010* *Exceptional*

**1984 Bin 707** *South Australia – Cabernet Sauvignon* **S.A.**
Crimson. Sweet blackberry/plummy fruit-driven aromas. Moderately concentrated but well-balanced palate with soft blackberry flavours, fine-grained tannins and a firm finish.
■ *84* *Now* *Exceptional*

**1985 Bin 707** *South Australia – Cabernet Sauvignon* **S.A.**
Deep crimson. Loose-knit cedar-wood/smoky aromas with touches of raspberry and aniseed. The palate is loose-knit with cedary fruit, fine textured tannins, good concentration and overall balance.
■ *90* *Now-2005* *Exceptional*

**1986 Bin 707** *South Australia – Cabernet Sauvignon* **S.A.**
Deep crimson. An absolute classic. Very intense cedar/meaty/nutty aromas and superb savoury fruit characters. Palate is rich and ripe with Christmas cake/prune-like flavours and touches of cedar and liquorice, lovely fine, sinewy tannins, integrated oak and marvellous length.
■-▲ *95* *Now-2015* *Exceptional*

**1987 Bin 707** *South Australia – Cabernet Sauvignon* **S.A.**
Deep crimson. Slightly volatile coconut/aniseed/tarry aromas. Fruit is beginning to fade with coconutty oak coming to the fore. There is an underlying austerity about the wine. Drink soon.
■ *75* *Now* *Exceptional*

**1988 Bin 707** *South Australia – Cabernet Sauvignon* **S.A.**
Deep crimson. Bracken/liquorice/aniseed/blackberry fruit. The palate is loose-knit with sweet blackcurrant-like flavours, grainy tannins, moderate concentration, and a firm finish.
■ *86* *Now-2005* *Exceptional*

**1989 Bin 707** *South Australia – Cabernet Sauvignon* **S.A.**
Deep crimson. An awkward wine with contrived cherry/overripe apple aromas and pronounced American oak. The palate is much nicer, but coconutty American oak dominates. High concentration, some good fruit-sweetness, but not really a cellaring prospect. Drink up.
■ *78* *Now* *Exceptional*

**1990 Bin 707** *South Australia – Cabernet Sauvignon* **S.A.**
Deep crimson. Intense cedar/blackcurrant/black olive aromas. Evolving palate with ripe fleshy blackcurrant dark chocolate fruit and well-seasoned cedary oak, ripe fine tannins and a firm finish. Brilliantly constructed wine, built for the long term.
■-▲ *94* *Now-2012* *Exceptional*

**1991 Bin 707** *South Australia – Cabernet Sauvignon* **S.A.**
Deep crimson. Cassis/vanillin aromas with touches of marmalade and cedar. The palate is fruit-sweet with plenty of cassis/vanillin flavours, fine-grained tannins, medium to high concentration and good length. May improve further but surprisingly simple.
■-▲ *88* *Now-2015* *Exceptional*

**1992 Bin 707** *South Australia – Cabernet Sauvignon* **S.A.**
Deep crimson. Smoky coconut/vanillin oak with sweet blackcurrant pastille nuances. Earlier drinking style with some juicy blackcurrant fruit. Slightly overpowering American oak. Fine, slightly bitter tannins.
■ *83* *Now-2008* *Exceptional*

**1993 Bin 707** *South Australia – Cabernet Sauvignon* **S.A.**
Deep crimson. A very big, muscular wine with cassis/blackcurrant aromas and some menthol notes. The palate is densely packed with blackcurrant/cedar/menthol flavours, fine oily/grainy tannins and good length. A strong powerful wine. Needs time to soften out. Will almost certainly improve.
■ *89* *2005-2015* *Exceptional*

**1994 Bin 707** *South Australia – Cabernet Sauvignon* **S.A.**
Deep crimson. Meaty, gamy, blackcurrant pastille aromas with touches of menthol and underlying oak. The palate is beautifully concentrated with ripe deep-set blackcurrant/aniseed flavours and finely structured tannins. Will develop into something quite special.
■ *93* *2005-2020* *Exceptional*

**1995 Bin 707** *South Australia – Cabernet Sauvignon* **S.A.**
Not made.

**1996 Bin 707** *South Australia – Cabernet Sauvignon* **S.A.**
Deep crimson/purple. Intense blackcurrant/cedar/vanillin aromas with plenty of savoury/meaty barrel ferment oak characters. The palate is strong and powerful with dense plush blackcurrant cedar fruit, some tropical/coconut/meaty flavours, lovely loose-knit, evenly proportioned, grainy tannins and excellent length. A perfectly balanced wine with all the hallmarks of a great long-term cellaring wine.
■ *98* *2005-2020* *Exceptional*

**1997 Bin 707** *South Australia – Cabernet Sauvignon* **S.A.**
Deep crimson. Youthful blackcurrant pastille aromas with touches of roasted meat and menthol. Evolving palate with rich, ripe blackcurrant/ginger fruit, well-seasoned American oak and pronounced gritty tannins. Has plenty of guts and concentration. Needs time to settle down.
■ *91* *2005-2020* *Exceptional*

**1998 Bin 707** *South Australia – Cabernet Sauvignon* **S.A.**
Intense plum/blackcurrant aromas and meaty/gamy complexity – all underpinned by well-seasoned American oak. The palate is very deep with blackcurrant/liquorice fruit and plenty of malty/coconutty oak characters, ripe– slightly lacy – fine-grained tannins, finishing long and flavoursome. A wine with power, complexity and excellent aging

potential. A quintessential *Bin 707*, almost unblemished and too correct for its own good!
■ *96* *2008-2020* *Exceptional*
**1999 Bin 707** *South Australia – Cabernet Sauvignon* **S.A.**
Deep crimson/opaque. Intense pure cassis aromas with savoury/malt oak and roasted nut complexity. Immensely concentrated wine with cassis/chocolaty flavours and malty oak nuances, ripe well-rounded tannins and superb length. Restrained power with tremendous balance and fruit purity.
■ *94* *2006-2018* *Exceptional*
**2000 Bin 707** *South Australia – Cabernet Sauvignon* **S.A.**
Not made
**1980 Bin 80A** *Coonawarra Cabernet – Kalimna Shiraz* **S.A.**
Brick red. Intense black cherry/liquorice/aniseed aromas. Developing palate with black cherry, slightly cordial-like flavours, moderate concentration and firm finish.
■ *83* *Now – 2010*
**1982 Bin 820** *Coonawarra Cabernet* **–** *Shiraz* **S.A.**
Brick red. Generous, warm blackcurrant pastille/coffee aromas and flavours with pithy fruit and soft ripe tannins. Not worth cellaring as unlikely to improve greatly.
■ *79* *Now*
**1990 Bin 90A** *Coonawarra Cabernet – Barossa Shiraz* **S.A.**
Deep crimson. Mint/choc-berry/menthol aromas with some cedar. The palate is quite deep and concentrated with minty/blackcurrant fruit and pronounced grainy tannins. Needs time to soften out.
■ *89* *Now-2015*
**1990 Bin 920** *Coonawarra – Cabernet Shiraz* **S.A.**
Deep crimson. Plush, plummy, berry fruit with plenty of liquorice. The palate is tightly packed with plum/berry fruits, fine-grained, grippy evenly proportioned tannins, excellent concentration, and length.
■ *93* *2005-2020*
**1994 Bin 94A** *South Australia – Chardonnay* **S.A.**
Pale yellow/gold. Luscious honeydew melon/pear/marmalade/peachy aromas with some cigar-smoke/bottle-age characters. Palate is fleshy and creamy with plenty of honeydew melon fruit, savoury oak background and good length. Will age fairly rapidly. Invest only to drink.
▼ *88* *Now*
**1995 Bin 95A** *South Australia – Chardonnay* **S.A.**
Pale yellow/gold. Tight peach/apricot fruit with some melon. The palate is highly concentrated with apricot/peachy/creamy flavours but a slightly oily finish. Drink soon. Nice wine.
▼ *90* *Now* *Distinguished*
**1983 Magill Estate** *Magill – Shiraz* **S.A.**
Brick red. Leather polish/mushroom-like aromas. Beginning to dry out. The palate is soft and silken with mushroomy flavours, fine tannins, but finishes a little short.
▼ *84* *Now* *Distinguished*
**1984 Magill Estate** *Magill – Shiraz* **S.A.**
Brick red. Nutty, slightly aldehydic aromas. The palate is flat with fading fruit. Probably the worst wine Penfolds has ever made. 'Rewards of Patience' tasting was a slightly better bottle than usual, but my advice is keep well away.
❍ *70* *Now* *Distinguished*
**1985 Magill Estate** *Magill – Shiraz* **S.A.**
Deep crimson. A sweet and sour wine with earthy but overdeveloped aromas. Restrained, mean wine with little fruit. A skeleton.
▼ *72* *Now* *Distinguished*
**1986 Magill Estate** *Magill – Shiraz* **S.A.**
Deep crimson. Cedar/cassis/mushroom aromas. Smells like claret! Cedar/mushroom-like flavours, slightly bitter tannins and a firm finish. Hard to like.
■ *80* *Now* *Distinguished*
**1987 Magill Estate** *Magill – Shiraz* **S.A.**
Deep crimson. Restrained liquorice/aniseed aromas with some prune characters. The palate has some flesh, liquorice/prune-like fruit, soft, but fine tannins and a relatively firm finish.
▼ *88* *Now-2005* *Distinguished*

*▼ = Weak* *■ = Moderate* *▲ = Strong* *☆ = Rare* *❍ = not saleble*

**1988 Magill Estate** *Magill – Shiraz* **S.A.**
Deep crimson. Rich, earthy, digestive biscuit/aniseed aromas. The palate is rich with plenty of sweet developed fruit, loose-knit grainy tannins and good length. A well-balanced wine with good complexity.
▼ *92* *Now-2006* *Distinguished*

**1989 Magill Estate** *Magill – Shiraz* **S.A.**
Crimson. Vegetal spearmint aromas. The palate is restrained and mean with vegetal capsicum/green pepper flavours, hard-edged tannins and firm finish. Drinkable… but not likable!
▼ *75* *Now* *Distinguished*

**1990 Magill Estate** *Magill – Shiraz* **S.A.**
Deep crimson. Leafy liquorice-like aromas with some crab apple nuances. The palate is leafy with some cedar/liquorice and vanillin undertones, pronounced tannins and marked acidity. A skewed wine.
■ *84* *Now* *Distinguished*

**1991 Magill Estate** *Magill – Shiraz* **S.A.**
Deep crimson. Ripe, plummy, aniseed aromas with hints of cedar/spice and molasses/chocolate. Plummy, aniseed/cedar flavours, high-pixel tannins and excellent length.
■ *93* *Now-2010* *Distinguished*

**1992 Magill Estate** *Magill – Shiraz* **S.A.**
Deep crimson. Spearmint/pepper/menthol aromas with some raspberry and coffee. The palate is quite green with spearmint/pepper/menthol aromas, some underlying oak, but bitter tannins and a short finish.
▼ *77* *Now-2005* *Distinguished*

**1993 Magill Estate** *Magill – Shiraz* **S.A.**
Crimson. Interesting and complex wine with mocha/chocolate/leafy aromas. Palate is loose-knit with chocolate/mocha fruit characters, a touch of leafiness, some developed leather notes, grainy tannins and a firm finish.
▼ *89* *Now-2005* *Distinguished*

**1994 Magill Estate** *Magill – Shiraz* **S.A.**
Deep crimson/purple. Fruit-sweet nougat/chocolate/cedar-wood aromas. The palate is generously proportioned with plenty of sweet, cedary fruit characters, fine loose-knit tannins, integrated oak and some earthiness but good length of flavour.
■ *91* *Now-2010* *Distinguished*

**1995 Magill Estate** *Magill – Shiraz* **S.A.**
Deep crimson. Raspberry/furniture polish/nutty aromas reminiscent of old library books. The palate is restrained with developing raspberry/furniture polish flavours, bitter tannins and medium length. A difficult wine. Drink soon.
▼ *79* *Now* *Distinguished*

**1996 Magill Estate** *Magill – Shiraz* **S.A.**
Deep crimson/purple. Cedar/blackberry aromas with some touches of earth. Lovely bright, earthy, blackberry fruit, cedary oak, fine-grained tannins and excellent length. A well-balanced wine with both restraint and power.
■ *94* *Now-2010* *Distinguished*

**1997 Magill Estate** *Magill – Shiraz* **S.A.**
Deep crimson/purple. Liquorice/cedar/blackcurrant pastille fruit with touches of Parma violet. The palate is quite ripe, with blackberry/liquorice/smoky/spiced fruit, moderate concentration, fine tannins and good length. A short-term prospect. Yet to market.
▼ *85* *Now-2008* *Distinguished*

**1998 Magill Estate** *Magill – Shiraz* **S.A.**
Intensely perfumed wine with plenty of violets, ginger and malty oak melded into a core of black cherry fruit. The palate is richly flavoured with blackberry/black olive/plum nuances, pronounced savoury cedar oak and fine, ripe, lacy tannins. This is an astonishingly good wine.
■ *98* *2006-2018* *Distinguished*

**1999 Magill Estate** *Magill – Shiraz* **S.A.**
Deep crimson. Intense aniseed liquorice aromas with plum menthol cedar nuances. Richly concentrated palate with plum/cedar fruit and some seaweed/aniseed nuances, fine slightly grippy tannins finishing quite firm and tight. Still very elemental.
■ *87* *2005-2012* *Distinguished*

**1997 RWT** *Barossa Valley – Shiraz* **S.A.**
Deep purple/crimson. Immense blackberry/liquorice/chocolate aromas. Richly flavoured, highly concentrated wine with sweet blackberry/ginger fruit soaking up the oak completely. Gripping tannins and a firm finish. An astonishingly good wine for the vintage. As the fruit settles down, tannins may appear a little green. In the meantime, plenty of baby fat. Yet to market.
■ *95* *2005-2015*

**1998 RWT** *Barossa Valley – Shiraz* **S.A.**
Intensely ripe deep-set plum/ prune/liquorice aromas and smoked/roasted almond, savoury oak characters. The palate is rich, powerful and highly concentrated with incredibly deep, beautifully direct, ripe plum/liquorice flavours, immense but fine tannins, lovely savoury oak and superb length. A brilliant foil to *Grange*.
■ *97* *2006-2018*

**1999 RWT** *Barossa Valley – Shiraz* **S.A.**
Deep crimson. Very complex smoky bacon/chocolate/*paneforte* aromas. Deep-set palate with plenty of choc-berry/nutty flavours and smoky nuances, well-integrated new oak, fine tannins finishing long and flavoursome.
■ *92* *2005-2015*

**1955 St Henri** *South Australia – Shiraz* **S.A.**
*Brick red. A curio really, and the only bottle I know in existence. Showed mushroomy sweet fruit aromas. Unmistakably Penfolds in style. Caused a fracas in Adelaide because we believed it to be the earliest* St Henri *under Penfolds ownership. A retailer in Adelaide gazumped us by announcing he had a half bottle of 1953* St Henri. *The Adelaide press loved it, but I don't think any one else in the world cared. Langton's has sold some bottles of 1896* St Henri *– when it was under different ownership.*
☆ *No score* *Now* *Excellent*

**1958 St Henri** *South Australia – Shiraz* **S.A.**
Brick red. Over developed orange/leather aromas with just a skerrick of fruit-sweetness. The palate beginning to dry out with some soapy, developed fruit, slightly astringent tannins and acidity coming to the fore. Interesting because it exists. Rare.
☆ *80* *Now* *Excellent*

**1959 St Henri** *South Australia – Shiraz* **S.A.**
Brick red. Earthy matchstick aromas with touches of leather and iodine. Some sweet fruit is still on the palate with marmalade/meaty flavours, soft tannins and medium length. Rare.
☆ *85* *Now* *Excellent*

**1961 St Henri** *South Australia – Shiraz* **S.A.**
Brick red. Meaty, aniseed aromas with some hessian/water bag characters. Soft, fleshy palate with vegetal, meaty flavours. Gripping tannins. Good length. This bottle in excellent condition. Rare. *Another bloody good bottle with mushroom/meaty/forest floor aromas and flavours, lacy, fine tannins, and plenty of flavour length. Remarkable.*
☆ *93* *Now* *Excellent*

**1962 St Henri** *South Australia – Shiraz* **S.A.**
Brick red. Leafy, almost vegetal aromas with some liquorice nuances. Seems overdeveloped? The palate is quite aggressive and bitter with little fruit. An experience rather than a pleasure! Rare.
☆ 76 Now Excellent

**1963 St Henri** *South Australia – Shiraz* **S.A.**
Brick red. Developed, sweet, soupy, demi-glace aromas with touches of tar. The palate is meaty and fruit-sweet, but green tannins and acidity are beginning to come through. A firm finish. Hanging on by its toe-nails. *Marmalade/leathery notes, but tannins seemed softer and riper. Drink up though.*
☆ *83* *Now* *Excellent*

**1964 St Henri** *South Australia – Shiraz* **S.A.**
Brick red. Earthy fungal/mushroomy aromas. Lightly structured wine with earthy flavours, loose-knit but furry tannins, moderate concentration

and medium length. Rare. *Very truffley/mushroomy wine, but acid is poking through and tannins are fading.*
☆ 79 Now Excellent

**1965 St Henri** *South Australia – Shiraz* **S.A.**
Brick red. Nutty sweet/molasses/gamy fruit. The palate is disjointed, almost sweet and sour, with developed, nutty, orange/chocolate flavours but a pronounced acid tang. *Had it now.*
■ 77 Now Excellent

**1966 St Henri** *South Australia – Shiraz* **S.A.**
Brick red. Menthol/chocolate/raspberry aromas and a touch of sweet fruit. The palate is more interesting, with concentrated menthol/ raspberry/aniseed flavours, firm tannins and good length.
■ 83 Now Excellent

**1967 St Henri** *South Australia – Shiraz* **S.A.**
Brick red. Nutty nougat/liquorice fruit with some meaty characters. Moderately concentrated palate with some developed, meaty, gamy, fruit flavours, slightly bitter tannins but good overall length.
■ 80 Now Excellent

**1968 St Henri** *South Australia – Shiraz* **S.A.**
Brick red. Leathery, dried out aromas and flavours. Fine, gritty tannins and acidity coming to the fore. Otherwise not bad! *Smells like mothballs/napthalene. Avoid.*
■ 72 Past Excellent

**1969 St Henri** *South Australia – Shiraz* **S.A.**
Brick red. Tea leaf aromas with plenty of volatility and a tired, dried-out palate.
■ 68 Past Excellent

**1970 St Henri** *South Australia – Shiraz* **S.A.**
Brick red. Sweet coffee/chocolate-like aromas with touches of leather. The palate is loose-knit and grainy with plenty of fleshy coffee/ chocolate flavours, marvellous concentration and length. Classic Penfolds stamp.
■ 93 Now Excellent

**1971 St Henri** *South Australia – Shiraz* **S.A.**
Brick red. High-pitched and complex sweet, nutty, liquorice/aniseed aromas. The palate is rich and ripe, developed and concentrated with plenty of sweet fruit flavours matched by big tannins. Superb length. An excellent foil to 1970 and a lovely wine. *Bloody beautiful wine with smoky meaty aromas and flavours, deep-set concentrated palate and superb flavour length. Underlying, bony tannins.*
▲ 94 Now Excellent

**1972 St Henri** *South Australia – Shiraz* **S.A.**
Brick red. Light, green/herbal fruit, a little medicinal. Fruit has faded on the palate, with dried out tannins. Quite skeletal.
■ 68 Past Excellent

**1973 St Henri** *South Australia – Shiraz* **S.A.**
Brick red. Tried two bottles – both bilgy, tainted, and tired.
■ 66 Past Excellent

**1974 St Henri** *South Australia – Shiraz* **S.A.**
Brick red. Tightly knit wine with developed tar/liquorice aromas. The palate is surprisingly generous and concentrated with come sweet tar/ liquorice flavours and fine tannins.
■ 80 Now Excellent

**1975 St Henri** *South Australia – Shiraz* **S.A.**
Brick red. Earthy mushroom/sweet/meaty aromas. The palate is squashy-soft and developed with plenty of sweet, earthy fruit, soft fine tannins, lovely concentration and length.
■ 93 Now Excellent

**1976 St Henri** *South Australia – Shiraz* **S.A.**
Brick red. Deep-set and ethereal wine with mature liquorice/earthy aromas. The palate is big and highly concentrated with ripe, developed, earthy liquorice/meaty fruit, powerful tannins and a persistent finish.
▲ 94 Now Excellent

**1977 St Henri** *South Australia – Shiraz* **S.A.**
Brick red. At the brink. Very complex, nutty aromas with a faint chlorine character. The palate saves the wine with some lovely, nutty,

sweet fruit flavours, structured, slightly furry tannins, good concentration and length.

■ 85 Now Excellent

**1978 St Henri** *South Australia – Shiraz* **S.A.**
Crimson brick. Meaty, game-like fruit with complex marmalade characters. The palate has plenty of sweet fruit, meaty, gamy flavours, good concentration and firm tannins.

■ 88 Now Excellent

**1979 St Henri** *South Australia – Shiraz* **S.A.**
Crimson brick. Intense and developed, coffee/chocolate aromas with hints of cedar. Palate is warm and generous with soft, fleshy chocolate/mocha flavours, grainy tannins and excellent length of flavour.

■ 92 Now Excellent

**1980 St Henri** *South Australia – Shiraz* **S.A.**
Crimson brick. Medicinal/menthol/herbal aromas and flavours. Sweet and sour palate with astringent tannins. *Some better bottles than this with cedar nuances and fine tannins. Definitely needs drinking up.*

■ 74 Now Excellent

**1981 St Henri** *South Australia – Shiraz* **S.A.**
Crimson brick. Fresh liquorice/gamy/aniseed aromas. The palate has plenty of sweet, gamy, liquorice/consommé fruit, lovely fine-grained tannins and concentration and a firm finish.

■ 93 Now Excellent

**1982 St Henri** *South Australia – Shiraz* **S.A.**
Crimson. Contrived cherry/cassis aromas with leathery, bilgy undertones. Palate is soft and fleshy, moderately concentrated, but beginning to fall apart.

■ 79 Now Excellent

**1983 St Henri** *South Australia – Shiraz* **S.A.**
Crimson. Tight and focused liquorice/meaty/slight tarry aromas. The palate is highly concentrated with liquorice/blackberry/meaty fruit characters, fine-grained tannins and excellent length. Lovely balance of age and youth.

■ 93 Now-2008 Excellent

**1984 St Henri** *South Australia – Shiraz* **S.A.**
Crimson. Coffee/caramel/earthy aromas with underlying liquorice/meaty tones. The palate is fruit-sweet but a little flat, with earthy, leafy characters and slightly bitter tannins. Beginning to fall.

■ 80 Now Excellent

**1985 St Henri** *South Australia – Shiraz* **S.A.**
Crimson. Loose-knit raspberry/wood-bark aromas with touches of aniseed. The palate is loose-knit with fine, furry but aggressive tannins, some raspberry, earthy flavours and a medium finish. Drink up.

■ 77 Now Excellent

**1986 St Henri** *South Australia – Shiraz* **S.A.**
Crimson. Intense sweet/meaty/prune-like aromas with touches of liquorice. The palate is sweet and fleshy with meaty, gamy fruit, fine-grained tannins, vibrant acidity and good length.

▲ 90 Now-2010 Excellent

**1987 St Henri** *South Australia – Shiraz* **S.A.**
Crimson. Leather/blackberry/black olive aromas and flavours. Moderately concentrated wine with slight oily characters and hard firm tannins. One to drink soon.

■ 83 Now Excellent

**1988 St Henri** *South Australia – Shiraz* **S.A.**
Deep crimson. Pruney, blackberry, ethereal aromas with slight contrived cassis characters. The palate is soft and fleshy with blackberry fruit, fine even tannins and good length. Well-balanced wine with plenty of fruit-sweetness.

■ 92 Now-2004 Excellent

**1989 St Henri** *South Australia – Shiraz* **S.A.**
Crimson. Sweet and green-looking wine with contrived cherry, herbal, creosote/tar aromas. The palate is quite hard-edged but loose-knit with cherry/tobacco flavours and some greenness. Firm finish. Drink now because this wine is going nowhere.

■ 76 Now Excellent

**1990 St Henri** *South Australia – Shiraz* **S.A.**
Deep crimson. Complex lanolin/berry aromas with some walnut nuances. Rich, ripe palate with plenty of fruit-sweetness, slightly lanolin/tarry complexity over ripe, berry fruit, fine ripe tannins, underlying oak, and plenty of length.
▲ *88* *Now-2010* *Excellent*

**1991 St Henri** *South Australia – Shiraz* **S.A.**
Deep crimson/purple. Very alcoholic with aniseed/liquorice/pure fruit aromas. The palate is loose-knit and grainy, almost oily, with some blackberry/aniseed fruit characters, good concentration but ultimately a little cumbersome. Could improve but perhaps a little disappointing.
▲ *85* *Now-2010* *Excellent*

**1992 St Henri** *South Australia – Shiraz* **S.A.**
Deep crimson. Raspberry/earthy low intensity wine. Easy but early drinking wine with moderate concentration, tight but ripe tannins and some earthy, raspberry flavours. Drink as soon as possible.
■ *80* *Now* *Excellent*

**1993 St Henri** *South Australia – Shiraz* **S.A.**
Deep crimson. A surprise for the vintage. Very deep, brooding wine with ripe, creamy, blackberry/liquorice/minty aromas. The palate is very concentrated with plenty of fleshy fruit, a lovely firm tannin structure and weight. Medium-term prospect however, with fruit probably hiding slightly green tannins.
■ *92* *Now-2005* *Excellent*

**1994 St Henri** *South Australia – Shiraz* **S.A.**
Deep crimson/purple. Raspberry/mulberry/blackberry/aniseed aromas. Beautifully focused. The palate is ripe with sweet raspberry/mulberry fruit, marvellous concentration, but firm astringent tannins. Could age well but there is a question mark over the overt tannin structure.
■ *89* *Now-2010* *Excellent*

**1995 St Henri** *South Australia – Shiraz* **S.A.**
Crimson/purple. A very early drinking but well made wine. Blackberry/creamy aromas with minty/eucalypt nuances. Loose-knit, but lovely, creamy blackberry-nip flavours, green-edged tannins and good length.
■ *84* *Now-2005* *Excellent*

**1996 St Henri** *South Australia – Shiraz* **S.A.**
Deep crimson/purple. A rich, ripe, exotic wine with plush tropical fruit, sweet blackberry/ginger spice aromas. The palate is extremely deep-set with lovely blackberry/ginger fruit, fine, ripe tannins and superb length. A classic year for *St Henri*.
▲ *96* *Now-2012* *Excellent*

**1997 St Henri** *South Australia – Shiraz* **S.A.**
Medium crimson. Loose-knit wine with raspberry/chocolate/meaty aromas. Plenty of fruit-sweetness on the palate with raspberry/chocolate flavours and touch of maturation walnut characters. Fine slightly pronounced tannins, medium concentration, but good length.
■ *83* *Now-2008* *Excellent*

**1998 St Henri** *South Australia – Shiraz* **S.A.**
Deep crimson. Richly perfumed sweet cherry/plum/mulberry fruit with hints of mushroom and liquorice. Deep-set concentrated palate with sweet cherry/plum/ chocolate/liquorice flavours, fine ripe tannins, and plenty of length. Tremendous fruit power.
■ *98* *2004-2018* *Excellent*

**1999 St Henri** *South Australia – Shiraz* **S.A.**
Medium deep crimson. Dark cherry/plum aromas with some mocha/game complexity. Sweet fruited dark cherry plum flavours, fine sinewy/dry tannins finishing firm and tight. Still evolving.
■ *85* *2006-2016* *Excellent*

**1951 Bin 1 Grange** *South Australia – Shiraz* **S.A.**
Fading medium brick red. Skeletal wine with little flesh and fading tannins. *Very rare bottle. (These were all hand-blown.) Some look to be in excellent condition. Many were not labelled until many years later – the bottles were originally binned as it was not a commercial release. This is why bottles can be in immaculate condition. At the time they were labelled, people were already appreciating the potential collector's value of this wine.*
☆ *No score* *Now* *Exceptional*

**1952 Bin 4 Grange** *South Australia – Shiraz* **S.A.**
Fading medium brick red. More lively than 1951, but both fruit and tannins fading. *This is purely a collector's item now – the first commercial release of* Grange. *Most have lost their fruit now and are very skeletal – hardly a wine now.*
☆ *No score Now* *Exceptional*

**1953 Bin 2 Grange** *South Australia – Shiraz* **S.A.**
Brick red. Extraordinary wine with complex leathery mushroom/polish/gamy/cedar aromas, soft silky palate with mushroom/meaty/cedary flavours and fine tannins. Still holding up well with core of sweet fruit. (Also *Bins 10 & 86C*). *Some bottles are still holding up but really this is academic now. This is a collector's item now.*
☆ *No score Now* *Exceptional*

**1954 Bin 11 Grange** *South Australia – Shiraz* **S.A.**
Medium brick. Fading wine with dried out fruit, virtually no tannin and pronounced acidity. (Also *Bin 12*). Collector's item now.
☆ *No score Now* *Exceptional*

**1955 Bin 95 Grange** *South Australia – Shiraz* **S.A.**
Crimson brick. Rich, perfumed, gamy, meaty, liquorice fruit with hints of allspice. The palate is rich and supple with cedar/meaty flavours, fine-grained tannins and excellent length. The wine is still lively and fresh. (Also *Bins 13, 14, 53, 54 & 148A*). *This wine is still holding very well but quality is erratic. The best come from cool cellars.*
☆ *95 Now* *Exceptional*

**1956 Bin 14 Grange** *South Australia – Shiraz* **S.A.**
Brick red. Still amazingly youthful in colour. Intense prune/liquorice aromas with touches of *paneforte* and soy. The palate is still vital with rich prune, plum, cedar and soy flavours, plenty of concentration, lacy tannins and a long finish. Classic wine with excellent fruit-sweetness. Wine came from the drives of Penfolds at Magill. A great example of why provenance is so important when it comes to aged wine. Score is academic. *Quality is now erratic. A collector's item now.*
☆ *No score Now* *Exceptional*

**1957 Bin 50 Grange** *South Australia – Shiraz* **S.A.**
Brick red. Intense cedar/meaty/malty aromas. Very tangy bright wine with cedary, meaty flavours, fine-grained, slightly gripping tannins, with acidity just at the fore, but excellent concentration, finishing firm and tight. Another example of good provenance. There is not such a thing as a great old vintage – only great old bottles. Score is academic. (Also *Bin 113*). Quality will be very erratic. A collectors item now.
☆ *No score Now* *Exceptional*

**1958 Bin 46 Grange** *South Australia – Shiraz* **S.A.**
Brick red. Overdeveloped dilute wine with dried out palate. (Also *Bins 46, 47 & 49*). *Saw two bottles at the Sydney Clinic – both looking better than this – but at the price, would rather buy two dozen 1976* Grange. *This is now an historical curio.*
☆ *No score Now* *Exceptional*

**1959 Bin 95 Grange** *South Australia – Shiraz* **S.A.**
Brick red. Verging on over-developed with coffee/spice fruit, fine-grained tannins and some fruit-sweetness. Variable bottles. (Also *Bins 46 & 49*). *Some very good bottles still hanging around, with roasted coffee/mocha/demi glace aromas and flavours. Plenty of sweet fruit. Consider anything below very high shoulder a compounded risk.*
▲ *No score Now* *Exceptional*

**1960 Bin 95 Grange** *South Australia – Shiraz* **S.A.**
Brick red. Very developed, earthy, mushroom consommé aromas and flavours with fine tannins and good fruit-sweetness. Bottles can be variable. *This remains true. There were a few fabulous wines at the clinic with roasted coffee/mocha flavours and plenty of fruit-sweetness.*
▲ *93 Now* *Exceptional*

**1961 Bin 95 Grange** *South Australia – Shiraz* **S.A.**
Brick red. Developed mushroomy aromas and flavours, some sweet fruit and soft tannins. *Interesting to see a few bottles with 'chalky' – sometimes gritty tannins. Still plenty of fruit-sweetness. The best bottles had some liquorice/sweet coffee aromas and flavours.*
▲ *No score Now* *Exceptional*

**1962 Bin 95 Grange** *South Australia – Shiraz* **S.A.**
Brick red. Cedary, sweet fruit aromas with plenty of sweet fruit, concentration and fine-grained tannins. *This is certainly losing its fruit power now. It still has some marmalade/apricot nuances but the tannins are beginning to poke through now.*
▲ *91* *Now* *Exceptional*

**1963 Bin 95 Grange** *South Australia – Shiraz* **S.A.**
Brick red. Loose-knit but deep-set, gamy, liquorice/honey-glaze aromas. The palate is rich and ripe with plenty of sweet fruit, gamy, prune/honeyed flavours, a ripe fine tannin structure, superb concentration and length. *The story of only good bottles here. When cellared correctly this wine is still superb with all the proverbials and exclamations intact. This is the best vintage of the 1960s.*
▲ *96* *Now-2006* *Exceptional*

**1964 Bin 95 Grange** *South Australia – Shiraz* **S.A.**
Brick red. Developed, earthy prune/cedar aromas. Earthy prune flavours with sinewy tannins, but beginning to dry out. *Showing quite a lot of menthol/leathery, sometimes floral, characters now. Chalky, sinewy tannins. Some still showing enough fruit-sweetness but should be drunk up now.*
■ *82* *Now* *Exceptional*

**1965 Bin 95 Grange** *South Australia – Shiraz* **S.A.**
Brick red. Complex gamy sweet-fruited aromas. The palate is highly concentrated with developed gamy, soupy flavours, loose-knit tannins and good length. *Still holding up well with some floral meaty tones but beginning to dry out. Drink up.*
▲ *86* *Now* *Exceptional*

**1966 Bin 95 Grange** *South Australia – Shiraz* **S.A.**
Brick red. Opulent coffee/nutmeg/old, dusty-cedar aromas. The palate is more structured with coffee/nutmeg flavours, chewy, grainy tannins and lovely length. Plenty of fruit-sweetness and concentration. *This wine is still holding up pretty well. The tannins are still quite chewy, chalky, and some of the bottles have developed subtle bitumen characters. I don't think this is going to improve now. Drink up.*
▲ *93* *Now* *Exceptional*

**1967 Bin 95 Grange** *South Australia – Shiraz* **S.A.**
Brick red. Intense mushroom/meaty aromas. The palate is still fresh with plenty of sweet fruit, fine-grained tannins and good length. *Tannins are drying but still showing mushroomy characters and some cinnamon. Need to drink up.*
■ *82* *Now* *Exceptional*

**1968 Bin 95 Grange** *South Australia – Shiraz* **S.A.**
Brick red. Fading wine with leathery, *sous bois* aromas. The palate is beginning to dry out with leathery, gamy, fruit flavours, fine tannins but acid coming to the fore. *Quite perfumed wine with floral/herbal/ demi glace notes and leafy tannins. Beginning to dry up but still drinking very well. Drink soon.*
■ *87* *Now* *Exceptional*

**1969 Bin 95 Grange** *South Australia – Shiraz* **S.A.**
Brick red. Cedar/mushroomy aromas with some polished leather notes. Touch of fruit-sweetness and cedar/leathery flavours and chalky tannins, finishing dry. Fading. *This is still holding – probably better than expected. It has some floral/leather/mushroomy notes and an oomph of fruit-sweetness to keep it alive.*
■ *No score* *Now* *Exceptional*

**1970 Bin 95 Grange** *South Australia – Shiraz* **S.A.**
Brick red. Gamy, herbal, smoked-oyster aromas. The palate is loose-knit with overdeveloped smoked-oyster/liquorice flavours, fine tannins and a firm finish. Really at its peak now. *Palate seems quite chalky. Most bottles have lost a lot of fruit-sweetness now.*
■ *82* *Now* *Exceptional*

**1971 Bin 95 Grange** *South Australia – Shiraz* **S.A.**
Brick red. Surely one of the greatest wines ever made. Exotic, fragrant aromas of gardenia and apricot. Touches of blackcurrant, strawberry and raspberries. Palate is silken and viscous with apricot/meaty flavours, ripe, sweet, supple tannins, superb concentration and length. A great experience! *I suspect this wine is beginning to fade in glory now. The fragrancy is giving in to mushroomy notes. Still has excellent flavour*

*length and will certainly last well until 2010. However it is in a new phase of its life. I am sure there are some great bottles around.*

▲ 94 Now-2010 Exceptional

**1972 Bin 95 Grange** *South Australia – Shiraz* **S.A.**

Brick red. Lively, sweet raspberry/apricot marmalade/blackberry fruit. The palate is well-preserved and vibrant with concentrated, sweet honeyed/apricot fruit, fine lacy tannins and excellent length. *There are fewer exceptional bottles these days. Apricot/mushroom/demi-glace aromas and fine slinky tannins, but becoming a touch skeletal/bony. Drink up now.*

■ 82 Now Exceptional

**1973 Bin 95 Grange** *South Australia – Shiraz* **S.A.**

Brick red. Sweet chamomile/earthy/apricot/cigar-box aromas. The palate is fleshy and sweet fruited with earthy, apricot flavours, slightly bitter but evenly proportioned tannins. *Beginning to fade now. Demi-glace/brothy aromas and flavours but tannins are still lacy. Definitely past its peak now.*

■ 90 Now Exceptional

**1974 Bin 95 Grange** *South Australia – Shiraz* **S.A.**

Brick red. Intense apricot/prune/vanillin/meaty aromas – quite opulent. Fleshy and lightly structured with prune apricot fruit, fine-grained tannins and a firm finish. *Showing deeper maturation characters with sweet leathery/all-spice aromas and flavours. Still hanging in there. Drink up.*

■ 88 Now Exceptional

**1975 Bin 95 Grange** *South Australia – Shiraz* **S.A.**

Brick red. Restrained, difficult wine with sweet burnished leather/meaty/liquorice aromas. The palate is thick and brooding with deep-set, leathery, almost one-dimensional fruit, high concentration and bitter, furry tannins, finishing firm. This is the kind of wine that goes on and on forever. It's a very unyielding wine, yet could open up and surprise us. Unfortunately this is unlikely to happen. *The wine is showing some demi-glace/apricot aromas and flavours with some menthol notes. The palate is still quite chalky/furry. I just can't see this wine softening out in the way that I hoped. Still a good drink but not great* Grange.

■ 83 Now-2010 Exceptional

**1976 Bin 95 Grange** *South Australia – Shiraz* **S.A.**

Deep crimson. Liquorice, earthy, meaty aromas with a touch of bilge. A soft and supple palate with liquorice/apple-skin flavours, high concentration, fine tannins and firm finish. This is not a great bottle. 1976 is supposedly a great *Grange* vintage. Poor corks have made this wine extremely variable. Clinic-ed wine is more likely to provide drinkers with better results. *The previous score did not do this wine justice. A lot of bottles with low levels have been triaged over the years. I have seen several bottles – most looking quite spectacular with very strong liquorice/gamy/meaty aromas and flavours, marvellous concentration and slinky tannins. In recent times, this vintage seems to overshadow the slightly more famous 1971 vintage.*

▲ 94 Now-2010 Exceptional

**1977 Bin 95 Grange** *South Australia – Shiraz* **S.A.**

Deep crimson. Intense, developed, and sweet, gamy fruit with a touch of tar. A well-rounded wine with complex roasted meat/gamy/tar flavours, loose-knit tannins, good concentration, and a firm finish. *Chocolate/praline aromas. Touches of demi glace and bitumen. The best bottles have plenty of succulent fruit, underpinned by chalky tannin structures. However this vintage can be quite varied. Be careful with lower levels as this has a major impact on quality.*

■ 88 Now-2010 Exceptional

**1978 Bin 95 Grange** *South Australia – Shiraz* **S.A.**

Deep crimson. Classical cedar-wood/sweet fruit/gamy aromas. The palate has plenty of sweet, developed apricot/gamy flavours, lovely gravelly tannins, high concentration and long finish. *Some good looking bottles still coming through. Holding up better than the 1979, with excellent concentration and flavour length. The tannin structures are still sublime.*

▲ 93 Now-2015 Exceptional

**1979 Bin 95 Grange** *South Australia – Shiraz* **S.A.**
Deep crimson. Quite youthful blackberry jam/aniseed aromas with developing sweet/gamy nuances. The palate is deep-set with apricot/cedary/blackberry fruit and massive, firm tannins. Not quite top-notch. *I saw many bottles that seemed as though they were quite developed. The blackberry confit characters have all but gone – giving way to secondary apricot/slightly leathery/menthol characters. Plenty of fruit-sweetness and solid tannin structures. Finishes bitter/metallic.*
▲ 90 Now-2010 Exceptional

**1980 Bin 95 Grange** *South Australia – Shiraz* **S.A.**
Deep crimson. Liquorice/tar/treacle/chocolate aromas. The palate is generous with chocolate/dark berry fruit, pronounced, but lacy tannins and a firm finish. Not very complex but still a good drink. *Some wonderful bottles coming through, showing more complexity than a few years back. A very chocolaty, satisfying wine that could well follow the 1963 vintage. Some demi-glace nuances.*
▲ 88 Now-2010 Exceptional

**1981 Bin 95 Grange** *South Australia – Shiraz* **S.A.**
Deep crimson. Complex red earth/*sous bois* aromas with touches of VA lift. The palate is highly pixilated with marked, slightly bitter, tannins and underlying cedary tones. Interesting for *Grange*. It's quite lean in style with more emphasis on texture than fruit. *Showing more complexity now and probably deserves better points. Aromas are fragrant with some choc-berry fruit characters. The tannins are still quite strong but the palate has certainly softened/loosened. Didn't notice the VA lift so much.*
▲ 80 Now-2010 Exceptional

**1982 Bin 95 Grange** *South Australia – Shiraz* **S.A.**
Deep crimson. Christmas cake/baked plum aromas with some contrived fruit characters. The palate has plenty of sweet contrived fruit favours, marked tannins and good length but it tastes a little overdeveloped. Quite an odd *Grange. This wine is so un-*Grange *like! The wine still smells and tastes the same – like a traditional Barossa wine. C'est magnifique – mais ce n'est pas* Grange.
■ 78 Now-2006 Exceptional

**1983 Bin 95 Grange** *South Australia – Shiraz* **S.A.**
Deep crimson. Very complex and intense apricot/blackberry/exotic scented aromas with touches of aniseed/liquorice. Beautifully constructed palate with abundant apricot/meaty fruit, excellent concentration and tannin definition. Will almost certainly develop down the same path as the 1971 vintage.
▲ 95 Now-2020 Exceptional

**1984 Bin 95 Grange** *South Australia – Shiraz* **S.A.**
Deep crimson. Prune/blackberry/cherry/briary aromas. The wine is quite forward, rather than complex, with developed fleshy prune fruit balanced by gripping tannins. Firm finish. At peak, but will hold for some years. *This is still holding well. Comparatively, this is still young* Grange. *In recent times, I have really enjoyed this wine. It is less opulent and overtly structured, yet it still has plenty of generosity and fruit-sweetness. It probably deserves a better reputation. It is far superior to the 1982, and is on par with the 1985 vintage.*
■ 88 Now-2006 Exceptional

**1985 Bin 95 Grange** *South Australia – Shiraz* **S.A.**
Deep crimson. Restrained, slightly leafy nuances, with meaty, blackberry fruit. The palate is cedary with a firm backbone of tannin. A very tight wine but could come round… *Pretty well how it is still looking. Tannins have softened, but there is still plenty of fruit-sweetness.*
■ 88 Now-2012 Exceptional

**1986 Bin 95 Grange** *South Australia – Shiraz* **S.A.**
Deep crimson/purple. Quintessential *Grange*. Sweet and complex chocolate/*paneforte*/prune-like fruit with some liquorice. The palate is richly flavoured and chocolaty with huge concentration. Fine but vice like tannins, balanced by sweet *paneforte*/apricot fruit and superb length. A blossoming wine.
▲ 98 2005-2020 Exceptional

**1987 Bin 95 Grange** *South Australia – Shiraz* **S.A.**
Deep crimson. Restrained, slightly lifted, leafy, briary aromas with hints of blackcurrant and tar. The palate is compact and grainy with

briary blackcurrant fruit, loose-knit harsh tannins and a firm finish. A compressed, rather unyielding *Grange*.

■ 83 Now-2010 *Exceptional*

**1988 Bin 95 Grange** *South Australia – Shiraz* **S.A.**
Deep crimson. Lifted gamy, coconutty aromas with American oak slightly overwhelming the fruit. The palate is rich and sappy with plenty of sweet fruit and oak, fine-grained tannins and a firm finish. Still looking quite youthful and awkward.

▲ 86 Now-2012 *Exceptional*

**1989 Bin 95 Grange** *South Australia – Shiraz* **S.A.**
Deep crimson. Contrived shaded fruit/cherry/apricot aromas. The palate is sweet-fruited and highly concentrated but has a quite harsh, bitter tannin backbone. Could improve.

▲ 85 Now-2015 *Exceptional*

**1990 Bin 95 Grange** *South Australia – Shiraz* **S.A.**
Deep crimson/purple. Intensely concentrated wine with strong prune/plum/dark chocolate aromas and some liquorice. Palate is rich, ripe and chocolaty with plum/blackberry nuances, a ripe, fine tannin structure, savoury slightly coconut oak, and great length. Classic *Grange*.

▲ 100 2005-2020 *Exceptional*

**1991 Bin 95 Grange** *South Australia – Shiraz* **S.A.**
Deep crimson. Deep-set and very complex malty/meaty/choc-berry/aniseed aromas. Seductively ripe flavoursome wine with malty/meaty/choc-berry flavours, balanced by fine gravel tannins, underscored by savoury, slightly tropical oak characters. Finishes slightly gritty but with plenty of length. Still a babe.

▲ 94 2005-2012 *Exceptional*

**1992 Bin 95 Grange** *South Australia – Shiraz* **S.A.**
Deep crimson/purple. Rather simple blackberry/cherry/cedary fruit aromas and flavours. Highly concentrated with plenty of sweet fruit, sinewy tannins and a firm finish. Early drinking *Grange*.

■ 84 2005-2015 *Exceptional*

**1993 Bin 95 Grange** *South Australia – Shiraz* **S.A.**
Deep crimson/purple. Intense blackberry/meaty/gamy aromas with menthol nuances. The palate is sweet-fruited with apricot/meaty/menthol flavours, loose-knit, gravelly tannins and excellent length. Nice balance between cool and warm. Very successful wine considering the vintage.

■ 95 2005-2015 *Exceptional*

**1994 Bin 95 Grange** *South Australia – Shiraz* **S.A.**
Deep crimson/purple. Elemental, disjointed wine with lovely deep-set choc-berry/gingersnap aromas and well-seasoned American oak. The palate is strong and powerful with deep-set, concentrated, sweet ripe fruit, cedary oak and a backbone of ripe grained tannins. In evolution.

■ 90 2005-2020 *Exceptional*

**1995 Bin 95 Grange** *South Australia – Shiraz* **S.A.**
Deep crimson/purple. Crushed aniseed/ginger/blackberry/oaky aromas. The palate is rich ripe and soupy with meaty, blackberry fruit flavours, some cedary, toasty oak and loose-knit rasping tannins. This is an early drinking *Grange*, possibly in the same mould as say 1992 or 1987.

■ 85 2002-2010 *Exceptional*

**1996 Bin 95 Grange** *South Australia – Shiraz* **S.A.**
Deep crimson. Highly defined meaty/gamy/plum/prune/liquorice aromas and coffee/chocolate nuances. The palate is decadently rich. Lashings of sweet fruit, deep-set choc-plum/prune/mocha/liquorice flavours. Supple, ripe but pronounced tannins. Plenty of underlying oak, building up to a firm finish. Certainly it is in the same class as the 1990 and 1991, with a cellar life of decades.

▲ 99 2008-2025 *Exceptional*

**1997 Bin 95 Grange** *South Australia – Shiraz* **S.A.**
Deep crimson. Very aromatic, complex wine with deep-set, roasted coffee/mocha, malty, chocolaty, liquorice aromas. Opulent, deceptively approachable palate with plush, coffee, mocha, gamy, fruit, supple almost fruit drenched tannins, with plenty of malty, oak concentration and length. Finishes with a tannin slick. Americans would describe this wine as 'having a lot of baby fat'. It is a delicious wine, even when very young. However it will become more restrained in the short to medium term, gaining more complexity as it comes out of its hole.

This is not great *Grange* – rather a gracious *Grange*. Probably more medium term – but very impressive for vintage.

■ *92* *2006-2018* *Exceptional*

**1998 Bin 95 Grange** *South Australia – Shiraz* **S.A.**

Deep crimson. Ripe opulent and explosive blackberry/meaty aromas, with touches of soy/malt characters. Lashings of fruit and oak. Lavish wine with plenty of fruit-sweetness, ripe rounded tannins, plenty of blackberry/soy characters and seasoned oak. Lovely plump wine. Finishes tremendously long with a slick of tannins. This is a very elemental wine with all the hallmarks of great *Grange*. Will certainly improve. Classic wine

▲ *100* *2010-2040* *Exceptional*

## PENLEY ESTATE

**1999 Hyland** *Coonawarra – Shiraz* **S.A.**

Medium crimson. Gamy, raspberry/blackberry aromas with touches of violets. Ripe succulent palate with blackberry/violet flavours and silken tannins, good concentration and length. Fruit driven style.

■ *88* *Now-2008*

**1989** *Coonawarra – Cabernet Sauvignon* **S.A.**

Medium crimson. Showing some developed cherry stone/leafy/lanolin aromas. Restrained medium concentrated palate with some cherry stone/meaty flavours, sinewy tannins, finishing dry and chalky.

■ *83* *Now*

**1990** *Coonawarra – Cabernet Sauvignon* **S.A.**

Medium deep crimson. Sweet coffee/mocha/meaty aromas with touches of vanillin. Tangy blackcurrant/mocha flavours. Touches of leather/ spice complexity. Fine grippy/rasping tannins, finishing firm and tight. Good core of fruit-sweetness. But medium term prospect.

■ *87* *Now-2008*

**1991** *Coonawarra – Cabernet Sauvignon* **S.A.**

Medium deep crimson. Very classical and complex cassis/cedar/ biscuity aromas. Well balanced elegant wine with classic cassis/cedar flavours, with underlying vanillin oak and finely grained tannins. Finishes firm.

■ *93* *Now-2010*

**1992** *Coonawarra – Cabernet Sauvignon* **S.A.**

Medium deep crimson. Immensely complex, sweet, leather/mocha/ demi glace aromas. Well poised palate with ripe blackcurrant/mocha/ leather/demi glace characters, fine grained but firm tannins, finishing long and minerally.

■ *90* *Now-2008*

**1993** *Coonawarra – Cabernet Sauvignon* **S.A.**

Medium deep crimson. Quite developed coffee/chocolate/prune/ bramble aromas with hint of tar. Demi glace/prune flavours, fine bitter tannins, some toffee/malty oak flavours tar, finishing firm and tight but good flavour length.

■ *85* *Now-2006*

**1994** *Coonawarra – Cabernet Sauvignon* **S.A.**

Deep crimson. Blackcurrant/chocolate aromas with liquorice/earthy undertones. Dense dark chocolate/bramble/berry flavours, pronounced gravelly tannins, plenty of concentration finishing quite firm and tight.

■ *89* *2004-2012*

**1995** *Coonawarra – Cabernet Sauvignon* **S.A.**

Crimson. Blackcurrant/mulberry/cedar aromas. Restrained palate with mulberry/cedar characters. Fine-grained tannins. Light to moderate concentration. Good length. Well made wine from very ordinary vintage.

■ *84* *Now*

**1996** *Coonawarra – Cabernet Sauvignon* **S.A.**

Deep crimson. Leafy-chocolate/meaty characters and some underlying savoury/mocha Silken wine with developed meaty/chocolaty flavours, ripe velveteen tannins finishing long and sweet. Touch of earthy notes.

■ *91* *Now-2008*

**1997** *Coonawarra – Cabernet Sauvignon* **S.A.**

Deep crimson. Intense blackcurrant/leafy aromas with some dark chocolate/raisin complexity. Blackcurrant /leafy flavours with savoury meaty notes, fine gravelly slightly grippy tannins, finishing quite firm but with plenty of fruit-sweetness and flavour length.

■ *88* *2004-2010*

**1998** *Coonawarra – Cabernet Sauvignon* **S.A.**

Deep crimson. Intense chocolate/cassis aromas with lavish but well seasoned malty/tropical/savoury oak. Ripe concentrated wine with lashings of choc-berry fruit flavours and touches of meaty mocha complexity, fine ripe tannins, plenty of concentration and length.

■ *93* *2005-2018*

## PETALUMA

**1996 Tiers** *Adelaide Hills – Chardonnay* **S.A.**

Pale yellow. Lemon curd/melon/peachy aromas with some toasty oak and a touch of leesy characters. Lemon curd/melon flavours with acid tang, some savoury, slightly grainy oak. Medium concentration, but good length.

■ *87* *Now*

**1997 Tiers** *Adelaide Hills – Chardonnay* **S.A.**

Pale yellow. Peach/matchstick, slight apricot/nectarine aromas with subtle, savoury oak, touches of lemon and roasted nuts. Very complex. Sweet lanolin/matchstick flavours, with plenty of apricots and dried fruits, malty, savoury oak, nuts and excellent length.

■ *90* *Now*

**1998 Tiers** *Adelaide Hills – Chardonnay* **S.A.**

Pale yellow. Refined pear/grapefruit aromas with bran/mealy/malt/ biscuity complexity. Well balanced wine with pear/grapefruit flavours and some meal/biscuity complexity, lovely creaminess across the mid palate, finishing very long and grapefruity.

■ *95* *Now-2008*

**1999 Tiers** *Adelaide Hills – Chardonnay* **S.A.**

Pale yellow. Quite floral delicate wine with apricot/lanolin aromas and some savoury oak characters. Restrained wine with some apricot/lanolin/ pear/chalky flavours, fine indelible acidity, with good persistency.

■ *89* *Now-2006*

**1992** *Adelaide Hills – Chardonnay* **S.A.**

Pale yellow/gold. Nougat/melon/peach/vanillin aromas. Richly flavoured with fleshy melon/peach slight lanolin fruit and vanillin, lovely creaminess across the mid-palate, attractive supporting oak, fine acid cut and good length. Classical.

■ *93* *Now* *Excellent*

**1997** *Adelaide Hills – Chardonnay* **S.A.**

Pale yellow/gold. Peach/pear/honeydew melon aromas with some biscuity oak. Peach/pear/honey dew flavours balanced by savoury, biscuity oak, fine acidity and length. Lovely wine.

■ *94* *Now* *Excellent*

**1998** *Adelaide Hills – Chardonnay* **S.A.**

Pale yellow. Lifted pear drop/melon/grapefruit aromas with touches of cashew, lemons and savoury oak. Deep-set melon/grapefruit flavours with some pear drop. Very tight wine with toasty oak, creaminess and complexity. Quite firm and tight (oak).

■ *87* *Now* *Excellent*

**1999** *Adelaide Hills – Chardonnay* **S.A.**

Pale yellow. Restrained butterscotch/mineral/leafy aromas with some vanilla nuances. Well balanced wine with restrained lanolin/pear flavours, some complex butterscotch characters and pronounced acidity. Good overall length.

■ *89* *Now-2006* *Excellent*

**2000** *Adelaide Hills – Chardonnay* **S.A.**

Medium yellow. Intense peach/crunchy pear aromas with yeasty/nougat complexity and plenty of savoury malt oak. Deep-set creamy concentrated melon/peach flavours with some savoury notes, plenty of concentration and length.

■ *91* *Now-2006* *Excellent*

**1999** *Adelaide Hills – Shiraz* **S.A.**

Medium deep crimson. Complex bitumen/lanolin/blackberry/leafy aromas. Deep-set leafy/bitumen flavours with some leafy nuances, grippy dry tannins, underlying oak, finishing dry and austere.

▼ *80* *Now-2006*

**2001 Forreston** *Adelaide Hills – Viognier* **S.A.**
Pale yellow. Intense perfumed aniseed/jasmine aromas with touches of apricot. Very tight linear wine with aniseed/jasmine/floral/limey flavours, fine long bright acidity, finishing tangy and long.
▼ *85* *Now-2005*

**1980** *Clare Valley – Riesling* **S.A.**
Gold/yellow. Perfumed, sweet, lemony, lime aromas with a touch of marmalade. Sweet lime/marmalade flavours, with underlying, tangy acidity and plenty of length. Holding up very well.
■ *90* *Now* *Excellent*

**1981** *Clare Valley – Riesling* **S.A.**
Gold. Very developed brassy/tobacco aromas. Broad, brassy, tropical fruit flavours, soft mineral acidity, but really at the end of its life.
■ *79* *Now* *Excellent*

**1982** *Clare Valley – Riesling* **S.A.**
Yellow gold. Sweet honey/pear aromas with touch of crème brulée. Incredibly complex and interesting palate with concentrated sweet honeyed/walnut/pear skin/lime flavours, plenty of mineral acidity finishing quite tight firm.
■ *92* *Now-2008* *Excellent*

**1983** *Clare Valley – Riesling* **S.A.**
Yellow/gold. Honeyed, kerosene aromas. Tightly structured with honeyed, bilgy flavours, hard acidity, some fruit-sweetness and medium length. Disappointing in the context.
■ *75* *Now* *Excellent*

**1984** *Clare Valley – Riesling* **S.A.**
Pale gold/yellow. Mineral/quartz, almost Germanic, slate/citrus/floral aromas. Lovely quartz/mineral/slate fruit characters with indelible acidity and excellent length. This wine is a classic. Will age further.
■ *94* *Now-2010* *Excellent*

**1985** *Clare Valley – Riesling* **S.A.**
Yellow/gold. Extraordinarily retarded wine with lime/cumquat/lemon-zest aromas. Limey, toasty flavours, a touch of lolly, pronounced, vital acidity with plenty of length.
■ *87* *Now* *Excellent*

**1986** *Clare Valley – Riesling* **S.A.**
Yellow/gold. Aromatic pine/lemon/honeyed aromas. The palate is bright with zesty lime/lemon/honey flavours, a hint sweet, lively acidity and good length.
■ *89* *Now* *Excellent*

**1987** *Clare Valley – Riesling* **S.A.**
Yellow gold. Complex lanolin/sour milk aromas with touches of lime and almonds. Fleshy and sweet-fruited palate with lanolin/tropical fruit flavours, underlying minerality and plenty of length. Ready to drink.
■ *88* *Now* *Excellent*

**1988** *Clare Valley – Riesling* **S.A.**
Yellow/gold. Complex straw/honeyed/herbal aromas and flavours. Some sweet and bitter straw/honey/lemon flavours, slightly grippy but good length.
■ *83* *Now* *Excellent*

**1989** *Clare Valley – Riesling* **S.A.**
Yellow/gold. Developed straw aromas with slightly oily, clove-like complexity. Sweet straw/clove-like flavours, a touch bitter, with hard acidity and medium length.
■ *80* *Now* *Excellent*

**1990** *Clare Valley – Riesling* **S.A.**
Yellow/gold. Intense, direct, citrus/lemongrass aromas – touches of spice and lavender. Well-balanced wine, showing plenty of restraint, but with sweet limey fruit and fine acid cut. Finishes long. Hint of toast.
■ *92* *Now-2005* *Excellent*

**1991** *Clare Valley – Riesling* **S.A.**
Yellow/gold. Perfumed, tropical, cumquat/toasty aromas. Fresh, toasty lime flavours with pronounced acidity and plenty of length.
■ *88* *Now-2005* *Excellent*

**1992** *Clare Valley – Riesling* **S.A.**
Yellow/gold. Developed and complex limey, straw/hay/clove aromas with a touch chocolate. Sweet-fruited, but developed straw/honeyed/hay flavours, fine, tangy acidity and plenty of length.
■ 83 Now *Excellent*

**1993** *Clare Valley – Riesling* **S.A.**
Yellow/gold. Developed crème brulée/caramel/earthy aromas. Rich, fleshy, but developed palate, with crème brulée flavours, fine acidity and medium finish. Early drinking wine.
■ 81 Now *Excellent*

**1994** *Clare Valley – Riesling* **S.A.**
Pale yellow/gold. Sweet lime/passionfruit/tropical fruit aromas with some toasty bottle-age complexity. This is a very tightly focused wine with classic juicy lime/lemon, fresh toasty flavours, fine natural acidity across the mid palate with an almost endless finish. Lovely wine.
■ 96 Now-2010 *Excellent*

**1995** *Clare Valley – Riesling* **S.A.**
Yellow/gold. Honey/crème brulée/grapefruit aromas – quite Chenin Blanc like. Honeyed, tropical fruit/grapefruit flavours with mouth-watering, mineral acidity, finishing lean and dry.
■ 86 Now-2007 *Excellent*

**1996** *Clare Valley – Riesling* **S.A.**
Pale yellow/gold. Sweet straw/honey and a touch of apricot, quite lifted and attractive. Tangy honey/straw-flavoured palate with plenty of fruit richness, all balanced by pronounced acidity, medium to high-concentration with good length. Early developing wine.
■ 84 Now-2005 *Excellent*

**1997** *Clare Valley – Riesling* **S.A.**
Pale yellow/gold/green tinge. Floral, fresh, lemon/pure fruit aromas. Beautifully focused wine with hints of lime and Gewürztraminer/spice. The wine is moderately concentrated but beautifully proportioned, with pure, zesty, lime/floral fruit, rapier-like acidity and superb length. A classic. Interestingly this wine looked quite awkward at release.
■ 98 Now-2010 *Excellent*

**1998** *Clare Valley – Riesling* **S.A.**
Pale yellow. Intense lemon curd/honey aromas already showing hints of development. The palate is developing with broad lemon/honey flavours, hard acidity but good overall length. Medium term prospect.
■ 85 Now-2005 *Excellent*

**1999** *Clare Valley – Riesling* **S.A.**
Pale gold/yellow. Pure, intense apple-blossom/floral/spice aromas. Very youthful and exuberant wine with apple/pear-skin flavours, immense concentration, fine linear acidity and good length. A bolder style.
■ 95 Now-2005 *Excellent*

**2000** *Clare Valley – Riesling* **S.A.**
Pale yellow. Classical slatey/lemony aromas with touch of sweet limes. Delicate palate with slatey/lemon grass characters, lovely fruit pure sweetness and mineral/quartz like acidity. Finishes clean and long. Superb definition.
■ 96 Now-2008 *Excellent*

**2001** *Clare Valley – Riesling* **S.A.**
Pale yellow. Intense pure lime/honeysuckle aromas. Fresh lively pure lime honeysuckle flavours, plenty of fruit-sweetness balanced by cutting acidity finishing long and thirst quenching. A classic wine.
■ 98 Now-2010 *Excellent*

**2002** *Clare Valley – Riesling* **S.A.**
Pale yellow. Very fine floral citrus aromas with some honeysuckle/chamomile nuances. The palate is concentrated and refined with pear/honeysuckle/chamomile flavours and crackling acidity. Excellent flavour length.
■ 97 Now-2015 *Excellent*

**1979** *Coonawarra – Cabernet Shiraz* **S.A.**
Brick red. At its peak. Fragrant mushroom/beefstock, slight violet aromas with some cedar nuances. Lovely, mature wine with mushroom beefstock and sweet American oak flavours. Fine lacy, supple tannins. Plenty of flavour length. Superb wine… much better than the last time!
■ 94 Now *Excellent*

**1980** *Coonawarra – Cabernet Shiraz* **S.A.**
Brick red. Meaty green pepper/leathery aromas. Sweet, leathery, green pepper flavours with fine tannins, plenty of concentration and length.
■ *86* *Now* *Excellent*

**1981** *Coonawarra – Cabernet Shiraz* **S.A.**
Brick red. Intensely perfumed and meaty, chocolaty, game aromas. Rich, ripe, gamy, chocolaty flavours, gravelly tannins, richness across the mid-palate, and plenty of length.
■ *93* *Now* *Excellent*

**1982** *Coonawarra – Cabernet Shiraz* **S.A.**
Crimson. Pure cassis/cedar mint aromas and flavours. Fine rasping tannins. Good concentration and flavour length. Underpowered finish.
■ *85* *Now* *Excellent*

**1983** *Coonawarra – Cabernet Shiraz* **S.A.**
Not made.

**1984** *Coonawarra – Cabernet Merlot* **S.A.**
Faded – undrinkable.
❍ No score *Past* *Excellent*

**1985** *Coonawarra – Cabernet Merlot* **S.A.**
Faded – undrinkable.
❍ No score *Past* *Excellent*

**1986** *Coonawarra – Cabernet Merlot* **S.A.**
Crimson. Restrained blackcurrant nutty earthy aromas with some chocolate. The palate is rich and balanced with dark chocolate blackcurrant flavours, fine-grained tannins, integrated oak, good concentration and length.
■ *92* *Now* *Excellent*

**1987** *Coonawarra – Cabernet Merlot* **S.A.**
Crimson brick. Herbal/cedar/capsicum aromas with touch of cassis aromas and flavours. Tannins are quite firm and bony although still some fruit-sweetness.
■ *85* *Now* *Excellent*

**1988** *Coonawarra – Cabernet Merlot* **S.A.**
Crimson. This wine is developing well. Briary blackcurrant pastille aromas with some truffle/menthol notes. Palate is rich and flavoursome with supple blackcurrant flavours, supple/chocolaty tannins and plenty of flavour length. This wine seems to get better as the years go by.
■ *91* *Now – 2008* *Excellent*

**1990** *Coonawarra – Cabernet Merlot* **S.A.**
Purple/crimson. Chocolate/blackcurrant aromas with some leafy complexity. Richly flavoured wine with choc-berry fruit flavours and some leafy/cedar characters, slightly gritty tannins, finishing dry and firm. Atypical wine.
■ *90* *Now-2010* *Excellent*

**1991** *Coonawarra – Cabernet Merlot* **S.A.**
Crimson. Smooth blackcurrant/mocha/violet aromas. A touch of cedar. Well balanced, smooth palate with choc-berry/mocha flavours. Fine velvety, lacy tannins. Plenty of length. Lovely wine. The best Petaluma.
■ *95* *Now-2006* *Excellent*

**1992** *Coonawarra – Cabernet Merlot* **S.A.**
Crimson. Black olive/cassis aromas. Concentrated almost soupy wine with strong aggressive tannins, but plenty of black olive cassis flavours and plenty of fruit-sweetness. Finishes with a slick of tannins.
■ *84* *Now-2007* *Excellent*

**1993** *Coonawarra – Cabernet Merlot* **S.A.**
Crimson. Elegant plum/blackcurrant fruits with biscuity oak. The palate is muscular and tight with restrained fruit, hard, sinewy tannins finishing firm. Not really satisfying.
■ *82* *Now-2005* *Excellent*

**1994** *Coonawarra – Cabernet Merlot* **S.A.**
Crimson. Briary cedar/prune aromas with touches of aniseed. The palate is quite gravelly and fruit-sweet with cedar/plum/prune flavours, fine grippy tannins and finishes long.
■ *90* *Now-2007* *Excellent*

**1995** *Coonawarra – Cabernet Merlot* **S.A.**
Deep crimson. Leafy/tobacco cassis aromas with touches of meat. Loose-knit slinky palate with leafy/tobacco/berry fruit flavours, fine

lacy tannins but quite firm at the finish. A very surprising, interesting and successful wine, considering vintage.

■ *88* *Now-2006* *Excellent*

**1996** *Coonawarra – Cabernet Merlot* **S.A.**

Deep crimson/purple. Classical style with ripe, beautifully focused, cassis/cedar aromas and touches of liquorice and aniseed. The palate is deep and sweet with blackcurrant/cedar flavours, fine, sweet tannins, plenty of concentration and length.

■ *98* *Now-2010* *Excellent*

**1997** *Coonawarra – Cabernet Merlot* **S.A.**

Crimson/purple. Raspberry/plum/violet aromas. Palate is restrained with plum/cedar flavours, fine-grained, slightly grippy tannins, integrated oak, and medium length.

■ *86* *Now-2006* *Excellent*

**1998** *Coonawarra – Cabernet Merlot* **S.A.**

Deep crimson. Intense ripe mulberry/plum/liquorice aromas with some cedar/minty complexity. The palate is concentrated with mulberry/plummy flavours, gravelly tannin structures, good concentration and flavour length. Probably an atypical vintage

■ *90* *Now-2010* *Excellent*

**1999** *Coonawarra – Cabernet Merlot* **S.A.**

Deep crimson. Intense plum/liquorice/mint aromas with some cedar/toasty characters. Richly flavoured palate with plummy/liquorice cedar flavours, fine grainy/grippy tannins, plenty of concentration and length. Lovely wine.

■ *94* *2004-2012* *Excellent*

**2000** *Coonawarra – Cabernet Merlot* **S.A.**

Deep crimson. Intense blackcurrant/cedar/violet aromas balanced with savoury new oak. Blackcurrant/cedar flavours intertwined with beautifully seasoned/smoky oak, fine grainy/supple tannins, building up firm and tight. Super wine.

■ *98* *2005-2012* *Excellent*

**1990** *Coonawarra – Merlot* **S.A.**

Crimson. Pure raspberry/cedar/almond aromas with touches of wholemeal. The palate is quite elegant with restrained raspberry/cedary flavours, fine loose-knit, slightly gripping, tannins and finishing firm.

■ *87* *Now-2005*

**1991** *Coonawarra – Merlot* **S.A.**

Crimson. Raspberry/plummy/currant fruit aromas. Stewed plummy, currant flavours with fine loose-knit, gripping tannins, medium concentration and finishing firm.

■ *84* *Now-2005*

**1992** *Coonawarra – Merlot* **S.A.**

Crimson. Lifted, plummy, chocolaty, fruit with savoury, malty oak. Dry, elegant palate with prune/chocolate flavours, some fruit-sweetness but sinewy, firm tannins.

■ *84* *Now-2005*

**1993** *Coonawarra – Merlot* **S.A.**

Deep crimson. Loose-knit, leafy blackcurrant/plum aromas with touch of cedar. Very plummy, Merlot fruit flavours, with lacy tannins and cedary oak. Of medium concentration and length.

■ *89* *Now-2005*

**1994** *Coonawarra – Merlot* **S.A.**

Deep crimson. Very muscular wine with elegant almond/dark cherry aromas with touch of liquorice and varnishy oak. The palate is tight and difficult with brooding, oily and deep fruit flavours and sinewy tannins. Finishes firm and dry. Very muscle bound.

■ *75* *Now-2006*

**1995** *Coonawarra – Merlot* **S.A.**

Crimson. Pronounced cedary, sappy oak over plummy, blackcurrant fruit. Sweet vanillin/cedary oak obscures plummy fruit, but fine-grained tannins, medium concentration and length. Successful wine for a crummy vintage.

■ *86* *Now-2005*

**1996** *Coonawarra – Merlot* **S.A.**

Deep crimson/purple. Complex, but still youthful, raspberry/apricot/cedar aromas with touches of blackcurrant. Elegantly proportioned palate with succulent raspberry/apricot/cedary flavours, savoury oak and fine tannins, finishing firm. A super wine.

■ *94* *2004-2010*

**1997** *Coonawarra – Merlot* **S.A.**

Crimson purple. Odd sour plum/pear aromas. Soft squashy wine with cherry/raspberry/plum characters, grainy slightly green tannins, drying but savoury oak, finishing firm.

■ *83* *2003-2010*

**1998** *Coonawarra – Merlot* **S.A.**

Crimson purple. Deep plum/chocolate aromas with plenty of malty/vanillin oak. Very ripe and direct. Rich, ripe plum/chocolate flavours – plenty of fruit-sweetness but underscored by a mass of fine pippy tannins. Finishes bitter.

■ *85* *2003-2010*

## PETER LEHMANN

**1998 Eight Songs** *Barossa Valley – Shiraz* **S.A.**

Medium deep crimson. Intense raspberry/prune and smoked meaty/savoury aromas. Well balanced wine with blackberry fruit, smoky/savoury oak flavours, some meaty complexity, fine ripe tannins and plenty of concentration and length

■ *91* *2004-2012*

**1998 Seven Surveys** *Barossa Valley* **–** *Mourvedre Shiraz Grenache* **S.A.**

Deep crimson. Redcurrant, slight herbal aromas. Touch of game/violet. Rich, chocolaty flavoured wine with herbal minty flavours. Fine, oaky wine. Pronounced grippy, leafy tannins. Finishes firm and rasping. Bail out.

■ *83* *Now -2006*

**1999 Seven Surveys** *Barossa Valley – Grenache Shiraz Mourvedre* **S.A.**

Deep crimson. Smoky matchstick aromas, plum tomato-leaf characters touch of dark chocolate. Rich, mouth-filling, supple wine with dark chocolate briary flavours. Supple tannins, building up quite grippy, finishing with a firm tannins slick.

■ *86* *Now-2006*

**1987 Stonewell** *Barossa Valley – Shiraz* **S.A.**

Deep brick red. Fruit-sweet, gamy, liquorice/toasty-coconut aromas with touches of meatiness. The palate is hard and grainy, medium-weighted and firm, with some gamy, toasty flavours, but a little mean.

■ *79* *Now* *Excellent*

**1988 Stonewell** *Barossa Valley – Shiraz* **S.A.**

Deep crimson. Intense black fruits, nutty, meaty aromas with some vanillin. The palate is well-developed with sweet, nutty, leathery flavours and fine, drying tannins. Acidity at the fore, medium concentration and length.

■ *81* *Now* *Excellent*

**1989 Stonewell** *Barossa Valley – Shiraz* **S.A.**

Deep crimson. Cranberry, slightly jammy, meaty, nutty aromas. The palate is rich and ripe with jammy, cranberry fruit flavours, a nutty complexity, grippy, green tannins, and a firm finish. Drink now.

■ *88* *Now-2004* *Excellent*

**1990 Stonewell** *Barossa Valley – Shiraz* **S.A.**

Deep crimson. Rich, perfumed, Christmas cake/pruney fruit with plush, sweet American oak. Warm generous palate with deep-set prune/Christmas cake/chocolate flavours, fine angular tannins, superb concentration and length. A classical Barossa style.

▲ *94* *Now-2010* *Excellent*

**1991 Stonewell** *Barossa Valley – Shiraz* **S.A.**

Deep crimson. Superb wine with complex dark chocolate/mocha aromas and raspberry pastille notes. Palate is deeply set with fine, dark chocolate/blackberry/mocha fruit flavours. Plenty of savoury/malty oak. Loose-knit tannins, finishing long and flavoursome. Lovely core of fruit-sweetness.

▲ *99* *Now-2008* *Excellent*

**1992 Stonewell** *Barossa Valley – Shiraz* **S.A.**

Medium deep crimson. Very successful wine for the vintage with pronounced blackberry/gamy fruit and fresh, but harder, oak profile.

The palate is angular in structure with plenty of sweet blackberry/meaty flavours, fine gripping tannins, pronounced new oak, but immense concentration and length.
■ 93 Now-2005 *Excellent*

**1993 Stonewell** *Barossa Valley – Shiraz* **S.A.**
Deep crimson. Perfumed raspberry/black cherry aromas with touches of cassis. Perhaps a little contrived. A lighter palate with red cherry/raspberry fruit flavours. Silky, slightly gripping tannins. Oak at the fore. Medium length. Early drinking style. Reminds me of the 1982 vintage.
■ 86 Now-2005 *Excellent*

**1994 Stonewell** *Barossa Valley – Shiraz* **S.A.**
Crimson/purple. Intense wine with beautifully focused blackberry/coffee/mocha fruit and touches of grilled bacon. Immensely concentrated and well-knitted wine with plush blackberry/savoury/bacon flavours, pronounced, slightly bitter tannins, but plenty of fruit-sweetness, concentration and length. Will evolve.
■-▲ 91 Now-2010 *Excellent*

**1995 Stonewell** *Barossa Valley – Shiraz* **S.A.**
Deep crimson. Intense, chocolaty, liquorice, sweet oaky flavours with gingersnap fruit. Quite structured, with skeletal but grippy tannins, and sweet American oak. Of good concentration but a medium-term wine.
■ 85 Now-2005 *Excellent*

**1996 Stonewell** *Barossa Valley – Shiraz* **S.A.**
Crimson. Absolute classic Barossa Shiraz showing all the hallmarks of regional provenance. Intense ripe blackberry/mulberry aromas balanced by perfectly pitched, spicy, malty oak. Palate is deeply set with superb choc-berry fruit flavours. Loose-knit gravelly/chocolaty tannins, beautifully seasoned malty, spicy oak, finishing with amazing length. Brilliant!
■-▲ 99 Now-2012 *Excellent*

**1997 Stonewell** *Barossa Valley – Shiraz* **S.A.**
Medium deep crimson. Intense chocolate/rum and raisin aromas and tropical/malty oak. Rich, ripe, plump, concentrated wine with choc-berry fruit, tropical malty oak, and strong gravelly tannins. Plenty of rum/raisiny flavour length but with an alcoholic finishes. Almost essence like.
■ 88 2004-2014 *Excellent*

**1998 Stonewell** *Barossa Valley – Shiraz* **S.A.**
Deep crimson. Elemental. Rich liquorice/gingersnap aromas with volumes of fruit and oak. Beautifully made wine with huge blackberry/gingersnap flavours, soft lacy tannins, plenty of new oak, but immense fruit-sweetness and depth, finishing quite firm and flavoursome. Very interesting, dense but superbly balanced wine.
■-▲ 95 2005-2014 *Excellent*

**1990 The Mentor** *Barossa Valley – Cabernet Sauvignon Shiraz Malbec* **S.A.**
Deep crimson. Iodine/blackcurrant/brambly/cherry-stone aromas with underlying dusty oak. Surprisingly angular wine with medium to high-concentration, blackcurrant/cedar flavours, fine-grained, compact tannins and finishing firm.
▼ 85 Now-2005

**1991 The Mentor** *Barossa Valley – Cabernet Sauvignon Shiraz Malbec* **S.A.**
Deep crimson. Cassis/plum/slight vegetal aromas with hints of liquorice. Ripe, grainy palate with pleasant, plummy, liquorice fruit, underlying oak, fine tannins and good length.
▼ 88 Now-2005

**1992 The Mentor** *Barossa Valley – Cabernet Sauvignon Shiraz Malbec***S.A.**
Crimson. A distinct Cabernet with its leafy blackcurrant/cigar box aromas. Nicely structured wine with blackcurrant/cedary flavours, fine-grained, but textured tannins, underlying oak and finishing firm. Elegant, but convincing style.
▼ 90 Now-2006

**1993 The Mentor** *Barossa Valley – Cabernet Sauvignon Shiraz Malbec* **S.A.**
Crimson. Leafy, green pea aromas with touches of aniseed. Sweet and sour palate with leafy green/vegetal flavours, almost contrived characters, medium concentration, but finishing tight and grippy. Pretty ordinary.
▼ *75* *Now*

**1994 The Mentor** *Barossa Valley – Cabernet Sauvignon Shiraz Malbec* **S.A.**
Crimson/purple. Vibrant and ripe wine with intense blackcurrant aromas with toasty, vanillin oak. The palate is richly flavoured with blackcurrant/cassis/chocolaty flavours, toasty new oak, plenty of fruit-sweetness and length. Lovely wine.
▼ *94* *Now-2008*

**1996 The Mentor** *Barossa Valley – Cabernet Sauvignon Shiraz Malbec* **S.A.**
Crimson/purple. Dark chocolate/coffee/blackcurrant/smoky tropical aromas. Richly flavoured, ripe, dark chocolate/blackcurrant fruit and smoky bacon/sappy oak, fine, slightly furry tannins, but lots of flavour and length.
▼ *89* *Now-2008*

**1998 The Mentor** *Barossa Valley – Cabernet Sauvignon Shiraz Malbec* **S.A.**
Medium deep crimson. Very barrel driven wine with malty/vanilla/chocolaty/mocha aromas over rich plummy fruit. Richly flavoured wine with deep-set malty/savoury oak and smooth plummy/mocha fruit, finely netted tannins, building up firm but good flavour length.
▼ *85* *2004-2010*

## PIERRO

**1996** *Margaret River – Cabernet* **W.A.**
Medium deep crimson. Fresh well-pitched almost decadent plummy/passionfruit/redcurrant aromas. Medium concentrated squashy palate with plummy/redcurrant flavours, fine ripe tannins with good length.
▼-■ *84* *Now-2008*

**1997** *Margaret River – Cabernet* **W.A.**
Crimson. Intense and pure, blackcurrant pastille aromas with touches of spice and cedar. Sweet-fruited blackberry pastille and vanillin/cedary oak, fine-pixel, even tannins, with a long fine finish.
▼-■ *91* *2002-2010*

**1998** *Margaret River – Cabernet* **W.A.**
Crimson/purple. Sweet raspberry/cranberry/cassis fruit aromas. Lovely blackcurrant/chocolaty/plummy flavours with plenty of fruit-sweetness, fine, almost silken tannins, underlying but well-seasoned oak and a long, savoury, sweet finish. A fruit-driven wine but lovely to drink.
▼-■ *93* *2002-2010*

**1999** *Margaret River – Cabernet* **W.A.**
Medium deep crimson. Very perfumed violet/plum/damson/liquorice aromas. Elegant loose-knit fruit-sweet wine with plenty of violet/damson flavours, underlying oak, fine sinewy tannins building up firm and tight at the finish.
▼-■ *88* *2004-2012*

**1996** *Margaret River – Chardonnay* **W.A.**
Yellow/gold. A complex, worked style with cashew nut/tobacco aromas and ripe peach. The palate is very fleshy with ripe/peach/melon fruit flavours, deep-set, new oak, balanced by pronounced acid. A nice wine.
■ *90* *Now-2005* *Outstanding*

**1997** *Margaret River – Chardonnay* **W.A.**
Yellow/gold. Developed, worked wine, with all the winemaker's artifice. Peachy, melon/butterscotch/roasted nut/savoury oak aromas. Rich, creamy, concentrated wine with savoury, vanillin oak, fine, cutting acidity and marvellous length.
■ *94* *Now-2007* *Outstanding*

**1998** *Margaret River – Chardonnay* **W.A.**
Pale yellow. Complex pear/melon/peach aromas, some touches of lime. Excellent intensity. Rich, ripe, squashy wine with pear/peach/melon flavours, toasted, nutty oak, touches of lime and roasted nuts, all woven together by a fine indelible acidity. Super concentration and length.
▲ *95* *Now-2007* *Outstanding*

**1999** *Margaret River – Chardonnay* **W.A.**
Pale yellow. Intense sweet lime/apricot aromas with touches of grapefruit. Some underlying toasty oak. Well balanced palate with roasted nut/apricot/grapefruit flavours, fine acidity, toasty savoury oak, plenty of concentration and length.
▲ *94* *Now-2008* *Outstanding*

**2000** *Margaret River – Chardonnay* **W.A.**
Pale yellow. Restrained and complex tropical fruit/guava/melon aromas with some nougat/malty oak. Rich and flavoursome palate with tropical/guava flavours, underlying malty/vanillin oak, fine well-pitched acidity finishing long and creamy.
▲ *92* *Now-2006* *Outstanding*

## PIKES

**1997 Reserve** *Clare Valley – Riesling* **S.A.**
Pale yellow. Lemon-custard with slight bottle age complexity. The palate is quite austere in structure with surprisingly developed, almost oily, fruit characters. Best to drink now.
▼-■ *83* *Now-2007*

**1998 Reserve** *Clare Valley – Riesling* **S.A.**
Pale yellow. Intense sweet-fruited wine with sweet/lime cordial/honeyed aromas. Sweet-fruited honey/baked apple flavours, fine, cutting, slightly austere acidity, finishing quite lean. Sweet and sour.
▼-■ *85* *Now-2005*

**2001 Reserve** *Clare Valley – Riesling* **S.A.**
Pale yellow. Intense floral/lime/lemon aromas with touch of oil skin. Loose-knit wine with lemon/apricot flavours, dry but long acidity finishing a touch grippy and tight.
▼-■ *84* *Now-2008*

**2000** *Clare Valley – Riesling* **S.A.**
Pale yellow. Intense powder-puff/ floral/jasmine/flowery aromas with hint of anise. Lovely vibrant, racy, mouth-quenching palate with lemony fruit and penetrating, but lively acidity, plenty of depth and length. Still quite elemental.
▼-■ *94* *Now-2010*

**2001** *Clare Valley – Riesling* **S.A.**
Pale yellow. Lime, slight herb garden, aromas. Concentrated and deep lime/citrus peel flavours, strong indelible acidity, finishing very long.
▼-■ *90* *Now-2010*

**1996** *Clare Valley – Shiraz* **S.A.**
Crimson. Minty, menthol, spicy, blackberry aromas. Ripe, highly concentrated palate with gripping tannins, sweetness of fruit and a firm finish. Showing excellent regional definition.
▼-■ *88* *Now*

**1998 Reserve** *Clare Valley – Shiraz* **S.A.**
Deep crimson. Quite an oak driven style with deep-set blackberry/mulberry aromas and tropical/malty oak over tones. Quite lavish and rich on the palate with deep-set blackberry/mulberry/white pepper flavours and malty savoury biscuity oak. Tannins are velvet building up quite firm at the finish. Still quite elemental.
▼-■ *89* *2004-2012*

**2000** *Clare Valley – Shiraz* **S.A.**
Medium deep crimson. Sweet plum/floral aromas. Touches of earth and aniseed. Well concentrated wine with sweet fruit/plum/floral flavours, fine loose-knit/lacy tannins, underlying oak and plenty of length.
▼-■ *91* *2005-2014*

## PIPERS BROOK VINEYARD

**1999 Reserve** *Northern Tasmania – Pinot Noir* **Tas.**
Medium crimson. Intense herb garden/spicy/cherry aromas – touch of menthol. Medium concentrated wine with cherry stone flavours, quite grippy tannins, and medium length.
▼-■ *80* *Now*

**2000 Reserve** *Northern Tasmania – Pinot Noir* **Tas.**
Medium crimson. Smoky/malty, oak aromas, over cherry, gunflint characters. Silky textured palate with cherry, gunflint flavours.

Fine tannins, malty oak, finishing long and flavoursome. Core of fruit-sweetness.

▼-■ *85* *Now-2006*

**2000 The Lyre** *Northern Tasmania – Pinot Noir* **Tas.**

Medium crimson. Gamy/smoky/black cherry, vanillin aromas. Dark cherry/smoky/gunflint flavours. Very tangy mid-palate but firm oak hard finish.

▼-■ *83* *Now*

**1997 Northern Tasmania -***Riesling* **Tas.**

Yellow/gold. Apricot/lemon-peel aromas with touches of tobacco and herbs. Exotic, fleshy wine with dried apricots and lemon-peel flavours, a touch of herb and honey, but tangy acidity and good length. Probably best to drink now.

▼-■ *83* *Now* *Distinguished*

**1998 Northern Tasmania -***Riesling* **Tas.**

Yellow/gold. Lemon curd/lime-like aromas with strong mineral-like characters. The palate is ripe with lemon/lime fruit characters, pronounced acid, immense concentration and length of flavour.

▼-■ *90* *Now-2005* *Distinguished*

**1999 Northern Tasmania -***Riesling* **Tas.**

Pale yellow. Lime/marmalade aromas and flavours with slight herb garden nuances, fine dry acidity, good mid-palate fruit-sweetness, finishing long and flavoursome.

▼-■ *86* *Now-2006* *Distinguished*

**2001 Northern Tasmania -***Riesling* **Tas.**

Pale yellow. Aromatic and quite floral wine with pear/jasmine aromas. Delicate wine with pear/jasmine/chamomile flavours, mineral acidity and good flavour length.

▼-■ *88* *Now-2008* *Distinguished*

**2001 Estate** *Pipers Brook – Riesling* **S.A.**

Pale colour. Aromatic and delicate lemony/apple/pear/Turkish Delight aromas. Delicate but beautifully balanced wine with lemony/pear flavours, fine, long, mineral acidity, finishing with lovely pure fruit-sweet flavours. Superb wine illustrating the underlying quality of vineyard site. Hurray!

▼-■ *95* *Now-2008*

## PLANTAGENET

**1995** *Great Southern – Cabernet* **W.A.**

Crimson/purple. Bright fruit, pure blackberry, raspberry aromas, underscored by vanillin oak and coffee complexity. The palate is fruit-sweet, with velvety tannins and underlying oak. Slightly contrived.

■ *84* *Now-2008* *Distinguished*

**1996** *Great Southern – Cabernet* **W.A.**

Crimson/purple. Intense, smoky, game/bacon, spicy, vanillin aromas with touches of blackcurrant. Medium to high concentration, smoky bacon/blackcurrant flavours, smooth velvety tannins and a long finish.

■ *91* *Now-2010* *Distinguished*

**1997** *Great Southern – Cabernet* **W.A.**

Deep crimson/purple. Beetroot/meaty/dark chocolate aromas with some gamy notes. Fine, dark chocolate/meaty fruit flavours with cedary oak, supple tannins and excellent length. Excellent cellaring style.

■ *93* *Now-2010* *Distinguished*

**1994** *Great Southern – Shiraz* **W.A.**

Deep crimson. Intensely focused chocolaty/savoury/meaty/dark berry aromas. Rich, ripe generous palate with seductive sweet, choc-berry/liquorice fruit flavours, lacy ripe tannins, underlying oak and superb length of flavour.

■ *93* *Now-2006*

**1995** *Great Southern – Shiraz* **W.A.**

Crimson. Rich, ripe, earthy, raspberry-like aromas with hints of gaminess. Almost Cote Rotie-like. Palate is moderately concentrated with ripe, raspberry/meaty flavours, good overall structure and length.

■ *95* *Now-2008*

**1996** *Great Southern – Shiraz* **W.A.**
Crimson/purple. Earthy, meaty, complex aromas and some vanillin. Richly textured wine with ripe, but pronounced, tannins, gamy almost funky palate, moderate concentration and length.
■ *89* *Now-2008*

**1999** *Great Southern – Shiraz* **W.A.**
Deep crimson. Intense cracked pepper/cloves/cool climate blackberry/ menthol aromas with some oak in the background. Well balanced palate with cool, cracked pepper/blackberry flavours, and excellent mid-palate richness, supported by sweet, vanillin oak and fine grainy-slightly grippy tannin structure. Finishes long and flavoursome.
■ *89* *Now-2008*

## PORT PHILLIP ESTATE

**2000 Reserve** *Mornington Peninsula – Shiraz* **Vic.**
Deep crimson. Beautifully restrained plum/liquorice aromas with chocolate/savoury undertones. Rich, spicy wine with plum/liquorice favours, fine sinewy tannins and some savoury/nutty nuances. Finishes firm and tight.
▼-■ *85* *Now-2008*

## PRINCE ALBERT

**1998** *Geelong – Pinot Noir* **Vic.**
Medium crimson. Developed polished leather/herbal/spice/undergrowth aromas. Well-flavoured wine with sappy mushroom/leather flavours, fine tannins and underlying oak. Finishes long.
▼ *82* *Now*

**2000** *Geelong – Pinot Noir* **Vic.**
Medium crimson. Exotic apricot/orange/clove aromas and flavours with plenty of plump fruit and underlying fine sinewy tannins finishing long and sweet. At peak.
▼ *87* *Now*

## RAY-MONDE

**1999** *Sunbury – Pinot Noir* **Vic.**
Medium crimson. Menthol/cherry/vegetal aromas with some underlying smoky oak. Menthol/cherry stone flavours, prickly acid, fine tannins. Finishes hard.
▼ *80* *Now*

## REDBANK

**1990 Sally's Paddock** *Pyrenees – Cabernet Shiraz Cabernet Franc Merlot* **Vic.**
Medium crimson. Restrained earthy/violet/redcurrant/cassis aromas. Restrained earthy/redcurrant flavours, medium concentration, fine loose-knit tannins, finishing leafy and long.
▼ *90* *Now-2008* *Excellent*

**1991 Sally's Paddock** *Pyrenees – Cabernet Shiraz Cabernet Franc Merlot* **Vic.**
Medium deep crimson. Sweet menthol/eucalypt aromas with some raspberry notes. Rich musky/raspberry/menthol flavours. Fine, well resolved tannins, with long violet/musky flavours. Finishing a touch bittersweet.
▼ *84* *Now* *Excellent*

**1992 Sally's Paddock** *Pyrenees – Cabernet Shiraz Cabernet Franc Merlot* **Vic.**
Medium deep crimson. Earthy/chocolate/cedar aromas with some leafy notes. Well structured palate with earthy/chocolate/leafy flavours. Fine velveteen, slightly bitter, tannins. Some fruit-sweetness and plenty of length.
▼ *86* *Now* *Excellent*

**1993 Sally's Paddock** *Pyrenees – Cabernet Shiraz Cabernet Franc Merlot* **Vic.**
Medium deep crimson. Lovely perfumed violet/rose petal aromas with some cassis notes. Interesting wine with violet/rose petal/musky flavours, and fine leafy/drying tannins. Finishing chalky but with plenty of flavour length.
▼ *87* *Now-2008* *Excellent*

**1994 Sally's Paddock** *Pyrenees – Cabernet Shiraz Cabernet Franc Merlot* **Vic.**
Medium Crimson. Sweet juicy fruit/blueberry/cassis aromas with some vanilla nuances. Blueberry/cassis flavours with touch of meaty complexity, fine grained, slightly bitter, tannins, with medium length. Nice burst of fruit-sweetness at the end.
▼ *87* *Now-2008* *Excellent*

**1995 Sally's Paddock** *Pyrenees – Cabernet Shiraz Cabernet Franc Merlot* **Vic.**
Medium deep crimson. Sweet fruited and aromatic lanolin/chocolate/prune/earthy aromas. Plump chocolate/prune/earthy flavours, fine supple tannins, finishing long and chocolaty.
▼ *85* *Now* *Excellent*

**1996 Sally's Paddock** *Pyrenees – Cabernet Shiraz Cabernet Franc Merlot* **Vic.**
Deep crimson. Menthol/mint chocolate/almond kernel aromas. Compact palate with cassis/earthy flavours, fine grained tannins, touch of vanilla finishing long. Restrained/elegant style.
▼ *83* *Now-2006* *Excellent*

**1997 Sally's Paddock** *Pyrenees – Cabernet Shiraz Cabernet Franc Merlot* **Vic.**
Deep crimson. Intense raspberry/gamy/cedar aromas with some seaweedy/consomme. Well concentrated, complex, earthy/cassis/cedar flavours with some consomme tones, fine but long rasping tannins which carry flavour right across the palate. Elegantly structured wine.
▼ *93* *2004-2010* *Excellent*

**1998 Sally's Paddock** *Pyrenees – Cabernet Shiraz Cabernet Franc Merlot* **Vic.**
Deep crimson. Intense youthful chocolate/blackcurrant/menthol aromas with hints of cedar/spice. Youthful, blackcurrant pastille/cedar/violet flavours, fine well resolved tannins which build up firm and gravelly, lovely fruit-sweetness and flavour length.
▼ *95* *2002-2012* *Excellent*

**1999 Sally's Paddock** *Pyrenees – Cabernet Shiraz Cabernet Franc Merlot* **Vic.**
Medium deep crimson. Leafy/undergrowth redcurrant aromas with hints of violet. Deeply concentrated wine with leafy/undergrowth redcurrant flavours, grainy/grippy tannins, building up firm but with a long fruit-sweet finish.
▼ *90* *2004-2012* *Excellent*

**2000 Sally's Paddock** *Pyrenees – Cabernet Shiraz Cabernet Franc Merlot* **Vic.**
Deep crimson. Intensely perfumed cassis/spearmint/mocha aromas. Smooth palate with cassis/mocha flavours and touches of spearmint and vanilla, fine lacy tannins, excellent concentration and length. Still extremely youthful with underlying complexity.
▼ *92* *2004-2012* *Excellent*

## ROCHFORD

**1999** *Macedon – Pinot Noir* **Vic.**
Medium light crimson. Developing apricot/cherry aromas with hints of tobacco. Seems a little underpowered. Light structured tobacco/apricot flavours, and bony dry tannins finishing short. Drink up.
▼ *76* *Now*

**2000** *Macedon – Pinot Noir* **Vic.**
Medium deep crimson. Intense dark brooding wine with strawberry/herb garden/French polish aromas. Plenty of ripe strawberry/dark cherry flavours, some sweet earthy undertones and long flavoursome finish.

## ROCHROCK

▼ *90* *Now-2006*

**1988 Basket Press** *Barossa Valley – Shiraz* **Vic.**
Medium full brick red. Developed, earthy, prune/chocolate/hazelnut aromas. Silky, concentrated palate with *paneforte*/hazelnut/chocolate flavours. Integrated oak. Fine-grained, even tannins. Excellent length.
▲ *92* *Now* *Outstanding*

mouth-filling cinnamon/dark cherry flavours, jam-packed with fruit-sweetness, fine lacy sweet tannins and plenty of length. Super wine.
▲ 93 Now-2012 *Outstanding*

**1994 Basket Press** *Barossa Valley – Shiraz* **S.A.**
Crimson/purple. Complex, earthy, liquorice/nutty/menthol aromas with touches of aniseed. Prune/Christmas cake flavours with menthol/ American oak, loose-knit, but ripe, textured tannins, plenty of fruit-sweetness and length.
▲ 88 2005-2015 *Outstanding*

**1996 Basket Press** *Barossa Valley – Shiraz* **S.A.**
Deep crimson. Complex wine on the cusp of age with fading raspberry/ mulberry characters and intense coffee/nutty nuances. The palate is sweet fruited and complex with restrained raspberry/mulberry/mocha flavours, fine but firm tannins finishing quite grippy and surprisingly lean. In an evolutionary state.
▲ 88 2004-2012 *Outstanding*

**1999 Basket Press** *Barossa Valley – Shiraz* **S.A.**
Medium crimson. Intense perfumed Turkish Delight/musky/plum/ chocolate aromas. Beautifully concentrated wine with blackberry/ Turkish Delight/plummy fruit intertwined with fine soft lacy/chocolaty tannins, finishing long and fruit-sweet. An incredibly well poised wine neither showing opulence or restraint.
▲ 99 2006-2020 *Outstanding*

**1996 Ebenezer** *Barossa Valley – Shiraz* **S.A.**
Deep crimson/opaque. Classic, pure and intense blackberry aromas with mint/savoury oak. Seductive, beautifully concentrated wine. Fine, dark chocolate/blackberry flavours, balanced by lovely fine pixilated chocolaty/textured tannins, underlying savoury oak, finishing long and fruit-sweet. Beautiful wine. American oak. Deep red soil over limestone.
▲ 100 2006-2020

**1996 Flaxman Valley** *Barossa Valley – Shiraz* **S.A.**
Deep crimson. Tight black cherry/chocolate/liquorice aromas, touch of liquorice. Richly flavoured, concentrated wine with plenty of black cherry/choc-berry flavours, balanced with dense fine fruit drenched tannins, finishing firm and drying. From Merv Steiner's vineyard near Eden Valley – flinty soils. French oak.
▲ 95 2006-2018

**1996 Moorooroo** *Barossa Valley – Shiraz* **S.A.**
Deep crimson. Smells like rain on a bitumen road. Some malty/tropical oak aromas and savoury miso/demi glace characters. The palate is rich and concentrated, with restrained *confit*/tarry fruit flavours, fine structured, almost drying tannins, finishing firm and tight. Moorooroo is near Kalimna – loamy brown red soils.
▲ 93 2004-2012

**1999 Rod and Spur** *Barossa Valley – Cabernet Shiraz* **S.A.**
Crimson. Intense fruit-driven wine with musky/chocolate/red cherry/ plum aromas and flavours. Fine, soft loose-knit tannins. Plenty of length.
■ 90 Now-2008

## ROSEMOUNT ESTATE

**1997 Rosemount Roxburgh** *Hunter Valley – Chardonnay* **N.S.W.**
Medium gold. Already quite developed butterscotch/brassy aromas and some meaty complexity. Brassy/butterscotch/tobacco flavours – very fat and developed. Drink now.
▼ 76 Now

**1999 Rosemount Roxburgh** *Hunter Valley – Chardonnay* **N.S.W.**
Medium yellow. Lifted quite old fashioned style with plenty of ripe melon aromas and pronounced new vanillin oak. Some straw bale complexity. Melon/lime/ vanilla flavours, fine grainy new oak characters, good concentration and length
▼ 85 Now

**1990 Show Reserve** *McLaren Vale – Shiraz* **S.A.**
Deep crimson. Rich, pruney, polished leather/Christmas cake aromas. Sweet prune/polish-like fruit, drying tannins, but all in balance and plenty of concentration and length. A lovely wine.
▼ 93 Now-2006

**1990 Show Reserve** *McLaren Vale – Shiraz* **S.A.**
Deep crimson. Rich, pruney, polished leather/Christmas cake aromas. Sweet prune/polish-like fruit, drying tannins, but all in balance and plenty of concentration and length. A lovely wine.
▼ *93* *Now-2006*

**1991 Show Reserve** *McLaren Vale – Shiraz* **S.A.**
Deep crimson. Tight liquorice/dried fruit/chocolaty aromas. The palate is deeply-set with rich choc-prune flavours, fine tannins, pronounced acidity but good length. Really beyond its peak.
▼ *86* *Now*

**1992 Balmoral** *McLaren Vale – Shiraz* **S.A.**
Deep crimson. Perfumed and complex dark chocolate/mocha/prune aromas with touches of violets. Rich sweet-fruited palate with squashy prune/chocolaty fruit and loose-knit, gravelly tannins. Quite delicious.
■ *94* *Now-2008*

**1993 Balmoral** *McLaren Vale – Shiraz* **S.A.**
Deep crimson. Coffee/prune/capsicum/raspberry aromas. The palate is green-edged with some developing, earthy, mocha/raspberry fruit, fine grippy tannins, medium concentration and length. A difficult wine.
■ *84* *Now-2005*

**1994 Balmoral** *McLaren Vale – Shiraz* **S.A.**
Deep crimson. Deep-set choc-liquorice aromas with savoury, slightly spicy oak. Rich, ripe fruit-sweet wine with plenty of choco/mocha fruit flavours, grainy tannins,and plenty of concentration and length.
■ *90* *Now-2008*

**1995 Balmoral** *McLaren Vale – Shiraz* **S.A.**
Deep crimson. Deep-set chocolate/mocha/blackberry aromas with hint of leather complexity. Ripe, well concentrated wine with choc-berry fruit, dense gravelly tannins, balanced by some savoury/nutty oak characters. Finishes firm and fruit-sweet.
▼-■ *89* *2003-2010*

**1996 Balmoral** *McLaren Vale – Shiraz* **S.A.**
Deep crimson/purple. Lifted, elemental, seductive wine with blackberry/ginger/liquorice aromas and underlying savoury, spicy oak. Incredibly concentrated wine with monumental blackberry/liquorice fruit, underlying spicy oak and fine high-pixel tannins, finishing firm. A great vintage.
■ *95* *2002-2012*

**1997 Balmoral** *McLaren Vale – Shiraz* **S.A.**
Deep crimson. Mocha/blackberry aromas with some cedar and spice complexity. The wine has plenty of sweet choc-berry fruit, underlying new oak, gravelly, well-structured tannins. Finishes quite firm and tight.
▼-■ *89* *2004-2012*

**1998 Balmoral** *McLaren Vale – Shiraz* **S.A.**
Deep crimson. Perfumed dark cherry/blackberry aromas with plenty of vanillin/meaty nuances and touches of spice aniseed. Beautifully concentrated wine with blackberry/ meaty/cedar/spice characters intertwined with beautifully ripe lacy tannins and superb length.
■ *97* *2004-2015*

**1999 Balmoral** *McLaren Vale – Shiraz* **S.A.**
Deep crimson. Meaty/cherry/blackberry aromas. Touches of gunsmoke/ lanolin and tropical well-seasoned American oak. Richly flavoured evenly structured wine with deep-set cherry/blackberry lanolin flavours, fine grained slightly grippy tannins, finishing firm and tight.
■ *88* *2004-2012*

**1995 Mountain Blue** *Mudgee – Shiraz Cabernet* **N.S.W.**
Crimson. Plum/bitumen/liquorice aromas, already showing a degree of bottle age. The palate is tarry and complex, with slightly bitter tannins.
▼-■ *80* *Now-2005*

**1996 Mountain Blue** *Mudgee – Shiraz Cabernet* **N.S.W.**
Deep crimson/purple. Intense raspberry/blackberry fruit aromas with hints of ginger and coconut. The palate is loose-knit with rich raspberry/blackberry fruit, pronounced tannins and underlying oak.
■ *92* *Now-2008*

**1997 Mountain Blue** *Mudgee – Shiraz Cabernet* **N.S.W.**
Deep crimson/purple. Plush wine with ultra-ripe liquorice/blackberry fruit and plenty of nutmeg/spicy smoky oak characters. The palate is thick and sweet-fruited with plenty of blackberry fruit, and smoky,

sappy oak, ripe, almost granular tannins, finishing firm. The oak is incredibly strong in this wine.

▼-■ *84* *2002-2008*

**1998 Mountain Blue** *Mudgee – Shiraz Cabernet* **N.S.W.**

Deep crimson. Very appealing liquorice, blackberry aromas with soy/malty oak characters. Rich, multi-layered wine with blackberry/chocolate/liquorice flavours, savoury cedar/malt oak, fine even tannins, finishing slightly grippy but with superb flavour length.

■ *94* *2006-2014*

**1999 Mountain Blue** *Mudgee – Shiraz Cabernet* **N.S.W.**

Deep crimson. Very complex and interesting smoked meat/charcuterie/menthol aromas. Menthol smoked meat/berry flavours with some underlying oak, fine sinewy tannins building up firm and tight.

▼-■ *82* *2004-2010*

## RYMILL

**1994** *Coonawarra – Cabernet Sauvignon* **S.A.**

Medium crimson/purple. Mulberry/chocolate/cedar aromas. Mulberry/chocolate flavours with strong cedary, sappy oak, pronounced green tannins and finishing firm.

▼ *84* *Now-2008*

**1995** *Coonawarra – Cabernet Sauvignon* **S.A.**

Crimson/purple. Intense blackcurrant/cedar aromas. Richly flavoured and loose-knit palate with blackcurrant/cedar flavours, medium to high concentration, fine grippy tannins and good length.

▼ *95* *Now-2005*

**1996** *Coonawarra – Cabernet Sauvignon* **S.A.**

Crimson/purple. Ripe choc-berry/liquorice/aniseed aromas. Rich, ripe, plush choc-berry fruit but with very pronounced, almost iron-like tannins. A firm finish.

▼ *88* *Now-2010*

**1997** *Coonawarra – Cabernet Sauvignon* **S.A.**

Crimson/purple. Leafy, slightly herbal, black cherry/spicy aromas. Soupy, mouth-filling wine with complex herbal, cherry/olive flavours, pronounced, slightly green, tannins, high concentration and medium length. Acidity is slightly at the fore.

▼ *82* *2002-2008*

**1999** *Coonawarra – Cabernet Sauvignon* **S.A.**

Deep crimson. Intense cassis/plum aromas with some earthy/cedar nuances. Well concentrated palate with blackcurrant/black olive flavours, fine sinewy tannins, finishing firm and tight.

▼ *85* *2004-2010*

**2000** *Coonawarra – Cabernet Sauvignon* **S.A.**

Medium deep crimson. Intense cassis/blackcurrant aromas with some leafy/seaweed nuances. Palate is well concentrated with cassis/blackcurrant/plum flavours and some cedar complexity, fine grained tannins and good flavour length.

▼ *88* *2004-2010*

**1994** *Coonawarra – Shiraz* **S.A.**

Deep crimson. Plum/apple-like fruit with touches of leaf. The palate is lean-fruited and slightly leathery with some underlying oak, fine-grained tannins and excellent length.

▼ *79* *Now-2005*

**1995** *Coonawarra – Shiraz* **S.A.**

Deep crimson. Leathery, gamy aromas with some touches of tar. The palate is lean and sinewy with gamy, leathery flavours but overall, quite closed and unyielding.

▼ *76* *Now*

**1996** *Coonawarra – Shiraz* **S.A.**

Deep crimson. Complex peppery, gamy, plum/aniseed aromas. Sweet, peppery, gamy fruit flavours but a gritty tannin structure, medium concentration and length.

▼ *80* *Now-2008*

**1997** *Coonawarra – Shiraz* **S.A.**

Deep crimson. Direct mulberry/blackberry fruit with touches of nectarine and pepper. The palate is soft and squashy with blackberry/mulberry/menthol flavours and fine-grained tannins.

▼ *85* *Now-2008*

**1998** *Coonawarra – Shiraz* **S.A.**
Deep crimson. Intense smoked meaty earthy/blackberry aromas. Beautifully constructed palate with ripe blackberry/mocha/earthy flavours, fine slinky/lacy tannins finishing long and cedary.
▼ *93* *Now-2008*

**1999** *Coonawarra – Shiraz* **S.A.**
Deep crimson. Lovely smoky/blackberry aromas with some mocha/ savoury nuances. Dense rich smoky blackberry/mocha flavours, plenty of underlying savoury oak, fine grippy/rasping tannins but good flavour length.
▼ *90* *2004-2010*

**2000** *Coonawarra – Shiraz* **S.A.**
Medium deep crimson. Highly strung, blackberry/red peppery aromas with touches of raspberry and cinnamon. Tightly knit wine with peppery blackberry/gamy flavours, and some spicy notes. Fine tannins, building up slightly chalky but excellent flavour length.
▼ *85* *Now-2008*

## SALTRAM

**1994 No. 1** *Barossa Valley – Shiraz* **S.A.**
Crimson. Cedary, chocolate aromas with some meaty, aniseed characters. Highly concentrated wine with chocolate/cedar flavours and touches of tar, pronounced new oak, and slightly unyielding tannins. A complex wine.
▼ *85* *Now-2008*

**1995 No. 1** *Barossa Valley – Shiraz* **S.A.**
Crimson. Sweet, plummy fruit with toasty, smoky bacon oak. The palate is strongly flavoured with smoky bacon oak but very sweet, solid, fruit underneath, ripe tannins and excellent length. Very well made wine, but a medium cellaring prospect.
▼ *91* *Now-2006*

**1996 No 1** *Barossa Valley – Shiraz* **S.A.**
Crimson. Intense smoky/meaty/blackberry aromas with plenty of complexity. The palate is highly concentrated with plenty of ripe mulberry/liquorice/aniseed flavours, meaty/oaky nuances, ripe dense tannin structure, finishing with a lick of drying tannins but plenty of flavour length.
■ *92* *Now-2008*

**1997 No. 1** *Barossa Valley – Shiraz* **S.A.**
Deep crimson/purple. Sweet, savoury, plummy aromas with plush American oak. The palate is ripe and sweet, with deep-set blackberry fruit and well-seasoned American oak, ripe tannins and plenty of length. Slightly 'painting-by-numbers'.
▼ *90* *2005-2015*

**1998 No 1** *Barossa Valley – Shiraz* **S.A.**
Crimson black. Leafy/dark chocolate/liquorice aromas with plenty of malty oak. Rich, thick, almost soupy wine with dark chocolate/ blackberry flavours, fine drying tannins, malty oak finishing quite chalky and firm. Still quite elemental.
■ *87* *2004-2012*

## SEPPELT

**1991 Dorrien** *Barossa Valley – Cabernet Sauvignon* **S.A.**
Deep crimson. Meaty, briary, chocolate with touches of primary blackcurrant and cedary oak. The palate is supple and well-balanced with classic blackcurrant/briar/cedar flavours, integrated oak, fine-grained, rounded tannins, superb depth and length.
■ *95* *Now-2020* *Distinguished*

**1992 Dorrien** *Barossa Valley – Cabernet Sauvignon* **S.A.**
Deep crimson. Deep, brooding wine with restrained blackberry/briar aromas and sumpy, deep-set new oak. The palate is soupy and thick with briary, prune-like fruit flavours, pronounced oak, gravelly tannins, plenty of concentration and flavour. Contrived, corporate looking wine.
■ *88* *Now-2008* *Distinguished*

**1993 Dorrien** *Barossa Valley – Cabernet Sauvignon* **S.A.**
Crimson. Plush dark chocolate/coconut/all-spice aromas. Dense, sweet-fruited wine with plush chocolate/prune flavours, pronounced American oak, ripe tannins, plenty of concentration and length.
▼-■ *91* *Now-2003* *Distinguished*

**1994 Dorrien** *Barossa Valley – Cabernet Sauvignon* **S.A.**
Black/purple. Intense liquorice/cedar fruit with plum/berry characters. Quite Merlot-like. Sweet liquorice/plummy fruit, lacy tannins, lovely concentration and length. A super wine.
■ *96* *2005-2020* *Distinguished*

**1996 Dorrien** *Barossa Valley – Cabernet Sauvignon* **S.A.**
Deep crimson. Intense, generous dark chocolate/violet aromas with some oak nuances. Immensely rich, concentrated wine with dark chocolate/berry flavours, strong fine grainy/pixilated tannins, plenty of concentration but very firm tannin finish. Very big wine.
■ *85* *2005-2015* *Distinguished*

**1997 Dorrien** *Barossa Valley – Cabernet Sauvignon* **S.A.**
Deep crimson. Cassis/mocha/liquorice aromas and flavours with strong malty oak nuances, plenty of concentration, ripe tannins, finishing firm and quite dry. Very well balanced wine with plenty of power. One of the twilight vintages, as this wine is to be discontinued… sadly
▼-■ *91* *2005-2016* *Distinguished*

**1991 Great Western Vineyard** *Grampians – Shiraz* **Vic.**
Deep crimson. Intense and developed chocolate/blackberry fruit with touches of liquorice/cumquat sweetness. Ripe concentrated wine with choc-berry, slight tarry/leathery fruit flavours, sinewy tannins and underlying savoury oak. Finishes firm and long.
■ *90* *Now-2008* *Distinguished*

**1993 Great Western Vineyard** *Grampians – Shiraz* **Vic.**
Crimson/purple. Prune/liquorice/menthol aromas. The palate is very cool-flavoured and quite hard with prune/Christmas cake/plummy fruit characters and aggressive/planky tannins. It has good concentration, but is like unravelled knitting!
▼-■ *81* *Now-2006* *Distinguished*

**1995 Great Western Vineyard** *Grampians – Shiraz* **Vic.**
Deep crimson. Menthol/choc-berry/plum aromas and flavours with lacy but hard, green edged, tannins – tapering off to a dry austere finish. Fruit is dipping out.
▼-■ *84* *2002-2008* *Distinguished*

**1996 Great Western Vineyard** *Grampians – Shiraz* **Vic.**
Crimson/purple. Intense, youthful, blackberry/pure fine chocolate flavours, savoury, malty American oak and plenty of meaty complexity. Palate is complex too, with rich, ripe deep-set chocolaty, blackberry fruit, balanced by well-seasoned new oak, and an even, velvety, plush tannin structure and superb length. A brilliant young wine.
■ *97* *2005-2020* *Distinguished*

**1998 St Peters Vineyard Great Western** *Grampians – Shiraz* **Vic.**
Deep crimson. Intense, pure, blackberry/aniseed aromas with underlying savoury chocolaty nuances. Richly flavoured wine, with choc-blackberry/aniseed flavours, pronounced gravelly tannins, underlying new oak, excellent concentration and length. Plenty of fruit-sweetness. Needs a little time to soften out.
■ *92* *2004-2012* *Distinguished*

**1878 -1903 Centenary Para Liqueur** *Barossa Valley* **S.A.**
*In 1878, Benno Seppelt laid down a puncheon of his finest wine – with instructions that it was not to be bottled and released for 100 years. Each year, Seppelt has carried on this tradition. Unlike many 100 year-old wines, these tawny port-style Para Liqueurs are fabulous curios and still drinking beautifully. They are palate-clinging wines with rancio leather/spice/raisined/prune/chocolate aromas and flavours. Some have a slight burnt orange/toffee complexity. Don't try to spit these wines out – as I tried – they are so unctuous and thick, it will dribble down your chin! These Paras will outlast us all. Drink them whenever.*

**1878 Centenary Para Liqueur** *Barossa Valley – Tawny* **S.A.**
Deep burnt umber colour. Very concentrated coffee/treacle aromas some bitter chocolate. Richly concentrated wine with burnt coffee

flavours. Very bitter, slightly earthy finish, but balanced by plenty of sweet fruit and flavour length.

■ *93* *Now – Keep*

**1879 Centenary Para Liqueur** *Barossa Valley – Tawny* **S.A.**
Deep burnt umber. Intense prune/dried apricot aromas with some liquorice nuances. Rich apricot/prune flavours and fine high tensile acidity and alcohol cut. Burnt, sinewy finish.

■ *94* *Now – Keep*

**1880 Centenary Para Liqueur** *Barossa Valley – Tawny* **S.A.**
Deep opaque colour. Intense black liquorice/roasted coffee/mocha aromas, with some leafy nuances. Well concentrated wine with smooth dark chocolate flavours and fine tannins, lovely rich viscosity, fine acidity, finishing with a lick of liquorice burnt chocolate.

■ *96* *Now – Keep*

**1881 Centenary Para Liqueur** *Barossa Valley – Tawny* **S.A.**
Lighter almost pale in this company. Medium tawny/red gold. Deep-set prune/dried apricot aromas with some rancio characters. A lighter skimpier wine – in this context! – with coffee/mocha flavours and some bittersweet characters. Good flavour length.

■ *87* *Now – Keep*

**1882 Centenary Para Liqueur** *Barossa Valley – Tawny* **S.A.**
Deep-set opaque black/red gold colour. Roasted coffee/charcoal/bitter chocolate aromas. Thick unctuous wine – almost the same as the 1884 – rich bitter chocolate/orange rind flavours, marked acidity and alcohol. Extraordinary curio.

■ *97* *Now – Keep*

**1883 Centenary Para Liqueur** *Barossa Valley – Tawny* **S.A.**
Deep-set brown/opaque colour with liquorice ground coffee aromas and touches of aniseed. Richly flavoured wine with ground coffee/mocha flavours, plenty of concentration, finishing long and sweet. Lovely wine.

■ *94* *Now – Keep*

**1884 Centenary Para Liqueur** *Barossa Valley – Tawny* **S.A.**
Thick solid/sumpy wine. Van Dyke brown/opaque black. Almost syrupy burnt coffee/molasses/dried apricot aromas with some liquorice characters. The thickest of all the *Paras* – so thick a spoon would stand up in it. Rich unctuous and decadent treacle/molasses flavours finishing with a bittersweet end. Remarkable.

■ *100* *Now – Keep*

**1885 Centenary Para Liqueur** *Barossa Valley – Tawny* **S.A.**
Not as viscous/oily as previous two vintages. Deep burnt umber/brown colour. Intense aniseed/molasses/bittersweet chocolate characters. Roasted coffee/prune chocolate with searing – almost crescendoing alcohol. Aniseed nuances. Bittersweet sinewy end.

■ *89* *Now – Keep*

**1886 Centenary Para Liqueur** *Barossa Valley – Tawny* **S.A.**
Deep Van Dyke brown/red gold. Burnt coffee aromas with some toffee/aniseed and dark chocolate nuances. Immensely concentrated treacle – like wine with burnt coffee/dark chocolate/molasses flavours, fine velveteen tannins, finishing dry and bittersweet.

■ *97* *Now – Keep*

**1887 Centenary Para Liqueur** *Barossa Valley – Tawny* **S.A.**
Van Dyke brown/molasses colour. Perfumed/lifted violet/aniseed/liquorice/prune/Christmas cake aromas Very thick almost solid wine. Viscous/oily but supple wine with aniseed/prune/chocolate flavours, slinky tannins with pronounced alcohol cut. Builds up quite firm and tight but excellent flavour length.

■ *93* *Now – Keep*

**1888 Centenary Para Liqueur** *Barossa Valley – Tawny* **S.A.**
Van Dyke brown/liquorice colour. Intense molasses/chocolate aromas with some aniseed/leafy nuances. Rich thick, unctuous wine with liquorice/molasses flavours. Acidity pokes through but plenty of depth and flavour length.

■ *91* *Now – Keep*

**1889 Centenary Para Liqueur** *Barossa Valley – Tawny* **S.A.**
Deep burnt umber. Intense savoury/nutty/liquorice/aniseed aromas. Alcohol very much to the fore. Quite alcoholic on the palate with deep-

set aniseed/liquorice/bittersweet chocolate/rancio/orange rind flavours, chocolaty tannins, finishing bitter but long.

■ *88* *Now – Keep*

**1890 Centenary Para Liqueur** *Barossa Valley – Tawny* **S.A.**
Deep umber colour. Liquorice/molasses/chocolaty aromas with some VA/aniseed. Richly flavoured high pitched wine with choc-liquorice flavours and some burnt bittersweet nuances. Not overtly powerful but excellent flavour length.

■ *93* *Now – Keep*

**1891 Centenary Para Liqueur** *Barossa Valley – Tawny* **S.A.**
Medium burnt umber colour. Rich and very concentrated chocolate/ molasses aromas. Deeply set wine with, viscous chocolate/coffee/ molasses flavours and some liquorice. Finishes long and velvety.

■ *91* *Now – Keep*

**1892 Centenary Para Liqueur** *Barossa Valley – Tawny* **S.A.**
Deep black/orange/umber colour. Orange rind/molasses/sweet fruit aromas with some aniseed. Bittersweet flavours. Quite sinewy in this company but enveloped in rich molasses fruit. Finishes drying but has good flavour length.

■ *87* *Now – Keep*

**1893 Centenary Para Liqueur** *Barossa Valley – Tawny* **S.A.**
Deep liquorice/red gold. Rich chocolate/treacle aromas with plenty of liquorice nuances. Rich chocolate/brown treacle/burnt sugar flavours and pronounced alcohol kick. Finishes long.

■ *92* *Now – Keep*

**1894 Centenary Para Liqueur** *Barossa Valley – Tawny* **S.A.**
Almost opaque/black liquorice colour. Intense and lifted liquorice/ aniseed/molasses aromas. Very classical for *Centenary*. Immensely concentrated wine with deep-set chocolate/burnt coffee flavours, long acidity and excellent alcohol cut. Finishes long and bittersweet. Superb!

■ *100* *Now – Keep*

**1895 Centenary Para Liqueur** *Barossa Valley – Tawny* **S.A.**
Deep umber. Intense molasses/dark chocolate aromas with some leafy/undergrowth/aniseed complexity. Richly flavoured wine with molasses/dark chocolate flavours and supple tannins. Builds up quite bittersweet and touch grippy, but excellent flavour length.

■ *91* *Now – Keep*

**1896 Centenary Para Liqueur** *Barossa Valley – Tawny* **S.A.**
Deep umber. Rich aromas of prune/Christmas cake and some molasses. Very sweet. Plenty of liquorice and VA lift. Highly concentrated bittersweet style, with prune/Christmas cake flavours, fine drying palate finishing savoury and bitter/sweet.

■ *90* *Now – Keep*

**1897 Centenary Para Liqueur** *Barossa Valley – Tawny* **S.A.**
Burnt umber/ red gold tinges. Perfumed violet/coffee/leafy/aniseed and liquorice aromas. Quite restrained in this company. Sweet coffee/ liquorice flavours, supple sweet flavours, builds up massively sweet and tangy at the finish. Excellent wine

■ *95* *Now – Keep*

**1898 Centenary Para Liqueur** *Barossa Valley – Tawny* **S.A.**
Deep Van Dyke brown, liquorice colour. Very intense and rich rancio/ chocolate/aniseed aromas. Quite an ethereal kick. Opulent and densely flavoured wine with deep layered rancio/chocolate flavours, and plenty of liquorice/aniseed complexity. Alcohol pulls flavours through the palate. This is an incredibly thick palate clinging wine with superb flavour length.

■ *98* *Now – Keep*

**1899 Centenary Para Liqueur** *Barossa Valley – Tawny* **S.A.**
Burnt umber colour. Perfumed and sweet prune/rum/burnt coffee aromas. Restrained bittersweet coffee flavours, fine slinky tannins, finishing quite savoury and bitter/charry. Not overtly concentrated in this context.

■ *89* *Now – Keep*

**1900 Centenary Para Liqueur** *Barossa Valley – Tawny* **S.A.**
Deep chocolate colour. Rancio/brassy aromas with some molasses/ burnt coffee. Richly flavoured and viscous with opulent rancio/burnt

coffee flavours, supple rich palate and plenty of flavour length. Bittersweet finish.

■ *95* *Now – Keep*

**1901 Centenary Para Liqueur** *Barossa Valley – Tawny* **S.A.**
Medium deep colour. Quite perfumed and elegant with charcoal/coffee aromas and some aniseed notes. Quite tight on the palate with acid poking through, but plenty of crème-brûlée flavours and alcoholic kick. Finishes long and savoury sweet.

■ *93* *Now – Keep*

**1902 Centenary Para Liqueur** *Barossa Valley – Tawny* **S.A.**
Burnt umber colour. Deep burnt chocolate/coffee aromas with some liquorice notes. Very concentrated wine with deep burnt coffee/ chocolate flavours, supple rich mid-palate with burnt chocolate finish. Excellent flavour length.

■ *89* *Now – Keep*

**1903 Centenary Para Liqueur** *Barossa Valley – Tawny* **S.A.**
Aromatic dried apricot/slightly floral aromas with some prune/ liquorice/dark chocolate. Rich smooth wine with chocolate/coffee flavours – some orange rind characters, finishes long and bittersweet.

■ *91* *Now – Keep*

## SEVILLE ESTATE

**1996** *Yarra Valley – Shiraz* **Vic.**
Crimson. Intense cracked pepper, Rhone-like/earthy aromas with an underlying purity of fruit. Restrained palate with moderate concentration, fine tannins and good length. Lighter style with moderate cellaring potential.

▼ *89* *Now*

**1997** *Yarra Valley – Shiraz* **Vic.**
Deep crimson. Developing mocha/brambly aromas. Dark cherry/ walnut/mocha flavours, fine firm tannin structures but plenty of concentration and length.

▼ *93* *Now-2008*

**2000** *Yarra Valley – Shiraz* **Vic.**
Deep crimson. Intense dark cherry/liquorice aromas with some savoury/malt oak characters and meaty nuances. Richly flavoured palate with dark cherry/liquorice fruit, plenty of fruit-sweetness, but sinewy long tannins building up firm. Good flavour length.

▼ *90* *2003-2008*

**1999** *Yarra Valley – Pinot Noir* **Vic.**
Medium light crimson. Brothy, slightly dilute strawberry/plum aromas with touches of spearmint. Lightly structured wine with some sweet cherry flavours and fine sinewy tannins.

▼ *78* *Now*

**2000** *Yarra Valley – Pinot Noir* **Vic.**
Medium crimson. Excellent complex strawberry/cherry/meaty/malt aromas. The palate is richly flavoured with strawberry/ red cherry flavours, plenty of gamy/malty complexity, silky tannins and length.

▼ *94* *Now-2006*

## ST HALLETT

**1990 Old Block** *Barossa Valley – Shiraz* **S.A.**
Deep crimson. Sweet, smoky, coconutty, tropical fruit with raspberry/ blackberry fruit and hints of leather. Ripely textured wine with sweet black cherry/currant/pure fruit flavours, underlying smoky, coconutty oak, lovely lacy tannins and excellent length. A super wine.

▲ *95* *Now-2010* *Excellent*

**1994 Old Block** *Barossa Valley – Shiraz* **S.A.**
Deep crimson/purple. Quite closed raspberry/earthy aromas with touches of tomato leaf. Richly flavoured wine with raspberry/earthy flavours, sinewy, gravelly tannins, underlying oak and plenty of length. Still in evolution.

■ *89* *2002-2012* *Excellent*

**1995 Old Block** *Barossa Valley – Shiraz* **S.A.**
Crimson. Quite restrained earthy, raspberry, chocolaty aromas. The palate is medium-bodied with earth/raspberry fruit and pronounced

oak. The tannins are a little bitter but sweet fruit obscures blemishes. Early drinking wine.

▼ *82* *Now-2005* *Excellent*

**1996 Old Block** *Barossa Valley – Shiraz* **S.A.**

Deep crimson/purple. Raspberry/liquorice/prune aromas with integrated oak. Rich and sweet-fruited wine with raspberry/liquorice/ meaty flavours, savoury oak and firm tannins. Will improve.

■ *89* *2004-2010* *Excellent*

**1997 Old Block** *Barossa Valley – Shiraz* **S.A.**

Deep crimson. A lighter, more refined style with classic mocha/prune aromas and meaty/smoky/flinty nuances. The palate is medium concentrated with restrained coffee/mocha fruit and complex meaty/smoky/bacon characters. Finishes long and sweet. Excellent wine for vintage.

▼ *91* *Now-2006* *Excellent*

**1998 Old Block** *Barossa Valley – Shiraz* **S.A.**

Deep crimson. Lifted tropical, smoked meaty/soupy wine. Plush wine with plenty of mulberry/meaty flavours and lashing of tropical/malt/ vanillin oak, ripe gravelly tannins, plenty of concentration, finishing savoury and long.

■ *89* *2004-2015* *Excellent*

**1999 Old Block** *Barossa Valley – Shiraz* **S.A.**

Deep crimson. Smoky charcoal/gamy blackberry aromas with some vanilla/malt nuances. Deep-set wine with mulberry/blackberry fruit and smoky/charcoal flavours, fine long -sinewy tannins, plenty of concentration and fruit-sweetness, building up firm.

■ *91* *2005-2016* *Excellent*

**2000 Old Block** *Barossa Valley – Shiraz* **S.A.**

Deep crimson. Profound rhubarb/prune/apricot with malt aromas. Sweet fruited palate with rhubarb/prune/apricot flavours, and deep-set malty/savoury oak. Ripe loose-knit tannins and plenty of length. Very attractive wine.

■ *93* *2005-2014* *Excellent*

## STONIER'S WINERY

**1998 Reserve** *Mornington Peninsula – Chardonnay* **Vic.**

Pale yellow. Ripe peach/pear aromas with touches of leesy, malty oak and nuts. Very nice. Worked style with plenty of leesy complexity, nutty, butterscotch flavours, with underlying pear fruit, a pronounced acid cut and a slightly malty finish. Quite a contrived style of wine ready for drinking.

■ *86* *Now*

**1999 Reserve** *Mornington Peninsula – Chardonnay* **Vic.**

Pale colour. White peach/lanolin/cheesy aromas with some nutty – almost amontillado – complexity. Well balanced wine with tropical/melon/cashew nut/lanolin complexity, fine long acidity finishing with plenty of length and fruit-sweetness.

■ *89* *Now-2004*

**2000 Reserve** *Mornington Peninsula – Chardonnay* **Vic.**

Pale colour. Sea breezy/lanolin/cashew nut/sweet melon aromas. Complex lanolin /cashew nut/melon flavours, lovely underlying savoury oak. Indelible acidity across the back palate but excellent concentration and length. Quite classical wine.

■ *93* *Now-2004*

**1997 Reserve** *Mornington Peninsula – Pinot Noir* **Vic.**

Medium crimson. Concentrated wine with deep-set, plum/strawberry flavours and underlying savoury oak. Richly flavoured with lovely plum/strawberry fruit flavours. Slightly gripping tannins. Firm finish.

■ *90* *Now*

**1998 Reserve** *Mornington Peninsula – Pinot Noir* **Vic.**

Medium crimson. Immensely concentrated, but beautifully balanced, with cherry stone/strawberry aromas and touches of liquorice. Deep-set strawberry/aniseed/liquorice flavours, savoury, malty oak, and a fine tannin grip. Finishes long. A very convincing wine. Yet to market.

■ *94* *Now-2004*

**1999 Reserve** *Mornington Peninsula – Pinot Noir* **Vic.**
Medium crimson. Weak fruited walnut/cherry/spice aromas with some leafy/perfumed characters. Palate is quite fleshy and supple with fine sweet tannins and moderate length.
■ *85* *Now-2005*

**2000 Reserve** *Mornington Peninsula – Pinot Noir* **Vic.**
Medium crimson. Intense floral/dark cherry/mint aromas with touches of plum/violet and some underlying oak. Slippery wine palate with cherry/plum flavours, savoury/vanillin oak, fine chewy tannins finishing long and sweet. Nice complex wine
■ *93* *Now-2005*

## TAHBILK

**1991 1860s Vines** *Nagambie Lakes – Shiraz* **Vic.**
Brick red. Complex meaty, gamy, prune aromas with touches of cedar and leather. Sweet-fruited, gamy palate with cedary, earthy nuances, lacy tannins and lovely length.
■ *94* *Now* *Outstanding*

**1992 1860s Vines** *Nagambie Lakes – Shiraz* **Vic.**
Medium crimson. Complex and developed gamy/beetroot/white pepper/sea breezy aromas. Quite tightly knit wine with gamy/beetroot/raspberry flavours, but almost impenetrable hard tack tannins on the middle palate. Plenty of meaty complexity.
■ *82* *Now-2010* *Outstanding*

**1994 1860s Vines** *Nagambie Lakes – Shiraz* **Vic.**
Medium crimson. Perfumed but very loose-knit raspberry/meaty/tomato leaf aromas and hints of mint/pepper. Raspberry/tomato leaf flavours on the palate with touches of pepper and spice, fine gravelly tannins building up to a firm but flavoursome finish.
■ *86* *2006-2014* *Outstanding*

**1995 1860s Vines** *Nagambie Lakes – Shiraz* **Vic.**
Medium crimson. Complex maturation style wine with sweet earthy/leafy/raspberry meaty aromas. Medium concentrated wine with leafy/raspberry fruit flavours. Fine, sinewy almost rasping tannins. Finishing firm and tight.
■ *83* *2005-2014* *Outstanding*

**1996 1860s Vines** *Nagambie Lakes – Shiraz* **Vic.**
Medium crimson. Complex cherry stone/raspberry/earthy aromas with some aniseed/chocolate. Medium concentrated but well balanced wine. Black cherry raspberry fruit flavours and some earthy/leather complexity. Very fine, long, slightly sinewy tannins. Finishing firm but with plenty of flavour length. A restrained style.
■ *89* *2004-2014* *Outstanding*

**1997 1860s Vines** *Nagambie Lakes – Shiraz* **Vic.**
Medium crimson. Intense black cherry/raspberry aromas with some leathery/aniseed nuances. Dark cherry/raspberry meaty flavours and loose-knit but gripping tannins. Plenty of sweet fruit of the front palate but finishes chalky firm dry.
■ *83* *2004-2010* *Outstanding*

**1998 1860s Vines** *Nagambie Lakes – Shiraz* **Vic.**
Medium deep crimson. Very elemental oak dominant tropical/malty aromas over mulberry/raspberry fruit. A little under-fruit-powered. Strong tropical/malty almost oily oak, some mulberry fruit, firm gripping tannins but plenty of length. Needs time to settle.
■ *85* *2006-2014* *Outstanding*

**1999 1860s Vines** *Nagambie Lakes – Shiraz* **Vic.**
Medium crimson. Beautifully perfumed, seductive rhubarb/mulberry/apricot aromas with touches of liquorice. Richly flavoured, seductive and squashy mulberry/rhubarb/apricot flavours. Long, fine, lacy, velveteen tannins, with plenty of length. Beautifully made wine.
■ *95* *2006-2020* *Outstanding*

**1994 1933 Vines** *Nagambie Lakes – Shiraz* **Vic.**
Medium crimson. Developed and perfumed plum apricot aromas with *sous bois*/ cedary complexity. Immensely complex and interesting wine with deep-set plummy apricot flavours, touches of raspberry and some earthy cedary undertones, fine sinewy tannins, building up firm and

tight. This wine is totally powered by fruit and maturation complexity. Absolutely wonderful wine showing power and restraint.

■ *100* *2006-2020*

**1996 1933 Vines** *Nagambie Lakes – Shiraz* **Vic.**
Medium crimson. Very complex mulberry/lanolin aromas with touches of plums and menthol. Complex developed mulberry/lanolin flavours and fine long sinewy tannins. Plenty of length and fruit-sweetness.

■ *90* *2006-2014*

**1997 1933 Vines** *Nagambie Lakes – Shiraz* **Vic.**
Medium crimson. Lifted complex raspberry/dark cherry aromas with malty meaty complexity. Ripe raspberry/dark cherry flavours, fine loose-knit grainy tannins, underlying oak finishing quite firm and tight.

■ *86* *2004-2014*

**1998 1933 Vines** *Nagambie Lakes – Shiraz* **Vic.**
Medium crimson. Perfumed plum/sweet fruit aromas with some cedar/spice nuances. Plum/redcurrant flavours with fine ripe tannins, building up firm and tight. Core of fruit-sweetness runs right through the wine. Excellent wine.

■ *93* *2005-2018*

**1999 1933 Vines** *Ngambie Lakes – Shiraz* **Vic.**
Deep crimson. Seductive and intense rhubarb plum/mulberry aromas with sweet liquorice nuances. Sweet fruited, seductive plum/raspberry, almost pear infused flavours. Fine but grippy tannins, finishing long and sweet. Needs time to meld, but very well balanced wine. The *Reserve Shiraz* is picked from Tahbilk's McLaughlin's Block which was planted in 1933. Fermented in century-old vats, followed by maturation in French oak for 19 months.

■ *92* *2006-2018*

**1991 Reserve** *Nagambie Lakes – Cabernet Sauvignon* **Vic.**
Medium deep crimson. Intense earthy/seaweed/iodine/black olive aromas with some raspberry/sweet plum undertones. Medium concentrated wine with developed earthy/seaweedy/blackcurrant fruit flavours, fine sinewy tannins, finishing quite firm/chalky. Elegant style.

■ *83* *Now*

**1992 Reserve** *Nagambie Lakes – Cabernet Sauvignon* **Vic.**
Medium crimson. Sweet cassis/plum/violet aromas with some malty savoury notes. Developed, earthy/cassis/liquorice flavours, with hazelnut/leather. Fine, gripping but long tannins. Finishing quite firm. Maturation style.

■ *84* *Now-2010*

**1993 Reserve** *Nagambie Lakes – Cabernet Sauvignon* **Vic.**
Medium crimson. Intense raspberry/plum fruit with touches of milk chocolate/malt. Raspberry/plum flavours with nutty complexity, fine grained but grippy tannins, finishing firm and tight.

■ *82* *Now-2010*

**1994 Reserve** *Nagambie Lakes – Cabernet Sauvignon* **Vic.**
Medium crimson. Developed complex perfumed cassis/raspberry aromas with some leafy apricot undertones. Cassis/mocha flavours with plenty of leafy complexity, fine grained tannins finishing quite grippy and tight.

■ *88* *Now-2010*

**1996 Reserve** *Nagambie Lakes – Cabernet Sauvignon* **Vic.**
Medium deep crimson. High pitched dark cherry/chocolate aromas with roasted coffee nuances. Dark cherry/cassis/chocolate flavours, ripe grainy tannins, medium concentration but good length.

■ *83* *Now-2010*

**1997 Reserve** *Nagambie Lakes – Cabernet Sauvignon* **Vic.**
Medium deep crimson. Intense choc-blackcurrant aromas with touches of cedar and spice. Choc-blackcurrant flavours with some brambly edges, fine pronounced grippy tannins, finishing long and flavoursome. Still quite youthful – will soften out.

■ *86* *2004-2012*

**1998 Reserve** *Nagambie Lakes – Cabernet Sauvignon* **Vic.**
Deep crimson. Chocolate/bramble/aniseed/minty/cassis aromas. Rich chocolate/mint/slight rum and raisin flavours, some savoury oak, and very lacy but almost bitter tannins.

■ *87* *2004-2012*

## TAHBILK

**1999 Reserve** *Nagambie Lakes – Cabernet Sauvignon* **Vic.**
Deep crimson. Beautifully perfumed dark cherry/apricot/minty/aniseed aromas. Complex wine with lovely dark cherry/apricot/almond flavours, fine slightly grippy tannins, but plenty of fruit flesh and length. Delicious wine.
■ *94* *2006-2014*

## TALTARNI

**1991** *Pyrenees – Cabernet Sauvignon* **Vic.**
Dark cherry/crimson. Earthy, peaty, chocolate/mocha aromas. Earthy, chocolate/cedary flavours, lovely concentration and mid-palate richness. Fine, even tannins and excellent length. At its peak.
▼ *94* *Now-2015* *Distinguished*

**1995** *Pyrenees – Cabernet Sauvignon* **Vic.**
Crimson/purple. Smoky, black olive, slight iodine-like aromas with touches of chocolate and coffee. Sweet, smoky, blackcurrant fruit, textured, almost gravelly, tannin structure, and high concentration, finishing firm. A restrained style.
▼ *88* *Now-2010* *Distinguished*

**1996** *Pyrenees – Cabernet Sauvignon* **Vic.**
Crimson/purple. Earthy, leather/black cherry fruit aromas with underlying subtle oak. The palate is restrained with leathery, black cherry fruits, grainy, slightly furry, tannins, but good fruit-sweetness. Ends with oily oak and a firm finish.
▼ *84* *Now-2010* *Distinguished*

**1998** *Pyrenees – Cabernet Sauvignon* **Vic.**
Medium deep crimson. Under-powered cassis/vanillin/mineral/leafy aromas. Restrained cassis/plum/vanilla/leafy flavours, medium concentration, fine grainy tannins and long finish.
▼ *84* *Now-2008* *Distinguished*

**1996** *Pyrenees – Shiraz* **Vic.**
Deep crimson/purple. Raspberry/blackberry/pepper-like fruit with lovely intensity. The palate is moderately concentrated with raspberry/peppery flavours, ripe, but fine tannins and good overall length. Excellent balance.
▼ *90* *Now-2005*

**1997** *Pyrenees – Shiraz* **Vic.**
Deep crimson. Tightly focused mulberry/blackberry/earthy fruit with some tropical/coconut characters. The palate is of medium concentration, with plenty of seductive, fleshy, mulberry/blackberry fruit, soft, ripe tannins and excellent length. Medium term.
▼ *91* *Now-2005*

**1998** *Pyrenees – Shiraz* **Vic.**
Medium crimson. Raspberry/matchstick aromas with touch of black pepper. Lightly structured wine with raspberry/matchstick flavours, fine netted tannins, slightly strong acidity, finishing quite firm.
▼ *79* *Now-2004*

**1999** *Pyrenees – Shiraz* **Vic.**
Medium crimson. Intense raspberry/lanolin/bitumen aromas. Elegant flavoured wine with raspberry/lanolin/cherry characters, chalky tannins but with a core of fruit-sweetness.
▼ *80* *Now-2006*

## TARRAWARRA

**1998** *Yarra Valley – Chardonnay* **Vic.**
Pale yellow. Intense grapefruit/melon/peach aromas. Lovely integrated, savoury oak and smoky nuances. Elegant and supple palate with melon/peach/grapefruit flavours, grainy tannins, savoury, malty oak, fine acid cut with plenty of concentration and life. Long finish. A nice wine.
▼ *95* *Now*

**2000** *Yarra Valley – Pinot Noir* **Vic.**
Medium crimson. Bright red cherry, plum, gamy aromas. Touches of ginger and savoury oak. Squashy, red cherry, plum flavours on the palate, underpinned by savoury oak, very fine tannins. Finishing dry and long.
▼ *87* *Now-2005*

## TATACHILLA

**1997 Foundation** *McLaren Vale – Shiraz* **S.A.**
Deep crimson. Barrel dominant wine with coconut/vanillin oak over some blackberry raspberry fruit. Ripe sweet fruit flavours and fine grained drying tannins. Over worked wine.
▼ *80* *2004-2012*

## TAYLORS

**1996 St Andrews** *Clare Valley – Riesling* **S.A.**
Pale yellow. Lime/mineral aromas with some biscuity/lanolin complexity. Tightly packed wine with lime/lemon flavours, fine indelible acidity, plenty of fruit-sweetness, tart but attenuated acidity, giving superb length of flavour. Very nice wine.
▼ *93* *Now-2008*

**1998 St Andrews** *Clare Valley – Shiraz* **S.A.**
Deep crimson. Deep-set blackberry/mulberry/liquorice aromas with touches of dark chocolate. The palate is deep and concentrated with blackberry/liquorice/mocha flavours, underlying oak, ripe well-textured tannins with plenty of length.
▼ *95* *2004-2010*

## T'GALLANT

**1994 Tribute** *Mornington Peninsula – Pinot Gris* **Vic.**
Pale yellow. Developed, sweet, apricot/floral aromas. Sweet, fleshy, apricot/floral flavours, with touches of spice, medium acidity and length. Beginning to broaden out.
▼ *85* *Now*

**1995 Tribute** *Mornington Peninsula – Pinot Gris* **Vic.**
Yellow/gold. Musky, violet/stone-fruit aromas showing some development. Sweet, fleshy, musk/apricot flavours, plenty of viscosity and fruit-sweetness, good concentration and length. Drink now.
▼ *84* *Now*

**1998 Tribute** *Mornington Peninsula – Pinot Gris* **Vic.**
Pale yellow. Intense ginger/spice/apricot aromas with touches of violet. Fresh violet/jasmine/apricot/Gewürztraminer flavours with fine acidity, plenty of concentration and length.
▼ *90* *Now*

**1999 Tribute** *Mornington Peninsula – Pinot Gris* **Vic.**
Pale yellow. Developed marmalade/peach/pear aromas. Musky/ marmalade/chalky flavours, some lanolin nuances, pronounced acidity and medium length. Showing some age now.
▼ *86* *Now*

**2000 Tribute** *Mornington Peninsula – Pinot Gris* **Vic.**
Pale yellow. Refined crunchy pear/apple/jasmine and some sea breezy notes. Spicy/ pear flavours with some chalky notes, mineral acidity finishing tangy and long.
▼ *90* *Now*

**1997** *Mornington Peninsula – Pinot Gris* **Vic.**
Pale yellow. Beautifully refined and scented ripe pear/floral/jasmine/ apricot Chinese gooseberry aromas. Well balanced wine with musky/ apricot/Chinese gooseberry flavours, fine minerally acidity, plenty of fruit-sweetness and length.
▼ *92* *Now*

## THREE RIVERS

**1991** *Barossa Valley – Shiraz* **S.A.**
Medium deep crimson. Dark cherry/juicy raspberry/lanolin/menthol aromas with some smoky oak characters. Beautifully balanced and mature wine with dark cherry/plum/raspberry flavours and plenty of smoked meaty complexity, lacy tannins, some menthol and savoury oak nuances, finishing slinky and long. Complete and ready to drink.
■ *97* *Now-2008*

**1992** *Barossa Valley – Shiraz* **S.A.**
Medium deep crimson. Very savoury gunpowder/smoky aromas intertwined with dark plum prune aromas and some malt oak. Well structured palate with dark plum/prune flavours and smoky undertones,

chalky but even tannins, finishing sinewy but with plenty of smoky briary flavours. Superb wine.

■ *94* *2004-2012*

**1993** *Barossa Valley – Shiraz* **S.A.**

Medium deep crimson. Chocolaty/mocha/malty aromas with touches of toffee and stubbier *confit*. Malty/toffee oak characters dominate with some chocolate/mocha flavours, fine gravelly tannin structures, finishing firm and tight, but with long vanilla/smoky black strap liquorice flavours.

■ *88* *Now-2008*

**1994** *Barossa Valley – Shiraz* **S.A.**

Medium deep crimson. Menthol/blackberry pastille aromas with some savoury/truffley/undergrowth notes. Well structured palate with menthol/blackberry pastille flavours, and deep-set menthol/savoury/tropical oak characters, sinewy tannins building up quite chalky but with excellent flavour length. Acidity pokes out slightly.

■ *92* *2004-2012*

**1995** *Barossa Valley – Shiraz* **S.A.**

Deep crimson. Plush developed wine with mulberry/apricot fruit with touches of sandalwood/cedar/smoky. Taut liquorice/mulberry/dark cherry fruit flavours with underlying chalky/velvet tannins and some menthol/vanilla/smoky oak. Finishes chocolaty with medium length.

■ *90* *Now-2010*

**1996** *Barossa Valley – Shiraz* **S.A.**

Deep crimson. Intense dark chocolate/prune/blackberry pastille/mulberry/menthol aromas with smoky bacon/malty oak and some aniseed tones. Tightly packed but richly flavoured wine with deep-set chocolate/blackberry fruit flavours and plenty of liquorice/aniseed nuances. Fine grained/granular tannins, underlying malty/menthol oak, finishing chalky firm but with long mulberry smoky flavours.

■ *95* *2006-2015*

**1995 RANDALL'S HILL** (second label of Three Rivers)
*Barossa Valley – Shiraz* **S.A.**

Deep crimson. Complex lanolin/liquorice/mulberry aromas with some choc-berry/bitumen characters. Loose-knit palate with liquorice/mulberry/dark cherry flavours and some menthol nuances, slinky tannins, savoury/cedar oak, finishing quite elegant and sinewy, but runnel of fruit-sweetness. Elegant style.

■ *91* *Now-2010*

## TIM ADAMS

**1994 Aberfeldy** *Clare Valley – Shiraz* **S.A.**

Deep crimson. Intense blackberry/raspberry/gamy aromas and underlying cedar oak characters. The palate has plenty of concentration and blackberry/raspberry/aniseed fruit flavours, all underpinned by cedary oak and dry chalky tannins. Finishes quite grippy and tight. A little unyielding.

■ *88* *2005-2012*

**1996 Aberfeldy** *Clare Valley – Shiraz* **S.A.**

Crimson/purple. Ripe fruit overlain with vanillin/liquorice/aniseed aromas. American oak at the fore. The palate is extremely complex with deep-set, spicy, blackberry-like flavours, classy oak, textured tannins and high concentration.

■ *93* *Now-2008*

**1997 Aberfeldy** *Clare Valley – Shiraz* **S.A.**

Medium crimson. Intense oak driven wine with sweet savoury/coconut/malty/soy/rum and raisin aromas. Richly flavoured wine with plenty of savoury/malty oak characters, over sweet, juicy fruit, velveteen tannins. Finishing firm and tight.

▼-■ *85* *2004-2012*

**1998 Aberfeldy** *Clare Valley – Shiraz* **S.A.**

Deep crimson. Intense choc-berry/liquorice aromas with touches of cedar. Richly flavoured choc-berry fruit with cedary vanillin oak, supple but strong tannins, plenty of concentration and length. Needs more time to develop but well balanced.

■ *89* *2005-2012*

**1999 Aberfeldy** *Clare Valley – Shiraz* **S.A.**
Medium deep crimson. Intense choc-berry aromas with plenty of savoury oak. Beautifully structured palate with deep-set choc-berry fruit flavours and malty oak characters. The tannins are soft and round but finish firm. Superb concentration and length.
■ *94* *2005-2018*

**2000** *Clare Valley – Cabernet Sauvignon* **S.A.**
Medium deep crimson. Restrained violet/blackcurrant pastille aromas with some aniseed notes. Compact palate with violet/blackcurrant pastille flavours, fine long sinewy tannins and underlying oak. Finishes firm and tight.
■ *91* *2004-2012*

**1992** *Clare Valley – Riesling* **S.A.**
Yellow gold. Fresh lemon/grapefruit//lanolin aromas. The palate is lively and well-balanced with lemon/grapefruit/wet stone/slatey flavours, fine quartz acidity building up firm and tight.
▼ *86* *Now-2006*

**1998** *Clare Valley – Riesling* **S.A.**
Pale yellow. Restrained mineral/quartz-like fruit. Slightly earthy, lime-like fruit flavours, marked acidity but balanced by fruit-sweetness. Could develop.
▼ *80* *Now-2005*

**1999** *Clare Valley – Riesling* **S.A.**
Pale yellow. Developed apricot/pear/oil-skin aromas. Sweet, developed palate with apricot slight earthy flavours, fine acidity and slight mushroomy finish.
▼ *77* *Now-2006*

**2000** *Clare Valley – Riesling* **S.A.**
Pale yellow. Lemon curd/slatey/mineral aromas. Palate is medium concentrated, almost lean, with lemon curd/slatey flavours that taper off towards the middle palate, leaving a dry austere finish. Could be worth cellaring for a few years.
▼ *83* *Now-2006*

**2001** *Clare Valley – Riesling* **S.A.**
Pale yellow. Lime marmalade/biscuity aromas. A quite lean, almost austere, palate with lime/lemony flavours and steely acidity.
▼ *86* *Now-2008*

**1996** *Clare Valley – Shiraz* **S.A.**
Crimson/purple. Intense menthol/eucalypt/coffee-like aromas. Tightly-knit palate with blackberry/menthol-like flavours, pronounced tannins and high concentration. Firm finish. Will improve.
▼ *84* *Now*

**1997** *Clare Valley – Shiraz* **S.A.**
Medium crimson. Complex raspberry/seabreezy/lanolin aromas. Leafy/briary raspberry lanolin flavours with core of fruit-sweetness, fine gripping tannins, finishing very firm and tight.
▼ *83* *Now-2008*

**1998** *Clare Valley – Shiraz* **S.A.**
Medium deep crimson. Intense sweet briary/menthol/minty aromas. Restrained leafy wine with briary/menthol flavours, sinewy tannins finishing firm and tight.
▼ *83* *Now-2008*

**1998** *Clare Valley – Shiraz* **S.A.**
Medium deep crimson. Intense sweet briary/menthol/minty aromas. Restrained leafy wine with briary/menthol flavours, sinewy tannins finishing firm and tight.
▼ *83* *Now-2008*

**1999** *Clare Valley – Shiraz* **S.A.**
Medium deep crimson. Perfumed, almost delicate, violet/aniseed/ cranberry aromas. Almost Cabernet profile with violet/iodine/seaweedy flavours and some liquorice, hard sinewy tannins, finishing firm and minty. Quite tough.
▼ *80* *Now-2008*

**2000** *Clare Valley – Shiraz* **S.A.**
Medium deep crimson. Menthol/dark chocolate aromas with leafy characters. Full flavoured wine with deep-set dark chocolate/briary/

menthol fruit, gravelly tannins, some savoury oak, finishing firm but with good flavour length.
▼ *87* *2004-2010*

## TIM KNAPPSTEIN

**1986** *Clare Valley – Riesling* **S.A.**
Yellow gold. Intense almost hot lime/honey/almond aromas. The palate is very complex with plenty of honey/biscuit/nutty flavours, fine bright acidity, and good length. Touch oily.
▼ *84* *Now-2006*

**1992** *Clare Valley – Riesling* **S.A.**
Yellow/gold. Fresh wine with vibrant lemon curd/macadamia nut-like aromas. Earthy, honeyed wine, slightly flat, a bit of marmalade, slight orange-peel/cheese characters, but soft, zingy acidity, and a fine finish.
▼ *89* *Now*

## TORBRECK

**1999 Descendant** *Barossa Valley – Shiraz Viognier* **S.A.**
Deep crimson. Aromatic wine with aniseed/plum/apricot/gardenia aromas. The palate is well structured with superb plum/apricot flavours, fine sinewy tannins, lovely concentration, finishing with plenty of aniseed/liquorice flavours.
■ *94* *2003-2010*

**2000 Descendant** *Barossa Valley – Shiraz Viognier* **S.A.**
Deep crimson. Beautiful and surprising wine with ripe mulberry/prune/apricot aromas with oak in the background. Superbly balanced wine with exotic mulberry/musky/apricot flavours, fine ripe slinky tannins and underlying oak. Finishes long and fruit-sweet. A wine that resonates in flavour.
■ *96* *2002-2008*

**1998 Run Rig** *Barossa Valley – Shiraz* **S.A.**
Deep crimson. Powerful ripe/blackberry/plum aromas with touches of liquorice and underlying malt oak characters. Richly flavoured deep-set palate with blackberry plum fruit flavours, slightly loose-knit, fine gravelly tannins, supported by malty oak characters.
■ *92* *2006-2015*

**1999 Run Rig** *Barossa Valley – Shiraz* **S.A.**
Deep crimson colour. Intense pure red cherry/raspberry/mulberry aromas with some malt characters. Highly concentrated mulberry/apricot flavours melded with savoury/malty oak, fine ripe loose-knit tannins, finishing firm with plenty of flavour length. Lovely wine.
■ *93* *2006-2018*

**1999 The Factor** *Barossa Valley – Shiraz Viognier* **S.A.**
Deep crimson. Highly pitched mulberrry/plum, perfumed violet aromas. Rich ripe mulberry/plum/dark chocolate flavours, fine tight slightly gravel tannins, finishing long. Needs time to evolve.
■ *89* *2005-2015*

**1999 The Steading** *Barossa Valley – Grenache Mourvedre Shiraz***S.A.**
Medium deep crimson. Intense chocolate/almond kernel aromas – some leafy complexity. Quite tough palate with chocolaty/leafy/herbal/raisiny palate, pronounced tannins, finishing firm and bitter.
▼ *77* *Now*

**2000 The Steading** *Barossa Valley – Grenache Mourvedre Shiraz***S.A.**
Medium deep crimson. Ethereal raspberry/lavender/chamomile aromas with touches of ginger. Rich, succulent wine with squashy raspberry/mulberry flavours and some musky/gamy notes, fine supple tannins with excellent flavour length. Finishes slightly firm.
▼ *89* *Now-2006*

**2001 Barossa Valley –** *Marsanne Viognier Rousanne* **S.A.**
Pale yellow. Floral aniseed/jasmine/peach aromas with some apricot nuances. Sweet fruited wine with peach/aniseed/jasmine/almond flavours, plenty of fruit-sweetness balanced by linear acidity. Finishes long and flavoursome. Previous vintage fell apart very quickly.
▼ *87* *Now*

## TREVOR JONES

**1998 Dry Grown** *Barossa Valley – Shiraz* **S.A.**
Crimson. Fruit intense wine with plenty of fruit-sweet liquorice/blackberry aromas and underlying oak. The palate is tightly structured with tangy mulberry/liquorice flavours, grainy tannins, malty/sappy oak and plenty of flavour length.
▼ *86* *2004-2010*

## TURKEY FLAT

**1999 Butcher's Block**
*Barossa Valley – Mourvedre Shiraz Grenache* **S.A.**
Medium deep crimson. Prune/leathery/mocha aromas. Rich leathery/roasted coffee flavours, with underlying walnutty flavours, pronounced drying almost furry tannins, finishing firm, but good flavour length.
▼ *80* *Now-2006*

**2000 Butcher's Block**
*Barossa Valley – Mourvedre Shiraz Grenache* **S.A.**
Medium deep crimson. Redcurrant/plum, slightly herbal, aromas. Soft plump wine with redcurrant/plum/pear flavours, fine ripe chocolaty tannins, plenty of concentration and length.
▼ *88* *Now-2005*

**1993** *Barossa Valley – Shiraz* **S.A.**
Crimson. Intense oak driven wine with strong mulberry/spicy/liquorice/incense aromas Good intensity. Well balanced wine with liquorice/mulberry flavours, slightly hard tannins, and underlying cedary, grainy oak. Finishes tight.
▼ *84* *Now-2008*

**1998** *Barossa Valley – Shiraz* **S.A.**
Deep crimson. Meaty/blackberry/chocolate fruit. The palate is well concentrated with plenty of chocolaty complexity, loose-knit/lacy tannin structure and excellent flavour length. Not mad about the aromas but could develop into a swan.
▼-■ *82* *2004-2008*

**1999** *Barossa Valley – Shiraz* **S.A.**
Deep crimson. Lead pencil/savoury/malty oak over cedar/blackberry/aniseed fruit. Interesting complex wine with blackberry/meaty/gamy fruit, pencil/malty oak, fine even tannins and good length.
▼-■ *88* *2004-2010*

## TWO HANDS

**2001 Brave Faces** *McLaren Vale – Shiraz Grenache* **S.A.**
Deep crimson. Exuberant/exotic spicy/mulberry musky/turkish delight aromas. Rich mulberry musky/turkish delight flavours, fine fruit drenched tannins, with savoury oak in background, finishes firm but plenty of flavour length.
▼-■ *90* *Now-2008*

**2001 Lily's Garden** *McLaren Vale – Shiraz* **S.A.**
Deep crimson. Intense dark cherry/musky/brambly aromas with plenty of savoury oak and some walnutty complexity. Concentrated and succulent dark cherry/musky/dried apricot flavours, superb savoury oak, slinky tannins, lovely fruit-sweetness and length.
▼-■ *92* *2004-2010*

## TYRRELL'S

**1992 Vat 1** *Hunter Valley – Semillon* **N.S.W.**
Yellow/gold. Sweet dried-apricot/melon/peach aromas with touches of smoke and limes. Sweet, fleshy, concentrated wine with peach/melon/apricot/limey flavours, with underlying oak, plenty of fruit-sweetness, balanced by fine thirst-quenching acidity, finishing long and dry.
▼-■ *90* *Now-2008* *Excellent*

**1993 Vat 1** *Hunter Valley – Semillon* **N.S.W.**
Pale yellow. Complex lanolin-like aromas with lemony, herbaceous characters. Beautifully balanced wine. Classically proportioned. Deep-set lemony, lanolin flavours and linear-like acidity. Will age brilliantly.
▼-■ *94* *Now-2015* *Excellent*

**1994 Vat 1** *Hunter Valley – Semillon* **N.S.W.**
Pale yellow. Lemony aromas with some developing honeyed characters. Tightly structured wine, citrus/honeyed flavours, pronounced acidity, good concentration and length. Still very tight and needs plenty of time to develop complexity.
▼-■ *91* *Now-2010* *Excellent*

**1995 Vat 1** *Hunter Valley – Semillon* **N.S.W.**
Pale yellow. Fresh and very youthful bitter-lemon/lime aromas with hints of honey. Limey, straw flavours with some honey, tangy acidity but medium concentration and length. Still quite austere and needs time to develop.
▼-■ *85* *Now-2010* *Excellent*

**1996 Vat 1** *Hunter Valley – Semillon* **N.S.W.**
Pale yellow. Lanolin/gunflint/citrus aromas. Complex lanolin/sweet-lemon fruit with some viscosity, pronounced cutting acidity and superb length of flavour. Will probably develop into a classic. Worth cellaring.
▼-■ *92* *Now-2008* *Excellent*

**1997 Vat 1** *Hunter Valley – Semillon* **N.S.W.**
Pale yellow. Intense Lemon rind /honeyed pear aromas. Tightly knit palate, lemon rind/skin flavours, touch phenolic, pronounced acidity but good concentration and flavour length. Finishes grassy.
▼-■ *87* *Now-2008* *Excellent*

**1998 Vat 1** *Hunter Valley – Semillon* **N.S.W.**
Pale yellow. Intense Lemon lime aromas with touch of grapefruit/ lanolin. Highly concentrated and tightly focused palate, with lime grapefruit flavours, fine, long acidity, core of fruit-sweetness on the middle, finishing long and flavoursome. Will develop well.
▼-■ *92* *2004-2010* *Excellent*

**1999 Vat 1** *Hunter Valley – Semillon* **N.S.W.**
Pale yellow, almost watery. Intense floral/lanolin/pear drop aromas. Very tight but concentrated floral/citrus fruit, lemony acidity and good length – all the hallmarks of a long-term cellaring proposition. Will almost certainly develop into a great Hunter Valley Semillon.
▼-■ *95* *2002-2015* *Excellent*

**1993 Vat 47** *Hunter Valley – Chardonnay* **N.S.W.**
Pale yellow. Youthful apple/melon-like aromas with a touch of yeasty, roasted nut complexity. Lean, slightly austere palate with apple/pear/ melon fruit, pronounced sherbety acidity and medium length. Very tight, mean wine, that could improve substantially with age.
▼-■ *84* *2003-2010* *Excellent*

**1995 Vat 47** *Hunter Valley – Chardonnay* **N.S.W.**
Pale yellow. Tight lemon curd/melon aromas with biscuity, nutty oak. Still quite youthful. Plenty of sweet, creamy, lemon curd/melon fruit flavours and underlying oak all pulled together by vibrant acidity. A well made wine.
▼-■ *92* *Now-2004* *Excellent*

**1996 Vat 47** *Hunter Valley – Chardonnay* **N.S.W.**
Pale yellow. Apple/pear aromas with underlying biscuity oak and touches of lanolin. Youthful, tight, apple/pear flavours, good concentration, zingy acidity and length. Early drinking wine.
▼-■ *89* *Now-2005* *Excellent*

**1997 Vat 47** *Hunter Valley – Chardonnay* **N.S.W.**
Yellow/gold. Intense oaky wine with background oak and butterscotch/ yeasty complexity. Creamy, but oaky, palate with melon/peach/ butterscotch flavours. A bit planky.
▼-■ *82* *Now-2010* *Excellent*

**1998 Vat 47** *Hunter Valley – Chardonnay* **N.S.W.**
Pale yellow. Lovely nectarine/peach aromas with touches of grapefruit – very pure and clean. Classically proportioned wine with plenty of grapefruit/nectarine fruit, subtle nutty, butterscotch characters, lovely dense fruit and plenty of length and flavour. A super wine.
■ *96* *Now-2010* *Excellent*

**1999 Vat 47** *Hunter Valley – Chardonnay* **N.S.W.**
Pale yellow. Tropical fruit/melon vanillin aromas, quite lifted and tight with some citrus-fruit characters. Tight, lemony fruit on the palate with high-pitched acidity. Very young, tight wine but should open up.
■ *83* *2002-2010* *Excellent*

**2000 Vat 47** *Hunter Valley – Chardonnay* **N.S.W.**
Pale yellow. Ripe melon/peach aromas with some toasty/savoury oak characters. Ripe melon/peach flavours with plenty of fruit-sweetness, some malty/vanillin oak finishing long and sweet.
■ *89* *Now-2008* *Excellent*

**2001 Vat 47** *Hunter Valley – Chardonnay* **N.S.W.**
Pale yellow. Melon/peach/malt/vanillin aromas with some roasted nut complexity. Classic melon/peach/butterscotch flavours, underlying savoury oak and roasted nut/leesy complexity, fine sparkling acidity finishing, quite tight and tangy.
■ *92* *Now-2010* *Excellent*

**1994 Vat 9** *Hunter Valley – Shiraz* **N.S.W.**
Crimson/purple. Smoky bacon/leather aromas with touches of earthiness, pepper and iodine. The palate is sweet and smoky with gamy, leathery, liquorice fruit, high concentration and firm tannins.
▼-■ *89* *Now-2010* *Distinguished*

**1995 Vat 9** *Hunter Valley – Shiraz* **N.S.W.**
Medium crimson. Wine already developing with cassis/leather aromas, plenty of sweet fruit but still a little simple. The palate is fleshy and deep with cassis/raspberry/leathery flavours, grainy, but textured and slightly pronounced, tannins. Needs to soften out a little, but still a medium-term wine.
▼-■ *83* *Now-2008* *Distinguished*

**1996 Vat 9** *Hunter Valley – Shiraz* **N.S.W.**
Deep crimson. Raspberry/mocha like aromas with touches of vanillin. Savoury fruit flavours of raspberry/mocha and cedar, very loose-knit tannins and nice savoury nuances, finishing quite firm but with plenty of flavour. Medium concentration but leaning towards elegant.
▼-■ *87* *Now-2007* *Distinguished*

**1997 Vat 9** *Hunter Valley – Shiraz* **N.S.W.**
Crimson. Ripe, spicy, raspberry/blackberry/earthy aromas with a nutty complexity. The palate is well-balanced and bright, with raspberry/blackberry/nutty/earthy flavours, grainy, gravelly tannins, finishing firm.
▼-■ *91* *Now-2010* *Distinguished*

**1998 Vat 9** *Hunter Valley – Shiraz* **N.S.W.**
Deep crimson. Restrained but complex lanolin/blackberry/walnut aromas and flavours, medium concentration, fine very drying tannnins with some underlying oak. Finishes firm and tight.
▼-■ *85* *Now-2010* *Distinguished*

**1999 Vat 9** *Hunter Valley – Shiraz* **N.S.W.**
Medium crimson. Developed, but sweet leafy/nutty aromas over bright cherry fruit characters. Dark cherry/chocolate flavours. Long, fine, lacy, slightly grippy, tannins, finishing firm but with plenty of flavour length. Very nice looking wine that should develop well. Maturation style.
▼-■ *89* *Now-2010* *Distinguished*

**2000 Vat 9** *Hunter Valley – Shiraz* **N.S.W.**
Medium deep crimson. Intense savoury leafy/raspberry/mulberry aromas with some smoky nuances. Ripe raspberry/mulberry fruit flavours, some leather/spice characters, fine sinewy tannins with plenty of length. Still quite youthful.
▼-■ *84* *Now-2010* *Distinguished*

## VASSE FELIX

**1995 Heytesbury** *Margaret River – Cabernet* **W.A.**
Medium crimson. Intense, meaty, chocolaty, blackcurrant aromas. Some feral/foxy notes. Rich, sweet, chocolaty, meaty flavours, some cedary oak. Fine-grained tannins. Medium length. Showing some development.
▼-■ *88* *Now-2008*

**1996 Heytesbury** *Margaret River – Cabernet* **W.A.**
Crimson/purple. Dark cherry/blackcurrant pastille aromas with some vanillin oak. Sweet-fruited well-balanced palate with cranberry/currant flavours, grippy, finely textured tannins, good concentration, and some complex seaweed characters. A firm finish.
▼-■ *91* *Now-2015*

**1997 Heytesbury** *Margaret River – Cabernet* **W.A.**
Deep crimson/purple. Perfumed blackcurrant/meaty/savoury aromas with hints of leafiness. Worked style with plenty of classy, new,

savoury, smoky oak, fine, leafy tannins and deep-set blackcurrant/meaty flavours. A firm finish. Delicious wine.
▼-■ *95* *2003-2012*

**1998 Heytesbury** *Margaret River – Cabernet* **W.A.**
Deep crimson/purple. Intense chocolaty, ripe, blackcurrant and sappy, savoury oak. Rich, ripe fruit with deep-set, plush, new, savoury, vanillin oak, gravelly tannins and excellent length. An 'essence of Cabernet' style, needing time to soften out.
▼-■ *89* *2005-2015*

**1999 Heytesbury** *Margaret River – Cabernet* **W.A.**
Deep crimson. Intense blackcurrant pastille aromas with touches of cedar and malt. Well balanced wine with blackcurrant/cedar flavours, fine grained tannins, underlying savoury oak, finishing firm and tight, but good length of flavour.
▼-■ *88* *2004-2012*

**2000 Heytesbury** *Margaret River – Cabernet* **W.A.**
Deep crimson. Complex earthy/cassis/choc-leafy aromas. Touches of aniseed and underlying savoury oak. Rich choc-berry fruit favours with fine sinewy tannins, savoury oak, building up to a firm finish.
▼-■ *87* *2004-2012*

**1994** *Margaret River – Cabernet* **W.A.**
Medium crimson. Sweet earthy/demi-glace/truffle aromas with underlying red berry fruit characters. Lovely sweet truffle/demi-glace flavours with hints of chocolate and raspberry, fine grained tannins, plenty of fruit-sweetness and length. Elegant well balanced wine.
■ *92* *Now-2010* *Distinguished*

**1995** *Margaret River – Cabernet* **W.A.**
Crimson/purple. Blackcurrant/cedar/mulberry aromas and flavours. Touches of chocolate, velvety tannins, cedary oak and plenty of length.
■ *90* *Now-2010* *Distinguished*

**1996** *Margaret River – Cabernet* **W.A.**
Crimson/purple. Cranberry/blackcurrant aromas with touches of tar and meaty complexity and some cedary oak. The palate is ripe and sweet-fruited with pure blackcurrant and cranberry fruit flavours, deep-set savoury oak and a firm finish.
■ *93* *2002-2012* *Distinguished*

**1997** *Margaret River – Cabernet* **W.A.**
Medium crimson. Complex miso soup/cassis aromas with touches of game and savoury oak. Plenty of sweet fruit. Complex gamy/cassis/raspberry flavours and some demi-glace nuances, fine tannins, underlying oak, finishing firm.
■ *88* *Now-2012* *Distinguished*

**1998** *Margaret River – Cabernet* **W.A.**
Crimson/purple. Blackberry jam/chocolate/cedar/spice aromas. Big, dense, wine with liquorice/blackcurrant/dark chocolate flavours, cedar-like oak, ripe, pronounced tannins and excellent length.
■ *93* *2002-2012* *Distinguished*

**1999** *Margaret River – Cabernet* **W.A.**
Medium deep crimson. Ripe choc-berry fruit with malty/vanillin undertones. Plenty of sweet fruit. Richly favoured wine with plenty of chocolate/ripe blackberry flavours, soft resolved almost velvet tannins, underlying oak, finishing long and flavoursome.
■ *94* *2004-2012* *Distinguished*

**2000** *Margaret River – Cabernet* **W.A.**
Deep crimson. Intense and generous choc-mint/cassis aromas with plenty of malty vanillin oak. Richly flavoured palate with choc-meaty characters, plenty of savoury oak, pronounced but ripe tannins, plenty of concentration and length. Good fruit-sweetness and length.
■ *88* *2004-2012* *Distinguished*

**1994** *Margaret River – Shiraz* **W.A.**
Crimson. Intense plummy, earthy, liquorice/vanilla bean aromas. Sweet-fruited palate with fleshy, dark plummy fruit, vanillin flavours, loose-knit, lacy tannins, medium concentration and length.
▼-■ *85* *Now*

**1995** *Margaret River – Shiraz* **W.A.**
Deep crimson. Ripe, sweet-fruited and complex wine with developed choc-berry/gamy/Christmas cake characters. Rich, ripe classically structured palate with choc-berry/plum fruit, slight tarry/tropical oak,

ripe gravelly tannins, finishing long and sweet. Showing some maturation. Delicious drink.

▼-■ *91* *Now-2010*

**1996** *Margaret River – Shiraz* **W.A.**

Purple/crimson. Very concentrated aniseed/vanillin aromas, almost ultra-ripe, with pronounced American oak. The palate is richly textured, but the oak destroys the fruit quality. Nonetheless, it is still a pretty good wine.

▼-■ *84* *Now*

**1997** *Margaret River – Shiraz* **W.A.**

Crimson/purple. Complex and intense dark chocolate/ blackberry/gamy aromas. A sweet, deep-set wine with dark chocolate/plummy fruit flavours, fine, firm tannins, but plenty of succulent fruit-sweetness. Endlessly long finish.

▼-■ *94* *Now*

**1998** *Margaret River – Shiraz* **W.A.**

Crimson/purple. Rich choc-berry/cedary fruit aromas. Generously proportioned wine with deep-set choc-berry fruit flavours, fine, slightly grippy tannins, but plenty of depth and good length.

▼-■ *88* *Now*

**1999** *Margaret River – Shiraz* **W.A.**

Deep crimson. Intense prune/gingersnap/chocolaty aromas with underlying oak. Deep-set generous palate with prune/ginger/mocha fruit flavours, fine quite pronounced and thick tannins, heaps of concentration, tropical cedary oak, finishing quite firm, but with plenty of fruit-sweetness and flavour length.

▼-■ *88* *2004-2010*

**2000** *Margaret River – Shiraz* **W.A.**

Deep crimson. Lovely direct blackberry/mulberry aromas with underlying mocha cinnamon oak. Richly flavoured wine with deep-set mulberry/meaty flavours bolstered up with tropical/cinnamon oak, ripe long gravelly tannins and plenty of length. Very well made wine which needs time to integrate.

▼-■ *92* *2004-2015*

## VERITAS

**1996 Hanisch Vineyard** *Barossa Valley – Shiraz* **S.A.**

Deep crimson/purple. Blackberry/creamy/brambly/fresh barnyard aromas. Rich, alcoholic, ripe palate with intense blackberry/liquorice, soupy, firm tannins, integrated oak and plenty of length. Complex but awkward wine.

■ *85* *Now-2006*

**1997 Hanisch Vineyard** *Barossa Valley – Shiraz* **S.A.**

Deep crimson. Intense raspberry essence/slight herb garden aromas and some choc-berry characters. Refined but well-concentrated raspberry/ herb flavours, fine rasping tannins finishing firm but with plenty of flavour length.

■ *91* *2004-2015*

**1998 Hanisch Vineyard** *Barossa Valley – Shiraz* **S.A.**

Deep crimson. Plush exotic wine with ultra-ripe liquorice/mulberry aromas, vanillin oak and apricot/chocolate complexity. Palate is rich and supple with intensely flavoured mulberry/liquorice/apricot fruit and aniseed nuances, underlying oak, ripe fine gravel tannins, finishing firm but with plenty of flavour length. Drop dead beautiful wine.

■ *99* *2006-2015*

**1999 Hanisch Vineyard** *Barossa Valley – Shiraz* **S.A.**

Deep crimson. Intense plum/liquorice/mulberry fruit with underlying malt oak. Deep-set plum/berry/chocolate flavours with some malty vanillin oak, massive pixilated tannin structure, building to a long tannin slick at the finish. This is a massively concentrated wine with plenty of flavour length.

■ *88* *2004-2014*

**2001 Heinrich** *Barossa Valley – Shiraz Mataro* **S.A.**

Medium crimson. Very perfumed musky/floral, almost gardenia, aromas with touch of aniseed. Highly tensioned wine with musky/ plum/aniseed flavours, fine tannins, pronounced acid cut, finishing firm but flavoursome.

■ *89* *2004-2012*

**1997 Heysen Vineyard** *Barossa Valley – Shiraz* **S.A.**
Deep crimson. Perfumed, dark chocolate/rose/gardenia/liquorice aromas all underpinned by new oak. Sweet liquorice/dark chocolate/malty flavours, fine grained tannins, building up quite grippy and alcoholic at the finish.
■ *87* *2005-2012*

**1998 Heysen Vineyard** *Barossa Valley – Shiraz* **S.A.**
Deep crimson. Perfumed musky/ripe apricot with some malty/biscuity oak. Deeply concentrated, almost essence-like palate, with deep-set dark chocolate/mulberry fruit and very attractive malty oak, fine lacy tannins finishing long and flavoursome. Superb wine.
■ *94* *2004-2012*

**1999 Heysen Vineyard** *Barossa Valley – Shiraz* **S.A.**
Deep crimson. Intense plum/mulberry aromas with malty oak nuances and miso/demi glace complexity. Richly concentrated wine with plum mulberry/dark cherry fruit, fine grippy/sinewy tannins balanced by plenty of malty/vanillin oak. Excellent length of flavour.
■ *90* *2005-2013*

## VIRGIN HILLS

**1992** *Macedon – Cabernet Shiraz Merlot Malbec* **Vic.**
Deep crimson. Complex mushroomy, meaty, aromas with some menthol notes with hints of leather and spice. Prune/sweet/soupy/mushroomy fruit flavours, finely textured tannins with good concentration and length. Probably the best it will ever be.
▼ *92* *Now-2005* *Distinguished*

**1994** *Macedon – Cabernet Shiraz Merlot Malbec* **Vic.**
Crimson/purple. Brambly, cassis, savoury oak. Restrained, elegant, leafy cassis fruit flavours with savoury oak flavours, very fine, silky tannins and excellent length. Needs to evolve.
▼ *84* *2003-2008* *Distinguished*

**1995** *Macedon – Cabernet Shiraz Merlot Malbec* **Vic.**
Medium crimson. Soupy, brothy, vegetal, cassis aromas. Light to medium concentration with leafy, brothy vegetal, cassis/menthol flavours, fine tannins and medium length. Showing some development but unlikely to improve.
▼ *79* *Now* *Distinguished*

**1997** *Macedon – Cabernet Shiraz Merlot Malbec* **Vic.**
Deep crimson/purple. Almost contrived confectionary aromas with some blackcurrants. Simple lolly fruit with fine-grained tannins, medium concentration and length.
▼ *75* *Now-2008* *Distinguished*

**1998** *Macedon – Cabernet Shiraz Merlot Malbec* **Vic.**
Medium crimson. Loose-knit red cherry/leafy/sweet fruit aromas. Restrained/tomato leaf/slightly soupy flavours and fine velveteen tannins and good length. Underpowered wine.
▼ *80* *Now-2008* *Distinguished*

## VOYAGER ESTATE

**1995 Tom Price** *Margaret River – Cabernet Sauvignon* **W.A.**
Deep crimson. Meaty menthol/beefy/demi glace aromas. Concentrated almost soupy palate with menthol/game/cassis flavours, underlying savoury oak, fine sinewy tannins finishing firm and tight. Nice core of fruit-sweetness but medium term.
▼ *85* *Now-2008*

**1998 Tom Price** *Margaret River – Cabernet Sauvignon* **W.A.**
Deep crimson. Intense quite complex blackcurrant/liquorice/brothy aromas – touches of mint. Choc-berry, minty flavours and savoury oak. Fine grained, slightly grippy tannins. Finishes quite leafy and firm. Some meaty complexity.
▼ *85* *2004-2012*

**1999 Tom Price** *Margaret River – Cabernet Sauvignon* **W.A.**
Medium crimson. Blackcurrant/earthy/minty aromas with some mocha notes. Strong earthy/menthol/sweet fruit flavours, with fine sinewy almost green edged tannins, finishing quite grippy.
▼ *83* *2004-2010*

**1998** *Margaret River – Cabernet Merlot* **W.A.**
Medium deep crimson. Intense and very complex dark cherry/toffee/mocha aromas. Rich flavoursome wine with deep-set dark cherry/blackcurrant/mocha (oak) flavours, long fine grained tannins with plenty of fruit-sweetness and length. Lovely wine.
▼ *93* *2004-2014*

**1999** *Margaret River – Chardonnay* **W.A.**
Pale medium yellow. Very ripe melon/peach aromas with strong malty slightly smoky oak with touches of roasted nuts and lanolin. Ripe melon/peach flavours, balanced with plenty of malty/savoury oak characters, fine slightly pronounced acidity, finishing long.
▼ *87* *Now*

**2000** *Margaret River – Chardonnay* **W.A.**
Pale colour. Intense peach/apricot/nougat aromas with beautiful savoury oak and roasted nut nuances. Quite aromatic and complex. Tightly knit on the palate with peachy/apricot flavours, underlying savoury oak, but just slightly green/tight, finishing long.
▼ *88* *Now*

**1999** *Margaret River – Shiraz* **W.A.**
Deep crimson. Lifted mocha/blackberry/minty aromas with underlying savoury oak. Supple and rich wine with mocha/blackberry flavours and chocolate/gravelly tannins, slightly minty, underlying savoury oak, with liquorice/tannin slick finish.
▼ *88* *Now-2008*

## WENDOUREE

**1991** *Clare Valley – Cabernet Malbec* **S.A.**
Dark crimson. Blackcurrant/liquorice/dark chocolate/mushroomy aromas. The palate is soupy, with mushroom demi glace/black chocolate/liquorice flavours, some cedary, leafy, green, pronounced tannins, and good length.
■ *89* *Now-2010* *Outstanding*

**1997** *Clare Valley – Cabernet Malbec* **S.A.**
Dark purple/crimson. Intense menthol/liquorice/earthy/chocolate aromas. Menthol/chocolate flavours, rasping, tough tannins, underlying spice and a firm finish. Very unyielding but could soften out.
■ *80* *Now-2010* *Outstanding*

**1998** *Clare Valley – Cabernet Malbec* **S.A.**
Deep crimson. Deep-set dark chocolate/leafy aromas. Fine dark chocolate/cassis flavours with some leafy/earthy nuances. Fine, very pronounced, rusty tannins, finishing firm and tight.
■ *86* *2004-2014* *Outstanding*

**1999** *Clare Valley – Cabernet Malbec* **S.A.**
Deep crimson. Lifted blackcurrant/black olive/menthol aromas. Sweet fruited blackcurrant/black olive/chocolate flavours with some savoury/menthol/seaweedy characters, fine sinewy tannins finishing very firm.
■ *86* *2004-2014* *Outstanding*

**1991** *Clare Valley – Cabernet Sauvignon* **S.A.**
Dark crimson. Menthol/chocolate/minty, almost iodine/salty. The palate is very austere with minty, menthol, raspberry fruit, rusty and pronounced tannins and medium length. Drink soon.
■ *81* *Now-2010* *Outstanding*

**1997** *Clare Valley – Cabernet Sauvignon* **S.A.**
Deep crimson/purple. Choc-mint, oily, menthol oak aromas. Sinewy, difficult wine with plenty of concentration but aggressive tannins. This could develop into something.
■ *76* *Now-2012* *Outstanding*

**1998** *Clare Valley – Cabernet Sauvignon* **S.A.**
Deep crimson. Choc-menthol aromas with touch eucalypt leaf. Intense deep choc-menthol/iodine flavours, plenty of fruit-sweetness, fine iron like tannins which build up to striking firmness. Idiosyncratic but fabulous wine.
▲ *93* *2004-2015* *Outstanding*

**1999** *Clare Valley – Cabernet Sauvignon* **S.A.**
Deep crimson. Intense ginger biscuit/chocolate/blackcurrant aromas with underlying savoury oak. Deeply concentrated ginger chocolaty

blackcurrant, black olive, menthol flavours, underlying savoury notes with strong sinewy tannins finishing firm and tight.

▲ 90 2006-2016 *Outstanding*

**1989** *Clare Valley – Shiraz* **S.A.**

Deep crimson. Developing meaty/blackberry aromas with some pure liquorice/minty nuances. Maturing meaty/blackberry/mint flavours with core of sweet fruit. Pronounced iron tannin structure. Finishing firm and very tight.

▲ 90 Now-2010 *Exceptional*

**1991** *Clare Valley – Shiraz* **S.A.**

Deep crimson. Strong but developed dark chocolate/bramble/dark cherry aromas. The palate is still elemental and brutish with strong fruit-sweet choc-berry fruit flavours and pronounced almost unyielding tannins profile. Finishes very firm and crisp with a long slick of tannins. Needs time to come around.

▲ 89 2005-2012 *Exceptional*

**1996** *Clare Valley – Shiraz* **S.A.**

Deep crimson/purple. Intense blackberry/anise aromas balanced by well-seasoned new oak. Complex palate with leafy berry fruit and marvellously high concentration, but with quite harsh tannins. Oak melds nicely. A cellaring style wine. Will almost certainly soften out.

▲ 85 Now-2010 *Exceptional*

**1997** *Clare Valley – Shiraz* **S.A.**

Purple/crimson. Complex and slightly cumbersome wine with leatherwood/liquorice/tomato leaf aromas with touches of tar. The palate is tough and unyielding but strongly flavoured with extractive tannins, but with a core of sweet fruit.

▲ 83 Now-2012 *Exceptional*

**1998** *Clare Valley – Shiraz* **S.A.**

Deep crimson. Intense aniseed/menthol/liquorice blackberry aromas with rusty nuances. Strongly flavoured wine with deep liquorice/ blackberry/mulberry fruit, fine iron like tannins structures, finishing very firm and tight.

▲ 94 2005-2012 *Exceptional*

**1999** *Clare Valley – Shiraz* **S.A.**

Medium deep crimson. Intense dark cherry, choc-leafy aromas – touch of menthol. Strong dark cherry stone/choc-leafy flavours, fine sinewy almost iron like tannins, finishing long and dry. Still very elemental and muscular.

▲ 90 2006-2018 *Exceptional*

**1997** *Clare Valley – Shiraz Malbec* **S.A.**

Crimson/purple. Grilled bacon/tar/liquorice aromas with touches of pepper. Very firm but flavoursome palate, with bacon/liquorice flavours and vice-like tannins. Finishes firm. Builds up in the glass.

■ 85 Now-2012 *Outstanding*

**1998** *Clare Valley – Shiraz Malbec* **S.A.**

Deep crimson. Lifted, but deeply set leafy/mulberry/prune/liquorice rusty aromas. Leafy raspberry/mulberry/seaweedy flavours with strong iron-like tannins running right across the palate. Finishes sinewy and tight with long slatey flavours.

▲ 93 2006-2018 *Outstanding*

**1999** *Clare Valley – Shiraz Malbec* **S.A.**

Deep crimson. Chocolate/bramble/mulberry aromas with touches of aniseed. Deeply set well-concentrated wine with sweet chocolate/prune/ mulberry flavours and plenty of liquorice, fine sinewy almost chewy tannins building up firm and tight.

■-▲ 92 2005-2015 *Outstanding*

**1997** *Clare Valley – Shiraz Mataro* **S.A.**

Crimson/purple. Menthol/aniseed/liquorice/blackberry fruit with touches of raspberry. The palate is soupy and developing with menthol/leather polish/blackberry/rusty flavours and fine, gripping, vice-like tannins. A solid fruit core.

■ 88 2002-2012 *Outstanding*

**1998** *Clare Valley – Shiraz Mataro* **S.A.**

Deep purple/crimson. Restrained peppercorn, leafy aromas with touches of liquorice. The palate is full-flavoured with blackberry/ pepper fruit, firm, fine tannins, good concentration and a firm finish.

■ 87 2003-2015 *Outstanding*

**1999** *Clare Valley – Shiraz Mataro* **S.A.**
Medium crimson. Red cherry/plum aromas.Touches of dark chocolate and aniseed. Restrained plum/cherry flavours. Fine, long sinew/rusty tannins finishing dry and firm.
■ *87* *2005-2015* *Outstanding*

## WIRRA WIRRA

**1998 R.S.W.** *McLaren Vale – Shiraz* **S.A.**
Medium deep crimson. Chocolate/leafy/cherry with underlying savoury notes. Moderately concentrated wine with cherry stone/chocolate flavours and fine slightly aggressive leafy tannins, but plenty of length of flavour and fruit-sweetness.
■ *84* *Now-2010*

**1999 R.S.W.** *McLaren Vale – Shiraz* **S.A.**
Deep crimson. High pitched ground coffee/choc-liquorice/blackberry pastille aromas with some malty nuances. Richly flavoured concentrated wine with coffee/chocolate flavours, fine grainy tannins and some malty oak. Finishes quite firm.
▼-■ *86* *2004-2012*

**1998 The Angelus** *McLaren Vale – Cabernet Sauvignon* **S.A.**
Deep crimson. Intense mocha/ground coffee aromas with touches of aniseed and blackcurrants. Ripe complex mocha/ground coffee flavours, loose-knit fine, slightly bitter, tannins, with pronounced acidity, plenty of concentration and length.
■ *89* *2004-2012*

**1999 The Angelus** *McLaren Vale – Cabernet Sauvignon* **S.A.**
Deep crimson. Sweet blackcurrant/cedar/mocha aromas with plenty of fruit-sweetness. Richly flavoured wine with sweet blackcurrant/mocha flavours, fine ripe sweet lacy tannins, plenty of fruit-sweetness finishing firm but with plenty of flavour length.
■ *92* *2004-2015*

## WOLF BLASS

**1991 Black Label** *South Australia – Cabernet* **S.A.**
Dark crimson. Choc-berry/coconut oaky aromas with touches of meatiness. Richly flavoured palate with generous chocolate/blackberry/liquorice fruit, substantial American oak, ripe tannins and excellent length. A classic Australian style.
■ *98* *Now-2008* *Excellent*

**1993 Black Label** *South Australia – Cabernet* **S.A.**
Deep crimson. Very scented wine with strong aromatic American oak and developing meaty, blackberry/cherry fruit. Plushly flavoured and concentrated wine with sweet, plummy, meaty fruit and strong menthol/coconut oak, sweet, grainy textured tannins and excellent length.
■ *93* *Now-2012* *Excellent*

**1994 Black Label** *South Australia – Cabernet* **S.A.**
Deep crimson/purple. Tightly knit prune/blackberry/dark chocolate aromas. Ripe, highly concentrated wine with prune/blackberry/dark chocolate flavours, slightly hard-edged oak, pronounced tannins and finishing firm. Will evolve.
■ *85* *Now-2014* *Excellent*

**1995 Black Label** *South Australia – Cabernet* **S.A.**
Crimson/purple. Pronounced new oak over meaty, gamy fruit. The menthol/coconut oak completely dominates the palate obscuring the fruit. Tastes like vanilla ice cream.
■ *74* *Now-2010* *Excellent*

**1996 Black Label South Australia –** *Cabernet Sauvignon Shiraz* **S.A.**
Deep crimson. Developed briary/tropical/menthol aromas with some savoury nuances. Dried plum/prune fruit intertwined with tropical/malty/menthol oak flavours, fine slightly grippy tannins with good overall flavour length. Oak too much at the fore.
■ *80* *2005-2014* *Excellent*

**1998 Black Label** *South Australia – Cabernet Sauvignon* **S.A.**
Deep crimson. Savoury/malty/blackcurrant/mocha aromas with touches of meaty complexity. Immensely concentrated wine with deep-set choc-berry/mocha flavours and plenty of well-seasoned malty oak,

long fine grained tannins, excellent concentration and fruit-sweetness, finishing with a tannin slick.
■ *91* *2004-2012* *Excellent*

**1998 Platinum** *South Australia – Shiraz* **S.A.**
Deep crimson. Intense choc-berry/vanillin aromas with some demi glace and savoury oak nuances. Well concentrated choc-berry flavours. Some menthol oak characters, dry gravelly tannins and good flavour length.
■ *89* *2004-2012*

## WYNNS COONAWARRA ESTATE

**1954 Black Label** *Coonawarra – Cabernet Sauvignon* **S.A.**
Brick red. Complex truffley, meaty, mushroom/chestnut aromas. Palate is fresh and complex with plenty of truffley mushroom/ chocolaty fruit, fine, lacy tannins and plenty of length. A superb old wine.
■ *96* *Now* *Distinguished*

**1959 Black Label** *Coonawarra – Cabernet Sauvignon* **S.A.**
Brick red. Earthy, choc-mint, chestnutty aromas with touches of polished leather. The palate is still vibrant with plenty of sweet fruit, earthy, chestnut/chocolaty flavours, fine, even, soft tannins and excellent length.
■ *93* *Now* *Distinguished*

**1960 Black Label** *Coonawarra – Cabernet Sauvignon* **S.A.**
Medium crimson. Intense, leafy, coffee aromas with touches of VA – smells like a Tawny port. Palate is drying up, with some earthy, maderised fruit and chalky tannins.
■ *81* *Now* *Distinguished*

**1966 Black Label** *Coonawarra – Cabernet Sauvignon* **S.A.**
Brick red. Earthy, chocolate/*paneforte* aromas. Richly flavoured wine with earthy, chocolaty flavours, ripe tannins and lacy, grainy tannins, lovely fruit-sweetness and a long finish. A remarkable wine.
■ *96* *Now* *Distinguished*

**1967 Black Label** *Coonawarra – Cabernet Sauvignon* **S.A.**
Brick red. Intense aniseed/liquorice/cassis/earthy aromas with smooth, deep-set chocolaty flavours, loose-knit, lacy tannins and medium length. Still holding up.
■ *88* *Now* *Distinguished*

**1973 Black Label** *Coonawarra – Cabernet Sauvignon* **S.A.**
Brick red. Intense raspberry/mocha aromas. Palate is very soapy; it is almost undrinkable.
■ *70* *Now* *Distinguished*

**1976 Black Label** *Coonawarra – Cabernet Sauvignon* **S.A.**
Brick red. Intense, sweet *paneforte*/leathery aromas with touches of cedar. Lovely, concentrated wine with cedary, mushroom flavours and touches of mocha, silky, fine, almost melting, tannins, finishing long and fine. Just brilliant.
■ *94* *Now* *Distinguished*

**1978 Black Label** *Coonawarra – Cabernet Sauvignon* **S.A.**
Medium brick red. Intense cedar/earthy/chocolate/mushroomy fruit. Mushroomy, cedar fruit flavours, fine-grained tannins, medium concentration and length.
■ *90* *Now* *Distinguished*

**1980 Black Label** *Coonawarra – Cabernet Sauvignon* **S.A.**
Medium brick red. Smoky coffee/chocolaty/green pepper/capsicum aromas. The palate is medium-concentrated with capsicum/chocolaty flavours, but chalky, dry tannins. Drink up.
■ *80* *Now* *Distinguished*

**1986 Black Label** *Coonawarra – Cabernet Sauvignon* **S.A.**
Deep crimson. Coffee/mocha/cedar aromas with touches of peppercorn and liquorice. Exotic, spicy, nutmeg/coffee/chocolaty flavours. Cedary oak, velvety tannins and excellent concentration and length. A classic.
▲ *95* *Now* *Distinguished*

**1988 Black Label** *Coonawarra – Cabernet Sauvignon* **S.A.**
Deep crimson. Coffee/mocha/raspberry/cassis aromas, perhaps a touch contrived. Intensely flavoured wine with deep-set coffee/mocha/ blackcurrant fruit, with touches of cedar and slightly firm, leafy tannins. Seems a little hollow.
■ *85* *Now-2008* *Distinguished*

**1990 Black Label** *Coonawarra – Cabernet Sauvignon* **S.A.**
Deep crimson. Iodine/black olive/blackcurrant aromas with hints of dark cherry and cedar. Plump black olive/curranty fruit flavours with quite hard, almost unyielding, fine, furry tannins, underlying oak and a firm finish. Not as good as it should be.
▲ *90* *Now-2006* *Distinguished*

**1991 Black Label** *Coonawarra – Cabernet Sauvignon* **S.A.**
Dark crimson. Rich and developed dark cherry/chocolate/leafy aromas. Ripe miso soup/reduced meaty/chocolate flavours, ripe, fine tannins, integrated oak, lovely concentration and length.
▲ *92* *Now – 2015* *Distinguished*

**1993 Black Label** *Coonawarra – Cabernet Sauvignon* **S.A.**
Deep crimson. Intense choc-*paneforte*/silage aromas with plenty of cassis nuances and oak. The palate is complex and deep, with smooth choc-berry fruit flavours propped up by smoky oak and balanced by fine, sinewy tannins. In the end, a bit of a mouthful.
■ *89* *Now-2005* *Distinguished*

**1996 Black Label** *Coonawarra – Cabernet Sauvignon* **S.A.**
Crimson/purple. Dense, immensely concentrated wine with strong raspberry/blackcurrant/tomato leaf aromas and some cedar. Richly flavoured palate. Blackcurrant/dark cherry fruit, massive grainy tannins and excellent length. Big brute of a wine that needs time to soften out.
▲ *89* *2005-2020* *Distinguished*

**1998 Black Label** *Coonawarra – Cabernet Sauvignon* **S.A.**
Deep crimson. Blackcurrant pastille/liquorice/slight meaty aromas with touches of vanillin. Choc-berry flavours with some meaty complexity, strong sinewy tannins, underlying oak, finishing very firm and tight. Touch bitter sweet.
■ *88* *Now-2010* *Distinguished*

**1999 Black Label** *Coonawarra – Cabernet Sauvignon* **S.A.**
Deep crimson. Liquorice/blackberry/black olive aromas and flavours. Immensely concentrated and elemental wine with strong fine sinewy tannins building up. Very firm and tight.
■ *91* *2003-2012* *Distinguished*

**2000 Black Label** *Coonawarra – Cabernet Sauvignon* **S.A.**
Medium crimson. Intense plum/red cherry/cassis aromas with some underlying oak. Well concentrated, mouth-filling wine with plum/cassis flavours, underlying malt oak, fine loose-knit chalky tannins, finishing long and sweet. Easy drinking wine but medium term cellaring prospect..
■ *88* *Now-2008*

**1982 John Riddoch** *Coonawarra – Cabernet Sauvignon* **S.A.**
Deep crimson. Roasted meaty, capsicum/green pepper/choc-berry fruit that is quite plush and complex. Ripe, meaty flavours, soft, ripe tannins with cherry/chocolate fruit flavours and some capsicum/green pepper, excellent fruit-sweetness and length.
▲ *90* *Now-2010* *Excellent*

**1990 John Riddoch** *Coonawarra – Cabernet Sauvignon* **S.A.**
Deep inky crimson. Still youthful, with pronounced choc-berry aromas, hints of liquorice and underlying vanillin oak. The palate is plush and powerful, with superb blackcurrant and fine dark chocolate flavours, balanced by well-seasoned savoury/vanillin oak and muscular fine-pixel tannins. A long-term wine.
▲ *98* *Now-2012* *Excellent*
*Excellent*

**1992 John Riddoch** *Coonawarra – Cabernet Sauvignon* **S.A.**
Purple crimson. Deep-set and pure blackberry/blackcurrant aromas with touches of aniseed and vanillin. Ripe, generous blackberry/cassis fruit, but loose-knit, fine gripping tannins, pronounced new oak and plenty of length.
▼-■ *88* *2004-2015* *Excellent*

**1993 John Riddoch** *Coonawarra – Cabernet Sauvignon* **S.A.**
Deep crimson/purple. Liquorice/blackcurrant/earthy aromas with plenty of cedar-wood. Well-knitted classical palate with squashy, cedar/blackcurrant/dark cherry flavours, ripe, but fine, slightly gravelly, tannins, cedary oak and good length.
▼-■ *92* *Now-2010* *Excellent*

**1994 John Riddoch** *Coonawarra – Cabernet Sauvignon* **S.A.**
Crimson/purple. Intense cedar/berry aromas with some pencil/oak characters. Deep-set, sappy, blackcurrant palate with velvety, slightly gripping tannins, pencil/cedary oak, plenty of mouth-feel and weight. Good length.
▼-■ *90* *Now-2012* *Excellent*

**1996 John Riddoch** *Coonawarra – Cabernet Sauvignon* **S.A.**
Crimson/purple. Power and restraint. Blackcurrant/sappy oak aromas with plenty of aniseed and liquorice. The palate is deep-set with blackcurrant/tarry flavours, sappy oak, massive velvety tannins and a firm finish. Still elemental and soupy, but should develop.
■ *88* *2005-2012* *Excellent*

**1997 John Riddoch** *Coonawarra – Cabernet Sauvignon* **S.A.**
Deep crimson. Developed meaty demi-glace/savoury aromas with some brambly fruit nuances. Well resolved palate with cassis/bramble/gamy flavours and demi glace/consomme complexity, fine slightly bitter tannins but lovely core of fruit-sweetness, vanillin oak, long flavoursome liquorice finish. Excellent concentration and length. Tannins build up at the end.
▼-■ *93* *2005-2018* *Excellent*

**1998 John Riddoch** *Coonawarra – Cabernet Sauvignon* **S.A.**
Deep crimson. Very deep blackcurrant/liquorice aromas, with almost perfectly pitched savoury/biscuity oak. Rich opulent wine with deep-set choc-cassis flavours and some liquorice nuances, fine grainy tannins, and touches of meaty/mocha complexity. Tannins build up firm but plenty of fruit-sweetness and length. Super wine.
■ *94* *2005-2015* *Excellent*

**1993 Michael** *Coonawarra – Shiraz* **S.A.**
Deep crimson. Savoury, smoky bacon/black cherry aromas with some blackberry, a touch herbal. The palate is quite opulent with blackberry/cherry fruit and savoury, green pepper/capsicum nuances. Slightly bitter, structured tannins and a firm finish. A medium term prospect.
▼-■ *85* *Now-2010*

**1994 Michael** *Coonawarra – Shiraz* **S.A.**
Deep crimson. Lavish smoky bacon/coconut oak aromas with underlying plum/liquorice fruit. The palate is still elemental and plush with lavish oak, sweet ripe tannins and prune/plummy fruit. Super concentration and length. Could evolve into a classic.
▼-■ *93* *Now-2012*

**1996 Michael** *Coonawarra – Shiraz* **S.A.**
Deep crimson. Intense earthy/chocolate/Christmas cake/gamy aromas. Elegantly proportioned palate with earthy/chocolate/plummy flavours matched with well seasoned oak, medium concentration, but gripping loose-knit tannins. Finishes quite firm but a little short on flavour.
■ *84* *2005-2012*

**1997 Michael** *Coonawarra – Shiraz* **S.A.**
Deep crimson. Blackberry pastille/chocolate aromas with some bitumen complexity. Well balanced wine with blackberry pastille/chocolate flavours, ripe tannins and underlying well seasoned tropical/coconut/malt nuances finishing long and flavoursome.
▼-■ *91* *2005-2010*

**1998 Michael** *Coonawarra – Shiraz* **S.A.**
Deep crimson. Lifted aniseed/choc-berry aromas with tropical malty oak characters. A very thick and concentrated wine with juicy, blackberry/chocolaty flavours, underlying smoky malty oak, ripe, dense tannins, and plenty of fruit-sweetness and length. Needs time to soften out. Excellent wine.
■ *92* *2005-2012*

**1995** *Coonawarra – Shiraz* **S.A.**
Crimson. Leafy blackberry/meaty aromas that are almost nettley. The palate is already developed with nettley, brambly flavours with fine tannins and medium length. Not really worth keeping for any length.
▼-■ *74* *Now*

**1996** *Coonawarra – Shiraz* **S.A.**
Deep crimson. Very loose-knit wine with menthol/spicy/plush raspberry/rhubarb aromas and flavours. Moderately concentrated palate with very fine-grained tannins and a firm finish.
■ *84* *Now-2008*

**1998** *Coonawarra – Shiraz* **S.A.**
Deep crimson. Profoundly deep choc-berry/liquorice aromas with some malty nuances. Rich ripe deep-set wine with choc-berry fruit flavours, ripe slinky tannins, underlying savoury oak finishing quite dry and chalky but with good flavour length.
■ *88* *Now-2008*

**1999** *Coonawarra – Shiraz* **S.A.**
Deep crimson. Aromatic mulberry/blueberry aromas with touches of vanillin. Deep-set juicy/mulberry flavours with some pepper characters, fine strong briary tannins, finishing long and flavoursome.
■ *87* *Now-2008*

**2000** *Coonawarra – Shiraz* **S.A.**
Medium deep crimson. Clear blackberry/plum aromas with some chocolate nuances. Well concentrated but tightly knit palate. Blackberry/plum flavours, some cedar/vanillin characters, velveteen tannins finishing with medium length.
▼-■ *84* *2004-2010*

## XANADU

**1991 Reserve** *Margaret River – Cabernet Reserve* **W.A.**
Dark crimson. Mulberry/chocolate/lanolin/slight menthol aromas with underlying oak. Well-balanced, concentrated wine with earthy, blackcurrant/cedar flavours, fine, sweet tannins, grainy, cedary oak, plenty of concentration, richness and length.
■ *94* *Now-2010* *Distinguished*

**1993 Reserve** *Margaret River – Cabernet Reserve* **W.A.**
Deep purple/crimson. Intense blackcurrant/coffee/cedary aromas with some spicy, malty characters. Very classical palate with cedar/ blackcurrant fruit, plenty of savoury oak with touches of spice and firm but fine tannins. Will build up over time.
■ *93* *Now-2012* *Distinguished*

**1994 Reserve** *Margaret River – Cabernet Reserve* **W.A.**
Crimson/purple. Intense, leafy blackcurrant aromas with some mintiness and black olives. Immense and dense wine with deep-set, leafy blackcurrant fruht, and cedary oak touches of menthol. A very muscular wine.
■ *92* *Now-2012* *Distinguished*

**1995 Reserve** *Margaret River – Cabernet Reserve* **W.A.**
Brick red. Cedar/cassis aromas with slightly sappy, overdone, 'polished' oak characters. The palate is quite austere with restrained cedar/ leathery/cassis flavours, powerful tannins and sappy oak. The core of sweet fruit balances it, just.
■ *86* *Now-2012* *Distinguished*

**1996 Lagan Estate Reserve** *Margaret River – Cabernet Reserve* **W.A.**
Deep crimson. Smoky lanolin/cassis aromas with complex slatey nuances. Lanolin/ smoky charcuterie flavours, fine sinewy – slightly bitter – tannins, plenty of fruit-sweetness and length.
■ *87* *2004-2010* *Distinguished*

**1997 Lagan Estate Reserve** *Margaret River – Cabernet Reserve* **W.A.**
Deep crimson. Intense black olive/blackcurrant/cedar/game aromas. Well concentrated palate with dark cherry/black olive flavours and some plummy/gamy nuances, fine grainy, slightly leafy tannins, finishing firm and tight.
■ *85* *2004-2010* *Distinguished*

**1999 Lagan Estate Reserve** *Margaret River – Cabernet Reserve* **W.A.**
Deep crimson. Lifted ginger/cassis aromas with touches of savoury/ malty oak. Deep-set choc-cassis flavours, pronounced grippy tannins, immense concentration and flavour length. Tannins are firmly structured – almost monstrous. Could tame down with age.
■ *89* *2004-2010* *Distinguished*

**2000 Lagan Estate Reserve** *Margaret River – Cabernet Merlot* **W.A.**
Deep medium crimson. Loose-knit plum/raspberry aromas with some flinty/smoky/lanolin nuances. Plummy/raspberry fruit flavours with pronounced sinewy tannins and underlying savoury oak. Finishes quite firm and tight.
■ *84* *2005-2012* *Distinguished*

## YALUMBA

**1993 The Menzies** *Coonawarra – Cabernet* **S.A.**
Deep crimson/purple. Prune/blackcurrant aromas with well-seasoned oak and hints of game. The palate is ripe and juicy with plenty of blackcurrant fruit flavours, ripe fine-grained tannins balanced by savoury oak. Finishes firm. Very successful for vintage.
▼-■ *92* *Now-2005*

**1994 The Menzies** *Coonawarra – Cabernet* **S.A.**
Deep crimson/purple. Classical blackcurrant/cedar aromas. Well-structured wine with choc-berry/cedar flavours, fine gravelly tannins, well-seasoned oak, medium concentration but good length. Will continue to evolve.
▼-■ *89* *Now*

**1995 The Menzies** *Coonawarra – Cabernet Sauvignon* **S.A.**
Deep crimson. Very floral cassis/ jasmine aromas with some savoury oak characters. Developing cassis game/ vegemite flavours, fine grainy but firm tannins, some underlying new oak, finishing long and sweet.
▼-■ *88* *2004-2010*

**1996 The Menzies** *Coonawarra – Cabernet* **S.A.**
Medium crimson. Plum/chocolaty aromas with some malty nuances. Sweet fruit flavoured wine with plum/chocolaty/herbal flavours, fine lacy tannins, finishing firm and tight.
▼-■ *82* *Now-2008*

**1997 The Menzies** *Coonawarra – Cabernet* **S.A.**
Deep crimson/purple. Intense blackcurrant pastille aromas with plenty of mulberries and vanillin. Sweet pastille/mulberry flavours with grainy, savoury oak, fine-grained, slightly grippy tannins and finishing firm. Needs time.
▼-■ *89* *2002-2012*

**1998 The Menzies** *Coonawarra – Cabernet Sauvignon* **S.A.**
Medium deep crimson. Very floral and quite delicate aniseed/violet/ rose petal aromas. Very pretty elegant wine with violet/aniseed/rose petal/cassis flavours, very fine sinewy tannins, finishing firm and tight.
▼-■ *91* *2005-2015*

**1999 The Menzies** *Coonawarra – Cabernet Sauvignon* **S.A.**
Medium crimson. Restrained violet/lavender/redcurrant aromas. Violet/lavender, almost sappy flavour, with strong impenetrable tannins, finishing very firm and gritty. Plenty of underlying fruit-sweetness but essentially quite austere. Might come around.
▼-■ *81* *2006-2015*

**1988 The Octavius** *Barossa Valley – Cabernet Sauvignon* **S.A.**
Deep crimson. Mocha/chocolate, slightly vegetal aromas with hints of liquorice and sappy oak. The palate is well developed with chocolate/ coffee, slightly sappy flavours, fine velvety, slightly green, tannins finishing firm.
■ *80* *Now-2005*

**1990 The Octavius** *Barossa Valley – Shiraz* **S.A.**
Crimson. Intense Christmas cake/gamy aromas with touches of malty/oak characters and liquorice/dried fruits. Rich, complex, deeply concentrated wine with prune/dried fruit/earthy flavours, lacy fine ripe tannins, underlying vanillin/malty oak finishing long and sweet.
■ *92* *Now-2010*

**1992 The Octavius** *Barossa Valley – Shiraz* **S.A.**
Deep crimson. Difficult year with developed prune/grilled bacon aromas, touch of aniseed – a little disjointed, with a hard, oily American oak background. The palate is rich with prune/blackberry/ sappy (oak)/aniseed flavours, soupy, thick tannins, finishing firm.
■ *84* *Now-2006*

**1993 The Octavius** *Barossa Valley – Shiraz* **S.A.**
Deep crimson. Aromatic black cherry/water bag aromas with touches of jam and smoky oak. Slightly under-fruited black cherry characters, with strong toasty bacon, almost sappy oak, fine, slightly gripping tannins, medium concentration and length.
■ *79* *Now-2004*

**1994 The Octavius** *Barossa Valley – Shiraz* **S.A.**
Deep crimson/purple. Classic new breed with very deep-set, brooding plum/prune/dark chocolate/*paneforte* aromas. The palate is deep and

thick, rich and ripe, with bright plum/prune/blackberry fruit, well-seasoned oak, fine, gravelly tannins and plenty of length. Good – could get even better.

■ *94* *2003-2013*

**1995 The Octavius** *Barossa Valley – Shiraz* **S.A.**

Deep crimson. Beautifully direct savoury liquorice/aniseed blackcurrant ginger aromas. Very structured palate with chocolaty/ meaty flavours and soy/liquorice nuances, drying tannins, plenty of savoury oak flavours , finishing chalky firm.

■ *90* *2005-2015*

**1996 The Octavius** *Barossa Valley – Shiraz* **S.A.**

Deep crimson/purple. Perfumed plum/cherry/rhubarb/tobacco/smoky aromas with touches of vanillin and toasty American oak. Plenty of sweet, plump, plum/berry/cherry fruit. Well-seasoned savoury oak. Ripe, textured tannins, massive concentration and excellent length. A sweet and savoury wine with outstanding balance and flavour.

■ *98* *2004-2014*

**1997 The Octavius** *Barossa Valley – Shiraz* **S.A.**

Medium deep crimson. Dark chocolate/dark cherry aromas with plenty of new malt/tropical oak characters. Deep-set dark choc-cherry flavours, firm gravelly tannins, plenty of tropical oak characters, finishing firm and drying.

■ *88* *2005-2015*

**1998 The Octavius** *Barossa Valley – Shiraz* **S.A.**

Deep crimson. Intense complex choc-berry musky aromas with prominent new oak. Fruit-sweet palate with chocolate/mocha/ mulberry fruit intertwined with strong new savoury/malty oak, fine grippy tannins, finishing firm and spicy. Nice wine.

■ *91* *2005-2012*

**1990 The Reserve** *Barossa Valley – Shiraz* **S.A.**

Deep crimson. Rich dark chocolate/minty sweet fruit aromas. Opulent palate with ultra-ripe dark chocolate/prune flavours, beautifully integrated oak, ripe lacy tannins and extraordinary length. Super wine.

■ *96* *Now-2010*

**1992 The Reserve** *Barossa Valley – Shiraz* **S.A.**

Deep crimson. Pure, intense, mocha/dark chocolate aromas. The palate is perfectly balanced with ripe, sweet, prune/chocolate fruit flavours, underlying oak and fine, slightly gripping tannins.

■ *94* *Now*

**1996 The Reserve** *South Australia* **–** *Cabernet Sauvignon Shiraz* **S.A.**

Deep crimson. Intense dark chocolate/mocha aromas with some herb garden/aniseed notes. Rich chocolaty/cedar//mocha/prune flavours, ripe gravelly/rolling tannins, plenty of concentration, finishing with a firm slick of tannins.

▲ *91* *2004-2012*

**1998 The Reserve** *South Australia* **–** *Cabernet Sauvignon Shiraz* **S.A.**

Medium deep crimson. Intense cinnamon/savoury oak with some briary/dark chocolate nuances. Deep-set wine with dark chocolate flavours intertwined with mocha/cinnamon/savoury oak, lacy tannins finishing firm but with good flavour length. An absolute classic.

▲ *95* *2005-2018*

**1990 The Signature** *South Australia – Cabernet Sauvignon Shiraz* **S.A.**

Deep crimson. Chocolaty, earthy, aromas with touches of gum leaf and tobacco. Plenty of fruit-sweetness on the palate. Deep-set choc-tobacco, earthy flavours balanced by fine gravelly tannins, finishing long.

▼-■ *94* *Now-2005*

**1991 The Signature** *South Australia – Cabernet Sauvignon Shiraz* **S.A.**

Deep crimson. Mocha/aniseed/vanillin aromas with touches of chocolate and meaty complexity. Vibrant palate with bright choc-plummy fruit flavours, but some green-edged, grippy tannins, and integrated oak, finishing firm.

▼-■ *88* *Now-2005*

**1992 The Signature** *South Australia – Cabernet Sauvignon Shiraz* **S.A.**

Deep crimson. Spearmint/eucalypt/choc-berry aromas and flavours with fine-grained, but slightly hard and pippy tannins, but good overall

concentration, finishing firm and tight. Can't see this going anywhere, so drink up. 100 per cent Barossa.
▼-■ 83 Now

**1993 The Signature** *South Australia – Cabernet Sauvignon Shiraz* **S.A.**
Medium deep crimson. Menthol/cassis aromas with some walnutty characters. Developed menthol/walnut/cassis/leathery flavours with strong grippy tannins, plenty of concentration and length.
▼-■ 85 2004-2012

**1994 The Signature** *South Australia – Cabernet Sauvignon Shiraz* **S.A.**
Deep crimson. Tightly focused wine with blackcurrant/vanillin/coconut oaky aromas with touches of meatiness. Richly flavoured palate with deep-set blackcurrant/chocolate fruit, pronounced oak, fine-grained, gravelly tannins and a long finish. Needs time.
▼-■ 91 Now-2010

**1996 The Signature** *South Australia – Cabernet Sauvignon Shiraz* **S.A.**
Deep crimson. Developed, sweet fruit, black olive/mocha aromas with some choc-berry characters. Developed, blackcurrant/mocha fruit flavours, with plenty of sweet meaty complexity. Tannins are sinewy and finish bitter, but good overall flavour length.
▼-■ 89 2004-2010

**1997 The Signature** *South Australia – Cabernet Sauvignon Shiraz* **S.A.**
Medium crimson. Aromatic but complex plum/rhubarb/cedar/vanilla aromas. Strong, sweet fruited wine with plum/rhubarb/liquorice flavours, dense but well structured tannins, underpinned by cedar/vanilla oak and plenty of flavour length.
▼-■ 89 2003-2012

**1998 The Signature** *South Australia – Cabernet Sauvignon Shiraz* **S.A.**
Deep crimson. Developing leather/spice/mocha/rich plum/chocolate aromas. Concentrated mocha/plum/chocolate flavours, strong dense tannins, underpinned by savoury/vanilla oak, finishing firm and oaky but with plenty of flavour length.
▼-■ 87 2004-2012

**1998 The Virgilius** *Eden Valley – Viognier* **S.A.**
Pale yellow/gold. Perfumed and exotic peach/apricot/nectarine/frangipani aromas. The palate is fleshy with peach/apricot, slightly aniseed flavours, plenty of mouth-feel and concentration with a fine acid cut. Excellent wine, but a early drinking proposition.
▼-■ 92 Now

**1999 The Virgilius** *Eden Valley – Viognier* **S.A.**
Pale yellow. Intense marmalade/lime aromas. Developed but tangy marmalade/lime flavours. Nice fruit-sweetness, finishing musky and long. Still nice to drink but prefer younger wine style.
▼-■ 90 Now

**2000 The Virgilius** *Eden Valley – Viognier* **S.A.**
Pale yellow. Very lifted rich musky/gardenia/apricot, almost fruit salad aromas with some savoury oak. Creamy slippery wine with musky/gardenia/apricot flavours, lovely fruit-sweetness, viscosity and length. Short term.
▼-■ 93 Now

**2001 The Virgilius** *Eden Valley – Viognier* **S.A.**
Pale yellow. Perfumed floral lime/pear aromas – some jasmine notes. Superbly balanced, slinky/slippery palate with juicy musky/pear flavours and quartz acidity, lovely concentration and long fine minerally finish. Wonderful wine.
▼-■ 96 Now-2004

## YARRA YERING

**1990 Dry Red No.1** *Yarra Valley – Cabernet* **Vic.**
Purple/crimson. Complex blackcurrant/prune/mushroomy aromas with some meaty, demi-glace characters. The palate is well rounded and velvety with pure, ripe fruit and meaty, savoury, miso flavours, ripe textured tannins and excellent length. Idiosyncratic but very fine.
■ 94 Now-2012 *Outstanding*

**1994 Dry Red No.1** *Yarra Valley – Cabernet* **Vic.**
Crimson/purple. Blackcurrant pastille/chocolaty fruit with meaty, bacon fruit. The palate is massively structured but very sweet and savoury with blackcurrant/bacon, savoury oak flavours, fine-grained, soupy tannins and good length. Idiosyncratic but very stylish.
■ *93* *Now-2012* *Outstanding*

**1993** *Yarra Valley – Pinot Noir* **Vic.**
Crimson/earthy. Matchstick, earthy, brothy, vegetal aromas. Weedy, vegetal/dark chocolate flavours, fine tannins but acidity coming to the fore. Fading wine.
■ *76* *Now* *Distinguished*

**1995** *Yarra Valley – Pinot Noir* **Vic.**
Crimson. Perfumed gamy, meaty, fennel/aniseed/dark cherry/chocolate aromas. Very complex and deep-set wine with gamy, cherry/aniseed fruit, sinewy tannins, underlying oak and quite firm.
■ *84* *Now-2008* *Distinguished*

**1996** *Yarra Valley – Pinot Noir* **Vic.**
Crimson/purple. Tight, perfumed, gamy, dark cherry/strawberry fruit aromas with underlying oak. The palate is rich and ripe with plenty of fruit, sweet strawberry/gamy notes, pronounced, rather hard, tannins make it a rather unyielding wine. May improve.
■ *80* *2005-2010* *Distinguished*

**1990 Dry Red No. 2** *Yarra Valley – Shiraz* **Vic.**
Deep crimson. Raspberry/blackberry/vanillin and sweet chocolate. Ripe, developed chocolaty, rhubarb/blackberry flavours, high concentration and firm tannins.
■ *90* *Now-2010* *Excellent*

**1991 Dry Red No. 2** *Yarra Valley – Shiraz* **Vic.**
Dark crimson. Leafy capsicum/green pepper aromas with some contrived blackberry fruit. Palate is soft and squashy, with leafy blackberry fruit, soft tannins, medium concentration and length. Drink soon.
■ *80* *Now* *Excellent*

**1994 Dry Red No. 2** *Yarra Valley – Shiraz* **Vic.**
Crimson/purple. Loose-knit style with blackberry jam, almost cordial-like fruit with touches of white pepper and cedar. Green pepper/cordial fruit characters, fine, loose tannins, medium concentration and length.
■ *78* *Now-2008* *Excellent*

## YERING STATION

**1999 Reserve** *Yarra Valley – Cabernet Sauvignon* **Vic.**
Deep crimson. Absolutely classic blackcurrant/cigarbox/black olive aromas with some iodine/seaweedy complexity. Palate is extremely well proportioned with deep-set blackcurrant/cedar flavours, fine grained tannins, underlying savoury oak and plenty of length of flavour. Still quite elemental but will build up over time gaining complexity and weight. This is a wonderful young Cabernet.
▼-■ *94* *2004-2012*

**2000 Reserve** *Yarra Valley – Cabernet Sauvignon* **Vic.**
Deep crimson. Very classy new cedar/nutty oak over blackcurrant/lead pencil fruit. Quite oak driven wine with malt/cedar oak, some cassis fruit, fine grainy slightly sinewy tannins finishing with medium length. Very Bordeaux like. Could blossom into something very special.
▼-■ *91* *2004-2015*

**1999 Reserve** *Yarra Valley – Chardonnay* **Vic.**
Pale yellow. Tangy, high tensile, melon/apricot/mineral aromas, with subtle new savoury/malty oak. Classic, beautifully focused palate with ripe melon/peach flavours and roasted nut complexity balanced with malty/savoury oak, finishing very long. A very impressive wine.
▼-■ *95* *Now-2007*

**1997 Reserve** *Yarra Valley – Pinot Noir* **Vic.**
Medium crimson. Intense cherry stone, bramble aromas, with underlying savoury characters. Well pitched palate, with tangy, cherry stone flavours and some brambly complexity, sinewy, leafy finishing quite grippy.
▼-■ *86* *Now-2006*

**1998 Reserve** *Yarra Valley – Pinot Noir* **Vic.**
Medium crimson. Intense vanilla, slightly stewed plum aromas with some cherry nuances. Well concentrated wine with plum/spicy favours,

fine silken tannins building up quite firm. Still quite savoury but losing varietal characters. Drink soon.

▼-■ 84 Now-2004

**2000 Reserve** *Yarra Valley – Pinot Noir* **Vic.**

Medium crimson. Intense red cherry/strawberry/plum aromas with underlying oak and some meaty complexity. Sweet fruited palate with complex red cherry/lanolin/gamy flavours, underlying savoury oak, fine long velveteen tannins, and plenty of length. Super complex wine.

▼-■ 94 Now-2007

## YERINGBERG

**1988** *Yarra Valley – Cabernet Blend* **Vic.**

Deep crimson. Dark cherry/chocolate/black berry/cassis aromas, showing lovely restraint. The palate is quite developed and cedary, with slightly oily tannins but enough chocolaty fruit to carry.

■ 80 Now-2005 *Outstanding*

**1990** *Yarra Valley – Cabernet Blend* **Vic.**

Medium crimson. Complex matchstick/blackcurrant/cedar aromas with touches of menthol. Classical wine with cedar/blackcurrant fruit, fine, even tannin structure, excellent concentration and length.

▲ 93 Now-2008 *Outstanding*

**1994** *Yarra Valley – Cabernet Blend* **Vic.**

Crimson. Leafy, smoky, blackcurrant aromas. Smoked oyster, blackcurrant, cedary flavours with fine, rasping, hard tannins, finishing firm.

▲ 78 Now-2010 *Outstanding*

**1995** *Yarra Valley – Cabernet Blend* **Vic.**

Crimson. Earthy, cassis aromas with very restrained oak. Elegant palate with cassis/earthy flavours, loose-knit, fine, lacy, slightly grippy tannins and medium length. Early drinking style.

■ 85 Now-2005 *Outstanding*

**1996** *Yarra Valley – Cabernet Blend* **Vic.**

Crimson. Blackcurrant pastille/earthy/almond aromas with a touch of leafiness. Medium concentrated wine with blackcurrant/earthy flavours, fine loose-knit tannins and a firm finish. Will build up.

▲ 85 Now-2010 *Outstanding*

**1997** *Yarra Valley – Cabernet Blend* **Vic.**

Deep crimson. Intense cherry/blackcurrant aromas with some malt oak tones. Classically proportioned wine with blackcurrant/cherry fruit flavours underscored by vanilla/spicy oak. Fine supple tannins, building firm and tight.

■ 90 2004-2010 *Outstanding*

**1998** *Yarra Valley – Cabernet Blend* **Vic.**

Deep crimson. Perfumed dark cherry/ rose petal/ aniseed aromas. Quite tight wine with dark cherry/violet/cedar spice flavours. Nice fruit-sweetness but very strong grippy tannins. Finishes firm and dry.

▲ 91 2004-2012 *Outstanding*

**1999** *Yarra Valley – Cabernet Blend* **Vic.**

Medium crimson. Restrained cherry/violet/chocolate aromas with some savoury notes. Medium concentrated wine with cherry/raspberry fruit flavours and touches of menthol. Fine but slightly green tannins finishing firm and tight. Core of fruit-sweetness runs through the wine.

▲ 87 2004-2012 *Outstanding*

**1999** *Yarra Valley – Chardonnay* **Vic.**

Pale yellow. Complex and elegant white peach/apricot/lanolin/chalky aromas. Restrained lanolin/chalky/white peach/apricot flavours, fine acidity and medium length. Elegant wine.

▲ 89 Now-2004

**2000** *Yarra Valley – Chardonnay* **Vic.**

Pale yellow. Floral/jasmine/pear/apricot aromas with underlying oak. Restrained wine with nutty/pear/apricot flavours, some fruit-sweetness on the middle palate, fine minerally acidity with good length. Likely to build up weight and complexity with age.

▲ 87 Now-2005

**1996** *Yarra Valley – Pinot Noir* **Vic.**

Medium crimson. Dark cherry aromas. Some spicy/French polish complexity. Richly flavoured wine. Dark cherry/spicy flavours. Some chocolate/mocha characters. Underlying oak, finishing with a tannin lick.

■ 89 Now-2006

**1998** *Yarra Valley – Pinot Noir* **Vic.**
Medium crimson. Apricot/strawberry fruit characters with touch of malty oak. Intensely flavoured apricot/strawberry fruit flavours, quite hard tannins, some vanillin oak, finishing quite firm and tight.
■ *86* *Now-2005*

## ZEMA ESTATE

**1996 Family Selection** *Coonawarra – Cabernet Sauvignon* **S.A.**
Deep crimson. Curious aromas. Dark cherry/leafy nettley aromas. A touch of vanillin. Palate is soupy wine dark cherry/leafy flavours, chocolaty tannins, some savoury oak background. Finishes quite firm.
■ *86* *Now-2010*

**1998 Family Selection** *Coonawarra – Cabernet Sauvignon* **S.A.**
Deep crimson. Aromatic red cherry aromas with hint of liquorice. Sweet red cherry/liquorice fruit, fine sinewy tannins, some tobacco/spice nuances, finishing firm and tight.
■ *83* *Now-2012*

**1999 Family Selection** *Coonawarra – Cabernet Sauvignon* **S.A.**
Deep crimson. Lovely chocolate/blackcurrant aromas, underpinned by mocha oak. Rich, ripe, blackcurrant/chocolate flavours, plenty of fruit-sweetness and concentration. Mocha/cedary oak, fine tannins, finishing firm.
■ *94* *2004-2012*

**2000** *Coonawarra – Cabernet Sauvignon* **S.A.**
Deep crimson. Very elemental but beautifully perfumed blackberry/liquorice/black olive aromas with underlying savoury oak. Very impressive palate with cassis/plum/liquorice flavours balanced by beautifully seasoned savoury biscuity oak, touches of ginger spice, plenty of concentration and length. A very polished elegant wine.
■ *97* *2005-2018*

**2000** *Coonawarra – Shiraz* **S.A.**
Medium deep crimson. Loose-knit, red cherry/raspberry aromas. Some savoury malty oak characters. Smoky/savoury oak over red cherry/raspberry fruit, sinewy tannins building up firm. Medium term drink.
■ *80* *Now-2008*

# ABOUT LANGTON'S

*For more than a decade, Langton's has been at the forefront of the Australian secondary wine market, building a respected international profile and wine industry presence. Through its focus on ultra-fine Australian wine, Langton's is recognised for raising the international investment profile and acceptance of Australian wine.*

The critically acclaimed *Langton's Classification of Australian Wine* and *Langton's Australian Fine Wine Buying and Investment Guide* are internationally recognised as authoritative investment tools.

Langton's offers more than 30,000 lots a year of fine and rare Australian and imported wines to private and trade buyers, nationally as well as internationally. Live and on-line auctions are conducted regularly in Melbourne, Sydney, and other centres. The introduction of a unique online wine auction service confirms Langton's as one of the leading secondary wine market institutions.

Langton's internet wine auction site *www.langtons.com.au* is the most advanced in the world – providing its national and international wine investment market with a valuable set of buying tools from electronic catalogues and live bidding services to 'informed opinion' and price data.

Langton's Fine Wine Auctions formed an important association with Christie's Australia in 1990. Langton's is also a partner in the Penfolds Wine Clinic program, a specialist recorking service for enthusiasts and investors.

Langton's Fine Wine Auction's has also held many important wine auction events in Australia since 1989, including 1991 'Classic Coonawarra', 1992 'Langton's Classification of Distinguished Australian Wine I', '1993 The Anders Josephson Collection', 1996 'Langton's Classification of Distinguished Australian Wine II', 1996 'Penfold's Red Wine Auction', 1997 'The Great Wine Estates of Western Australia I', 1998 'Shiraz Australia', 1999 'The Great Wine Estates of Western Australia II', 1999 'Golden Summers A Vintage Australian Decade 1990-1999', 1999 'The Golden Century – 1900-1999', 2000 'Langton's Classification of Australian Wine III', 2001 'Rich Rare and Red – Coonawarra Masterpieces – Barrel Series V', 2001 'Penfold's Grange Online Wine Auction', 2001 'The Great Wine Estates of Western Australia III', and 2002 'Shiraz Australia II'.

**Stewart Langton**

In 1987, Stewart Langton established his own specialist wine auction house in Melbourne. It was considered a risky venture at the time.

Two years later, he was joined by Andrew Caillard MW, and together they set up a Sydney auction house in 1989.

Stewart has brought many innovations to the wine auction business. He was the first to introduce the Silent Bid Auction to Australia and the first to establish a national wine auction service.

In 1990, Christie's, the world's largest wine auctioneers, approached Stewart to form a business alliance with Langton's, a unique relationship forged by common interests and aspirations.

Langton's was established with a long term objective: to become a great antipodean wine auction house. The launch of *www.langtons.com.au* is another step in that direction.

Stewart Langton is proprietor of Langton's Wine Bar and Restaurant, a Melbourne dining insititution. He is also a director of the Mansion Group, a wine and tourism company.

**Andrew Caillard**

Andrew Caillard is a specialist wine auctioneer and has been an executive partner of Langton's Fine Wine Auctions since 1988. Andrew has strong historical family links with the Australian wine industry – his great-great grandfather was John Reynell, the man who introduced grapevines to South Australia.

Andrew began his career in wine in Bordeaux, Germany, and the U.K. In 1983, he attended Roseworthy Agricultural College, now the University of Adelaide, South Australia. He has worked the vintage at Brokenwood, Hunter Valley, New South Wales, and Petaluma, Adelaide Hills, South Australia.

In 1993, he was awarded the highly prized Madame Bollinger Medal for excellence in wine tasting, becoming only the fifth Australian to pass the Master of Wine exam. In 2002, at the time of writing, there are only 11 Masters of Wine in Australia.

As an author and wine reviewer, Andrew has written widely on wine and wine investment. He pens *Langton's Australian Fine Wine Buying and Investment Guide* and has co-authored *Penfolds Rewards of Patience*. He is a regular tasting panellist with *Wine Magazine* and also writes for *The Wine Magazine* (Australia) and *Decanter* (U.K.) and other publications.

**Tamara Grischy**

Tamara is Langton's senior valuation expert and marketing manager. Tamara graduated in wine marketing at the University of Adelaide in 1992 and earned a Bachelor of Business from the University of Technology, Sydney in 1995. She gained practical wine experience at Peter Lehmann, Brokenwood (a virtual wine-making university) and McWilliams in the Hunter Valley, New South Wales.

In 1994, Tamara joined Langton's as an auction manager and valuer, leaving in 1997 to work at Wairu River Wines in Marlborough, New Zealand. In 1998, she returned to Langton's in Melbourne, moving to an executive role in marketing and planning. Her responsibilities include a key role in wine valuations, communicating specialist wine knowledge to clients, as well as overseeing all aspects of marketing.

Tamara is a member of *The Wine Magazine* tasting panel. As a project leader, she has been actively involved in the development of Langton's online facility. She is currently studying for an MBA at Swinburne University in Melbourne.

**Kate Clarke**

Kate Clarke, valuation specialist, has a background in science and viticulture, with a BSc in biochemistry from Flinders University, Adelaide (1995), and a second degree in Agricultural Science (viticulture) from the University of Adelaide (1998). Kate grew up on a farm near Mt Gambier in South Australia, close to Coonawarra. She has worked vintage in Coonawarra and McLaren Vale.


## ACKNOWLEDGEMENTS

Thank you to the wonderful team at Langton's who are largely responsible for our successes and reputation – Tamara Grischy, Georgia Weatherhead, Ann Burgess, Elizabeth Elliot, Ross Marshall, Ron Ridge, Les Lamos, Matt and Patrick Langton in Melbourne, and Kate Clarke, Tracy Bramford, Alan Bouch, and Joe Bugden in Sydney. Thanks also to my friends on the *Gourmet-Traveller Wine Magazine* tasting panel – Peter Forrestal, Huon Hooke, Peter Bourne, Nick Bullied MW, and Sophie Otton. So too Scott Reid, Mike Dyson, and Mark McCabe for their valuable contributions. And to boffins – Stewart Button, Peter Jordan, and James Foggarty; the gang at Media21, especially Stephen Balme, and editor, Peter Ching. Also to the Caillard boys – Alex, Toby and Dominic – who have all learned happily to use a corkscrew. They may see an age when such devices are no longer necessary. More certain however is the day we can share a bottle. Finally to Bobby Caillard and Lain Langton, who bear the brunt of our adventures and misadventures.